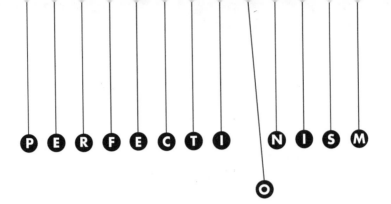

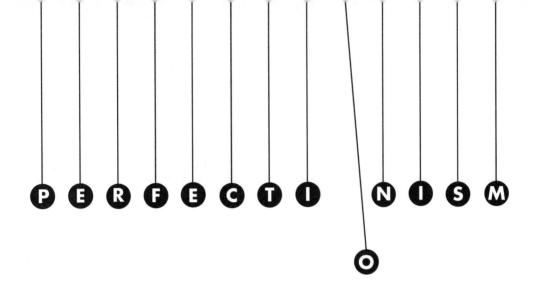

PERFECTIONISM

Theory, Research, and Treatment

Edited by Gordon L. Flett and Paul L. Hewitt

AMERICAN PSYCHOLOGICAL ASSOCIATION

WASHINGTON, DC

Published by
American Psychological Association
750 First Street, NE
Washington, DC 20002
www.apa.org

To order
APA Order Department
P.O. Box 92984
Washington, DC 20090-2984

Tel: (800) 374-2721; Direct: (202) 336-5510
Fax: (202) 336-5502; TDD/TTY: (202) 336-6123
Online: www.apa.org/books/
Email: order@apa.org

In the U.K., Europe, Africa, and the Middle East, copies may be ordered from
American Psychological Association
3 Henrietta Street
Covent Garden, London
WC2E 8LU England

Typeset in Century Schoolbook by EPS Group Inc., Easton, MD

Printer: United Book Press, Inc., Baltimore, MD
Cover Designer: Nini Sarmiento, NiDesign, Baltimore, MD
Technical/Production Editor: Casey Ann Reever

The opinions and statements published are the responsibility of the authors, and such opinions and statements do not necessarily represent the policies of the American Psychological Association.

Library of Congress Cataloging-in-Publication Data

Perfectionism : theory, research, and treatment / edited by Gordon L. Flett and Paul L. Hewitt.
    p. cm.
   Includes bibliographical references and index.
   ISBN 1-55798-842-0
    1. Perfectionism (Personality trait)   I. Flett, Gordon L.
II. Hewitt, Paul L. (Paul Louis)

   BF698.35.P47 P37 2002
   155.2'32—dc21

                            2001056664

British Library Cataloguing-in-Publication Data
A CIP record is available from the British Library.

Printed in the United States of America
First Edition

This book is dedicated to my wife Kathy
and to our daughters Hayley and Alison,
and to the memory of Tom Martin
—Gordon L. Flett

This work is dedicated to my wife Barbara
and to our children Harrison, J. C., Jackson, and Maclean
—Paul L. Hewitt

Contents

Contributors

Lynn E. Alden, PhD, Department of Psychology, University of British Columbia, Vancouver

Jeffrey S. Ashby, PhD, Department of Counseling and Psychological Services, Georgia State University, Atlanta

Aaron T. Beck, MD, Department of Psychiatry, University of Pennsylvania, Philadelphia

Kirk R. Blankstein, PhD, Department of Psychology, University of Toronto at Mississauga, Ontario

Sidney J. Blatt, PhD, Departments of Psychiatry and Psychology, Yale University School of Medicine, New Haven, CT

Gary P. Brown, PhD, Psychology Department, Paterson Centre, St. Mary's Hospital, London

Jennifer D. Campbell, PhD, Department of Psychology, University of British Columbia, Vancouver

Sarah J. Cockell, PhD, Eating Disorders Clinic, St. Paul's Hospital, Vancouver, British Columbia

Brian J. Cox, PhD, Department of Psychiatry, University of Manitoba, Winnipeg

Patricia Marten DiBartolo, PhD, Department of Psychology, Smith College, Northampton, MA

Adam Di Paula, PhD, Department of Psychology, University of British Columbia, Vancouver

David M. Dunkley, PhD, Department of Psychology, McGill University, Montreal, Quebec

Albert Ellis, PhD, President, Albert Ellis Institute, New York

Murray W. Enns, MD, FRCPC, Department of Psychiatry, University of Manitoba, Winnipeg

Gordon L. Flett, PhD, Department of Psychology, York University, Ontario

Carol A. Flynn, PhD, Department of Psychology, University of British Columbia, Vancouver

Randy O. Frost, PhD, Department of Psychology, Smith College, Northampton, MA

Elliot M. Goldner, MD, FRCPC, Mental Health Evaluation and Community Consultation Unit, University of British Columbia, Vancouver

A. Marie Habke, PhD, Department of Psychology, University of British Columbia, Vancouver

Paul L. Hewitt, PhD, Department of Psychology, University of British Columbia, Vancouver

Silvana Macdonald, PhD, Department of Psychology, York University, Ontario

Tanna M. B. Mellings, PhD, Department of Psychology, University of British Columbia, Vancouver

Joan M. Oliver, PhD, Department of Psychology,
St. Louis University, St. Louis, MO

Wayne D. Parker, PhD, Director of Research and Evaluation
Virginia G. Piper Charitable Trust, Scottsdale, AZ

Kenneth G. Rice, PhD, Department of Counseling, Educational
Psychology, and Special Education, Michigan State University,
East Lansing

Andrew G. Ryder, PhD, Department of Psychology, University of
British Columbia, Vancouver

Robert B. Slaney, PhD, Department of Counselor Education, Counseling
Psychology, and Rehabilitation Services, Pennsylvania State
University, University Park

Suja Srikameswaran, PhD, Department of Psychology, University of
British Columbia, Vancouver

June Price Tangney, PhD, Department of Psychology, George Mason
University, Fairfax, VA

David C. Zuroff, PhD, Department of Psychology, McGill University,
Montreal, Quebec

Preface

A strong case can be made for the claim that perfectionism is endemic to Western culture. Popular phrases such as "No one is perfect" and "Learn from your mistakes" reflect the attention paid to trying to be as perfect as possible and to keep flaws and shortcomings to a minimum. Some authors have even suggested that everyone wants to be perfect. Was Alfred Adler (1956) correct when he suggested that the striving for perfection is a basic part of the human response to feelings of inadequacy and inferiority?

To our knowledge, this book represents the first attempt to integrate contemporary theory and research on the nature of perfectionism. It presents the work of many of the leading investigators in the field in one volume. The authors have reported some of this work in previous book chapters and journal articles, but this volume also includes extensive descriptions of newer work, including some studies that are described in print for the first time.

Our empirical work has been guided by concerns about the debilitating nature of perfectionism, and most of the offerings in this volume focus on perfectionism as maladaptive. Some authors have expressed concern that current research in this field does not place enough emphasis on the positive aspects of perfectionism and that a focus on perfectionism and psychopathology promotes a negative view of perfectionism. Perhaps the most vexing question in this area involves how to understand highly talented perfectionists who have attributes that are seemingly adaptive yet who come to experience significant impairment and find themselves in dire need of assistance. Just how does perfectionism as a core aspect of personality come to be associated with distress, both for individual perfectionists and for their family members? Several contributors to this volume address this issue, either directly or indirectly, by identifying factors that are associated consistently with maladaptive forms of perfectionism.

Over the years we have been interviewed by members of the media, and they continue to ask some basic questions that have yet to be addressed by perfectionism researchers. In the current volume, answers are not forthcoming to such questions as, To what extent is perfectionism a part of daily life? Are there cultural differences in perfectionism? Do people become more or less perfectionistic as they get older? Do women and men differ in the salience and importance attached to perfectionism? The dearth of information on those key issues underscores that much work remains to be done in this area. At the same time, we can take some solace from the many issues and questions that are addressed at length in this book. Those questions include, How is perfectionism assessed and conceptualized? How does perfectionism develop? What is the role of emotion in perfectionism? When is perfectionism irrational? Which aspects of perfectionism are adaptive and under what circumstances? How is perfectionism linked to stress? Why are perfectionists anxious? What interpersonal problems are associated with perfectionism?

Our primary goal for this book is to provide a source that will be useful for readers who are interested in contemporary research developments as well as for readers who seek insights that can be used to decrease levels of perfectionism among people they encounter in applied settings. Thus, the book is clearly geared toward clinicians and counselors who encounter distressed perfectionists on a regular basis. It is also aimed at educators who are concerned about perfectionistic students. Although no extensive research has been conducted on perfectionism from a treatment perspective, this volume includes theoretical insights and some empirical research about the difficulties associated with treating perfectionists. A focus on treatment reflects the growing need for basic information about how to help distressed perfectionists.

We are pleased that virtually all the authors whom we contacted accepted our invitation to contribute a chapter to this book. The various contributors may differ in their conceptualizations of the nature of perfectionism, but they share a common recognition of the importance and significance of research and theory on the perfectionism construct.

This book is divided into four parts. The first part serves as an introduction to some basic themes in the perfectionism field, beginning with chapter 1, in which we provide an overview of definitional issues, conceptual issues, and treatment considerations. In chapter 2, Murray W. Enns and Brian J. Cox provide a description and critical assessment of existing perfectionism measures. Enns and Cox provide a balanced account of those measures and point to areas for further investigation. Chapter 3, by Robert B. Slaney, Kenneth G. Rice, and Jeffrey S. Ashby, adds to this focus on assessment by providing a description of the development, structure, and research applications of the Almost Perfect Scale. The inclusion of a discrepancy component is an intriguing aspect of this measure; the role of discrepancies in perfectionism is important at both the applied and theoretical levels.

In chapter 4, we and our colleagues Joan M. Oliver and Silvana Macdonald provide an extended analysis of factors that contribute to the development of perfectionism and associated problems in parental stress. We also outline an initial model of the development of perfectionism, one that is based on the notion that numerous factors beyond those related to parental attributes contribute to the development of perfectionism. Chapter 5, by Wayne D. Parker, adds to the developmental focus of this segment of the book by providing an overview of his research on the nature and correlates of perfectionism in gifted children. Parker's research compares and contrasts the aspects of adaptive versus maladaptive perfectionism and shows that only a subset of gifted children are characterized by maladaptive perfectionism.

The second part of this book examines the role of social, motivational, emotional, and cognitive factors in perfectionism. It broadens the analysis of perfectionism by assessing the key correlates and processes that underscore this personality construct. In chapter 6, A. Marie Habke and Carol A. Flynn provide a comprehensive evaluation of the role of perfectionism factors in interpersonal processes and outcomes. Research in this area shows the relevance of perfectionism in relationship problems and the potential difficulties associated with perfectionistic self-presentation. In chapter 7, Jennifer D. Campbell and Adam Di Paula illustrate the potential usefulness of examining specific facets of perfectionism and provide some much-needed data on the link between perfectionism and motivational constructs. In chapter 8, June Price Tangney discusses the link between perfectionism and self-conscious emotions; she focuses on the role of shame in social forms of perfectionism. In chapter 9, Albert Ellis provides his unique reflections on the link between irrational beliefs and perfectionism. He includes an expanded account of some specific processes that are involved in irrational beliefs and perfectionism and associated treatment implications. As Ellis notes, his chapter represents his most detailed assessment of the link between perfectionism and irrational beliefs. The focus on cognitive factors is elaborated further in chapter 10, in which Gary P. Brown and Aaron T. Beck provide an updated account of the role of dysfunctional attitudes and perfectionism in depression, supplementing Beck's classic work in this area.

The third part of the book focuses primarily on the important association between perfectionism and life stress and how the two combine to produce adjustment difficulties. In chapter 11, we provide an extended analysis of the role of stress processes in an attempt to identify the specific mechanisms involved in the association between perfectionism and various forms of maladjustment; our particular focus is on stress and depression. A key aspect of our proposed model is the link between perfectionism and stress generation. The association between perfectionism and stress is further evaluated in chapter 12, in which Kirk R. Blankstein and David M. Dunkley assess the role of coping, stress, and social support as mediating and moderating factors in the association between perfectionism and distress.

The final part of this book focuses on perfectionism as it relates to clinical disorders in the therapeutic context. This segment begins in chapter 13, in which Elliot M. Goldner, Sarah J. Cockell, and Suja Srikameswaran provide a cogent summary of the voluminous literature on perfectionism and eating disorders, followed by an initial model of the role of various dimensions in perfectionism. In chapter 14, Randy O. Frost and Patricia Martin DiBartolo provide an insightful analysis of the role of various dimensions of perfectionism in anxiety and obsessive–compulsive disorder and associated traits. Next, Lynn E. Alden, Andrew G. Ryder, and Tanna M. B. Mellings summarize the role of perfectionism in social fears and advance their two-factor theory of perfectionism and social anxiety in chapter 15. Finally, in chapter 16, Sidney J. Blatt and David C. Zuroff conclude the volume by discussing issues involved in the treatment of perfectionism and their innovative empirical research in this area.

We thank the many people who have provided suggestions that have shaped the contents of this book. In particular, we express our gratitude to fellow contributors Lynn Alden and Kirk Blankstein as well as to Avi Besser, Clarry Lay, and William McCown. We also would like to thank our many graduate and undergraduate students over the years for their creative input and diligence and Glen Flett for his photography. Finally, we acknowledge the expert tutelage, guidance, and patience of our APA team, including Acquisitions Editor Margaret Schlegel, Development Editor Kristine Enderle, and Production Editor Casey Reever.

It is our hope that publication of this book will serve as an impetus for further research on the assessment, nature, and treatment of dysfunctional forms of perfectionism. Although many important developments have occurred, as suggested earlier, the reader will see that many issues still need to be addressed, especially with regard to the treatment of dysfunctional forms of perfectionism. We eagerly look forward to the developments in this field as we progress through the 21st century.

Reference

Adler, A. (1956). The neurotic disposition. In H. L. Ansbacher & R. R. Ansbacher (Eds.), *The individual psychology of Alfred Adler* (pp. 239–262). New York: Harper.

Part I

Conceptual Issues, Assessment, and Developmental Patterns

1 _____

Perfectionism and Maladjustment: An Overview of Theoretical, Definitional, and Treatment Issues

Gordon L. Flett and Paul L. Hewitt

What is perfectionism? On the surface, this question does not seem difficult to answer. *Perfectionism* is the striving for flawlessness, and *extreme perfectionists* are people who want to be perfect in all aspects of their lives. If we asked several leading researchers to define perfectionism, however, their answers would probably be somewhat different and would vary according to how they view perfectionism and the factors they emphasize.

In part, this diversity reflects the fact that research and theory on perfectionism have increased exponentially over the past two decades; a survey of PsychLit references using the term *perfectionism* illustrates this point. According to our search, 102 publications with the term were published in the 1980s, compared with 336 publications in the 1990s (i.e., an increase of almost 330 percent).

Although this increased attention has led to a better understanding of the perfectionism construct, people who are relatively new to this field are now faced with many different conceptualizations and definitions. One purpose of this introductory chapter, then, is to provide an overview of the numerous approaches to the study of perfectionism and related conceptual issues, some of which are represented in this book. As our discussion progresses, we hope that it will become more obvious that the manner in which perfectionism is conceptualized and assessed has a direct bearing on the findings obtained from research that investigates the role of perfectionism in maladjustment.

This chapter also discusses such issues as the negative and positive aspects of perfectionism and the conceptual and empirical significance of distinguishing the actual standards that influence behavior versus the evaluative reactions involving the attainment of these standards. It concludes with a summary of research on perfectionism from a treatment perspective as well as a description of some of the problems associated with treating perfectionists either for the perfectionism itself, or related disorders. First, however, we begin by describing some case studies to illustrate the various forms of distress that can be associated with perfectionism.

Case Studies of Perfectionism and Maladjustment

Descriptive case studies have provided excellent accounts of the link between perfectionism and maladjustment. Case studies of troubled perfectionists abound in the psychological and psychiatric literatures, and they can be regarded as indirect evidence of the pervasiveness of dysfunctional forms of perfectionism. Examples include those of the troubled adolescents with a history of suicidality described by Hewitt, Flett, and Weber (1994) and of the three gifted people who killed themselves, described by Blatt (1995). Blatt concluded that

> these accounts of Vincent Foster, Alasdair Clayre, and Denny Hansen are typical of numerous examples of talented, ambitious, and successful individuals who are driven by intense needs for perfection and plagued by intense self-scrutiny, self-doubt, and self-criticism. (p. 1005)

Other case examples illustrate perfectionism directed toward others. A unique case is that of the perfectionistic professor who was so distressed about making a mistake in his textbook that he eventually killed his wife (see Lombardi, Florentino, & Lombardi, 1998). Flett and Hewitt (in press) also described a case in which a woman endured physical abuse from her perfectionistic husband for many years. When asked about her husband's perfectionism, the woman said

> Perfectionism played a big part in the abuse I experienced. I had to be the perfect wife, and I would get hit when I did not meet my husband's expectations. One time when I didn't answer the phone fast enough for his liking, he grabbed me by my hair, picked me up, and threw me across the room and against the wall. Another time I was cut and severely injured when he pulled me through a door in a fit of rage. And this usually occurred when he felt that I was not meeting his standards. I had to keep the house looking perfect and act the role of the perfect wife. The real irony is that he often said that the only mistake that he ever made was marrying me.

This account suggests that other-oriented perfectionism in the batterer may contribute to a sense of socially prescribed perfectionism and attendant feelings of helplessness in his abused partner.

Although some case studies focus on other-oriented perfectionism, most case histories illustrate the associations among perfectionism, personal distress, and evaluations of the self. Perfectionism has caused substantial distress for a number of popular performers, including Alanis Morissette, Barbra Streisand, and Donny Osmond. As we illustrated in an earlier study with professional performers, perfectionism may be a boon to performance, but it is also associated with reduced performance satisfaction (Mor, Day, Flett, & Hewitt, 1995).

Some of the most poignant case studies focus on the suicidal tendencies of perfectionists. For instance, renowned philosopher Ludwig Wittgenstein had lifelong problems with dysphoria and suicidal urges. Hughes

(1993) attributed Wittgenstein's difficulties to several aspects of his character, including perfectionism. Hughes noted that Wittgenstein

> had imbibed in his father's house an absolute sense of morality, a strict sense of duty and of probity. He was to remain with a keen sense of guilt in sometimes seemingly minor matters; he displayed the highest ideals for himself ("*Of course* I want to be perfect" [Rhees, 1981, p. 50]) he once exclaimed. . . . (p. 88)

Hughes observed that Wittgenstein's perfectionism coexisted with other obsessive traits, a nervous temperament, and interpersonal problems. Perhaps Wittgenstein's perfectionism accounts for his academic interest in the nature of ideals and idealism.

Author Sylvia Plath is arguably the perfectionist who has received the most attention. Her brief, brilliant career was cut short when she took her own life in 1962. Plath experienced severe levels of depression and a sense of self-hatred that is documented in her works and her journals. Plath was an exacting perfectionist who judged both herself and others by exceedingly high standards (see Shulman, 1998; Van Pelt, 1997). In fact, Plath's final work focused on the possibility of finding perfection in death and reflected her admission that she had "lived under the shadow of fear: fear that I would fall short of some abstract perfection" (Plath, 1982, p. 178).

Other perfectionists are less famous but still provide us with clear illustrations of the potential problems associated with perfectionism. Burns and Beck (1978) described the case of a young woman who experienced unremitting depression and various bouts of self-harm, including wrist-slashing and an intentional pill overdose. They concluded that her problem stemmed from exceedingly perfectionistic, all-or-none standards. They noted that

> she developed depressive reactions whenever she perceived her performance as being less than perfect. The blue mood and panic she then experienced seemed to convince her that it was, in fact, terrible to be imperfect because she felt terrible. When the depressive symptoms evolved, she experienced increasing lethargy and inactivity and began to withdraw from normal activities. Then she would interpret her decreased productivity as further evidence of her own inadequacy and worthlessness. Thus, the vicious cycle of depressive thoughts, feelings, and behaviors would continue to feed itself. (p. 120)

This excerpt contains the interesting and as yet untested idea that perfectionists interpret their depressive symptoms as symbols of failure; this interpretation may contribute to a tendency for them to become even further depressed about their depression.

Flanagan (1993) outlined the history of Mr. G, who was an attorney who suffered for many years as a result of chronic procrastination and indecision. Flanagan determined that Mr. G did not have major depression or dysthymia; rather, he had a personality disorder not otherwise specified with obsessive–compulsive, dependent, passive–aggressive, and narcissistic features. Flanagan was able to determine that perfectionism lay behind Mr. G's negative thoughts and behavioral deficits; she noted that

> without too much searching, we discovered that he believed he had to be perfect. . . . Over many weeks we examined and reexamined how much of his behavior could be explained by this acquired understanding. For example, he compensated for the conviction that he was unlovable by believing that he had to be perfect, and thus he invariably dressed impeccably but often took several hours to decide what to wear. In his attempts to never make any mistakes or reveal any flaws, he avoided making any commitments at all, procrastinating at work and keeping all conversations superficially entertaining. (pp. 825–826)

We have found that this tendency to overcompensate by trying to be perfect is a common theme among distressed people. In that sense, perfectionism can be seen as an ill-advised coping response to an already imperfect situation.

The need to compensate by striving for perfection is also evident in the case of Samuel, an 18-year-old Orthodox Jew (see Sorotzkin, 1998) who used his outward achievements and superior intelligence to compensate for his increasing tendency to engage in inappropriate sexual acts at strip clubs as well as his growing sense of "unbearable tension and inner turmoil" (p. 93). Sorotzkin felt that Samuel's perfectionism was a direct reflection of being raised by a cold and distant mother and a father who was hypercritical, overcontrolling, and physically abusive.

Maltsberger (1998) described the characteristics of Robert Salter, a 22-year-old law student who attempted suicide by plunging 200 feet off a bridge. Maltsberger noted that Salter had experienced severe anxiety and depression for several years; the symptoms became more severe once he started law school and experienced the pressures associated with the law school environment. Once again, perfectionism was seen as playing a key role. Maltsberger observed, "Highly competitive and perfectionistic, Robert found his coursework extremely difficult; he felt inferior to and jealous of his classmates" (p. 226). (Ellis discusses the apparent link between perfectionism and negative social comparisons at length in chapter 9, this volume.)

The importance of perfectionism and hypercompetitiveness also is represented in a case study of an elite gymnast identified as "Susan" (see Krane, Greenleaf, & Snow, 1997). Susan endangered herself by continuing to compete when seriously injured, engaging in unhealthy eating practices, overtraining, and not heeding the advice of medical experts. Perfectionism was seen as being central to her difficulties. Krane et al. (1997) stated that Susan was pressured to be perfect by her coaches and her parents and that she incorporated this pressure into her own personal goals to be perfect. The authors noted that

> this was evident when Susan stated: "as I progressed with skills, the way I stayed content was to learn something new, and to practice and perfect it." Susan's constant quest for perfection was often described as:

"Nothing ever was perfect. I mean, I always could be able to do something better." (p. 62)

This quest for perfectionism resulted in chronic self-doubt and anxiety. Susan acknowledged, "I never gave myself credit. Behind everything I was scared to death because I could not manage to be perfect" (Krane et al., 1997, p. 63). This case study shows us that any attempt to examine perfectionism from a motivational perspective must incorporate the notion that certain people are, indeed, "driven" to be perfect and their excessive goal orientation can become an obsession.

Most of the case studies described thus far have involved people experiencing depression and related forms of distress. Other cases illustrate the role of perfectionism in obsessive–compulsive disorder (OCD), although those cases require that some *thing,* rather than some *person* (i.e., the self or others), be perfect. That distinction may be important in the perfectionism that is evident in some disorders (e.g., OCD and obsessive–compulsive personality disorder) than in others (e.g., depression and narcissistic personality disorder).

Tallis (1996) provided brief but compelling accounts of three people with OCD who displayed compulsive washing even though they did not experience phobic, illness-related anxieties reflecting contamination fears. Tallis (1996) concluded that all three cases' compulsive washing could be attributed to perfectionism. Two of the people engaged in compulsive washing so that they could keep their possessions in perfect condition: One person wanted his compact discs and musical instruments to remain in pristine condition, whereas the other person engaged in washing to protect the perfect condition of his golf clothes and equipment. The third person was described as a 28-year-old woman with an excessive washing compulsion that included 12 hours of washing without being able to stop. Her goal was to complete the perfect wash and maintain a state of perfect cleanliness.

Another comprehensive account of a troubled perfectionist was provided by Reilly (1998), who used cognitive therapy to treat "Jane," a 28-year-old woman who attempted suicide by drug overdose on at least two occasions, including during the course of treatment. She was diagnosed with major depressive disorder and generalized anxiety disorder. Reilly (1998) reported that Jane experienced perfectionistic dysfunctional attitudes, self-criticism, and a preponderance of automatic thoughts about her inability to live up to socially prescribed pressures to be perfect. This woman's socially prescribed perfectionism also was accompanied by high levels of perceived responsibility, interpersonal sensitivity, hopelessness, and perceived deficits in coping and problem-solving ability.

The cases described above illustrate the link between perfectionism and maladjustment. In addition, several cases suggest that perfectionists may be highly capable people and that in some cases, relentless striving and high performance is an attempt to compensate for perceived deficits in the self. Unfortunately, these compelling, representative studies have not yet been supplemented with epidemiological studies of the incidence and prevalence of dysfunctional perfectionism in community samples, so we can only wonder about the extent to which perfectionism is a problem in the lives of people from the general community.

More recently, we obtained some insight into this issue while attempting to recruit participants from Vancouver for a group treatment study of perfectionism being led by the second author of this chapter (see Hewitt, Flynn, Mikail, & Flett, 2000). The initial goal was to identify at least 30 people with significant impairment resulting from perfectionism. To our amazement, 60 potential participants were recruited from the community within just 3 days, and another 250 individuals were placed on the waiting list. The surprising response led us to believe that the problematic aspects of perfectionism may be quite underestimated.

Although perfectionism may have some positive aspects, as we indicated in the preface of this book, our collaborative research over the past 12 years has focused on the negative aspects of this personality orientation. We believe that perfectionism is associated with significant levels of impairment and distress not only for perfectionists but for their family members as well. Indeed, this book focuses primarily on the adjustment problems associated with perfectionism and examines contemporary research and theory on perfectionism in light of such significant problems as anxiety, depression, suicide, and eating disorders. We now turn to a discussion of current conceptualizations of the perfectionism construct.

Conceptualizations of Perfectionism

As suggested earlier, some key differences exist among researchers in how perfectionism is defined and conceptualized. One way to distinguish among various conceptualizations is according to whether perfectionism is treated as unidimensional or multidimensional. Historically, the "unidimensional camp" has included a focus on cognitive factors in the form of irrational beliefs (Ellis, 1962) or dysfunctional attitudes (Burns, 1980; Weissman & Beck, 1978). A unidimensional approach also has predominated in the eating disorder literature, where most studies have used the six-item Perfectionism subscale of the Eating Disorder Inventory (EDI; Garner, Olmstead, & Polivy, 1983). More recently, Rheaume and associates suggested the need to return to a unidimensional conceptualization and have designed a unidimensional measure (see Rheaume, Freeston, & Ladouceur, 1995; Rheaume et al., 2000).

Dimensions of Perfectionism

A strong case can be made for the claim that one of the most significant developments in this field is the discovery that the perfectionism construct is multidimensional; that is, it has both personal and interpersonal aspects. The advent of two measures that share the same name, the Multidimensional Perfectionism Scale (MPS; Frost, Marten, Lahart, & Rosenblate, 1990; Hewitt & Flett, 1990, 1991) was significant because it promoted the notion that because perfectionism is a complex, multidimensional entity, unidimensional approaches may miss some key aspects of this personality orientation.

Frost et al. (1990) developed a six-factor measure that assesses four aspects of perfectionism directed toward the self (i.e., high personal standards, doubts about actions, concern over mistakes, and organization) and two aspects of perfectionism that reflect the perceived presence of parental demands on the self (i.e., high parental expectations and parental criticism). Frost et al. suggested that a total score could be derived from their instrument, but they suggested dropping organization from the total because of its relatively low correlations with the other five dimensions.

We identified dimensions involving perfectionism directed toward either the self (i.e., self-oriented perfectionism) or others (i.e., other-oriented perfectionism) as well as a third dimension that involves the generalized belief or perception that others are imposing unrealistic demands on the self (i.e., socially prescribed perfectionism; see Hewitt & Flett, 1989, 1991). In earlier developmental work, we also used the separate dimensions of perfectionistic motivation and world-oriented perfectionism (see Hewitt & Flett, 1990). The perfectionistic motivation concept subsequently was incorporated into the self-oriented perfectionism dimension described above. The concept of world-oriented perfectionism is a global concept (i.e., a belief in the need for perfect solutions to broad problems) that Jones (1969) introduced in his work on specific irrational beliefs.

The creation of multidimensional measures led some researchers to reexamine unidimensional measures to see whether it is possible to identify subfactors. For instance, Joiner and Schmidt (1995) conducted a factor analysis of the six items on the EDI Perfectionism subscale and found two factors. The first factor had item content that tapped self-oriented perfectionism, and the second factor had item content that tapped socially prescribed perfectionism.

Negative and Positive Perfectionism

Some authors (e.g., Slaney, Ashby, & Trippi, 1995) have suggested that the perfectionism field has the same general bias that characterizes psychology in general—that is, a tendency to focus on negative aspects without recognizing the positive aspects of the construct. Additional ways of conceptualizing perfectionism have emerged from attempts to identify positive aspects of the construct. Originally, Hamachek (1978) suggested the need for a refined approach that included the distinction between *normal* and *neurotic* perfectionism. Normal perfectionism is defined as striving for reasonable and realistic standards that leads to a sense of self-satisfaction and enhanced self-esteem; neurotic perfectionism is a tendency to strive for excessively high standards and is motivated by fears of failure and concern about disappointing others.

Similarly, other authors have distinguished between *positive* and *neg-*

Exhibit 1.1.   Perfectionism Terms and Definitions

Active perfectionism—Action tendency resulting from high standards that motivate behavior

Concern over mistakes—A tendency to have a negative reaction to mistakes, anticipate disapproval, and interpret mistakes as equivalent to failure

Discrepancy—Perceived inability to meet high standards set for the self

Doubts about actions—Extent to which a person doubts his or her ability to accomplish a task

High personal standards—Setting high standards of great importance imposed on the self

Maladaptive evaluation concerns—Negative aspects of perfectionism reflecting concern over mistakes, doubts about actions, parental criticism and expectations, and socially prescribed perfectionism

Negative perfectionism—Perfectionistic behavior that is a function of negative reinforcement and avoidance tendencies

Neurotic perfectionism—Striving for excessively high standards due to fears of failure and concerns about disappointing others

Normal perfectionism—Striving for reasonable and realistic standards that leads to self-satisfaction and enhanced self-esteem

Organization—Belief in the importance of neatness and order

Other-oriented perfectionism—Exceedingly high standards for other people

Parental criticism—Belief that parents are overly harsh

Parental expectations—Belief that parents set very high standards for the self

Passive perfectionism—Inaction due to excess concern over mistakes, doubts about action, and dilatory tendencies

Perfectionism cognitions—Automatic thoughts that reflect the need to be perfect and awareness of imperfections

Perfectionistic self-presentation—A style involving the need to appear perfect or avoid appearing imperfect to others

Positive achievement strivings—Positive aspects of perfectionism that reflect high personal standards, self-oriented perfectionism, other-oriented perfectionism, and organization

Positive perfectionism—Perfectionistic behavior that is a function of positive reinforcement and approach tendencies

Self-oriented perfectionism—High personal standards and motivation to attain perfection

Socially prescribed perfectionism—Perception of unrealistically high standards being imposed on the self

World-oriented perfectionism—The belief that precise, correct, and perfect solutions to all human and world problems exist

---

measure of body esteem were administered. The correlational analyses indicated that the association between neurotic perfectionism and neuroticism was exceptionally high ($r = .75$) and surpassed the correlations between neurotic perfectionism and the perfectionism dimensions assessed by the MPS. At an empirical and conceptual level, we believe that it is best to distinguish neuroticism and perfectionism when seeking to identify neurotic forms of perfectionism; it is important that perfectionism measures are not contaminated with items that mix perfectionistic tendencies with distress reactions and emotional tendencies associated with the fail-ure to attain perfection. If the NPQ is correlated with measures of anxiety and depression, then it is likely that the correlations are inflated due to shared-item overlap in the measures. This concern about item content may apply to several measures described in the perfectionism literature.

Distinguishing Between Perfectionism and the Attainment of Perfection

Another key issue in our field involves the need to recognize (both concep-tually and empirically) the distinction between perfectionistic standards and the attainment of those standards. When we constructed our MPS (see Hewitt & Flett, 1991), we tried as much as possible to focus on item content that referred to levels of personal and social standards and did not refer to assessments of how near or far the respondent was from being perfect. An important test for future trait measures of perfectionism is whether the items focus on the perfectionistic standards per se and do not make explicit reference to whether the standards have been attained.

Regarding this issue, Slaney and associates have opted to include a separate measure of discrepancy as part of their Almost Perfect Scale–Revised (Slaney, Rice, Mobley, Trippi, & Ashby, 2001; see Slaney, Rice, and Ashby, chapter 3, this volume). Discrepancy involves the person's percep-tion of the extent to which perfectionistic standards have been reached. Clearly, perceptions of discrepancy play an important role in the experi-ence of distress (see Higgins, 1987), and Slaney and his colleagues are to be commended for including a focus on this concept. Indeed, the case stud-ies of troubled perfectionists that were outlined earlier include many ref-erences to the distress associated with the failure to attain perfection.

According to Slaney and his associates, the Discrepancy subscale is a central aspect of the perfectionism construct; it is the key factor in deter-mining whether perfectionism is adaptive or maladaptive. We believe that it is important to measure perceived discrepancies, and we are in the pro-cess of developing a multidimensional discrepancy measure that will ac-company our MPS. We feel that definitions of perfectionism, however, should be restricted to perfectionistic strivings and that individual differ-ences in perceived discrepancies should be seen as part of a related but distinct construct that emphasizes self-evaluation.

Discrepancies and trait perfectionism can differ in several respects. For instance, one key difference between perfectionism and self-evaluation involves temporal factors. Whereas perfectionism is regarded as a rela-tively stable personality construct, discrepancies can and should fluctuate substantially as an ongoing function of performance feedback, life expe-riences, and so on.

Our suggestion to regard perfectionism and discrepancy as distinct concepts is in keeping with the results of a study by Hankin, Roberts, and Gotlib (1997), who examined the empirical association between dimen-sions of perfectionism and self-discrepancies in a sample of 115 high school students. They found that self-oriented perfectionism was not correlated with measures of actual–ideal and actual–ought discrepancies. They found a small but significant positive correlation, however, between socially prescribed perfectionism and actual–ideal discrepancies. Socially prescribed perfectionism was not associated significantly with greater actual–ought discrepancies. In their discussion section, Hankin et al. (1997) suggested that the perfectionism dimensions and self-discrepancies might differ conceptually and empirically in important ways because perfectionism, as conceptualized in our MPS, assesses "the magnitude of individuals' self-standards regardless of their ability to meet them" (p. 675).

The need to distinguish between perfectionism and self-evaluation is also evident in research on perfectionism and self-efficacy. Experimental investigations of standard setting and self-efficacy are based on the premise that it is desirable and meaningful to distinguish between standards and a person's perceived ability to meet those standards (Wallace & Alden, 1991). Indeed, the two-factor model of social anxiety outlined by Alden, Ryder, and Mellings (chapter 15, this volume) maintains this distinction between perfectionism and efficacy judgments.

The potential usefulness of distinguishing perfectionism and self-evaluative tendencies is illustrated further by research on perfectionism, self-esteem, and depression. Recent studies by Rice, Ashby, and associates have evaluated the possibility that self-esteem mediates the link between perfectionism and depression (Preusser, Rice, & Ashby, 1994; Rice, Ashby, & Slaney, 1998). Although evidence of mediational effects has been mixed at times, a clear implication of the research is that it is possible and theoretically meaningful to distinguish perfectionism and the valence of self-judgments. We believe it is equally meaningful to distinguish between perfectionism and appraisals of the extent to which perfection has been achieved.

Generalized Perfectionism Versus Specific Domains of Perfectionism

At present, most of the research in the perfectionism field has focused primarily on individual trait differences in generalized forms of perfectionism. One assumption implicit in this focus on trait perfectionism is that extreme perfectionists are those who pursue extreme standards across a variety of life domains (e.g., achievement, interpersonal relationships, and appearance). That assumption needs to be evaluated in empirical research. Perhaps maladaptive and adaptive forms of perfectionism differ in that adaptive perfectionism is circumscribed and limited to one or two life domains, whereas maladaptive perfectionism is global and overgeneralized, involving all aspects of the self. A related issue that needs to be tested is the possibility that a state component to perfectionism is activated in specific situations. With one exception (see Saboonchi & Lundh, 1999), the issue has not received empirical attention.

Recently, some researchers have begun to explore the feasibility of examining the nature and correlates of perfectionism in specific life domains. Mitchelson and Burns (1998) modified the MPS (Hewitt & Flett, 1991) by asking respondents to indicate their levels of perfectionism at home and at work. They found meaningful individual differences in domain-specific forms of perfectionism. Comparisons showed that levels of self-oriented, other-oriented, and socially prescribed perfectionism were significantly higher in the work context than at home.

Research in our laboratory has investigated the usefulness of domain-specific measures as predictors of postpartum adjustment difficulties in new parents (see Flett, Hewitt, Berk, & Besser, 2001). Specifically, we created a measure of concern about parenting mistakes by making slight modifications to the Concern Over Mistakes subscale of the Frost et al. (1990) MPS. We have found that this measure of concern over parenting mistakes is a mediator of the link between more general measures of trait perfectionism and postpartum adjustment (see Flett et al., 2001).

A different way of examining the specificity issue is to assess the levels of perfectionism associated with certain people in a person's life. Randolph and Dykman (1998) modified the MPS (Hewitt & Flett, 1991) to assess perceived levels of perfectionism in parents. Similarly, Habke, Hewitt, and Flett (1999) used a modified version of our MPS that enabled participants to evaluate levels of perfectionism in their spouses. The studies illustrate the feasibility of using an approach that measures perfectionism in specific "target" people as a supplement to the general tendency to focus on global forms of perfectionism.

Maladaptive Versus Adaptive Perfectionism

A full discussion of the maladaptive perfectionism versus adaptive perfectionism issue is beyond the scope of this introductory chapter. Interested readers are referred to other sources that have addressed this issue, including several chapters in this book (see chapters 2, 3, 5, 12, and 14).

As noted earlier, some researchers have suggested that the various perfectionism dimensions differ in their link with adjustment difficulties: Some components are described as neurotic, or maladaptive, and other components are described as normal, or adaptive (Hamachek, 1978). Regarding trait measures, dimensions of perfectionism such as self-oriented perfectionism and high personal standards have been described as adaptive, whereas dimensions such as socially prescribed perfectionism and excessive concern over mistakes have been described as maladaptive. This distinction stems back to observations that a key distinction can be made between normal and neurotic perfectionists or satisfied and dissatisfied perfectionists (Hamachek, 1978; Slaney et al., 1995; Terry-Short et al., 1995).

The distinction between adaptive and maladaptive perfectionism has been accepted without criticism by some researchers, who have incorporated this distinction into their empirical work. We believe that this issue is far from resolved, however, because a number of related issues have not been evaluated. Three issues are outlined below.

Adaptive perfectionism or conscientiousness? In many respects, adaptive forms of perfectionism appear to reflect the broad personality trait of conscientiousness. Indeed, past research has confirmed that self-oriented perfectionism is associated with conscientiousness and its various facets, including competence, order, dutifulness, achievement striving, self-discipline, and deliberation (Hill, McIntire, & Bacharach, 1997).

To what degree does adaptive perfectionism overlap with conscientiousness? Comparative research on adaptive perfectionism versus conscientiousness is lacking at present, and it is clearly needed. Our view is that self-oriented perfectionism is a more extreme form of striving that is related to but goes well beyond conscientiousness. Items that assess self-oriented forms of perfectionism need to be evaluated to determine whether they enable researchers to make the subtle but important distinction between people with high levels of conscientiousness and people who take it a step further and demand absolute perfection from the self.

One indication that adaptive perfectionism is linked closely with conscientiousness is provided by research on organization, as assessed by the Frost et al. (1990) MPS. Frost et al. recommended that scores on the Organization subscale not be included as part of a total score because the subscale had low correlations with the other perfectionism dimensions assessed by their MPS. The issue of whether organization should be considered part of the perfectionism construct remains to be resolved and is beyond the scope of our discussion. For our purposes, however, it should be noted that a tendency to be organized is a key aspect of the conscientiousness construct (see Hogan & Ones, 1997). Also, when clusters of adaptive versus maladaptive perfectionists have been identified, a high level of organization is a definitive feature of the adaptive perfectionist group (see Parker, 1997; Rice & Mirzadeh, 2000). This finding raises concerns that adaptive perfectionism in some people may actually reflect conscientiousness and an achievement-oriented work style rather than perfectionism per se.

Continuity or discontinuity? Research on people with adaptive versus maladaptive perfectionism has used cluster analyses to identify people who fit in the two groups (Parker, 1997; Rice & Mirzadeh, 2000). Thus, it is assumed that different types of perfectionists differ qualitatively in their characteristics; that is, categories of perfectionists exist, and discontinuities can be identified.

The alternative to this approach is the view that the essential differences in perfectionism are primarily dimensional in nature: People differ in *degrees* of perfectionism, rather than in *kinds* of perfectionism. At present, it has not been determined whether continuities or discontinuities exist because a full taxometric investigation of this issue has yet to be conducted in the perfectionism field. Similar tests in the depression field consistently favor a dimensional approach over a categorical approach (see Flett, Vredenburg, & Krames, 1997; Ruscio & Ruscio, 2000). Similarly, research on the nature of attachment styles has shown that attachment styles should be regarded as dimensions, rather than categories (Fraley & Waller, 1998).

Until this issue is resolved in the perfectionism field, some cautions should be kept in mind. First, when researchers compare groups of people with adaptive versus maladaptive perfectionism on certain variables, it is important to first compare total levels of perfectionism in the groups, especially on attributes that both groups share, such as high personal standards. If the tests of perfectionistic groups show that one group has higher levels of perfectionism on common attributes, as has been found in at least two samples (see Parker, 1997; Rice & Mirzadeh, 2000; Sample 1), then it cannot be ruled out that the differences are quantitative rather than qualitative in nature and reflect absolute differences in levels of perfectionism. If so, it is conceivable that maladaptive perfectionism is a more extreme form of perfectionism and that high levels of perfectionism are associated with vulnerability to adjustment problems.

Adaptive perfectionism and life stress. To us, the most important question involving adaptive perfectionism is: What happens to people with adaptive perfectionism when they inevitably encounter life problems? Our work on a diathesis–stress approach has been based on the notion that certain dimensions of perfectionism result in depression when perfectionistic people encounter life difficulties that highlight the fact that things are not perfect (see Hewitt and Flett, chapter 11, this volume). This view is in keeping with research (Abramson, Alloy, & Metalsky, 1990) on attributional style that posits that how a person explains negative events becomes relevant when life stressors are experienced.

Although research outcomes have not always supported the diathesis–stress model of perfectionism and depression, enough findings in the literature show that a supposedly adaptive dimension of perfectionism (i.e., self-oriented perfectionism) can be linked with dysphoria when combined with the experience of negative life events (Flett, Hewitt, Blankstein, & Mosher, 1995; Hewitt & Flett, 1993; Hewitt, Flett, & Ediger, 1996; Joiner & Schmidt, 1995). Adaptive aspects of perfectionism also are associated with symptoms of anxiety when people experience ego-involving situations that threaten the self (Flett, Hewitt, Endler, & Tassone, 1994–1995). The findings underscore the need for a comprehensive evaluation of environmental factors and life circumstances when seeking to determine the adaptiveness or maladaptiveness of perfectionism.

Treatment Considerations

Except for the informative studies conducted by Blatt and Zuroff (chapter 16, this volume) and their colleagues, little systematic research on the role of perfectionism in treatment has taken place. Their findings are based on further analyses of the data from the National Institute of Mental Health's Treatment of Depression Collaborative Research Program (for a description, see Elkin, 1994). They have obtained an impressive series of findings indicating that perfectionism (as assessed by the Dysfunctional Attitudes Scale [DAS]; Weissman & Beck, 1978) is associated with poor treatment response and problems with establishing a good working alliance between the therapist and client. The findings hold across several different types of treatment, including cognitive–behavioral therapy, interpersonal therapy, and pharmacotherapy.

This segment of our introductory chapter expands on this theme by summarizing the results of several other investigations showing that perfectionistic tendencies are difficult to treat and that perfectionism is a personality style associated with a negative treatment outcome. Our description examines perfectionism in the context of drug treatments, cognitive therapy, and emotion-oriented therapy.

Pharmacological Therapy

Reda, Carpiniello, Secchiaroli, and Blanco (1985) reported the outcomes experienced by 60 depressed patients who received antidepressant medication and were examined over four years. The patients were administered the DAS (Weissman & Beck, 1978) when first admitted to the hospital and when they were released. Also, a subset of half of the patients was reassessed one year after discharge. Reda et al. found that although many dysfunctional attitudes were significantly reduced as depression remitted, certain dysfunctional attitudes proved to be resistant to change, including perfectionistic beliefs reflecting the theme that mistakes should never be made. Moreover, those beliefs were still quite evident among the subset of patients who were reassessed one year after discharge. Self-presentational concerns also persisted and were represented by dysfunctional attitudes such as "It is shameful to display weaknesses."

Scott and associates investigated the role of perfectionistic attitudes in bipolar depression and hypomanic states and confirmed that perfectionistic attitudes are linked with bipolar depression (Scott, 2001; Scott, Stanton, Garland, & Ferrier, 2000). Their findings are consistent with previous evidence indicating that trait aspects of perfectionism are associated with chronic symptoms of bipolar depression (Hewitt, Flett, Norton, & Flynn, 1998). In addition, however, Scott (2001) reported that perfectionism was associated with several other variables that predicted nonadherence to medication and poor treatment outcome. Thus, contrary to the general view that perfectionists are conscientious, Scott's data suggest that perfectionism may undermine adherence to certain forms of treatment. Perhaps the treatment regime conflicts with the perfectionists' acknowledged need for personal control (Flett, Hewitt, Blankstein, & Mosher, 1995) or the regime, on a daily basis, confronts the person with his or her own perceived shortcomings and inability to cope effectively (see Hewitt et al., 2001).

Cognitive–Behavioral Therapy

Tallis (1996) noted that the three patients with OCD who displayed compulsive washing despite the absence of phobic and illness anxiety all had a poor response to cognitive therapy. Better outcomes resulted from a behavioral approach that focused on exposure and response prevention, but the obtained improvements were marginal at best; in addition, all three patients required extensive follow-up treatment on an inpatient or outpatient basis.

The negative outcomes described in the case studies reported by Tallis (1996) contrast with the positive outcome reported by Freeston (2001). Freeston provided a detailed analysis of the recovery process and cognitive–behavioral treatment of a 14-year-old boy from Quebec who had OCD. He had various cleanliness rituals in which the underlying goal was perfectionism, and that goal had to be achieved with certainty; thus, brushing his teeth would take 20 minutes, showering would take 90 minutes, and his bedtime routine would take 60 to 90 minutes. The client experienced related academic and interpersonal problems stemming from his belief that his behavior should be perfect and that if negative outcomes occurred, he was responsible. Cognitive–behavioral treatment eventually led to reductions in target behaviors (e.g., excessive tooth brushing), and the client's level of obsessive–compulsive symptoms decreased from the severe to the moderate range. Freeston (2001) concluded that the use of a behavioral intervention focused on a clear target (i.e., reduced tooth brushing) facilitated improvement.

Ferguson and Rodway (1994) also provided evidence indicating that cognitive–behavioral treatments may be effective in treating perfectionism and associated problems. Cognitive activities included cognitive restructuring, which focused on coping statements, and bibliotherapy. Behavioral treatments included role playing and relaxation exercises. Ferguson and Rodway provided separate data and case summaries for each of their nine clients, seven of whom showed reductions in levels of perfectionism (as assessed by the Burns Perfectionism Scale; Burns, 1980) following the intervention. The study is difficult to interpret, however, because it did not include a no-treatment control group. Another concern in interpreting this study is that close inspection of the results reveals that three of the nine participants began the study with relatively low levels of perfectionism.

Rector, Zuroff, and Segal (1999) examined how cognitive therapy combined with individual-difference factors to predict treatment response among depressed patients. Certain findings in the research were quite consistent with the general themes emerging from Blatt and Zuroff's research program. That is, dysfunctional attitudes reflecting perfectionism had a negative impact on the ability to form an early therapeutic alliance.

Mixed evidence of the efficacy of cognitive restructuring emerged from a recent study by DiBartolo, Frost, Dixon, and Almodovar (2001). The purpose of the study was to determine whether a cognitive intervention could lead to improvements in cognition and negative affect when participants were faced with the task of giving a speech. The investigators identified students who were high or low in concern over mistakes as assessed by Frost and colleagues' (1990) MPS. Participants were then exposed to a cognitive-restructuring condition or a distraction condition. The cognitive intervention lasted for approximately 8 minutes and included three components:

1. addressing probability overestimation (i.e., estimating the likelihood that feared expectations would actually occur and how often the feared expectation actually happened in the past)
2. decatastrophizing the feared outcome (i.e., comparing the horribleness of the feared outcome to serious life events, such as death of a loved one, failing a course)
3. identifying a coping thought or statement that could be used to alleviate anxiety during the speech task. The distraction task involved identifying specific letters in a written passage.

DiBartolo et al. (2001) found that students scoring high in Concern Over Mistakes benefited more from the cognitive intervention than did students scoring low in Concern Over Mistakes, but the results varied, depending on the measure in question. Cognitive restructuring was successful in reducing probability estimates that the most feared outcomes would actually occur, and levels of self-reported anxiety became significantly lower as well. Cognitive restructuring, however, did not result in reductions on a global measure of negative affect (i.e., the Positive and Negative Affect Schedule; Watson, Clark, & Tellegen, 1988), nor did it reduce negative thoughts about the speech. The investigators suggested that improvements were not found on all outcome measures because the intervention may have been too specific and too brief—it lasted for only 8 minutes.

The results of a follow-up assessment between 1 and 2 weeks after the laboratory component of the experiment clearly illustrated the negative aspects of perfectionism (DiBartolo et al., 2001). Group comparisons of participants high or low in concern over mistakes showed that the participants with high concern over mistakes, regardless of experimental condition, reported that they were still bothered by continuing thoughts about the speech and their performance and did not enjoy giving the speech. They also rated themselves more negatively on their ability to communicate.

Emotion-Focused Therapy

Although emotion-focused therapy has not been used extensively as a form of treatment for perfectionists, a recent case study (Greenberg & Bolger, 2001) suggests that emotion-focused therapy may be quite effective for alleviating some of the emotional pain that distressed perfectionists experience. Greenberg and Bolger reported a case study of a 40-year-old woman who was raised by alcoholic parents who were also physically abusive. It was acknowledged that this client had a strong need for maternal approval and a high need for control. This client identified perfectionism as a central problem:

Client: And so I get my standards from other people's behavior, and in turn I expect that they judge me. I always wanted to be viewed as having things in order. But it would be good for me to get beyond that. I would really like to be able to know what I really feel is important and not to be worried about what other people think. And to get rid of all the negative conversations I have with myself.

Therapist: To give yourself permission to be who you are and not what other people think.

Client (weeping): Probably to give myself permission to make mistakes.

Therapist: What's there right now?

Client: I feel sad because I don't know where I have learned this message so much that I can't make mistakes, that I have to be perfect.

Therapist: This is very deep sadness.

Client: Yes, for myself.

Therapist: How does this feel to be sad for yourself?

Client: It feels okay, but I wish I could go beyond it and say it's alright to feel sad, you don't have to be perfect all the time. It's okay to make mistakes. It doesn't mean that you have lost control. (Greenberg & Bolger, 2001, p. 206)

Greenberg and Bolger outlined a three-step treatment process to address psychological pain. The first goal of emotion-oriented therapy is to focus on developing a heightened sense of emotional awareness. The second goal is to learn how to soothe and comfort the self; presumably, doing so helps combat the tendency of perfectionists to be highly self-critical and addresses the low self-acceptance of certain perfectionists. The third and final goal in alleviating the emotional pain of perfectionists—and others in distress—is to substitute adaptive emotions for distressing emotions.

Psychodynamic–Interpersonal Treatment

Blatt (1992), in an analysis of data from the Menninger Psychotherapy Research Project, completed one of the first major studies to address treatment of perfectionistic behavior. In general, Blatt found that people with strong perfectionistic tendencies responded better to long-term, intensive, psychodynamically oriented treatments than to either short-term treatments (Blatt & Ford, 1994) or other forms of therapy (see Blatt and Zuroff, chapter 16, this volume). According to Blatt, Quinlan, Pilkonis, and Shea (1995), therapists are attempting to change personality structure when dealing with perfectionism issues, and that goal necessitates a longer time frame and more exhaustive treatment protocols than can be accomplished in short-term therapy.

Some work has been reported on short-term, psychodynamically based group psychotherapy for perfectionists, however. Fredtoft, Poulsen, Bauer, and Malm (1996) used an object-relations perspective to focus on issues pertaining to separation from significant others in treating both dependency-related issues and perfectionism. They suggested that a short-term, focused, psychodynamic orientation can yield changes in perfectionistic behavior.

The treatment approach developed by the second author and described in Hewitt et al. (2001) takes a psychodynamic, interpersonal approach in both individual and group formats in treating perfectionism. Essentially, the focus is not on perfectionistic behavior (i.e., excessive standards, punitive self-evaluation, and so forth) per se, but rather on the interpersonal precursors (e.g., the need for approval or respect or forestalling abandonment) that drive the perfectionistic behavior and the process-related variables that create difficulties in the therapeutic alliance (Flynn, 2001). Preliminary findings suggest that the approach decreases perfectionistic behavior and the attendant distress symptoms as rated by patients, significant others, and therapists; it may hold some promise in alleviating some of the difficulties experienced by perfectionists.

Difficulties in Treating Perfectionists

It has already been suggested by authors such as Blatt and Zuroff that perfectionism is associated with a relatively poor working alliance between the perfectionist and the therapist. Another pernicious problem associated with treating perfectionists is that the perfectionists themselves often cling to their standards because of the perceived benefits and rewards associated with striving toward perfectionistic goals. Those advantages are identified by perfectionists despite the fact that clear disadvantages can also be recognized. Beck, Rush, Shaw, and Emery (1979) discussed the pros and cons of perfectionism in reporting the case of a woman who held the basic assumption that she had to be perfect in order to be happy. The patient listed four advantages associated with giving up this belief:

1. Attempting to do new things that were previously avoided
2. Being able to be more open and expressive with others so that new friendships could develop
3. Being less anxious about making mistakes or less depressed because a mistake was made
4. Being able to accept the reality that she is not a perfect person.

This person, however, identified the following three disadvantages of giving up this belief:

> a. I've been able to do exceptionally well in school and on my job.
> b. What I do, I do well.
> c. Because I avoid a lot of things, I've avoided a lot of trouble and problems. (Beck et al., 1979, p. 263)

Beck et al. indicated that the next treatment step was for the therapist to help the patient examine the perceived disadvantages of giving up the belief that happiness depends on being perfect. They noted that having a person list the advantages and disadvantages associated with a dysfunctional belief is a surprisingly effective way of bringing about long-term changes in how problems are handled. Clearly, an important treatment goal for troubled perfectionists is to have them come to the realization that many negative consequences can be associated with perfectionism and excessively high standards may need to be lowered.

Sorotzkin (1998) identified two other significant problems in the context of his analysis of the complex problems associated with treating perfectionism in religious adolescents. First, Sorotzkin noted that the all-or-none thinking of perfectionists can prove to be a problem in their evaluations of treatment progress. Perfectionists must learn to cherish small improvements and view treatment as a gradual process that unfolds over time. Sorotzkin observed,

> This is more difficult than it sounds since it is very painful for someone with a poor self-image to give up the dream of glory inherent in perfection for the, as yet never experienced, joy of gradual emotion growth. (p. 91)

Another significant problem identified by Sorotzkin (1998) involves the tendency for perfectionists to strive for perfectionistic goals as part of the treatment process. Specifically, he observed that "as they become more knowledgeable about psychological issues, they may also become perfectionistic in the process of therapy, by trying to become the perfect emotional specimen (i.e., by not having any anxieties, conflicts, or fears)" (p. 92). Indeed, we have suggested elsewhere that perfectionists may have unrealistic coping goals and standards that may undermine their recovery progress (Hewitt & Flett, 1996). Some support for this possibility is provided by a recent case study of a patient who tried to assume the identity of the perfect patient (see Hirsch & Hayward, 1998). In this instance, the authors noted that the very problem that led this person to require treatment also was useful in his recovery because he was quite conscientious; the important caveat here, however, is that the key to this person's recovery was that he learned to be less of a perfectionist.

Finally, one of the major difficulties in treatment of perfectionistic people involves the effect of the patient's perfectionistic behavior on the therapist. One of the most dramatic experiences for therapists in the group-treatment study for perfectionism discussed earlier (Flynn, 2001; Hewitt et al., 2001) was the level of hostility of the patients. This finding is consistent both with the clinical experience of the second author and with numerous findings indicating that perfectionists tend to fall in the hostile–dominant quadrant of the interpersonal circumplex (e.g., Flynn, Hewitt, Broughton, & Flett, 1998; Hill, Zrull, & Turlington, 1997). Socially prescribed perfectionism also has been linked with borderline personality disorder (Hewitt, Flett, & Turnbull, 1994) and the attendant feelings of rage and demandingness that sometimes are expressed by people with this diagnosis (Benjamin, 1996). The tendency for certain perfectionists to be hostile and extrapunitive underscores the clear need for well-trained therapists and for an emphasis on the process of psychotherapy.

Furthermore, other important transference-related characteristics of perfectionistic people can infuse the therapeutic situation and both color and potentially impede the progress of therapy unless handled appropriately. Expectations of the therapist being perfect, attempting to be the perfect patient, perceived excessive demands of the therapist, and comparing one's progress with other patients of the therapist are examples of issues pertaining to perfectionism that have arisen in the second author's treatment of perfectionists. Moreover, the level of distress and the depth of psychopathology can place significant demands on the therapeutic relationship and the therapist.

Future Directions for Treatment Research

One obvious limitation of existing research on perfectionism in the treatment context is that perfectionism has not been studied as a multidimensional construct; instead, most research has treated perfectionism as a monolithic entity. An important goal for future researchers is to devise methodologically sound studies that compare the various dimensions of the perfectionism construct in terms of their relative ability to predict treatment outcomes.

Another important feature of treatment research is that perfectionism should be an explicit focus of the intervention: Pretest and posttest measures of perfectionism should be included to evaluate treatment progress. Trait measures, such as the MPS instruments (Frost et al., 1990; Hewitt & Flett, 1991), should be used, but perfectionism measures that are more amenable to state changes in cognition and affect, such as the Perfectionism Cognitions Inventory (see Flett et al., 1998), should also be considered.

Our own research in this area is focusing extensively on the interpersonal aspects of perfectionism and emphasizes perfectionistic self-presentation. As stated, perfectionistic self-presentation has some important implications at the interpersonal level. For instance, people with high levels of perfectionistic self-presentation are less willing to seek help, in part because the act of seeking help can be construed as an open admission of failure to important others (Nadler, 1983); that admission poses a great threat to a person's self-esteem. Also, high levels of perfectionistic self-presentation in the context of therapy may undermine treatment because the client may be unwilling to reveal intimate aspects of his or her self; that reluctance contributes to the experience of distress and undermines the treatment process (Habke, Hewitt, & Flett, 2001; Hewitt et al., 2001).

In this regard, Sorotzkin (1998) analyzed the motives associated with perfectionistic self-presentation in the therapeutic context. He suggested that, at least in the initial stages of treatment, certain perfectionists

> have little interest in emotional growth or integration of affect since they had long ago been compelled to abandon natural emotional re-

sponsiveness in favor of desirable behaviors. They are really striving to look perfect more than to be perfect since they "know" how bad they really are. But, consistent with their early life experience, how they look to others is what really counts. (p. 91)

Conclusion

The purpose of this chapter was to provide an overview of some of the theoretical, definitional, and treatment issues that we believe are central to an understanding of perfectionism. The chapters that follow contain many rich theoretical insights that should pave the way for a great deal of new research in the years to come.

Clearly, it is an exciting time to be studying this personality style, and we hope that this book will serve as a useful guide for subsequent research and interventions designed to help perfectionists in need of assistance.

References

Abramson, L. Y., Alloy, L. B., & Metalsky, G. I. (1990). The hopelessness theory of depression: Current status and future directions. In N. L. Stein & B. Levanthal (Eds.), *Psychological and biological approaches to emotion* (pp. 333–358). Hillsdale, NJ: Erlbaum.

Beck, A. T., Rush, A. J., Shaw, B. F., & Emery, G. (1979). *Cognitive therapy of depression.* New York: Guilford.

Benjamin, L. (1996). *Interpersonal diagnosis and treatment of personality disorders.* New York: Guilford.

Blatt, S. J. (1992). The differential effect of psychotherapy and psychoanalysis on anaclitic and introjective patients: The Menninger Psychotherapy Research Project revisited. *Journal of the American Psychoanalytic Association, 40,* 691–724.

Blatt, S. J. (1995). The destructiveness of perfectionism: Implications for the treatment of depression. *American Psychologist, 50,* 1003–1020.

Blatt, S. J., & Ford, R. (1994). *Therapeutic change: An object relations perspective.* New York: Plenum.

Blatt, S. J., Quinlan, D. M., Pilkonis, P. A., & Shea, M. T. (1995). Impact of perfectionism and need for approval on the brief treatment of depression: The National Institute of Mental Health Treatment of Depression Collaborative Research Program revisited. *Journal of Consulting and Clinical Psychology, 63,* 125–132.

Burns, D. (1980, November). The perfectionist's script for self-defeat. *Psychology Today,* 34–51.

Burns, D., & Beck, A. T. (1978). Cognitive behavior modification of mood disorders. In J. P. Foreyt & D. P. Rathjen (Eds.), *Cognitive behavior therapy: Research and application* (pp. 109–139). New York: Plenum.

Davis, C. (1997). Normal and neurotic perfectionism in eating disorders: An interactive model. *International Journal of Eating Disorders, 22,* 421–426.

DiBartolo, P. M., Frost, R. O., Dixon, A., & Almodovar, S. (2001). Can cognitive restructuring reduce the disruption associated with perfectionistic concerns? *Behavior Therapy, 32,* 167–184.

Elkin, I. (1994). The NIMH Treatment of Depression Collaborative Research Program: Where we began and where we are. In A. E. Bergin & S. L. Garfield (Eds.), *Handbook of psychotherapy and behavior change* (4th ed., pp. 114–139). New York: Wiley.

Ellis, A. (1962). *Reason and emotion in psychotherapy.* New York: Lyle Stuart.

Eysenck, H. J., & Eysenck, S. B. G. (1991). *Manual for the Eysenck Personality Scales.* London: Hodder & Stoughton.

Ferguson, K. L., & Rodway, M. R. (1994). Cognitive behavioral treatment of perfectionism: Initial validation studies. *Research on Social Work Practice, 4,* 283–308.

Flanagan, C. M. (1993). Treating neurotic problems that do not respond to psychodynamic therapies. *Hospital and Community Psychiatry, 44,* 824–826.

Flett, G. L., & Hewitt, P. L. (in press). Personality factors and substance abuse in relationship violence and child abuse: A review and theoretical analysis. In C. Wekerle & A. M. Wall (Eds.), *The violence and addiction equation: Theoretical and clinical issues in substance abuse and relationship violence.* Philadelphia: Brunner/Mazel.

Flett, G. L., Hewitt, P. L., Berk, L., & Besser, A. (2001, July). *Perfectionism cognitions and concern over parenting mistakes in postpartum depression.* In P. L. Hewitt (Chair), *Perfectionism and depression.* Symposium conducted at the World Congress of Behavioral and Cognitive Therapies, Vancouver, British Columbia, Canada.

Flett, G. L., Hewitt, P. L., Blankstein, K. R., & Gray, L. (1998). Psychological distress and the frequency of perfectionistic thinking. *Journal of Personality and Social Psychology, 75,* 1363–1381.

Flett, G. L., Hewitt, P. L., Blankstein, K. R., & Mosher, S. W. (1995). Perfectionism, life events, and depression: A test of a diathesis-stress model. *Current Psychology, 14,* 112–137.

Flett, G. L., Hewitt, P. L., Endler, N. S., & Tassone, C. (1994–1995). Perfectionism and components of state and trait anxiety. *Current Psychology, 13,* 326–350.

Flett, G. L., Vredenburg, K., & Krames, L. (1997). The continuity of depression in clinical and nonclinical samples. *Psychological Bulletin, 121,* 395–416.

Flynn, C. A. (2001). *The impact of protective perfectionistic self-presentation on group psychotherapy process and outcome.* Unpublished dissertation, University of British Columbia, Vancouver.

Flynn, C. A., Hewitt, P. L., Broughton, R., & Flett, G. L. (1998, August). *Mapping perfectionism dimensions onto the interpersonal circumplex.* Poster presented at the annual meeting of the American Psychological Association, San Francisco.

Fraley, R. C., & Waller, N. G. (1998). Adult attachment patterns: A test of the typological model. In J. A. Simpson & W. S. Rholes (Eds.), *Attachment theory and close relationships* (pp. 77–114). New York: Guilford.

Fredtoft, T., Poulsen, S., Bauer, M., & Malm, M. (1996). Dependency and perfectionism: Short term dynamic group psychotherapy for university students. *Psychodynamic Counselling, 24,* 476–497.

Freeston, M. H. (2001). Cognitive–behavioral treatment of a 14-year-old teenager with obsessive–compulsive disorder. *Behavioural and Cognitive Psychotherapy, 29,* 71–84.

Frost, R. O., Marten, P., Lahart, C., & Rosenblate, R. (1990). The dimensions of perfectionism. *Cognitive Therapy and Research, 14,* 449–468.

Frost, R. O., Turcotte, T. A., Heimberg, R. G., Mattia, J. I., Holt, C. S., & Hope, D. A. (1995). Reactions to mistakes among subjects high and low in perfectionistic concern over mistakes. *Cognitive Therapy and Research, 19,* 195–206.

Garner, D. M., Olmstead, M. P., & Polivy, J. (1983). Development and validation of a multidimensional eating disorder inventory for anorexia nervosa and bulimia. *International Journal of Eating Disorders, 2,* 15–34.

Greenberg, L. S., & Bolger, E. (2001). An emotion-focused approach to the overregulation of emotion and emotional pain. *Journal of Clinical Psychology, 57,* 197–211.

Habke, A. M., Hewitt, P. L., & Flett, G. L. (1999). Perfectionism and sexual satisfaction in intimate relationships. *Journal of Psychopathology and Behavioral Assessment, 21,* 307–322.

Habke, A. M., Hewitt, P. L., & Flett, G. L. (2001). *Perfectionistic self-presentation and implications for psychotherapy: Cognitive appraisals, affect, and arousal.* Unpublished manuscript.

Hamachek, D. E. (1978). Psychodynamics of normal and neurotic perfectionism. *Psychology, 15,* 27–33.

Hankin, B. L., Roberts, J., & Gotlib, I. H. (1997). Elevated self-standards and emotional distress during adolescence: Emotional specificity and gender differences. *Cognitive Therapy and Research, 21,* 663–679.

Hewitt, P. L., & Flett, G. L. (1989). The Multidimensional Perfectionism Scale: Development and validation [Abstract]. *Canadian Psychology, 30,* 339.

Hewitt, P. L., & Flett, G. L. (1990). Perfectionism and depression: A multidimensional analysis. *Journal of Social Behavior and Personality, 5,* 423–438.

Hewitt, P. L., & Flett, G. L. (1991). Perfectionism in the self and social contexts: Conceptualization, assessment, and association with psychopathology. *Journal of Personality and Social Psychology, 60,* 456–470.

Hewitt, P. L., & Flett, G. L. (1993). Dimensions of perfectionism, daily stress, and depression: A test of the specific vulnerability issue. *Journal of Abnormal Psychology, 102,* 58–65.

Hewitt, P. L., & Flett, G. L. (1996). Personality traits and the coping process. In M. Zeidner & N. S. Endler (Eds.), *Handbook of coping* (pp. 410–433). London: Wiley.

Hewitt, P. L., Flett, G. L., & Ediger, E. (1995). Perfectionism traits and perfectionistic self-presentation in eating disorder attitudes, characteristics, and symptoms. *International Journal of Eating Disorders, 18,* 317–326.

Hewitt, P. L., Flett, G. L., & Ediger, E. (1996). Perfectionism and depression: Longitudinal assessment of a specific vulnerability hypothesis. *Journal of Abnormal Psychology, 105,* 276–280.

Hewitt, P. L., Flett, G. L., Norton, G. R., & Flynn, C. A. (1998). Dimensions of perfectionism and chronic symptoms of unipolar and bipolar depression. *Canadian Journal of Behavioural Science, 30,* 234–242.

Hewitt, P. L., Flett, G. L., Sherry, S. B., Habke, A. M., Parkin, M., Lam, R. W., McMurtry, B., Ediger, E., Fairlie, P., & Stein, M. (2001). *The interpersonal expression of perfection: Perfectionistic self-presentation and psychological distress.* Manuscript submitted for publication.

Hewitt, P. L., Flett, G. L., & Turnbull, W. (1994). Borderline personality disorder: An investigation with the Multidimensional Perfectionism Scale. *European Journal of Psychological Assessment, 10,* 28–33.

Hewitt, P. L., Flett, G. L., & Weber, C. (1994). Perfectionism, hopelessness, and suicide ideation. *Cognitive Therapy and Research, 18,* 439–460.

Hewitt, P. L., Flynn, C., Mikail, S. F., & Flett, G. L. (2000). Treatment of vulnerability factors in depression: Perfectionism dimensions [Abstract]. *Canadian Psychology, 41,* 61.

Hewitt, P. L., Flynn, C. A., Mikail, S. F., & Flett, G. L. (2001). *Evaluation of a psychodynamic/interpersonal approach to the treatment of perfectionism.* Unpublished manuscript.

Higgins, E. T. (1987). Self-discrepancy: A theory relating self and affect. *Psychological Review, 94,* 319–340.

Hill, R. W., McIntire, K., & Bacharach, V. R. (1997). Perfectionism and the big five factors. *Journal of Social Behavior and Personality, 12,* 257–270.

Hill, R. W., Zrull, M. C., & Turlington, S. (1997). Perfectionism and interpersonal problems. *Journal of Personality Assessment, 69,* 81–103.

Hirsch, C. R., & Hayward, P. (1998). The perfect patient: Cognitive-behavioural therapy for perfectionism. *Behavioural and Cognitive Psychotherapy, 26,* 359–364.

Hogan, J., & Ones, D. S. (1997). Conscientiousness and integrity at work. In R. Hogan, J. Johnson, & S. Briggs (Eds.), *Handbook of personality psychology* (pp. 849–870). New York: Academic Press.

Hughes, J. C. (1993). Wittgenstein's dysphoria. *Integrative Psychiatry, 9,* 86–91.

Joiner, T. E., Jr., & Schmidt, N. B. (1995). Dimensions of perfectionism, life stress, and depressed and anxious symptoms: Prospective support for diathesis-stress but not specific vulnerability among male undergraduates. *Journal of Social and Clinical Psychology, 14,* 165–183.

Jones, R. G. (1969). A factorial measure of Ellis' irrational beliefs system, with personality and maladjustment correlates. *Dissertation Abstracts, 29,* 4379–B (UMI No. 69-6443).

Krane, V., Greenleaf, C. A., & Snow, J. (1997). Reaching for gold and the price of glory: A motivational case study of an elite gymnast. *Journal of Sport and Exercise Psychology, 19,* 53–71.

Lombardi, D. N., Florentino, M. C., & Lombardi, A. J. (1998). Perfectionism and abnormal behavior. *Individual Psychology, 54,* 61–71.

Maltsberger, J. T. (1998). Robert Salter: Attempted suicide by jumping from a high bridge. *Suicide and Life-Threatening Behavior, 28,* 226–228.

Mitchelson, J., & Burns, L. R. (1998). Career mothers and perfectionism: Stress at work and at home. *Personality and Individual Differences, 25,* 477–485.

Mitzman, S. F., Slade, P. D., & Dewey, M. E. (1994). Preliminary development of a questionnaire designed to measure neurotic perfectionism in the eating disorders. *Journal of Clinical Psychology, 50,* 516–522.

Mor, S., Day, H. I., Flett, G. L., & Hewitt, P. L. (1995). Perfectionism, control, and components of performance anxiety in professional performers. *Cognitive Therapy and Research, 19,* 207–225.

Nadler, A. (1983). Personal characteristics and help-seeking. In B. M. Depaulo, A. Nadler, & J. D. Fisher (Eds.), *New directions in help-seeking: Vol. 2 Help-seeking* (pp. 303–340). San Diego, CA: Academic Press.

Parker, W. D. (1997). An empirical typology of perfectionism in academically talented children. *American Educational Research Journal, 34,* 545–562.

Plath, S. (1982). *The journal of Sylvia Plath.* New York: Dial Press.

Preusser, K. J., Rice, K. G., & Ashby, J. S. (1994). The role of self-esteem in mediating the perfectionism–depression connection. *Journal of College Student Development, 35,* 88–93.

Randolph, J. J., & Dykman, B. M. (1998). Perceptions of parenting and depression-proneness in the offspring: Dysfunctional attitudes as a mediating mechanism. *Cognitive Therapy and Research, 22,* 377–400.

Rector, N. A., Zuroff, D. C., & Segal, Z. V. (1999). Cognitive change and the therapeutic alliance: The role of technical and nontechnical factors in cognitive therapy. *Psychotherapy, 36,* 320–328.

Reda, M. A., Carpiniello, B., Secchiaroli, L., & Blanco, S. (1985). Thinking, depression, and antidepressants: Modified and unmodified depressive beliefs during treatment with amitriptyline. *Cognitive Therapy and Research, 9,* 135–143.

Reilly, C. E. (1998). Cognitive therapy for the suicidal patient: A case study. *Perspectives in Psychiatric Care, 34,* 26–36.

Rheaume, J., Freeston, M. H., & Ladouceur, R. (1995, July). *Functional and dysfunctional perfectionism: Construct validity of a new instrument.* Paper presented at the World Congress of Behavioral and Cognitive Therapy, Copenhagen, Denmark.

Rheaume, J., Freeston, M. H., Ladouceur, R., Bouchard, C., Gallant, L., Talbot, F., & Vallieres, A. (2000). Functional and dysfunctional perfectionists: Are they different on compulsive-like behaviors? *Behaviour Research and Therapy, 38,* 119–128.

Rhees, R. (1981). *Ludwig Wittgenstein: The duty of genius.* London: Cape.

Rice, K. G., Ashby, J. S., & Slaney, R. B. (1998). Self-esteem as a mediator between perfectionism and depression: A structural equations analysis. *Journal of Counseling Psychology, 45,* 304–314.

Rice, K. G., & Mirzadeh, S. A. (2000). Perfectionism, attachment, and adjustment. *Journal of Counseling Psychology, 47,* 238–250.

Ruscio, J., & Ruscio, A. M. (2000). Informing the continuity controversy: A taxometric analysis of depression. *Journal of Abnormal Psychology, 109,* 473–487.

Saboonchi, F., & Lundh, L.-G. (1999). State perfectionism and its relation to trait perfectionism, type of situation, priming, and being observed. *Scandinavian Journal of Behaviour Therapy, 28,* 154–166.

Scott, J. (2001, July). *Cognitive vulnerability in clients with bipolar disorders: Implications for life events research and for treatment interventions.* Paper presented at the World Congress of Cognitive and Behavior Therapies, Vancouver, British Columbia, Canada.

Scott, J., Stanton, B., Garland, A., & Ferrier, I. N. (2000). Cognitive vulnerability in patients with bipolar disorder. *Psychological Medicine, 30,* 467–472.

Shulman, E. (1998). Vulnerability factors in Sylvia Plath's suicide. *Death Studies, 22,* 597–613.

Slade, P. D., & Owens, R. G. (1998). A dual process model of perfectionism based on reinforcement theory. *Behavior Modification, 22,* 372–390.

Slaney, R. B., Ashby, J. S., & Trippi, J. (1995). Perfectionism: Its measurement and career relevance. *Journal of Career Assessment, 3,* 279–297.

Slaney, R. B., Rice, K. G., Mobley, M., Trippi, J., & Ashby, J. S. (2001). The Almost Perfect Scale–Revised. *Measurement and Evaluation in Counseling and Development, 34*, 130–145.

Sorotzkin, B. (1998). Understanding and treating perfectionism in religious adolescents. *Psychotherapy, 35*, 87–95.

Tallis, F. (1996). Compulsive washing in the absence of phobic and illness anxiety. *Behaviour Research and Therapy, 34*, 361–362.

Terry-Short, L. A., Owens, R. G., Slade, P. D., & Dewey, M. E. (1995). Positive and negative perfectionism. *Personality and Individual Differences, 18*, 663–668.

Van Pelt, T. (1997). Symptomatic perfectionism: Ideal ego and ego ideal in the *Journals of Sylvia Plath. Literature and Psychology, 43*, 47–64.

Wallace, S. T., & Alden, L. E. (1991). A comparison of social standards and perceived ability in anxious and nonanxious men. *Cognitive Therapy and Research, 15*, 237–254.

Watson, D., Clark, L. A., & Tellegen, A. (1988). Development and validation of brief measures of Positive and Negative Affect: The PANAS scales. *Journal of Personality and Social Psychology, 54*, 1063–1070.

Weissman, A. N., & Beck, A. T. (1978, October). *Development and validation of the Dysfunctional Attitudes Scale*. Paper presented at the annual meeting of the Association for the Advancement of Behavior Therapy, Chicago.

2

The Nature and Assessment of Perfectionism: A Critical Analysis

Murray W. Enns and Brian J. Cox

This chapter reviews and compares the various instruments that have been developed to measure the perfectionism construct. To date, the assessment of perfectionism has relied almost exclusively on self-report measures. The first part of the chapter describes each perfectionism scale, provides an overview of the conceptualization and process of scale development, and summarizes the evidence for the reliability and validity of each instrument. The second part reviews the relationship between perfectionism measures and higher order personality factors, including new clinical data from our own studies. The order of discussion of perfectionism measures in the chapter generally follows the chronological order of their appearance in the psychological and psychiatric literature.

Burns Perfectionism Scale

David Burns's (1980) perfectionism scale was one of the earliest instruments developed specifically to provide a quantitative measure of the perfectionism construct. Burns described his conceptualization of a perfectionist as that of a person "whose standards are high beyond reach or reason . . . who strains compulsively and unremittingly toward impossible goals and who measures his own worth entirely in terms of productivity and accomplishment" (p. 34). Burns asserted that this kind of perfectionism could be associated with various mood problems, lowered life and career satisfaction, and decreased productivity (Burns, 1983). The Burns Perfectionism Scale (BPS) is thus clearly intended to measure a maladaptive characteristic. Burns's 10-item scale was derived from Weissman and Beck's (1978) Dysfunctional Attitudes Scale, which purports to measure self-defeating attitudes associated with clinical depression and anxiety. The BPS consists of 10 statements; the respondent is asked to indicate on a 5-point scale the degree to which he or she agrees or disagrees with each statement (e.g., "If I don't set the highest standards for myself, I am likely to end up a second-rate person").

Hewitt and Dyck (1986) provided preliminary evidence of the reliability and validity of the BPS. They reported good 2-month test–retest reliability (r = .63) and reasonable internal consistency (α = .70). They also provided some evidence of construct validity; the authors found a modest but significant correlation between BPS scores and the number of yes-rated perfectionistic words on a dichotomous rating scale composed of 24 perfectionistic adjectives (r = .23; N = 197). Hewitt, Mittelstaedt, and Wollert (1989) reported evidence of the convergent and discriminant validity of the BPS in a study of 52 college students. The BPS showed a large correlation with each of two measures having conceptually similar content (high standards and high self-expectations) but only a moderate correlation with measures of depression and self-blame.[1] Another study involving 150 undergraduate students reported a correlation of .52 between the BPS and the Self-Criticism scale of the Depressive Experiences Questionnaire (DEQ; Blatt, D'Afflitti, & Quinlan, 1976) but a correlation of only .15 between the BPS and the Dependency scale of the DEQ (Hewitt & Flett, 1990).

Two brief reports (Broday, 1988; Broday & Sedlacek, 1988) considered whether any of the BPS items should be eliminated. Following principal-components factor analysis, Broday and Sedlacek suggested that items 5 and 7 (apparently statements reflecting healthy rather than neurotic attitudes) could be removed, thereby increasing the factor validity without losing internal consistency. They also reported good 2-week test–retest reliability for the BPS (r = .74).

Several studies, all using college undergraduates for participants, have provided evidence of the predictive validity of the BPS. A 2-month prospective study of 105 students found a significant correlation between self-reported stressful life events and depression for perfectionists, but not for nonperfectionists (Hewitt & Dyck, 1986). The study failed to show that Time 1 BPS scores were associated with depression at Time 2, however. Another study used a mood-induction procedure in 47 participants to determine whether perfectionism would predict mood reactions in response to failure (Hewitt et al., 1989). The authors reported that BPS scores did indeed predict mood reactions, but only for tasks identified as important. A correlational study with 162 participants examined the relationship among BPS scores, self-reported stressful life events, and the dependent variables neuroticism and trait anxiety (Flett, Hewitt, & Dyck, 1989). The analyses indicated that BPS perfectionism interacted with major life events to predict trait anxiety and neuroticism. Finally, a cross-sectional study of 50 participants found that BPS perfectionism interacted with generalized performance importance (a measure of the importance of performing well across numerous areas of activity) to predict Beck Depression Inventory (BDI; Beck, Steer, & Garbin, 1988) scores (Hewitt, Mittelstaedt, & Flett, 1990).

Conclusions

The BPS is a brief, easy-to-use measure of perfectionism. Its development from a clearly psychopathological perspective (i.e., its assumption that per-

---

[1]In describing the size of correlations, the criteria of Cohen (1992) are used throughout the chapter: small r = .10; medium r = .30; large r = .50.

fectionistic attitudes are, by their nature, dysfunctional) and the unidimensional nature of the construct are notable weaknesses. Few studies demonstrate the reliability and validity of the scale, and their findings are generally modest. Also, for a scale designed to measure pathological perfectionism, few clinical studies of the scale have been conducted.

Perfectionism Instruments Developed for Eating Disorders

Neurotic perfectionism has been hypothesized to be a major predisposing factor contributing to the development of eating disorders (e.g., Bruch, 1978; Slade, 1982). As such, several psychometric instruments developed for the assessment of eating disorders (or eating behavior) have incorporated a perfectionism rating scale, including the Eating Disorders Inventory (EDI; Garner, Olmstead, & Polivy, 1983), the Neurotic Perfectionism Questionnaire (NPQ; Mitzman, Slade, & Dewey, 1994), and the Setting Conditions for Anorexia Nervosa Scale (SCANS; Slade & Dewey, 1986).

Eating Disorders Inventory

The authors of the EDI noted that previously developed eating disorder scales tended to be strongly focused on symptoms and behavioral patterns seen in the eating disorders. The EDI was developed with the intention of assessing a wide range of psychological variables relevant to anorexia nervosa and bulimia (Garner et al., 1983). The EDI subscales measure drive for thinness, bulimia, body dissatisfaction, ineffectiveness, perfectionism, interpersonal distrust, interoceptive awareness, and maturity fears. The EDI Perfectionism subscale (EDI-P) consists of six statements (e.g., "Only outstanding performance is good enough in my family"), all of which are positively keyed. Participants respond to each statement on a 6-point scale ranging from *never* to *always*. The maximum score on each item is 3; the three least perfectionistic responses (*never*, *rarely*, and *sometimes*) all are given no score (0).

In their original validation studies (Garner et al., 1983), the authors reported data from EDI scores in 113 patients with anorexia nervosa and 577 female comparison participants (university students). Reliability coefficients (α) were .82 for the patients with anorexia and .73 for the comparison participants; test–retest reliability was not reported. Further comparison samples included 17 patients who had recovered from anorexia and 166 male college students. Participants with anorexia nervosa scored significantly higher than all comparison groups on the EDI-P. As further evidence of criterion validity, the authors reported a moderate correlation ($r = .47$) between clinician ratings of perfectionism and the EDI-P. Scores in 65 participants showed a moderate to large correlation ($r = .51$) with the Interpersonal Sensitivity subscale of the Hopkins Symptom Check List (Derogatis, Lipman, Rickels, Uhlenhuth, & Covi, 1974), and showed reasonable discriminant validity with a variety of other self-report measures.

Subsequent reports have provided further data on the psychometric properties of the EDI-P. Wear and Pratz (1987) reported respectable three-week test—retest reliability (r = .88) for the EDI-P in a sample of 70 university students. Crowther, Lilly, Crawford, and Shepherd (1992) conducted a one-year follow-up study of the EDI in a group of 282 adult women. The EDI-P's test—retest reliability (r) was .65 for the total sample and .70 for the subgroup with eating problems. Raciti and Norcross (1987) reported internal consistency (α) of .79 in a sample of 238 female college students. A principal-components analysis of the EDI scores of the participants resulted in retention of five of the original six EDI-P items in the perfectionism factor. A study of younger participants (ages 11 to 18 years) found relatively poor internal consistency for the EDI-P in males (n = 169, α = .62) and moderate internal consistency for females (n = 354, α = .70; Shore & Porter, 1990). Another factor analytic study of the EDI (Welch, Hall, & Norring, 1990) was conducted in 271 patients with eating disorders. An eight-factor solution resulted in all six of the original EDI-P items loading significantly and uniquely on a separate factor. Internal consistency was somewhat lower than Garner's original data (α = .72).

In line with the clinical evidence used to develop the EDI, studies using this instrument have consistently shown higher scores on the EDI-P in patients with anorexia than in control participants (e.g., Bastiani, Rao, Weltzin, & Kaye, 1995; Cooper, Cooper, & Fairburn, 1985; Srinivasagam et al., 1995; Szabo & Blanche, 1997). Several of those studies also have noted that the elevated EDI-P scores persist after recovery of the eating disorder (Bastiani et al., 1995; Srinivasagam et al., 1995; Szabo & Blanche, 1997). Studies that simultaneously used other perfectionism measures along with the EDI provided evidence of the concurrent validity of the EDI-P measure; patients with anorexia had elevated EDI-P scores as well as elevations of most of the subscales of the Multidimensional Perfectionism Scales (MPS) of Frost and colleagues (Frost, Marten, Lahart, & Rosenblate, 1990) and Hewitt and Flett (1991b) (Bastiani et al., 1995; Srinivasagam et al., 1995).

The EDI-P consists of only six items; however, Joiner and Schmidt (1995) noted that half of the items appear to reflect self-oriented perfectionism and the other reflect socially prescribed perfectionism (especially pertaining to the family of origin). The subtypes are congruent with two of the three dimensions of perfectionism measured by the Hewitt and Flett MPS (Hewitt & Flett, 1991b). This two-factor model for the EDI-P was assessed by confirmatory factor analysis in a group of 174 undergraduate students. The goodness of fit for the two-factor model was very good and was statistically superior to that of the one-factor model (Joiner & Schmidt, 1995).

Several reports have provided evidence of the predictive validity of the EDI-P. Joiner and Schmidt (1995) reported a three-week follow-up study of 174 students designed to investigate diathesis—stress and specific-vulnerability hypotheses about the relationships among perfectionism, life stress, and depression. Their results demonstrated an interaction between the two dimensions of perfectionism and life stress: They predicted increases in depressive symptoms in males but not in females (i.e., the specific-vulnerability hypothesis was not supported). A 10-year follow-up study of 459 women examined the predictive value of the EDI-P (and other bulimia-related indicators). EDI-P scores at the index assessment were moderately predictive of bulimic symptoms at follow up ($r = .25$; Joiner, Heatherton, & Keel, 1997). A further study of a diathesis-stress model was reported by the same principal investigator (Joiner, Heatherton, Rudd, & Schmidt, 1997). A total of 890 women from two nonclinical samples participated. As the authors had predicted, EDI-P served as a risk factor for bulimic symptoms for women who perceived themselves as overweight but not for women who did not perceive themselves as overweight.

Conclusions. The EDI has become one of the most popular instruments for assessing eating behaviors and eating disorders. With only six items, the EDI-P is an extremely brief measure of perfectionism, and most of the studies reviewed indicated that it had satisfactory internal consistency and test-retest reliability. Despite its brevity, the EDI-P actually may consist of two 3-item factors. One could legitimately question, however, whether factors with only three items are sufficient to assess fairly broad constructs like self-oriented and socially prescribed perfectionism. The EDI rarely has been used in psychopathological conditions other than eating disorders; as such, one cannot be confident of its reliability and validity in other clinical contexts. Moreover, the diagnostic specificity of the subscales has not been established. Within the spectrum of eating disturbances, evidence points to the concurrent and predictive validity of the EDI-P. Studies using the EDI-P have used it as part of the entire (i.e., 64-item) EDI; it has not been established whether the six EDI-P items could be used on their own as a brief measure of the perfectionism construct.

Setting Conditions for Anorexia Nervosa Scale (SCANS)

The SCANS was developed on the basis of the functional–analytic model of anorexia and bulimia nervosa proposed by Slade (1982). The model posits that the combination of perfectionism and general dissatisfaction (with life and oneself) constitute crucial "setting conditions" that can lead to an intense need for bodily control and, ultimately, an eating disorder. The SCANS was intended to function as a screening instrument to identify people at risk for developing anorexia nervosa, perhaps before the development of overt symptoms (Slade & Dewey, 1986). The authors of the scale began with questionnaire items designed to assess five constructs: dissatisfaction, perfectionism, social/personal anxiety, adolescent problems, and need for control (perfectionism and dissatisfaction were considered the "major constructs").

The participants in the study development sample included 227 11th- and 12th-grade girls, 141 female college students, and 354 nursing students, 93% of whom were female (Slade & Dewey, 1986). Two principal-components analyses involving the first two groups, then the third group, were conducted; in each instance the solution was limited to five factors. The resulting solutions were similar, but because two of the perfectionism items were cross-loaded, they were excluded from the final version of the SCANS Perfectionism subscale (SCANS-P). The SCANS-P has four items (eight positively and four negatively keyed). Each item consists of a statement with a 5-point Likert-type response format (e.g., "Think of a person who tries to be perfect in their work. Is this person: very much like you; much like you; somewhat like you; very little like you; not at all like you"). The authors reported relatively poor consistency of the SCANS-P (α = .66). They also compared their three sample groups without eating disorders to a group of patients with anorexia nervosa (n = 20) and a group of patients with bulimia nervosa (n = 20). As predicted, SCANS-P scores were significantly higher in both groups of patients with eating disorders than in the groups without eating disorders.

Slade, Dewey, Kiemle, and Newton (1990) provided further normative data on the SCANS by administering the scale to 1,163 nonpatient female participants and 106 mixed-diagnosis patients with eating disorders; again, the patients' SCANS-P scores were significantly higher than those of the control group. Normative data for younger participants (ages 11 to 16 years, n = 462) were provided in a separate report (Waller, Wood, Miller, & Slade, 1992), which also demonstrated relatively poor internal consistency for the SCANS-P (α = .65). Evidence of the discriminant validity of the SCANS-P was provided in a study of 148 participants; there was no significant correlation with the Eysenck Personality Questionnaire (EPQ; Eysenck & Eysenck, 1975) measures of Neuroticism and Extroversion, and only a modest inverse correlation with psychoticism was found (Slade, Butler, & Newton, 1989). The absence of a significant correlation with neuroticism is somewhat surprising; however, the authors predicted that the combination of elevated perfectionism scores with elevated general dissatisfaction would be associated with psychopathology.

Two further reports provided evidence of the validity of the SCANS-P. Kiemle, Slade, and Dewey (1987) found that elevated SCANS-P scores (along with dissatisfaction) contributed to the identification of a group of students with abnormal eating attitudes and weight preoccupation (as measured by other eating disorder instruments and an interview measure). Owens and Slade (1987) predicted and found elevated SCANS-P scores in a group of 35 female distance runners relative to a control group.

Conclusions. The psychometric properties of the SCANS-P are not yet well studied. Published normative data are based on adequate numbers of participants, but on only small groups of participants with eating disorders; normative data for other groups are unavailable. The reported internal consistency of the scale is fairly low, and predictive validity has not been well established. Further study of the psychometric properties of the SCANS-P is clearly indicated before its use can be advocated.

Neurotic Perfectionism Questionnaire

The NPQ is a relatively recent development for the psychometric assessment of perfectionism (Mitzman et al., 1994). As the name implies, the scale is intended to tap potentially maladaptive aspects of perfectionism, particularly those thought to be linked with eating disorders. Scale development began with 66 items "generated from clinical and research material" (Mitzman et al., 1994, p. 517), and the item pool was reduced to 42 items on the basis of two principal components analyses, followed by elimination of items that were not highly correlated with both the SCANS-P and SCANS Dissatisfaction scales. Each item of the NPQ is a statement to which participants respond on a 5-point scale (1 = *strongly disagree*, 5 = *strongly agree*). The authors reported a high degree of internal consistency (= .95); they also reported that the NPQ discriminated well between control participants and patients with eating disorders.

Only one other report using the NPQ was identified in a literature search (Davis, 1997); that study involved 123 patients with eating disorders who completed the NPQ as well as the Hewitt and Flett MPS and a measure of "body esteem." The NPQ showed large correlations with self-oriented perfectionism (*r* = .54) and socially prescribed perfectionism (*r* = .69), and it showed a large inverse relationship with body esteem (*r* = −.57). The questionnaire was related minimally to other-oriented perfectionism (*r* = .16). The findings provide preliminary evidence of convergent and discriminant validity.

Conclusions. The NPQ was designed to tap an interesting and potentially important aspect of perfectionism, but one wonders whether such a long scale is needed to assess a single dimension or aspect of perfectionism. The NPQ requires much further study to establish its reliability and validity.

Frost Multidimensional Perfectionism Scale

In developing their MPS, Frost and colleagues (1990) noted the varied and nonspecific definitions of perfectionism in previous work. As a result of their review of perfectionism literature, they emphasized several features of perfectionism that had been identified as important, including excessively high personal standards; excessive concern over mistakes in performance; doubting of the quality of one's performance; the role of the expectations and evaluation of one's parents; and an exaggerated emphasis on precision, order, and organization.

Scale development began with a group of 67 items derived from a variety of sources. The sources included two existing measures of perfectionism (the BPS and the EDI-P) and a measure of obsessionality, but a large number of new items were developed for the scale. Potential items for the scale were selected on the basis of conceptual fit with each of the five dimensions outlined above. All items consisted of a statement to which participants responded by indicating their agreement on a 5-point Likert-type scale ranging from *strongly disagree* to *strongly agree*. Reliability analyses and two factor analyses conducted in samples of female undergraduate students (N = 232 and N = 178, respectively) resulted in a reduction of the number of items to 35, with a six-factor solution (the results of the second factor analysis closely replicated the first). The final six subscales included Concern Over Mistakes (CM; nine items, e.g., "I should be upset if I make a mistake"), Organization (O; six items, e.g., "Neatness is very important to me"), Parental Criticism (PC; four items, e.g., "I never felt like I could meet my parents' standards"), Parental Expectations (PE; five items, e.g., "My parents wanted me to be the best at everything"), Personal Standards (PS; seven items, e.g., "I have extremely high goals"), and Doubts About Actions (DA; four items, e.g., "Even when I do something very carefully, I often feel that it is not quite right"). Internal consistencies (α) for the subscales ranged from .77 to .93. A "total perfectionism score" was generated by adding subscale scores (except for the O subscale, which showed the weakest intercorrelation with the other subscales). The resulting total perfectionism scores showed large correlations with other perfectionism measures in a group of 84 female undergraduates (BPS, r = .85; EDI-P, r = .59). In each instance, the CM subscale showed the strongest relationship with the concurrent perfectionism measure.

In their initial report, Frost and colleagues included studies of normal participants in evaluating the relationship between MPS scores and measures of several psychopathological symptoms hypothesized to be related to perfectionism. They found that perfectionism was broadly related to numerous kinds of psychiatric symptomology (as measured by the Brief Symptom Inventory; Derogatis & Melisaratos, 1983). As predicted, perfectionism showed a stronger relationship with self-criticism than dependency (as measured by the DEQ). Total perfectionism, CM, and DA also showed moderate to large correlations with measures of guilt (Situational Guilt Scale; Klass, 1987), obsessive–compulsive symptoms (Maudsley Obsessive Compulsive Inventory [MOCI]; Rachman & Hodgson, 1980), and procrastination (Procrastination Assessment Scale Students; Solomon & Rothblum, 1984). A brief report by Clavin, Clavin, Gayton, and Broida (1996) found the same pattern of correlations between Frost MPS scores and the MOCI in a sample of 41 men. Collectively, the findings provided preliminary support for the construct, convergent, and discriminant validity of the Frost MPS.

Several subsequent papers have reported psychometric studies of the Frost MPS. Parker and Adkins (1995a) noted that Frost and colleagues had developed the MPS using an all-female sample from an "elite" university (i.e., Smith College). As a result, they conducted a study of the Frost MPS using a mixed-gender sample of college students (University of Alabama, n = 143; Birmingham Southern College, n = 135). The mean values obtained for the MPS subscales in Parker and Adkins' sample were remarkably different from the values reported by Frost, Lahart, and Rosenblate (1991). In particular, potentially adaptive aspects of perfectionism (PS and O) were higher in the Smith College sample, and several potentially maladaptive aspects of perfectionism (CM, PC, and DA) were higher in the Parker and Adkins sample. Those interesting observations suggest that further investigations of the relevance of social–cultural context in the assessment of perfectionism are warranted. The authors also reported internal consistencies (α) of the Frost MPS subscales ranging from .57 for PE to .95 for O. A factor analysis of their data provided strong confirmation of the factor structure suggested by Frost et al. (1990).

Parker and Stumpf (1995) also examined the psychometric properties of the Frost MPS in a sample of academically talented sixth-grade children (N = 855). The mean scores reported in their paper are closely comparable to the results of Frost et al. (1991). Internal consistency (α) of the Perfectionism subscales ranged from .67 for DA to .90 for O. A confirmatory factor analysis showed an acceptable degree of fit to the Frost et al. (1990) factor structure.

The Frost MPS has been used quite widely in studying various kinds of psychopathological symptoms and diagnostic groups, including indecisiveness, obsessive–compulsive symptoms, depressed mood in response to mistakes, chronic fatigue, social phobia, erectile dysfunction, eating disorders, and suicidal ideation. This chapter presents only a concise overview of selected studies.

A series of reports has convincingly demonstrated a substantial relationship between Frost's dimensions of perfectionism and obsessive–compulsive phenomena. Comparisons of obsessive–compulsive patients and subclinical obsessive–compulsive participants to (noncompulsive) control participants demonstrated elevated levels of total perfectionism, CM, and DA (Frost & Steketee, 1997; Frost, Steketee, Cohn, & Griess, 1994). Correlations of the Frost MPS subscales have been observed with measures of indecisiveness (Frost & Shows, 1993; Gayton, Clavin, Clavin, & Broida, 1994) and obsessive–compulsive symptoms (Rheaume, Freeston, Dugas, Letarte, & Ladouceur, 1995). The subscales that most consistently have shown moderate to large correlations with obsessional phenomena are CM and DA. As a result of those and other studies, the Obsessive Compulsive Cognitions Working Group (1997) included perfectionism as one of six central belief domains of importance in obsessive–compulsive disorder.

Several reports (see Frost, Heimberg, Holt, Mattia, & Neubauer, 1993; Minarik & Ahrens, 1996) have documented strong correlations between the Frost MPS subscales and depressive symptoms, typically measured with the BDI. Total perfectionism, CM, and DA have generally shown moderate to large correlations with BDI scores, whereas other subscales (e.g., PS) have shown smaller (or even inverse) relationships with the BDI.

As noted earlier, perfectionism is believed to be a central personality vulnerability factor for eating disorders. As predicted, several studies have demonstrated a strong relationship between abnormal eating behavior or eating disorders and the Frost MPS subscales (Bastiani et al., 1995; Minarik & Ahrens, 1996; Srinivasagam et al., 1995). Although most of the subscales have shown associations with eating pathology, once again the CM and DA scales show the largest effects.

The CM and DA subscales showed moderate to large correlations with social anxiety and general psychopathology in social phobia (Juster et al., 1996), whereas CM also showed a relationship with Stroop interference on socially threatening words in people with social phobia (Lundh & Ost, 1996). Evidence regarding the relationship between the Frost MPS and other psychopathological symptoms may be found in the following references: reactions to mistakes (Frost et al., 1995), suicidal preoccupation (Adkins & Parker, 1996), sexual dysfunction (DiBartolo & Barlow, 1996), and chronic fatigue (Magnusson, Nias, & White, 1996).

Conclusions

Collectively the studies reviewed above provide compelling evidence of the construct, concurrent, and discriminant validity of the Frost MPS. The Frost MPS is a reasonably brief, comprehensive, and psychometrically sound measure of six dimensions of the perfectionism construct. Studies with large samples of participants have provided evidence of adequate internal consistency of the subscales, although some later studies reported lower estimates of α than did the original report of Frost and colleagues (1990). Unfortunately, we were unable to find any published reports of the test–retest reliability of the scale. The strong correlations observed between some Frost MPS subscales and BDI scores also raise the possibility of affective-state dependency. Relationships (predicted on the basis of clinical observation and experience) between perfectionism and a wide variety of psychopathological symptoms have been confirmed using the Frost MPS; however, longitudinal studies demonstrating the predictive power of the Frost MPS have yet to be published. A broad relationship between the Frost MPS dimensions and psychopathology appears to exist, but evidence of the diagnostic specificity of those dimensions has been limited.

Hewitt and Flett Multidimensional Perfectionism Scale

In developing their MPS, Hewitt and Flett (1991b) observed that existing measures (and conceptualizations) of perfectionism focused exclusively on self-directed cognitions. They asserted that perfectionism has interpersonal aspects that are important in personal adjustment. Hewitt and Flett described three essential components of perfectionistic behavior: self-oriented perfectionism (the setting of excessively high standards and "perfectionistic motivation" for oneself), socially prescribed perfectionism (the perception that others hold excessively high standards for oneself), and other-oriented perfectionism (holding unrealistic standards of performance or behavior for significant others). The principal distinction among the three dimensions of perfectionism lies in the source and direction of the perfectionistic behavior. The Hewitt and Flett MPS bears the same name as the instrument of Frost et al. (1990), but the "dimensions" of perfectionism to which the authors refer are distinctly different.

The initial step in developing the Hewitt and Flett MPS was to generate a large pool of items reflecting the three dimensions of perfectionism (Hewitt & Flett, 1991b); they compiled a total of 122 potential items that could be rated for agreement on a 7-point scale. The items were administered to a group of 156 university students, and items were selected on the basis of mean scores (2.5 to 5.5), strong correlations with the respective subscale, and weak correlations with other subscales and social desirability. The result was a 45-item instrument with 15 items assessing each of the proposed dimensions: self-oriented perfectionism (SOP; e.g., "I must always be successful at school or work"), socially prescribed perfectionism (SPP; e.g., "The people around me expect me to succeed at everything I do"), and other-oriented perfectionism (OOP; e.g., "I do not have very high standards for those around me"; reverse-keyed item). Internal consistency (α) was reported as .86 for SOP, .82 for OOP, and .87 for SPP. Three-month test–retest reliabilities were reported for a sample of 34 participants; the r values were .88 for SOP, .85 for OOP, and .75 for SPP.

Several additional studies of the validity of the MPS were included in Hewitt and Flett's (1991b) original report. Principal-components analyses using large groups of university students ($N = 1,106$) and psychiatric patients ($N = 263$) both resulted in three-factor solutions closely corresponding to the original item assignments. Self-ratings of the three dimensions of perfectionism were significantly correlated with observer ratings of the same dimensions in a subset of the students; similarly, self-ratings of the perfectionism dimensions were significantly correlated with clinicians' ratings in a subset of the psychiatric patients.

Several samples of participants were used to assess the convergent and discriminant validity of the MPS. The MPS subscales were compared against a variety of personality measures, the Symptom Checklist subscales (SCL-90; Derogatis, 1983), and measures of performance standards. SOP was related to a number of self-related personality measures. OOP was related most strongly to other-directed traits, such as authoritarianism, dominance, and a tendency to blame others. SPP correlated significantly with fear of negative evaluation, need for approval, and external locus of control. In general, SPP showed the strongest relationship to the SCL-90 symptom scales. Finally, 77 mixed-diagnosis psychiatric patients completed the MPS and the Millon Clinical Multiaxial Inventory (MCMI; Millon, 1983). SPP again showed the strongest pattern of correlations with clinical symptom subscales. SPP was related to schizoid, avoidant, and passive–aggressive dimensions, and OOP was related principally to Cluster B (i.e., histrionic, narcissistic, and antisocial) personality traits. Normative data from each sample also were provided in the original report.

Hewitt, Flett, Turnbull-Donovan, and Mikail (1991) provided further evidence of the reliability and validity of the MPS in psychiatric samples as well as normative data for a sample of psychiatric patients ($N = 387$). Test–retest reliability (r) of the MPS was somewhat lower in a subgroup of 49 psychiatric patients than in the student group, ranging from .60 (for SPP) to .69 (for SOP). The most striking difference between the psychiatric patients' scores and the scores from the community sample was elevated

SPP in the former group. This observation is consistent with earlier findings and with the elements of disturbed social relations and learned helplessness in the SPP subscale (Hewitt & Flett, 1991b). Concurrent validity was assessed in a group of 60 psychiatric patients who completed the MPS in addition to the BPS and a measure of self-punitive tendencies (the Attitudes Toward Self Scale [ATSS]; Carver, LaVoie, Kuhl, & Ganellen, 1988). SOP and SPP both showed significant correlations with the ATSS subscales and the BPS, whereas OOP did not.

Since those early reports, the Hewitt and Flett MPS has been used extensively in studies examining a wide range of clinical groups and a wide variety of psychopathological symptoms, including studies of depression, suicidal ideation, several indices of social adjustment, anxiety, eating disorders, obsessional phenomena, self-esteem, and various personality traits. Because the intent of this section is to document evidence of the predictive and concurrent validity of the MPS, it presents only a selective review of some of the major findings.

Both cross-sectional and longitudinal studies have demonstrated a relationship between depression and MPS subscale scores. Hewitt and Flett (1991a) compared patients with unipolar depression ($n = 22$), patients with anxiety disorder ($n = 13$), and control participants ($n = 22$). Elevated levels of SPP were found in both patient groups, but only the group with depression showed elevated SOP scores. The results suggested that elevated levels of SOP may be more specific to depression.

Several reports have described tests of diathesis–stress and specific-vulnerability models. Hewitt and Flett (1993) obtained partial support for a specific-vulnerability hypothesis in a cross-sectional study of samples of depressed patients ($n = 51$) and mixed-diagnosis psychiatric patients ($n = 94$). In both samples, SOP interacted only with achievement stressors to predict depression; SPP interacted with interpersonal stress to predict depression in the mixed sample, but contrary to the hypothesis, SPP interacted with achievement stress in the second sample to predict depression. A three-month prospective follow-up study of 173 undergraduates found support for a general diathesis–stress model (Flett, Hewitt, Blankstein, & Mosher, 1995). SOP (at Time 1) predicted increases in depression symptoms at Time 2 among people who had experienced a major life event. Another longitudinal assessment study involving 103 patients with mood disorders found partial support for a specific-vulnerability hypothesis (Hewitt, Flett, & Ediger, 1996). The participants completed a measure of depression and the MPS at Time 1 and measures of stress and depression four months later. SOP interacted only with achievement stress to predict depression at Time 2; SPP predicted Time 2 depression as a main effect, but it did not show an interaction with stressors. Together, the results of the studies suggest that the dimensions of perfectionism measured by the MPS may act as vulnerability factors for depression.

Hewitt, Flett, and Turnbull-Donovan (1992) hypothesized that both SOP and SPP would be related to suicidal ideation. Several studies using adult samples of psychiatric patients, college students, or both have confirmed the predicted relationship between suicidal ideation and SPP (Dean

& Range, 1996; Hewitt, Flett, & Turnbull-Donovan, 1992; Hewitt, Flett, & Weber, 1994). Of those studies, only one confirmed the predicted association between SOP and suicidal ideation (Hewitt et al., 1994). The authors of that study observed that SOP and SPP were related to suicidal ideation in samples of both psychiatric patients (n = 91) and college students (n = 160). Furthermore, they found that both SOP and SPP moderated the association between life stress and suicidal ideation. A modified version of the MPS, the Child–Adolescent Perfectionism Scale (CAPS; Flett, Hewitt, Boucher, Davidson, & Munro, 1997), was used in a study of suicidal ideation in 66 adolescent psychiatric inpatients (Hewitt, Newton, Flett, & Callander, 1997). The results showed that SPP (along with hopelessness) accounted for unique variance in suicidal ideation. Collectively, the findings indicate that SPP is consistently associated with suicidal ideation; longitudinal studies to establish whether the MPS dimensions act as risk factors for suicidal behavior are needed.

The authors began development of the MPS with the contention that perfectionism has interpersonal aspects that are important in adjustment difficulties. In accordance with this contention, it has been hypothesized that interpersonal aspects of perfectionism (SPP and OOP) would be associated with various kinds of psychosocial difficulties. Flett, Hewitt, and Hallett (1994) observed that high levels of SPP were associated with the frequency and intensity of professional distress and low job satisfaction in a group of 62 teachers. Hewitt, Flett, and Mikail (1995) found that the relationship and family adjustment of 83 pain patients was associated with their spouse's levels of OOP. Higher SPP was associated with several social adjustment problems, such as loneliness, fear of negative evaluation, lower levels of social self-esteem, and lower self-perceived social skills in a group of 105 university students (Flett, Hewitt, & De Rosa, 1996). Another report involving two samples of college students indicated that higher SPP was associated with negative self-perception of social problem-solving ability (Flett, Hewitt, Blankstein, Solnik, & Van Brunschot, 1996). Finally, a comparison of people with social phobia (n = 28) and matched control participants found higher levels of SPP in the phobic group (Bieling & Alden, 1997). Thus, the prediction of an association between interpersonal aspects of perfectionism and social maladjustment has been confirmed.

Evidence of the predictive validity of the MPS has been found in relation to a wide variety of other disorders and symptom measures: self-esteem (Flett, Hewitt, Blankstein, & O'Brien, 1991; Preusser, Rice, & Ashby, 1994), procrastination (Flett, Blankstein, Hewitt, & Koledin, 1992; Saddler & Sacks, 1993), personality traits (Ferrari & Mautz, 1997; Flett, Hewitt, Blankstein, & Dynin, 1994; Hewitt, Flett, & Turnbull, 1992), anxiety and fears (Blankstein, Flett, Hewitt, & Eng, 1993; Flett, Hewitt, Endler, & Tassone, 1994–1995), and eating disorders (Hewitt, Flett, & Ediger, 1995).

Conclusions

The Hewitt and Flett MPS is a brief and reliable psychometric measure that was developed with a sophisticated multidimensional conceptualization of the perfectionism construct. Convergent and discriminant validity of the subscales have been clearly demonstrated, and several studies have demonstrated the predictive validity of the MPS subscales in a wide range of psychopathological conditions. The SPP subscale appears to have the broadest association with various forms of psychopathology; however, the SOP and OOP scales have shown some unique and relatively more specific associations with psychiatric and psychological syndromes (e.g., SOP and specific vulnerability to depression when confronted with achievement-related negative life events). Further studies of the OOP dimension in various social contexts (e.g., marital therapy and organizational contexts) are warranted. The broader and generally stronger association between SPP and psychopathology (compared with the other perfectionism dimensions) may reflect the general importance of a person's perception of excessive expectations from others. Alternatively, the SOP dimension may have both adaptive and maladaptive aspects, thus "diluting" the association between SOP and psychological problems. The Hewitt and Flett MPS is a useful instrument for the assessment of perfectionism, and it has contributed to an increased understanding of the nature of perfectionism.

MPS Comparisons

The MPS instruments of Hewitt and Flett (1991b) and Frost and colleagues (1990) are the two most widely studied and used measures of perfectionism. As described earlier, the two scales were developed from rather different perspectives. Parker and Adkins (1995b) commented that the Frost MPS has a strong intrapersonal focus, whereas the Hewitt and Flett MPS has a stronger interpersonal emphasis.

What is the relationship between the perfectionism dimensions measured by the two instruments? Four studies using different populations of participants have directly compared the MPS subscale scores. They include a study of 553 college students (Frost et al., 1993), a second study of 261 college students (Flett, Sawatzky, & Hewitt, 1995), a study of 60 mixed-diagnosis psychiatric patients (Hewitt, Flett, & Blankstein, 1991), and a study of 145 patients with major depressive disorder (Enns & Cox, 1999). The results are compiled in Table 2.1.

In summary, the four samples show a fairly consistent pattern of interrelationships. SOP appears to be most strongly related to CM and PS, and it is the only Hewitt and Flett MPS dimension that shows a consistent (albeit modest) association with O. These observations support the contention that the SOP dimension taps both adaptive and maladaptive aspects of perfectionism directed toward the self. SPP appears to be related to most of the Frost perfectionism subscales, particularly in the two psychiatric samples; the only notable exception is the lack of relationship with O. This finding mirrors the broad relationship that SPP has shown with various kinds of psychopathology. SPP also is the Hewitt and Flett MPS dimension that shows the most consistently strong relationship with PE and PC. This result is in keeping with the interpersonal quality of the

Table 2.1. Correlations Between Multidimensional Perfectionism Subscales in College Student and Psychiatric Samples From Four Studies

Frost MPS	Hewitt and Flett MPS[a]					
	Self-oriented		Socially prescribed		Other-oriented	
Concern Over Mistakes	.38	.53	.49	.59	.22	.42
	.52	.52	.65	.70	.18	.41
Doubts About Actions	.16	.23	.28	.37	.01	.07
	.24	.43	.48	.46	.01	.32
Personal Standards	.62	.61	.16	.28	.33	.39
	.64	.66	.49	.38	.42	.40
Parental Expectations	.24	.27	.49	.57	.19	.17
	.47	.46	.67	.49	.40	.26
Parental Criticism	.07	.18	.49	.53	.10	.07
	.38	.33	.47	.49	.22	.18
Organization	.29	.26	−.01	.01	.07	.14
	.15	.27	.30	−.02	.04	.15

Note. The values in the table correspond to the following studies:

- Upper left: Frost et al. (1993); college student sample ($N = 553$).
- Upper right: Flett et al. (1995); college student sample ($N = 261$).
- Lower left: Hewitt et al. (1991); mixed-diagnosis psychiatric sample ($N = 60$).
- Lower right: Enns and Cox (1999); depressed sample ($N = 145$).

[a]According to Cohen (1992), correlations of .10, .30, and .50 represent small, medium, and large effects, respectively.

underlying construct of this subscale. OOP appears to relate most strongly to CM and PS; however, the pattern is not as strong as for SOP. O does not appear to relate closely to any of the other MPS dimensions, a finding that corroborates the reasoning that Frost and colleagues (1990) used in excluding O items from their measure of total perfectionism. Taken together, the findings provide additional support for the concurrent validity of the two MPS scales. Although a few subscale correlations are large (e.g., CM and SPP; PS and SOP), most relationships are moderate in size, suggesting that the underlying perfectionism dimensions and constructs are fairly distinct.

Almost Perfect Scale

Clinically derived conceptualizations of perfectionism have tended to emphasize the significant psychopathological implications of the high standard setting of perfectionists (e.g., Burns, 1980; Hollender, 1965; Pacht, 1984). Slaney, Ashby, and Trippi (1995) contended that the development of both MPS scales (Hewitt & Flett, 1991b; Frost et al., 1990) was based on a view of perfectionism as an essentially negative or problematic trait. In their description of the development of the Almost Perfect Scale (APS), Slaney et al. (1995) emphasized their intention to explore and measure the construct of perfectionism from an "unbiased perspective," allowing for "the possibility that perfectionism might have both positive and negative aspects" (p. 281). Following a qualitative study of a group of perfectionists (Slaney & Ashby, 1996) and a review of the perfectionism literature, Slaney and colleagues began the development of the APS. They used 62 items intended to assess high personal standards, orderliness and organization, interpersonal relationship difficulties, potential difficulties in counseling relationships, anxiety, and procrastination (see Slaney & Johnson, 1992). Two exploratory factor analyses resulted in a reduction of the number of items to 32 and four interpretable factors, which the researchers labeled Standards and Order (12 items), Relationships (12 items), Procrastination (4 items), and Anxiety (4 items). The APS consists of statements that are rated on a 7-point Likert-type scale that ranges from *strongly disagree* to *strongly agree*. The following statements are representative items: "I like to always be organized and disciplined" (Standards and Order), "I feel uncomfortable in intimate relationships" (Relationships), "I tend to put things off for as long as I can" (Procrastination), and "I often feel anxious when I strive to complete a task" (Anxiety).

Some of the items in the APS, particularly the Relationships subscale, appear to lack face validity for inclusion in a perfectionism measure; for example, many perfectionistic people may endorse an item such as "I find it hard to talk about my feelings." The statements have little explicit connection with perfectionism, however, and there is little reason to believe such statements are specific to perfectionism.

Coefficients of internal consistency (α) for the APS subscales were reported for the sample of 1,425 college students who participated in the scale development project as follows: Standards and Order, .85; Relationships, .82; Anxiety, .71; and Procrastination, .80 (Johnson & Slaney, 1996). The authors also reported test–retest reliabilities for two samples. The r values from the first sample ($n = 58$, testing interval of 2 weeks) were as follows: Standards and Order, .92; Relationships, .90; Anxiety, .81; and Procrastination, .86. For the second sample ($n = 86$, testing interval of 4 weeks), the r values were Standards and Order, .81; Relationships, .87; Anxiety, .79; and Procrastination, .81.

Preliminary evidence for the discriminant validity of the APS scale was derived from a comparison of perfectionistic ($n = 106$) and nonperfectionistic ($n = 106$) men and women (Johnson & Slaney, 1996). As predicted, the group of perfectionists scored higher than the nonperfectionists on the Standards and Order scale and the Anxiety scale. Scores on the Relationships scale, however, did not differ between groups, and the perfectionists scored lower than the nonperfectionists on the Procrastination scale. As a further test of the scale's validity, the authors conducted a comparison of two groups of counseling clients, those with "problematic perfectionism" ($n = 25$) and those with "nonproblematic perfectionism" ($n = 26$). The two groups did not differ on the Standards and Order scale or the Relationships scale. As predicted, however, problematic perfectionists scored higher than nonproblematic perfectionists on the Anxiety and Procrastination scales. Because problematic perfectionism was identified by clinicians on the basis of perfectionism interfering with task completion, the results provided evidence of the concurrent validity of the Procrastination scale. This study also reported moderate-sized correlations between the APS scales and conceptually similar scales; for example, the Anxiety scale correlated .47 with Spielberger's Trait Anxiety Inventory (Spielberger, Gorsuch, & Lushene, 1970).

Slaney and colleagues (1995) conducted a separate study of the APS in 167 undergraduate students and reported correlations between the APS subscales and the subscales of the Frost MPS (1990) and the Hewitt and Flett MPS (1991a). They found some support for the concurrent validity of the APS. The APS Standards and Order subscale most closely correlated with Hewitt and Flett's SOP ($r = .60$) and Frost's PS ($r = .54$) and O scales ($r = .76$). The APS Anxiety and Procrastination subscales were most strongly correlated with Frost's DA scale ($r = .57$ and .35, respectively).

Additional evidence of the discriminant validity of the APS comes from Ashby, Mangine, and Slaney (1995), who compared the APS scores of 36 adult children of alcoholics (ACOAs) from a counseling service with those of 173 control participants (university students). Scores on the three subscales intended to measure maladaptive aspects of perfectionism (i.e., Procrastination, Anxiety, and Relationship Problems) were higher for the ACOA participants than for the control participants.

As noted earlier, two consecutive exploratory factor analyses were used in developing the APS. Slaney et al. (1995) reevaluated the factor structure of the APS using confirmatory factor analysis of APS scores from a sample of 568 undergraduate students. The results indicated that a six-factor model had slightly, but significantly better, fit to the data than the original four-factor solution.

Since the publication of the early studies on the APS, Slaney and colleagues have expanded and revised the APS to include a Discrepancy subscale (12 items designed to measure distress caused by the discrepancy between performance and standards), and they have separated the subscales for Standards and Order (APS-R; Slaney, Mobley, Trippi, Ashby, & Johnson, 1996). The concept intended to be measured in the Discrepancy subscale of the APS-R appears to closely mirror the concepts described in self-discrepancy theory (Higgins, 1987; Strauman, 1989); a comparison of the APS-R with a self-discrepancy measure would be an appropriate future investigation. (See Slaney, Rice, & Ashby, chapter 3, in this volume, for additional data and discussion of the APS.)

Conclusions

The APS was developed from a counseling perspective; it therefore is based on somewhat different assumptions about the nature of perfectionism and attempts to discriminate between adaptive and maladaptive aspects of the perfectionism construct. As such, it represents an interesting and potentially valuable addition to the collection of perfectionism measures reviewed in this chapter. Because the scale was developed quite recently, published data on it are relatively limited at this time. The subscales appear to be acceptably reliable and internally consistent. Available data provide moderately positive support for the concurrent and discriminant validity of the scale, but predictive validity has not been well demonstrated. Although three of the four APS subscales were developed to assess maladaptive aspects of perfectionism (i.e., relationship problems, anxiety, and procrastination), those factors are not likely to be specific to perfectionism; one might expect elevation of those factors in a wide range of perfectionistic and nonperfectionistic people. Furthermore, the Relationship scale failed to distinguish between perfectionists and nonperfectionists and between problematic and nonproblematic perfectionists (Johnson & Slaney, 1996). Further studies on the APS-R are awaited. The discrepancy scale of the APS-R may capture an important maladaptive aspect of the perfectionism construct.

Perfectionism Cognitions Inventory

The perfectionism measures reviewed above are all intended to capture perfectionism as a personality trait. Flett, Hewitt, Blankstein, and Gray (1998) more recently reported on the development of a questionnaire designed to assess the frequency of automatic thoughts involving perfectionism. The Perfectionism Cognitions Inventory (PCI) is a 25-item questionnaire consisting of a list of perfectionistic thoughts (e.g., "I can't stand to make mistakes" and "My work should be flawless"). Respondents are asked to indicate how frequently, if at all, the thoughts occurred to them in the past week on a scale ranging from *not at all* (0) to *all of the time* (4).

Flett et al. (1998) reported a series of studies of the PCI that provided evidence of adequate psychometric properties. A high level of internal consistency was found in a sample of 234 college students (α = .96), although a fairly high mean interitem correlation (α = .49) may indicate some degree of redundancy of items. Correlational analyses provided evidence of the convergent and discriminant validity of the scale. Additional studies in samples of college students confirmed that the frequency of perfectionistic thoughts measured with the PCI accounted for unique variance in distress, over and above the level of distress explained by trait perfectionism dimensions.

The PCI assesses perfectionism from a unique, cognitive perspective. Further research on this measure, including studies in clinical populations, are indicated. The relationship of this measure with other cognitive constructs, such as rumination and self-focused attention, also requires further study.

Adaptive and Maladaptive Perfectionism

Perfectionism has been conceptualized in a variety of ways, ranging from unidimensional, maladaptive perspectives to multidimensional perspectives that focus on numerous facets of a wide perfectionism construct. The evidence reviewed above indicates that perfectionism includes a variety of interrelated traits, some of which are generally adaptive and others of which are associated with maladjustment. In fact, a distinction between "normal" (i.e., adaptive) and "neurotic" (i.e., maladaptive) perfectionism was suggested by clinical writers before psychometric measures of perfectionism had been established (Adler, 1956; Hamachek, 1978; Hollender, 1965). On the basis of clinical experience and anecdotal evidence, Hamachek (1978) described a variety of differences between neurotic perfectionism and normal perfectionism. Table 2.2 summarizes the differences between adaptive and maladaptive perfectionism that Hamachek and other early writers on perfectionism (e.g., Adler, 1956; Burns, 1980; Hollender, 1965; Pacht, 1984) suggested.

A review of the content of the various perfectionism measures described in this chapter indicates that existing measures tap many of the facets of adaptive and maladaptive perfectionism outlined in Table 2.2, although none of the instruments explicitly measures both adaptive and maladaptive perfectionism. Several of the authors of perfectionism measures, however, have made explicit efforts to identify the maladaptive com-

Table 2.2. Differences Between Maladaptive ("Neurotic") and Adaptive ("Normal") Perfectionism

Maladaptive perfectionism	Adaptive perfectionism
Unable to experience pleasure from labors	Able to experience satisfaction or pleasure
Inflexibly high standards	Standards modified in accordance with the situation
Unrealistically or unreasonably high standards	Achievable standards
Overly generalized high standards	High standards are matched to the person's limitations and strengths
Fear of failure	Striving for success
Focus on avoiding error	Focus on doing things right
Tense/anxious attitude toward tasks	Relaxed but careful attitude
Large gap between performance and standards	Reasonable match between attainable performance and standards
Sense of self-worth dependent on performance	Sense of self independent of performance
Associated with procrastination	Timely completion of tasks
Motivation to avoid negative consequences	Motivation to achieve positive feedback/ rewards
Goals attained for self-enhancement	Goals attained for enhancement of the society
Failure associated with harsh self criticism	Failure associated with disappointment and renewed efforts
Black and white thinking: perfection versus failure	Balanced thinking
Belief that one *should* excel	*Desire* to excel
"Compulsive" tendencies and doubting	Reasonable certainty about actions

Note. Table derived from Adler (1956), Burns (1980), Hamachek (1978), Hollender (1965), and Pacht (1984).

ponents of perfectionism. For example, Johnson and Slaney (1996) sought to distinguish maladaptive perfectionism on the basis of its association with procrastination, anxiety, and relationship problems. A revised version of Slaney's Almost Perfect Scale (APS-R; Slaney et al., 1996) added a Discrepancy subscale designed to measure distress caused by the discrepancy between standards and performance. Similarly, Slade, Newton, Butler, and Murphy (1991) identified people as "neurotic or dissatisfied perfectionists" on the basis of cutoff scores on two SCANS subscales, namely, Perfectionism and General Dissatisfaction. The NPQ is intended to measure only the maladaptive aspect of perfectionism; items were selected on the basis of correlations with the same two subscales of the SCANS (Mitzman et al., 1994).

In developing their MPS, Frost and colleagues (1990) did not specifically intend to measure adaptive and maladaptive perfectionism, but they stated their belief that a central aspect of perfectionism, the setting of and striving for high standards, was not of itself pathological. In their study comparing the Frost MPS with the Hewitt and Flett MPS, Frost et al. (1993) reported a factor analysis of the subscale scores of the two MPSs. The two-factor solution represented two conceptually unambiguous factors, which they labeled *maladaptive evaluation concerns* (including CM, PE, PC, DA, and SPP) and *positive striving* (including PS, O, SOP, and OOP). Slaney and colleagues (1995) also reported a factor analysis of perfectionism subscale scores that included the subscales of the two MPSs plus the subscales of the APS. Again, a two-factor solution into adaptive perfectionism and maladaptive perfectionism was suggested; the MPS subscales loaded on the same factors as in the earlier report, whereas the APS dimensions loaded on adaptive (Standards and Order) and maladaptive (Relationships, Anxiety, and Procrastination) perfectionism.

One study that began with the intention of measuring perfectionism explicitly defined in terms of positive versus negative outcomes also suggested a clear distinction between positive and negative perfectionism (Terry-Short, Owens, Slade, & Dewey, 1995). After inspecting several established measures of perfectionism, Terry-Short and colleagues devised a new, 40-item questionnaire with a deliberate balance of items assessing positive versus negative perfectionism and personal versus socially prescribed perfectionism. Factor analysis of the scores of 255 women yielded a three-factor solution, which the authors labeled *negative perfectionism* (containing both personal and social items), *positive personal perfectionism,* and *positive social perfectionism.* When the number of factors was limited to two, a clear distinction between positive and negative perfectionism resulted (overriding the social–personal distinction). As yet, no further evidence of the reliability or validity of this scale has been reported.

Adaptive and maladaptive aspects of perfectionism appear to be distinguishable both conceptually and statistically. As indicated in the preceding paragraphs, the distinguishing characteristics of maladaptive perfectionism may be numerous and diverse. Studies using multidimensional measures of perfectionism (as reviewed) have already demonstrated that different maladaptive aspects of perfectionism are relevant to various different forms of psychopathology. Continued investigation using sophisticated multidimensional measures of perfectionism are needed to further clarify these complex issues.

Perfectionism and Higher Order Personality Factors

Investigations of the relationship between perfectionism and higher order personality factors, or "source traits," may shed light on the possible origins of perfectionism. Early discussions of the origins of perfectionism emphasized the role of neuroticism. For example, it was asserted that perfectionism arises, in part, from a neurotic need to please significant others, fear of failure, and characterologically based anxiety and self-doubt (Adler, 1956; Hamachek, 1978). Several investigators have empirically examined the relationship between neuroticism and perfectionism using correlational analyses. Flett et al. (1989) found a small but significant correlation between the BPS and EPI neuroticism in a group of 162 students ($r = .16$); extraversion was not associated with BPS scores. Slade et al. (1989) observed that the SCANS-P was not significantly correlated with EPQ neuroticism or extraversion in a group of 123 students; a small inverse relationship between SCANS-P and EPQ psychoticism was reported. Hewitt, Flett, and Blankstein (1991) tested the hypothesis that SOP and SPP (but not OOP) would be associated with neuroticism in samples of students ($n = 107$) and psychiatric patients ($n = 76$). They observed moderate-sized correlations between EPQ neuroticism and the predicted perfectionism scales in both populations. (OOP was not associated with neuroticism, and none of the perfectionism subscales showed a consistent relationship with extraversion.) Frost et al. (1993) used a different measure of positive and negative affectivity (PANAS; Watson, Clark, & Tellegen, 1988) in their comparison of the two MPS measures. In a group of 553 students, they observed small to moderate correlations ($r = .21$ to $.28$) between negative affectivity and the CM, PC, DA, and SPP subscales; SOP showed only a small, nonsignificant correlation with negative affectivity. Positive affectivity was correlated with PS, O, and SOP.

In recent years, the Big Five[2] model of personality has gained favor as a higher order factor structure to characterize and better understand other personality constructs (Costa & McCrae, 1992a, 1992b). In our search of the literature, we were able to find two reports describing perfectionism in relation to the Big Five model. Hill, McIntire, and Bacharach (1997) studied the relationship between the Hewitt and Flett MPS dimensions and the five-factor model using the NEO-Personality Inventory–Revised (NEO-PI-R; Costa & McCrae, 1992a) in a group of 214 undergraduate students. SOP showed a large correlation with conscientiousness; at the facet level, achievement striving, dutifulness, and self-discipline were

---

[2]The five factor model includes neuroticism, extraversion, openness, agreeableness, and conscientiousness.

the strongest contributors to this relationship. Adaptive aspects of SOP are reflected in those associations. SOP showed only a small correlation with neuroticism, notably the facets of anxiety and angry hostility. A small negative correlation between SOP and agreeableness also was noted. The latter associations appear to reflect potentially maladaptive aspects of SOP. In contrast, SPP showed the strongest association with neuroticism (notably the depression facet), but it lacked an association with any of the adaptive traits in the five-factor model. The third MPS dimension, OOP, showed a moderate-sized negative correlation with agreeableness and a small correlation with conscientiousness; the inverse relationship with agreeableness, along with an association with the angry–hostility facet of neuroticism, may reflect the potential of the high-OOP person for interpersonal problems stemming from competitiveness, willingness to express anger, and self-centered or narcissistic attitudes (Costa & McCrae, 1992a; Hill et al., 1997).

Parker and Stumpf (1995) examined the correlations between the Frost MPS subscales and NEO-Five Factor Inventory scores (NEO-FFI; Costa & McCrae, 1992a) in a large sample of academically talented sixth-grade children (n = 855). The most noteworthy relationships included moderate-sized correlations between neuroticism and several perfectionism subscales (i.e., CM, DA, and PC). Conscientiousness showed a moderate-sized correlation with PS and a large correlation with O. Thus, the Frost MPS dimensions showed clear differential relationships with higher order personality factors. The Frost MPS dimensions showing the strongest relationship with neuroticism are, not surprisingly, the same dimensions that showed strong relationships with psychopathological symptoms in other studies.

These interesting observations provided the impetus for a further exploration of the relationship between the Big Five factors and perfectionism. We sought to replicate and extend the findings of Hill and colleagues (1997) and Parker and Stumpf (1995) by comparing both MPS measures with the five-factor model in a clinical sample.

The participants for our investigation were a large series of nonpsychotic outpatients who had been referred to a mood and anxiety disorders clinic for an assessment. The referral sources were general practitioners (64%), psychiatrists (16%), and recruitment by newspaper advertisement for participation in clinical trials (20%). Before their clinical interview, participants completed a demographic questionnaire, the two MPS measures, and the NEO-FFI (Costa & McCrae, 1992a). A total of 281 patients (58% women) with an average age of 41 (SD = 13) participated. They were diagnosed on the basis of all clinically available information using the criteria of the *Diagnostic and Statistical Manual of Mental Disorders, 4th edition* (American Psychiatric Association, 1994). Their primary diagnoses were major depressive disorder (51%), dysthymia (12%), bipolar disorder (6%), panic disorder (16%), other anxiety disorders (5%), substance abuse (2%), and other Axis I and II diagnoses (8%). Table 2.3 presents the observed correlations between the MPS subscales and the Big Five factors.

The patterns of relationships between the Hewitt and Flett MPS and

Table 2.3. Correlations Between Multidimensional Perfectionism Scales (MPS) and NEO-Five Factor Inventory (NEO-FFI) Scales

	NEO-FFI Scales				
	Neuroticism	Extraversion	Openness	Agreeableness	Conscientiousness
Hewitt and Flett (1991b) MPS					
Self-Oriented	.17	−.11	.10	−.16	.22
Socially Prescribed	.36	−.22	.10	−.38	−.11
Other-Oriented	.06	−.17	.03	−.39	.07
Frost et al. (1990) MPS					
Concern Over Mistakes	.58	−.29	.00	−.32	−.21
Doubts About Actions	.57	−.35	.01	−.21	−.40
Parental Criticism	.27	−.05	.20	−.23	−.02
Parental Expectations	.15	.04	.20	−.07	.08
Personal Standards	.11	.06	.17	−.07	.30
Organization	−.14	.01	−.13	−.03	.51

Note. $N = 281$, mixed-diagnosis psychiatric outpatients.

the Big Five factors are rather similar to those observed by Hill et al. (1997) in their student sample. SOP showed a stronger correlation with neuroticism and a weaker correlation with conscientiousness in our psychiatric sample, suggesting that SOP plays a less adaptive role in patients with psychiatric disturbance. In comparison to studies involving student samples, SPP showed a stronger correlation with neuroticism and a stronger negative association with both agreeableness and conscientiousness—again emphasizing a more maladaptive role of interpersonal perfectionism in psychiatric patients.

The Frost MPS subscales also showed widely discrepant relationships with the Big Five factors. This finding is most apparent in their relationships with neuroticism and conscientiousness. The correlation (r) between the Frost MPS subscales and neuroticism ranged from .58 for CM to a small inverse correlation with O ($-.14$). The correlation between Frost MPS subscales and conscientiousness followed almost exactly the reverse order: O showed a large correlation with conscientiousness ($r = .51$) and a substantial inverse relationship with both CM and DA ($r = -.21$ and $-.40$, respectively). CM and DA also showed inverse relationships with extraversion and agreeableness, consistent with their association with psychopathological symptoms. Further comparisons of the Frost MPS and higher order personality factors using the lower order facets of the NEO-PI-R may help further characterize the Frost MPS dimensions.

Conclusion

Several self-report instruments have been developed for the assessment and quantification of perfectionism in the past 20 years, but the perfectionism concepts underlying the different measures vary considerably. The instruments themselves range from brief, simple, unidimensional measures (such as the BPS) to more elaborate, multidimensional measures, such as the Hewitt and Flett MPS, the Frost MPS, and Slaney's APS. To date, the two MPS measures have shown the greatest evidence of validity in a wide range of clinical and nonclinical populations. The APS was developed recently and therefore has been far less widely used and validated. Several features of the APS-R, notably the Discrepancy scale, may be useful in efforts to discriminate between adaptive and maladaptive aspects of perfectionism. Clear delineation of the positive and negative aspects of perfectionism may be helpful in optimizing risk assessment for psychopathology or predicting relapse versus successful coping following development of clinical disorders.

Areas for further development include clarification of the relationships between perfectionism constructs and related lower order constructs (e.g., the relationship between concern over mistakes and self-criticism or the relationship between SPP and dependency). Measures of a number of personality traits, such as neuroticism, dependency, and self-criticism, have been demonstrated to be affective-state dependent (i.e., elevated scores occur in association with current depressive syndromes; Enns & Cox,

1997). To date, none of the perfectionism scales have been tested for affective-state dependency; such tests would help further our understanding of the relationship between perfectionism and depression.

We were unable to identify any interview measures of perfectionism in the psychological or psychiatric literature. Given the strong evidence for the validity of several existing self-report measures (including predictive validity), it is uncertain whether an observer rating of perfectionism would provide sufficient incremental benefit over self-report measures to justify the additional time and effort required. A significant association between perfectionism and psychopathology has been demonstrated, and perfectionism also may adversely affect clinical treatment outcomes (Blatt, Quinlan, Pilkonis, & Shea, 1995). It therefore would be useful to demonstrate whether existing perfectionism measures are able to detect clinical change during the course of cognitive–behavioral therapy or other forms of treatment, such as psychodynamically oriented therapy (Blatt, 1995).

References

Adkins, K. K., & Parker, W. D. (1996). Perfectionism and suicidal preoccupation. *Journal of Personality, 64,* 529–543.

Adler, A. (1956). The neurotic disposition. In H. L. Ansbacher & R. R. Ansbacher (Eds.), *The individual psychology of Alfred Adler*. New York: Harper.

American Psychiatric Association. (1994). *Diagnostic and Statistical Manual of Mental Disorders* (4th ed.). Washington, DC: Author.

Ashby, J. S., Mangine, J. D., & Slaney, R. B. (1995). An investigation of perfectionism in a university sample of adult children of alcoholics. *Journal of College Student Development, 36,* 452–455.

Bastiani, A. M., Rao, R., Weltzin, T. E., & Kaye, W. H. (1995). Perfectionism in anorexia nervosa. *International Journal of Eating Disorders, 17,* 147–152.

Beck, A. T., Steer, R. A., & Garbin, M. G. (1988). Psychometric properties of the Beck Depression Inventory: 25 years of evaluation. *Clinical Psychology Review, 8,* 77–100.

Bieling, P. J., & Alden, L. E. (1997). The consequences of perfectionism for patients with social phobia. *British Journal of Clinical Psychology, 36,* 387–395.

Blankstein, K. R., Flett, G. L., Hewitt, P. L., & Eng, A. (1993). Dimensions of perfectionism and irrational fears: An examination with the fear survey schedule. *Personality and Individual Differences, 15,* 323–328.

Blatt, S. J. (1995). The destructiveness of perfectionism: Implications for the treatment of depression. *American Psychologist, 50,* 1003–1020.

Blatt, S. J., D'Afflitti, J. P., & Quinlan, D. M. (1976). Experiences of depression in normal young adults. *Journal of Abnormal Psychology, 85,* 383–389.

Blatt, S. J., Quinlan, D. M., Pilkonis, P. A., & Shea, M. T. (1995). Impact of perfectionism and need for approval on the brief treatment of depression: The NIMH treatment of depression collaborative research program revisited. *Journal of Consulting and Clinical Psychology, 63,* 125–132.

Broday, S. F. (1988). A shortened version of the Burns Perfectionism Scale. *Psychological Reports, 62,* 70.

Broday, S. F., & Sedlacek, W. E. (1988). Factor analysis and reliability of the Burns Perfectionism Scale. *Psychological Reports, 62,* 806.

Bruch, H. (1978). *The golden cage*. New York: Basic Books.

Burns, D. (1980, November). The perfectionist's script for self-defeat. *Psychology Today,* 34–51.

Burns, D. D. (1983). The spouse who is a perfectionist. *Medical Aspects of Human Sexuality, 17,* 219–230.

Carver, C. S., LaVoie, L., Kuhl, J., & Ganellen, R. J. (1988). Cognitive concomitants of depression: A further examination of the roles of generalization, high standards and self-criticism. *Journal of Social and Clinical Psychology, 7,* 350–365.

Clavin, S. L., Clavin, R. H., Gayton, W. F., & Broida, J. (1996). Continued validation of the Multidimensional Perfectionism Scale. *Psychological Reports, 78,* 732–734.

Cohen, J. (1992). A power primer. *Psychological Bulletin, 112,* 155–159.

Cooper, Z., Cooper, P. J., & Fairburn, C. G. (1985). The specificity of the Eating Disorder Inventory. *British Journal of Clinical Psychology, 24,* 129–130.

Costa, P. T., Jr., & McCrae, R. R. (1992a). *Revised NEO Personality Inventory (NEO-PI–R) and NEO Five Factor Inventory (NEO-FFI) professional manual.* Odessa, FL: Psychological Assessment Resources.

Costa, P. T., & McCrae, R. R. (1992b). Four ways five factors are basic. *Personality and Individual Differences, 13,* 653–665.

Crowther, J. H., Lilly, R. S., Crawford, P. A., & Shepherd, K. L. (1992). The stability of the Eating Disorder Inventory. *International Journal of Eating Disorders, 12,* 97–101.

Davis, C. (1997). Normal and neurotic perfectionism in eating disorders: An interactive model. *International Journal of Eating Disorders, 22,* 421–426.

Dean, P. J., & Range, L. M. (1996). The escape theory of suicide and perfectionism in college students. *Death Studies, 20,* 415–424.

Derogatis, L. R. (1983). *Manual for the SCL-90.* Towson, MD: Clinical Psychometric Research.

Derogatis, L. R., Lipman, R., Rickels, K., Uhlenhuth, E. H., & Covi, L. (1974). The Hopkins Symptom Checklist: A self report symptom inventory. *Behavioral Science, 19,* 1–15.

Derogatis, L. R., & Melisaratos, N. (1983). The Brief Symptom Inventory: An introductory report. *Psychological Medicine, 13,* 595–605.

DiBartolo, P. M., & Barlow, D. H. (1996). Perfectionism, marital satisfaction and contributory factors to sexual dysfunction in men with erectile disorder and their spouses. *Archives of Sexual Behavior, 25,* 581–588.

Enns, M. W., & Cox, B. J. (1997). Personality dimensions and depression: Review and commentary. *Canadian Journal of Psychiatry, 42,* 274–284.

Enns, M. W., & Cox, B. J. (1999). Perfectionism and depression symptom severity in major depressive disorder. *Behaviour Research and Therapy, 37,* 783–794.

Eysenck, H. J., & Eysenck, S. B. G. (1975). *Manual for the Eysenck Personality Questionnaire.* London: Hodder & Stoughton.

Ferrari, J. R., & Mautz, W. T. (1997). Predicting perfectionism: Applying tests of rigidity. *Journal of Clinical Psychology, 53,* 1–6.

Flett, G. L., Blankstein, K. R., Hewitt, P. L., & Koledin, S. (1992). Components of perfectionism and procrastination in college students. *Social Behavior and Personality, 20,* 85–94.

Flett, G. L., Hewitt, P. L., Blankstein, K. R., & Dynin, C. B. (1994). Dimensions of perfectionism and type A behaviour. *Personality and Individual Differences, 16,* 477–485.

Flett, G. L., Hewitt, P. L., Blankstein, K. R., & Gray, L. (1998). Psychological distress and the frequency of perfectionistic thinking. *Journal of Personality and Social Psychology, 75,* 1363–1381.

Flett, G. L., Hewitt, P. L., Blankstein, K. R., & Mosher, S. W. (1995). Perfectionism, life events and depressive symptoms: A test of a diathesis–stress model. *Current Psychology, 14,* 112–137.

Flett, G. L., Hewitt, P. L., Blankstein, K. R., & O'Brien, S. (1991). Perfectionism and learned resourcefulness in depression and self-esteem. *Personality and Individual Differences, 12,* 61–68.

Flett, G. L., Hewitt, P. L., Blankstein, K. R., Solnik, M., & Van Brunschot, M. (1996). Perfectionism, social problem solving ability, and psychological distress. *Journal of Rational–Emotive and Cognitive Behavior Therapy, 14,* 245–274.

Flett, G. L., Hewitt, P. L., Boucher, D. J., Davidson, L. A., & Munro, Y. (1997). *The Child–Adolescent Perfectionism Scale: Development, validation and association with adjustment.* Unpublished manuscript, York University, Toronto, Ontario, Canada.

Flett, G. L., Hewitt, P. L., & De Rosa, T. (1996). Dimensions of perfectionism, psychosocial adjustment and social skills. *Personality and Individual Differences, 20,* 143–150.

Flett, G. L., Hewitt, P. L., & Dyck, D. G. (1989). Self-oriented perfectionism, neuroticism and anxiety. *Personality and Individual Differences, 10,* 731–735.

Flett, G. L., Hewitt, P. L., Endler, N. S., & Tassone, C. (1994–1995). Perfectionism and components of state and trait anxiety. *Current Psychology, 13,* 326–350.

Flett, G. L., Hewitt, P. L., & Hallett, C. J. (1994). Perfectionism and job stress in teachers. *Canadian Journal of School Psychology, 11,* 32–42.

Flett, G. L., Sawatzky, D. L., & Hewitt, P. L. (1995). Dimensions of perfectionism and goal commitment: A further comparison of two perfectionism measures. *Journal of Psychopathology and Behavioral Assessment, 17,* 111–124.

Frost, R. O., Heimberg, R. G., Holt, C. S., Mattia, J. I., & Neubauer, A. L. (1993). A comparison of two measures of perfectionism. *Personality and Individual Differences, 14,* 119–126.

Frost, R. O., Lahart, C., & Rosenblate, R. (1991). The development of perfectionism: A study of daughters and their parents. *Cognitive Therapy and Research, 15,* 469–489.

Frost, R. O., Marten, P., Lahart, C., & Rosenblate, R. (1990). The dimensions of perfectionism. *Cognitive Therapy and Research, 4,* 449–468.

Frost, R. O., & Shows, D. L. (1993). The nature and measurement of compulsive indecisiveness. *Behaviour Research and Therapy, 7,* 683–692.

Frost, R. O., & Steketee, G. (1997). Perfectionism in obsessive–compulsive disorder patients. *Behaviour Research and Therapy, 35,* 291–296.

Frost, R. O., Steketee, G., Cohn, L., & Griess, K. (1994). Personality traits in subclinical and non-obsessive compulsive volunteers and their parents. *Behaviour Research and Therapy, 32,* 47–56.

Frost, R. O., Turcotte, T. A., Heimberg, R. G., Mattia, J. I., Holt, C. S., & Hope, D. A. (1995). Reactions to mistakes among subjects high and low in perfectionistic concern over mistakes. *Cognitive Therapy and Research, 19,* 195–205.

Garner, D. M., Olmstead, M. P., & Polivy, J. (1983). Development and validation of a multidimensional eating disorder inventory for anorexia nervosa and bulimia. *International Journal of Eating Disorders, 2,* 15–34.

Gayton, W. F., Clavin, R. H., Clavin, S. L., & Broida, J. (1994). Further validation of the indecisiveness scale. *Psychological Reports, 75,* 1631–1634.

Hamachek, D. E. (1978). Psychodynamics of normal and neurotic perfectionism. *Psychology, 15,* 27–33.

Hewitt, P. L., & Dyck, D. G. (1986). Perfectionism, stress and vulnerability to depression. *Cognitive Therapy and Research, 10,* 137–142.

Hewitt, P. L., & Flett, G. L. (1990). Perfectionism and depression: A multidimensional analysis. *Journal of Social Behavior and Personality, 5,* 423–438.

Hewitt, P. L., & Flett, G. L. (1991a). Dimensions of perfectionism in unipolar depression. *Journal of Abnormal Psychology, 100,* 98–101.

Hewitt, P. L., & Flett, G. L. (1991b). Perfectionism in the self and social contexts: Conceptualization, assessment and association with psychopathology. *Journal of Personality and Social Psychology, 60,* 456–470.

Hewitt, P. L., & Flett, G. L. (1993). Dimensions of perfectionism, daily stress and depression: A test of the specific vulnerability hypothesis. *Journal of Abnormal Psychology, 102,* 58–65.

Hewitt, P. L., Flett, P. L., & Blankstein, K. R. (1991). Perfectionism and neuroticism in psychiatric patients and college students. *Personality and Individual Differences, 12,* 61–68.

Hewitt, P. L., Flett, G. L., & Ediger, E. (1995). Perfectionism traits and perfectionistic self-presentation in eating disorder attitudes, characteristics and symptoms. *International Journal of Eating Disorders, 18,* 317–326.

Hewitt, P. L., Flett, G. L., & Ediger, E. (1996). Perfectionism and depression: Longitudinal assessment of a specific vulnerability hypothesis. *Journal of Abnormal Psychology, 105,* 276–280.

Hewitt, P. L., Flett, G. L., & Mikail, S. F. (1995). Perfectionism and relationship adjustment in pain patients and their spouses. *Journal of Family Psychology, 9,* 335–347.

Hewitt, P. L., Flett, G. L., & Turnbull, W. (1992). Perfectionism and multiphasic personality inventory (MMPI) indices of personality disorder. *Journal of Psychopathology and Behavioral Assessment, 14,* 323–335.

Hewitt, P. L., Flett, G. L., & Turnbull-Donovan, W. (1992). Perfectionism and suicide potential. *British Journal of Clinical Psychology, 9,* 181–190.

Hewitt, P. L., Flett, G. L., Turnbull-Donovan, W., & Mikail, S. F. (1991). The Multidimensional Perfectionism Scale: Reliability, validity and psychometric properties in psychiatric samples. *Psychological Assessment, 3,* 464–468.

Hewitt, P. L., Flett, G. L., & Weber, C. (1994). Dimensions of perfectionism and suicide ideation. *Cognitive Therapy and Research, 18,* 439–460.

Hewitt, P. L., Mittelstaedt, W. M., & Flett, G. L. (1990). Self-oriented perfectionism and generalized performance importance in depression. *Individual Psychology, 46,* 67–73.

Hewitt, P. L., Mittelstaedt, W. M., & Wollert, R. (1989). Validation of a measure of perfectionism. *Journal of Personality Assessment, 53,* 133–144.

Hewitt, P. L., Newton, J., Flett, G. L., & Callander, L. (1997). Perfectionism and suicide ideation in adolescent psychiatric patients. *Journal of Abnormal Child Psychology, 25,* 95–101.

Higgins, E. T. (1987). Self-discrepancy: A theory relating self and affect. *Psychological Review, 94,* 319–340.

Hill, R. W., McIntire, K., & Bacharach, V. R. (1997). Perfectionism and the big five factors. *Journal of Social Behavior and Personality, 12,* 257–270.

Hollender, M. H. (1965). Perfectionism. *Comprehensive Psychiatry, 6,* 94–103.

Johnson, D. P., & Slaney, R. B. (1996). Perfectionism: Scale development and a study of perfectionistic clients in counselling. *Journal of College Student Development, 37,* 29–41.

Joiner, T. E., Jr., Heatherton, T. F., & Keel, P. K. (1997). Ten-year stability and predictive validity of five bulimia related indicators. *American Journal of Psychiatry, 154,* 1133–1138.

Joiner, T. E., Jr., Heatherton, T. F., Rudd, M. D., & Schmidt, N. B. (1997). Perfectionism, perceived weight status and bulimic symptoms: Two studies testing a diathesis–stress model. *Journal of Abnormal Psychology, 106,* 145–153.

Joiner, T. E., Jr., & Schmidt, N. B. (1995). Dimension of perfectionism, life stress, and depressed and anxious symptoms. *Journal of Social and Clinical Psychology, 14,* 165–183.

Juster, H. R., Heimberg, R. G., Frost, R. O., Holt, C. S., Mattia, J. I., & Faccenda, K. (1996). Social phobia and perfectionism. *Personality and Individual Differences, 21,* 403–410.

Kiemle, G., Slade, P. D., & Dewey, M. E. (1987). Factors associated with abnormal eating attitudes and behaviors: Screening individuals at risk of developing an eating disorder. *International Journal of Eating Disorders, 6,* 713–724.

Klass, E. T. (1987). Situational approach to assessment of guilt: Development and validation of a self-report measure. *Journal of Psychopathology and Behavioral Assessment, 9,* 35–48.

Lundh, L.-G., & Ost, L.-G. (1996). Stroop interference, self-focus and perfectionism in social phobics. *Personality and Individual Differences, 20,* 725–731.

Magnusson, A. E., Nias, D. K., & White, P. D. (1996). Is perfectionism associated with fatigue? *Journal of Psychosomatic Research, 41,* 377–383.

Millon, T. (1983). *Millon Clinical Multiaxial Inventory.* Minneapolis: National Computer Systems.

Minarik, M. L., & Ahrens, A. H. (1996). Relations of eating behavior and symptoms of depression and anxiety to dimensions of perfectionism among undergraduate women. *Cognitive Therapy and Research, 20,* 155–169.

Mitzman, S. F., Slade, P. D., & Dewey, M. E. (1994). Preliminary development of a questionnaire designed to measure neurotic perfectionism in the eating disorders. *Journal of Clinical Psychology, 50,* 516–522.

Obsessive Compulsive Cognitions Working Group. (1997). Cognitive assessment of obsessive compulsive disorder. *Behaviour Research and Therapy, 35,* 667–681.

Owens, R. G., & Slade, P. D. (1987). Running and anorexia nervosa: An empirical study. *International Journal of Eating Disorders, 6,* 771–775.

Pacht, A. R. (1984). Reflections on perfection. *American Psychologist, 39,* 386–390.

Parker, W. D., & Adkins, K. K. (1995a). A psychometric examination of the Multidimensional

Perfectionism Scale. *Journal of Psychopathology and Behavioral Assessment, 17,* 323–334.

Parker, W. D., & Adkins, K. K. (1995b). Perfectionism and the gifted. *Roeper Review, 17,* 173–176.

Parker, W. D., & Stumpf, H. (1995). An examination of the Multidimensional Perfectionism Scale with a sample of academically talented children. *Journal of Psychoeducational Assessment, 13,* 372–383.

Preusser, K. J., Rice, K. G., & Ashby, J. S. (1994). The role of self esteem in mediating the perfectionism–depression connection. *Journal of College Student Development, 35,* 88–93.

Rachman, S. J., & Hodgson, R. J. (1980). *Obsessions and compulsions.* Englewood Cliffs, NJ: Prentice Hall.

Raciti, M. C., & Norcross, J. C. (1987). The EAT and EDI: Screening, interrelationships and psychometrics. *International Journal of Eating Disorders, 6,* 579–586.

Rheaume, J., Freeston, M. H., Dugas, M. J., Letarte, H., & Ladouceur, R. (1995). Perfectionism, responsibility and obsessive compulsive symptoms. *Behaviour Research and Therapy, 33,* 785–794.

Saddler, C. D., & Sacks, L. A. (1993). Multidimensional perfectionism and academic procrastination: Relationships with depression in university students. *Psychological Reports, 73,* 863–871.

Shore, R. A., & Porter, J. E. (1990). Normative and reliability data for 11 to 18 year olds on the Eating Disorders Inventory. *International Journal of Eating Disorders, 9,* 201–207.

Slade, P. D. (1982). Towards a functional analysis of anorexia nervosa and bulimia nervosa. *British Journal of Clinical Psychology, 21,* 167–179.

Slade, P. D., Butler, N., & Newton, T. L. (1989). A short note on the relationship between the Setting Conditions for Anorexia Scale (SCANS) and the Eysenck Personality Questionnaire (EPA). *Personality and Individual Differences, 10,* 801–802.

Slade, P. D., & Dewey, M. E. (1986). Development and preliminary validation of SCANS: A screening instrument for identifying individuals at risk of developing anorexia and bulimia nervosa. *International Journal of Eating Disorders, 5,* 517–538.

Slade, P. D., Dewey, M. E., Kiemle, G., & Newton, T. L. (1990). Update on SCANS. *International Journal of Eating Disorders, 9,* 583–584.

Slade, P. D., Newton, T. L., Butler, N. M., & Murphy, P. (1991). An experimental analysis of perfectionism and dissatisfaction. *British Journal of Clinical Psychology, 30,* 169–176.

Slaney, R. B., & Ashby, J. S. (1996). Perfectionists: Study of a criterion group. *Journal of Counselling and Development, 74,* 393–398.

Slaney, R. B., & Johnson, D. G. (1992). *The Almost Perfect Scale.* Unpublished manuscript, The Pennsylvania State University.

Slaney, R. B., Ashby, J. S., & Trippi, J. (1995). Perfectionism: Its measurement and career relevance. *Journal of Career Assessment, 3,* 279–297.

Slaney, R. B., Mobley, M., Trippi, J., Ashby, J. S., & Johnson, D. P. (1996). *Almost Perfect Scale–Revised.* Unpublished manuscript, Pennsylvania State University.

Solomon, L. J., & Rothblum, E. D. (1984). Academic procrastination: Frequency and cognitive–behavioral correlates. *Journal of Counseling Psychology, 31,* 503–509.

Spielberger, C. B., Gorsuch, R. L., & Lushene, R. E. (1970). *Manual for the State–Trait Anxiety Inventory.* Palo Alto, CA: Consulting Psychologists Press.

Srinivasagam, N. M., Kaye, W. H., Plotnicov, K. H., Greeno, C., Weltzin, T. E., & Rao, R. (1995). Persistent perfectionism, symmetry and exactness after long term recovery from anorexia nervosa. *American Journal of Psychiatry, 152,* 1630–1634.

Strauman, T. J. (1989). Self-discrepancies in clinical depression and social phobia: Cognitive structures that underlie emotional disorders? *Journal of Abnormal Psychology, 98,* 14–22.

Szabo, C. P., & Blanche, M. J. T. (1997). Perfectionism in anorexia nervosa. *American Journal of Psychiatry, 154,* 132.

Terry-Short, L. A., Owens, R. G., Slade, P. D., & Dewey, M. E. (1995). Positive and negative perfectionism. *Personality and Individual Differences, 18,* 663–668.

Waller, G., Wood, A., Miller, J., & Slade, P. D. (1992). The development of neurotic perfectionism: A risk factor for unhealthy eating attitudes. *British Review of Bulimia and Anorexia Nervosa, 6,* 57–62.

Watson, D., Clark, L. A., & Tellegen, A. (1988). Development and validation of brief measures of positive and negative affect: The PANAS scales. *Journal of Personality and Social Psychology, 54,* 1063–1070.

Wear, R. W., & Pratz, O. (1987). Test–retest reliability for the Eating Disorder Inventory. *International Journal of Eating Disorders, 6,* 767–769.

Weissman, A. N., & Beck, A. T. (1978). *Development and validation of the Dysfunctional Attitudes Scale.* Paper presented at the annual meeting of the Association for the Advancement of Behavior Therapy, Chicago.

Welch, G., Hall, A., & Norring, C. (1990). The factor structure of the Eating Disorder Inventory in a patient setting. *International Journal of Eating Disorders, 9,* 79–85.

3

A Programmatic Approach to Measuring Perfectionism: The Almost Perfect Scales

Robert B. Slaney, Kenneth G. Rice,
and Jeffrey S. Ashby

This chapter describes the efforts of several researchers to understand, define, and measure the construct of perfectionism. It focuses initially on the early development of the Almost Perfect Scale (APS), which was designed to measure the components of perfectionism. The chapter reports data on initial studies on the APS as well as data that led to the reconsideration and eventual revision of the scale to produce the Almost Perfect Scale–Revised (APS–R; Slaney, Rice, Mobley, Trippi, & Ashby, 2001). It presents the revision procedures and current studies on the APS–R, along with some of the clinical implications derived from the research, and it concludes by outlining some possible directions for future research.

The idea for the development of the APS evolved from supervising two doctoral students who each had a client whose psychological concerns were not easily classifiable. Both clients were doing well academically in a university environment that valued academic performance, but they were apparently unable to derive any sense of accomplishment or pleasure from their successes. In fact, they seemed to have clear tendencies to interpret their performances as signs of failure as opposed to success. The clients' academic performances, although at a high level that would have pleased most undergraduates, were not pleasing the clients. It became clear that the students' goals or standards differed from their perceptions of their performance. The perceived difference between their standards and their performance seemed like a potentially important source of their unhappiness. Given the students' high standards, the difference also seemed conceptually related to the construct of perfectionism, although the basis of that relationship was decidedly vague at that time.

Those early observations developed into a series of discussions with students and colleagues and, eventually, to a review of the available literature on perfectionism. This early review predated the scales by Frost and his colleagues (Frost, Marten, Lahart, & Rosenblate, 1990) and Hewitt and Flett (1991) and revealed a fragmented and primarily anecdotal literature. That review made it clear, however, that being perfectionistic was generally seen as problematic, if not pathological.

A research team was formed at Pennsylvania State University that consisted of students and faculty who were interested in studying perfectionism. Four issues were clear from the outset:

1. The research program had two main goals: to initially develop a conceptually and psychometrically adequate measure of perfectionism and to use that measure to explore the clinical implications of perfectionism.
2. The research program was to include both quantitative and qualitative or interview studies.
3. The construct was conceived of as being multidimensional and phenomenological.
4. The construct might have positive as well as negative dimensions.

Research on the Almost Perfect Scale

One student, Doug Johnson, became particularly interested in perfectionism and launched a dissertation on the topic. He, along with others, had been instrumental in developing and refining items to construct potential scales to measure the dimensions the literature review had suggested were central to perfectionism. More specifically, the construct seemed to involve five dimensions: (a) having high standards, (b) being orderly, (c) being anxious, (d) having tendencies to procrastinate, and (e) having problems with interpersonal relationships. Because of the interest in therapy and the implications of interpersonal problems for therapy, another dimension addressing interpersonal problems in counseling was added. Johnson's (1993) dissertation involved the initial analyses of the newly developed items as well as a comparison of two groups of perfectionistic clients who were in counseling. His results were published in Johnson and Slaney (1996).

The Johnson and Slaney study provided the initial reliability and validity data and support for the scale that had been named the Almost Perfect Scale (Slaney & Johnson, 1992). Following two separate principal-components analyses on a total sample of 1,425 participants, a four-factor structure emerged from the APS. The four factors accounted for 84% and 86% of the variance, respectively. The scales were a combined Standards and Order scale (12 items); an Anxiety scale (4 items); a combined Interpersonal and Counseling Relationship scale (12 items); and a Procrastination scale (4 items). Internal consistency coefficients (α) for the scales ranged from .71 for the Anxiety scale to .85 for the Standards and Order scale. Test–retest correlations (r) for a four-week period ($N = 86$) ranged from .79 for the Anxiety scale to .86 for the Standards and Order scale. Johnson and Slaney (1996) also compared the APS scores of 106 participants whose self-ratings indicated that they were perfectionists with those of 106 self-rated nonperfectionists. As expected, perfectionists had significantly higher Standards and Order scores than nonperfectionists; perfectionists also had higher Anxiety scores. Contrary to expectations, however, nonperfectionists had significantly higher Procrastination scores and the groups did not differ on their Relationship scores.

In the second part of their study, Johnson and Slaney (1996) compared two groups of perfectionistic clients who were in counseling. The therapists and the clients all agreed that the clients were perfectionistic. The clients were divided into those who reported that their perfectionism was problematic and those who reported that it was not problematic; the division also involved client and therapist agreement. The two groups did not differ on the APS Standards and Order or Relationship subscales, nor did they differ on a measure of ordinary orderliness, suggesting that having high standards and being orderly were not necessarily problematic. The group whose perfectionism was problematic did report significantly higher scores on the APS Anxiety and Procrastination subscales as well as on a measure of trait anxiety (Spielberger, Gorsuch, Lushene, Vagg, & Jacobs, 1983) and a measure of obsessiveness (Sandler & Hazari, 1960).

Slaney, Ashby, and Trippi (1995) examined the relationship among the APS, Frost et al.'s (1990) Multidimensional Perfectionism Scale (MPS), and Hewitt and Flett's (1991) MPS. The authors conducted a principal-components factor analysis that included the subscales of each instrument. The analysis resulted in a two-factor solution similar to the two factors found by Frost, Heimberg, Holt, Mattia, and Neubauer (1993), which they had labeled *adaptive* and *maladaptive*. The APS's Standards and Order scale had the highest structure coefficient on the adaptive factor (.89), suggesting that the scale may measure aspects of perfectionism that are not necessarily negative or maladaptive. The other APS scales loaded on the maladaptive factor. Slaney et al. (1995) also examined the relationship among the APS subscales, the subscales of the other perfectionism measures, and measures of depression and worry.

In the second part of their study, Slaney et al. (1995) used a confirmatory factor analysis (CFA) to test the goodness of fit (GFI) for the four-factor structure of the APS against the original six-factor structure, which had posited separate Standards and Order scales and separate scales for interpersonal and counseling relationships. The results narrowly supported the six-factor solution as providing the best fit for the data. Although both the four- and six-factor solutions met numerous criteria for fit (e.g., *df* ratio <2.0), the six-factor model had a slightly higher GFI and adjusted GFI than the four-factor model. The chi-square difference between the four-factor and six-factor models also was statistically significant.

In the first interview study, Slaney and Ashby (1996) questioned the apparent negative bias of the perfectionism literature and argued for a different approach to studying the construct. Their study involved interviewing a criterion group of 37 perfectionists. No definitions of perfectionism were provided; the participants either defined themselves as perfectionistic or were defined by others who knew them well. Slaney and Ashby found that when the participants described themselves or defined perfectionism, the central importance of high personal standards was clearly expressed. Orderliness frequently accompanied high standards. Slaney and Ashby noted that although participants' evaluations of their perfectionism were rather positive, most also found it distressing to some degree. None of the participants who were asked said they would give it up, however. The results seemed consistent with the contention that perfectionism has positive as well as negative aspects.

Slaney, Chadha, Mobley, and Kennedy (2000) used the APS and an interview format similar to that used by Slaney and Ashby (1996) to further explore the meaning of the perfectionism construct in India. In the first part of their study, the researchers administered the APS to 321 Hindu students at the University of Delhi. Results of a CFA based on Johnson and Slaney's (1996) four-factor APS structure provided a good fit for the data gathered in India. The APS means and standard deviations for the Indian students also were quite similar to those found in the U.S. sample except that the Indian students more frequently expressed concerns about interpersonal relationships. The Indian students who rated themselves higher on perfectionism were, like the U.S. students, significantly higher on the Standards and Order scale than were those who did not rate themselves highly on perfectionism. Unlike the U.S. students, however, Indian students who rated themselves as higher on perfectionism did not have higher Anxiety scores than the comparison group. In addition, no differences on the Procrastination scale were found, whereas in the U.S. sample the group with higher self-ratings had lower Procrastination scores.

In the second part of their study, Slaney et al. (2000) interviewed five volunteer graduate students and University of Delhi faculty members who considered themselves perfectionists. Both in the articulation of the core or essence of perfectionism and in their definitions of perfectionism, the participants identified having high standards for performance as primary and placed secondary emphasis on orderliness or neatness. All of the participants evaluated their perfectionism positively, although most also acknowledged that it was accompanied by distress. In sum, the results were similar to those of Slaney and Ashby (1996) and supported the contention that the construct of perfectionism, as measured by the APS, has relevance for Indian university students and faculty.

In another interview study, Slaney, Suddarth, Rice, Ashby, and Mobley (1999) used the APS and the Penn State Worry Questionnaire (PSWQ; Meyer, Miller, Metzger, & Borkovec, 1990) to identify people who might fit Hamachek's (1978) description of "normal" and "neurotic" perfectionists. The researchers interviewed 36 participants drawn from a large sample, who scored above the median on the APS Standards and Order scale and either above (i.e., neurotic) or below (i.e., normal) the median on the PSWQ. The interview format was a revised version of the one used in Slaney and Ashby (1996). The results of the study were consistent with Slaney and Ashby in that participants again identified high standards for performance as a basic part of the definition of perfectionism, often accompanied by a sense of neatness or orderliness. The results also were consistent with Hamachek's (1978) description of normal and neurotic perfectionism: Participants in the normal (i.e., low-worry) group seemed to evaluate their perfectionism in a more positive light than those in the neurotic (i.e., high-worry) group did. Participants in the high-worry group reported greater distress related to their perfectionism. The participants in both groups generally tended to be self-critical and were decidedly reluctant to give up their perfectionism.

Research Applications With the APS

Ashby, Mangine, and Slaney (1995) used the APS to investigate perfectionism in a university sample of adult children of alcoholics (ACOAs). To test the hypothesis, frequently found in the anecdotal literature, that perfectionism is embedded in the ACOA personality profile, the authors administered the APS to a clinical sample of university counseling center clients identified by their therapists as dealing with ACOA issues and to a nonclinical comparison group of university students. Ashby et al. (1995) found that ACOAs had significantly higher Relationship, Procrastination, and Anxiety scores than the students in the nonclinical sample. As in Johnson and Slaney (1996), the ACOAs did not differ significantly from the comparison group on the Standards and Order scale.

Rice, Ashby, and Preusser (1996) used the APS to identify perfectionists and subsequently investigate their relationships with their parents. The authors noted that the scale could be used to identify perfectionists who might later be classified as normal or adaptive because the APS Standards and Order scale was not confounded by self-critical evaluations or other maladaptive tendencies. Using median splits on the APS Standards and Order scale and the Frost et al. (1990) Concern Over Mistakes scale, the authors identified normal perfectionists (i.e., those scoring above the median on Standards and Order and below the median on Concern Over Mistakes) and neurotic perfectionists (i.e., those scoring above the median on Standards and Order and on Concern Over Mistakes). Compared with normal perfectionists, neurotic perfectionists reported significantly higher levels of parental criticism and parental expectations. Regression analyses showed that self-esteem in normal perfectionists was positively influenced by greater parental expectations and inversely associated with overprotective fathers. For neurotic perfectionists, self-esteem was inversely associated with overprotective mothers and positively influenced by greater parental expectations.

Rice, Ashby, and Slaney (1998) conducted structural equation analyses of perfectionism, self-esteem, and depression. Similar to Hamachek (1978) and Preusser, Rice, and Ashby (1994), Rice et al. (1998) suggested that depression may be an indirect result of perfectionism, occurring through the effect perfectionism has on self-esteem. They hypothesized that self-esteem would mediate the perfectionism–depression association (i.e., that the predictive power of perfectionism would diminish significantly when accounting for self-esteem). Rice et al. randomly split the sample ($N = 489$)

so that half could be used for measurement and initial theoretical model testing and the other half could be used to cross-validate the results found with the first group.

Rice et al. (1998) used the APS and the Frost et al. (1990) MPS to measure two constructs of adaptive and maladaptive perfectionism defined a priori. They argued that the APS Standards and Order subscale, along with the Personal Standards and Organization subscales from the Frost et al. measure, would load onto "adaptive perfectionism." The remaining subscales from both measures were expected to load onto "maladaptive perfectionism." The results of a CFA were generally consistent with those expectations, except for the Procrastination scale, which loaded on both dimensions.

Rice et al. (1998) tested a series of nested structural models to determine whether self-esteem mediated the association between perfectionism and depression for either or both perfectionism dimensions. They found the most support for a model that maintained both the direct effects and the indirect effects (through self-esteem) of maladaptive perfectionism on depression while excluding adaptive perfectionism from the model. That is, adaptive perfectionism appeared to play a nonsignificant role in self-esteem and depression; maladaptive perfectionism was a decisive predictor of both low self-esteem and depression. A significant interaction between self-esteem and maladaptive perfectionism also was found. At high levels of maladaptive perfectionism, depression was increased by low self-esteem. High self-esteem, however, appeared to buffer the depressogenic effects of maladaptive perfectionism. Thus, people who endorsed characteristics typical of maladaptive perfectionism but who also experienced robust self-esteem were unlikely to be depressed. Participants with low self-esteem were unlikely to be depressed unless they also were maladaptive perfectionists. Those with high self-esteem were unlikely to be depressed regardless of their degree of maladaptive perfectionism.

The data from the APS, as well as data from other scales, seemed to suggest that two higher order dimensions of perfectionism exist, similar perhaps to the adaptive and maladaptive dimensions suggested by Frost et al. (1993) and Slaney et al. (1995) or to the normal and neurotic dimensions posited by Hamachek (1978). The APS results suggested that the combined Standards and Order dimensions represented the adaptive, or normal, dimension of perfectionism rather well. The interview data clearly suggested that having high standards was more central to participants' definitions of perfectionism than was orderliness; however, the data also suggested that the maladaptive, or neurotic, dimension needed further consideration and clarification. For example, data from both the quantitative and qualitative studies indicated that Procrastination scores were not positively related to having high standards or perceiving oneself as perfectionistic. The data for the Relationship scale seemed more equivocal: The quantitative data offered few links to perfectionism, but the interviews suggested that women, in particular, felt that their relationships were negatively affected by their high standards. Anxiety did seem to be related to having high standards in U.S. samples, but that finding was not replicated in the Indian sample in Slaney et al. (2000).

The data (especially on the maladaptive dimensions of perfectionism) raised the question of whether the APS subscales adequately captured the major defining dimensions of perfectionism. Clearly, the possession of high standards for one's performance has proven to be the dimension of perfectionism about which there is near unanimity in dictionary definitions, the literature, scale development, and interview studies. Far less agreement, however, can be found about the negative dimensions. Relative to the APS, it can be argued that although anxiety might be seen as an effect, a concomitant, or even a cause of perfectionism, its prevalence in many psychological disorders argues against it as a defining aspect of perfectionism. Although problems with relationships and procrastination also might be described as the result, a concomitant, or even a cause of perfectionism, neither characteristic was supported by the research as an essential negative aspect of perfectionism. Having thereby qualified or eliminated all the negative scales of the original APS, it remained for the research team to carefully consider how to conceptualize the defining negative aspects of perfectionism. After extensive thought and discussions with students and colleagues, the research team settled on the concept of *discrepancy*, which was defined as the perception that one consistently fails to meet the high standards one has set for oneself. To the research team, the concept of discrepancy did seem to be basic to perfectionism and to potentially capture the essential defining negative dimension of the construct. Revision of the APS therefore seemed necessary, and new items that measured the concept of discrepancy were developed. A second goal was to clarify and strengthen the Standards dimension of the APS; the Order dimension was judged to be adequate.

The Almost Perfect Scale–Revised

The revision of the APS resulted in the Almost Perfect Scale–Revised (Slaney, Mobley, Trippi, Ashby, & Johnson, 1996) and led to a rigorous, multisite psychometric study. For the revision, the research team, through multiple meetings, discussions, sample items, and revisions, finally agreed on 7 additional items to measure the Standards dimension and 20 new items designed to capture the concept of discrepancy. Approximately 809 undergraduates at three universities participated in the validation and cross-validation efforts for the APS–R. Participants responded to the APS–R and the Hewitt and Flett (1991) MPS and provided additional information about their psychological and academic functioning. Maximum-likelihood CFA was selected to analyze the item response data for the APS–R because CFA allows the a priori specification of item–factor associations and controls measurement error, thereby disattenuating results that would otherwise be affected by error variance. Slaney et al. (2001) specified, a priori, which items they believed would be good indicators of the three perfectionism subscales (i.e., Standards, Order, and

Discrepancy). In addition to the item analyses, Slaney et al. examined the construct intercorrelations between the perfectionism measures to assess further convergent validity. To further assess discriminant and concurrent validity, they also examined correlations between the APS–R dimensions and outcome indicators such as self-esteem, depression, and grade point average (GPA).

In the initial CFA study, Slaney et al. (2001) used 39 APS–R items (the 27 new items plus the 12 items from the original APS Standards and Order scale) and constrained them to load onto the three hypothesized factors: Standards, Order, and Discrepancy. Slaney et al. conducted a conservative series of data analysis steps aimed at delimiting the most psychometrically sound items and thus more finely approximating the constructs of interest. For example, items with low structure coefficients on their respective factors (i.e., <.45) were eliminated. Items were also eliminated if statistically indicated modifications revealed that they tapped more than one of the dimensions. Eventually, 7 items were retained to be indicators of Standards, 4 items indicated Order, and 13 items indicated Discrepancy. Five of the Standards items were new items from the revision process, and two of the older items were retained.

The 24 items and the three-factor model that emerged from the CFA on the data from the validation sample were then tested with a separate, cross-validation sample. Again, a conservative and rigorous approach was taken with the multiple-group analyses, in which the model and the results from the validation sample were "constrained" to be invariant from the results observed in the cross-validation sample. Essentially, the tests consisted of nested-model analyses comparing one model, in which the results (model and parameter estimates) were permitted to be freely estimated (different) for both samples, with another model, in which the results were forced to be identical between the samples. A conspicuously low structure coefficient for one of the Discrepancy items emerged in those analyses. After eliminating that item, statistically comparing the nested models supported the invariance of results from the validation to cross-validation samples; strong support was demonstrated for the psychometric integrity of the APS–R items and the three-factor structure. Indeed, this 23-item, three-structure solution received substantial support in a final administration of the measure to a third sample of students.

Final CFA statistics of the validation sample revealed that APS–R item structure coefficients ranged from .49 to .83, indicating excellent convergent validity. Tests of Cronbach's coefficient alphas indicated that the factors evidenced strong internal consistency for order (.86), standards (.85), and discrepancy (.92). Factor intercorrelations for the APS–R revealed only modest or nonsignificant correlations between Standards and Order (.41), between Standards and Discrepancy (−.07), and between Order and Discrepancy (−.05), and between the APS–R and the Hewitt and Flett (1991) MPS scales. The highest correlations between perfectionism dimensions were .45 (between Discrepancy and Socially Prescribed Perfectionism) and .55 (between Standards and Self-Oriented Perfectionism).

Moreover, the APS–R factors correlated in expected directions with potential outcomes of perfectionism. In fact, the CFA revealed that the APS–R and Hewitt and Flett factors related in different ways to self-esteem, depression, and GPA. Self-Oriented Perfectionism and Socially Prescribed Perfectionism, from Hewitt and Flett's MPS, were significantly correlated with the Beck Depression Inventory (BDI; Beck, 1978; .14 and .39, respectively). Socially Prescribed Perfectionism also was negatively correlated with self-esteem (−.31) and GPA (−.09). Standards and, to a lesser degree, Order on the APS–R were unrelated to depression (−.10 and .03, respectively), modestly and positively related to self-esteem (.19 and .14), and more strongly and positively correlated with GPA (.34 and .09). Discrepancy was significantly correlated with depression (.49) and inversely associated with self-esteem (−.44) and GPA (−.23). The analyses provided excellent support for the discriminant and concurrent validity of the APS–R scores. That is, the APS–R appears to tap unique dimensions of perfectionism and predict relevant healthy as well as maladaptive psychological and achievement outcomes.

Additional evidence of convergent and discriminant validity for the APS–R emerged in a recent study by Ashby and Rice (in press). They surveyed 260 undergraduates and gathered data using the APS–R, the Dysfunctional Attitudes Scale (DAS; Weissman & Beck, 1978), and self-esteem. Factor analyses of the DAS have consistently revealed two attitudinal dimensions: the Need for Approval and the Perfectionism subscales. The DAS Perfectionism subscale has been a central focus of Blatt's data analyses from the National Institute of Mental Health Treatment of Depression Collaborative Research Program (e.g., Blatt, Quinlan, Pilkonis, & Shea, 1995; Blatt, Zuroff, Quinlan, & Pilkonis, 1996; Blatt & Zuroff, chapter 16, this volume). Ashby and Rice sought to determine the association between the DAS Perfectionism subscale and the APS–R subscales, suspecting that the DAS Perfectionism subscale would correlate significantly with APS–R Discrepancy (both as indicators of maladaptive perfectionism) but would be unrelated to APS–R indicators of adaptive perfectionism (Standards and Order). They also hypothesized that the DAS and APS–R would be significant predictors of self-esteem.

Ashby and Rice conducted an initial CFA of the APS–R items and found support for the cross-validation of the measurement structure of the APS–R similar to that observed by Slaney et al. (2001). For example, structure coefficients ranged from .50 to .86, and the intercorrelations of the APS–R factors ranged from .18 to .51. Ashby and Rice then examined, through the CFA, the construct interrelations between the APS–R perfectionism factors and the DAS Perfectionism subscale. The analyses were conceived to demonstrate the discriminant validity of the APS–R from the DAS Perfectionism subscale. They found that the APS–R Discrepancy subscale and the DAS Perfectionism subscale were significantly correlated ($r = .61$). The DAS Perfectionism subscale was not correlated with Standards ($r = .09$) or Order ($r = .08$).

The perfectionism factors were then used as predictors of self-esteem in a structural equations analysis. The analysis simultaneously controlled for the effects of all other predictors when examining the importance of individual predictors. Ashby and Rice found that the APS–R Order factor was not a significant predictor of self-esteem (standardized path coefficient = .09); however, Standards was a significant positive predictor of self-esteem (.25), whereas Discrepancy and DAS Perfectionism both were significant negative predictors (−.31 and −.45, respectively). Thus, the strongest predictors of low self-esteem were the maladaptive perfectionism factors, although Standards evidenced a positive (i.e., adaptive) relationship with self-esteem. The significant associations emerged after controlling for the effects of other predictors, indicating that the perfectionism factors accounted for unique variation in self-esteem.

Ashby and his colleagues have conducted a series of additional studies involving the APS–R. Ashby and Kottman (1996) used the 66th percentile on the Standards scale to distinguish between perfectionists and nonperfectionists. Adaptive and maladaptive perfectionists were identified by using a median split on the Discrepancy scale. Adaptive perfectionists were defined as those with high standards and low Discrepancy scores. Maladaptive perfectionists (i.e., those with high Standards and Discrepancy scores) had significantly higher levels of inferiority than adaptive perfectionists, as measured by the Comparative Feeling of Inferiority Index (Strano & Dixon, 1990). Ashby and Kottman suggested that, from an Adlerian perspective, maladaptive perfectionists may be fleeing inferiority, whereas adaptive perfectionists may be pursuing superiority.

Ashby and Huffman (1999) investigated the relationship between religiosity and perfectionism in university students. An item assessing the importance of religion was used to divide participants into more and less religious groups. They found that more highly religious people had higher Standards scale scores than did less highly religious people, but they did not have higher scores on any of the maladaptive dimensions measured by the original APS and the APS–R (i.e., Discrepancy, Procrastination, Anxiety, and Relationship Concerns). Their results seem to support Timpe's (1989) contention that religiosity may be related to the positive dimensions of perfectionism. Specifically, the significant correlations between intrinsic religiosity and the APS–R high Standards and Order subscales are consistent with Bergin, Stinchfield, Gaskin, Masters, and Sullivan's (1988) notion that intrinsic religiosity may be a vehicle for positive dimensions of perfectionism, particularly higher standards.

Ashby, Kottman, and DeGraaf (1999) compared adaptive perfectionists, maladaptive perfectionists, and nonperfectionists on measures of leisure attitudes and satisfaction. Using median splits on the APS–R Standards and Discrepancy scales, they found significant differences between nonperfectionists and both adaptive and maladaptive perfectionists. Specifically, although perfectionists scored higher on positive beliefs about and value placed on leisure, they scored significantly lower on measures of freedom, enjoyment, and involvement in leisure. No significant differences were found between the two types of perfectionists. Ashby et al. suggest that their results may indicate that although perfectionists approach leisure activities believing in their benefits, setting and striving toward high standards in pursuing those activities may limit their enjoyment and sense of freedom.

Ashby, Kottman, and Schoen (1998) compared a clinical sample of people being treated for eating disorders with a comparison group of undergraduate women on the APS–R and the Frost MPS. They found that women with eating disorders had significantly higher scores than those in the comparison group on a factor representing maladaptive perfectionism (including the Discrepancy, Relationship, Anxiety, and Procrastination scales of the APS and APS–R). The groups did not differ significantly on a factor representing adaptive perfectionism (which included the APS–R Standards and Order scales). Significant positive correlations also were found between the maladaptive perfectionism factor and several subscales of the Eating Disorder Inventory (EDI), including Body Dissatisfaction (r = .47), Ineffectiveness (r = .63), Perfectionism (r = .52), Interoceptive Awareness (r = .48), and Interpersonal Distrust (r = .72). No significant correlations between the adaptive perfectionism factor and any EDI subscales were found.

Kottman and Ashby (1999) investigated the relationship between perfectionism and social interest, which is generally seen as the Adlerian criterion for mental health. The authors distinguished between perfectionists and nonperfectionists by labeling those participants who scored above the 66th percentile on the APS–R Standards scale as perfectionists. The researchers then divided the perfectionists into adaptive and maladaptive groups on the basis of a median split on the APS–R Discrepancy subscale. No significant differences were found among the three groups (i.e., adaptive perfectionists, maladaptive perfectionists, and nonperfectionists) on a measure of social interest. The authors suggested that perfectionists may be applying their high standards in striving to feel connected with others. They saw this explanation as consistent with the Slaney and Ashby (1996) finding that perfectionists reported that their perfectionism affected their relationships—some positively and some negatively.

Finally, Ashby, Bieschke, and Slaney (1997) used the APS–R to compare adaptive, maladaptive, and nonperfectionists on self-efficacy in career decision making. Using the Career Decision-Making Self-Efficacy Scale (Taylor & Betz, 1983), the authors found significantly higher Accurate Self-Appraisal, Goal Selection, Making Plans for the Future, and Problem-Solving scale scores for adaptive perfectionists than for maladaptive perfectionists. The adaptive perfectionists scored significantly higher on Self-Appraisal, Goal Selection, Making Plans for the Future, Problem Solving, and Gathering Occupational Information than did the nonperfectionists. The authors suggested that adaptive perfectionists may differ from nonperfectionists on career decision-making self-efficacy because they are accustomed to setting high standards and striving toward them. They also suggested that adaptive and maladaptive perfectionists may differ in this area because of the manner in which they attempt to fulfill their high personal standards in career choices.

Additional data have been produced through a series of dissertations completed at Penn State. In the first dissertation to use the APS–R, Barbara Suddarth subjected the responses of 197 undergraduates to the Frost et al. (1990) MPS scales, the Hewitt and Flett (1991) MPS scales, and the APS–R to a principal-components factor analysis with an orthogonal rotation (see Suddarth & Slaney, 2001). Three orthogonal factors emerged. Factor 1, which Suddarth and Slaney (2001) called Unhealthy Perfectionism, was composed of the Concern for Mistakes, Parental Expectations, Parental Criticism, and Doubts About Actions scales from Frost et al.; the Socially Prescribed Perfectionism scale from Hewitt and Flett; and the APS–R Discrepancy scale. Factor 2 was called Healthy Perfectionism and was composed of the Personal Standards scale from Frost et al., the Self-Oriented and Other-Oriented Perfectionism scales from Hewitt and Flett, and the APS–R Standards scale. Factor 3 was called Orderliness and was made up of the Organization scale from Frost et al. and the Order scale of the APS–R. Suddarth and Slaney's (2001) findings were consistent with the results of Frost et al. (1993) and Slaney et al. (1995) in finding adaptive and maladaptive factors, although they also found an Orderliness factor.

In a series of simultaneous regression analyses, Suddarth and Slaney found that the Unhealthy Perfectionism factor was a significant and positive predictor of trait anxiety, severity of psychological symptoms, and external locus of control and a negative predictor of self-acceptance and existentiality. Healthy Perfectionism and Orderliness generally accounted for negligible variance in the host of dependent variables.

Melora Braver's (1996) dissertation examined the relationship among the APS–R scales and measures of achievement, distress, efficacy, self-criticism, and obsessive–compulsive behaviors. Braver (1996) gathered data from 336 undergraduates and found that Standards scores were positively correlated with GPA ($r = .31$) and SAT scores ($r = .24$). The Standards scale also was related substantively to the Efficacy subscale of the Depressive Experiences Questionnaire (DEQ; $r = .61$) and weakly related to the DEQ Self-Criticism subscale ($r = .12$). Participants scoring highest on Standards reported the lowest levels of distress. In contrast, Discrepancy was positively related to Self-Criticism ($r = .67$) and Distress ($r = .60$), and Discrepancy and Self-Criticism each contributed uniquely to the prediction of distress. For obsessive–compulsive behavior, two interactions were significant: High Standards and high Order predicted average obsessive–compulsive behavior; Standards and Discrepancy were associated with low behavior when Standards scores were high, with average behavior when Standards and Discrepancy scores were low, and with high behavior when levels of Standards were low and Discrepancy was high. No results indicated that high Order scores were related to high obsessive–compulsive behavior scores.

John Wade's (1997) dissertation explored the relationship between measures of perfectionism and status as an ACOA. Wade (1997) was curious about whether the Ashby et al. (1995) results might have been based on differences between participants who were in treatment and participants who were not. From a sample of 246 undergraduates, Wade chose a group of ACOAs, a second group who were from dysfunctional families but were not ACOAs, and a third group who were neither ACOAs nor from dysfunctional families. Wade looked for differences on the APS–R, the Frost et al. (1990) scales, and the DAS Perfectionism and Need for Approval subscales (Weissman & Beck, 1978). Contrary to the predictions about the relationships between ACOA status and perfectionism found in the anecdotal literature, Wade found no differences across groups on any of the scales. Wade cited other studies on college-age participants that had also failed to find differences related to ACOA status and questioned the accuracy of the clear sets of descriptors of ACOAs found in the anecdotal literature.

For Wade's entire sample, the respective correlations with the DAS Perfectionism and Need for Approval subscales were .59 and .45 (respectively) for the APS–R Discrepancy scale, .19 and .07 for the Standards scale, and .15 and −.05 for the Order scale. The most striking correlations between the Frost scales and the APS–R scales were between Organization and Order ($r = .86$), Concern Over Mistakes and Discrepancy ($r = .70$), Personal Standards and Standards ($r = .59$), and Personal Standards and Discrepancy ($r = .44$). The correlations between GPA and Standards, Order, and Discrepancy were .43, .12, and .00, respectively.

Mary Ann McNally Lacour (1997) investigated the relationship between eating disorders and perfectionism with 194 undergraduate women. She used the APS–R, the subscales of the Silencing the Self Scale (STSS; Jack & Dill, 1992), and her adapted version of the Eating Attitudes Test (EAT-26; Garner, Olmstead, Bohr, & Garfinkel, 1982). McNally Lacour concluded that the factor structures she found for the EAT-26 differed substantively for her nonclinical sample. She named her factors Weight Concern, Worry of Others, and Control. She then used the APS–R and STSS and their interaction in a series of stepwise multiple regressions to predict scores on her EAT-26 factors. Discrepancy accounted for the most variance in predicting weight concerns. For Control, the interaction of Discrepancy and the STSS accounted for the greatest amount of variance. No statistically significant results were found for the Worry of Others scale. As suspected, Discrepancy, but not Standards or Order, was involved in predicting scores on scales measuring concern with eating.

Michael Mobley (1998) became highly involved in research on perfectionism while a doctoral student at Penn State. He had had a central role in the data gathering and data analyses of the APS–R. Noting that the available research on perfectionism has almost exclusively involved majority samples, Mobley (1998) did his dissertation on the APS–R using 251 African American undergraduates. He performed a single-group CFA on their responses. The results indicated that the three-factor structure of the APS–R model provided a good fit and that the structure coefficients were almost all greater than .50. Mobley then performed a multiple-group CFA that simultaneously compared his sample with a large, predominantly White sample; he found similar support for the factor structure of the APS–R. His results suggest that the APS–R is appropriate for use with African American university students.

Andrew Shea's (1999) dissertation explored the implications of perfectionism for relationships. More specifically, he developed a 40-item scale entitled the Dyadic APS–R, which was based on the APS–R and was designed to examine the interpersonal implications of imposing one's perfectionistic standards on one's partner or significant other. Shea's participants were 327 university students. A principal-components analysis of the 40 items indicated that the three-factor structure mirrored the structure of the original scale without exception. His final scale was composed of 30 items whose structure coefficients all met or exceeded the criterion of .50. Reliability coefficients ranged from .83 to .93, indicating acceptable internal consistency. In a second part of his study, Shea analyzed the responses of 63 sets of couples to a variety of dependent variables and found that the Dyadic APS–R Discrepancy was the best predictor of relationship satisfaction. Although more research is clearly needed, the Dyadic APS–R seems like a promising addition to the currently available measures of perfectionism.

Denise Accordino's dissertation explored the relationship between the APS–R and measures of achievement, achievement motivation, depression, and self-esteem in 123 high school students (see Accordino, Accordino, & Slaney, 2000). Using multiple regression analyses, Accordino and her colleagues found that the High Standards scale of the APS–R significantly predicted academic achievement and achievement motivation. The APS–R Discrepancy scale was related to increased levels of depression and lower levels of self-esteem. Accordino's study indicates that the use of the APS–R can be usefully extended to high school students. In a similar vein, Vandiver and Worrell (in press) successfully extended the use of the APS–R to academically talented middle-school students. Their study indicates that the reliability and validity of the APS–R is quite acceptable with these participants.

Studies Completed Recently or in Progress

In addition to the studies described above, other research is ongoing in the laboratories of this chapter's authors. The following sections present a brief overview of this research.

Slaney and colleagues. The Penn State research team has now turned its attention to examining the clinical implications of having different scores on particular APS–R subscales. More specifically, participants who have high Standards scores and either low or high Discrepancy scores have been the focus of attention in the most recent set of structured interviews.

Data also have been gathered from the Indian Institute of Technology–Delhi, a highly selective technical training institute in India. With the collaboration of Dr. Dil Bagh Kaur, a faculty member at the institute, demographic data have been gathered along with data on the APS–R and the BDI. Hour-long interviews of selected students with high Standards scores and either high or low Discrepancy scores also have been conducted. Additional studies involving perfectionism and students in India and at Penn State are also presently under way.

Two dissertations and a study by the current Penn State research team will investigate different aspects of the relationships among perfectionism, gender roles, and interpersonal relationships.

Rice and colleagues. Rice and his colleagues have been investigating adaptive and maladaptive dimensions of perfectionism in an ongoing series of studies. Some of their work has focused on the possible precursors of perfectionism and the connection between perfectionism and aspects of self-development, such as narcissism. Rice and Dellwo (in press) found that both adaptive and maladaptive perfectionism appeared to be linked to two aspects of self-development identified by Kohut and Wolf (1978). Kohut has argued that healthy self-development emerges when children have caretakers who admire their children and serve as useful objects of idealization for them. Problems in self-development resulting in narcissistic self structures occur when either or both of those functions are chronically absent or insufficient.

Rice and Dellwo (in press) found that narcissism was associated with derailments in the grandiose–admiration sector of self-development; derailments in the idealized parental-image sector were significantly associated with maladaptive perfectionism, however, whereas a healthy idealization was significantly associated with adaptive perfectionism. Rice and Dellwo created adaptive and maladaptive perfectionism dimensions that incorporated the idealization component and found that those dimensions related in different ways to a host of outcomes. For example, for a large sample of undergraduates, maladaptive perfectionism was a strong predictor of depression, low self-esteem, poor social adjustment, and poor academic integration, but it was unrelated to GPA. Conversely, adaptive perfectionism was not significantly associated with depression, self-esteem, or social adjustment, but it was a significant predictor of academic integration and GPA.

In recent research, Rice and his associates have investigated the link between perfectionism and different indicators of coping, as well as the stability and change in perfectionism–adjustment associations over time (Rice & Dellwo, 2001). For example, Rice and Lapsley (2001) found that adaptive perfectionists reported greater use of problem-focused coping and less use of dysfunctional coping than did maladaptive perfectionists. They suggested that the organizational features of adaptive perfectionism dispose a person to adopt the sort of planning and other active coping activities that are characteristic of problem-focused coping. Furthermore, they suggested that the development of adaptive perfectionism holds broad promise as a factor in coping with stressful events or experiences, whereas maladaptive perfectionism may be considered a potential risk factor under similar circumstances. Rice and Lapsley (2001) did not find that coping mediated the relationship between perfectionism and emotional adjustment, although perfectionism did mediate the association between dysfunctional coping and emotional adjustment. They also found support for an indirect link between problem-focused coping and adjustment through perfectionism. One implication of the findings is that helping to decrease

problematic coping strategies may be necessary, but not sufficient, in helping perfectionists feel more emotionally adjusted. They suggested the utility of adding interventions geared toward reducing maladaptive perfectionism (e.g., decreasing excessive worry about making mistakes by
challenging and revising cognitive distortions) or enhancing adaptive perfectionism (e.g., teaching strategies for improved organization and helping
students develop higher yet reasonable standards) to augment interventions aimed at coping skills.

Ashby and colleagues. Ashby and his colleagues continue to investigate the differences among adaptive perfectionists, maladaptive perfectionists, and nonperfectionists. One recent study (Kottman et al., 1999)
compared the Adlerian personality priorities of adaptive perfectionists
(i.e., people with high Standards and low Discrepancy scores), maladaptive
perfectionists (i.e., people with high Standards and high Discrepancy
scores), and nonperfectionists (i.e., people without high Standards scores).
Kottman and colleagues found that both types of perfectionists scored
higher than nonperfectionists on the Achieving Personality priority. Maladaptive perfectionists, however, scored higher than either the adaptive
perfectionists or the nonperfectionists on the Outdoing priority. The results suggest that although both groups of perfectionists are striving to
achieve, maladaptive perfectionists may be more inclined than adaptive
perfectionists to use social comparison as a measure of achievement.

In a follow-up study, Ashby, LoCicero, and Kenny (in press) investigated the relationship between the Adlerian concept of psychological birth
order and perfectionism. They found that maladaptive perfectionists and
nonperfectionists had significantly higher scores on a measure of middle-
child characteristics (e.g., feeling less important than siblings) than adaptive perfectionists. Additionally, nonperfectionists had significantly higher
scores than maladaptive perfectionists on a measure of youngest child
characteristics (e.g., having others do for them).

Another study investigated the relationship between perfectionism
and self-efficacy. Using the same procedure as Kottman et al. (1999) to
form groups of perfectionists and nonperfectionists, LoCicero and Ashby
(2000) found that adaptive perfectionists scored significantly higher than
both maladaptive perfectionists and nonperfectionists on measures of general self-efficacy and social self-efficacy. The authors suggest that having
high standards may contribute to self-efficacy and that the high standards
of maladaptive perfectionists may moderate the expected deleterious effects of their self-critical attitudes (as represented in their APS–R Discrepancy scores). A follow-up study is looking more specifically at career
self-efficacy and perfectionism.

Ashby, Slaney, and Mangine (1996) investigated the relationship between multidimensional perfectionism and the five-factor model of personality. Using the APS–R and the NEO (Costa & McCrae, 1985), the authors
found that the APS–R Standards and Order scales were significantly associated with conscientiousness and the scales representing the more maladaptive components of perfectionism (e.g., Discrepancy, Anxiety, and Pro-

crastination) were associated with neuroticism. The data suggest that the five-factor model is reasonably related to the various aspects of perfectionism.

In a replication and extension of Rice et al.'s (1998) investigation of perfectionism, self-esteem, and depression, Ashby et al. (2001) investigated the relationship among maladaptive perfectionism, shame, and depression. Structural equation modeling was used to replicate a model wherein maladaptive perfectionism was negatively associated with self-esteem and positively associated with depression, with self-esteem mediating the effects of maladaptive perfectionism on depression. Additional models showed that the path from maladaptive perfectionism to depression was partially mediated by shame. The results support Blatt's (1995) contention that perfectionists' depression may be related to feelings of shame.

Finally, several additional studies have investigated the differences between maladaptive perfectionists, adaptive perfectionists, and nonperfectionists on a number of variables. For instance, Periasamy, Ashby, and LoCicero (1999) found that adaptive perfectionists and maladaptive perfectionists had significantly higher scores on a measure of internal locus of control than nonperfectionists did and that maladaptive perfectionists had significantly higher scores for external locus of control by powerful others than did both adaptive perfectionists and nonperfectionists. Rahotep, Ashby, Periasamy, Kenny, and Pak (2000) found that maladaptive perfectionists, adaptive perfectionists, and nonperfectionists differed significantly on a variety of Rogerian personality variables (as measured by the Feelings, Reactions, and Beliefs Survey; Cartwright & Mori, 1988). Specifically, both adaptive and maladaptive perfectionists scored higher on a measure of focusing conscious attention than nonperfectionists, and adaptive perfectionists scored higher than maladaptive perfectionists and nonperfectionists on a measure of the fully functioning person. LoCicero et al. (2001) investigated perfectionism in middle-school students and found that adaptive perfectionists had significantly higher levels of academic confidence, family support, peer acceptance, and responsibility than nonperfectionists; adaptive perfectionists had significantly higher levels of social confidence than both nonperfectionists and maladaptive perfectionists.

In an investigation of perfectionism and ego defense styles, Edge et al. (2001) found that adaptive perfectionists had significantly lower scores on immature defenses such as denial, acting out, passive aggression, and projection than maladaptive perfectionists. In an investigation of perfectionism and epistemological style, Martin et al. (2001) found that nonperfectionists scored significantly lower on a measure of evaluativism than either maladaptive or adaptive perfectionists; maladaptive perfectionists scored significantly higher on a measure of relativism than both adaptive perfectionists and nonperfectionists. Bruner et al. (2001) compared adaptive perfectionists, maladaptive perfectionists, and nonperfectionists on obsessive–compulsive behaviors and found that compared with adaptive perfectionists, maladaptive perfectionists engaged in more checking, indecision and double-checking, and doubting behaviors. They also found that adaptive perfectionists had significantly lower scores on slowness than both maladaptive perfectionists and nonperfectionists.

Summary of the Research With the APS and APS–R

The initial version of the APS was based on the constructs that the literature seemed to suggest were related to perfectionism. That literature, in turn, was largely anecdotal and portrayed perfectionism as a primarily negative trait. Early studies using the APS suggested that having high standards for performance and a sense of orderliness, in that order, were central to perfectionism, as the literature suggested; however, the studies did not indicate that those aspects of perfectionism were problematic. In addition, although the literature was quite clear that perfectionism was negative in some basic way, it offered a decided lack of clarity about what the essential negative aspects were. For the APS, procrastination was not found to be positively related to having high standards, as suggested, and relationship problems seemed unrelated according to the APS Relationship scale. The early interview study (Slaney & Ashby, 1996) provided additional support for the centrality of the Standards and Order scales and indicated that perfectionism has both negative and positive aspects, as Hamachek (1978) had suggested. In addition, although Slaney and Ashby's study suggested that perfectionism was seen as causing distress, the participants indicated that they generally had no inclination to give up their perfectionism, regardless of the stress.

As research on the APS developed, it became increasingly clear that the construct was multidimensional and that some of the dimensions were positive, whereas others were negative. It also was becoming evident that the APS subscales did not capture what appeared to be the defining negative aspect of perfectionism. The unavoidable conclusion seemed to be that there was a need, first, to rethink the negative aspects of perfectionism and, second, to revise the scale according to that reconsideration. That reconsideration and revision resulted in the APS–R (Slaney et al., 2001).

Although the research on the APS–R is very much a work in progress, the early studies on the measure seem promising. The factor structure of the scale has been solidly supported by the initial confirmatory analyses, and a growing number of studies report measures of internal consistency that support the reliability of the subscales. The relationships between the Standards and Order scales suggest that the two scales are consistently, positively, and moderately correlated, as they were in the APS, where they were combined in one scale. The research also indicates that of the two dimensions, the standards dimension is more central to perfectionism, both conceptually and empirically. Although a range of values has been found, the correlations between the Standards and Discrepancy scales suggest that their relationship is typically negative—sometimes positive— but consistently negligible. That is, these dimensions seem independent and therefore are a psychometric aspect of the APS–R that has potential implications for clinical studies and, quite probably, implications for treatment studies.

A growing number of studies provide an evolving nomological network indicating that the Standards scale, in particular, seems to be modestly, but consistently and positively, related to self-esteem and to measures of academic achievement such as GPA, SAT scores, and efficacy (as measured by the DEQ, for example). It makes intuitive sense that the Standards scale is related to achievement. The Discrepancy scale seems clearly, positively, and substantively related to a variety of scales measuring negative psychological states; measures of depression, anxiety, and distress are perhaps the most prominent. Discrepancy often is negatively related to measures of achievement and to positive psychological measures, such as self-esteem, results that also seem reasonable. It appears that the Order scale measures something like normal orderliness but is not related to obsessive–compulsive features of personality, as was initially suspected. Although additional studies may be needed, it does appear that progress has been made toward reaching the first major goal of developing a conceptually and psychometrically adequate measure of perfectionism.

Clinical Implications of the Research

Perhaps the most striking implication from the above research is that having high standards for achievement does not seem to be related to the problematic aspects of perfectionism. Indeed, the standards construct of the APS–R has been repeatedly related to measures of achievement and self-esteem (Braver, 1996; Rice et al., 1998). It does not appear that lowering one's standards, as the early literature suggested, is a necessary or appropriate goal. In fact, it appears that self-esteem may be enhanced by increasing personal standards and that low self-esteem may be the result of lower standards. This point seems related to the second interview study (Slaney et al., 1999), in which the participants were asked about their reluctance to give up an attribute that caused them stress. The dominant themes from their responses were (a) that their perfectionism was so basic to who they were that they could not imagine giving it up and (b) that it was a positive, although sometimes stressful, attribute that was closely related to their achievement and success. Thus, it is not high personal standards per se that contribute to poor emotional adjustment; rather, it may be the responses that people have to their perceptions that they consistently fail to meet their own standards that lead to emotional difficulties. If, as it appears, the participants in the interview studies were reluctant to give up their high standards, then it may be that attempts to help clients discriminate between Standards and Discrepancy in their own thinking about their perfectionism would be helpful. The research on the APS and APS–R also suggests that possession of a normal sense of orderliness, as measured by the APS–R Order construct, is not problematic or in need of remediation, nor is it as central a construct in perfectionism as are Standards and Discrepancy.

The results of Rice et al. (1998) imply that for clients presenting with depression and maladaptive perfectionism, interventions could be directed toward enhancing self-esteem, which appears to diminish the effects of maladaptive perfectionism on depression. This possibility seems even clearer in the research relating the APS–R and self-esteem. One way to help such clients might be to educate them about the different components of perfectionism and help them become more aware of their options regarding perfectionism and the likely consequences of their choices. Clients may derive self-satisfaction by adhering to adaptive perfectionism while relinquishing the maladaptive aspects of perfectionism. Perfectionism also can be addressed in preventive activities. For example, psychoeducational interventions on the topic of perfectionism can be provided to the community or to people making stressful transitions to situations that may exacerbate perfectionism–distress associations (e.g., the transition to college for late adolescents; the transition into career positions with increasing responsibilities or demands; and marriage, parenthood, or other long-term relationship commitments).

The research on the APS–R clearly indicates that the discrepancy construct is consistently and substantively related to negative psychological states; conversely, it is negatively related to positive states and measures of achievement. The broad clinical implications would appear to be that future treatment studies should focus on the construct of discrepancy and explore treatments designed to decrease the perceived difference between one's standards and one's performance. Clearly, different theoretical perspectives will suggest different approaches. The most obvious challenge, however, may be to decrease the experiences of dissatisfaction, angst, or unhappiness while indicating that the maintenance of standards for performance is possible, reasonable, and even desirable. This approach seems necessary because the possession of high standards for one's performance is basic to the fabric of U.S. and Western societies and seems highly related to the reluctance of interview participants to give up their perfectionism.

The assumption that support for high standards of achievement is basic to the U.S. and other Western cultures raises an important question for clinicians: How widespread is the feeling that a discrepancy exists between one's standards for performance and one's actual performance? Particularly with regard to academic or career achievements, the message often seems to be that doing one's best is all that is called for. The apparent benevolence of this message masks the fact that consistently doing one's best is a high standard indeed. This message often is combined with the particularly American-sounding message that one can achieve anything given determination, hard work, and other similarly touted virtues. Issues such as how much achievement is enough, how one can achieve a reasonable balance in life, or how one might react when avenues of achievement are blocked, and so forth, are less frequently addressed. In sum, it seems quite possible that some feelings of discrepancy may be ingrained in rather large segments of the population. How large that segment is and how much unhappiness results seem to be important issues. A closely related question is whether a sense of discrepancy is an affliction that is particularly relevant to academic and career pursuits, particularly to professionals or the competent among us. Finally, is perfectionism a useful diagnostic category unto itself, or is it more logically subsumed under some other category, such as depression or anxiety?

Several studies that have explored Adlerian explanations for differences between adaptive and maladaptive perfectionism (Ashby & Kottman, 1996; Ashby et al., in press; Kottman & Ashby, 1999) suggest that an important distinction between adaptive and maladaptive perfectionism may rest in how perfectionists use their perfectionism. From an Adlerian perspective, the adaptive perfectionist, who experiences less distress related to perfectionism and is striving for high standards, may be appropriately pursuing superiority, a sign of mental health according to Adler (1956). This view is consistent with interview participants' general perceptions that their perfectionism, though stressful, was related to achievement and success (Slaney et al., 1999). In contrast, maladaptive perfectionists may pursue high standards to avoid feelings of inferiority. The avoidance may be manifest in the need to outdo others and may be related to a family atmosphere in which love and acceptance are based on performance.

Rice and Dellwo (in press) and Rice and Mirzadeh (2000) also emphasize the importance of the family in their research on the relationship between early experiences with parents and the development of perfectionism. On the basis of self psychology (Kohut & Wolf, 1978) and attachment theory, Rice and colleagues suggested that perfectionism may develop in a context of harsh and excessively critical parent–child relationships. Because excessively critical parents may be particularly difficult to idealize, children from such families may be predisposed to develop maladaptive perfectionism. Alternatively, parents who maintain high standards but also remain emotionally accessible, responsive, and supportive of their children may facilitate the development of adaptive perfectionistic tendencies. One therapeutic implication of the Rice and Dellwo (in press) study is that perfectionists may be more likely to develop idealizing–hungry transferences (Kohut & Wolf, 1978) in psychotherapy that, with adequate intervention, ultimately may yield the development of adaptive perfectionistic characteristics. Indeed, the transference dynamics that maladaptive perfectionists bring to therapy may be one reason why clients experience poor outcomes in short-term psychotherapy and better outcomes in long-term psychotherapy (Blatt, 1995; Blatt et al., 1996).

Rice's suggestions also have implications for interpersonal relationships; the interview studies, in particular, seemed to suggest that interpersonal relationships are affected by perfectionism, most frequently in a negative manner. Women seemed to indicate this with greater clarity than men, although the reasons for this difference are unclear. The theme of competition was particularly clear in the Indian men who were interviewed. Although the latter results can be seen as merely suggestive, the issue of how the various aspects of perfectionism are related to interpersonal relationships is an interesting and important topic for future work.

It may be that perfectionism plays out differently according to gender roles.

Implications for Future Research

A number of the clinical implications described above lead logically to suggestions for future research. For example, future studies could address the question of whether helping clients delineate the negative and positive aspects of perfectionism might help convey the message that high standards and orderliness are not necessarily problematic and need not be treated or given up. At the same time, various therapeutic approaches to reducing the phenomenological sense of discrepancy in clients who feel highly distressed might be usefully explored. How would such studies relate to Blatt et al.'s (1995, 1996) findings on the difficulty of treating "perfectionists" in short-term psychotherapy? At this point, no studies have carefully addressed the basis of the phenomenological sense of discrepancy. For example, are there people whose assessments of their degree of discrepancy represent accurate self-evaluations that are based on some reasonable set of external criteria or judgments, or are those estimates strictly internal? Are some people with low standards simply unconcerned about achievement? What are participants like who have low standards and high discrepancy scores?

Although it has not been articulated as such, perfectionism tends to be construed as a relatively static personality characteristic. Indeed, in one study, Blatt et al. (1995) concluded that pretreatment and posttreatment perfectionism scores (as measured by the DAS subscale) were significantly correlated ($r = .65$). In another study, Blatt et al. (1996) stated that brief psychotherapy may be insufficient to change "well-entrenched negative mental representations of self and other" (p. 169). To our knowledge, however, no forthright examination of the stability or change in higher or second-order perfectionism dimensions has taken place. Thus, it may be the case that certain dimensions of perfectionism are impervious to change, regardless of time of intervention, whereas other dimensions may fluctuate over time and in response to interventions. It seems plausible to hypothesize that Discrepancy, as measured by the APS–R, could be affected through psychotherapeutic intervention, but not high Standards and Order. Indeed, it may prove to be the case that focused interventions should attend to shoring up or maintaining Standards and Order while diminishing the strength of the Discrepancy dimension in depressed clients.

A related question is whether the dimensions of perfectionism are pervasive personality characteristics or specific to certain situations or issues. Thus far, perfectionism—more accurately, its components—has been treated as if it is a general attribute of personality. The interview studies, however, indicate that academic and career pursuits are typically areas in which participants' Standards, Order, and Discrepancy have the greatest relevance. Would the relationships and predictions from those scales be improved if they were designed to focus on specific areas or activities? For example, should scales be developed to measure individual perceptions of standards, order, and discrepancy in academic, career, interpersonal, athletic, or more specific domains of life, similar to Bandura's conceptualization of self-efficacy?

Finally, longitudinal research on the implications of perfectionism for mental health could address the specificity of perfectionism. For example, perfectionism may only become destructive (Blatt, 1995) when stress occurs in specific perfectionism-relevant domains. Some perfectionists may be "primed" for self-destructive or depressogenic reactions as a result of a disappointing job performance, whereas others may have difficulties after a disappointing social interaction. Adaptive perfectionism may be found to be an important predictor of current academic functioning or social functioning that, in turn, may protect people from later stress-induced emotional difficulties. Likewise, early detection of maladaptive perfectionism and low self-esteem could be used in prevention programming to reduce the risk for later depression. Interventions aimed at enhancing self-esteem could ultimately buffer the deleterious effects that maladaptive perfectionism has on depression (Rice et al., 1998). Clearly, these issues and those mentioned above provide fertile ground for future research.

A major purpose in writing this chapter was to describe the development and refinement of the APS–R and to encourage research on perfectionism, in general, and with the APS–R, in particular. The measure has been rigorously evaluated on its psychometric qualities and predictive capabilities. At this point, several thousand research participants have provided data on the APS and APS–R, including undergraduate, clinical, and cross-cultural samples. The APS–R extends our thinking about perfectionism in ways that address psychological strengths (or protective factors) as well as limitations (or risk factors). The APS–R has emerged as an efficient and psychometrically sound instrument that could prove useful as a screening or treatment progress measure for the clinician. The measure taps potential individual resources as well as concerns that would be of interest to practitioners in a variety of settings (e.g., student affairs professionals, school counselors, and parent education trainers). Finally, the APS–R can serve as a sound measure of perfectionism for the interested personality or clinical researcher. It is our hope that others find the complementary advantages of the APS–R for the science and practice of psychology as conceptually interesting and potentially useful as we have.

References

Accordino, D. B., Accordino, M. P., & Slaney, R. B. (2000). An investigation of perfectionism, mental health, achievement and achievement motivation in adolescents. *Psychology in the Schools, 37,* 535–545.

Adler, A. (1956). *The Individual Psychology of Alfred Adler.* H. Ansbacher & R. Ansbacher, Eds. New York: Basic Books.

Ashby, J., Bieschke, K., & Slaney, R. B. (1997, August). *Multidimensional perfectionism and career decision-making self-efficacy.* Poster presented at the annual meeting of the American Psychological Association, Chicago.

Ashby, J., & Huffman, J. (1999). Religious orientation and multidimensional perfectionism: Relationship and implications. *Counseling and Values, 43,* 178–188.

Ashby, J., & Kottman, T. (1996). Inferiority as a distinction between normal and neurotic perfectionism. *Individual Psychology, 52,* 237–245.

Ashby, J., Kottman, T., & DeGraaf, D. (1999). Leisure satisfaction and attitudes of perfectionists: Implications for therapeutic recreation professionals. *Therapeutic Recreation Journal, 33,* 142–151.

Ashby, J., Kottman, T., & Schoen, E. (1998). Perfectionism and eating disorders reconsidered. *Journal of Mental Health Counseling, 20,* 261–271.

Ashby, J., LoCicero, K. A., & Kenny, M. C. (in press). Perfectionism and psychological birth order. *Individual Psychology.*

Ashby, J., Mangine, J. D., & Slaney, R. B. (1995). An investigation of perfectionism in a university sample of adult children of alcoholics. *Journal of College Student Development, 36,* 452–455.

Ashby, J., & Rice, K. G. (in press). Multidimensional perfectionism, dysfunctional attitudes, and self-esteem: A structural equations analysis. *Journal of Counseling and Development.*

Ashby, J. S., Rice, K. G., Kenny, M. C., Bruner, L. P., Edge, C. A., Blasko, L. S., & Martin, J. L. (2001, August). *Perfectionism, shame, self-esteem, and depression: A structural equations analysis.* Poster presented at the annual meeting of the American Psychological Association, San Francisco.

Ashby, J., Slaney, R. B., & Mangine, J. D. (1996, August). *An investigation of the relationship between perfectionism and the Big-Five factor structure.* Poster presented at the annual meeting of the American Psychological Association, Toronto, Ontario, Canada.

Beck, A. T. (1978). *Depression inventory.* Philadelphia: Center for Cognitive Therapy.

Bergin, A. E., Stinchfield, R. D., Gaskin, T. A., Masters, K. S., & Sullivan, C. E. (1988). Religious life-styles and mental health: An exploratory study. *Journal of Counseling Psychology, 35,* 91–98.

Blatt, S. J. (1995). The destructiveness of perfectionism: Implications for the treatment of depression. *American Psychologist, 50,* 1003–1020.

Blatt, S. J., Quinlan, D. M., Pilkonis, P. A., & Shea, M. T. (1995). Impact of perfectionism and need for approval on the brief treatment of depression: The National Institute of Mental Health Treatment of Depression Collaborative Research Program revisited. *Journal of Consulting and Clinical Psychology, 63,* 125–132.

Blatt, S. J., Zuroff, D. C., Quinlan, D. M., & Pilkonis, P. A. (1996). Interpersonal factors in brief treatment of depression: Further analyses of the National Institute of Mental Health Treatment of Depression Collaborative Research Program. *Journal of Consulting and Clinical Psychology, 64,* 162–171.

Braver, M. L. (1996). Distinguishing normal and pathological perfectionism in college students: Dimensions of the Almost Perfect Scale–Revised and patterns of relationship with academic performance and psychological functioning. *Dissertation Abstracts International, 57,* 12B. (UMI No. 7716)

Bruner, L. P., Ashby, J. S., Blasco, L. S., Edge, C. A., LoCicero, K. A., Martin, J. L., & Kenny, M. C. (2001, August). *Multidimensional perfectionism and obsessive–compulsive behaviors.* Poster presented at the annual meeting of the American Psychological Association, San Francisco.

Cartwright, D., & Mori, C. (1988). Scales for assessing aspects of the person. *Person Centered Review, 3,* 176–194.

Costa, P. T., & McCrae, R. R. (1985). *The NEO Personality Inventory manual.* Odessa, FL: Psychological Assessment Resources.

Edge, C. A., Ashby, J. S., Blasco, L. S., Bruner, L. P., Martin, J. L., & Kenny, M. C. (2001, August). *Multidimensional perfectionism and ego defense styles.* Poster presented at the annual meeting of the American Psychological Association, San Francisco.

Frost, R. O., Heimberg, R. G., Holt, C. S., Mattia, J. I., & Neubauer, A. L. (1993). A comparison of two measures of perfectionism. *Personality and Individual Differences, 14,* 119–126.

Frost, R. O., Marten, P., Lahart, C., & Rosenblate, R. (1990). The dimensions of perfectionism. *Cognitive Therapy and Research, 14,* 449–468.

Garner, D. M., Olmstead, M. P., Bohr, Y., & Garfinkel, P. E. (1982). The Eating Attitudes Test: Psychometric features and clinical correlates. *Psychological Medicine, 12,* 871–878.

Hamachek, D. E. (1978). Psychodynamics of normal and neurotic perfectionism. *Psychology, 15,* 27–33.

Hewitt, P. L., & Flett, G. L. (1991). Perfectionism in the self and social contexts: Conceptualization, assessment, and association with psychopathology. *Journal of Personality and Social Psychology, 60,* 456–470.

Jack, D. C., & Dill, D. (1992). The Silencing the Self Scale: Schema of intimacy associated with depression in women. *Psychology of Women Quarterly, 16,* 97–106.

Johnson, D. P. (1993). An investigation of the construct validity of a measure of perfectionism: The Slaney, Johnson, Sternberg questionnaire. *Dissertation Abstracts International, 53,* 7B. (UMI No. 3756)

Johnson, D. P., & Slaney, R. B. (1996). Perfectionism: Scale development and a study of perfectionists in counseling. *Journal of College Student Development, 37,* 29–41.

Kohut, H., & Wolf, E. S. (1978). The disorders of the self and their treatment: An outline. *International Journal of Psycho-Analysis, 59,* 413–425.

Kottman, T., & Ashby, J. (1999). Social interest and multidimensional perfectionism. *Journal of Individual Psychology, 55,* 176–185.

Kottman, T., Ashby, J. S., Schoen, E., LoCicero, K., Stoltz, K., & Periasamy, S. (1999, August). *Multidimensional perfectionism and Adlerian personality priorities.* Poster presented at the annual meeting of the American Psychological Association, Boston.

Lacour, M.-A. McNally (1997). Creating a model to predict eating disturbances in women from the components of perfectionism and self-silencing. *Dissertation Abstracts International, 58,* 12B. (UMI No. 6814)

LoCicero, K. A., & Ashby, J. S. (2000). Multidimensional perfectionism and self-reported self-efficacy in college students. *Journal of College Student Psychotherapy, 15,* 47–56.

LoCicero, K. A., Blasko, L. S., Ashby, J. S., Bruner, L. P., Martin, J. L., & Edge. C. A. (2001, August). *Multidimensional perfectionism and coping resources in middle school students.* Poster presented at the annual meeting of the American Psychological Association, San Francisco.

Martin, J. L., Ashby, J. S., Bruner, L. P., Edge, C. A., Blasco, L. S., & Kenney, M. C. (2001, August). *Multidimensional perfectionism and epistemological style.* Poster presented at the annual meeting of the American Psychological Association, San Francisco.

Meyer, T., Miller, M., Metzger, R. L., & Borkovec, T. (1990). Development and validation of the Penn State Worry Questionnaire. *Behaviour Research and Therapy, 28,* 487–495.

Mobley, M. (1998). Construct validity of the Almost Perfect Scale–Revised: Academic performance and differential standards among African-American college students. *Dissertation Abstracts International, 60,* 1B. (UMI No. 412)

Periasamy, S., Ashby, J. S., & LoCicero, K. (1999, August). *Multidimensional perfectionism and locus of control.* Poster presented at the annual meeting of the American Psychological Association, Boston.

Preusser, K. J., Rice, K. G., & Ashby, J. S. (1994). The role of self-esteem in mediating the perfectionism–depression connection. *Journal of College Student Development, 35,* 88–93.

Rahotep, S., Ashby, J. S., Periasamy, S., Kenny, M. C., & Pak, L. (2000, August). *Multidimensional perfectionism and Rogerian personality characteristics.* Poster presented at the annual meeting of the American Psychological Association, Washington, DC.

Rice, K. G., Ashby, J. S., & Preusser, K. J. (1996). Perfectionism, relationships with parents, and self-esteem. *Individual Psychology, 52,* 246–260.

Rice, K. G., Ashby, J. S., & Slaney, R. B. (1998). Self-esteem as a mediator between perfectionism and depression: A structural equations analysis. *Journal of Counseling Psychology, 45,* 304–314.

Rice, K. G., & Dellwo, J. P. (in press). Perfectionism and self-development: Implications for college adjustment. *Journal of Counseling and Development.*

Rice, K. G., & Dellwo, J. P. (2001). Within-semester stability and adjustment correlates of the Multidimensional Perfectionism Scale. *Measurement and Evaluation in Counseling and Development, 34,* 146–156.

Rice, K. G., & Lapsley, D. K. (2001). Perfectionism, coping, and emotional adjustment. *Journal of College Student Development, 42,* 157–168.

Rice, K. G., & Mirzadeh, S. A. (2000). Perfectionism, attachment, and adjustment. *Journal of Counseling Psychology, 47,* 238–250.

Sandler, J., & Hazari, A. (1960). The "obsessional": On the psychological classification of obsessional character traits and symptoms. *British Journal of Medical Psychology, 33,* 113–122.

Shea, A. J. (1999). *Associations between perfectionism and relationship satisfaction.* Unpublished doctoral dissertation, Pennsylvania State University, State College.

Slaney, R. B., & Ashby, J. A. (1996). Perfectionists: Study of a criterion group. *Journal of Counseling and Development, 74,* 393–398.

Slaney, R. B., Ashby, J. S., & Trippi, J. (1995). Perfectionism: Its measurement and career relevance. *Journal of Career Assessment, 3,* 279–297.

Slaney, R. B., Chadha, N., Mobley, M., & Kennedy, S. (2000). Perfectionism in Asian Indians: Exploring the meaning of the construct in India. *Counseling Psychologist, 28,* 10–31.

Slaney, R. B., & Johnson, D. G. (1992). *The Almost Perfect Scale.* Unpublished manuscript, Pennsylvania State University, State College.

Slaney, R. B., Mobley, M., Trippi, J., Ashby, J. S., & Johnson, D. G. (1996). *Almost Perfect Scale–Revised.* Unpublished manuscript, Pennsylvania State University, State College.

Slaney, R. B., Rice, K. G., Mobley, M., Trippi, J., & Ashby, J. S. (2001). The Almost Perfect Scale–Revised. *Measurement and Evaluation in Counseling and Development, 34,* 130–145.

Slaney, R. B., Suddarth, B. H., Rice, K. G., Ashby, J. S., & Mobley, M. (1999). *Perfectionism: Interviews with "normal" and "neurotic" perfectionists.* Unpublished manuscript, Pennsylvania State University, State College.

Spielberger, C. D., Gorsuch, R. L., Lushene, R. E., Vagg, R. C., & Jacobs, G. S. (1983). *Manual for the State–Trait Anxiety Inventory.* Palo Alto, CA: Consulting Psychologists.

Strano, D. A., & Dixon, P. N. (1990). The comparative feeling of inferiority index. *Individual Psychology, 46,* 29–42.

Suddarth, B. H., & Slaney, R. B. (2001). An investigation of the dimensions of perfectionism in college students. *Measurement and Evaluation in Counseling and Development, 34,* 157–165.

Taylor, K. M., & Betz, N. E. (1983). Applications of self-efficacy theory to the understanding and treatment of career indecision. *Journal of Vocational Behavior, 22,* 63–81.

Timpe, R. L. (1989). Ritualization and ritualisms in religious development: A psychosocial perspective. *Journal of Psychology and Theology, 11,* 311–317.

Vandiver, B. J., & Worrell, F. C. (in press). The reliability and validity of scores on the Almost Perfect Scale–Revised with academically talented middle school students. *Journal of Secondary Gifted Education.*

Wade, J. C. (1997). Perfectionism in adult children of alcoholics, adult children from dysfunctional but non-alcoholic families, and adults from non-dysfunctional families. *Dissertation Abstracts International, 58,* 7B. (UMI No. 3937).

Weissman, A. N., & Beck, A. T. (1978, August). *Development and validation of the Dysfunctional Attitude Scale: A preliminary investigation.* Paper presented at the 86th annual meeting of the American Psychological Association, Toronto, Ontario, Canada.

4 ⎯⎯⎯⎯⎯⎯⎯⎯⎯⎯⎯⎯⎯⎯⎯⎯

Perfectionism in Children and Their Parents: A Developmental Analysis

Gordon L. Flett, Paul L. Hewitt, Joan M. Oliver, and Silvana Macdonald

One of the best ways to obtain insight into the nature of any personality construct is to examine the factors and processes that contribute to its development. In the case of perfectionism, numerous theoretical accounts describe its origins. Unfortunately, those accounts have not been followed by extensive empirical work, so research on the development of perfectionism is still in its early stages.

This chapter provides a comprehensive overview of perfectionism from a developmental perspective. The first part reviews past theoretical statements, with a particular emphasis on the role of family factors; it describes various models of the development of perfectionism and related research on the family environment of perfectionists. Those models are then incorporated into an integrative, transactional model that takes into account the array of factors that contribute to perfectionism. The model examines the various dimensions of perfectionism in terms of processes involving factors both outside the self (i.e., family and cultural environment) and within the self. Implicit in this model is the recognition that many factors may contribute to the development of perfectionism; the different factors have important implications for possible differences among types of perfectionists.

The final part of our chapter examines the consequences of perfectionism in the family; it presents the argument that perfectionistic parents have a distinct set of characteristics that may put their children at risk for negative outcomes. The section describes recent research in our laboratory that examines the maladaptive beliefs, behaviors, and emotional functioning of perfectionistic parents with young children. Our research shows that certain dimensions of perfectionism are associated with parenting stress, distress, and a diminished sense of worth in the parenting role. We conclude with a discussion of the implications of these findings and an outline of directions for future research.

Models of the Development of Perfectionism

Past theorists have identified various family histories that may contribute
to the development of perfectionism. We have labeled those models the
social expectations model, the *social learning* model, the *social reaction*
model, and the *anxious rearing* model.

Social Expectations Model

Both Hamachek (1978) and Missildine (1963) discussed the development
of perfectionism in response to contingent parental approval; that is, the
child learns that parental approval is forthcoming if the child is perfect.
This idea is derived from Rogers's (1951) work on conditions of worth.
Rogers maintained that children are prone to low self-esteem when parental approval is contingent on meeting parental expectations. In the case
of perfectionism, it is believed that the parental standards are quite high,
and this emphasis is reflected in the content of perfectionism instruments
such as the Frost Multidimensional Perfectionism Scale (MPS), which has
a Parental Expectations subscale (Frost, Marten, Lahart, & Rosenblate,
1990).

Implicit in the social expectations model is the notion that children
who are not capable of meeting parental expectations will experience a
chronic sense of helplessness and hopelessness as a result of their inability
to meet the standards imposed on them. In general, exposure to conditions
that foster a sense of conditional self-worth also increases the likelihood
that a state of helplessness will develop (see Burhans & Dweck, 1995;
Chorpita & Barlow, 1998). A sense of contingent self-worth is a central
aspect of socially prescribed perfectionism, as described by Hewitt and
Flett (1991). People who score high on measures of socially prescribed
perfectionism and who tend to endorse such statements as "The better I
do, the better I am expected to do" are likely to have been exposed to
conditions of contingent self-worth, and they are highly vulnerable to feelings of helplessness in response to negative feedback from others.

Whereas Frost and associates focused specifically on parental expectations, Hewitt and Flett (1991) conceptualized socially prescribed perfectionism in a manner that includes the influence of family members but
involves broader societal pressures as well. A focus on a more generalized
view of socially prescribed perfectionism has implications for the concept
of contingent self-worth, because such a perspective would include contingent regard not only from family members but also from other people,
including peers and teachers. At a broad level, this view could involve
contingent regard from society as a whole (e.g., the societal ideal of having
the perfect physical appearance).

Recent research by Dweck and associates has shown that feedback
that focuses on the attributes of a child rather than the achievement process can promote a sense of contingent self-worth (Kamins & Dweck, 1999;
Mueller & Dweck, 1998). Remarkably, this research has shown that even

positive feedback about personal characteristics (e.g., high intelligence) can foster a sense of contingent self-worth (see Kamins & Dweck, 1999) and in turn create a vulnerability to experiencing helplessness that is activated once the positive feedback is no longer experienced and is instead replaced by negative feedback.

Dweck and associates' finding may have particular significance for high-achieving perfectionists. We maintain that people with high levels of perfectionism, including forms of perfectionism that have been identified by some authors as adaptive (e.g., self-oriented perfectionism) will be vulnerable to adjustment problems if their perfectionism is based on a sense of contingent self-worth. This prediction is in keeping with research showing that self-oriented perfectionists who experience achievement failures are prone to experience depression (Hewitt & Flett, 1993; Hewitt, Flett, & Ediger, 1996). It is likely that self-oriented perfectionists viewed failure as a reflection of their personal characteristics and felt a sense of personal inadequacy.

The social expectations model historically has focused on excessively high parental expectations; at the other end of the spectrum, however, the lack of any expectations also may be problematic. Hamachek (1978) suggested that perfectionism can develop when a child has not been presented with any parental input or guidelines. Several adults in treatment have indicated that they adopted perfectionism as a way of dealing with parental neglect. In this situation, children set high expectations for themselves as a way of coping with the absence of clear standards and expectations and their uncertainty about whether a particular behavior is punishable or likely to be rewarded. To our knowledge, the link between perfectionism in the child and parental neglect or inattention has not been empirically tested.

Social Learning Model

The social learning model focuses on the role of imitation of the perfectionism that presumably resides in parents. Children with perfectionistic parents will have a tendency to imitate their parents. Social learning also will take place as a result of the developmental tendency for young children to have an idealized notion of their parents; many children will want to be like their seemingly "perfect" parents.

The possible role of social learning in the acquisition of perfectionistic tendencies was demonstrated in classic research conducted by Bandura and his colleagues (for a summary, see Bandura, 1986). Their research demonstrates that children tend to imitate and embrace the evaluative standards modeled by others; this pattern extends to imitating the self-evaluative tendencies of adults. For example, in the Bandura and Kupers (1964) experiment, children were exposed to an adult model who had high or low standards that had to be met in order to engage in self-reward. Bandura and Kupers found that children exposed to models who rewarded themselves only after meeting high standards were unlikely to reward themselves unless they met high standards as well. In contrast, children exposed to models who rewarded themselves for meeting lower standards imitated that pattern of self-reinforcement.

In related research, Bandura, Grusec, and Menlove (1967) conducted an experiment that simultaneously examined several factors involved in social learning. They found that the most extreme, stringent style of self-reward is evident among children who experience an adult model with unrealistic standards, an adult model who does not indulge the child, and nonexposure to peers who reward themselves for relatively low levels of performance. Bandura et al. (1967) conducted this research to demonstrate the many factors that may influence the setting of high standards and related aspects of self-evaluation.

Perfectionism researchers have indirectly tested the social learning perspective by examining levels of perfectionism in parents and their children. If imitation exists, then perfectionism should "run in the family." Frost, Lahart, and Rosenblate (1991) examined the link between two samples of undergraduate women ($N = 41$ and $N = 63$) and their mothers and fathers. All participants completed the Frost MPS. The student participants provided ratings of parental characteristics, and levels of psychological distress among the students were assessed in one of the samples. The results indicated that perfectionism in mothers was associated with perfectionism in daughters. No significant association was found between perfectionism in fathers and daughters, but the perceived harshness of the father, as rated by the daughter, was associated with perfectionism in daughters. Analyses involving the measures of psychological distress in daughters found that their distress was correlated with perfectionism in mothers. Modeling is one explanation for the link between perfectionism in mothers and daughters.

Chang (2000) examined perfectionism scores on the Frost MPS in 195 students and their parents. The sample was predominantly female and consisted of 134 students and 153 mothers. Chang (2000) found that levels of perfectionism in students and their parents were correlated significantly ($r = .25$). Unfortunately, the results focused only on the total perfectionism scores and were not reported separately for various perfectionism dimensions.

Vieth and Trull (1999) conducted related research. They used the Hewitt and Flett MPS (Hewitt & Flett, 1991) to examine levels of perfectionism in 188 university students and their parents. The MPS measures self-oriented perfectionism, other-oriented perfectionism (i.e., high standards for others), and socially prescribed perfectionism (i.e., the perception that others demand perfection from oneself). Vieth and Trull found that self-oriented perfectionism in daughters was correlated with self-oriented perfectionism in mothers ($r = .31$) but not in fathers. Self-oriented perfectionism in sons was associated positively with self-oriented perfectionism in fathers ($r = .46$), but it was associated negatively with self-oriented perfectionism in mothers ($r = -.28$). No significant correlations were found for levels of other-oriented perfectionism. Finally, socially prescribed perfectionism was correlated in daughters and mothers. The data suggest that the role of imitation in perfectionism may be specific to perfectionism in the same-sexed parent; at the same time, however, it must be acknowledged that direct tests of the role of social learning in perfectionism have not been conducted.

We have explored the role of social learning not only by examining levels of perfectionism in parents and their children but also by asking research participants to complete the Hewitt and Flett MPS both for themselves and as they expect it would be completed by their parents. That is, we asked participants to provide their subjective views of levels of perfectionism in their parents. In one recent study, Flynn, Hewitt, Flett, and Caelian (2001) had 119 students complete the MPS for themselves and their parents; they also completed the Moos Family Environment Scale (Moos & Moos, 1986), the Parental Bonding Index (Parker, Tupling, & Brown, 1979), and the Parent Behavior Form (see Kelly & Worell, 1976). The findings involving perceptions of parenting behaviors are reported in subsequent sections of this chapter. Regarding participants' own perfectionism and perceived perfectionism in their parents, the highest correlations were between corresponding dimensions. For instance, participants' own self-oriented perfectionism scores were correlated most highly with their mothers' and fathers' self-oriented perfectionism, as rated by the participant. This finding held for all three MPS dimensions. In addition, a significant association was found between participants' socially prescribed perfectionism and perceptions of mothers' other-oriented perfectionism. The data suggest that social learning processes operate in perfectionism, especially in empirical research with an explicit focus on perceived levels of perfectionism in parents.

In general it would appear that perfectionism in children is associated with ratings of parental perfectionism; modeling may be relevant in this regard, but the possible influence of genetic factors cannot be ascertained from this research. Clearly, further research is needed to directly investigate the role of imitation in the development of perfectionism. The original experiments conducted by Bandura and colleagues, however, strongly indicate that social learning is a key element.

Social Reaction Model

Other models of the development of perfectionism also can be identified. We maintain that it is important to test a model that we refer to as the *social reaction* model. The model is based on the premise that children who become perfectionistic have been exposed to a harsh environment, which can come in many forms, including exposure to physical abuse; psychological maltreatment, including love withdrawal and exposure to shame; or a chaotic family environment. The child may react or respond to that environment by becoming perfectionistic, almost as a coping mechanism. Perfectionism as a social reaction or response to adversity can involve several interrelated goals. The child can become perfectionistic in an attempt to escape from or to minimize further abuse or to reduce exposure to shame and humiliation (e.g., "If I am perfect, no one will hurt me"). Alternatively, the child may become perfectionistic as a way of trying to establish a sense of control and predictability in an unpredictable environment. One aspect of this reaction is that it is in response to a lack of consistency on the part of parents and other caregivers.

It should be evident that a substantial overlap exists between the social expectation and the social reaction models. We felt that the models should be viewed separately, however, because the social reaction model involves elements of harshness and punitive tendencies that do not necessarily exist in all families that promote perfectionism through high expectations. A subsequent section of this chapter describes research on various parenting dimensions that suggests the need to distinguish high expectations from hostile reactions. The social expectations model would involve the control dimension of parenting, but the social reaction model would involve extrapunitive forms of hostility and lack of warmth, which is a different parenting dimension.

Relatively few studies have directly tested the social reaction model of the development of perfectionism; however, the evidence from research on people with eating disorders is consistent with the notion that some people become perfectionistic as a way of coping with a hostile environment (Kaner, Bulik, & Sullivan, 1993; Kinzl, Traweger, Guenther, & Biebl, 1994; Lindberg & Distad, 1985; Schaaf & McCanne, 1994; Tobin & Griffing, 1996; Zlotnick et al., 1996). For instance, Zlotnick et al. (1996) examined scores on the Eating Disorder Inventory (EDI) as a function of whether participants had a history of sexual abuse. The female participants were in one of four groups (i.e., psychiatric patients with a history of sexual abuse, psychiatric patients with no history of sexual abuse, bulimic patients, and anorexic patients). Examination of the EDI subscale scores indicated that patients with a history of sexual abuse had significantly elevated levels of perfectionism. Similarly, Kaner et al. (1993) examined levels of perfectionism on the EDI as a function of whether bulimic women did or did not have a history of being battered. Bulimic women with a history of being battered had higher levels of perfectionism than did bulimic women without a history of being battered, who, in turn, had higher perfectionism scores than a nonbattered group without a history of bulimia. Finally, Schaaf and McCanne (1994) assessed levels of perfectionism in a sample of women that included sexually abused college students, physically abused college students, and nonabused college students. Relative to controls, scores on the Perfectionism subscale were elevated in both abused groups, but only participants with a history of physical abuse had significantly higher scores. Interestingly, the EDI Perfectionism subscale was one of the few EDI subscales to yield a significant group difference.

We also have been able to identify anecdotal case histories that are consistent with a social reaction model. For instance, in their paper on adolescent victims of incest, Lindberg and Distad (1985) described the case of a 14-year-old girl who had been abused by her grandfather for 10 years and neglected by her alcoholic mother and father. Regarding the girl's characteristics, they observed that

> She was regarded as bright, friendly and "bubbly" to the casual observer. In addition, she was considered perfectionistic and tended to intellectualize her trauma. Pondering abstract questions related to her incest or expressing the need to act or think "perfectly" may have allowed her to temporarily escape feelings of despair, bitterness, and worthlessness. This girl's relief was temporary. She had also made six major suicide attempts. (p. 523)

Frost et al.'s (1991) study, described earlier, provided empirical evidence consistent with the social reaction model. In addition to completing measures of perfectionism, both the parents and the students were asked to provide ratings of parental harshness. The results indicated that maternal harshness (as rated by mothers and daughters) was associated with perfectionism in daughters. Similarly, the perceived harshness of the father, as rated by the daughter, was associated with perfectionism in daughters. The link between parental harshness and daughter's perfectionism suggests that some daughters may have developed perfectionistic tendencies as a way of coping with their parents' hostile expectations. Given that concern with making mistakes is the central element measured by the Frost perfectionism measure, it follows that the desire to minimize mistakes is the primary focus when people have adopted perfectionism in an attempt to cope.

Anxious Rearing Model

A fourth model, the anxious rearing model, constitutes another pathway to the development of perfectionism. To our knowledge, no published research on perfectionism has tested the possibility that perfectionistic strivings and an anxious overconcern with mistakes reflects a history of being exposed to anxious parents who promote a focus on mistakes and the negative consequences of making mistakes. The focus of parenting in the anxious rearing model is exposure to parental worry about being imperfect. Overprotection may come in the specific form of the parent continually reminding the child of the need to be on the "lookout" for possible mistakes in the future that may pose a threat to the child's emotional or physical well-being, including reminders of how they may be judged negatively by other people. This anxious rearing promotes the development of perfectionistic tendencies and a future orientation that involves the need to avoid threats associated with anticipated mistakes.

Research on the development of anxiety disorders is just now beginning to look at the role of exposure to anxious parenting. Extensive research has shown that people with anxiety disorders report a lack of parental care or too much overprotection, but it is only recently that investigators have focused specifically on the possible role of anxious rearing in promoting the development of anxious cognitions (see Barrett, Rapee, Dadds, & Ryan, 1996). In one such investigation, Gruner, Muris, and Merckelbach (1999) developed a measure of anxious rearing and administered it to a sample of school children. They found that reported exposure to anxious rearing accounted for unique variance in a variety of anxiety indices (e.g., social phobia, separation anxiety, and generalized anxiety) over and above a measure of perceived parental rejection. The content of the Anxious Rearing scale included such items as "Your parents worry about you making a mistake."

We administered this measure of anxious rearing and Hewitt and Flett MPS to a sample of 117 university students. Our findings confirmed that socially prescribed perfectionism was associated significantly with anxious parental rearing ($r = .30$, $p < .01$; see Flett, Sherry, & Hewitt, 2001). Self-oriented and other-oriented perfectionism were not associated with anxious parental rearing in this sample.

Clearly, the anxious rearing model merits further investigation. Exposure to anxious rearing may account, in part, for the consistent link between certain dimensions of perfectionism and anxiety as well as for the evidence described in subsequent sections of this chapter on the link between perfectionism and fearfulness.

The Family Environment of Perfectionists

A shared theme in each of the models outlined above is that perfectionistic children are exposed to a particular type of family environment that has contributed to their perfectionism. Slaney and Ashby (1996) recently provided evidence of the role of the family. They asked 37 perfectionists to indicate the origins of their perfectionism; most participants identified their family environments as important. Thirty perfectionists indicated that their perfectionism came from their parents; women mentioned both parents, and men identified their fathers. Twelve perfectionists, however, indicated that their perfectionism originated from the self, four respondents identified their grandparents, and four identified their siblings.

Research on the family environments of people with eating disorders has provided empirical evidence of the link between perfectionism and family environment variables. Much of this research derives from the claims of Minuchin and colleagues (Minuchin, Rosman, & Baker, 1978) that patients with eating disorders come from a controlling and perfectionistic family environment that emphasizes rigid adherence to rules and the attainment of high goals.

For instance, Head and Williamson (1990) examined personality and family environment variables in participants who met diagnostic criteria for bulimia. They obtained evidence of the existence of an achievement-oriented family environment that was associated with high levels of perfectionism and paranoid characteristics. Brookings and Wilson (1994) examined the link between perceptions of family environment and the EDI Perfectionism subscale in 137 female undergraduates. Perfectionistic women indicated that their family environments were high in conflict, control, and achievement orientation and emphasized morality and religion. The family environments also were rated as low in cohesion, expressiveness, and independence, as assessed by the Moos Family Environment Scale.

Graber, Brooks-Gunn, Paikoff, and Warren (1994) examined the correlates of eating problems in a sample of adolescent girls. Perfectionism was included as one of the predictor variables and was assessed with the EDI. The pattern of correlations indicated that perfectionism was associated with lower family cohesion and greater family conflict. It also was associated with a range of adjustment difficulties, including higher reported levels of aggression, delinquency, hyperactivity, and depressive symptoms.

Collectively, the results from the studies vary somewhat, but they provide general support for the hypothesized family environment of perfectionists. Additional data have been provided in research on depression and more general forms of distress. Richter, Eisemann, and Perris (1994) investigated the link between dysfunctional attitudes and retrospective accounts of parental child-rearing behavior in a sample of diagnosed depressives. A perfectionism factor was derived from a German version of the Dysfunctional Attitudes Scale (Weissman & Beck, 1978). People with high levels of perfectionism were more likely to report maternal rejection and shaming behavior and low levels of maternal tolerance and affection. Perfectionism also was associated with lower paternal tolerance and affection, but greater paternal overprotection. The link with shame is consistent with indications that perfectionists have a self-reported history of being shamed by others (Wyatt & Gilbert, 1998).

Recently, Richter, Eisemann, and Richter (2000) assessed the association between the same perfectionism factor and recollections of parental behavior in a sample of 540 adult volunteers without a history of mental disorder. Reports of parental behavior were assessed with the EMBU (Swedish acronym for "own memories concerning upbringing"; Perris, Jacobsson, Lindstrom, von Knorring, & Perris, 1980), which includes subscale measures of Rejection, Emotional Warmth, and Overprotection. The analyses found no significant associations between perfectionism and recalled parenting behaviors among men; however, perfectionism in women was associated with low Emotional Warmth from mothers and fathers.

Rickner and Tan (1994) examined the correlates of perfectionism in a mixed sample of Protestant clergy and teachers from public and Christian high schools. The perfectionism measure was the Frost MPS, which was only examined in terms of total scores on all six subscales. Participants also completed measures of situational guilt, psychological distress, and the Family of Origin Scale (Hovestadt, Anderson, Piercy, Cochran, & Fine, 1985), which assesses self-perceived health in the family, focusing on the aspects of the family that promote autonomy and intimacy. Correlational analyses confirmed that perfectionism was associated with guilt, psychological distress, and a maladjusted family of origin ($r = -.38$, $p < .0001$), correlations that reflected a lack of intimacy and autonomy.

Earlier, we described a study by Flynn et al. (2001) in which 119 students completed the Hewitt and Flett MPS for both themselves and their parents, in addition to completing the Moos Family Environment Scale and related measures. Analyses with the MPS showed that socially pre-scribed perfectionism was the only dimension associated with the family environment variables. Higher levels of socially prescribed perfectionism were associated with lower levels of cohesion, expressiveness, indepen-dence, intellectual, and active–recreational personal growth. Socially pre-scribed perfectionism also was associated with increased conflict, achieve-ment, and control.

Finally, two recent Australian studies support the link between a con-trolling family environment and the development of perfectionism. Findlay and Watts (1998) examined the correlations between the Hewitt and Flett MPS and family variables in 201 university students. They found that perfectionism was associated with parental overprotection, low parental care, and relatively poor health in the family of origin. Foy (1998) inves-tigated dimensions of perfectionism and parental control in a sample of 207 university students, who completed 13 measures of familial style. Two latent constructs representing parental psychological control and parental behavioral control were derived from the measures. Self-oriented perfec-tionism was associated with parental psychological control and behavioral control, whereas socially prescribed perfectionism was associated with pa-rental psychological control.

All the studies described above were based on the participants' sub-jective views of the family environment. Empirical investigations with ob-jective measures of the family environment are lacking, for the most part, and need to be undertaken in subsequent research. Existing research also is limited because most investigations of family environment factors have not used multidimensional measures of perfectionism.

Toward an Integrated Model of the Development of Perfectionism

One premise guiding our analysis of the development of perfectionism is that different developmental pathways to perfectionism exist and that per-fectionists differ in salient ways that reflect, in part, the perfectionism dimensions (i.e., self-oriented, other-oriented, or socially prescribed) most relevant to the individual (see Flett & Hewitt, chapter 1, this volume, for a description of those dimensions). Although our developmental analysis places a great deal of emphasis on the role of social expectations of per-fection, as a reflection of level of the parent's controllingness, we maintain that the analysis must be extended to include a separate dimension of parental harshness, as reflected by the social response model. Note that analyses of parenting behavior have consistently identified a dimension that is associated with the level of parental controlling and demanding behavior and a second dimension that reflects the presence or absence of parental acceptance and warmth (Maccoby & Martin, 1983; Schaefer,

1959). Both dimensions are perceptible to children and adolescents as they are growing up (Amato, 1990).

We believe that the two salient parenting dimensions are highly relevant in the development of perfectionism. Moreover, it is important to distinguish between these orthogonal dimensions because doing so points to the possibility that different kinds of socially prescribed perfectionists may exist. The parental expectations variable will range from exceedingly high expectations and an overcontrolling orientation to exceedingly low expectations and lack of control or involvement. The parenting warmth variable can range from extreme harshness to extreme warmth; it reflects both the valence and intensity of a parent's evaluation of the child, such that some parents are extremely negative in expressed evaluations of their children, whereas other parents are moderate, and others are extremely positive.

Various combinations of those variables should contribute to some subtle yet potentially important differences among perfectionists. Some children experience high parental expectations, but their parents are relatively warm and accepting, or are at least average in parental warmth, to the extent that they do not respond with harsh criticism when the child does not meet high expectations. This description likely applies to most controlling parents, who simply want the best for their child. Another possibility is that of parents who want perfect children but are inconsistent with their rewards and punishments.

Those two types of parents are quite different from another subset of demanding parents, who not only expect perfectionism but also respond with criticism, punishment, or a lack of warmth and acceptance when their impossibly high expectations are not met. Such parents are highly controlling and express a variety of negative emotions when their children are imperfect; they are unlikely to respond with positive affect when children come close to meeting unrealistic expectancies.

A third possibility is that some children will experience high parental expectations (i.e., high controllingness), but those expectations are accompanied by overly positive responses from the parent that reflect the parent's idealization of the child. This pattern will contribute to a form of narcissistic perfectionism. Narcissistic perfectionists not only strive for perfection but feel that they are quite capable of attaining that goal (see Hewitt & Flett, 1991). Millon (1998) has suggested that such "elitist narcissists" have developed their tendencies in response to overly positive evaluations received from their parents.

At this point, we have not distinguished between *actual* characteristics of demanding parents and *perceived* characteristics of demanding parents as determined by the people exposed to those parents. In our model, both actual and perceived characteristics of parents are significant. This issue is key when considering socially prescribed perfectionism, which may be based on actual exposure to demanding parents, perceived exposure to demanding parents, or both.

Important implications follow from the possibility that some socially prescribed perfectionists perceive that they have been exposed to high parental expectations but low to moderate criticism, whereas other socially prescribed perfectionists perceive both high expectancies and parental criticism. Socially prescribed perfectionists who encounter parental harshness should be distinguishable according to their levels of emotional adjustment. High expectations, in conjunction with a lack of warmth, is a condition known as *affectionless control* (see Parker, Tupling, & Brown, 1979), which is directly implicated in the development of anxiety and depression (see Chorpita & Barlow, 1998; Masia & Morris, 1998). For instance, work by Oliver and her colleagues (Oliver & Berger, 1992; Oliver & Paull, 1995; Oliver, Raftery, Reeb, & Delaney, 1993) has confirmed that depression is associated with perceptions of parents as being overly restrictive and lacking in affection. Blatt and Homann (1992) have identified affectionless control as central in the development of self-critical depression, and they postulate a close link between self-criticism and factors that reflect socially prescribed perfectionism. Specifically, they observed that

> introjectively depressed patients . . . are driven by the danger of loss of parental approval for failing to meet stern and harsh parental standards and expectations. The child's struggles toward separation, individuation, and self-definition are thwarted by the internalized judgments of one or both parents and their tendencies to be intrusive and controlling. (p. 80)

Conceptual analyses (e.g., Blatt, 1995) and empirical investigations have confirmed the link between socially prescribed perfectionism and self-criticism (Hewitt & Flett, 1993).

Rice, Ashby, and Preusser (1996) studied perfectionism and affectionless control by examining scores on the Parental Bonding Instrument (PBI; Parker et al., 1979) in a mixed sample of "normal" perfectionists and "neurotic" perfectionists. Participants were deemed to be perfectionists on the basis of their scores on the Almost Perfect Scale; they then were categorized as neurotic perfectionists if they had elevated scores on the Concern Over Mistakes subscale of the Frost MPS. This study found no significant group differences on the PBI measures of parental overprotection (i.e., control) and care (i.e., warmth), but the study is limited because it did not include a comparison group of nonperfectionists.

More recently, Stöber (1998) reported data on perfectionism and affectionless control from parents as part of his investigation of the psychometric properties of the Frost MPS. A sample of 243 German university students completed the perfectionism measure and a translated version of the PBI. Stöber reported that numerous dimensions of perfectionism assessed by Frost et al. (1990) were associated with reports of parental overprotection (i.e., control) and lack of parental care (i.e., nonwarmth), suggesting a link between perfectionism and affectionless control.

As noted earlier, the Flynn et al. (2001) study of perfectionism in students and perceived parental behaviors included the PBI and several measures of control as part of the 13 scales on the Parent Behavior Form (Kelly & Worell, 1976). The results showed that socially prescribed perfectionism in men and women was associated with affectionless control from both the mother and the father. Other findings varied as a function of gender: For instance, a perceived lack of care from the father was associated with other-oriented perfectionism in men but not in women. Also, overprotection from both parents was associated with self-oriented and other-oriented perfectionism in men, but overprotection from fathers was associated with self-oriented and other-oriented perfectionism in women.

Both similarities and differences were found in adult children's perceptions of their mothers and fathers. Self-oriented perfectionism in adult children was not associated with mothers' perceived behaviors, but it was associated with decreased acceptance and higher levels of perceived rejection from fathers as well as strict, punitive, and hostile control. Other-oriented perfectionism was associated with increased hostile rejection and control on the part of mothers and fathers. Finally, consistent with the findings for affectionless control, socially prescribed perfectionism was associated with increased hostile rejection from both mothers and fathers.

In related research, Hickinbottom and Thompson (1999) examined the associations among the Hewitt and Flett MPS, the PBI, and a parent-specific version of the Inventory of Interpersonal Problems (IIP; Horowitz, Rosenberg, Baer, Ureno, & Villasenor, 1988) in a sample of 242 undergraduate students. Self-oriented perfectionism in women was associated with overprotection from mothers and fathers, as assessed by the PBI. The same associations were not evident among men. In addition, analyses of IIP scores showed that self-oriented perfectionism in women was associated with autocratic, intrusive, and vindictive tendencies from both mothers and fathers.

Other-oriented perfectionism was not associated with the parental bonding measures in Hickinbottom and Thompson's (1999) sample. Weak positive associations were found between other-oriented perfectionism and autocratic, intrusive tendencies of mothers. The strongest associations for both women and men were found with socially prescribed perfectionism. The PBI analyses showed that socially prescribed perfectionism was associated with a reported pattern of affectionless control (i.e., high overprotection and low care) from both parents; it also was associated with autocratic, intrusive, and vindictive tendencies from mothers and fathers.

Randolph and Dykman (1998) tested the link between perfectionism and affectionless control by having a sample of students complete a battery of measures that included the PBI and a parent-specific measure of perfectionism. That is, Randolph and Dykman (1998) reworded the Socially Prescribed Perfectionism subscale of the Hewitt and Flett MPS to refer specifically to one's parents (e.g., "My father expects me to be perfect"). They found that being the target of socially prescribed perfectionism from both parents was associated with overcontrol, low perceived care, and exposure to parental criticism. Similarly, Flynn et al. (2001) found that parents seen as high in other-oriented perfectionism also were perceived to be high in control and low in care.

The findings generally are consistent with earlier work on exposure to demanding parents who lack warmth that was conducted by Cole and

Rehm (1986). They tested predictions derived from Rehm's self-control model by assessing parental standards and parental reward of their children. The participants were the families of 15 children with depression, 15 clinic children with other forms of dysfunction, and 15 nonclinic control children. The results of behavioral interactions showed that the mothers of the depressed children and the control children both had exacting standards for their children, but the mothers of depressed children also reinforced their children at much lower rates. Thus, the perfectionistic demands of those mothers were associated with less warmth and acceptance, again illustrating the need to consider both parenting dimensions.

Mediational Models Involving Perfectionism and Parental Bonding

A key feature of the Randolph and Dykman (1998) study is that it was designed to test a mediational model that was based on the assumption that exposure to a perfectionistic parent contributed to the development of dysfunctional, perfectionistic attitudes and subsequent proneness to depression in the children of perfectionistic parents. They tested this model by administering measures of perceived parental perfectionism, other parenting variables (i.e., critical parenting, low care, and parental overprotection), dysfunctional attitudes, depression, and proneness to depression to a sample of 247 undergraduate students. Randolph and Dykman found that perceived exposure to socially prescribed perfectionism from one's parents was associated with dysfunctional attitudes and subsequent proneness to depression; this proposed sequence held even when controlling for depressive symptoms and other forms of psychological distress. Ratings of socially prescribed perfectionism from parents also were associated directly with depression.

A new study by Clara, Enns, and Cox (2001) used the same measures as in Randolph and Dykman (1998), including the scale assessing perceived exposure to socially prescribed perfectionism from parents. Again, socially prescribed perfectionism from parents was associated with a maladaptive perfectionism factor that, in turn, was associated with depression proneness. The study thus provided additional evidence of mediation.

These findings described above are clearly in keeping with the notion that exposure to perfectionistic and critical parenting will contribute to depression in the children of perfectionistic parents. At the social cognitive level, joint exposure to excessive parental control and parental punitiveness also should have significant implications for perfectionists' internal working models of other people. Socially prescribed perfectionists who perceive being exposed to high levels of affectionless control will be likely to develop a negative working model of others, reflecting their sense of hostility and the perception that the people who have imposed perfectionistic demands on them cannot be trusted to be warm and responsive and, indeed, may induce feelings of shame in the self.

A second mediational model involving perfectionism, parental bonding, and depression was tested recently by Enns, Cox, and Larsen (2000).

They found that socially prescribed perfectionism and concern over mistakes mediated the association between lack of maternal care and depression in clinically depressed women. In addition, socially prescribed perfectionism and concern over mistakes mediated the link between paternal overprotection and depression in clinically depressed men. At a more basic level, analyses of the zero-order correlations showed that socially prescribed perfectionism and self-oriented perfectionism in women were associated with affectionless control from mothers and fathers. Only socially prescribed perfectionism in men, however, was associated with affectionless control from mothers and fathers. Unfortunately, other-oriented perfectionism was not assessed in this study.

Collectively, the studies outlined above suggest that exposure to perfectionism, in conjunction with perceived affectionless control from parents, may play a central role in the etiology of depression. Unfortunately, existing research is cross-sectional and correlational in nature; longitudinal investigations are needed to clarify the developmental role of parental factors in perfectionism.

The section that follows further explores the role of family factors in perfectionism by examining the link between perfectionism and attachment style. The research points to a link between socially prescribed perfectionism and insecure attachment.

Perfectionism and Attachment Styles

At present, the literature contains little data on perfectionism and attachment styles. The first published study that we could locate was conducted by Brennan and Shaver (1995); unfortunately, they used the EDI Perfectionism subscale, which is limited by its unidimensional nature. They examined the responses of 242 students and found small but significant correlations between the EDI Perfectionism subscale and measures of avoidant attachment style ($r = .13$), lack of a secure attachment style ($r = -.14$), and ambivalence and fear of abandonment ($r = .16$). They also reported a positive association between perfectionism and compulsive self-reliance ($r = .20$).

Andersson and Perris (2000) investigated attachment styles and perfectionism in two convenience samples of adults without a history of psychiatric disorder. The perfectionism measure in this study was a subscale factor derived from the Dysfunctional Attitudes Scale (DAS; Weissman & Beck, 1978); the measures of attachment were the Attachment Styles Questionnaire (ASQ; Feeney, Noller, & Hanrahan, 1994) and the Adult Attachment Scale (AAS; Collins & Read, 1990). The ASQ provides five subscales, including a Confidence scale, which measures secure attachment, and four subscales that measure insecure attachment (i.e., Discomfort, Need for Approval, Preoccupation With Relationships, and Relationships as Secondary). The AAS measures comfort with closeness, anxiety in relationships, and feelings about the dependability of others. Andersson and Perris (2000) found that all the DAS subscales (including the perfectionism measure and measures of depressogenic information processing and self-esteem depending on others' approval) were associated with the various measures of insecure attachment. Thus, perfectionism was strongly associated with attachment variables such as relationship preoccupation and need for approval.

Rice and Mirzadeh (2000) conducted two studies in which they assessed the link between the Frost MPS and the Mother and Father subscales of the Inventory of Parent and Peer Attachment (Armsden & Greenberg, 1987). Rice and Mirzadeh used cluster analyses to identify three groups of perfectionists: nonperfectionists, adaptive perfectionists, and maladaptive perfectionists. The latter two groups differed in that the maladaptive perfectionism group tended to have elevated scores on all the Frost MPS subscales (i.e., Personal Standards, Organization, Doubts About Actions, Concern Over Mistakes, Parental Expectations, and Parental Criticism), whereas the adaptive perfectionism group tended to have elevated scores on the Personal Standards and Organization subscales. Comparative analyses of the perfectionism groups showed that the adaptive perfectionists had more secure attachment to both parents. This finding is not surprising, given that the two perfectionism groups already differed in parental criticism; the maladaptive perfectionism group was characterized by high parental criticism, which is a factor antithetical to the development of a secure, strong attachment bond.

Recently, we conducted a series of studies that examined attachment styles and dimensions of perfectionism (see Flett, Hewitt, Mosher, Sherry, Macdonald, & Sawatzky, 2001). Our first study used both a continuous measure of adult attachment styles (Becker, Billings, Eveleth, & Gilbert, 1997) and the fourfold categorical framework outlined by Bartholomew and colleagues (see Bartholomew, 1990; Bartholomew & Horowitz, 1991). This model yields a fourfold classification scheme that is based on a positive versus negative model of the self as it relates to dependence and a positive versus negative view of others as it relates to avoidance. The four attachment-style categories in this framework are secure (i.e., positive view of self and others), preoccupied (i.e., negative view of self and positive view of others), fearful (i.e., negative view of self and others), and dismissing (i.e., positive view of self and negative view of others).

A total of 265 students were provided with paragraphs describing the four attachment styles from the Relationship Style Questionnaire (Bartholomew & Horowitz, 1991) and were asked to select which one applied to them. The continuous measure assessed three attachment dimensions (i.e., secure, preoccupied, and fearful). Our results indicated that participants who categorized themselves as preoccupied or fearful had substantially higher levels of socially prescribed perfectionism than did those with a secure attachment style (mean = 49.76). No significant differences were found involving self-oriented or other-oriented perfectionism. The correlational results with the continuous measure of attachment styles confirmed this pattern. Socially prescribed perfectionism was associated jointly with fearful and preoccupied attachment dimensions, whereas self-oriented and other-oriented perfectionism were not associated with the attachment style measures. The same results emerged in a second sample of 66 dating couples. Once again, socially prescribed perfectionism was associated with measures of fearful and preoccupied attachment for both men and women; the associations held after controlling for variance resulting from trait neuroticism.

The link between socially prescribed perfectionism and fearful and preoccupied styles of attachment has several implications for cognitive processes, emotional styles, and interpersonal tendencies. In terms of cognitive processes, socially prescribed perfectionism is distinct from the other perfectionism dimensions in that it appears to represent, at least in part, an internalization of early experiences with significant others. The effects of insecure attachment to parents should persist in the form of working models (Bowlby, 1969) or relational schemata (Baldwin, 1992) that involve ready access to episodic memories of past overcontrolling or critical behavior from others (see Crittenden, 1994) as well as a tendency to view current or future interactions in a manner that provokes feelings of hostility and anxiety.

As for emotional styles, it is widely established that people with insecure attachments are prone to experiencing a wide range of negative affects; anxiety and hostility are especially predominant. Although those negative emotions are experienced, they may not be openly expressed. Crittenden (1994) has suggested that some children who have a fearful–avoidant style develop a "defended" form of attachment that involves an unwillingness to express negative emotions for fear of arousing the ire of adult caregivers. Crittenden observed that such children may learn to express overly positive, false affect and present a false sense of self that allows the expression only of feelings that are deemed acceptable by caregivers. Given that socially prescribed perfectionism is associated with fearful and avoidant forms of attachment, it follows that some perfectionists will experience intense negative affect but will attempt to mask it in an effort to gain social approval or avoid further disapproval and shame. Our recent research suggests that some people will take this behavior to the extreme by engaging in a perfectionistic form of self-presentation that may take many forms, including false displays of positive emotions and nondisplays of negative emotions. This perfectionistic self-presentation also is linked with insecure attachment styles.

Finally, regarding interpersonal implications, socially prescribed perfectionists have a strong desire for approval and contact with others, but as the current results indicate, that desire occurs in the context of an insecure attachment style and social avoidance behaviors. Melges (1982) suggested that people who are overly concerned with social evaluations come to develop ambivalent attachment patterns because they desire to be with others yet remain highly fearful of negative reactions. According to Melges (1982), this form of attachment leads to "desynchronized transactions" (p. 231) and a lack of reciprocal intimacy between people. If so, then socially prescribed perfectionists with an insecure attachment style should be at risk for relationship difficulties; such interpersonal problems have been documented in recent studies (see Hewitt, Flett, & Mikail, 1995; Hill, Zrull, & Turlington, 1997).

Statements involving socially prescribed perfectionism and insecure forms of attachment must be qualified by the possibility that different kinds of socially prescribed perfectionists exist. Examination of our categorical data revealed that some socially prescribed perfectionists assign themselves to the preoccupied attachment category, and other socially prescribed perfectionists assign themselves to the fearful category. At present, the link between perfectionism and attachment style has not been assessed through attachment interviews, and it is evident that the replicability of our findings needs to be explored with more rigorous measures. The self-report data, however, are in keeping with our view that some socially prescribed perfectionists are relatively dependent and wish to approach the people they seek approval from; given their preoccupied attachment style, perfectionists of this type should experience significant separation anxiety when lacking contact with significant others, who are regarded as powerful and potent sources of social approval. In contrast, other socially prescribed perfectionists have exceedingly negative working models of others; their cynicism and hostility reflect exposure to abuse or lack of acceptance and warmth from caregivers. Perfectionists in this group are most likely to display a false self and misrepresent their true emotions in an attempt to avoid punitive responses from others. Finally, because the component of attachment that involves a positive or negative working model of others is indeed dimensional in nature (Bartholomew, 1990), some socially prescribed perfectionists will have a neutral or mixed view of others that involves elements of interpersonal approach and interpersonal avoidance; the predominance of the approach tendency versus the avoidance tendency is likely to vary, depending on the people they encounter and the situations they experience, but insecure attachment is at the root of their behavior.

Salience and Frequency of Evaluation in Perfectionistic Families

Most developmental accounts of perfectionism focus on how a person comes to have a high or low score on various perfectionism dimensions; it should be evident from our analysis of perfectionism and attachment styles that we have adopted a similar approach. In addition to focusing on levels of perfectionism, however, it is also important in developmental analyses to include an emphasis on the *salience* of perfectionistic standards. One of the most important functions of being raised in a perfectionistic family may be to promote not only a constant emphasis on the attainment of standards but also a preoccupation with evaluating how near or how far family members are from being perfect. Numerous case descriptions make it clear that perfectionists are highly evaluative people. They may evaluate themselves (i.e., self-oriented perfectionism) or other people (i.e., other-oriented perfectionism), or they may be cognitively preoccupied with evaluations from others (i.e., socially prescribed perfectionism). Whatever the case, this tendency is most likely to be fostered in highly evaluative families that constantly appraise the "goodness" or "badness" of family members, acquaintances, material goods, and life in general. We maintain that perfectionists are highly attuned to evaluative feedback and engage frequently in forms of self-assessment; this characteristic reflects, at least in part, a history of being exposed to environments that increase the salience of evaluation and the need for evaluation. The schemata of extreme perfectionists therefore are highly evaluative.

A Caution About the Development of Perfectionism

If we were to end this chapter here, we would be providing only a limited account of the development of perfectionism, but one that would be consistent with the restricted scope of many developmental theories prior to the 1970s. More recent accounts, such as Sameroff's (1975) transactional model or other sophisticated models (e.g., Belsky, 1984; Bronfenbrenner, 1979), acknowledge that although parental inputs play an important role, it is important to take into account the role of other people in the child's environment (i.e., peers and teachers) as well as societal and cultural factors that may promote perfectionism. Cultures that emphasize a need to meet prescribed expectations may play an important role. A strong case can be made for the position that social construction plays a vital role in the development of perfectionism; subtle and more obvious cues may promote a tendency for certain people to increase their preoccupation with attaining impossible standards.

The notion of the social construction of perfectionism has particular implications for interpretations of socially prescribed perfectionism. Socially prescribed perfectionism may reflect the perceived or actual pressures imposed on the self by significant others; however, it is possible and even advisable to regard socially prescribed perfectionism from a global, societal perspective that involves cultural pressures to measure up to unrealistic expectancies. Those cultural pressures often have been seen in people's quest for the perfect body and the "tyranny of perfection" (see Glassner, 1992), but cultural pressures need not be restricted to the physical self. Cultural pressures to be perfect also should apply, at a minimum, to achievement goals and interpersonal goals.

Most important, in addition to cultural factors, any model of the development of perfectionism also must include the role of child characteristics (i.e., temperament). Any such model must acknowledge the child's role in self-socialization (see Bell & Chapman, 1986), including active goal setting and seeking of achievement-related information in achievement situations. A key issue in self-socialization, as it relates to perfectionism, is whether the child who is being pressured to strive for perfection then goes on to internalize perfectionistic values or actively rejects pressures to be perfect, rebelling against those who are trying to impose perfectionistic demands on him or her.

Figure 4.1 illustrates a preliminary model that outlines the various

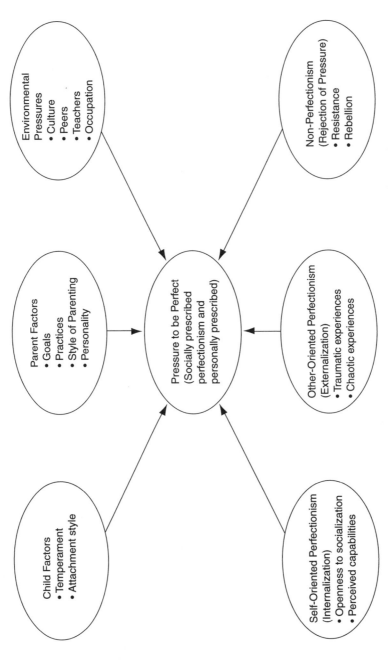

Figure 4.1.   Preliminary model of the development of perfectionism.

factors contributing to perfectionism. The model illustrates our main contention that numerous factors contribute to perfectionism and that it is important to be mindful of the heterogeneity that should exist among any group of perfectionists in terms of both the most salient perfectionism dimensions and the factors and processes that contributed to those differences. The heterogeneity reflects the influence of a complex and diverse array of factors, including processes that originate in the parent, the child, and the broader social environment. The model also accounts for the role of ongoing life experiences and social contexts (e.g., competitive and demanding school and job environments) that further promote the development of perfectionism. We hope that the model will serve as a useful heuristic device for future research on the development of perfectionism.

Parent, Environment, and Self Factors

The main premise of our preliminary model is that at least three categories of factors may exert perfectionistic pressures on a person: parental factors, environmental pressures, and factors originating within the self (i.e., temperament, achievement needs, and attachment style).

Parent Factors

The parental variables shown in Figure 4.1 incorporate some important distinctions that Darling and Steinberg (1993) made in their integrative model of parenting style. Darling and Steinberg made a compelling case for the need to distinguish among parenting goals and values, specific parenting practices (i.e., specific behaviors in specific situations), and general parenting style (i.e., parenting attitudes and the emotional climate in which behavior is expressed). Those distinctions are particularly relevant to the development of perfectionism. We maintain that perfectionism is likely to develop not only when children are exposed to authoritarian parenting and an emotional climate that emphasizes the negative consequences of making mistakes but also when parents engage in specific behaviors designed to promote perfectionism (e.g., placing children in demanding situations that emphasize the attainment of standards and meeting expectations) and when parents express perfectionistic goals and standards.

The parents' perfectionistic goals and standards can be examined according to their level, their importance, and their type. Some parents have unreasonably high goals and strong values that emphasize the need to be perfect, whereas other parents have more realistic and reasonable goals and place less importance on the need for children to be perfect. Perfectionism is more likely to develop when exposed to high parental standards that are quite important (i.e., that are highly valued by the parent and/or the child); however, the type of goal is also important. The motivational literature makes a clear distinction between goals that are focused on learning and goals that are focused on performance. Learning goals tend to involve learning for the sake of learning, and performance goals involve a focus on performing in order to obtain rewards and approval from others; the latter tend to involve high levels of ego involvement and excessive social comparison. A parental focus on performance goals is likely to result in a form of perfectionism that develops in response to ego threats and concerns about self-esteem.

Ablard and Parker (1997) recently examined the link between parental goals and the development of perfectionism; they showed that the particular type of expectancy that a parent expresses may be a key determinant of subsequent perfectionism. In their study of gifted children, they found that maladaptive perfectionism was associated with exposure to parents who endorsed performance goals rather than learning goals. Separate analyses for mothers and fathers found that the tendency to emphasize performance goals was associated with a high concern over mistakes among mothers but not among fathers.

In addition to the parenting goals already mentioned, the personality of parents is important, especially if the parent is an extreme perfectionist. Perfectionistic parents may play a role by serving as a model that can be imitated, as indicated by the social learning model. Social learning processes operate when the mother or father is a perfectionist and the child seeks to emulate his or her parent. Here, we qualify the social learning model by adding the caveat that social learning may involve various dimensions of perfectionism—the child may imitate the parent's self-oriented perfectionism, other-oriented perfectionism, and expressed concerns and fears involving socially prescribed pressures imposed on the self.

Child Factors

An important aspect of our model of the development of perfectionism is that the child is not seen as entirely reactive and influenced by parental factors or cultural pressures to be perfect. In fact, our model is more in keeping with the classic views of theorists such as Adler (1956) and Horney (1950), who regarded the development of perfectionism as the child's active response to feelings of inferiority and neurotic difficulties. The role of external pressures (both parental and social) is reflected clearly in the development of socially prescribed perfectionism. The lack of parental responsiveness also will contribute to the insecure attachment styles associated with socially prescribed perfectionism. The development of perfectionism, however, requires the child to actively translate those pressures by internalizing the demands into pressures on the self (i.e., self-oriented perfectionism) or externalizing the demands in the form of pressure on others (i.e., other-oriented perfectionism).

The need to include factors reflecting self-socialization and personal influences becomes especially evident when one considers the nature of the perfectionism dimensions assessed by the MPS (Hewitt & Flett, 1991). If a person is to develop a high level of self-oriented perfectionism, he or she must internalize socially imposed standards at some point. This notion of incorporating social pressures into the self system as a form of self-socialization is in keeping with developmental work on the self-concept. For instance, in research on self-concept development, Harter (1990) used path-analytic procedures on data from a sample of 8- to 15-year-olds to determine that perceptions of regard from others and concerns with approval precede development of a sense of self-regard.

As shown in Figure 4.1, several key factors determine whether pressures to be perfect develop into self-oriented and other-oriented perfectionism. One key factor is the child's openness to socialization. Research on the development of conscience shows that some children are more open to socialization and the subsequent internalization of values; the difference is partly a reflection of individual differences in temperament (see Kochanska, 1997; Kochanska & Askan, 1995). Self-oriented perfectionism is most likely to develop when the child is open to parental and societal influence, as reflected by a strong need for approval and recognition.

Another key factor is the person's perceived or actual ability to attain perfectionism, including the personal history of achievement successes versus failures in school settings. A tendency to be a self-oriented perfectionist would be especially irrational if a person has had no realistic possibility of attaining perfectionism and has experienced limited success in achievement situations; people are more likely to increase their personal goals as they experience success and gain an increased sense of personal capability (Bandura & Cervone, 1986; Locke, 1996). By extension, then, it follows that perfectionists will be most likely to strive for personal goals of perfectionism in areas that involve feelings of competence and foster the sense that perfection is possible.

The presence and awareness of individual differences in ability will take on added significance for contributing to the development of perfectionism as children mature cognitively. As children grow older and approach adolescence, they become more aware of the constancy and relative stability of ability and realize that their level of performance has long-standing implications for the self (Ruble & Flett, 1988).

Temperament is particularly important. Unfortunately, any attempt to examine the role of possible temperamental factors in perfectionism must remain highly speculative at this point because of the paucity of data in this area. To our knowledge, the only published research on the subject was conducted by Richter et al. (2000), who examined the extent to which dysfunctional attitudes involving perfectionism are associated with the dimensions of temperament posited by Cloninger (1986). They found that perfectionism in healthy adults was associated with elevated levels of harm avoidance in both men and women. Perfectionism in men also was associated with reduced levels of novelty seeking.

We believe that perfectionists have a temperament that is characterized by high levels of emotionality, including high fearfulness, along with high levels of persistence. Fearfulness and task persistence are elements of temperament that can be detected among infants (Martin, Wisenbaker, & Huttunen, 1994); those aspects of temperament influence a child's sensitivity to rewards and punishments (Rothbart, Ahadi, & Hershey, 1994). Temperament may account, at least in part, for several characteristics of perfectionists, including fear of failure, concern about mistakes, intolerance of criticism, need for social approval, and tenacious achievement striving (Flett, Hewitt, Endler, & Tassone, 1994–1995; Frost et al., 1990; Hewitt & Flett, 1991).

We have obtained indirect evidence of the hypothesized link between perfectionism and a fearful temperament by examining the correlations between the Hewitt and Flett MPS and self-reported measures of behavioral inhibition and behavioral activation. Carver and White (1994) created brief measures to assess functioning of the behavioral inhibition system (BIS) and behavioral activation system (BAS), as outlined by Gray (1982). The BIS and BAS are believed to reflect physiological functioning. The BIS is associated with the experience of negative affects, such as fear, sadness, and frustration, and is attuned to signals of punishment and nonreward. In contrast, the BAS is associated with the experience of positive affects: It involves an appetitive orientation that is attuned to signals of reward, lack of punishment, and escape from punishment (Gray, 1982). Certain models of temperament have incorporated sensitivity to those cues (see Rothbart & Derryberry, 1981).

Carver and White (1994) developed one general BIS measure and three measures of BAS activation (i.e., reward, drive, and fun seeking). Recently, we examined the association between those measures and the three MPS subscales in a sample of 71 undergraduates. All three MPS measures were correlated strongly with the BIS measure (r values ranged from .50 to .61). In addition, self-oriented perfectionism was associated positively with BAS measures of drive and reward ($r = .29$ in both instances). Thus, perfectionists may be characterized by sensitivity involving both the BIS and BAS, but the predominant focus is on a fearful sensitivity to signals of punishment and nonreward, consistent with the possible presence of a fearful temperament. If this temperament style is involved in perfectionism, budding perfectionists will be highly sensitive to parental feedback, especially if it is perceived as punishment or nonreward.

Environmental Factors

The model displayed in Figure 4.1 incorporates environmental pressures to be perfect. At a general level, the pressure to be perfect should be stronger in individualistic cultures that emphasize personal achievements and goals. Unfortunately, little research on perfectionism has been conducted from a cross-cultural perspective. It suffices to say at this point that although personal pressures to be perfect may be greater in individualistic cultures, those pressures are not irrelevant in collectivist cultures. One possibility is that socially prescribed pressures may be more salient in collectivist cultures that emphasize the self in relation to others.

As noted above, one reflection of the impact of societal factors in perfectionism is the sociocultural emphasis on extreme thinness as the ideal body image. It has been widely recognized that women in North American societies are under great pressure to conform to the "perfect" body image, even though the prescribed weight is extremely idealistic and unrealistic for most women (Brownell, 1991). The importance of those pressures is reflected by observations that increases in rates of bulimia may occur because "high performance expectations have interacted with pressures induced by the glamorization of thinness in Western societies" (Dorian & Garfinkel, 1999, p. 188).

It is worth reiterating that pressures resulting from school and work environments are no less important; however, virtually no research has been conducted on the role of specific environmental contexts in promoting perfectionism, including competitive school environments and demanding job environments. It is expected that peer interactions will be found to play a vital role in the development and maintenance of perfectionism. One recent developmental model posits that the influence of parents on the long-term development of personality is overstated and that peers have a substantial influence on a child's personality characteristics, especially during adolescence (Harris, 1995). Peers may influence the development of perfectionism in a variety of ways that reflect the importance that peers place on meeting expectations and standards, the importance of obtaining social approval, and the creation of a competitive environment that emphasizes frequent social comparisons with normative standards as the focus.

The Internalization, Externalization, or Rejection of the Pressure to Be Perfect

Once a significant pressure to be perfect exists, it still remains to be determined whether that pressure will be incorporated into a coherent self-view and view of others. As shown in the lower half of Figure 4.1, we maintain that some people will develop self-oriented or other-oriented perfectionism, or both, in response to the pressure they experience. Other people may reject the pressure, especially socially prescribed perfectionism, and will display a pattern of behavior characterized by reactance and rebellion, consistent with engaging in reactance as a response to perceived threats involving control and loss of freedom (Brehm & Brehm, 1981). Rejection of pressure may occur for a variety of reasons, including a personal inability to attain perfection and a strong desire to be distinct from a perfectionistic parent who may have personality characteristics and associated forms of behavior that the child has come to despise. Although the pressure to be perfect will not lead to self-oriented or other-oriented perfectionism in some people, they may still be quite cognizant of socially prescribed pressures, and their internal working models of the self in relation to others will reflect the profound sense of hostility, resentment, and frustrative nonreward that commonly are experienced when someone perceives that he or she is being unfairly treated.

At the conceptual level, our decision to incorporate the notion of reactance and attendant feelings of hostility is based, in part, on hearing many people tell us that their parents were perfectionists who tried to impose perfectionistic expectations on them. Such people felt almost compelled to reject those parental pressures, sometimes resulting in extreme, self-destructive behavior. Empirically, little evidence links perfectionism and reactance, although our initial data has confirmed that a link does indeed exist. Recently, we had a sample of university students complete the Hewitt and Flett MPS and a multidimensional measure of reactance (Hong & Page, 1989). Our preliminary analyses indicate that socially prescribed perfectionism is associated with all facets of reactance, including resisting advice from others and having an emotional response when choices have been constricted. The association between socially prescribed perfectionism and reactance has significant implications for clinical and counseling interventions because general research has shown that some people experience the reactance phenomenon in treatment settings when they feel a loss of freedom and feel controlled (Dowd & Wallbrown, 1993).

Returning to our preliminary model, a complex set of factors will determine whether the pressure to be perfect does develop subsequently into self-oriented perfectionism:

1. Whether the child is open to socialization and has a strong desire to please others by striving for perfection
2. Whether the child is exposed to a self-oriented perfectionist and wishes to emulate him or her
3. Whether the family environment emphasizes the achievement of high standards
4. Whether the child has skills and abilities in at least one domain that suggest that perfection is possible
5. Whether the child has a temperament characterized by extreme persistence and some degree of fearfulness.

What factors and processes contribute to the development of other-oriented perfectionism as a way of externalizing the pressure? First, other-oriented perfectionism is more likely when children have been raised in a family setting that is extremely evaluative in nature, with a clear emphasis on the importance of everyone striving for perfection. Thus, other-oriented perfectionists will be evaluative, rather than descriptive, in their external orientation and will be high in the need to evaluate (see Jarvis & Petty, 1996). Other-oriented perfectionism is also more likely to emerge to the extent that children have been exposed to harsh and controlling parents; however, such children have maintained the narcissistic self-view that they are capable of attaining perfection and that it is therefore entirely reasonable to demand perfection from others.

We also believe that a great deal of defensiveness is associated with other-oriented perfectionism. Anecdotally, we have found that high levels of other-oriented perfectionism are common among highly capable people who have experienced traumatic events, often in a chaotic setting. Their other-oriented perfectionism often takes the form of exceedingly high expectations of the levels of support that ought to be provided by other people, a belief that is reflected on the Hewitt and Flett MPS by such items as "The people who matter to me should never let me down." In many instances, the exceedingly high expectations for others often seem to reflect a desire to compensate for a history or perception of being mistreated or disappointed by others.

Key Periods of Development

Although space does not permit a full analysis here, our model also allows for the role of life contexts throughout the entire life cycle. That is, the development of perfectionism is regarded as an ongoing process that does not rely solely on the early experiences of children. To be sure, early experiences are important. Parental factors have a strong impact early on, but it is difficult to separate those factors from the role of temperament and other factors. Key periods in the development of perfectionism include the early stages of childhood, during which it has been suggested that most children are characterized to some degree by the just-right phenomenon (which includes an increasing compulsion to do things perfectly; see Evans et al., 1997), and the stage of adolescence, which includes heightened levels of self-consciousness. Presumably, the impact of socially prescribed pressures to be perfect are magnified substantially during adolescence, when social evaluations become increasingly important.

Our main purpose in outlining this preliminary model is to encourage additional research on the numerous factors that may contribute to the development of perfectionism. We now describe current research that further examines the implications of being exposed to a perfectionistic parent.

Characteristics and Consequences of Perfectionism in Parents

The first segment of this chapter has focused primarily on the factors in the family that contribute to the development of perfectionism in children. When examining the consequences of perfectionism, however, it is important to consider the personal costs of perfectionism for parents who are perfectionists. The remainder of this chapter focuses on perfectionism in parents. As a personality construct, perfectionism should generalize across situations and life roles. In theory, people with extremely high levels of perfectionism not only will want to have perfect appearance and be perfect at their work but also will want to be the perfect parents of perfect children, to the extent that is possible.

The following sections examine the correlates and consequences of perfectionism in parents, focusing on the initial results from a program of research designed to examine the parenting beliefs and behaviors of perfectionists. A description of research on perfectionism in parenting stress and distress follows.

Numerous authors have described the parental quest for perfection.

The notion of the perfect parent is perhaps most prominent in the sociological literature. Authors have commented on the quest to be the perfect mother and the inherent problems associated with this goal. In fact, Chodorow and Contratto (1989) criticized several feminist authors who seemed to promote the image of the perfect mother as the antithesis of the tendency to blame mothers for negative child outcomes. They reminded readers that the overidealization of the possibilities of motherhood is inherently dangerous because no parent can be perfect.

Regarding the link between perfectionism and parental stress, Sophie Freud, granddaughter of Sigmund Freud, discussed the pressures associated with striving for parental perfection, including her own experiences in attempting to achieve this goal. Regarding her own perfectionistic parenting goals, Freud (1988) noted that

> Little did I realize at that distant time what hubris was involved in these presumptuous goals. Not trying to be the best possible parent within one's limited ability is thoughtless, unkind, and irresponsible. Yet reaching for perfection in the rearing of one's children is a self-defeating goal that can only lead to disaster. (p. 171)

Freud went on to document the problems encountered by several parents who created a maladaptive family environment in attempting to strive for perfection and perfect outcomes for their children. She described a friend in the following manner:

> "I have to protect you against your own mistakes," a friend of mine used to say to her children. "I have to control you for your own good." She would hound them into doing their homework, bribe them into good academic performance, coerce them into practicing their musical instruments, shame them into learning foreign languages. She would show them affection only if they met her expectations. Her children have become accomplished and successful professionals. Yet their sense of self-worth depends on their achievement, which they pursue relentlessly, while their self-esteem continues to elude them. They will never forgive her for loving them conditionally and for having been such a controlling mother. (p. 181)

Of course, many of Freud's observations are in keeping with our earlier discussion of the family factors that contribute to the development of perfectionism. The literature abounds with similar examples. Regarding the early parenting behavior of perfectionistic parents, Missildine (1963) provided an account of a troubled young woman named Leslie. He noted that Leslie's early childhood took place in the following atmosphere:

> When Leslie was born, her mother was determined, as a good and dutiful mother, to see to it that Leslie was a perfect baby. She set up rigid rules and regulations for herself and Leslie. All routines, such as bathing and feeding, were meticulous and on schedule. Bowel training was begun when she was only three months old. As the child grew older,

much attention was given every aspect of her life: diction, posture, cleanliness, demeanor, obedience, choice of playmates, studies—and her reading, television programs, school homework and social manners. Her dress, physical status and appearance were sources of endless concern. (p. 86)

This description highlights the overcontrolling nature that may characterize perfectionistic parents and the subsequent impact on children. What seems to be lacking in most accounts is an analysis of how perfectionistic tendencies among parents not only may influence their children but also may contribute to stress and distress in the parents.

The sections that follow report research on several issues that pertain to perfectionism in parents, including the parenting beliefs and parenting behaviors of perfectionists. We investigate the extent to which perfectionistic parents have unrealistic parenting attitudes and how those attitudes become expressed in parenting behaviors that are less than ideal. Finally, we examine the possibility that striving to be the perfect parent is associated with poor adjustment to the parenting role, as reflected by elevated levels of parental stress and low parenting satisfaction.

Perfectionism and Parental Attitudes

In her classic work, Baumrind (1971) identified three parenting styles that reflect qualitatively different forms of parental control: *authoritarian* parenting (i.e., controlling and harsh), *permissive* parenting (i.e., noninvolved and neglectful), and *authoritative* parenting (i.e., control with reason). Numerous studies have confirmed that both the authoritarian and permissive orientations are associated with poor child outcomes (see Flett, Hewitt, & Singer, 1995). Flett et al. explored perfectionism and reported parenting styles by administering the Hewitt and Flett MPS and the Parental Authority Styles Questionnaire (PASQ; Buri, 1991) to 100 university students. It was found that socially prescribed perfectionism in men was associated with reported exposure to authoritarian parenting from the mother and father; however, parental authoritarianism was not associated with socially prescribed perfectionism in women. The parenting measures were not associated with self-oriented or other-oriented perfectionism.

Macdonald, Martin, Flett, and Hewitt (1995) also examined the link between perfectionism and reported parenting styles. A sample of 125 university students, composed primarily of women, completed both the Frost and the Hewitt and Flett versions of the MPS along with a measure of perceived parenting styles (Dornbusch, Ritter, Leiderman, Roberts, & Fraleigh, 1987). They also completed a measure of family satisfaction. Results from this study indicated that all the perfectionism measures were associated with reports of exposure to authoritarian parents. Few significant correlations were found between perfectionism and the indices of permissive and authoritative parenting. Additional analyses indicated that low family satisfaction was associated with the absence of authoritative parenting and the presence of authoritarian parenting. The perfectionism measures also were associated with low family satisfaction, and concern over mistakes and socially prescribed perfectionism predicted unique variance in family satisfaction, over and above variance attributable to perceived parenting style measures.

Additional unpublished data on the link between perfectionism and parenting tendencies were collected by Wintre and Sugar (2000) as part of their investigation on parental relationships and the transition to university. They administered the MPS, the PASQ (Buri, 1991), a measure of perceived parental support, and a measure of perceived parental reciprocity to 170 first-year students at York University. The Parental Reciprocity Scale (Wintre, Yaffe, & Crowley, 1995) provides separate measures of reciprocity from the mother and father in addition to a total score. Parental reciprocity involves the perception that a mutual relationship exists between the parent and child such that both viewpoints are acknowledged and respected. Parental reciprocity is associated with higher levels of academic, social, and emotional adjustment among students (Wintre & Sugar, 2000). The antithesis of parental reciprocity is the existence of a unidirectional relationship, in which an authoritarian parent fails to acknowledge the child; such relationships are associated with resentment and conflict.

The results showed that self-oriented and other-oriented perfectionism were not correlated significantly with the parenting variables that Wintre and Sugar (2000) assessed. Socially prescribed perfectionism in both women and men, however, was associated with the presence of authoritarian parenting and a lack of authoritative parenting from both parents. In addition, socially prescribed perfectionism was linked with a lack of perceived support from parents and low levels of perceived reciprocity from both parents.

The finding that socially prescribed perfectionism is associated with a relative lack of perceived reciprocity from parents has some potentially important implications for a child's internalization of perfectionism parental standards. Research on socialization processes has shown that children are more likely to internalize parental tendencies when parents respond in a positive, responsive manner and when children experience reciprocal relationships of shared positive affect (Kochanska & Aksan, 1995; Maccoby & Martin, 1983). The lack of reciprocity associated with socially prescribed perfectionism suggests that certain people with high levels of socially prescribed perfectionism will find it difficult to internalize perfectionistic standards and may instead show a form of reactance in which those standards are rejected and not accepted at a personal level. Such a response would be likely among people who perceive that they simply lack the characteristics and capabilities needed to attain perfection and therefore see external demands for perfection as arbitrary and punitive. We have incorporated this notion into Figure 4.1 by indicating that some people will come to reject pressures being placed on them. Nevertheless, perceived exposure to imposed standards of perfection will continue to be distressing and stressful regardless of whether they become internalized.

Beliefs of Perfectionistic Parents

The studies described above are limited by the fact that students were asked to rate their parents' characteristics. What findings emerge under a direct focus on actual parents and their beliefs? Some insights are provided in a study by Roehling and Robin (1986), who examined the correlates of the Family Beliefs Inventory (FBI) in 30 distressed families of troubled adolescents. The FBI provides measures of unreasonable parental beliefs involving a variety of themes, including perfectionism (e.g., that teenagers should behave in a flawless manner). Scores on the measure of family beliefs for the mother, father, and adolescent were compared with the beliefs of members of families in which the adolescent did not have an identified adjustment problem. They found that the fathers of distressed adolescents had more extreme, unrealistic beliefs involving themes of the importance of their child being perfect and obedient. The data suggest that other-oriented perfectionism in fathers is associated with adolescent adjustment problems.

Macdonald, Flett, and Hewitt (2001) extended this work on perfectionistic beliefs in parents by conducting an analysis of the link between trait perfectionism and parenting attitudes as part of a larger investigation. A sample of 56 mothers and their children, who ranged in age from 14 to 28 months, were recruited. Mothers completed a battery of measures that included the Hewitt and Flett MPS, the Parent Expectations subscale of the Parent Behavior Checklist (Fox, 1992), and the self-report version of the Child-Rearing Practices Report (CRPR; Rickel & Biasatti, 1982), which was originally developed by Block (1981). The CRPR has 18 items that measure parental nurturance and 22 items that measure parental restrictiveness toward the child (i.e., overly controlling orientation). Correlational analyses revealed no significant correlations between the MPS and the measures of maternal expectations and maternal nurturance. Beliefs reflecting maternal restrictiveness, however, were associated with self-oriented perfectionism ($r = .39$, $p < .01$) and with socially prescribed perfectionism ($r = .35$, $p < .01$). A marginally significant correlation was found between other-oriented perfectionism and maternal restrictiveness ($r = .24$, $p < .08$). Thus, all three perfectionism dimensions were associated with maternal attitudes involving a cognitive orientation toward restrictiveness and controlling behaviors.

Perfectionism and Parenting Behaviors

Another important question is whether perfectionism can be detected by analyzing the overt actions of perfectionistic parents. Hyson, Hirsh-Pasek, Rescorla, Cone, and Martell-Boinske (1991) provided initial evidence of perfectionistic parenting behavior. Hyson et al. interviewed 90 mothers of preschoolers and observed each mother's directive, controlling, perfectionistic, and critical behavior during two tasks requiring interaction between the mother and child. Cluster analyses of the ratings revealed an identifiable subset of 29 mothers who exhibited high frequencies of criticism, directiveness, control, and perfectionistic behaviors. Hyson et al. concluded that those mothers were most likely to put unwarranted pressure on their children, a finding that is consistent with the anecdotal evidence we presented earlier.

Sockett-Dimarco, Landy, Flett, and Hewitt (2001) further evaluated the link between parental behaviors and trait perfectionism in parents. Their investigation focused on emotional availability as revealed by the behaviors of 31 parents who were participating in a preventive parenting program for families at risk. Emotional availability involves the extent to which emotional features of the parent–child relationship promote healthy development (see Biringen, 2000). Parents in our study completed the Hewitt and Flett MPS and were videotaped with their children (mean age 4.0 years) during a 35-minute interaction sequence that included both a free-play segment and structured-task segments (i.e., a task in which the parent teaches the child). The videotaped interactions in this study subsequently were scored with the Emotional Availability Scales (Biringen & Robinson, 1991; Biringen, Robinson, & Emde, 1989). The parents' behaviors were coded according to the parents' sensitivity to their children (i.e., flexible responsiveness to the child's cues) and level of intrusiveness (i.e., degree of overcontrol and interference with the child's autonomy).

Analyses found no significant differences involving self-oriented perfectionism, but an effect that approached conventional levels of significance was found on the sensitivity measure ($p < .06$). Parents with high levels of self-oriented perfectionism exhibited fewer sensitive responses. Additional analyses found that other-oriented perfectionism was not associated with significant differences in intrusiveness, but other-oriented perfectionists, relative to nonperfectionists, exhibited significantly lower levels of sensitive parenting behaviors. Finally, parents with a high level of socially prescribed perfectionism expressed behaviors reflecting both greater intrusiveness and lower sensitivity.

In addition to examining perfectionism and parenting attitudes, the Macdonald et al. (2001) study described above also included behavioral interactions between mothers and their children. Mothers were videotaped while interacting with their children during a 5-minute free-play period, followed by a 5-minute period involving a teaching task. Specifically, each mother–child dyad was presented with a jigsaw puzzle, and the mother was asked to teach her child how to put the puzzle together because it would be difficult for the child to complete it on his or her own. Observations were coded in several categories, including the number of critical responses and the number of supportive responses that mothers expressed toward their children. Trained observers also made global ratings of each mother on a variety of dimensions, including parental sensitivity, control, and emotional support. Analyses yielded no significant effects involving parental sensitivity and emotional support, in contrast to the findings reported above; however, self-oriented perfectionism was associated with higher ratings of parental control ($r = .28$, $p < .05$). This finding is in keeping with the link between self-oriented perfectionism and restrictive parenting attitudes that was reported above.

Evidence for a possible mediational model starts to emerge when we consider the finding from the Macdonald et al. (2001) study that perfectionism was associated with beliefs reflecting maternal restrictiveness. Other data from this study indicate that beliefs involving maternal restrictiveness are associated with controlling and intrusive maternal behaviors, as determined by observer ratings (Macdonald, 1998). These findings suggest the possibility that trait perfectionism in parents can be regarded as a distal factor that is associated with intrusive parenting through its association with restrictive beliefs. Perfectionism also may contribute to intrusive parenting through a link with parenting stress and distress, but it is first necessary to establish an empirical link between perfectionism and parenting stress and distress. Research on this issue is described in the following section.

Stress and Distress in the Perfectionistic Parent

Given the extensive link between perfectionism and stress (Hewitt & Flett, chapter 11, this volume), one would have every reason to expect that parents who feel pressure to be perfect will also experience significant stress and distress. We have argued elsewhere that perfectionists are prone to experience stress, in part because of the difficulties associated with pursuing extremely high goals. Perfectionists have characteristics that will lead to stress enhancement and may indeed generate stress for themselves in a variety of ways. Finally, perfectionists also may anticipate future stress, a trait that, in part, may reflect a propensity on the part of perfectionists to be chronic worriers. These observations all point to a link between perfectionism and parenting stress.

What kinds of emotional outcomes are experienced by perfectionistic parents? If certain dimensions of perfectionism are indeed maladaptive and if trait perfectionism generalizes across life domains, then it follows that perfectionistic parents should be susceptible to parenting stress and related forms of negative affectivity. Our initial work in this area has indicated that socially prescribed perfectionism is a particularly maladaptive orientation. Parents who are firmly convinced that perfectionism is expected of them tend to report a number of adjustment difficulties.

A focus on emotional adjustment of perfectionistic parents is one element of our major research project on personality predictors of postpartum distress (see Flett, Besser, & Hewitt, 2001; Flett & Hewitt, 1997). Women and men making the transition to parenthood were asked to complete a variety of personality measures (i.e., measures of perfectionism, dependency, self-criticism, autonomy, and sociotropy) and measures of negative and positive affect when the mothers-to-be were in the final month of pregnancy. A total of 181 families participated in our first prospective study. The same participants completed a battery of measures at 1 and 3 months postpartum, including measures of negative and positive affect. The Parenting Sense of Competence Scale (see Gibaud-Wallston & Wandersman, 1978; Johnston & Mash, 1989), which has two subscales measuring parenting efficacy and parenting satisfaction, was administered at 3 months postpartum. We found for both mothers and fathers that socially prescribed perfectionism measured prior to the child's birth was a significant predictor of parenting dissatisfaction and high postpartum levels of negative affect. Structural equation modeling also indicated that perceived parenting competence mediated the link between the personality vulnerability factors and postpartum levels of negative affect, after controlling for levels of affect prior to the child's birth.

Several implications follow from these findings. First, a group of personality factors, including socially prescribed perfectionism, seem to operate as vulnerability factors for postpartum distress. In addition, consistent with previous research by Cutrona and Troutman (1986), a new parent's sense of competence in the parenting role is a key mediator of this association. The finding implies that interventions designed to boost parenting confidence may protect new parents from experiencing increases in levels of negative affect and decreases in level of positive affect.

Our postpartum project also included an assessment of pathological worry, as assessed by the Penn State Worry Questionnaire (Meyer, Miller, Metzger, & Borkovec, 1990). We found that worry during the pregnancy and postpartum periods was associated with self-oriented and socially prescribed perfectionism in mothers and fathers. The link between pathological worry and perfectionism in parents is interesting because it appears that the association between perfectionism and fearfulness is a central theme not only in this chapter but also in several other chapters in this book. Data reported in this chapter suggest that dimensions of perfectionism are associated with an anxious attachment style, BIS functioning that reflects an anxious orientation, and persistent worry in parents. It seems reasonable to suggest that much of the behavior of perfectionists reflects a sensitivity to anxiety; for instance, the controlling behaviors of perfectionistic parents may be motivated by a desire to avoid feared outcomes.

The preliminary results of another prospective study (Flett, Hewitt, Endler, Pickering, & Berk, 2001) of personality and postpartum adjustment provide support for this observation. We are in the midst of an investigation of personality, coping, and adjustment in parents making the transition to parenthood. One aspect of our study includes the development of a measure of concern over parenting mistakes adapted from the Frost et al. (1990) measure. Analyses of the data from the pregnancy period indicate that an excessive concern with making parenting mistakes is associated with stress and distress. Concern over parenting mistakes in expectant mothers and their partners is associated with greater perceived stress, emotion-oriented coping, anxiety, depression, and a ruminative response orientation when depressed.

Another study has further explored the link between concern over parenting mistakes and postpartum depression in new mothers (see Flett, Hewitt, Berk, & Besser, 2001). This investigation involved administering the Hewitt and Flett MPS, the Perfectionism Cognitions Inventory, the

Concern Over Parenting Mistakes Scale, and the Edinburgh Postnatal Depression Scale (Cox, Holden, & Sagovsky, 1987) to new mothers. Our analyses showed that both concern over parenting mistakes and perfectionism cognitions were associated with postpartum depression. Moreover, structural equation modeling indicated that both concern over parenting mistakes and perfectionism cognitions mediated the link between trait levels of socially prescribed perfectionism and postpartum depression. Collectively, the findings point to the potential usefulness of cognitive interventions that focus on alleviating the distress associated with concern over parenting mistakes and automatic thoughts involving the need to be perfect.

Perfectionism and Stress in Parents of Preschoolers

The negative correlates of socially prescribed perfectionism in parents continue to be evident when the focus shifts to adjustment in parents of preschoolers. Henderson, Macdonald, Flett, and Hewitt (1997) investigated the correlates of trait perfectionism in a sample of 82 mothers of preschoolers. The mean age of their children was 3.2 years. The parents completed the Hewitt and Flett MPS; a host of other measures, including those measuring depression, anxiety, pathological worry; and the McMaster Family Assessment Device (FAD; Epstein, Baldwin, & Bishop, 1983). The FAD measures general family functioning as well as functioning in the areas of problem solving, communication, roles, affective responsiveness, affective involvement, and behavioral control. The Problem-Solving scale measures the family's ability to resolve problems at a level that maintains effective family functioning. The Communication scale assesses whether family communication is clear and direct as opposed to indirect and vague, and the Roles scale measures whether the family has established patterns of behavior for completing family tasks. The Affective Responsiveness scale assesses whether family members respond to situations with the appropriate quality and quantity of emotion, and Affective Involvement measures the degree to which family members are involved and interested in the activities of other family members. Finally, the Behavioral Control scale assesses the way in which the family expresses and maintains standards of behavior in the family unit. Parents in this study also completed measures of parenting self-efficacy and satisfaction as well as a 10-item parenting esteem scale that we constructed by modifying Rosenberg's (1965) measure of general self-esteem.

We found that socially prescribed perfectionism is associated with extensive problems with family functioning. Analyses of the FAD measures showed that socially prescribed perfectionism in the parent was associated with poor functioning and low scores on the Roles, Affective Responsiveness, Affective Involvement, and Behavior Control scales. Socially prescribed perfectionism also was associated with low levels of parenting satisfaction and parenting self-esteem. Additional results indicated that other-oriented perfectionism was associated with family adjustment problems in a variety of domains.

Analyses with the measures of psychological distress confirmed that socially prescribed perfectionism in mothers of young children is associated with depression, anxiety, and chronic worry. In addition, self-oriented perfectionism in mothers of young children is associated with chronic worry.

Finally, in another recent study, Delavar (1998) examined the correlates of perfectionism in a sample of 58 parents with at least one child age 10 or younger. This study confirmed the association between socially prescribed perfectionism and parenting dissatisfaction ($r = .27$, $p < .05$). In addition, associations were found between dimensions of perfectionism and a brief measure of parenting stress created by Berry and Jones (1995). We found that scores on this measure were correlated with both self-oriented perfectionism ($r = .28$, $p < .05$) and socially prescribed perfectionism ($r = .32$, $p < .05$).

Delavar's (1998) results are consistent with recent research by Mitchelson and Burns (1998), who examined the link between perfectionism and parenting stress in 66 career mothers. The measure of parental stress was taken from the short form of the Parenting Stress Index (Abidin, 1983). Perfectionism was assessed with the Hewitt and Flett MPS and with measures of positive perfectionism and negative perfectionism scales created by Terry-Short, Owens, Slade, and Dewey (1995). The results indicated that higher levels of parenting stress were associated with elevated levels of self-oriented perfectionism ($r = .33$, $p < .001$), socially prescribed perfectionism ($r = .43$, $p < .001$), and negative perfectionism ($r = .39$, $p < .001$). A particular aspect of the Mitchelson and Burns study was that the MPS was adapted to assess perfectionism in specific situations (i.e., at home versus work) rather than as a general dispositional trait. Analyses with the modified versions of the MPS indicated that mothers reported greater perfectionism at work than at home.

Taken together, the results of these studies indicate that aspects of perfectionism in general—socially prescribed perfectionism and concern over parenting mistakes in particular—are associated with parenting stress, dissatisfaction, and distress. One limitation of the studies conducted thus far, however, is that all the data have been in the form of self-reports; observer ratings of the stress and distress of mothers and fathers have not been obtained. The lack of behavioral ratings may mask certain findings. For instance, perhaps the extrapunitive tendencies associated with other-oriented perfectionism (i.e., the tendency to be critical of others) will be linked with family conflict when studies are conducted with multiple informants, including the people who live with such demanding people as other-oriented perfectionists. Also, consistent with a broad developmental approach, objective measures of child outcomes and child characteristics need to be obtained.

Treatment Implications

A full analysis of the treatment implications of our model and research findings is beyond the scope of this chapter. Given the general lack of research on perfectionism and parenting, it is not surprising that no empirical research has studied the extent to which the parenting stress of perfectionists can be reduced by treatment interventions. In general, research on the treatment of parenting stress is scant, but the research that does exist suggests that levels of parenting stress can be reduced by cognitive–behavioral therapies that include an explicit focus on parent education and instruction (for a review, see Deater-Deckard, 1998). Our findings suggest that those interventions should include an explicit focus on perfectionistic tendencies, including the destructive effects of being too concerned about making mistakes and an omnipresent sense of pressure on the self to be a perfect parent. The findings from our most recent research indicate that perfectionistic mothers and fathers also will benefit by being taught adaptive forms of coping and problem solving that will boost their sense of confidence and efficacy in the parenting role.

Directions for Future Research

Although our work on the attitudes and behaviors of perfectionistic parents has provided us with several new insights, we must reiterate that work in this area is in its initial stages. It is evident that future research may take numerous directions as we work toward testing a comprehensive model of perfectionism in the parent. Consistent with our previous observations, it will be important in future research to distinguish parents who expect perfection from their children but are moderate to high in acceptance from parents who are both controlling and rejecting in their perfectionistic demands.

It is also evident that a host of potential factors may serve to mediate or moderate the link between perfectionism, parenting styles, and outcomes, not the least of which is the skill and temperament of the child in the family. Another factor that is likely to be important is the affective disposition of the parent. A growing number of studies indicate that psychological distress in the parent is associated with inappropriate parenting behaviors and poor child outcomes (Downey & Coyne, 1990; Fleming, Ruble, Flett, & Shaul, 1988). The experience of psychological distress may contribute to poor parenting in myriad ways; see Dix (1991) for a comprehensive review of the role of negative and positive affect in parenting. Elements of trait perfectionism, such as socially prescribed perfectionism and overconcern with making mistakes, may prove to be an important variable in parenting to the extent that they contribute to chronic forms of dysphoria, worry, and anger which, in turn, influence parenting attitudes and behaviors. Similarly, research needs to examine more fully the role of parenting self-efficacy as a mediator of the link between perfectionism and parenting, given our initial results indicating that socially prescribed perfectionism is associated consistently with negative appraisals of parenting competence. Perfectionistic parents will be especially prone to distress to the extent that they see themselves as relatively incapable of attaining perfect parenting and have a persistent focus on the discrepancy between their parenting characteristics and their unfulfilled images of the ideal parent.

References

Abidin, R. R. (1983). *Parenting Stress Index*. Odessa, FL: Psychological Assessment Resources.

Ablard, K. E., & Parker, W. D. (1997). Parents' achievement goals and perfectionism in their academically talented children. *Journal of Youth and Adolescence, 26,* 651–667.

Adler, A. (1956). The neurotic disposition. In H. L. Ansbacher & R. R. Ansbacher (Eds.), *The individual psychology of Alfred Adler* (pp. 239–262). New York: Harper.

Amato, P. R. (1990). Dimensions of the family environment as perceived by children: A multidimensional scaling analysis. *Journal of the Marriage and the Family, 52,* 613–620.

Andersson, P., & Perris, C. (2000). Attachment styles and dysfunctional assumptions in adults. *Clinical Psychology and Psychotherapy, 7,* 47–53.

Armsden, G. C., & Greenberg, M. T. (1987). The Inventory of Parent and Peer Attachment: Individual differences and their relationship to psychological well-being in adolescence. *Journal of Youth and Adolescence, 16,* 427–453.

Baldwin, M. W. (1992). Relational schemas and the processing of social information. *Psychological Bulletin, 112,* 461–484.

Bandura, A. (1986). *Social foundations of thought and action: A social cognitive theory*. Englewood Cliffs, NJ: Prentice Hall.

Bandura, A., & Cervone, D. (1986). Differential engagement of self-reactive influences in cognitive motivation. *Organizational Behavior and Human Decision Processes, 38,* 92–113.

Bandura, A., Grusec, J. E., & Menlove, F. L. (1967). Observational learning as a function of symbolization and incentive set. *Child Development, 37,* 499–506.

Bandura, A., & Kupers, C. J. (1964). Transmission of patterns of self-reinforcement through modeling. *Journal of Abnormal and Social Psychology, 69,* 1–9.

Barrett, P. M., Rapee, R. M., Dadds, M. R., & Ryan, S. M. (1996). Family enhancement of cognitive style in anxious and aggressive children: Threat bias and the FEAR effect. *Journal of Abnormal Psychology, 24,* 187–203.

Bartholomew, K. (1990). Avoidance of intimacy: An attachment perspective. *Journal of Social and Personal Relationships, 7,* 147–178.

Bartholomew, K., & Horowitz, L. M. (1991). Attachment styles among young adults: A test of a four-category model. *Journal of Personality and Social Psychology, 61,* 226–244.

Baumrind, D. H. (1971). Current patterns of parental authority. *Developmental Psychology Monographs, 4*(1, Pt. 2).

Becker, T. E., Billings, R. S., Eveleth, D. M., & Gilbert, N. W. (1997). Validity of three attachment style scales: Exploratory and confirmatory evidence. *Educational and Psychological Measurement, 57,* 477–493.

Bell, R. Q., & Chapman, M. (1986). Child effects in studies using experimental or brief longitudinal approaches to socialization. *Developmental Psychology, 22,* 595–603.

Belsky, J. (1984). The determinants of parenting: A process model. *Child Development, 55,* 83–96.

Berry, J., & Jones, W. (1995). The Parent Stress Scale: Initial psychometric evidence. *Journal of Social and Personal Relationships, 12,* 463–472.

Biringen, Z. (2000). Emotional availability: Conceptualization and research findings. *American Journal of Orthopsychiatry, 70,* 104–114.

Biringen, Z., & Robinson, J. (1991). Emotional availability in mother–child interactions: A reconceptualization for research. *American Journal of Orthopsychiatry, 61,* 258–271.

Biringen, Z., Robinson, J., & Emde, R. N. (1989). *The Emotional Availability Scales*. Unpublished manuscript, University of Colorado Health Sciences Center, Department of Psychiatry, Denver.

Blatt, S. J. (1995). The destructiveness of perfectionism: Implications for the treatment of depression. *American Psychologist, 50,* 1003–1020.

Blatt, S. J., & Homann, E. (1992). Parent–child interaction in the etiology of dependent and self-critical depression. *Clinical Psychology Review, 12,* 47–91.

Block, J. (1981). *The Child-Rearing Practices Report (CRPR): A set of Q-items for the description of parental socialization attitudes and values.* Santa Cruz: University of California.

Bowlby, J. (1969). *Attachment and loss: Vol. 1. Attachment.* New York: Basic Books.

Brehm, S. S., & Brehm, J. M. (1981). *Psychological reactance: A theory of freedom and control.* San Diego, CA: Academic Press.

Brennan, K. A., & Shaver, P. R. (1995). Dimensions of adult attachment, affect regulation, and relationship functioning. *Personality and Social Psychology Bulletin, 21,* 267–283.

Bronfenbrenner, U. (1979). *The ecology of human development.* Cambridge, MA: Harvard University Press.

Brookings, J. B., & Wilson, J. F. (1994). Personality and the family–environment predictors of self-reported eating attitudes and behaviors. *Journal of Personality Assessment, 63,* 313–326.

Brownell, K. D. (1991). Dieting and the search for the perfect body: Where physiology and culture collide. *Behavior Therapy, 22,* 1–22.

Burhans, K. K., & Dweck, C. S. (1995). Helplessness in early childhood: The role of contingent worth. *Child Development, 66,* 1719–1738.

Buri, J. R. (1991). Parental authority questionnaire. *Journal of Personality Assessment, 57,* 110–119.

Carver, C. S., & White, T. L. (1994). Behavioral inhibition, behavioral activation, and affective responses to impending reward and punishment: The BIS/BAS Scales. *Journal of Personality and Social Psychology, 67,* 319–333.

Chang, E. C. (2000). Perfectionism as a predictor of positive and negative psychological outcomes: Examining a mediational model in younger and older adults. *Journal of Counseling Psychology, 47,* 18–26.

Chodorow, N. J., & Contratto, S. (1989). The fantasy of the perfect mother. In N. J. Chodorow (Ed.), *Feminism and psychoanalytic theory* (pp. 79–96). New Haven, CT: Yale University Press.

Chorpita, B. F., & Barlow, D. H. (1998). The development of anxiety: The role of control in the early environment. *Psychological Bulletin, 124,* 3–21.

Clara, I. P., Enns, M. W., & Cox, B. J. (2001, July). *Origins of perfectionism.* Poster presented at the World Congress of Behavioral and Cognitive Therapies, Vancouver, British Columbia, Canada.

Cloninger, C. R. (1986). A unified biosocial theory of personality and its role in the development of anxiety states. *Psychiatric Developments, 3,* 167–226.

Cole, D. A., & Rehm, L. P. (1986). Family interaction patterns and childhood depression. *Journal of Abnormal Child Psychology, 14,* 297–314.

Collins, N. L., & Read, S. J. (1990). Adult attachment, working models, and relationship quality in dating couples. *Journal of Personality and Social Psychology, 58,* 644–666.

Cox, J. L., Holden, J. M., & Sagovsky, R. (1987). Detection of postnatal depression: Development of the 10-item Edinburgh Postnatal Depression Scale. *British Journal of Psychiatry, 150,* 782–786.

Crittenden, P. M. (1994). Peering into the black box: An exploratory treatise on the development of self in young children. In D. Cicchetti & S. L. Toth (Eds.), *Rochester Symposium on Developmental Psychology: Vol. 5: Disorders and dysfunctions of the self* (pp. 79–148). Rochester, NY: University of Rochester Press.

Cutrona, C. E., & Troutman, B. (1986). Social support, infant temperament, and parenting self-efficacy: A mediational model of postpartum depression. *Child Development, 58,* 1507–1518.

Darling, N., & Steinberg, L. (1993). Parenting style as context: An integrative model. *Psychological Bulletin, 113,* 487–496.

Deater-Deckard, K. (1998). Parenting stress and child adjustment: Some old hypotheses and new questions. *Clinical Psychology: Science and Practice, 5,* 314–332.

Delavar, M. (1998). *Perfectionism, coping styles, and parenting stress.* Unpublished honors thesis, York University, Toronto.

Dix, T. (1991). The affective organization of parenting: Adaptive and maladaptive processes. *Psychological Bulletin, 110,* 3–26.

Dorian, B. J., & Garfinkel, P. E. (1999). The contributions of epidemiologic studies to the etiology and treatment of the eating disorders. *Psychiatric Annals, 29,* 187–192.

Dornbusch, S. M., Ritter, P. L., Leiderman, P. H., Roberts, D. F., & Fraleigh, M. J. (1987). The relation of parenting style to adolescent school performance. *Child Development, 58,* 1244–1257.

Dowd, E. T., & Wallbrown, F. (1993). Motivational components of client reactance. *Journal of Counseling and Development, 71,* 533–538.

Downey, G., & Coyne, J. C. (1990). Children of depressed parents: An integrative review. *Psychological Bulletin, 108,* 50–76.

Enns, M. W., Cox, B. J., & Larsen, D. K. (2000). Perceptions of parental bonding and symptom severity in adults with depression: Mediation by personality dimensions. *Canadian Journal of Psychiatry, 45,* 263–268.

Epstein, N. B., Baldwin, L. M., & Bishop, D. S. (1983). The McMaster Family Assessment Device. *Journal of Marital and Family Therapy, 9,* 171–182.

Evans, D. W., Leckman, J. F., Carter, A., Reznick, J. S., Henshaw, D., King, R. A., & Pauls, D. (1997). Ritual, habit, and perfectionism: The prevalence and development of compulsive-like behavior in normal young children. *Child Development, 68,* 58–68.

Feeney, J. A., Noller, P., & Hanrahan, M. (1994). Assessing adult attachment. In M. B. Sperling & W. H. Berman (Eds.), *Attachment in adults: Clinical and developmental perspectives* (pp. 128–153). New York: Guilford.

Findlay, B., & Watts, S. (1998). Psychological correlates of perfectionism [Abstract]. *Australian Journal of Psychology, 50,* 67.

Fleming, A. S., Ruble, D. N., Flett, G. L., & Shaul, D. (1988). Postpartum adjustment in first-time mothers: Relations between mood, maternal attitudes, and mother–infant interactions. *Developmental Psychology, 24,* 71–81.

Flett, G. L., Besser, A., & Hewitt, P. L. (2001). *Personality vulnerability factors, parenting competence, and positive and negative affect in new mothers and fathers.* Manuscript submitted for publication.

Flett, G. L., & Hewitt, P. L. (1997). Personality, childcare stress, social support, and parenting satisfaction in new parents [Abstract]. *Canadian Psychology, 38,* 159.

Flett, G. L., Hewitt, P. L., Berk, L., & Besser, A. (2001, July). Perfectionism cognitions and concern over parenting mistakes in postpartum depression. In P. L. Hewitt (Chair), *Perfectionism and depression.* Symposium presented at the World Congress of Behavioral and Cognitive Therapies, Vancouver, British Columbia, Canada.

Flett, G. L., Hewitt, P. L., Endler, N. S., Pickering, L., & Berk, L. (2001). *Personality, stress, and coping with the birth of the first child.* Unpublished manuscript.

Flett, G. L., Hewitt, P. L., Endler, N. S., & Tassone, C. (1994–1995). Perfectionism and components of state and trait anxiety. *Current Psychology, 13,* 326–350.

Flett, G. L., Hewitt, P. L., Mosher, S. W., Sherry, S. B., Macdonald, S., & Sawatzky, D. L. (2001, August). *Dimensions of perfectionism and attachment style.* Paper presented at the annual meeting of the American Psychological Society, Toronto, Ontario, Canada.

Flett, G. L., Hewitt, P. L., & Singer, A. (1995). Perfectionism and parental authority styles. *Individual Psychology, 51,* 50–60.

Flett, G. L., Sherry, S. B., & Hewitt, P. L. (2001). *Perfectionism, parental punitiveness, and anxious parental rearing.* Unpublished manuscript.

Flynn, C. A., Hewitt, P. L., Flett, G. L., & Caelian, C. (2001). *The development of perfectionism: Parental behavior and cultural influences.* Unpublished manuscript.

Fox, R. A. (1992). Development of an instrument to measure the behaviors and expectations of parents of young children. *Journal of Pediatric Psychology, 17,* 231–239.

Foy, S. N. (1998). Multidimensional perfectionism and perceived parental psychological control and behavioral control [Abstract]. *Australian Journal of Psychology, 50,* 84.

Freud, S. (1988). *My three mothers and other passions.* New York: New York University Press.

Frost, R. O., Lahart, C., & Rosenblate, R. (1991). The development of perfectionism: A study of daughters and their parents. *Cognitive Therapy and Research, 15,* 469–489.

Frost, R. O., Marten, P., Lahart, C., & Rosenblate, R. (1990). The dimensions of perfectionism. *Cognitive Therapy and Research, 14,* 449–468.

Gibaud-Wallston, J., & Wandersman, L. P. (1978, August). *Development and utility of the Parenting Sense of Competence Scale.* Paper presented at the annual meeting of the American Psychological Association, Toronto, Ontario, Canada.

Glassner, B. (1992). *Bodies: The tyranny of perfection.* Los Angeles: Lowell House.

Graber, J. A., Brooks-Gunn, J., Paikoff, R. L., & Warren, M. P. (1994). Prediction of eating problems: An 8-year study of adolescent girls. *Developmental Psychology, 30,* 823–834.

Gray, J. A. (1982). *The neuropsychology of anxiety: An inquiry into the functions of the septo-hippocampal system.* New York: Oxford University Press.

Gruner, K., Muris, P., & Merckelbach, H. (1999). The relationship between anxious rearing behaviors and anxiety disorders symptomatology in normal children. *Journal of Behavior Therapy and Experimental Psychiatry, 30,* 27–35.

Hamachek, D. E. (1978). Psychodynamics of normal and neurotic perfectionism. *Psychology, 15,* 27–33.

Harris, J. R. (1995). Where is the child's environment? A group socialization theory of development. *Psychological Review, 102,* 458–489.

Harter, S. (1990). Causes, correlates and the functional role of global self-worth: A life-span perspective. In R. J. Sternberg & J. Kolligian, Jr. (Eds.), *Competence considered* (pp. 67–97). New Haven, CT: Yale University Press.

Head, S. B., & Williamson, D. A. (1990). Association of family environment and personality disturbances in bulimia nervosa. *International Journal of Eating Disorders, 9,* 667–674.

Henderson, K., Macdonald, S., Flett, G. L., & Hewitt, P. L. (1997, August). *Perfectionism and family adjustment in parents of preschool children.* Paper presented at the 105th annual convention of the American Psychological Association, Chicago.

Hewitt, P. L., & Flett, G. L. (1991). Perfectionism in the self and social contexts: Conceptualization, assessment, and association with psychopathology. *Journal of Personality and Social Psychology, 60,* 456–470.

Hewitt, P. L., & Flett, G. L. (1993). Dimensions of perfectionism, daily stress, and depression: A test of the specific vulnerability hypothesis. *Journal of Abnormal Psychology, 102,* 58–65.

Hewitt, P. L., Flett, G. L., & Ediger, E. (1996). Perfectionism and depression: Longitudinal assessment of a specific vulnerability hypothesis. *Journal of Abnormal Psychology, 105,* 276–280.

Hewitt, P. L., Flett, G. L., & Mikail, S. F. (1995). Perfectionism and family adjustment in pain patients and their spouses. *Journal of Family Psychology, 9,* 335–347.

Hickinbottom, S. L. J., & Thompson, J. M. (1999, August). *Parents and perfectionism: Adults' memories and perceptions.* Poster presented at the 107th annual convention of the American Psychological Association, Boston.

Hill, R. W., Zrull, M. C., & Turlington, S. (1997). Perfectionism and interpersonal problems. *Journal of Personality Assessment, 69,* 81–103.

Hong, S.-M., & Page, S. (1989). A psychological reactance scale: Development, factor structure, and reliability. *Psychological Reports, 64,* 1323–1326.

Horney, K. (1950). *Neurosis and human growth.* New York: Norton.

Horowitz, L. M., Rosenberg, S. E., Baer, B. A., Ureno, G., & Villasenor, V. S. (1988). Inventory of Interpersonal Problems: Psychometric properties and clinical applications. *Journal of Consulting and Clinical Psychology, 56,* 885–896.

Hovestadt, A. J., Anderson, W. T., Piercy, F. P., Cochran, S. W., & Fine, M. (1985). A family of origin scale. *Journal of Marital and Family Therapy, 11,* 287–297.

Hyson, M. C., Hirsh-Pasek, K., Rescorla, L., Cone, J., & Martell-Boinske, L. (1991). Ingredients of parental "pressure" in early childhood. *Journal of Applied Developmental Psychology, 12,* 347–365.

Jarvis, W. B. G., & Petty, R. E. (1996). The need to evaluate. *Journal of Personality and Social Psychology, 70,* 172–194.

Johnston, C. J., & Mash, E. J. (1989). A measure of parenting satisfaction and efficacy. *Journal of Clinical Child Psychology, 18,* 167–175.

Kamins, M. L., & Dweck, C. S. (1999). Person versus process praise and criticism: Implications for contingent self-worth and coping. *Developmental Psychology, 35,* 835–847.

Kaner, A., Bulik, C. M., & Sullivan, P. F. (1993). Abuse in adult relationships of bulimic women. *Journal of Interpersonal Violence, 8,* 52–63.

Kelly, J. A., & Worell, L. (1976). Parent behaviors related to masculine, feminine, and androgynous sex role orientations. *Journal of Consulting and Clinical Psychology, 44,* 843–851.

Kinzl, J. F., Traweger, C., Guenther, V., & Biebl, W. (1994). Family background and sexual abuse associated with eating disorders. *American Journal of Psychiatry, 151,* 1127–1131.

Kochanska, G. (1997). Multiple pathways to conscience for children with different temperaments: From toddlerhood to age 5. *Developmental Psychology, 33,* 228–240.

Kochanska, G., & Askan, N. (1995). Mother–child mutually positive affect, the quality of child compliance to requests and prohibitions, and maternal control as correlates of early internalization. *Child Development, 66,* 236–254.

Lindberg, F. H., & Distad, L. J. (1985). Survival responses to incest: Adolescents in crisis. *Child Abuse and Neglect, 9,* 521–526.

Locke, E. A. (1996). Motivation through conscious goal setting. *Applied and Preventive Psychology, 5,* 117–124.

Maccoby, E. E., & Martin, J. A. (1983). Socialization in the context of the family: Parent–child interaction. In E. M. Hetherington (Ed.), *Handbook of child psychology: Vol. 4 Socialization, personality, and social development* (pp. 1–101). New York: Wiley.

Macdonald, S. (1998). An examination of parents' expectations, attitudes, scaffolding behaviours, and children's developmental outcomes. *Dissertation Abstracts International, 59,* 5B. (UMI No. 2457)

Macdonald, S., Flett, G. L., & Hewitt, P. L. (2001). *Perfectionism, parenting attitudes, and parenting behaviors toward young children.* Unpublished manuscript.

Macdonald, S., Martin, T. R., Flett, G. L., & Hewitt, P. L. (1995). Perfectionism, parenting styles, and family satisfaction [Abstract]. *Canadian Psychology, 36,* 239.

Martin, R. P., Wisenbaker, J., & Huttunen, M. (1994). Review of factor analytic studies of temperament measures based on the Thomas-Chess structural model: Implications for the big five. In C. F. Halverson, G. A. Kohnstamm, & R. P. Martin (Eds.), *The developing structure of temperament and personality from infancy to adulthood* (pp. 157–172). Hillsdale, NJ: Erlbaum.

Masia, C. L., & Morris, T. L. (1998). Parental factors associated with social anxiety: Methodological limitations and suggestions for integrated behavioral research. *Clinical Psychology: Science and Practice, 5,* 211–228.

Melges, F. T. (1982). Emotion spirals and interpersonal expectations. In F. T. Melges (Ed.), *Time and the inner future: A temporal approach to psychiatric disorders* (pp. 219–238). New York: Wiley.

Meyer, T. J., Miller, M. L., Metzger, R. L., & Borkovec, T. D. (1990). Development and validation of the Penn State Worry Questionnaire. *Behaviour Research and Therapy, 28,* 487–495.

Millon, T. (1998). DSM narcissistic personality disorder: Historical reflections and future directions. In E. F. Ronningstam (Ed.), *Disorders of narcissism: Diagnostic, clinical, and empirical implications* (pp. 75–101). Washington, DC: American Psychiatric Association.

Minuchin, S., Rosman, B. L., & Baker, L. (1978). *Psychosomatic families: Anorexia nervosa in context.* Cambridge, MA: Harvard University Press.

Missildine, W. H. (1963). Perfectionism—If you must strive to "do better." In W. H. Missildine (Ed.), *Your inner child of the past* (pp. 75–90). New York: Pocket Books.

Mitchelson, J., & Burns, L. R. (1998). Career mothers and perfectionism: Stress at work and at home. *Personality and Individual Differences, 25,* 477–485.

Moos, R. H., & Moos, B. H. (1986). *Family Environment Scale Manual* (2nd ed). Palo Alto, CA: Consulting Psychologists Press, Inc.

Mueller, C. M., & Dweck, C. S. (1998). Praise for intelligence can undermine children's motivation and performance. *Journal of Personality and Social Psychology, 75,* 33–50.

Oliver, J. M., & Berger, L. S. (1992). Depression, parent–offspring relationships, and cognitive vulnerability. *Journal of Social Behavior and Personality, 7,* 415–429.

Oliver, J. M., & Paull, J. C. (1995). Self-esteem and self-efficacy: Perceived parenting and family climate; and depression in university students. *Journal of Clinical Psychology, 51,* 467–481.

Oliver, J. M., Raftery, M., Reeb, A., & Delaney, P. (1993). Perceptions of parent–offspring relationships as functions of depression in offspring: "Affectionless control," "negative bias," and "depressive realism." *Journal of Social Behavior and Personality, 8,* 405–424.

Parker, G., Tupling, H., & Brown, L. B. (1979). A parental bonding instrument. *British Journal of Medical Psychology, 52,* 1–10.

Perris, C., Jacobsson, L., Lindstrom, H., von Knorring, L., & Perris, H. (1980). Development of a new inventory for assessing memories of a parental rearing behaviour. *Acta Psychiatrica Scandinavica, 61,* 265–274.

Randolph, J. J., & Dykman, B. M. (1998). Perceptions of parenting and depression-proneness in the offspring: Dysfunctional attitudes as a mediating mechanism. *Cognitive Therapy and Research, 22,* 377–400.

Rice, K. G., Ashby, J. S., & Preusser, K. J. (1996). Perfectionism, relationships with parents, and self-esteem. *Individual Psychology, 52,* 246–260.

Rice, K. G., & Mirzadeh, S. A. (2000). Perfectionism, attachment, and adjustment. *Journal of Counseling Psychology, 47,* 238–250.

Richter, J., Eisemann, M., & Perris, C. (1994). The relation between perceived parental rearing and dysfunctional attitudes in unipolar depressive inpatients. *Clinical Psychology and Psychotherapy, 1,* 82–86.

Richter, J., Eisemann, M., & Richter, G. (2000). Temperament, character and perceived parental rearing in healthy adults: Two related concepts? *Psychopathology, 33,* 36–42.

Rickel, A. U., & Biasatti, L. L. (1982). Modification of the Block Child Rearing Practices Report. *Journal of Clinical Psychology, 38,* 129–134.

Rickner, R. G., & Tan, S.-Y. (1994). Psychopathology, guilt, perfectionism and family of origin functioning among Protestant clergy. *Journal of Psychology and Theology, 22,* 29–38.

Roehling, P. V., & Robin, A. L. (1986). Development and validation of the Family Beliefs Inventory: A measure of unrealistic beliefs among parents and adolescents. *Journal of Consulting and Clinical Psychology, 54,* 693–697.

Rogers, C. R. (1951). *Client-centered therapy: Its current practice, implications and theory.* Boston: Houghton-Mifflin.

Rosenberg, M. (1965). *Society and the adolescent child.* Princeton, NJ: Princeton University Press.

Rothbart, M. K., Ahadi, S. A., & Hershey, K. L. (1994). Temperament and social behavior in children. *Merrill-Palmer Quarterly, 40,* 21–39.

Rothbart, M. K., & Derryberry, D. (1981). Development of individual differences in temperament. In M. E. Lamb & A. L. Brown (Eds.), *Advances in developmental psychology* (Vol. 1, pp. 37–86). Hillsdale, NJ: Erlbaum.

Ruble, D. N., & Flett, G. L. (1988). Conflicting goals in self-evaluative information-seeking: Development and ability level analyses. *Child Development, 59,* 97–106.

Sameroff, A. J. (1975). Transactional relations in early social models. *Human Development, 18,* 65–79.

Schaaf, K. K., & McCanne, T. R. (1994). Childhood abuse, body image disturbance, and eating disorders. *Child Abuse and Neglect, 18,* 607–615.

Schaefer, E. (1959). A circumplex model for maternal behavior. *Journal of Abnormal and Child Psychology, 59,* 226–253.

Slaney, R. B., & Ashby, J. S. (1996). Perfectionists: Study of a criterion group. *Journal of Counseling and Development, 74,* 393–398.

Sockett-Dimarco, N., Landy, S., Flett, G. L., & Hewitt, P. L. (2001). *Perfectionism, parental insensitivity, and parental intrusiveness.* Unpublished manuscript.

Stöber, J. (1998). The Frost Multidimensional Perfectionism Scale revisited: More perfect with four (instead of six) dimensions. *Personality and Individual Differences, 24,* 481–491.

Terry-Short, L. A., Owens, R. G., Slade, P. D., & Dewey, M. E. (1995). Positive and negative perfectionism. *Personality and Individual Differences, 18,* 663–668.

Tobin, D. L., & Griffing, A. S. (1996). Coping, sexual abuse, and compensatory behaviour. *International Journal of Eating Disorders, 20,* 143–148.

Vieth, A. Z., & Trull, T. J. (1999). Family patterns of perfectionism: An examination of college students and their parents. *Journal of Personality Assessment, 72,* 49–67.

Weissman, A. N., & Beck, A. T. (1978, November). *Development and validation of the Dysfunctional Attitude Scale: A preliminary investigation.* Paper presented at the annual meeting of the Association for the Advancement of Behavior Therapy, Chicago, IL.

Wintre, M. G., & Sugar, L. A. (2000). Relationships with parents, personality, and the university transition. *Journal of College Student Development, 41,* 202–214.

Wintre, M. G., Yaffe, M., & Crowley, J. (1995). Perception of Parental Reciprocity Scale (POPRS): Development and validation with adolescents and young adults. *Social Development, 4,* 129–48.

Wyatt, R., & Gilbert, P. (1998). Dimensions of perfectionism: A study exploring their relationship with perceived social rank and status. *Personality and Individual Differences, 24,* 71–79.

Zlotnick, C., Hohlstein, L. A., Shea, M. T., Pearlstein, T., Recupero, P., & Bidadi, K. (1996). The relationship between sexual abuse and eating pathology. *International Journal of Eating Disorders, 20,* 129–134.

5

Perfectionism and Adjustment in Gifted Children

Wayne D. Parker

At the Olympic games a hurdler is in his blocks, coiled, waiting for the starter's gun to discharge. He has trained hours daily for a race that will last just seconds. He knows that to win a medal, he must have an excellent start and maintain almost perfect form. Is this a healthy striving for excellence, or a neurotic preoccupation with perfection? The same question can be asked of any striving for excellence, from the competitive pianist who has practiced the same piece for months to master the technique and phrasing, to the mathematically talented child who feels a need to be the highest scorer in a national math contest, to an author on the 17th rewrite of a short story.

When dealing with students of typical ability, this question is usually easy to answer: Striving for excellence is unhealthy when the goals are unrealistically high. When dealing with students who are gifted, however, it is much more difficult to determine what goals are unrealistic. Among Olympic athletes it is understood that one must be obsessed with competing and approaching perfection in technique to even make the team. Are attainable goals approaching perfection unhealthy if they are consuming, or is this obsession a necessary element of a desirable attainment of excellence?

These questions have been under exploration at the Center for Talented Youth of Johns Hopkins University in a series of studies examining perfectionistic needs among academically talented youth. The participants in this line of research are among the brightest students in the country, almost all scoring at or above the 99.5 percentile for their age on either the Math or Verbal subtest (or both) of the Secondary School Admission Test (SSAT; see Mills & Barnett, 1992) in the fifth or sixth grade or the Scholastic Aptitude Test (SAT; see Stanley, 1985) in the seventh grade.

This chapter outlines a program of research clearly showing that it is possible to distinguish between gifted students with adaptive and maladaptive forms of perfectionism. It describes methods used to define the two forms of perfectionism and compares adaptive and maladaptive perfectionism in terms of associated differences in personality traits and self characteristics, including an analysis of the long-term stability of perfectionism in gifted children. The chapter concludes with an overview of the characteristics of parents of children with adaptive versus maladaptive perfectionism.

Measurement

The Frost Multidimensional Perfectionism Scale (MPS; Frost, Marten, La-hart, & Rosenblate, 1990) was chosen to measure perfectionism in the students; it originally was developed with female college students. Parker and Stumpf (1995) addressed the utility of this scale with a large sample of academically talented sixth graders. Frost et al. (1990) reported an internal reliability of .90 for the total score, with the coefficient alphas of the subscales ranging from .77 to .93. Among these much younger students (Parker & Stumpf, 1995), the internal reliability for the total score was .87, with subscale reliability ranging from .67 to .90. The matrix of inter-correlations of MPS subscales was consistent between the two samples, and a confirmatory factor analysis demonstrated an acceptable degree of fit.

To allow the results to be easily interpretable to those familiar with the Hewitt and Flett (1991) Multidimensional Perfectionism Scale (MPS), both the Frost et al. (1990) MPS and Hewitt and Flett's MPS were administered to 117 gifted seventh graders (Parker, 1996). The correlations between the two instruments presented in Table 5.1, are the same correlations obtained among college students (Frost, Heimberg, Holt, Mattia, & Neubauer, 1993). The two correlational matrices are highly similar, with the correlation produced by the correlational pairs of seventh-grade results

Table 5.1. Correlations Between the Frost et al. (1990) and Hewitt and Flett (1991) Multidimensional Perfectionism Scales (MPS)

Frost et al. MPS subscale	Hewitt and Flett MPS Perfectionism Subscale		
	Self-oriented	Socially prescribed	Other-oriented
Concern Over Mistakes	.52***	.52***	.45***
	[.38]	[.49]	[.22]
Personal Standards	.67***	.15	.33***
	[.62]	[.16]	[.33]
Parental Expectations	.26***	.60***	.14
	[.24]	[.49]	[.19]
Parental Criticism	.12	.72***	.13
	[.07]	[.49]	[.10]
Doubts About Actions	.03	.36***	.08
	[.16]	[.28]	[.01]
Organization	.31***	−.01	.27***
	[.29]	[−.11]	[.07]
Total	.55***	.71***	.40***
	[.49]	[.57]	[.28]

Note. The first correlations are for seventh grade students at the Center for Talented Youth, Baltimore, MD ($N = 117$). The bracketed correlations are those reported by Frost et al. (1990) for college students.

and college results equal to .92. Frost et al. (1993) reported a varimax solution of the nine subscales of the two MPSs with college students that yielded two factors: The first represents maladaptive evaluation concerns, and the other represents positive strivings. When the factor structure of the seventh graders was compared with the Frost et al. (1993) target, the congruence coefficient was an excellent .99; the congruence coefficient for the first factor was .99, and it was .98 for the second factor.

Perfectionistic Types and the Incidence of Perfectionism

In light of the factor analytic evidence that both maladaptive and adaptive forms of perfectionism might exist, a cluster analytic study was conducted to determine the number of perfectionistic types and their characteristics (Parker, 1997). A total of 820 academically talented sixth-grade students from a nationally gathered sample were administered the MPS (Frost et al., 1990). This sample was 63% male and 87% White; Asian students constituted the only large racial and ethnic minority representation (10% of the sample). The children tended to come from well-educated families, with 79% of fathers and 76% of mothers having at least a bachelor's degree, and 51% of fathers and 40% of mothers possessing advanced degrees.

To assist in the interpretation of the results of the planned cluster analysis, 565 members of the sample took the Adjective Check List (ACL; Gough & Heilbrun, 1983), 568 took the NEO-Five Factor Inventory (NEO-FFI; Costa & McCrae, 1992), 811 took the Rosenberg Self-Esteem Scale (Rosenberg, 1965), and 409 took the Brief Symptom Inventory (BSI; Derogatis, 1993). The ACL consists of 300 adjectives and adjectival phrases to which a person responds with a self-evaluation. Using the validity index to detect random responding, 506 ACLs scored in the range that allowed them to be safely assumed to be valid. The NEO-FFI is a 60-item short form of the NEO Personality Inventory–Revised (NEO-PI-R; Costa & McCrae, 1992) that measures the domains of the five-factor model of personality (Neuroticism, Extraversion, Openness to Experience, Agreeableness, and Conscientiousness). This instrument, traditionally used only with adults, has been demonstrated to be appropriate for use with academically talented youth (Parker & Stumpf, 1998). The Rosenberg Self-Esteem Scale is the most widely used unidimensional measure of self-concept (Blascovich & Tomaka, 1991). The BSI is a 53-item, self-report, Likert-scale, symptom inventory that is a shortened version of the Symptom Checklist–90 (SCL-90-R; Derogatis & Cleary, 1977); it has been judged to be among the best screening instruments for maladjustment (Edwards, Yarvis, Mueller, Zingale, & Wagman, 1978; Waskow & Parloff, 1975) and has been widely used in psychiatric research and clinical screening.

Four hundred students were randomly selected, and their MPS subtest scores were analyzed with hierarchical cluster analysis using Ward's method and squared Euclidian distances. A three-cluster solution was indicated on the basis of the change in the agglomeration coefficient (Hair,

Anderson, Tatham, & Black, 1992). The cluster centroids from the hierarchical cluster analysis then were used as the initial seed points in a nonhierarchical cluster analysis for the same 400 students to give greater precision to the results. As a cross-validation of the cluster solution, a second nonhierarchical cluster analysis was performed on the scores of the remaining 420 students. This analysis, which was based on both the cluster centroids and the percentage membership in each cluster, was highly similar to the initial results. Differences between final cluster centers were tested by analysis of variance, and differences for each subscale across clusters in both the initial and cross-validation subsamples all were significant at the $p < .000$ level.

With this validation of the cluster solution, the final cluster centers from the original subsample of 400 students were used to determine cluster membership for the entire sample. This process yielded 248 students (30.2%) in Cluster 1, 344 students (42.0%) in Cluster 2, and 228 students (27.8%) in Cluster 3. Mean MPS scores by cluster group as well as the univariate F tests by cluster groups are presented in Table 5.2. All differences across clusters for MPS scores were statistically significant, and effect sizes were of sufficient magnitude to be meaningful. Scores for the Concern Over Mistakes and Organization subscales and total score had the greatest impact in differentiating among the groups. In the Tukey post hoc testing, all pairwise comparisons were statistically significant for all MPS variables except for the difference between Clusters 1 and 2 on the Parental Expectations subscale.

Self-descriptions of the ACL were analyzed to assist in understanding how members of the three cluster groups saw themselves. A pool of statistically significant ($p < .01$) descriptors was generated for each cluster group; the descriptors with the largest correlations for each group are shown in Table 5.3. In addition, the ACL-scaled scores were produced, and the model of a relationship between the ACL scaled scores and membership in the MPS cluster groups was statistically significant.

To understand differences between the clusters from the perspective of the five-factor model of personality, NEO-FFI scores were analyzed through multiple discriminant analysis by MPS group membership; the means and standard deviations of the NEO-FFI raw scores, by cluster membership and univariate F test results, are presented in Table 5.4. Conscientiousness had the greatest impact, accounting for 23% of the variance in group membership, with the other NEO-FFI scores each accounting for less than 10% of the variance. When the discriminant functions were examined, the first discriminant function accounted for more than 80% of the between-groups variance, and the NEO-FFI scores with loadings of at least .40 on the function were Conscientiousness and Extraversion. The other three scores (Neuroticism, Agreeableness, and Openness) had similar loadings on the second discriminant function. The composite potency index (Perrault, Behrman, & Armstrong, 1979), a relative measure of the discriminating power of a variable across all significant functions, indicated that the most important component of perfectionism is Conscien-

Table 5.2. Multidimensional Perfectionism Scale (Frost et al., 1990) Raw Score Means and Standard Deviations by Cluster Group

	Cluster 1		Cluster 2		Cluster 3			
	M	SD	M	SD	M	SD	F	r^2
Concern Over Mistakes	16.1	3.3	15.1	3.3	25.1	5.0	518.44[abc]	.56
Personal Standards	20.2	3.7	24.0	4.0	26.5	3.9	161.76[abc]	.28
Parental Expectations	12.4	3.3	12.7	3.4	16.9	4.0	117.78[bc]	.22
Parental Criticism	6.6	2.2	5.8	2.1	8.8	3.2	106.91[abc]	.21
Doubts About Actions	8.8	2.4	7.8	2.4	10.8	3.1	87.23[abc]	.18
Organization	16.1	4.1	25.3	2.9	21.5	4.6	409.87[abc]	.50
Total	60.0	8.9	66.8	7.8	83.1	11.1	396.40[abc]	.49

Note. $df = 1,817$; all F tests statistically significant at $p < .0000$.
[a]Tukey pairs were significant for Clusters 1 and 2.
[b]Tukey pairs were significant for Clusters 1 and 3.
[c]Tukey pairs were significant for Clusters 2 and 3.

Table 5.3.   ACL Self-Descriptions of Each Cluster Group With Correlations to Cluster-Group Membership

Group 1		Group 2		Group 3	
Sees Self As	Does Not See Self As	Sees Self As	Does Not See Self As	Sees Self As	Does Not See Self As
Careless (.22)	Organized (−.29)	Organized (.34)	Careless (−.22)	Gloomy (.13)	Attractive (−.14)
Disorderly (.19)	Mature (−.20)	Attractive (.20)	Disorderly (−.16)	Hostile (.13)	Good looking (−.14)
Distractible (.17)	Precise (−.18)	Reliable (.19)	Distractible (−.14)	Hurried (.12)	Jolly (−.12)
Slipshod (.17)	Practical (−.17)	Strong (.19)	Irresponsible (−.13)	Dull (.12)	Kind (−.12)
Forgetful (.13)	Ambitious (−.16)	Understanding (.17)	Lazy (−.13)	Stingy (.12)	Relaxed (−.12)
Rattlebrained (.12)	Reliable (−.16)	Conscientious (.16)	Hostile (−.12)		
	Responsible (−.16)	Sociable (.16)	Absent minded (−.12)		
	Clear thinking (−.15)	Self-confident (.15)	Resentful (−.12)		
	Dependable (−.15)	Thorough (.14)	Withdrawn (−.12)		
	Efficient (−.15)	Outgoing (.14)			
	Thorough (−.15)				

Note. N = 506 (Group 1, n = 147; Group 2, n = 219; Group 3, n = 140). From Parker (1997). An empirical typology of perfectionism in academically talented children. *American Educational Research Journal, 34*, 545–562. Copyright © 1997 by the American Educational Research Association. Reprinted with permission.

Table 5.4. NEO-Five Factor Inventory (Costa & McCrae, 1992) Raw Score Means and Standard Deviations by Cluster Group

Factor	Cluster 1		Cluster 2		Cluster 3		F	p	r^2
	M	SD	M	SD	M	SD			
Neuroticism	19.9	7.2	18.2	7.3	22.3	8.2	14.42[abc]	.000	.05
Extraversion	30.5	7.3	32.7	5.5	30.4	6.3	9.00[ac]	.000	.03
Openness	26.3	6.1	26.7	5.6	27.9	5.8	3.25[b]	.04	.01
Agreeableness	29.7	5.7	31.9	5.4	28.6	5.8	18.79[ac]	.000	.06
Conscientiousness	25.4	6.5	33.9	6.1	29.7	7.1	84.02[abc]	.000	.23

Note. $N = 568$ (Group 1, $n = 169$; Group 2, $n = 234$; Group 3, $n = 165$); F tests $df = 2,565$.
[a]Tukey pairs were significant for Clusters 1 and 2.
[b]Tukey pairs were significant for Clusters 1 and 3.
[c]Tukey pairs were significant for Clusters 2 and 3.
Copyright © 1997 by the American Educational Research Association. Reprinted with permission.

tiousness (.79), followed in order by Agreeableness (.18), Neuroticism (.14), Extraversion (.09), and Openness (.03).

Scores on the Rosenberg Self-Esteem Scale were compared across the three clusters. The highest self-esteem scores were obtained by Cluster 2; the lowest scores, by Cluster 3. Additional analyses yielded a group difference in levels of depression, with children in Cluster 3 scoring significantly higher on depression than children in Cluster 2.

According to these results, Cluster 1, which comprised 38% of the sample, would appear to consist of *nonperfectionists*. On the MPS, they were characterized by low Personal Standards, low perceived Parental Expectations, low Organization, and low total score. This finding is reinforced by the NEO-FFI, on which this group had the lowest score on Conscientiousness. Their characteristic descriptors on the ACL indicated a self-perception of disorganization and unreliability. Schuler (1997) found that this group tends to have a high percentage diagnosed as gifted learning disabled.

Cluster 2 was the largest cluster, comprising 42% of the sample. Students in this group described themselves in quite positive terms, and their self-characterizations were confirmed by their parents' reports. On the MPS their scores demonstrated low Concern Over Mistakes, Parental Criticism, and Doubts About Actions and high scores on Organization. All other MPS scores, including total score, were moderate. This cluster demonstrated a moderately high level of Personal Standards, probably indicative of focused and realistically high standards. On the NEO-FFI this group of students scored as the least neurotic, the most extroverted, the most agreeable, and the most conscientious. The ACL descriptors suggested people who are organized, dependable, and socially skilled. Their ACL scaled scores indicated students who are conscientious, achievement oriented, well-adjusted, and socially at ease. It appears that this group of students could be characterized as *healthy* perfectionists whose perfectionistic strivings motivate them to successfully achieve.

The Cluster 3 students, comprising 25% of the sample, had the most extreme scores on the MPS. They scored highest on Concern Over Mistakes, Personal Standards, Parental Expectations, Parental Criticism, Doubts About Actions, and total MPS score. On the NEO-FFI, they scored highest on Neuroticism and Openness to Experience and lowest on Agreeableness. These students also produced the fewest and least intense ACL descriptors. The characteristic descriptors that were produced, however, were consistent with the NEO-FFI results, suggesting people who were anxious and disagreeable. These results were underscored by the ACL scaled scores, which suggested that members of this cluster tend to be socially detached, anxious, moody, and predisposed to be overly competitive. This cluster may be characterized as *dysfunctional* perfectionists.

To understand the clusters from the perspective of the Hewitt and Flett MPS (1991), we analyzed the data set with results from both MPS instruments, which was previously described (Parker, 1996). Each student was assigned to one of the clusters on the basis of scores on the Frost et al. (1990) MPS, and Hewitt and Flett (1991) MPS scores were examined by cluster. The distribution of this sample by types did not significantly differ from the distribution in the original sample that produced the typology. The model of a relationship between the three Hewitt and Flett (1991) MPS scores and membership in the three cluster groups was statistically significant. All three univariate F tests were likewise significant at the $p < .000$ level. Group membership accounted for 29% of the variance in Self-Oriented Perfectionism, 25% of the variance in Socially Prescribed Perfectionism, and a more modest, 16% of the variance in Other-Oriented Perfectionism. The nonperfectionists scored relatively low on the Self-Oriented and Other-Oriented Perfectionism scales, the healthy perfectionists scored relatively low on the Socially Prescribed Perfectionism scale, and the dysfunctional perfectionists scored relatively high on all three scales. Table 5.5 presents a summary of means and standard deviations on the Hewitt and Flett MPS by cluster membership.

The Longitudinal Stability of Perfectionism

The longitudinal stability of perfectionism was of particular interest, so the participants in the Parker (1997) study were retested almost four years later (Parker & Stumpf, 1999a). The MPS was readministered to 317 of the original 820 participants. No significant differences in MPS scores were found between the retained participants and those who either dropped out or who could not be located. Using Cohen's d to measure effect sizes, moderate increases were found on Parental Expectations, Parental Criticism, and total score. Mild increases were found on Concern Over Mistakes and Personal Standards, a mild decrease was found on Organization, and Doubts About Actions was essentially unchanged. Correlations of the MPS subscales between the 1994 and 1998 administrations ranged from a low of .28 (Concern Over Mistakes) to a high of .53 (Organization), with a median correlation for the six subscales of .39. The correlation for the total score was .42. These findings are particularly noteworthy given the general lack of research on the test–retest reliability of the subscales (for a discussion, see Enns & Cox, chapter 2, this volume).

The four-year retest also was analyzed according to the previously described typology (Parker, 1997). The retest was analyzed using the z-score cluster centroids from the original study. The healthy perfectionists

Table 5.5. Mean Scores and Standard Deviations on the Hewitt and Flett (1991) Multidimensional Perfectionism Scale by Cluster Group

Perfectionism scale	Cluster 1		Cluster 2		Cluster 3	
	M	SD	M	SD	M	SD
Self-Oriented	53.9	9.4	64.7	11.3	73.9	14.5
Other-Oriented	46.9	9.0	52.8	8.2	58.2	12.8
Socially Prescribed	48.2	13.4	42.4	7.2	57.3	12.0

Note. $N = 119$ (Cluster 1, $n = 34$; Cluster 2, $n = 52$; Cluster 3, $n = 33$).

(Cluster 2) were the most stable over time: Nearly 63% of the original Cluster 2 members retained Cluster 2 membership. Of the remaining original Cluster 2 members, about 14 percent shifted to nonperfectionists and almost 24% joined the dysfunctional perfectionistic group. The next most stable group was the dysfunctional perfectionists: Almost 56% retained cluster membership. More of the remainder changed to healthy perfectionists (26%) than became nonperfectionists (19%). The nonperfectionists were the least stable group: 41% remained in the group, and fairly equal numbers migrated to the other two clusters. Clearly, the findings of these analyses point to the need for future research that seeks to identify factors that predict shifts from healthy perfectionism to dysfunctional perfectionism, and vice versa.

Following exploratory factor analyses of the MPS at the item level, Stöber (1998) argued that most of the items of the Concern Over Mistakes and Doubts About Actions scales, on the one hand, and the Parental Expectations and Parental Criticism scales, on the other, essentially measure only one factor each. This structure is believed to represent a parsimonious description of perfectionism that is more robust than the six scales defined by the scoring key across various populations. It is unclear, however, how those factors are related to the constructs of healthy and dysfunctional perfectionism. Are healthy and unhealthy perfectionism opposite poles of a single trait, or are they separate factors representing two different constructs?

To help answer that question, Stumpf and Parker (2000) performed a hierarchical structural analysis of the MPS. The six scales produced the four factors described by Stöber. A second-order solution yielded two factors, one representing healthy perfectionism (positive loadings on Personal Standards and Organization scales) and the other representing unhealthy perfectionism (positive loadings on the Concern Over Mistakes, Parental Expectations, Parental Criticism, and Doubts About Actions scales). Healthy perfectionism was correlated with conscientiousness; unhealthy perfectionism was correlated with a lack of self-esteem. Healthy and unhealthy perfectionism appear not to be poles of one continuum, but distinct, independent factors that are embedded in the personality in different ways.

Within the nonempirical literature on gifted students, many writers have expressed concern about the predisposition of the gifted to be perfectionistic (e.g., Adderholt-Elliott, 1987; Clark, 1983; Roedell, 1984). Much of this literature contains an implicit syllogism that gifted children are predisposed to perfectionism, that perfectionism produces maladjustment, and that therefore, the gifted are inordinately predisposed to certain types of maladjustment, including depression, suicide, and eating disorders. This belief is quite pervasive among educators of the gifted, despite Terman's (1925) finding, later confirmed by many other researchers (e.g., Gallucci, 1988; Richardson & Benbow, 1990), that gifted children tend to have superior adjustment.

To determine whether perfectionism is more common among academically talented students, Parker and Mills (1996) administered the Frost

MPS to 600 gifted sixth-grade students from a national talent search and a comparison group of 418 sixth graders from the same schools that had provided the gifted sample. The use of a comparison group of similar socioeconomic status was seen by the investigators as critically important. Students who are identified as academically talented tend to come from more affluent environments; were this group to be compared to students of more typical ability and social class, it would be difficult to tease apart the differential effects of ability and class on obtained group differences. The means and standard deviations by group and by gender within group are presented in Table 5.6.

The scores were analyzed with univariate F tests using group-by-gender models. To help control Type I error, a conservative technique, such

Table 5.6.   Frost Multidimensional Perfectionism Scale (Frost et al., 1990) Scores for Sixth-Grade Academically Talented and Comparison Group Students

Scale	Academically talented		Comparison	
	M	SD	M	SD
Concern Over Mistakes				
Total	18.09	5.61	18.10	5.86
Male	18.19	5.70	18.81	5.67
Female	17.88	5.46	17.18	5.99
Personal Standards				
Total	23.49	4.66	22.99	4.55
Male	23.35	4.64	23.27	4.45
Female	23.77	4.69	22.61	4.67
Parental Expectations				
Total	13.77	4.09	13.53	3.94
Male	13.73	4.02	13.95	3.85
Female	13.85	4.22	12.98	3.99
Parental Criticism				
Total	6.79	2.68	7.08	3.09
Male	6.86	2.68	7.22	3.07
Female	6.66	2.68	6.91	3.12
Doubts About Actions				
Total	8.95	2.74	9.38	3.22
Male	8.88	2.72	9.64	3.23
Female	9.09	2.77	9.03	3.19
Organization				
Total	20.91	5.41	22.42	5.17
Male	20.48	5.39	21.55	5.06
Female	21.75	5.37	23.56	5.11
Total score				
Total	71.09	13.63	71.08	15.05
Male	71.01	13.73	72.89	14.58
Female	71.25	13.47	68.71	15.38

Note.   Academically talented group, $N = 600$ (male, $n = 399$; female, $n = 201$). Comparison group, $N = 418$ (male, $n = 237$; female, $n = 181$).

as a Bonferroni correction, would typically be used. Because the authors doubted the conventional wisdom that the gifted were more perfectionistic, a liberal statistical standard of testing the seven group-by-gender models without Bonferroni correction was used. Even using this liberal standard, few differences were found between the academically talented sixth graders and their comparison group. All but one of the differences that distinguished gifted students from comparison students indicated greater perfectionism in the comparison group, and the differences found had such small effect sizes as to be inconsequential.

Statistically significant interactions were obtained for the Parental Expectations and Doubts About Actions subscales as well as the total score. The Parental Expectations interaction indicated that the comparison-group girls scored lower than the comparison-group boys, whose results were similar to all the academically talented students. On the Doubts About Actions subscale, the comparison-group boys scored higher than the other three subgroups, who produced comparable scores. The total score indicated that the gifted boys and girls produced similar results, which were higher than those of the comparison-group girls but lower than those of the comparison-group boys. The Concern Over Mistakes subscale yielded a statistically significant result only for gender, with boys scoring higher than girls independent of group membership. The Organization subscale produced statistically significant results for both main effects: Girls scored higher than boys, and the comparison group scored higher than the gifted group. The effect sizes for the differences were small, with the group-by-gender model for Organization accounting for 4% of the variance, and the total score, Concern Over Mistakes, Parental Expectations, and Doubts About Actions each only accounting for 1% of the variance.

The students' results also were examined using the previously described typology (Parker, 1997). Chi-square analyses by group and by gender were computed. Statistical significance by gender was demonstrated, with results indicating that girls are more likely than boys to be healthy perfectionists and boys more likely than girls to be nonperfectionists. A similar analysis by academic ability group was not statistically significant, indicating no difference between the gifted group and the comparison group of more typical abilities.

To determine whether the distinction between healthy and unhealthy perfectionism is highly culture bound, the MPS was administered to 142 gifted students and 77 typical students in the Czech Republic (Parker, Portesova, & Stumpf, in press). In that sample, the structure of both the cluster analytic typology and the hierarchical structure analysis found in gifted American students were replicated. Three full-factorial multiple analyses of variance were performed: one for the six scale scores, one for the four first-order factors, and one for the two second-order factors. Scale scores produced no significant interaction, but the main effects of both gender and group were significant. Personal Standards was significant for gender (boys scored higher than girls) and for group; Concern Over Mistakes, Parental Criticism, and Organization scores were lower for gifted students than for nongifted students. For the first-order factors, only group was significant, with Factor 1 (Concern Over Mistakes and Doubts About Actions) and Factor 2 (Organization) lower for gifted students. For the second-order factors, only group was significant, with unhealthy perfectionism higher for the typical students than for the gifted.

When the typology of perfectionism was examined among the gifted Czech students, 37% were nonperfectionists, 35% were healthy perfectionists, and 28% were dysfunctional perfectionists. In the nongifted Czech comparison group, 20% were nonperfectionists, 35% were healthy perfectionists, and 45% were dysfunctional perfectionists. The distribution between the two subsamples differed significantly; in addition, the type distribution was different from what was found in samples of gifted American students.

In the Czech study, the relationship between MPS scores and parent-reported presence or absence of student allergies, asthma, migraine headaches, attention deficit disorder, eating disorders, depression, and history of emotional problems was assessed, and the relationships were found to be fairly weak. Asthma was related to parental pressures, and depression was related to Concerns Over Mistakes, but the effect sizes were quite small. The strongest and most consistent result was found with migraine headaches, which were negatively related to high personal standards and a healthy pursuit of excellence.

Parents of Gifted Students and Perfectionism

Parents of gifted students have been accused of "hothousing," or pushing their children to achieve at exceptional levels at quite early ages (Elkind, 1981; Gallagher & Coché, 1987). Although evidence indicates that parents' support for high achievement is important and, in moderation, facilitates achievement in children (Stevenson & Baker, 1987), researchers have expressed great concern that parents' unrealistic expectations create pressure and foster performance anxiety in their children (Sigel, 1987). Thus, it was of considerable interest to investigate the role of parents in the development of perfectionistic strivings in their children.

A study by Parker and Stumpf (1999b) consisted of administering the Frost MPS to 578 gifted sixth graders and their parents. A previous study by Frost, Lahart, and Rosenblate (1991) had used two fairly small samples of college women, both of which had indicated that mothers' perfectionism, but not fathers', was associated with increased perfectionism in the college women. In the much younger sample studied by Parker and Stumpf (1999b), the effect sizes of parental impact on perfectionism were strikingly small, with parents typically accounting for less than 4% of the variance in their children's scores. Mothers' level of perfectionism had a greater relationship to children of either sex than did the fathers' level of perfectionism. Mothers and daughters were most closely related, followed by mothers and sons. The greater impact of mothers was based principally on the relationship of the Personal Standards scores of mothers and their children, indicating that mothers who set high goals and standards for themselves tend to have children who do the same. The main impact of fathers on perfectionism in their children was the development of Organization (O). Children's O scores were mildly correlated with most of their fathers' subscale scores, but they were only correlated with the mothers' O scores and not the mothers' other MPS subscales. This finding suggests that perfectionistic fathers tend to produce children who are preoccupied with order and structure.

Ablard and Parker (1997) investigated the impact of parents' goals for their children on the development of perfectionistic types in these children. Dweck and her colleagues (Dweck, 1986; Dweck & Leggett, 1988; Heyman & Dweck, 1992) have described two types of achievement goals that parents possess for their children. The *learning-goal orientation* is possessed by parents who primarily encourage their children to understand the material, enjoy learning, and seek challenges. In contrast, the *performance goal orientation* characterizes parents who emphasize external indicators of academic success, such as grades and test scores. Ablard and Parker (1997) demonstrated that most parents of the gifted have a learning-goal orientation and that children of parents with a performance-goal orientation were significantly more likely to manifest the dysfunctional perfectionistic type (Parker, 1997).

Conclusion

This line of research has indicated that among gifted children, perfectionistic strivings are more likely to stimulate healthy achievement needs than to be associated with personal or academic maladjustment. The findings do not, however, mean that perfectionism is not a problem for some children. Maladaptive perfectionism is associated with a variety of negative attributes, including negative appraisals of personality characteristics, elevated neuroticism, and reduced agreeableness. Moreover, analyses of cluster membership indicate that some children shift over time from the adaptive perfectionism group to the dysfunctional perfectionism group.

Several unanswered questions are currently being pursued in our laboratory; they include the relationship between styles of parenting and resulting perfectionism in children, the impact of culture on the development of perfectionism in the gifted, the role of perfectionism in the development of childhood psychosomatic disorders, and the extent to which dysfunctional perfectionism is a predictor of later significant adult maladjustment. Of particular interest is the role of perfectionism in the development of depression and suicidal ideation and a better understanding of the precursors and development trajectory of dysfunctional, unhealthy perfectionism.

References

Ablard, K. E., & Parker, W. D. (1997). Parents' achievement goals and perfectionism in their academically talented children. *Journal of Youth and Adolescence, 26,* 651–667.

Adderholt-Elliott, M. (1987). *Perfectionism: What's bad about being too good?* Minneapolis, MN: Free Spirit.

Blascovich, J., & Tomaka, J. (1991). Measures of self-esteem. In J. P. Robinson, P. R. Shaver, & L. S. Wrightsman (Eds.), *Measures of personality and social psychology attitudes: Vol. 1. Measures of social psychological attitudes* (pp. 115–160). San Diego, CA: Academic Press.

Clark, B. (1983). *Growing up gifted* (2nd ed.). Columbus, OH: Charles E. Merrill.

Costa, P. T., Jr., & McCrae, R. R. (1992). *Revised NEO Personality Inventory (NEO-PI-R) and NEO Five Factor Inventory (NEO-FFI) professional manual.* Odessa, FL: Psychological Assessment Resources.

Derogatis, L. R. (1993). *Brief Symptom Inventory (BSI): Administration, scoring, and procedures manual.* Minneapolis, MN: National Computer Systems.

Derogatis, L. R., & Cleary, P. A. (1977). Confirmation of the dimensional structure of the SCL-90-R: A study in construct validation. *Journal of Clinical Psychology, 33,* 981–989.

Dweck, C. S. (1986). Motivational processes affecting learning. *American Psychologist, 41,* 1040–1048.

Dweck, C. S., & Leggett, E. L. (1988). A social–cognitive approach to motivation and personality. *Psychological Review, 95,* 256–273.

Edwards, D. W., Yarvis, R. M., Mueller, D. P., Zingale, H. C., & Wagman, W. J. (1978). Test-taking and the stability of adjustment scales: Can we assess patient deterioration? *Evaluation Quarterly, 2,* 275–291.

Elkind, D. (1981). *The hurried child: Growing up too fast, too soon.* Reading, MA: Addison-Wesley.

Frost, R. O., Heimberg, R. G., Holt, C. S., Mattia, J. I., & Neubauer, A. L. (1993). A comparison of two measures of perfectionism. *Personality and Individual Differences, 14,* 119–126.

Frost, R. O., Lahart, C., & Rosenblate, R. (1991). The development of perfectionism: A study of daughters and their parents. *Cognitive Therapy and Research, 15,* 245–261.

Frost, R. O., Marten, P., Lahart, C., & Rosenblate, R. (1990). The dimensions of perfectionism. *Cognitive Therapy and Research, 14,* 449–468.

Gallagher, J. M., & Coché, J. (1987). Hothousing: The clinical and educational concerns over pressuring young children. *Early Childhood Research Quarterly, 2,* 203–210.

Gallucci, N. T. (1988). Emotional adjustment of gifted children. *Gifted Child Quarterly, 32,* 273–276.

Gough, H. G., & Heilbrun, A. B. (1983). *The Adjective Check List manual.* Palo Alto, CA: Consulting Psychologists Press.

Hair, J. F., Jr., Anderson, R. E., Tatham, R. L., & Black, W. C. (1992). *Multivariate data analysis with readings.* New York: Macmillan.

Hewitt, P. L., & Flett, G. L. (1991). Perfectionism in the self and social contexts: Conceptualization, assessment, and association with psychopathology. *Journal of Personality and Social Psychology, 60,* 456–470.

Heyman, G. D., & Dweck, C. S. (1992). Achievement goals and intrinsic motivation: Their relation and their role in adaptive motivation. *Motivation and Emotion, 16,* 231–247.

Mills, C. J., & Barnett, L. B. (1992). The use of the Secondary School Admission Test (SSAT) to identify academically talented elementary school students. *Gifted Child Quarterly, 36,* 155–159.

Parker, W. D. (1996). [A comparison of two measures of perfectionism in academically talented youth]. Unpublished raw data.

Parker, W. D. (1997). An empirical typology of perfectionism in academically talented children. *American Educational Research Journal, 34,* 545–562.

Parker, W. D., & Mills, C. J. (1996). The incidence of perfectionism in gifted students. *Gifted Child Quarterly, 40,* 194–199.

Parker, W. D., Portesova, S., & Stumpf, H. (in press). Perfectionism in gifted and typical Czech students. *Journal for Education of the Gifted.*

Parker, W. D., & Stumpf, H. (1995). An examination of the Multidimensional Perfectionism Scale with a sample of academically talented children. *Journal of Psychoeducational Assessment, 13,* 372–383.

Parker, W. D., & Stumpf, H. (1998). A validation of the Five-Factor Model of personality in academically talented youth across observers and instruments. *Personality and Individual Differences, 25,* 1005–1025.

Parker, W. D., & Stumpf, H. (1999a). *The longitudinal stability of perfectionism in gifted students*. Unpublished manuscript, Center for Talented Youth, Johns Hopkins University, Baltimore.

Parker, W. D., & Stumpf, H. (1999b). *Perfectionism in academically talented children and their parents*. Unpublished manuscript, Center for Talented Youth, Johns Hopkins University, Baltimore.

Perrault, W. D., Behrman, D. N., & Armstrong, G. M. (1979). Alternative approaches for interpretation of multiple discriminant analysis in marketing research. *Journal of Business Research, 7,* 151–173.

Richardson, T. M., & Benbow, C. P. (1990). Long-term effects of acceleration on the social–emotional adjustment of mathematically precocious youth. *Journal of Educational Psychology, 82,* 464–470.

Roedell, W. C. (1984). Vulnerabilities of highly gifted children. *Roeper Review, 6,* 127–130.

Rosenberg, M. (1965). *Society and the adolescent self-image*. Princeton, NJ: Princeton University Press.

Schuler, P. A. (1997). *Characteristics and perceptions of perfectionism in gifted adolescents in a rural school environment*. Unpublished doctoral dissertation, University of Connecticut, Storrs.

Sigel, I. E. (1987). Does hothousing rob children of their childhood? *Early Childhood Research Quarterly, 2,* 211–225.

Stanley, J. C. (1985). Finding intellectually talented youths and helping them educationally. *Journal of Special Education, 19,* 363–372.

Stevenson, D. L., & Baker, D. P. (1987). The family–school relation and the child's school performance. *Child Development, 58,* 1348–1357.

Stöber, J. (1998). The Frost Multidimensional Perfectionism Scale revisited: More perfect with four (instead of six) dimensions. *Personality and Individual Differences, 24,* 481–491.

Stumpf, H., & Parker, W. D. (2000). A hierarchical structural analysis of perfectionism and its relation to other personality characteristics. *Personality and Individual Differences, 28,* 837–852.

Terman, L. M. (1925). *Genetic studies of genius: Vol. 1. Mental and physical traits of a thousand gifted children*. Stanford, CA: Stanford University Press.

Waskow, I., & Parloff, M. (Eds.). (1975). *Psychotherapy change measures*. Rockville, MD: National Institute of Mental Health.

Part II

Elements of Perfectionism: Social, Motivational, Emotional, and Cognitive Factors

6

Interpersonal Aspects of Trait Perfectionism

A. Marie Habke and Carol A. Flynn

> To be perfect would require an individual to be an automaton without charm, without character, without vitality, and almost without any redeeming qualities. . . . The human quality in each of us comes from our imperfections, from all of those "defects" that give us our unique personalities and make us real people. Without those "defects" we are cold, sterile, and, indeed, unlovable. (Pacht, 1984, p. 386)

With the above description, Pacht made it clear that a "perfect" individual would not be interpersonally popular. But what of the person who, although not perfect, aims for or expects perfection? The wealth of research available to date and reviewed throughout this volume demonstrates an important role for perfectionism in the experience of such intrapersonal states as depression, anxiety, and hopelessness. Do perfectionists also experience *interpersonal* difficulties? Although the question has received less attention in the literature, theorists and researchers are beginning to suggest that this is indeed the case. Pursuit of the implications of perfectionism in relationships is consistent with current conceptualizations of perfectionism that recognize the existence of interpersonal dimensions of this personality construct. Hewitt and Flett (1991b) described two interpersonal dimensions of perfectionism: *other-oriented perfectionism,* in which the person has perfectionistic expectations for close others, and *socially prescribed perfectionism,* in which the person feels as though others expect perfection from him or her. Similarly, Frost, Marten, Lahart, and Rosenblate (1990) included subscales of parental expectations and parental criticism that are clearly interpersonal in nature, although they do not specifically describe their dimensions as interpersonal.

The notion of interpersonal consequences of perfectionism is not entirely new. Burns and Beck (1978) discussed perfectionists' anticipated rejection and hypersensitivity to criticism as factors in disturbed interpersonal relationships; this characteristic has been hypothesized to be related to a "disclosure phobia" that promotes social withdrawal (Frost et al., 1995). Other theorists have focused more on emotional, cognitive, and behavioral outcomes of perfectionism (e.g., Hamachek, 1978; Pacht, 1984). In exploring some of those symptoms, however, we can begin to elucidate interpersonal effects. For example, in his summary of behavioral symptoms, Hamachek (1978) outlined two behaviors that have marked interpersonal qualities: face-saving behavior and shyness. As discussed later in this chapter, both behaviors result in limited social contact and decreased intimacy in social relationships. Other evidence of interpersonal difficulties can be derived from case histories presented in key papers. Blatt (1995) described several high-profile suicide cases that seem to have a basis in perfectionism. The following selection of quotations suggests the interpersonal problems faced by perfectionistic individuals:

- "[His] private life was like his professional life 'turbulent'" and noted "more for conquest than for stability."
- "[He was] an embittered, isolated, and angry scholar."
- "[He] had become intense and judgmental—rigid, arrogant, and moralistic toward his colleagues." (p. 1005)

Likewise, Sorotzkin's (1985) case description of "Dan" centers on his client's interpersonal problems both with classmates and with establishing a close working relationship with the therapist. Thus, perfectionism theorists have identified, if not clarified, the interpersonal impact of trait perfectionism.

Such interpersonal distress may be related to perfectionism in two ways. Most obviously, perfectionism, whether self-directed or interpersonal, may affect relationships by working indirectly, through promotion of intrapersonal pathology. For example, perfectionism is strongly predictive of high levels of depression (Hewitt & Flett, 1991a), and depression itself is clearly related to negative interpersonal interactions (Ruscher & Gotlib, 1988; Schmaling & Jacobson, 1990). Perfectionism also may have direct effects on interpersonal relationships, however, by limiting or impairing social contacts. For example, researchers have noted that perfectionists are likely to avoid relationships because of expectations of being hurt for failing to be perfect (Blatt, 1995). Similarly, perfectionism may affect the quality of the relationships that are maintained, perhaps by stimulating more aversive behaviors from others (Flett, Hewitt, Garshowitz, & Martin, 1997).

Although research addresses the relation between perfectionism and interpersonal functioning to a lesser extent than it does the relation between perfectionism and intrapersonal pathology, this chapter seeks to review what is known about perfectionistic traits and relationships. To place our discussion in an interpersonal context, we first review the relations between the dimensions of perfectionism and other interpersonal personality traits and personality disorders. Although we do not suggest a causal link between such personality variables and perfectionism, the information allows for a clear understanding of the interpersonal milieu of people who score high on those dimensions. We then consider the ways in which perfectionism works in interpersonal relationships, either indirectly, by affecting factors known to be related to social impairment, or directly, by working within the relationship itself.

Relations Between Perfectionism and Interpersonal Facets of Personality

In exploring the relationship between trait perfectionism and interpersonal functioning, we can consider its association with several factors that are known to have interpersonal impact. Among those factors are "normal" variations in personality and more extreme variants of personality or personality disorders. This section reviews the research linking perfectionism to each of these constructs.

"Normal" Personality

In the study of normal personality, one conceptual model has come to the fore in recent years. The five-factor model has been established by numerous researchers using a variety of techniques (e.g., Costa & McCrae, 1988; Tupes & Christal, 1961). Factor analyses repeatedly distinguish five primary personality factors: Neuroticism, Extraversion, Agreeableness, Conscientiousness, and Openness (sometimes called Culture or Intellect). These factors seem to capture our self-descriptions, descriptions of others ranging from spouses to strangers, and psychological assessments of personality (Costa & McCrae, 1992; McCrae & Costa, 1987).

Hill, McIntire, and Bacharach (1997) examined links between perfectionism and the five-factor model. The team gave Hewitt and Flett's (1991b) Multidimensional Perfectionism Scale (MPS-H&F) and the NEO Personality Inventory—Revised (NEO-PI-R; Costa & McCrae, 1992) to a sample of 214 undergraduate students. Because the factors of Extraversion and Agreeableness are most salient in describing interpersonal style, the associations between these two factors and the three dimensions of perfectionism provide the focus for this section. At the bivariate level, self-oriented perfectionism was positively correlated only with the intrapersonal factor of Conscientiousness. Similarly, the sole significant correlation with socially prescribed perfectionism was with the intrapersonal factor of Neuroticism. Other-oriented perfectionism, however, was inversely associated with Agreeableness, suggesting interpersonal hostility.

Hill, McIntire, et al. (1997) further explored these associations by using regression analyses to predict each perfectionism dimension from the five-factor scores. For self-oriented perfectionism, both Neuroticism and Conscientiousness were positive predictors of perfectionism, whereas Agreeableness was a negative predictor. Inspection of the facet scales of each of the five factors indicated that the facets of angry hostility and vulnerability in the Neuroticism factor and dutifulness and achievement striving in the Conscientiousness factor were most responsible for the positive associations. The positive link with angry hostility and the negative association with Agreeableness both reflect the potentially hostile inter-personal nature of self-oriented perfectionism.[1] Other-oriented perfection-ism was predicted similarly by high scores on the Conscientiousness factor and low Agreeableness scores. The facets of achievement striving in Con-scientiousness and compliance and modesty in Agreeableness were most responsible for these associations. Thus, other-oriented perfectionists ex-perience high levels of achievement striving and are interpersonally hos-tile, as reflected by their low levels of compliance and lack of modesty.

In contrast, socially prescribed perfectionism was linked exclusively to the intrapersonal distress factor of Neuroticism, particularly to the facet of depression. This finding appears to contradict claims of the interper-sonal nature of this dimension. However, it may be that the links between socially prescribed perfectionism and neuroticism or distress are so strong that they overwhelm the interpersonal associations. Indeed, past work on socially prescribed perfectionism has repeatedly demonstrated strong links to many forms of psychopathology, especially depression (Hewitt & Flett, 1991a; Hewitt, Flett, & Ediger, 1995, 1996; Hewitt, Flett, & Turnbull-Donovan, 1992). Partialing out the effect of depression may il-luminate the true interpersonal nature of this dimension. It is also inter-esting to note that the theoretically *intrapersonal* dimension of self-oriented perfectionism exhibits a modest negative association with the interpersonal factor of Agreeableness. Although the focus for self-oriented perfectionists may be on their own goals and achievement motivation, it appears that their behavior, expressions of frustration or, perhaps, meth-ods of reaching their goals, may have an adverse impact on interpersonal relationships.

Perfectionism and Disordered Personality

Among the earliest studies to investigate the impact of perfectionism on interpersonal relationships were those that explored the associations be-tween perfectionism and personality disorders. Although a controversial area, many theorists have proposed that personality disorders have im-portant interpersonal precursors that define features and consequences (Clarkin & Lenzenweger, 1996). For example, both psychodynamic and interpersonal models propose that personality disorders develop through and are maintained by problematic early relationships (Benjamin, 1996a; Kernberg, 1996). Perhaps more relevant to our discussion is the fact that many classification systems use interpersonal problems as defining fea-tures. Millon and Davis (1996) proposed that the self–other polarity is an important defining feature for several disorders. Disorders such as narcis-sism and antisocial personality have an excessive focus and reliance on

---

[1]Hill, McIntire, et al.'s (1997) discussion suggests that self-oriented perfectionism is modestly *positively* associated with Agreeableness and that this association may temper the expression of angry hostility. The data provided in their Results section, however, do not match this interpretation. Both at bivariate and regression levels of analysis, self-oriented perfectionism is indicated to be *negatively* linked to Agreeableness.

the self, whereas in other disorders, such as dependent and histrionic personality, people seek reinforcement from others and have strong needs for support and attention. Benjamin (1996b) provided interpersonal summaries of the defining features of each personality disorder. For dependent personality, she wrote,

> The baseline position is of marked submissiveness to a dominant other person who is supposed to provide unending nurturance and guidance. The wish is to maintain connection to that person even if it means tolerating abuse. The DPD believes that he or she is instrumentally incompetent, and this means that he or she cannot survive without the dominant other person. (p. 226)

Thus, associations between perfectionism and personality disorders provide insight into interpersonal styles linked to various forms of perfectionism.

Hewitt, Flett, and their colleagues have used several measures of personality disorder to test correlations with their perfectionism dimensions. In an initial study (Hewitt & Flett, 1991b), 77 adult psychiatric patients completed both the MPS-H&F and the Millon Clinical Multiaxial Inventory (MCMI; Millon, 1983). As anticipated, other-oriented perfectionism was correlated positively with both Narcissistic and Antisocial subscales as well as with a third "dramatic cluster" style, histrionic. Consistent with predictions based on NEO-PI-R findings that linked neuroticism and both Borderline Personality Disorder (BPD) and Passive–Aggressive Personality Disorder (Wiggins & Pincus, 1989), socially prescribed perfectionism was strongly correlated with both Borderline and Passive–Aggressive subscales of the MCMI. Socially prescribed perfectionism also was correlated positively with Schizoid, Avoidant, and Schizotypal subscales and negatively with the Compulsive subscale. It is noteworthy that self-oriented perfectionism was not significantly related to any of the MCMI personality patterns. This finding supports the notion that the primary thrust of self-oriented perfectionism is intrapsychic, rather than a result of problematic interpersonal patterns. Associations between this perfectionism dimension and interpersonal measures may simply reflect the interpersonal consequences of strong motivation and achievement-driven behavior. For example, in a second study reported in this paper (Hewitt & Flett, 1991b), undergraduate students who scored higher than others in the sample on self-oriented perfectionism also tended to report more narcissistic tendencies on the Narcissistic Personality Inventory (Raskin & Terry, 1988), especially on the Authority and Entitlement subscales. Other-oriented perfectionism, however, was more strongly related to narcissism and to interpersonal aspects of narcissism, such as exploitativeness.

In a second article, Hewitt, Flett, and Turnbull-Donovan (1992) reported similar, although not identical, findings using the Minnesota Multiphasic Personality Inventory–Personality Disorder Scales (MMPI-PDS; Morey, Waugh, & Blashfield, 1985). For instance, self-oriented perfectionism was not significantly correlated with any of the personality disorder scales at the bivariate level. Other-oriented perfectionism continued to show strong links to narcissistic traits as well as a negative correlation with dependent characteristics. Finally, socially prescribed perfectionism maintained strong connections with both odd−eccentric cluster traits (paranoid and schizotypal) and anxious−fearful cluster traits (avoidant, compulsive, dependent, and passive−aggressive). One difference was that socially prescribed perfectionism was correlated positively with the MMPI-PDS Compulsive scale and negatively associated with the MCMI scale, although those differences were not unexpected given the discrepancies in conceptualizations of each disorder in the two personality inventories. Perhaps the most striking difference between the MCMI and MMPI-PDS findings was that socially prescribed perfectionism failed to correlate significantly with the MMPI-PDS borderline scale.

In a third investigation, Hewitt, Flett, and Turnbull-Donovan (1994) sought to clarify whether socially prescribed perfectionism was linked to borderline personality traits. They compared perfectionism scores from groups of female borderline inpatients, psychiatric patients, and nonpsychiatric controls. As expected, the patients with BPD reported significantly higher levels of socially prescribed perfectionism than either of the comparison groups did. Many borderline traits can be well understood in light of underlying socially prescribed perfectionism. For example, it makes sense for someone who believes that others have impossibly high expectations of them to experience other-directed anger. It also would be logical for such people to have labile mood and experience feelings of depression and hopelessness, which in turn could lead to the suicidal tendencies so often manifested by people with BPD.

In exploring the connections between the various perfectionism dimensions and personality disorders, it becomes clear that perfectionism is linked to a variety of personality disorders that may lead to different interpersonal problems. In particular, other-oriented perfectionism is associated with dramatic cluster traits, especially narcissism, which could lead to aggressive conflicts with others, in which the perfectionistic person plays a domineering and exploitive role. In contrast, the socially prescribed perfectionist is characterized by both odd−eccentric and anxious−fearful cluster traits; as a result, it is likely that they will avoid social contact and conflict. However, this perfectionism dimension also can be linked to the intense emotions and interpersonal disarray of the borderline personality. Although self-oriented perfectionism is not as clearly connected to the rigid styles of any particular personality disorder, some research indicates that the interpersonal behavior of self-oriented perfectionists can create conflict, as through the display of mildly narcissistic characteristics (Hewitt & Flett, 1991b).

Effects of Perfectionism on Interpersonal Functioning

The above review illuminates the perfectionist's approach to his or her social environment and suggests that perfectionists are likely to experience interpersonal strain in several ways. The following sections examine the evidence that supports an association between perfectionism and interpersonal difficulties. We first consider the indirect ways in which perfectionism might affect relationships by assessing links to other important variables known to be related to impaired social functioning. That is, we explore how perfectionism may promote interpersonal impairment by influencing the way in which the social environment is perceived and through relations with various forms of psychopathology, such as depression and social anxiety, that are also related to interpersonal problems. Next, we turn to the direct effects of perfectionism on three important areas of interpersonal functioning: interpersonal behavior, functioning in intimate relationships, and interactions in a therapeutic setting.

Indirect Effects

Social perception. It has long been suggested that perfectionism has deep roots in the interpersonal environment; many theorists have proposed that early relationships with parents are pivotal in generating perfectionistic ideals (Hamachek, 1978; Horney, 1950). Indeed, Pacht (1984) suggested that the pursuit of parental love lies at the root of perfectionistic strivings; some recent empirical evidence supports a role for parental styles and family variables in predicting levels of perfectionism (Flett, Hewitt, & Singer, 1995; Flynn, Hewitt, & Flett, 1996). Those factors seem to be reflected in the social flavor of many perfectionistic traits and behaviors. For example, Blatt (1995) suggested that perfectionists experience feelings of vulnerability and inferiority and constantly seek to avoid failure and gain approval from others. That is, interpersonal acceptance and assumptions regarding the unavailability of such acceptance in the absence of perfection may be at the root of much of perfectionistic behavior. This idea is in keeping with Baldwin and Sinclair's (1996) suggestion that people who feel that acceptance is conditional on performance will be more reactive to even minor successes and failures.

Consider then, perfectionists' view of their social world. They would seem to see the social world as threatening, containing many people who are judgmental and easily dissatisfied with a less than perfect performance. They also may be prone to feeling helpless to affect social outcomes (Flett, Hewitt, Blankstein, & Mosher, 1995). Socially prescribed perfectionism may be particularly potent, because the person who perceives others to have expectations that he or she cannot meet is especially vulnerable to fears of the social consequences of failure or of being imperfect, such as being criticized or looking foolish to others (Blankstein, Flett, Hewitt, & Eng, 1993). Those fears may explain the socially prescribed perfectionist's propensity to feeling socially inadequate (Flett, Hewitt, & DeRosa, 1996).

Reactions to such fears and to feelings of threat from the environment would seem to take one of two social forms. First, it is possible that a perfectionistic person would feel it necessary to seek the approval of others. That is, they may work especially hard in social relationships to avoid rejection. Some evidence indicates that those high in sociotropy, or the need for social approval, engage in defense mechanisms that are interpersonally neutral or positive, such as denial, repression, or reaction formation (Lobel, Kashtan, & Winch, 1987) and have relatively positive interactions with peers and close others (see Blatt & Zuroff, 1992). Such an orientation, however, may make perfectionistic people particularly prone to the negative effects of social failure. Whittal and Dobson (1991) found that people high in a need for approval experienced increases in depressed mood in reaction to negative feedback about performance; their finding is mirrored in the effect of failure on state anxiety for those high in perfectionism (Flett, Hewitt, Endler, & Tassone, 1994–1995). Similarly, those high in perfectionistic concern over mistakes (akin to self-oriented perfectionism) respond to mistakes with feelings that others will see them as less intelligent (Frost et al., 1995).

Social withdrawal is a second route for perfectionists fearful of the social environment. That is, they may not seek social contact but instead distance themselves from social relationships. This pattern is consistent with the separation between need for approval or dependency and perfectionistic self-criticism suggested by some authors (Blatt, Quinlan, Pilkonis, & Shea, 1995). Such self-critical or autonomous orientations are likely to be related to interpersonal relationships that are superficial, distant, and less emotionally involved (Blatt et al., 1995). Blatt and Zuroff (1992) reviewed a large number of studies that have found high self-criticism to be related to an unwillingness to self-disclose in relationships, to less positive self- and observer ratings of social interactions with peers, and to perceptions of peers as less supportive and cooperative. Emotional withdrawal from relationships, resulting in self-concealment, has been related to weak social support systems in general that extend to an avoidance of professional help out of a fear of self-disclosure (Larson & Chastain, 1990). The absence of supportive others (Cohen & Wills, 1985; Kessler & Essex, 1982) —or the perception of their absence (MacFarlane, Norman, Steiner, & Roy, 1984; Wethington & Kessler, 1986)—is related to an increased vulnerability to stress. Preliminary research suggests that perceptions of not being able to count on others are particularly common for those high in socially prescribed perfectionism (Hewitt, Habke, & Flynn, 1995).

To date, research suggests that perfectionists experience both a desire for social relationships and autonomous self-criticism. Hewitt and Flett (1993) used the Sociotropy–Autonomy Scale (Beck, Epstein, Harrison, & Emery, 1983) and the Self-Criticism–Dependency Scale (Barnett & Gotlib, 1988) and found that self-oriented perfectionism was related to both social measures (sociotropy and dependency) as well as to both individual measures (autonomy and self-criticism). Socially prescribed perfectionism was related to both social measures but only to the individual measure of self-criticism. Using a different measure of sociotropy and autonomy, Flett et al. (1997) found that both dimensions of perfectionism were related to both dimensions. Because dependency and self-criticism often are proposed as being quite separate (see Blatt & Zuroff, 1992), the concurrent presence of both orientations within the perfectionism dimensions does require further research. The results, however, seem to point to the perfectionists' bind in being concerned about social relationships but experiencing them as unreliable or conflictual.

Psychopathology. Given other work in this volume, there is no need to review the relations between perfectionism and psychopathological states such as depression or anxiety. Certainly, it makes sense that perfectionists are prone to those syndromes, given some of the cognitive assumptions about their social world. It is of value to remember, however, that those syndromes may be part of the pathway to perfectionists' interpersonal problems. That is, perfectionism may affect interpersonal relationships by working through psychopathological syndromes. Horowitz and Vitkus (1986) supported an interpersonal focus for psychopathology: They suggested that in an interpersonal environment, symptoms of depression or social anxiety can be seen as generating behaviors from others that reinforce the symptom and lead to frustration for the helper when symptoms do not change. If such frustration is repeated, then disturbances in relationships should be expected.

A sampling of the literature is all that is necessary to establish a link between depression or social anxiety and interpersonal functioning, showing that these syndromes are detrimental in the social world. First, it has been shown that both depression and social anxiety are related to cognitive strain in social situations that is likely to interfere with smooth interpersonal interactions. For example, people with depression are more likely to perceive a discrepancy between their standards and their efficacy for interpersonal behavior than are those who are not depressed (Kanfer & Zeiss, 1983) and to rate themselves as less socially competent (Gotlib & Meltzer, 1987).[2] Similarly, people who are socially anxious were found to rate their own ability lower than nonanxious individuals in several studies (Alden, Bieling, & Wallace, 1994; Wallace & Alden, 1991).

Second, evidence indicates that depression and social anxiety are directly related to impairments in relationships. For example, compared with people without depression, people with depression have been shown to be less socially skilled (Jacobson & Anderson, 1982), to engage in fewer social interactions, and to have a lower quality of interactions (Nezlek & Imbrie, 1994); they also demonstrate more negative behavior, including hostility (Schmaling & Jacobson, 1990), and less positive behavior (Ruscher & Gotlib, 1988) in intimate relationships. People who are socially anxious see themselves as socially avoidant and nonassertive (Alden & Phillips, 1990) and, in fact, are rated as being less involved and open in interactions than individuals who are not socially anxious (Reno & Kenny, 1992), particularly when they face potential evaluation (DePaulo, Epstein, & LeMay, 1990). Thus, we see that perfectionism, through its influence on emotional states, contributes to the experience of interpersonal distress.

---

[2]This finding may reflect the depressives' failure to overestimate their behavior, as nondepressed people tend to do (Ducharme & Bachelor, 1993; Edison & Adams, 1992).

Direct Effects

Although we have little information about how perfectionism translates into social behavior, growing evidence supports a direct role for perfectionism in interpersonal relationships. This section reviews that research. First, we consider the research that links perfectionistic traits to predictors and measures of interpersonal problems and supports the proposition that perfectionists display behaviors and attitudes consistent with both the hostile–dominant and submissive styles described earlier. Then we review findings that show impaired functioning in intimate relationships, including evaluations of both relationship satisfaction and behaviors directed toward an intimate partner. Finally, we present new research on the role of perfectionism in a therapeutic setting.

Perfectionism displayed in the interpersonal context. As with other sections in this chapter, this one begins with an examination of associations between trait perfectionism and a prominent conceptualization of interpersonal problems. The interpersonal circumplex has been derived from neo-Sullivanian theory, which focuses on interpersonal exchanges of love and status (Wiggins, Trapnell, & Phillips, 1988). The circumplex is divided into quadrants by the axes of love–nurturance and status–dominance; dividing the circumplex into octants creates more highly defined groupings. Although not intended to map all relevant personality traits, the circumplex model provides a useful measure of interpersonal personality characteristics.

To date, only two investigations have explored how current models of perfectionism relate to the interpersonal circumplex; of those, only one has been published (Hill, Zrull, & Turlington, 1997). Hill, Zrull, and Turlington (1997) studied the association of the MPS-H&F and two models of the interpersonal circumplex: the Interpersonal Adjective Scale–Revised (IAS-R; Wiggins, Trapnell, & Phillips, 1988) and the Inventory of Interpersonal Problems (IIP; Horowitz, Rosenberg, Baer, Ureno, & Villasenor, 1988; circumplex scales from Alden, Wiggins, & Pincus, 1990). The IIP circumplex is discussed here because it focuses on interpersonal problems or dysfunction; in contrast, the IAS-R assesses interpersonal personality traits. Hill et al.'s study concluded that all three forms of perfectionism in men were tied to dominant and hostile personality traits, specifically the octants of "domineering" and "vindictive." These sections reflect problems with control, manipulation, suspicion, and lack of empathy. In women, a different pattern emerged, in which each form of perfectionism was associated with a different set of problem areas. Self-oriented perfectionism was not correlated strongly with any particular octant, although it was most related to "overly nurturant." The authors concluded that this form of trait perfectionism was not significantly tied to interpersonal distress. Other-oriented perfectionism in women demonstrated similar relationships to those displayed by men; that is, strong links to domineering and vindictive problem areas. Finally, socially prescribed perfectionism in women was positively correlated with all interpersonal problem domains and reflected the greatest degree of interpersonal distress.

The second study to investigate perfectionism and the interpersonal circumplex included two additional measures of perfectionism along with the MPS-H&F (Flynn, Hewitt, Broughton, & Flett, 1998). Frost, Marten, Lahart, and Rosenblate (1990) have developed a scale also entitled the Multidimensional Perfectionism Scale (MPS-Frost); it assesses six dimensions of perfectionism: Concern Over Mistakes, Personal Standards, Doubts About Actions, Organization, Parental Expectations, and Parental Criticism. The third measure included in this study was the Personal Styles Inventory (PSI; Robins et al., 1994). Although the scale can be divided into several factors, the study focused on the Perfectionism subscale.

As in the Hill, Zrull, and Turlington (1997) study, interpersonal circumplexes were constructed using both the IAS-R and the IIP. Forty-seven male and 68 female university undergraduates participated in this project. Considering first the IAS-R–derived circumplex, results for the MPS-H&F were quite comparable to those reported by Hill, Zrull, et al. (1997) except that socially prescribed perfectionism fell into the "arrogant" octant for women in this sample. Once again, most of the perfectionism subscales were located in the hostile–dominant quadrant. The sole exception was self-oriented perfectionism, which was associated with agreeableness and gregariousness in women. Results for the PSI Perfectionism subscale were similar to those reported above. Once again, for men, this measure was linked to hostile–dominant characteristics, whereas for women it was localized in the hostile–submissive quadrant. IIP circumplex results emphasized male perfectionists' difficulties with being domineering and female perfectionists' struggles with problems of dominance and coldness.

Findings from the MPS-Frost were quite distinct from those discussed thus far. All subscales on this measure were plotted on the "agreeable" half of the circumplex. Once again, scores for men suggested slightly more dominant traits and suggested submissiveness for women, but the only subscale to show a clear trend was for Personal Standards, which was associated with increased submissiveness. Figure 6.1 illustrates the positioning of these subscales compared with Hewitt and Flett's measures on the IAS-R–generated interpersonal circumplex. Vector angles represent the type of association between each perfectionism dimension and the axes of dominance–submission and hostility–agreeableness. Vector length suggests the strength of the association.

These results suggest several major conclusions. First, the associations reported by both Hill, Zrull, et al. (1997) and Flynn et al. (1998) demonstrate the interpersonal nature of most subscales and measures of perfectionism. In addition, strong evidence supports the multidimensional nature of perfectionism, given that at least one perfectionism subscale or measure was located in each octant of the interpersonal circumplex. Second, clear gender differences exist: Factors such as self-oriented perfectionism were linked to agreeable characteristics in women and to hostile traits in men. Similarly, many perfectionism dimensions have been linked to dominant behavior in men and submissive traits in women. These dif-

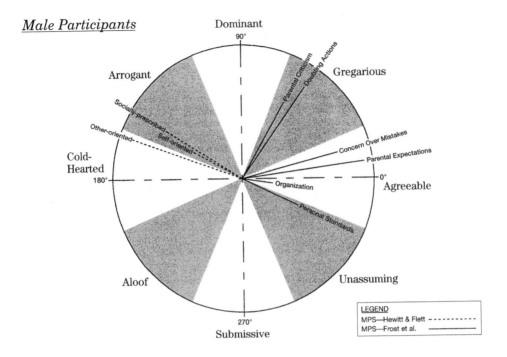

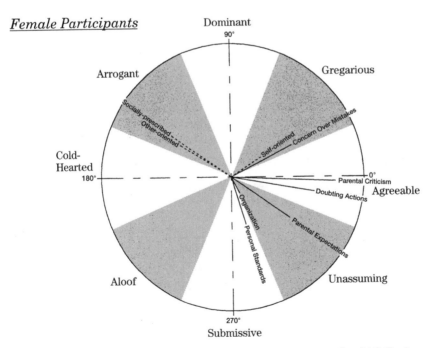

Figure 6.1. Locations of perfectionism dimensions on the IAS-R circumplex.

ferences may highlight cultural gender stereotypes for "perfect" men and women, or they may suggest different interpersonal coping strategies for each gender (i.e., social avoidance in women and domineering behavior in men). Finally, the variability between scales devised by different research-ers is an important consideration. In particular, perfectionism as con-strued by Hewitt and Flett seems to access a dominant and hostile inter-personal style that is quite distinct from the more agreeable traits tapped into by the MPS-Frost.

A variety of studies have supported the idea that perfectionism has an interpersonal expression that can create difficulties in interactions and relationships; clearly, expressions differ for each of the different dimen-sions. As suggested by the results described above, other-oriented perfec-tionism is consistently related to behaviors with a hostile–dominant tone. Other-oriented perfectionists not only tend to be more authoritarian, ex-ploitive, dominant, and likely to engage in other-directed blame (Hewitt & Flett, 1991b), they also display the Type A characteristics of impatience and competitiveness[3] (Flett, Hewitt, Blankstein, & Dynin, 1994). In ad-dition, other-oriented perfectionism is the only dimension to be positively associated with assertiveness (Flett et al., 1996). Although it is possible that this dimension represents an appropriate self-confidence, it seems equally likely that it has hostile or aggressive overtones. Thus, consistent with the conceptualization of other-oriented perfectionists as concerned with the behavior of others, we see these other-oriented perfectionists en-gaged in behaviors that are strongly other-directed.

The data on self-oriented and socially prescribed perfectionism are less clearly supportive of a picture of hostile interactions. For example, self-oriented perfectionism is strongly related to competitiveness and impatience–irritability (Flett et al., 1994) as well as to feelings of entitle-ment (Hewitt & Flett, 1991b). It does not relate to styles such as domi-nance or authoritarianism, as might be expected (Hewitt & Flett, 1991b). Indeed, one study found that people high in self-oriented perfectionism are especially nurturing in relationships (Flett et al., 1996); unfortunately, that study did not report on gender differences. It is possible that the predominantly female sample was demonstrating the warmth of female self-oriented perfectionists noted earlier (Flynn et al., 1998; Hill, Zrull, et al., 1997). Again, the reasons for gender differences are unclear, but they may reflect attempts to match gender-based stereotypes of dominance for men and nurturance for women (Flynn et al., 1998). Although the nature of their interpersonal problems is vague, several studies have indicated that interpersonal relationships are a focus for self-oriented perfectionists. For example, self-oriented perfectionism is correlated with sociotropy and dependency (Flett et al., 1997; Hewitt & Flett, 1993) and is accompanied by reports of high levels of stressful interpersonal life events (Hewitt et al., 1996) and trait anxiety surrounding social evaluation (Flett et al., 1994–1995).

---

[3]This study used two samples; other-oriented perfectionism was associated with the Competitiveness factor only for males in one sample.

The data on socially prescribed perfectionism are similarly mixed involving both hostile–dominant and submissive presentations. This dimension again is related to impatience and competitiveness (Flett et al., 1994) as well as to other-directed blame (Hewitt & Flett, 1991b). In addition, socially prescribed perfectionism is significantly related to tendencies to be overcontrolled and overly responsible in relationships (Hewitt et al., 2001), both of which may require a considerable degree of directiveness or disagreeableness. Socially prescribed perfectionists, however, also have problems being too submissive and nonassertive in relationships (Hewitt et al., 2001) and present with social anxiety and withdrawal.[4] These individuals fear negative evaluation and desperately seek the approval of others (Flett et al., 1994; Hewitt & Flett, 1991b). They report many interpersonal fears, including fears of criticism, of looking foolish, and of people in authority (Blankstein et al., 1993) and admit to a reluctance to talk about their emotions (Flett et al., 1996). Those insecurities may be especially painful given the importance of relationships to socially prescribed perfectionists as demonstrated by high scores on measures of sociotropy and dependency (Flett et al., 1997; Hewitt & Flett, 1993). To the extent that a person displays such a mixed presentation of aggression and withdrawal, it seems logical to posit that they will have difficulty establishing the mutual attachment in interpersonal relationships that they desire.

Two lines of research provide preliminary support that perfectionists engage in negative behaviors in their social environment. In a recent study, Flett and his colleagues (1997) recruited a mixed-gender sample of undergraduates ($N = 176$) and administered both the MPS-H&F and the Inventory of Negative Social Interactions (Lakey, Tardiff, & Drew, 1994), which measures the frequency of negative interpersonal behaviors directed toward the self, such as criticism, betrayal, or a lack of recognition. Results showed positive correlations between such negative interactions and both self-oriented and socially prescribed perfectionism. These findings suggest that the aversive style of perfectionists may stimulate negative responses from the social environment. Although it is possible that the findings reflect a more negative perception or interpretation of behaviors that is not necessarily veridical, it is likely that such perceptions, in turn, will affect social relationships in damaging ways; perceptions of criticism may stimulate either an aggressive or a withdrawal response from the perfectionist, who already may be prone to such patterns of behavior. Clearly, further research is needed in this area, but the results are intriguing.

A second line of research on interpersonal interactions supports the proclivity for perfectionists (or at least socially prescribed perfectionists) to engage in social behaviors that impede intimacy. Hobden and Pliner (1995) recently assessed the use of self-handicapping in relation to levels of perfectionism. Self-handicapping refers to actions or choices that occur

---

[4]This last study controlled for gender and therefore suggests that the findings are not simply a result of sex differences in the ways in which socially prescribed perfectionism is expressed, as suggested by Hill et al. (1997).

prior to a performance that maximize the chance that failure will be attributed externally and success will be attributed internally (Berglas & Jones, 1978); it is a display of an impediment to performance that should divert the observer from making attributions that would blame the performer (Sheppard & Arkin, 1990).

The researchers provided participants with an experience of either success or failure and then asked them to choose music labeled either *performance-impairing* or *performance-enhancing* to listen to while taking a second test. The music choice was made under either public or private conditions (i.e., with or without the experimenter present). The results showed that participants high in socially prescribed perfectionism self-handicapped more in public conditions than did those low in this dimension. That is, when they were at risk of being judged for a failure, socially prescribed perfectionists made sure the judge could excuse that failure by attributing it to the "performance-impairing" music that was playing. This finding supports the notion that socially prescribed perfectionists work to secure the good opinion of others and is consistent with Sorotzkin's (1985) suggestion that perfectionists seek a socially acceptable "face" to protect against rejection and to secure admiration and acceptance.

Recent work suggests that a desire for a presentation of perfection can be identified and reliably measured. Hewitt and his colleagues (2001) suggested that perfectionistic self-presentation consists of a desire to avoid the appearance of imperfection as well as the desire to promote an image of perfection. The different dimensions show strong associations with the trait dimensions of perfectionism, although they also can be distinguished as unique constructs. The implications of such self-presentation are clear with regard to securing meaningful relationships; not only are the façades difficult to maintain, they also decrease the chance of emotional intimacy that is vital for close and satisfying relationships.

Functioning in intimate relationships. When considering the issue of adjustment in relationships, the most obvious conclusion must be that perfectionists are prone to poor-quality relationships. A wealth of literature links marital distress to neurotic styles (Bentler & Newcomb, 1978; Kelly & Conley, 1987; Russell & Wells, 1994a, 1994b) and clinical syndromes such as depression (Fincham & Bradbury, 1992; Ulrich-Jakubowski, Russell, & O'Hara, 1988). Perfectionism affects intimate relationships, as shown by findings that both socially prescribed and other-oriented perfectionism are related to lower sexual satisfaction (Habke, Hewitt, & Flett, 1999), a factor highly related to global ratings of marital adjustment (Cupach & Comstock, 1990; Woody, D'Souza, & Crain, 1994). In addition, we know that neurotic styles and syndromes such as depression also are related to distress in the spouse (Bouras, Vanger, & Bridges, 1986), making it probable that perfectionism will be related to spousal distress. This hypothesis is consistent with studies linking spousal behaviors, including those reflecting other-oriented perfectionism (e.g., commanding their partner or complaining about something their partner did), to marital distress (Jacobson, Waldron, & Moore, 1980). Even self-oriented perfectionism has been related to negative coping styles in relationships, such as criticism, sarcasm, and revenge (Hewitt, Flett, & Mikail, 1993).

Eighty-three pain patients (both men and women) and their spouses were part of a research project by Hewitt, Flett, and Mikail (1995). Both partners completed measures of perfectionism, relationship adjustment, depression, and pain. Results demonstrated that although patients' own perfectionism did not relate to adjustment, those with a partner who was high in other-oriented perfectionism had poorer dyadic adjustment and a greater number of family difficulties than patients whose partners were not perfectionistic. This result held after controlling for patient depression. Participants with a partner who was high in other-oriented perfectionism also felt less supported by their mate. The partner's ratings of other-oriented perfectionism were not related to their own relationship satisfaction, a result suggesting that the target of unrealistic expectations suffers in the relationship, not the perfectionist. Although the patients' other-oriented perfectionism was not reflected in their partner's dissatisfaction, the authors suggested that the self-absorption needed to cope with pain and depression may result in less outward expression of expectations. Another research project expands on those results by examining the relations between perfectionism, relationship adjustment, and relationship interactions.

Relationship adjustment. Habke and her colleagues (Habke, Hewitt, Fehr, Callander, & Flett, 1997) administered the MPS-H&F and the Dyadic Adjustment Scale (DAS; Spanier, 1976) to a community sample of 74 married and cohabiting couples.[5] The DAS measures overall adjustment and provides subscale ratings of Affectional Expression, a sense of togetherness (Cohesion), tendencies to agree with each other (Consensus), and Satisfaction With the Relationship. The socially prescribed and other-oriented perfectionism subscales were reworded to focus specifically on the spouse rather than on generalized others. For example, the item "The better I do, the better I am expected to do" was rephrased to read "The better I do, the better my spouse expects me to do," and the item "I am not likely to criticize someone for giving up too easily" became "I am not likely to criticize my spouse for giving up too easily" to reflect socially prescribed perfectionism and other-oriented perfectionism, respectively. The change helps address some findings that perfectionism measured by a nonspecific focus on generalized others is not necessarily reflected in increased standards either perceived from or placed on specific others (Alden et al., 1994).

Because of the dyadic structure of the data, Habke et al. (1997) ran analyses separately for men and women. For women, the feeling that their partner held unrealistic expectations for them was related to lower overall adjustment in the relationship and to lower Affection, Cohesion, and Satisfaction subscale ratings. The results were similar for men, although Co-

---

[5]Fewer than half of the participants were married, but the couples had been together an average of 4.0 years (*SD* = 5.94).

hesion subscale scores were not significantly linked to this form of perfectionism, whereas those from the Consensus subscale were.[6] A similar sample (Hewitt & Flett, 1997) generally supported these results, although ratings of high expectations for her mate were related to lower marital satisfaction for women. This result is consistent with an earlier research finding that unrealistic expectations for the spouse or the relationship are associated with marital distress (Eidelson & Epstein, 1982).

The use of couples allows us to consider dyadic adjustment and the partner's perfectionism. For both men and women, it appears that poorer adjustment is related to their partner's socially prescribed perfectionism. That is, having a spouse who feels one expects a lot from him or her is related to one's own feelings of dissatisfaction in the marriage. It is possible that dissatisfaction is communicated in ways that are interpreted as expectations. That this interpretation may be accurate is suggested by positive correlations between ratings of what the spouse expects and what the spouse actually admitted to expecting of his or her partner in this sample.

The finding that both self and partner perfectionistic traits are related to ratings of dissatisfaction leads to the question of which traits are the strongest predictors. Habke et al. (1997) ran regression analyses with perfectionism dimensions from both partners. Because of the influence of depression on marital adjustment, depression was entered as a control variable. The results suggest two general patterns.

First, it is clear that socially prescribed perfectionism is an important predictor of relationship satisfaction. For both men and women, dyadic adjustment is uniquely predicted by self- and partner ratings of perceived expectations. That is, those who were dissatisfied in their relationship were more likely to feel that their partner expected a lot from them and to have a partner who believed the same thing.[7] Marriages that are particularly distressed may be characterized by poor communication patterns that leave each partner with assumptions about their mate's expectations. Also, to the extent that socially prescribed perfectionism is related to a desire to self-present in a protective manner, such perfectionists' marriages may be less intimate. Finally, as posited by Clark, Pataki, and Carver (1996), being the target of socially prescribed perfectionists' attempts at self-presentation may weaken the sense of trust in another with a growing awareness of the discrepancy between the self-portrayal and the actual self.

The second pattern demonstrates that self-oriented perfectionism is important as a predictor of positive marital adjustment. For both men and women, having high expectations for the self was a unique predictor of greater satisfaction. Possibly, high expectations for the self leave one feeling that failure should be attributed to the self, not to the relationship—in other words, "I am unhappy with myself, not my relationship." It also

---

[6]The results are described in Habke et al. (1997).

[7]The second sample noted earlier showed strong effects of women's perfectionism on both their own and their mate's satisfaction but no effect of men's perfectionism.

is possible that having such standards encourages one to work harder at a relationship. Although socially prescribed perfectionism would leave one feeling ineffective in making changes that would satisfy his or her partner, self-oriented perfectionism might actually prompt constructive attempts to rectify problems or concerns in the relationship. Finally, controlling for depression may partial out the self-oriented perfectionists who are currently distressed and more likely to be expressing dissatisfaction with their marriage.

Unlike the earlier study with pain patients, other-oriented perfectionism did not play a particularly important role in adjustment in Habke et al.'s (1997) study. In the only case in which other-oriented perfectionism was related to the partner's satisfaction with the relationship, it was a predictor of positive adjustment: Men with mates who admitted to high standards for their partner had higher ratings of marital satisfaction. It is possible that this result may reflect the effect of direct communication in intimate relationships. Some people with other-oriented perfectionism may be open about their expectations, a characteristic that may serve to "clear the air" and allow for positive changes in the relationship. It also is possible that having high expectations for someone who is able to attempt to fulfill those expectations may reflect pride in one's partner, in contrast to a blaming and demanding style, when the partner is unable even to try to reach those expectations, as in the case of the chronic pain patient.

Relationship interactions. To further understand the expression of perfectionism in intimate relationships, Habke et al. (1997) asked participants to indicate at least three problems in their marriage. From those lists, two difficulties were chosen, and the couple was required to discuss each problem for 5 minutes. The interactions were videotaped and then coded for behavior according to Halweg and Conrad's (1983) *Interaction Coding System*. The behavioral categories were combined to reflect patterns of negative behavior and of positive behavior. Negative behaviors included criticism, negative solutions, and disagreements; positive behaviors included positive solutions, agreements, and acceptance. The behaviors were considered first in terms of their frequency across both problem discussions; however, it is possible that it is not the frequency of either positive or negative behaviors that is important, but rather the tone of the interaction. Thus, the analyses were repeated using the proportion of negative behaviors in the interactions (see also Ruscher & Gotlib, 1988).

Correlations between negative behaviors over both interactions and own and partner's perfectionism, mood, and adjustment were generated (Table 6.1). Consistent with other research suggesting that behavior in an interaction may be especially tied to the husband's personality (Newton, Kiecolt-Glaser, Glaser, & Malarkey, 1995), husbands' perfectionism scores were better predictors of both their own and their partner's behavior than were wives' scores. The same pattern was evident for positive behaviors. Regression results demonstrated that husbands' trait perfectionism contributed a significant amount of explained variance to predictions of the

Table 6.1. Correlations Between Negative Behaviors and Perfectionism and Dyadic Adjustment

	Negative behaviors			
	Husbands		Wives	
	Frequency	Proportion	Frequency	Proportion
	Husbands			
Perfectionism				
Self-oriented	.09	.04	.07	.01
Expects of spouse	.26*	.39***	.18	.14
Perceived expectations from wife	.13	.26*	.30**	.37***
Dyadic adjustment	−.13	−.17	−.13	−.19
	Wives			
Perfectionism				
Self-oriented	.11	.04	.14	.05
Expects of spouse	−.08	.04	.19	.12
Perceived expectations from husband	−.10	−.08	−.05	.14
Dyadic adjustment	−.03	−.08	−.20	−.29**

*$p > .05$. **$p > .01$. ***$p > .001$.

proportion of negative behaviors from both themselves and their partners and to the frequency of their own positive behaviors. In particular, husbands' self-reported expectations for their partners explained unique variance in the proportion of their negative behaviors as well as frequency of positive behaviors. That is, husbands who had high expectations for their partner were more argumentative and critical and were less positive when interacting with their spouses than the husbands with low expectations were.

Husbands' socially prescribed perfectionism also showed a unique link to wives' negative behavior as well as a trend toward a negative relation with wives' positive behaviors. That is, husbands who believed that their partner expected a lot from them had wives who were more negative and less positive than the wives of husbands who did not hold this belief. At least two possible explanations exist for this finding. First, given that women are sensitive to their partner's expressions of hostility (Gaelick, Bodenhausen, & Wyer, 1985), they may be sensitive to their partner's perceptions of them and behave more negatively in response to being perceived as critical or demanding. In fact, perceptions of being labeled in that way may be interpreted as hostility, which is commonly reciprocated in interactions (Gaelick et al., 1985). It also is possible, however, that a woman's behaviors during an interaction might represent evidence of her mate's accuracy in his perceptions; it is possible that men might be reporting perceptions arising from similar situations in the relationship in which their partners acted in comparably demanding and argumentative ways. This notion is supported by correlations suggesting that men are relatively (although not perfectly) good predictors of their mate's level of expectations for them.[8]

Another interesting finding was that self-oriented perfectionism contributed uniquely to the frequency of men's positive behaviors. Although it is possible that those men scoring high in this dimension act more positively in a testing situation because of a desire to be seen as perfect, recent research on perfectionistic self-presentation (Hewitt et al., 2001) suggested that this pattern should be as true or more so for those high in socially prescribed perfectionism. Evidently, that was not the case; rather, Habke et al.'s (1997) result supports the contention that self-oriented perfectionism actually may confer some benefits in relationships, at least to the extent that it encourages one to be the "perfect" spouse.

To forestall at least two possible objections to the data, Habke et al. (1997) evaluated alternative ways to explain the data. One objection was that participants may have simply reciprocated the behavior of their partner during the interaction; however, when the partner's behavior (frequency or proportion, as appropriate) was entered as a control variable, the relations with the perfectionism dimensions still held, even though the other's behavior did explain a great deal of the variance in the subject's behavior. Second, it is possible that interactional behaviors are the result of mood (Hautzinger, Linden, & Hoffman, 1982; Kowalik & Gotlib, 1987) or marital adjustment (Fincham & Bradbury, 1990; Jacobson, Follette, & Waggoner-McDonald, 1982), rather than perfectionism. Indeed, controlling for both partners' hostility, depression, and marital adjustment scores, men's perfectionism scores did not predict significant variance in their partner's negative behavior. Husbands' proportion of negative behavior and lower frequencies of positive behavior, however, continued to be predicted by his expectations for his mate. That is, men with high expectations of their partner acted more negatively and less positively than their counterparts with low expectations did, over and above the influences of their own or their mate's mood, dyadic satisfaction, and hostility. The patterns held true even when first controlling for the length of the relationship.

Functioning in the therapeutic context. In addition to supportive others, relationships with mental health professionals often are critical during times of stress. The willingness to seek out and to engage in such relationships would seem to be particularly important for perfectionists, given their high rates of psychopathology. A recent study, however, found that perfectionism was clearly related to a lower tolerance of the stigma associated with seeking help and with less willingness to be open about personal issues (Nielsen et al., 1997). This finding was particularly true for participants high in socially prescribed perfectionism. Regression analyses confirmed that socially prescribed perfectionism is a unique predictor of low stigma tolerance and less openness, even when considering the in-

---

[8]The correlation for men was .44 ($p < .001$); for women, it was .23 ($p < .05$), suggesting that women are somewhat less accurate at predicting their partner's perfectionism.

fluence of gender, ethnicity, current depression, and past help-seeking behavior. Other-oriented perfectionism was the only perfectionism trait to be associated with lower confidence in mental health professionals. Such perfectionists are likely to be more skeptical and, perhaps, more confrontational in a therapy setting than other clients. Thus, even in the contemplation stage, perfectionists may experience considerable anxiety about the process of therapy.

For those that move beyond contemplation to presenting for help, the fact that so many perfectionism dimensions lie in the hostile–dominant and hostile–submissive quadrants of the interpersonal circumplex has important implications. Interpersonal problems associated with hostility predict less therapeutic progress within sessions (Gurtman, 1996); problems in the vindictive, cold, and dominating octants, in which most dimensions of perfectionism were located, are least likely to be discussed, and even when they are discussed in therapy, they show little improvement (Horowitz, Rosenberg, & Bartholomew, 1993). In addition, hostile dominance has been related to such therapeutic liabilities as a present orientation, impulsivity, and difficulties with intimacy as well as poor *emotional resonance* (i.e., a sense that patient and therapist are not relating well; Gurtman, 1996). Supporting this finding, Muran, Segal, Samstag, and Crawford (1994) assessed interpersonal style using the IIP prior to treatment and asked patients to complete the Working Alliance Inventory (Horvath & Greenberg, 1989) following three sessions of short-term cognitive–behavioral therapy. Only friendly–submissive traits were positively associated with working alliance; personality styles such as narcissistic, histrionic, and antisocial, which we linked to other-oriented perfectionism, were strongly associated with poor therapeutic alliance. Because most perfectionism dimensions are associated with high levels of hostility, the results of the studies described above do not bode well for rapid therapeutic improvement.

A recently completed study of people seeking therapy at a variety of different outpatient settings offers some evidence that perfectionism is significantly related to a more distressing experience of the therapeutic relationship itself (Habke, 1997). Participants completed standardized measures of perfectionism, appraisals of their social behaviors (the Behavioral Ratings of Social Competence; Lewinsohn, Mischel, Chaplin, & Barton, 1980), and emotional status (Positive Affect–Negative Affect Scales [PANAS]; Watson, Clark, & Tellegen, 1988). They then were asked to provide some information on two situations in their life in which they made a mistake or did not cope well; those events formed the backbone of a discussion with a clinical interviewer. Three general areas were considered. First, the cognitive response of perfectionists was assessed by determining their appraisals of their own and the interviewer's expectations and satisfaction with their own performance. Second, the affective response to self-disclosure was assessed by self-report of anxiety and distress to determine whether perfectionists find self-disclosure of shortcomings distressing. Finally, one behavioral response to clinical interactions was measured through opportunities to claim handicaps to performance.

The results suggested that perfectionism was associated with an experience of the therapeutic interview as aversive. Prior to the interview, self-oriented perfectionism was related to negative mood and to negative assessments of the ability to interact in ways that are socially competent. Other-oriented perfectionism was a unique predictor of higher ratings of social competence in the upcoming interaction, suggesting that this dimension may offer some degree of protection from this distressing situation. Following the clinical interview, the influence of socially prescribed perfectionism was most apparent. This dimension was uniquely associated with postinterview negative mood and with lower ratings of participants' own social competence during the interview. Furthermore, it was related to the impression that the clinician was dissatisfied with participants' performance and liked them less than she would like most people completing the same interview.

Behaviorally, consistent with Hobden and Pliner (1995), socially prescribed perfectionism seemed to be the trait dimension most related to self-handicapping. Prior to the interview, participants scoring high on this dimension (compared with those scoring low) were more likely to claim that something would impair their performance, such as unusual stress or outside influences. Among participants who self-handicapped, those scoring high on socially prescribed perfectionism also claimed a greater degree of disability; that is, they indicated that the performance-impairing factor they mentioned was likely to have a large impact on what they would do during the interview. Although socially prescribed perfectionism did not predict who would attempt to excuse their behavior following the interview, it did predict level of disability claimed by those who chose to excuse their behavior.

Taken together, the results suggest that trait dimensions of perfectionism may play an important role in the experience of a therapeutic relationship. Although that role may be shared by other variables, such as mood or social anxiety, perfectionism continues to be an important predictor of a distressed therapeutic relationship: Regression analyses controlling for those variables reduced the relations between trait perfectionism and the study variables but, on the whole, did not eliminate them. Those high in perfectionism arrive with a fair degree of anticipatory anxiety, low expectations of their own abilities, and expectations that they will disappoint their therapist. This distress and distrust of the therapist may interfere with the formation of a constructive working relationship, as has been clearly demonstrated in previous research (Moras & Strupp, 1982; Muran, Segal, Samstag, & Crawford, 1994; Piper et al., 1991). That is, the patients appear to come into therapy handicapped in regard to forming the early therapeutic alliance that is an important determinant of outcome (Kotokovic & Tracey, 1990). Such an impairment in the early stages of the alliance is further demonstrated by interviewers' ratings of how much they liked the patient and how willing they would be to have the patient as a client. Even after controlling for interaction anxiety and depression, negative relations were found between both the interviewer ratings and socially prescribed perfectionism. Thus, like Gurtman (1996), we see impairment in emotional resonance with the therapist and problems with intimacy in the alliance, both of which are associated with hostile–dominant interpersonal styles.

Summary

Taken together, the studies described above support earlier work on the impaired interpersonal relationships that plague perfectionists and provide some insight into the mechanisms by which such impairment might occur. Perfectionists, or at least male perfectionists high on the interpersonal dimensions, seem to engage in negative behaviors as well as to stimulate negative behavior on the part of their intimate others. Similarly, perfectionists seem to interpret a therapeutic interaction as threatening and to engage in self-protective behaviors, although the pattern varies with the different dimensions. Other-oriented perfectionism seems to be reflected in hostile–dominant behavior; socially prescribed perfectionism is reflected in attitudes and behaviors that are self-critical and self-protective. Clearly, it would be useful to measure perceptions in intimate relationships and interactional style in therapeutic relationships; we can only call for further research in this area.

Conclusion and Directions for Future Research

Given the empirical support reviewed here, it seems reasonable to conclude that perfectionism is related to difficult interpersonal styles and interpersonal problems, including distressed interpersonal relationships. We are beginning to establish that perfectionism is expressed negatively in interactions with others, has a negative impact on a person's confidence in interactions, and leads to perceptions of others as critical. Consider then, the following portraits of perfectionists:

> Sam scores high on measures of socially prescribed perfectionism. He is somewhat depressed most of the time and anxious much of the time, particularly about what others might think of him. He believes that others, such as his parents or supervisors, have expectations of him that he cannot possibly meet; those perceived expectations make him prone to being irritable or aggressive in interactions with others. However, the fears of being judged negatively (and his need to be accepted) also prompt Sam to avoid social relationships or to act in ways that can protect him from being rejected. He does not want to consider therapy as a way to help him with his problems because he is fearful of the therapist and what he or she might expect.
>
> Sally is high in other-oriented perfectionism: She expects others to be perfect. Unlike Sam, she is pretty confident about herself and does not experience depression or anxiety. Others find Sally difficult, however, because of her hostile–aggressive style; she tends to be impatient and authoritarian. Her husband is particularly frustrated because

Sally is not supportive and is often hostile and critical. She is skeptical about therapy because she does not trust the therapist.

John is a self-oriented perfectionist: He is driven to achieve goals that are forever out of reach, and he often feels stressed. He can be very short and hostile with people in general and is generally self-absorbed. With his wife, however, he is more careful to be supportive and accepting. He is ambivalent about therapy.

Sam, Sally, and John each face interpersonal challenges because of their generally hostile style, and they face unique challenges in specific relationships. They also present challenges to researchers and clinicians. For example, why are self-oriented perfectionists like John able to avoid some of the interpersonal problems experienced by others? Is Sally's negative behavior a direct expression of her expectations for her husband, or is it associated with a generally argumentative style that might hold true across other relationships? What part does Sam's perfectionistic self-presentation play in his interpersonal problems? Finally, perhaps most important, what can be done in a therapeutic setting to help perfectionists deal with the personal and interpersonal consequences of their perfectionistic traits? Future studies in this burgeoning area of research will need to address those and other key questions.

Clearly, significant advances have been made in recognizing the interpersonal nature of perfectionism and its ramifications within the interpersonal context. However, research relating to the interpersonal facets of perfectionism remains in the early stages. A few new directions already have been mentioned in this chapter. For example, Hewitt and his colleagues are exploring the interpersonal styles with which people create an image of perfection for those around them. Identification of specific behaviors involved with perfectionistic self-presentation could assist clinicians in targeting those issues in therapy and provide greater insight into the daily interactions of perfectionists.

Given the interpersonal consequences of perfectionism, it also would be interesting to consider the interpersonal precursors of this personality trait. Specifically, various forms of perfectionism may be linked to different attachment styles in infancy and in adulthood. Results in each of the interpersonal contexts described in this chapter suggest additional avenues of study. For example, perfectionism in men and women appears to be differentially associated with higher levels of dominance and submission. It will be important to replicate those findings and to explore why such a difference may exist. Flynn et al. (1998) suggested that people of each gender may attempt to fit their sociocultural stereotype. Work on the impact of perfectionism in couples may wish to explore *how* perfectionism interferes with intimacy and cohesion. For example, does perfectionism influence the selection of a partner, and does it interfere with effective communication and coping with stress within the relationship?

Within the therapy context, it also will be important to discern mechanisms by which perfectionism interferes with therapy outcome. Recent work by Zuroff et al. (2000) suggested that perfectionism interferes with clients' ability to augment their contribution to the therapeutic alliance over time. In other words, perfectionists have difficulty engaging more deeply with their therapists and with the process of therapy. Questions remain regarding *why* perfectionists experience this difficulty and *how* they avoid increasing intimacy in therapy. Given the difficulties experienced by perfectionists in interpersonal contexts, it would be fascinating to investigate whether they are capable of engaging in group psychotherapy.

Finally, our understanding of interpersonal processes is best expanded when a variety of perspectives is represented. The series of studies on perfectionism in couples provides an excellent example of research considering the perspective of the perfectionist, the person with whom they interact (in this case, the spouse), and an objective observer. This model of research also could be applied to casual social interactions as well as to the therapy context.

The ideas represented here demonstrate just a few of the potential directions for subsequent research on the interpersonal nature of perfectionism. Other contexts could be explored, such as the workplace and parent–child interactions. Much work remains to be done in this fascinating and far-reaching branch of perfectionism research.

References

Alden, L. E., Bieling, P. J., & Wallace, S. T. (1994). Perfectionism in an interpersonal context: A self-regulation analysis of dysphoria and social anxiety. *Cognitive Therapy and Research, 18,* 297–316.

Alden, L., & Phillips, N. (1990). An interpersonal analysis of social anxiety and depression. *Cognitive Therapy and Research, 14,* 499–513.

Alden, L. E., Wiggins, J. S., & Pincus, A. L. (1990). Construction of the circumplex scales for the Inventory of Interpersonal Problems. *Journal of Personality Assessment, 55,* 521–536.

Baldwin, M. W., & Sinclair, L. (1996). Self-esteem and "if . . . then" contingencies of interpersonal acceptance. *Journal of Personality and Social Psychology, 71,* 1130–1141.

Barnett, P., & Gotlib, I. H. (1988). *Personality and depression: New scales and a model of relationships.* Paper presented at the annual convention of the Canadian Psychological Association, Montreal, Quebec, Canada.

Beck, A. T., Epstein, N., Harrison, R. P., & Emery, G. (1983). *Development of the Sociotropy–Autonomy Scale: A measure of personality factors in psychopathology.* Unpublished manuscript, University of Pennsylvania, Philadelphia.

Benjamin, L. S. (1996a). An interpersonal theory of personality disorders. In J. F. Clarkin & M. F. Lenzenweger (Eds.), *Major theories of personality disorder* (pp. 141–220). New York: Guilford.

Benjamin, L. S. (1996b). *Interpersonal diagnosis and treatment of personality disorders.* New York: Guilford.

Bentler, P. M., & Newcomb, M. D. (1978). Longitudinal study of marital success and failure. *Journal of Consulting and Clinical Psychology, 46,* 1053–1070.

Berglas, S., & Jones, E. E. (1978). Drug choice as a self-handicapping strategy in response to noncontingent success. *Journal of Personality and Social Psychology, 36,* 405–417.

Blankstein, K. R., Flett, G. L., Hewitt, P. L., & Eng, A. (1993). Dimensions of perfectionism and irrational fears: An examination with the Fear Survey Schedule. *Personality and Individual Differences, 15,* 323–328.

Blatt, S. J. (1995). The destructiveness of perfectionism: Implications for the treatment of depression. *American Psychologist, 50,* 1003–1020.

Blatt, S. J., Quinlan, D. M., Pilkonis, P. A., & Shea, M. T. (1995). Impact of perfectionism and need for approval on the brief treatment of depression: The National Institute of Mental Health Treatment of Depression Collaborative Research Program revisited. *Journal of Consulting and Clinical Psychology, 63,* 125–132.

Blatt, S. J., & Zuroff, D. C. (1992). Interpersonal relatedness and self-definition: Two prototypes for depression. *Clinical Psychology Review, 12,* 527–562.

Bouras, N., Vanger, P., & Bridges, P. K. (1986). Marital problems in chronically depressed and physically ill patients and their spouses. *Comprehensive Psychiatry, 27,* 127–130.

Burns, D. D., & Beck, A. T. (1978). Cognitive behavior modification of mood disorders. In J. P. Foreyt & D. P. Rathjen (Eds.), *Cognitive behavior therapy* (pp. 109–134). New York: Plenum.

Clark, M. S., Pataki, S. P., & Carver, V. H. (1996). Some thoughts and findings on self-presentation of emotions in relationships. In G. J. O. Fletcher & J. Fitness (Eds.), *Knowledge structures in close relationships: A social psychological analysis* (pp. 247–274). Mahwah, NJ: Erlbaum.

Clarkin, J. F., & Lenzenweger, M. F. (1996). *Major theories of personality disorder.* New York: Guilford.

Cohen, S., & Wills, T. (1985). Stress, social support, and the buffering hypothesis. *Psychological Bulletin, 98,* 310–357.

Costa, P. T., & McCrae, R. R. (1988). From catalog to classification: Murray's needs and the Five Factor Model. *Journal of Personality and Social Psychology, 55,* 258–265.

Costa, P. T., & McCrae, R. R. (1992). Four ways five factors are basic. *Personality and Individual Differences, 13,* 653–665.

Cupach, W. R., & Comstock, J. (1990). Satisfaction with sexual communication in marriage: Links to sexual satisfaction and dyadic adjustment. *Journal of Social and Personal Relationships, 7,* 179–186.

DePaulo, B. M., Epstein, J. A., & LeMay, C. S. (1990). Responses of the socially anxious to the prospect of interpersonal evaluation. *Journal of Personality, 58,* 623–640.

Ducharme, J., & Bachelor, A. (1993). Perception of social functioning in dysphoria. *Cognitive Therapy and Research, 17,* 53–70.

Edison, J. D., & Adams, H. E. (1992). Depression, self-focus, and social interaction. *Journal of Psychopathology & Behavioral Assessment, 14,* 1–19.

Eidelson, R. J., & Epstein, N. (1982). Cognition and relationship maladjustment: Development of a measure of dysfunctional relationship beliefs. *Journal of Consulting and Clinical Psychology, 50,* 715–720.

Fincham, F. D., & Bradbury, T. (1990). Social support in marriage: The role of social cognition. *Journal of Social and Clinical Psychology, 9,* 31–42.

Fincham, F. D., & Bradbury, T. N. (1992). Assessing attributions in marriage: The relationship attribution measure. *Journal of Personality and Social Psychology, 62,* 457–468.

Flett, G. L., Hewitt, P. L., Blankstein, K. R., & Dynin, C. B. (1994). Dimensions of perfectionism and Type A behavior. *Personality and Individual Differences, 16,* 477–485.

Flett, G. L., Hewitt, P. L., Blankstein, K. R., & Mosher, S. W. (1995). Perfectionism, life events, and depressive symptoms: A test of a diathesis–stress model. *Current Psychology, 14,* 112–137.

Flett, G. L., Hewitt, P. L., & DeRosa, T. (1996). Dimensions of perfectionism, psychosocial adjustment, and social skills. *Personality and Individual Differences, 20,* 143–150.

Flett, G. L., Hewitt, P. L., Endler, N. S., & Tassone, C. (1994–1995). Perfectionism and components of state and trait anxiety. *Current Psychology, 13,* 326–350.

Flett, G. L., Hewitt, P. L., Garshowitz, M., & Martin, T. R. (1997). Personality, negative social interactions, and depressive symptoms. *Canadian Journal of Behavioral Science, 29,* 28–37.

Flett, G. L., Hewitt, P. L., & Singer, A. (1995). Perfectionism and parental authority styles. *Individual Psychology, 51,* 50–60.

Flynn, C. A., Hewitt, P. L., Broughton, R., & Flett, G. L. (1998, August). *Mapping perfectionism dimensions onto the interpersonal circumplex.* Poster session presented at the annual meeting of the American Psychological Association, San Francisco.

Flynn, C. A., Hewitt, P. L., & Flett, G. L. (1996). Perfectionism and family relationships from a cross-cultural perspective [Abstract]. *Journal of International Psychology, 31,* 250.

Frost, R. O., Marten, P., Lahart, C., & Rosenblate, R. (1990). The dimensions of perfectionism. *Cognitive Therapy and Research, 14,* 449–468.

Frost, R. O., Turcotte, T. A., Heimberg, R. G., Mattia, J. I., Holt, C. S., & Hope, D. A. (1995). Reactions to mistakes among subjects high and low in perfectionistic concern over mistakes. *Cognitive Therapy and Research, 19,* 195–205.

Gaelick, L., Bodenhausen, G. V., & Wyer, R. S. (1985). Emotional communication in close relationships. *Journal of Personality and Social Psychology, 49,* 1246–1265.

Gotlib, I. H., & Meltzer, S. J. (1987). Depression and the perception of social skill in dyadic interaction. *Cognitive Therapy and Research, 11,* 41–54.

Gurtman, M. B. (1996). Interpersonal problems and the psychotherapy context: The construct validity of the Inventory of Interpersonal Problems. *Psychological Assessment, 8,* 241–255.

Habke, A. M. (1997). The manifestations of perfectionistic self-presentation in a clinical sample. *Dissertation Abstracts International, 59,* 02B. (UMI No. 872).

Habke, A. M., Hewitt, P. L., Fehr, B., Callander, L., & Flett, G. L. (1997). Perfectionism and behavior in marital interactions [Abstract]. *Canadian Psychology, 38,* 75.

Habke, A. M., Hewitt, P. L., & Flett, G. L. (1999). Perfectionism and sexual satisfaction in intimate relationships. *Journal of Psychopathology and Behavioral Assessment, 21,* 307–322.

Halweg, K., & Conrad, M. (1983). *Coding Manual: Interaction Coding System.* Unpublished manuscript.

Hamachek, D. E. (1978). Psychodynamics of normal and neurotic perfectionism. *Psychology, 15,* 27–33.

Hautzinger, M., Linden, M., & Hoffman, N. (1982). Distressed couples with and without a depressed partner: An analysis of their verbal interaction. *Journal of Behavior Therapy and Experimental Psychiatry, 13,* 307–314.

Hewitt, P. L., & Flett, G. L. (1991a). Dimensions of perfectionism in unipolar depression. *Journal of Abnormal Psychology, 100,* 98–101.

Hewitt, P. L., & Flett, G. L. (1991b). Perfectionism in the self and social contexts: Conceptualization, assessment, and association with psychopathology. *Journal of Personality and Social Psychology, 60,* 456–470.

Hewitt, P. L., & Flett, G. L. (1993). Dimensions of perfectionism, daily stress, and depression: A test of the specific vulnerability hypothesis. *Journal of Abnormal Psychology, 102,* 58–65.

Hewitt, P. L., & Flett, G. L. (1997, August). *Perfectionism traits, perfectionistic self-presentation and dyadic adjustment.* Paper presented at the annual convention of the American Psychological Association, Chicago.

Hewitt, P. L., Flett, G. L., & Ediger, E. (1995). Perfectionism traits and perfectionistic self-presentation in eating disorder attitudes, characteristics, and symptoms. *International Journal of Eating Disorders, 18,* 317–326.

Hewitt, P. L., Flett, G. L., & Ediger, E. (1996). Perfectionism and depression: Longitudinal assessment of a specific vulnerability hypothesis. *Journal of Abnormal Psychology, 105,* 276–280.

Hewitt, P. L., Flett, G. L., & Mikail, S. F. (1993). *Perfectionism in the marital context.* Unpublished manuscript.

Hewitt, P. L., Flett, G. L., & Mikail, S. F. (1995). Perfectionism and relationship adjustment in pain patients and their spouses. *Journal of Family Psychology, 9,* 335–347.

Hewitt, P. L., Flett, G. L., Sherry, S. B., Habke, A. M., Parkin, M., Lam, R. W., McMurtry, B., Ediger, E., Fairlie, P., & Stein, M. (2001). *The interpersonal expression of perfectionism: Perfectionistic self-presentation and psychological distress.* Manuscript submitted for publication.

Hewitt, P. L., Flett, G. L., & Turnbull-Donovan, W. (1992). Perfectionism and suicide potential. *British Journal of Clinical Psychology, 31,* 181–190.

Hewitt, P. L., Flett, G. L., & Turnbull-Donovan, W. (1994). Borderline personality disorder: An investigation with the Multidimensional Perfectionism Scale. *European Journal of Psychological Assessment, 10,* 28–33.

Hewitt, P. L., Habke, A. M., & Flynn, C. A. (1995). [Perfectionism and social support]. Unpublished raw data.

Hill, R. W., McIntire, K., & Bacharach, V. R. (1997). Perfectionism and the Big Five factors. *Journal of Social Behavior and Personality, 12,* 257–270.

Hill, R. W., Zrull, M. C., & Turlington, S. (1997). Perfectionism and interpersonal problems. *Journal of Personality Assessment, 69,* 81–103.

Hobden, K., & Pliner, P. (1995). Self-handicapping and dimensions of perfectionism: Self-presentation vs. self-protection. *Journal of Research in Personality, 29,* 461–474.

Horney, K. (1950). *Neurosis and human growth.* New York: Norton.

Horowitz, L. M., Rosenberg, S. E., Baer, B. A., Ureno, G., & Villasenor, V. S. (1988). Inventory of Interpersonal Problems: Psychometric properties and clinical applications. *Journal of Consulting and Clinical Psychology, 56,* 885–892.

Horowitz, L. M., Rosenberg, S. E., & Bartholomew, K. (1993). Interpersonal problems, attachment styles, and outcome in brief dynamic psychotherapy. *Journal of Consulting and Clinical Psychology, 61,* 549–560.

Horowitz, L. M., & Vitkus, J. (1986). The interpersonal basis of psychiatric symptoms. Special issues: Personality assessment in the '80s: Issues and advances. *Clinical Psychology Review, 6,* 443–469.

Horvath, A. O., & Greenberg, L. S. (1989). Development and validation of the Working Alliance Inventory. *Journal of Counseling Psychology, 36,* 223–233.

Jacobson, N. S., & Anderson, E. A. (1982). Interpersonal skill and depression in college students: An analysis of the timing of self-disclosures. *Behavior Therapy, 13,* 271–282.

Jacobson, N. S., Follette, W., & Waggoner-McDonald, D. (1982). Reactivity to positive and negative behavior in distressed and nondistressed married couples. *Journal of Consulting and Clinical Psychology, 50,* 706–714.

Jacobson, N., Waldron, H., & Moore, D. (1980). Toward a behavioral profile of marital distress. *Journal of Consulting and Clinical Psychology, 48,* 696–703.

Kanfer, R., & Zeiss, A. M. (1983). Depression, interpersonal standard setting, and judgments of self-efficacy. *Journal of Abnormal Psychology, 92,* 319–329.

Kelly, E. L., & Conley, J. J. (1987). Personality and computability: A prospective analysis of marital stability and marital satisfaction. *Journal of Personality and Social Psychology, 52,* 27–40.

Kernberg, O. F. (1996). A psychoanalytic theory of personality disorders. In J. F. Clarkin & M. F. Lenzenweger (Eds.), *Major theories of personality disorder* (pp. 106–140). New York: Guilford.

Kessler, R. C., & Essex, M. (1982). Marital status and depression: The role of coping resources. *Social Forces, 61,* 484–507.

Kotokovic, A. M., & Tracey, T. J. (1990). Working alliance in the early phase of counseling. *Journal of Counseling Psychology, 37,* 16–21.

Kowalik, D. L., & Gotlib, I. H. (1987). Depression and marital interaction: Concordance between intent and perception of communication. *Journal of Abnormal Psychology, 96,* 127–134.

Lakey, B., Tardiff, T. A., & Drew, J. B. (1994). Negative social interactions: Assessment and relations to social support, cognition, and psychological distress. *Journal of Social and Clinical Psychology, 13,* 1046–1053.

Larson, D. G., & Chastain, R. L. (1990). Self-concealment: Conceptualization, measurement, and health implications. *Journal of Social and Clinical Psychology, 9,* 439–455.

Lewinsohn, P. M., Mischel, W., Chaplin, W., & Barton, R. (1980). Social competence and depression: The role of illusory self-perceptions. *Journal of Abnormal Psychology, 89,* 203–212.

Lobel, T. E., Kashtan, O., & Winch, G. L. (1987). The relationship between defense mechanisms, trait anxiety and need for approval. *Personality and Individual Differences, 8,* 17–23.

MacFarlane, A., Norman, G., Steiner, D., & Roy, R. (1984). Characteristics and correlates of effective and ineffective social supports. *Journal of Psychosomatic Research, 28,* 501–540.

McCrae, R. R., & Costa, P. T. (1987). Validation of the Five-Factor model of personality across instruments and observers. *Journal of Personality and Social Psychology, 52,* 81–90.

Millon, T. (1983). *Millon Clinical Multiaxial Inventory.* Minneapolis, MN: National Computer Systems.

Millon, T., & Davis, R. D. (1996). An evolutionary theory of personality disorders. In J. F. Clarkin & M. F. Lenzenweger (Eds.), *Major theories of personality disorder* (pp. 221–356). New York: Guilford.

Moras, K., & Strupp, H. H. (1982). Pretherapy interpersonal relations, patient's alliance, and outcome in brief therapy. *Archives of General Psychiatry, 39,* 405–409.

Morey, L. C., Waugh, M. H., & Blashfield, R. K. (1985). MMPI scales for *DSM-III* personality disorders: Their derivation and correlates. *Journal of Personality Assessment, 49,* 245–251.

Muran, J. C., Segal, Z. V., Samstag, L., & Crawford, C. E. (1994). Patient pretreatment interpersonal problems and therapeutic alliance in short-term cognitive therapy. *Journal of Consulting and Clinical Psychology, 62,* 185–190.

Newton, T. L., Kiecolt-Glaser, J. K., Glaser, R., & Malarkey, W. B. (1995). Conflict and withdrawal during marital interaction: The roles of hostility and defensiveness. *Personality and Social Psychology Bulletin, 21,* 512–524.

Nezlek, J. B., & Imbrie, M. (1994). Depression and everyday social interaction. *Journal of Personality & Social Psychology, 67,* 1101–1111.

Nielsen, A. D., Hewitt, P. L., Han, H., Habke, A. M., Cockell, S. J., Stager, G., & Flett, G. L. (1997, June). *Perfectionistic self-presentation and attitudes toward professional help-seeking.* Poster presented at the annual meeting of the Canadian Psychological Association, Toronto, Ontario, Canada.

Pacht, A. R. (1984). Reflections on perfection. *American Psychologist, 29,* 386–390.

Piper, W. E., Azim, H. F., Joyce, A. S., McCallum, M., Nixon, G. W., & Segal, P. S. (1991). Quality of object relations versus interpersonal functioning as predictors of therapeutic alliance and psychotherapy outcome. *Journal of Nervous and Mental Disease, 179,* 432–438.

Raskin, R., & Terry, H. (1988). A principal-components analysis of the Narcissistic Personality Inventory and further evidence of its construct validity. *Journal of Personality and Social Psychology, 54,* 890–902.

Reno, R. R., & Kenny, D. A. (1992). Effects of self-consciousness and social anxiety on self among unacquainted individuals: An application of the Social Relations Model. *Journal of Personality, 60,* 79–94.

Robins, C. J., Ladd, J., Welkowitz, J., Blaney, P. H., Diaz, R., & Kutcher, G. S. (1994). The Personal Style Inventory: Preliminary validation studies. *Journal of Psychopathology and Behavioral Assessment, 16,* 277–300.

Ruscher, S. M., & Gotlib, I. H. (1988). Marital interaction patterns of couples with and without a depressed partner. *Behavior Therapy, 19,* 455–470.

Russell, R. J., & Wells, P. A. (1994a). Personality and quality of marriage. *British Journal of Psychology, 85,* 161–168.

Russell, R. J., & Wells, P. A. (1994b). Predictors of happiness in married couples. *Personality and Individual Differences, 17,* 313–321.

Schmaling, K. B., & Jacobson, N. S. (1990). Marital interaction and depression. *Journal of Abnormal Psychology, 99,* 229–236.

Sheppard, J. A., & Arkin, R. M. (1990). Shyness and self-presentation. In W. R. Crozier (Ed.), *Shyness and embarrassment: Perspectives from social psychology* (pp. 286–314). New York: Cambridge University Press.

Sorotzkin, B. (1985). The quest for perfection: Avoiding guilt or avoiding shame? *Psychotherapy, 22,* 564–571.

Spanier, G. (1976). Measuring dyadic adjustment: New scales for assessing the quality of marriage and similar dyads. *Journal of Marriage and the Family, 38,* 15–28.

Tupes, E. C., & Christal, R. E. (1961). *Recurrent personality factors based on trait ratings* (U.S. Air Force Technical Report No. 61-97). Lackland Air Force Base, TX: U.S. Air Force Aeronautical Systems Division.

Ulrich-Jakubowski, D., Russell, D. W., & O'Hara, M. W. (1988). Marital adjustment difficulties: Cause or consequence of depressive symptomatology. *Journal of Social and Clinical Psychology, 7,* 312–318.

Wallace, S. T., & Alden, L. E. (1991). A comparison of social standards and perceived ability in anxious and nonanxious men. *Cognitive Therapy and Research, 15,* 237–254.

Watson, D., Clark, L. A., & Tellegen, A. (1988). Development and validation of brief measures of positive and negative affect: The PANAS Scales. *Journal of Personality and Social Psychology, 54,* 1063–1070.

Wethington, E., & Kessler, R. C. (1986). Perceived support, received support, and adjustment to stressful life events. *Journal of Health and Social Behavior, 27,* 78–89.

Whittal, M., & Dobson, K. S. (1991). An investigation of the temporal relationship between anxiety and depression as a consequence of cognitive vulnerability to interpersonal evaluation. *Canadian Journal of Behavioral Science, 23,* 391–398.

Wiggins, J. S., & Pincus, A. L. (1989). Conceptions of personality disorders and dimensions of personality. *Psychological Assessment, 1,* 305–316.

Wiggins, J. S., Trapnell, P. D., & Phillips, N. (1988). Psychometric and geometric characteristics of the Revised Interpersonal Adjective Scale (IAS-R). *Multivariate Behavioral Research, 23,* 517–530.

Woody, J. D., D'Souza, H. J., & Crain, D. D. (1994). Sexual functioning in clinical couples: Discriminant validity of the Sexual Interaction System Scale. *American Journal of Family Therapy, 22,* 291–303.

Zuroff, D. C., Blatt, S. J., Sotsky, S. M., Krupnick, J. L., Martin, D. J., Salislow, C. A., III, & Simmens, S. (2000). Relation of therapeutic alliance and perfectionism to outcome in brief outpatient treatment of depression. *Journal of Consulting and Clinical Psychology, 68,* 114–124.

7

Perfectionistic Self-Beliefs: Their Relation to Personality and Goal Pursuit

Jennifer D. Campbell and Adam Di Paula

The authors of this chapter view perfectionism as a constellation of self-beliefs that reside in the self-concept. Those self-beliefs are important to other components of the self-concept, motivation, and goal pursuit. Theories involving the self-concept have changed dramatically during the past 20 years or so (Markus & Wurf, 1987). Whereas early theorists tended to view the self-concept as a unitary, monolithic entity and typically focused their research on a single aspect of the self-concept (e.g., self-esteem), present-day theorists rely on a multifaceted construal that generally equates the self-concept with a cognitive schema. In the contemporary literature on the self, the self-concept is conceptualized as a dynamic, extensive, organized knowledge structure that contains beliefs, evaluations, and memories about the self and controls the processing of information relevant to the self (e.g., Greenwald & Pratkanis, 1984; Kihlstrom et al., 1988).

The current conceptualization of the self-concept allows one to distinguish the contents of this schema from its structural aspects. The contents are vast and include, for example, beliefs about one's specific attributes (e.g., personality traits, physical characteristics, and abilities) as well as one's roles, values, motives, standards, and personal goals. Also resident in the contents are beliefs that involve evaluation of the self, such as the perceived positivity of one's specific attributes and self-esteem, which is a global self-evaluation that is the product of viewing the self as an attitude object.

Structural characteristics of the self-concept generally focus on how the contents are organized. Examples include the number of independent dimensions underlying the organization (Linville, 1985, 1987); the extent to which the dimensions are psychologically integrated (Donahue, Robins, Roberts, & John, 1993); the extent to which positive and negative self-aspects reside in different dimensions (Showers, 1992); and the extent to which the contents are clearly and confidently defined, internally consistent, and temporally stable (Campbell, 1990).

In this chapter, we first articulate a set of self-beliefs that define perfectionism; we then examine the relations between those beliefs and several personality traits, including the "Big-Five" dimensions, traits that tap emotional states and dispositions (i.e., depression and negative and positive affectivity), self-evaluation (i.e., self-esteem), the structure of the self-concept (i.e., self-concept clarity and goal instability), and action versus state orientation (as described by Kuhl's 1994 Action Control scales). We subsequently focus on the role of perfectionistic self-beliefs in the self-regulation of goal-directed behavior and describe a longitudinal study that investigated the relation between perfectionistic self-beliefs and academic and social goal pursuit over the course of an academic year.

Self-Beliefs That Define Perfectionism

In early work, Hollander (1965) described the *perfectionist* as a person who sets rigid, unrealistically high standards and engages in "all-or-none" thinking when evaluating his or her performance. Thus, a contingency is created in which success is perceived only if a high standard has been reached and performance in the service of that standard is flawless. Subsequent theorists have continued to view this stringent evaluative style as the central aspect of perfectionism; they also have converged on the notion that perfectionists overgeneralize failure experiences (e.g., Burns, 1980; Hamachek, 1978; Pacht, 1985). For the perfectionist, failure to meet one standard implies a failure to meet any of the self's standards. This portrayal of perfectionism would seem to be a recipe for self-defeat, and it is perhaps not surprising that research has shown perfectionism to be associated with depression, anxiety, low self-esteem (Burns & Beck, 1978; Hamachek, 1978; Missildine, 1963), suicide (Burns, 1980), coronary-prone behavior (Smith & Brehm, 1981), and alcoholism (Pacht, 1985).

Measures of Perfectionism

Burns's (1980) Perfectionism Scale is the first published scale for measuring perfectionism for which substantial reliability and validity information is available. The items conform closely to the conceptualization outlined above, and the validity evidence includes studies showing direct but moderate correlations between Burns's scale and depression (e.g., Hewitt & Flett, 1990) and anxiety (e.g., Flett, Hewitt, & Dyck, 1989). The scale also has been shown to moderate the relations between stress and anxiety (Flett et al., 1989) and depression (Hewitt & Dyck, 1986) such that stress is a better predictor of anxiety and depression among those high in perfectionism.

To refine and expand its various components, recent theorists have developed multidimensional measures of perfectionism. Frost, Marten, Lahart, and Rosenblate's (1990) Multidimensional Perfectionism Scale (MPS) yields five interrelated factors, or subscales, that can be summed to form a total perfectionism score. The subscales measure the extent to which the person (a) is concerned over making mistakes, (b) sets high personal standards, (c) feels criticized by his or her parents, (d) feels that his or her parents have high expectations for him- or herself, and (e) doubts his or her ability to perform actions.

Hewitt and Flett (1991) developed an MPS that distinguishes several types of perfectionism. The Self-Oriented Perfectionism scale of their MPS assesses the extent to which people set rigid, exacting standards for themselves and contains items similar to those in Burns's (1980) scale and in Frost et al.'s (1990) Personal Standards subscale (e.g., "I strive to be the best at everything I do"). Hewitt and Flett's Socially Prescribed Perfectionism scale assesses the extent to which high rigid standards are perceived to be imposed by others, coupled with the belief that others will reject the self if such standards are not attained. The scale items tend to overlap with the Frost et al. subscales of Concern Over Mistakes (e.g., "People around me think I am still competent even if I make a mistake"), Parental Criticism (e.g., "The better I do, the better I am expected to do"), Parental Expectations (e.g., "My family expects me to be perfect"), and Doubt About Actions (e.g., "It is difficult to meet others' expectations of me"). The Self-Oriented and Socially Prescribed Perfectionism scales are positively correlated, but the magnitude of the correlation (.20 to .40) warrants viewing them as measuring largely independent forms of perfectionism.

With the advent of multidimensional scales, evidence has emerged suggesting that perfectionism may have positive as well as negative consequences. Frost et al. (1990) reported that their Personal Standards subscale correlated negatively with procrastination and positively with self-efficacy (whereas their other subscales either correlated in the opposite direction or were not correlated with procrastination and self-efficacy). Hewitt and Flett's (1991) scales also have yielded divergent outcomes. Self-oriented perfectionism is positively correlated with positive affect but is uncorrelated with negative affect, whereas socially prescribed perfectionism is positively correlated with negative affect but uncorrelated with positive affect (Frost, Heimberg, Holt, Mattia, & Neubauer, 1993). In addition, Flett, Hewitt, Blankstein, and O'Brien (1991) reported that socially prescribed perfectionism is positively correlated with depression, whereas self-oriented perfectionism is uncorrelated with depression.

Although self-oriented perfectionism has been shown to relate to positive outcomes, recent evidence shows that self-oriented perfectionism may act as a vulnerability factor in depression. Several studies have found that self-oriented perfectionism predicts depression among those experiencing achievement stressors (Hewitt & Flett, 1993; Hewitt, Flett, & Ediger, 1996). Thus, the beliefs of the self-oriented perfectionist may precipitate negative outcomes when negative life events are experienced.

In sum, it appears that different specific self-beliefs relevant to perfectionism, although often correlated with one another, exhibit divergent patterns of associations with other traits or behaviors theoretically implicated by the perfectionism construct. To better understand the concomitants of the different self-beliefs, we conducted a fine-grained analysis of

Hewitt and Flett's (1991) Self-Oriented and Socially Prescribed Perfectionism scales. We chose the Hewitt and Flett scales because the distinction between self-directed and other-directed beliefs is important both in
research on the self-concept (see, e.g., Higgins's 1987 work on ideal standards vs. ought standards) and in research on the self-regulation of goal-
directed behavior (see, e.g., Deci and Ryan's 1985 work on intrinsic vs.
extrinsic motivation). It is also the case that the items in Hewitt and
Flett's scales conceptually capture most of the item content in Frost et al.'s
(1990) scales. Indeed, when Frost et al. (1993) factor analyzed their subscales together with the Hewitt and Flett scales, only two factors emerged.
One factor contained the Hewitt and Flett Self-Oriented Perfectionism
scale and the Frost et al. Personal Standards subscale. The second factor
contained the Hewitt and Flett Socially Prescribed Perfectionism scale and
the remaining Frost et al. subscales (Concern Over Mistakes, Parental
Criticism, Parental Expectations, and Doubts About Actions).

Personality Correlates of Perfectionistic Self-Beliefs

In examining the Socially Prescribed Perfectionism scale, we perceived at
least two distinct types of self-beliefs represented in the items. One is the
belief that being loved and accepted by others is contingent on high
achievement. The second is the belief that others hold high standards or
expectations for the self. We also detected two distinct types of self-beliefs
in the Self-Oriented Perfectionism scale. One is the belief that it is important to be perfect, and the other is the belief that one actively strives
for perfection. The latter belief involves a core volitional component largely
missing from the other beliefs and reflects Hewitt and Flett's intention to
assess the motivational and behavioral aspects of perfectionism in addition
to the cognitive aspects.
    To determine whether our perceptions were reflected in the factor
structure underlying the scales, we administered the Self-Oriented and
Socially Prescribed Perfectionism scales along with a set of other individual difference measures to a sample of 243 undergraduates at the beginning of an academic year. The factor analyses of the two 15-item scales
each yielded two factors with eigenvalues greater than 1 and generally
confirmed our perceptions regarding item content. On the basis of the factor loadings, we created two subscales measuring socially prescribed perfection:

- Conditional Acceptance (five items, $\alpha = .71$), which reflects the belief that being loved and accepted by others is contingent on high
  achievement (e.g., "Others will like me, even if I don't excel at
  everything")
- Others' High Standards (six items, $\alpha = .75$), which reflects the belief that others hold high standards or expectations for the self
  (e.g., "People expect nothing less than perfection from me").

We also created two self-oriented subscales:

- Importance of Being Perfect (five items, $\alpha = .80$), which reflects the belief that it is important to be perfect (e.g., "It is very important that I am perfect in everything I attempt")
- Perfectionistic Striving (five items, $\alpha = .73$), which reflects the perception that one actively strives for perfection ("I strive to be as perfect as I can be").

The four remaining items of the Socially Prescribed scale and the five remaining items of the Self-Oriented scale were not used in the construction of the subscales because they loaded similarly on both factors.

The two socially prescribed perfection subscales were interrelated ($r = .36$), as were the two self-oriented subscales ($r = .43$). In addition, the Others' High Standards subscale was positively correlated with both the Perfectionistic Striving subscale ($r = .18$) and the Importance of Being Perfect subscale ($r = .50$). In contrast, although the Conditional Acceptance subscale of socially prescribed perfectionism also was positively correlated with the Importance of Being Perfect subscale ($r = .29$), it was negatively correlated with the Perfectionistic Striving subscale ($r = -.25$) of self-oriented perfectionism. Thus, differentiating the item content of Hewitt and Flett's Socially Prescribed Perfection and Self-Oriented Perfectionism scales highlights the fact that believing that other people's love and acceptance is contingent on performance appears to inhibit socially prescribed perfectionists from actively striving for superior performance.

We then correlated the Socially Prescribed and Self-Oriented Perfectionism scales and each of their subscales with a battery of individual-difference measures, including the Rosenberg Self-Esteem Inventory (Rosenberg, 1965); the Beck Depression Inventory (Beck, 1967); the abbreviated Five-Factor Inventory measures of Neuroticism, Extraversion, Agreeableness, Conscientiousness, and Openness to Experience (Costa & McCrae, 1989); and the dispositional measures of positive affectivity and negative affectivity (Watson, Clark, & Tellegen, 1988). To assess structural components of the self-concept, we administered the Self-Concept Clarity Scale (Campbell et al., 1996), which assesses the extent to which the contents of the self-concept are clearly and confidently defined, internally consistent, and temporally stable, and the Goal Instability Scale (Robbins, Payne, & Chartrand, 1990). Finally, we included Kuhl's (1994) Action Control Scale (ACS), which assesses dispositions that are especially relevant to goal-directed behavior. The ACS yields three subscales that measure the facility with which goal-directed behavior can be (a) initiated (Decision-Related subscale), (b) sustained (Performance-Related subscale), and (c) changed in the face of unpleasant experiences, particularly failure (Failure-Related subscale). The correlations are presented in Table 7.1.

We first focus on the correlates of the Hewitt and Flett Socially Prescribed Perfectionism scale (see Table 7.1, column 1). Some of the individual-difference measures examined here have been included in earlier research, and our correlations generally replicate that research (Hew-

Table 7.1. Correlations Between Perfectionism Measures and Individual-Difference Measures

	Socially Prescribed Perfectionism			Self-Oriented Perfectionism		
	Total scale	Conditional Acceptance subscale	Others' High Standards subscale	Total scale	Importance of Being Perfect subscale	Perfectionistic Striving subscale
Self-esteem	-.32***	-.54***	-.07	-.03	-.16*	.22**
Depression	.32***	.40***	.18**	-.03	.06	-.25***
Neuroticism	.30***	.43***	.10	-.02	.12	-.19**
Extraversion	-.18**	-.30***	-.04	.01	-.01	.24***
Agreeableness	-.35***	-.34***	-.24***	.06	-.09	.12
Conscientiousness	.00	-.13*	.10	.32***	.30***	.49***
Openness	-.15*	-.26***	-.03	.02	-.04	.15*
Negative affect	.35***	.44***	.13	-.06	.11	-.15*
Positive affect	-.13*	-.32***	.04	.07	.04	.30***
Self-concept clarity	-.26***	-.39***	-.08	.06	-.03	.25***
Goal instability	.26***	.36***	.09	-.16*	-.08	-.42***
Action control subscales						
Failure-related	-.21***	-.26***	-.11	-.16*	-.24***	.02
Performance-related	-.04	-.14*	.01	.14*	.14*	.20**
Decision-related	-.17**	-.22***	-.08	.15*	.10	.30***

Note. $N = 226–238$.
*$p < .05$. **$p < .01$. ***$p < .001$.

itt & Flett, 1991). That is, Socially Prescribed Perfectionism was positively correlated with depression, neuroticism, and negative affectivity and was negatively correlated with self-esteem, extraversion, agreeableness, positive affectivity, and openness to experience. The individual-difference measures examined here for the first time reveal additional correlates that are theoretically consistent with the construct of socially prescribed perfectionism. The Socially Prescribed Perfectionism scale was reliably associated with a lack of clarity in the self-concept, goal instability, and Kuhl's Decision-Related and Failure-Related subscales, a result indicating that socially prescribed perfectionism is associated with an inability to initiate and change goal-directed behavior.

More striking, however, are the correlations with the two subscales we constructed from the socially prescribed items (see Table 7.1, columns 2 and 3). The deleterious concomitants of socially prescribed perfectionism outlined above appear to derive almost exclusively from the perception that one's acceptance by others is conditional on attaining superior performance. The Conditional Acceptance subscale consistently showed associations with the other traits that are in the same direction but are higher in magnitude than those shown with the total Socially Prescribed scale. In contrast, the other component of socially prescribed perfectionism, the belief that others have high expectations for the self, does not appear in and of itself to be an important factor in accounting for the problematic aspects of socially prescribed perfectionism. This finding may have occurred because the item content of the Others' High Standards subscale is moot with respect to whether the standards perceived to be held by others have been internalized by the person. For example, people who agree with the item "People expect nothing less than perfection from me" may or may not accept others' expectations as constituting reasonable self-standards. Indeed, it is possible that those who perceive others as having exceedingly high standards for the self may simply resent those others, a possibility supported by the significant correlation between the Others' High Standards subscale and low levels of agreeableness (e.g., hostility).

We now turn to the correlates of Hewitt and Flett's Self-Oriented Perfectionism scale. Consistent with prior research, the total scale was not correlated substantially with any of the individual-difference measures with the exception of conscientiousness. Again, however, an examination of the two subscales revealed a divergent pattern: Perfectionistic Striving was generally associated with traits indicating positive adjustment, whereas the Importance of Being Perfect was either uncorrelated or was negatively correlated with these traits. The Perfectionistic Striving subscale was reliably associated with lower levels of anxiety and depression and with higher levels of self-esteem, self-concept clarity, goal stability, extraversion, positive affect, conscientiousness, and the ability to initiate and sustain goal-directed behavior. This result is consistent with recent research showing that Frost et al.'s (1990) Personal Standards subscale is associated with the tendency to stay focused on attaining goals and planful action (Stöber, 1998). Although the Importance of Being Perfect subscale also was associated with higher conscientiousness and the ability to sustain goal-directed behavior (to a lesser degree, however, than the Perfectionistic Striving subscale), it was negatively correlated with self-esteem and the ability to change goal-directed behavior in the face of failure.

Given this divergence between the correlates of the Perfectionistic Striving and Importance of Being Perfect subscales, the effect of combining the two types of self-beliefs in the Self-Oriented Perfectionism scale may be to mask the positive consequences of perfectionistic striving for adjustment and goal-directed behavior. Our data are mute with respect to the stress–diathesis model, the notion that perfectionistic striving makes people vulnerable to negative outcomes in times of acute stress or failure (Hewitt & Flett, 1993; Hewitt et al., 1996). In that connection, it is worth noting that, although perfectionistic striving was related to the ability to initiate and sustain goal-directed behavior, it was not related to the ability to effectively change goal-directed behavior in the face of failure. Pursuing perfection may not bestow psychological benefits when that pursuit takes place in the face of failure (Klinger, 1977).

From this analysis one can draw several conclusions regarding the negative and positive consequences of perfectionism. First, the previously demonstrated negative consequences of socially prescribed perfectionism appear to be primarily a result of perceptions that acceptance by others is conditional on the attainment of high performance. The perception that others have high standards for the self does not, in isolation, appear to be critical. Second, the emphasis on actively striving to achieve perfection may be a core factor underlying the positive consequences of perfectionism that have emerged in the literature. Finally, although the belief that it is important to be perfect may cause a person to be more conscientious, it also appears to contribute to lower levels of self-esteem and a reluctance to alter goal-directed behavior when confronted with failure.

Perfectionistic Self-Beliefs and Goal Pursuit

Kuhl's Action Control Scales tap different aspects of goal-directed behavior. Our analysis of the scales suggested that perceptions of conditional acceptance may impair effective goal pursuit, whereas beliefs about perfectionistic striving may facilitate such pursuit. Because the perfectionism construct is so intimately linked to goal pursuit (indeed, Hewitt and Flett developed their scales in part to emphasize the behavioral component of perfectionism), we explored more directly the impact of the two types of self-beliefs on actual goal-directed behavior and thought (see Flett, Sawatzky, & Hewitt, 1995, for research on perfectionism and goal commitment).

Our initial data suggested that perceptions of conditional acceptance might seriously impede active, effortful goal pursuit despite the fact that perceptions of acceptance contingent on achievement should serve to increase the subjective importance of such achievement. An important distinction in the literature on persistence is potentially useful in understanding this apparent contradiction. Although persistence is usually referenced in terms of behavioral pursuit (active efforts to achieve a goal), one influential conceptualization of persistence emphasizes the cognitive processes that can occur after behavioral pursuit has ended (Lewin, 1951; Zeigarnik, 1938). That is, despite the fact that the person has stopped pursuing a goal behaviorally, he or she may cognitively persist at that goal, keeping the goal and goal-related thoughts activated in memory with intrusive, repetitive thoughts (i.e., rumination).

The Conditional Acceptance subscale was strongly associated with anxiety, low self-esteem, and negative affect in addition to the traits reflecting deficits in goal pursuit (Kuhl's ACS). This pattern suggests that the anxiety attached to beliefs about conditional acceptance may interfere with behavioral goal pursuit while increasing goal-related rumination. We therefore anticipated that the Conditional Acceptance subscale would be associated with lower levels of behavioral pursuit and higher levels of rumination. The Perfectionist Striving subscale, in contrast, was associated with lower levels of anxiety and higher scores on Kuhl's scales, indicating more effective behavioral goal pursuit. We therefore anticipated that this subscale would be associated with higher levels of behavioral pursuit and lower levels of rumination.

Another important determinant of goal-directed behavior is the motivational basis for the goal. Deci and Ryan (1985) documented the importance of the extent to which goals are self-determined. That is, people may pursue goals for purely intrinsic reasons (e.g., pleasure), for identified reasons (i.e., they freely endorse the goal), for introjected reasons (i.e., they would feel guilty or anxious if they did not pursue the goal), or for external reasons (i.e., rewards). Deci and Ryan showed that behavioral pursuit depends on the extent to which goals are self-determined, with higher levels of self-determination (i.e., intrinsic and identified) leading to more behavioral pursuit than lower levels (i.e., introjected and external).

Our initial study indicated that the Conditional Acceptance and Perfectionist Striving subscales were correlated in opposite directions with two other traits that are likely to be associated with self-determination. Conditional Acceptance was negatively correlated with self-concept clarity and positively correlated with goal instability, whereas Perfectionist Striving showed the opposite pattern. High goal instability suggests that the person has chosen goals for external reasons and changes goals in response to altering external demands and pressures. Low self-concept clarity also suggests lower levels of self-determination in that selecting goals that correspond to one's interests, values, and talents requires adequate self-knowledge. We therefore anticipated that Conditional Acceptance would be associated with lower levels of self-determination and that Perfectionistic Striving would be associated with higher levels of self-determination.

These hypotheses were examined in the context of a larger investigation of the determinants of goal-directed behavior. We recruited a subsample of 83 undergraduates who had participated in our initial study. The study took place in two parts.

At Time 1 (which took place 3 to 4 weeks after participants completed the initial study), participants listed five academic and five social goals they wanted to attain during the current academic year. They were instructed to list concrete goals so that they would be able to evaluate their goal progress 5 months later (see below); progress evaluation would be difficult with abstract goals, such as "to be happy."

Participants evaluated their goals on several dimensions, including their degree of goal efficacy. Efficacy beliefs (or expectations) regarding goals have been shown to have a powerful impact on goal-directed behavior (e.g., Bandura, 1989). Participants rated each of their goals for the extent they believed they would achieve the goal during the academic year. The ratings were averaged across the goals to create a Goal-Efficacy score. The resulting 10-item scale was internally consistent ($\alpha = .75$).

Participants also rated each goal for the extent to which it was self-determined (Ryan, Sheldon, Kasser, & Deci, 1996; Sheldon & Kasser, 1995). They rated the extent to which they were pursuing each goal for "external" reasons, "introjected" reasons, "identified" reasons, and "intrinsic" reasons. Those reasons form a self-determination continuum—the order (i.e., external, introjected, identified, and intrinsic) reflects relatively low to relatively high levels of self-determination. A Self-Determination score was calculated for each participant according to the guidelines of Sheldon and Kasser (1995). First, the external and intrinsic ratings were doubled. Second, the sum of the 10 external and 10 introjected ratings was subtracted from the sum of the 10 identified and 10 intrinsic ratings ($\alpha = .79$).

Five months later (Time 2), participants reported on their goal progress. They also completed the Rosenberg Self-Esteem Inventory and the Self-Concept Clarity Scale (Campbell et al., 1996) again. The measures allowed us to examine the effect over time that the perfectionistic self-beliefs, as well as the efficacy beliefs, goal self-determination, and goal progress, had on both the evaluation components (self-esteem) and knowledge components (self-concept clarity) of the self-concept. Participants also completed the Beck Depression Inventory again to enhance our ability to compare our results with those of other perfectionism studies, many of which have examined the association between perfectionism and depression.

Participants answered several items assessing cognitive and behavioral goal persistence. For each goal, participants indicated the degree to which they were satisfied with their progress toward the goal. The responses were averaged across the 10 goals to create a reliable Satisfaction With Goal Progress measure ($\alpha = .71$). For each goal, effortful pursuit and rumination were measured using two items. Participants indicated their degree of active goal pursuit over the past 5 months, their current degree of active goal pursuit, the degree to which they had experienced ruminative thoughts (i.e., intrusive, unwanted thoughts) regarding the goal over the past 5 months, and the degree to which they currently were ruminating about the goal. Because the items assessing past and current effortful pursuit were highly correlated and the items assessing past and current rumination were highly correlated, they were averaged across the 10 goals to create two measures: Effortful Goal Pursuit (α = .82) and Goal Rumination (α = .89).

Participants also indicated whether they had abandoned any of their goals. The number of goals that participants abandoned formed the Goal Abandonment index. We focused on goal abandonment, as opposed to goal attainment, because a lack of goal attainment is ambiguous with respect to whether participants were continuing to persist toward the goal.

We first examined the associations between the four perfectionism subscales, participants' goal efficacy, and reasons for goal pursuit assessed at Time 1. The Conditional Acceptance subscale was negatively correlated with Goal Efficacy, r (80) = $-.30$, $p < .01$, indicating that perceptions of conditional acceptance were associated with a lack of efficacy regarding goal attainment. As anticipated, Conditional Acceptance also was negatively correlated with Self-Determination, r (81) = $-.37$, $p < .01$, indicating that people who believe that acceptance by others is conditional on achievement tend to pursue goals for relatively external reasons. Although the Perfectionistic Striving subscale was positively correlated with Goal Efficacy and Self-Determination, the correlations were small and unreliable. Neither of the other two perfectionism subscales (Others' High Standards and Importance of Being Perfect) were significantly correlated with Goal Efficacy or Self-Determination ($p > .12$ for both subscales).

We then correlated the four perfectionism subscales as well as the Time 1 measures of Goal Efficacy and Self-Determination with the four measures of goal persistence: Effortful Goal Pursuit, Goal Rumination, Goal Progress, and Goal Abandonment (Table 7.2). Goal Efficacy and Self-Determination were positively correlated with Effortful Goal Pursuit and Goal Progress and negatively correlated with Goal Rumination and Goal Abandonment. The correlations replicate earlier research and serve to highlight the importance of efficacy as well as the motivational basis for pursuing goals.

We anticipated that perceptions of conditional acceptance and perfectionistic striving would be related to the measures of goal persistence, but

Table 7.2. Correlations Between Goal Measures and Measures of Goal Efficacy, Self-Determination, and Perfectionism

Scale	Effortful Goal Pursuit	Goal Rumination	Satisfaction With Goal Progress	Goal Abandonment
Goal Efficacy	.43***	−.43***	.47***	−.33**
Self-Determination	.37***	−.55***	.27*	−.10
Conditional Acceptance	−.32**	.36***	−.39***	.32**
Others' High Standards	.03	.11	.04	.13
Perfectionistic Striving	.41***	−.01	.30**	−.14
Importance of Being Perfect	.05	.20	.00	.15

Note. N = 76–79.
*$p < .05$. **$p < .01$. ***$p < .001$.

in opposite directions. As expected, perceptions of conditional acceptance were reliably associated with reduced Effortful Goal Pursuit and lower levels of Satisfaction With Goal Progress. The measure also was correlated positively with Goal Abandonment and with higher levels of Goal Rumination. Those results, in conjunction with those of our initial study, yield a coherent portrait of the deleterious consequences of believing that one's acceptance by others is contingent on good performance. Such beliefs not only are associated with concurrent measures of psychological distress, low levels of self-esteem, and self-concept confusion but also predict less effective pursuit of one's goals.

In contrast, Perfectionistic Striving was correlated with high levels of Effortful Goal Pursuit and Satisfaction With Goal Progress, indicating effective goal pursuit. At the same time, the subscale was uncorrelated with the measures of Goal Rumination and Goal Abandonment. The other two perfectionism subscales, Others' High Standards and the Importance of Being Perfect, which were generally uncorrelated with the personality measures in our earlier study, were not associated with any of the persistence measures in this study.

Although the correlations in Table 7.2 suggest that perceptions of conditional acceptance have several deleterious consequences for effective goal pursuit, the Conditional Acceptance subscale also was negatively associated with Goal Efficacy and Self-Determination, two important predictors of goal pursuit measured at Time 1. It is possible that feelings of conditional acceptance do not negatively affect goal pursuit directly but are associated with less effective goal pursuit only insofar as those feelings cause low Goal Efficacy and low Self-Determination. To assess whether feelings of conditional acceptance had a direct effect on goal pursuit over and above its indirect effect through low levels of efficacy and goal self-determination, we conducted hierarchical regressions for each of the four goal-persistence measures. In each analysis, we first entered Goal Efficacy and Self-Determination. Second, we entered the Conditional Acceptance measure, noting the incremental variance accounted for by this measure after the effects of efficacy and self-determination were controlled.

The analyses indicated that feelings of conditional acceptance exerted direct as well as indirect effects on Goal Rumination, Satisfaction With Goal Progress, and Goal Abandonment, accounting for 3%, 6%, and 5% additional variance, respectively (all Fs > 3.88, all p < .05). Conditional Acceptance also added 2% incremental variance in the prediction of Effortful Goal Pursuit, an increment that did not quite reach conventional levels of statistical significance. The data therefore suggest that, although feelings of conditional acceptance inhibit effective goal pursuit by undermining efficacy and self-determination, they also create a direct vulnerability to ineffective goal pursuit.

We conducted comparable analyses examining the effects of perfectionistic striving on the two measures of goal persistence with which the subscale exhibited reliable zero-order correlations: Effortful Goal Pursuit and Satisfaction With Goal Progress. As above, we entered Perfectionistic Striving in the regression after controlling for the effects of Goal Efficacy and Self-Determination. The analyses indicated strong direct as well as indirect effects for the impact of perfectionistic striving. The measure accounted for 12% incremental variance in Effortful Goal Pursuit ($F = 11.88$, $p < .01$) and 6% incremental variance in Satisfaction With Goal Progress ($F = 5.71, p < .02$). Thus, a behavioral orientation of striving for perfection appears to directly promote effective goal pursuit as well as enhancing feelings of efficacy and self-determination.

The analysis suggests that those who perceived their acceptance by others as conditional on performance are more likely to experience intrusive ruminations regarding their goals but are less likely to actively pursue their goals. In contrast, those who focus on perfectionistic striving are more likely to actively pursue their goals without incurring the potential cost of increased rumination. Those conclusions, however, are based solely on self-report data and would be strengthened by demonstrating how perceptions of conditional worth and perfectionistic striving affect a more objective indicator of goal performance.

We had such an indicator in our study: A subset of participants (86%) gave us access to their final grade point average (GPA) for the academic year over which the study took place. We used GPA as an objective indicator of academic goal performance and examined its relation to Conditional Acceptance and Perfectionistic Striving. Both subscales were reliably correlated with GPA; Conditional Acceptance was associated negatively with GPA ($r = -.36$, $p < .01$), and Perfectionistic Striving was positively correlated with GPA ($r = .30$, $p < .05$). The other two subscales (Others' High Standards and the Importance of Being Perfect) were uncorrelated with GPA. To examine the extent to which the impact of those beliefs had direct as well as indirect effects on GPA through more effective self-regulation, we also computed partial correlations, controlling for Effortful Goal Pursuit and Goal Rumination of only the academic goals. The partial correlation with the Conditional Acceptance subscale was $-.28$, $p < .02$, whereas the partial correlation with the Perfectionistic Striving subscale was $.21, p < .10$. Thus, it appears that the two types of perfectionistic beliefs (as assessed at the beginning of the academic year) exerted direct as well as indirect effects on participants' academic performance across the academic year.

In addition to exploring how perceptions of conditional worth and perfectionistic striving influence goal pursuit, we were interested in the extent to which the two types of perfectionistic beliefs might affect changes in the self-concept over time. We therefore examined the correlations between the subscales and participants' scores on self-esteem and self-concept clarity taken at Time 2, controlling for their scores at Time 1. We also examined changes in depression over the course of the study, given that depression has been a focal measure in the perfectionism literature. The analyses did not indicate any reliable associations between perfectionistic beliefs at Time 1 and changes in depression or self-esteem over time. The lack of a direct association between perfectionist striving and changes in depression over time is consistent with Hewitt and Flett's earlier research on self-oriented perfectionism, which yielded no direct correlations with subsequent depression, only interactions with stress. Perfectionistic striving may not lead to changes in depression unless an achievement stressor interacts with perfectionistic striving.

Reliable partial correlations were obtained between those beliefs and changes in self-concept clarity, however. People who scored higher on the Conditional Acceptance subscale showed significant decreases in self-concept clarity over time (partial $r = -.25$, $p < .05$), whereas people who scored higher on the Perfectionistic Striving subscales showed significant increases in self-concept clarity over time (partial $r = .44$, $p < .01$). Thus, although these perfectionistic beliefs were not associated with changes in the evaluative components of the self-concept, they were associated with changes in the structure, such that Conditional Acceptance decreased and Perfectionistic Striving increased self-concept clarity.

Conclusion

The construct of perfectionism has evolved over the past decade or so from being one that focused quite specifically on the deleterious consequences of holding excessively high, rigid standards for the self to one that focuses on the positive and negative consequences of an interrelated constellation of specific self-beliefs. Those self-beliefs are concerned with the interplay between one's own standards, the standards for the self held by significant others, the perceived ability to attain these standards, and how the attainment of those standards affects self-evaluation and perceived acceptance by others.

Research, including that reported here, increasingly indicates that standard setting per se may have little to do with the negative concomitants of perfectionism. First, several studies have demonstrated a paradox with respect to psychological distress and standard setting. For example, although people who are dysphoric or socially anxious describe themselves and others as perfectionistic, they do not differ in the standards they actually set for themselves or in the actual standards they believe others use to evaluate them (Ahrens, Zeiss, & Kanfer, 1988; Alden, Bieling, & Wallace, 1994; Kanfer & Zeiss, 1983; Wallace & Alden, 1991). Alden et al. (1994) also reported that participants scoring higher on the Socially Prescribed Perfectionism scale did not differ in their objective ratings of others' expectations of them in a specific social context. One interpretation of that pattern is that people who are dysphoric or socially anxious (and those who score higher on the Socially Prescribed Perfectionism scale), compared with their nonanxious counterparts, may view the same set of social expectations as more demanding. That is, perfectionism may have more to do with low efficacy—the belief that standards are not likely to be attained—than with the standards per se.

Our data further suggest that even perceiving that others' standards are too demanding or unattainable may not be the most critical factor in the psychological distress that people high in socially prescribed perfectionism show. Our data revealed that depression, neuroticism, low self-esteem, and negative affect were much more strongly associated with beliefs about conditional acceptance than with the belief that others' standards were excessively high. Indeed, the strongest correlate of the Other's High Standards subscale was low agreeableness, suggesting that this belief is more strongly related to externally directed hostility than to internal distress.

Baldwin and Sinclair (1996) recently provided additional evidence that the belief that acceptance is conditional on being successful is an important aspect of low self-esteem. Rather than relying on self-reports concerning that belief, they used a lexical decision task to compute reaction times to words related to acceptance and rejection (e.g., cherished, abandoned) after presentation of primes related to success and failure (e.g., win, lose). They reported that for low self-esteem participants—but not high self-esteem participants—failure activated rejection and success (nonsignificantly) activated success. This finding is consistent with classic theories of psychological functioning, which highlight the strong connection between beliefs of conditional acceptance and low self-esteem (e.g., Rogers, 1951).

Our data further suggest that beliefs about conditional acceptance affect the regulation of goal-directed behavior in important ways. Despite the fact that such regulation is closely linked with the construct of perfectionism, few studies have examined the impact of perfectionism on goal-directed behavior. Scores on the Conditional Acceptance subscale reliably predicted the extent to which participants actively pursued, abandoned, ruminated about, or were satisfied with their progress on a set of academic and social goals they enumerated at the beginning of the academic year. In addition, Conditional Acceptance scores were a negative predictor of participants' GPA, an objective measure of success in pursuit of academic goals. This predictive ability was, in part, a result of the fact that beliefs about conditional acceptance were quite strongly correlated with the extent to which participants' goals were self-determined and the participants felt efficacious about their ability to attain them.

The painful irony of maintaining perceptions of conditional acceptance is apparent in both its direct and indirect effects on goal pursuit. A person believes he or she will be accepted by others only if some standard is reached (e.g., obtaining high grades). Yet, this belief is associated with adopting goals for which one feels little or no identification—goals that are chosen specifically to gain approval and thus lack the sense of personal commitment that is so critical for effective performance. Rather than engaging in effortful goal pursuit, the person engages in excessive rumination, thereby undermining the attainment of the standard viewed as so necessary for acceptance. Perfectionistic strivers follow quite a different path: Those who place an emphasis on striving for perfection engage in more effortful pursuit of their goals, derive more satisfaction from their goal progress, and attain better academic outcomes (in terms of GPA) than do people who do not place an emphasis on striving for perfection.

Thus, the psychological and behavioral consequences of perfectionism appear to depend on the particular set of perfectionistic self-beliefs that one chooses to examine among the constellation of available measures. The two beliefs that we have highlighted appear to mirror a highly important motivational distinction. The correlates of beliefs about conditional acceptance suggest a primary motive to avoid failure. That is, concern about others' rejection was coupled with low self-esteem, negative affect (negative affectivity, depression, neuroticism), a lack of certainty or clarity about one's attributes and goals, low efficacy, rumination, goals adopted for introjected or external reasons, and a tendency to be dissatisfied with goal progress or to abandon declared goals. These concomitants all suggest a far stronger concern with minimizing failure than with achieving success. In contrast, the belief that one pursues or strives for perfection suggests a primary motive to achieve success; people with this belief evidence little concern about rejection (the negative correlation with the Conditional Acceptance subscale), high self-esteem, positive affect, greater certainty about one's attributes and goals, high efficacy, self-determined goals, and an active pursuit and satisfaction with progress on declared goals. Although both motives (and perfectionism) indicate a strong focus on standards and performance, the divergent consequences of the two motives on psychological well-being and the regulation of goal-directed behavior suggest that the motivational distinction may be a critical one in refining our understanding of perfectionism.

References

Ahrens, A. H., Zeiss, A. M., & Kanfer, R. (1988). Depressive deficits in interpersonal standards, self-efficacy, and social comparison. *Cognitive Therapy and Research, 12,* 53–67.

Alden, L. E., Bieling, P. J., & Wallace, S. T. (1994). Perfectionism in an interpersonal context: A self-regulation analysis of dysphoria and social anxiety. *Cognitive Therapy and Research, 18,* 1–20.

Baldwin, M. W., & Sinclair, L. (1996). Self-esteem and "if . . . then" contingencies of interpersonal acceptance. *Journal of Personality and Social Psychology, 71,* 1130–1141.

Bandura, A. (1989). Self-regulation of motivation and action through internal standards and goal systems. In L. Pervin (Ed.), *Goal concepts in personality and social psychology* (pp. 19–85). Hillsdale, NJ: Erlbaum.

Beck, A. T. (1967). *Depression: Clinical, experimental, and theoretical aspects.* New York: Harper & Row.

Burns, D. D. (1980, November). The perfectionist's script for self-defeat. *Psychology Today,* 34–51.

Burns, D. D., & Beck, A. T. (1978). Cognitive behavior modification of mood disorders. In J. P. Foreyt & D. P. Rathjen (Eds.), *Cognitive behavior therapy* (pp. 109–134). New York: Plenum.

Campbell, J. D. (1990). Self-esteem and clarity of the self-concept. *Journal of Personality and Social Psychology, 59,* 538–549.

Campbell, J. D., Trapnell, P. D., Heine, S. J., Katz, I. M., Lavallee, L. F., & Lehman, D. R. (1996). Self-concept clarity: Measurement, personality correlates, and cultural boundaries. *Journal of Personality and Social Psychology, 70,* 141–156.

Costa, P. T., Jr., & McCrae, R. R. (1989). *The NEO-PI/FFI manual supplement.* Odessa, FL: Psychological Assessment Resources.

Deci, E. L., & Ryan, R. M. (1985). *Intrinsic motivation and self-determination in human behavior.* New York: Plenum.

Donahue, E. M., Robins, R. W., Roberts, B. W., & John, O. P. (1993). The divided self:

Concurrent and longitudinal effects of psychological adjustment and social roles on self-concept differentiation. *Journal of Personality and Social Psychology, 64,* 834–846.

Flett, G. L., Hewitt, P. L., Blankstein, K. R., & O'Brien, S. (1991). Perfectionism and learned resourcefulness in depression and self-esteem. *Personality and Individual Differences, 12,* 61–68.

Flett, G. L., Hewitt, P. L., & Dyck, D. G. (1989). Self-oriented perfectionism, neuroticism, and anxiety. *Personality and Individual Differences, 10,* 731–735.

Flett, G. L., Sawatzky, D. L., & Hewitt, P. L. (1995). Dimensions of perfectionism and goal commitment: A further comparison of two perfectionism measures. *Journal of Psychopathology and Behavioral Assessment, 17,* 111–124.

Frost, R. O., Heimberg, R. G., Holt, C. S., Mattia, J. I., & Neubauer, A. L. (1993). A comparison of two measures of perfectionism. *Personality and Individual Differences, 14,* 119–126.

Frost, R. O., Marten, P., Lahart, C., & Rosenblate, R. (1990). The dimensions of perfectionism. *Cognitive Therapy and Research, 14,* 449–468.

Greenwald, A. G., & Pratkanis, A. R. (1984). The self. In R. S. Wyer & T. K. Srull (Eds.), *Handbook of social cognition* (Vol. 3, pp. 129–178). Hillsdale, NJ: Erlbaum.

Hamachek, D. E. (1978). Psychodynamics of normal and neurotic perfectionism. *Psychology, 15,* 27–33.

Hewitt, P. L., & Dyck, D. G. (1986). Perfectionism, stress, and vulnerability to depression. *Cognitive Therapy and Research, 10,* 137–142.

Hewitt, P. L., & Flett, G. L. (1990). Perfectionism and depression: A multidimensional analysis. *Journal of Social Behavior and Personality, 5,* 423–438.

Hewitt, P. L., & Flett, G. L. (1991). Perfectionism in the self and social contexts: Conceptualization, assessment, and association with psychology. *Journal of Personality and Social Psychology, 60,* 456–470.

Hewitt, P. L., & Flett, G. L. (1993). Dimensions of perfectionism, daily stress, and depression: A test of the specific vulnerability hypothesis. *Journal of Abnormal Psychology, 102,* 58–65.

Hewitt, P. L., Flett, G. L., & Ediger, E. (1996). Perfectionism and depression: Longitudinal assessment of a specific vulnerability hypothesis. *Journal of Abnormal Psychology, 105,* 276–280.

Higgins, E. T. (1987). Self-discrepancy: A theory relating self and affect. *Psychological Review, 94,* 310–340.

Hollander, M. H. (1965). Perfectionism. *Comprehensive Psychiatry, 6,* 94–103.

Kanfer, R., & Zeiss, A. M. (1983). Standards and self-efficacy in depression. *Journal of Abnormal Psychology, 92,* 319–329.

Kihlstrom, J. F., Cantor, N., Albright, J. S., Chew, B. R., Klein, S. B., & Niedenthal, P. M. (1988). Information processing and the study of the self. In L. Berkowitz (Ed.), *Advances in experimental social psychology* (Vol. 21, pp. 159–187). San Diego, CA: Academic Press.

Klinger, E. (1977). *Meaning and void: Inner experience and the incentives in people's lives.* Minneapolis: University of Minnesota Press.

Kuhl, J. (1994). Action versus state orientation: Psychometric properties of the Action Control Scale (ACS-90). In J. Kuhl & J. Beckmann (Eds.), *Volition and personality: Action versus state orientation* (pp. 47–60). Seattle, WA: Hogrefe & Huber.

Lewin, K. (1951). *Field theory in social science.* New York: Harper.

Linville, P. W. (1985). Self-complexity and affective extremity: Don't put all of your eggs in one cognitive basket. *Social Cognition, 3,* 94–120.

Linville, P. W. (1987). Self-complexity as a cognitive buffer against stress-related illness and depression. *Journal of Personality and Social Psychology, 52,* 663–676.

Markus, H. R., & Wurf, E. (1987). The dynamic self-concept: A social psychological perspective. *Annual Review of Psychology, 38,* 299–337.

Missildine, W. H. (1963). *Your inner child of the past.* New York: Simon & Schuster.

Pacht, A. R. (1985). Reflections on perfection. *American Psychologist, 39,* 386–390.

Robbins, S. B., Payne, E. C., & Chartrand, J. M. (1990). Goal instability and later life adjustment. *Psychology and Aging, 5,* 447–450.

Rogers, C. R. (1951). *Client-centered therapy: Its current practice, implications, and theory.* Boston: Houghton-Mifflin.

Rosenberg, M. (1965). *Society and the adolescent self-image.* Princeton, NJ: Princeton University Press.

Ryan, R. M., Sheldon, K. M., Kasser, T., & Deci, E. L. (1996). All goals are not created equal: An organismic perspective on the nature of goals and their regulation. In P. Gollwitzer & J. Bargh (Eds.), *The psychology of action: Linking cognition and motivation to behavior* (pp. 7–26). New York: Guilford.

Sheldon, K. M., & Kasser, T. (1995). Coherence and congruence: Two aspects of personality integration. *Journal of Personality and Social Psychology, 68,* 531–543.

Showers, C. (1992). Compartmentalization of positive and negative self-knowledge: Keeping bad apples out of the bunch. *Journal of Personality and Social Psychology, 62,* 1036–1049.

Smith, T. W., & Brehm, S. S. (1981). Cognitive correlates of the Type A coronary-prone behavior pattern. *Motivation and Emotion, 3,* 215–223.

Stöber, J. (1998). The Frost Multidimensional Perfectionism Scale revisited: More perfect with four (instead of six) dimensions. *Personality and Individual Differences, 24,* 481–491.

Wallace, S. T., & Alden, L. E. (1991). A comparison of social standards and perceived ability in anxious and nonanxious men. *Cognitive Therapy and Research, 15,* 237–254.

Watson, D., Clark, A. L., & Tellegen, A. (1988). Development and validation of brief measures of positive and negative affect: The PANAS scales. *Journal of Personality and Social Psychology, 54,* 1063–1070.

Zeigarnik, B. (1938). On finished and unfinished tasks. In W. D. Ellis (Ed.), *A source book of gestalt psychology* (pp. 300–314). New York: Harcourt, Brace, & World.

8

Perfectionism and the Self-Conscious Emotions: Shame, Guilt, Embarrassment, and Pride

June Price Tangney

Inquiry into the dynamics of perfectionism naturally leads to a consideration of the self-conscious emotions. The family of self-conscious emotions —shame, guilt, embarrassment, and pride—are fundamentally emotions of evaluation, specifically with respect to the self. That is, each involve, as a central feature, some form of self-reflection and self-evaluation. This self-evaluation may be implicit or explicit, consciously experienced or silently transpiring below conscious awareness. But these emotions are, by definition, about the self. For example, when good things happen, we may feel a range of positive emotions—joy, happiness, satisfaction, or contentment. But we feel pride in our *own* positive attributes or actions. By the same token, when bad things happen, we may feel any one of several negative emotions—grief, sadness, fear, anxiety, annoyance, or anger, for example. We feel ashamed, guilty, or embarrassed, however, when *we* fail to reach some standard for performance, when *we* transgress and stray from standards of moral conduct, or when *we* violate social norms. In one way or another, the self is the evaluative object of those self-conscious emotions.[1]

Perfectionists are apt to be especially familiar with the self-conscious emotions because they focus so much energy on self-evaluation. Perfectionists do not just set high, often rigid, standards for themselves in a particular domain; they are oriented toward the process of evaluation. Life is a series of quizzes, tests, and final exams, and their name is always at the top of the report card.

This chapter focuses on emotional aspects of perfectionism. Because people frequently confuse shame with embarrassment and (especially) shame with guilt, I begin with a brief description of the phenomenology of the self-conscious emotions, underscoring the distinctions among them. I then explore the affective implications of "living with a report card" on a day-to-day basis.

---

[1]Even in those situations when we feel shame or embarrassment over another person's behavior, that person is almost invariably someone with whom we are closely affiliated or identified (e.g., a family member, friend, or colleague closely associated with the self). We experience shame because that person is part of our self definition.

Shame Versus Guilt

Psychologists agree that shame and guilt are emotions to be reckoned with, but more often than not, their conceptions of shame and guilt tend to be imprecise. In the clinical literature, especially, it is not uncommon to see psychologists refer to "feelings of shame and guilt" or to discuss the "effects of shame and guilt" without making any distinction between the two emotions. Conversely, in everyday conversation the average person rarely speaks of his or her own shame. People are inclined to entirely avoid the term *shame*, referring instead to *guilt* when they mean shame, guilt, or some combination of the two.

When people do distinguish between shame and guilt, they often refer to differences in the content or structure of events eliciting those emotions. The assumption is that certain kinds of situations lead to shame, whereas other kinds of situations lead to guilt. For example, a long-standing notion is that shame is a more public emotion than guilt. Benedict (1946), for example, conceptualized shame as an emotion arising from public exposure and disapproval of some shortcoming or transgression, in contrast to the more private experience of guilt arising from self-generated pangs of conscience. Similarly, Gehm and Scherer (1988) asserted that

> Shame is usually dependent on the public exposure of one's frailty or failing, whereas guilt may be something that remains a secret with us, no one else knowing of our breach of social norms or of our responsibility for an immoral act. (p. 74)

As it turns out, surprisingly little empirical support exists for this widely held public–private distinction. For example, in a recent study of children's and adults' descriptions of personal shame and guilt experiences (Tangney, Marschall, Rosenberg, Barlow, & Wagner, 1994), no difference was found in the frequency with which shame and guilt experiences occurred in public contexts. Both shame and guilt were most often experienced in the presence of others, and no difference was found in the likelihood of "solitary" guilt versus solitary shame experiences. Similarly, in an independent study of adults' narrative accounts of personal shame, guilt, and embarrassment experiences (Tangney, Miller, Flicker, & Barlow, 1996), no evidence indicated that shame was the more public emotion. In fact, in this study shame was somewhat more likely (18.2%) than guilt (10.4%) to occur outside of the presence of an observing audience.

Shame and guilt do not differ substantially in the types of transgressions or failures that elicit them, either. Analyses of personal shame and guilt experiences described by both children and adults have revealed few, if any, "classic" shame-inducing or guilt-inducing situations (Tangney, 1992; Tangney et al., 1994). Most types of events (e.g., lying, cheating, stealing, failing to help another, disobeying parents) were cited by some people in connection with feelings of shame and by other people in connection with guilt. Some evidence indicated that nonmoral failures and shortcomings (e.g., socially inappropriate behavior or dress) may be more likely to elicit shame. Even so, failures in work, school, or sport settings and violations of social conventions were cited by a significant number of children and adults in connection with guilt.

So what *is* the difference between shame and guilt? The weight of evidence now appears to support Helen Block Lewis's (1971) influential distinction between the two closely related emotions. From Lewis's perspective, the crux of the difference between shame and guilt lies not in the type of transgression or circumstances of the situation that elicits the emotions but rather in the way in which the events are construed. Is one's focus on one's self or on one's behavior?

According to Lewis, when people feel guilt, our key concern is with a particular behavior. Feelings of guilt involve a negative evaluation of some specific behavior (or failure to act)—a feeling that "I *did* that horrible *thing*." With this focus on a specific behavior comes a sense of tension, remorse, and regret. People in the midst of a guilt experience often report a nagging focus or preoccupation with the specific transgression—thinking of it over and over, wishing they had behaved differently or could somehow undo the bad deed that was done. Thus, the press of guilt is toward reparation. People experiencing guilt often are motivated to confess, apologize, or atone.

In contrast, when people feel shame, our key concern is with our self, as a person. Feelings of shame involve a painful negative scrutiny of the entire self—a feeling that "*I* am an unworthy, incompetent, or bad person." People in the midst of a shame experience often report a sense of shrinking or of "being small." They feel worthless and powerless, and they feel exposed. Although shame does not necessarily involve an actual observing audience present to witness one's shortcomings, people often imagine how their defective self would appear to others. As in guilt, feelings of shame can arise from a specific behavior or transgression, but the processes involved in shame extend beyond those involved in guilt. The "bad behavior" is taken not simply as a local transgression, requiring reparation or apology; rather, the offending or objectionable behavior is seen as a reflection, more generally, of a defective, objectionable self. Not surprisingly, shame often leads to a desire to escape or to hide—to sink into the floor and disappear.

In sum, what matters is not so much what was done (or not done). Rather, what matters is whether people focus on themselves (i.e., their character) or their behavior. In turn, this differential emphasis on self ("*I* did that horrible thing") versus behavior ("I *did* that horrible *thing*") is associated with different phenomenological experiences that we call shame and guilt, respectively.

Embarrassment

Miller (1995) defined *embarrassment* as "an aversive state of mortification, abashment, and chagrin that follows public social predicaments" (p. 322). In fact, embarrassment appears to be the most "social" of the self-conscious emotions. Unlike shame and guilt, it occurs almost without exception in the company of other people (Parrott & Smith, 1991; Tangney et al., 1996). Beyond this public feature of embarrassment, however, few situational factors consistently define an embarrassing situation. Miller (1992; see also Cupach & Metts, 1992) has attempted to catalog the types of situations that cause people to feel embarrassment. At the top of the list are "normative public deficiencies," such as tripping in front of a large class, forgetting someone's name, and making unintended bodily noises. They are the sorts of clumsy, absent-minded, or hapless behaviors that one typically thinks of as embarrassing. In addition, however, Miller's catalog includes a broad range of circumstances, such as awkward social interactions, conspicuousness in the absence of any deficiency, "team transgressions" (embarrassed by a member of one's group), and "empathic" embarrassment.

A common question concerns the distinction between embarrassment and shame. Is there a difference between the two emotions, or are they pretty much the same affective experience? Although some theorists have essentially equated the two emotions (Izard, 1977; Kaufman, 1989; Lewis, 1971), a more dominant view is that shame and embarrassment can be distinguished according to intensity of affect (e.g., Borg, Staufenbiel, & Scherer, 1988), severity of transgression (Buss, 1980; Lewis, 1992; Ortony, Clore, & Collins, 1988), or both. Shame is generally seen as a more intense emotion than embarrassment, resulting from more serious failures and moral transgressions. Embarrassment, in contrast, is thought to arise in response to relatively trivial social transgressions or untoward interactions.

In recent years, several researchers have conducted studies to systematically compare shame and embarrassment (Babcock & Sabini, 1990; Manstead & Tetlock, 1989; Miller & Tangney, 1994; Mosher & White, 1981; Tangney et al., 1996). Together, the studies suggest that shame and embarrassment are indeed quite different emotions—more distinct, even, than shame and guilt! For example, in a study comparing young adults' personal shame, guilt, and embarrassment experiences, Tangney et al. (1996) found that compared with embarrassment, shame was a more intense, painful emotion that involved a greater sense of moral transgression. Even with intensity and morality controlled, however, shame and embarrassment differed markedly along a range of affective, cognitive, and motivational dimensions. For example, shamed participants felt greater responsibility and regret. They felt more angry and disgusted with themselves and believed that others, too, felt anger toward them. In contrast, embarrassment events involved more humor and occurred more suddenly and with a greater sense of surprise. Embarrassment also was accompanied by more obvious physiological changes (e.g., blushing) and by a greater sense of exposure and conspicuousness. Conversely, little support was found for Modigliani's (1968) assumption (see also Klass, 1990; Shott, 1979) that embarrassment results more from losses of perceived approval from others than from changes in self-appraisal.

Pride

Mascolo and Fischer (1995) defined *pride* as an emotion "generated by appraisals that one is responsible for a socially valued outcome or for being a socially valued person" (p. 66). From their perspective, pride enhances people's self-worth and encourages future behavior that conforms to social standards of worth or merit (see also Barrett, 1995).

Both Tangney (1990) and Lewis (1992) have suggested that two types of pride may exist. Paralleling the self-versus-behavior distinction of guilt and shame, Tangney (1990) distinguished between pride in self (i.e., *alpha pride*) and pride in behavior (i.e., *beta pride*). In a similar vein, Lewis (1992) distinguished between pride and hubris: According to Lewis, pride is experienced when one's success is attributed to a specific action or behavior; hubris (or pridefulness) arises when success is attributed to the global self.

Lewis (1993) viewed *hubris* as a largely maladaptive reaction: It is "something dislikeable and to be avoided" (p. 570) in part because hubristic people may distort and invent situations to sustain this positive but transient emotion. Furthermore, Lewis observed, people do not like those who are hubristic. It is worth noting, however, that most of Lewis's discussions focus on hubris as a trait (i.e., tendencies to experience hubris frequently across multiple situations), rather than as a state (e.g., momentary feelings of pride in self). Whether momentary (and, possibly, well-deserved) experiences of hubris are maladaptive or socially annoying remains an open question.

Perfectionism and the "Self-Evaluative," Self-Conscious Emotions

Shame, guilt, embarrassment, and pride are emotions of self-evaluation. People experience those emotions when they evaluate aspects of our self (e.g., core personality characteristics; abilities; behaviors; or closely associated, identity-defining others) in reference to some set of standards.

Although everyone self-evaluates with some regularity, perfectionists make it a full-time job. Perfectionists not only set unusually high standards for themselves. They invest a great deal of time and energy into the process of evaluation itself as a result of at least two factors. First, perfectionists are inclined to develop rigid, inflexible notions of success and failure. Success is an all-or-nothing matter; that is, to qualify as a success, the job, product, or performance must be perfect in all respects, so careful scrutiny is required. A quick scan will not do—evaluation must be comprehensive and complete. Second, perfectionists are inclined to require superior performance across multiple domains. Compared with the average person, they tend to be rather indiscriminate, demanding perfection even in areas in which high performance does not really matter. Whereas most people have the ability to "lay back" and take a break from self-evaluation when doing so is appropriate, the perfectionist never really takes a vacation from the "report card." In short, perfectionists grade themselves hard, often, and with considerable vigor.

What are the affective implications of living with a report card on a daily basis? One could speculate that as a result of all this self-evaluation, perfectionists might be especially prone to emotions of self-evaluation. Their emotional life may be disproportionately occupied with feelings of shame, guilt, embarrassment, and pride. Furthermore, negative self-evaluative emotions may be especially salient in perfectionists' experience. Because they evaluate themselves against unusually high, often unrealistic standards, perfectionists substantially broaden the range of outcomes that they would classify as failures. Thus, perfectionists may be particularly well-acquainted with negative self-evaluative emotions.

Moreover, perfectionists may be especially vulnerable to feelings of shame. Perfectionists hold a set of assumptions regarding the meaning and implications of their mistakes and failures that naturally leads them down the path to feelings of shame and disgrace. First, perfectionists are inclined to engage in all-or-nothing thinking (Hewitt, Flett, Turnbull-Donovan, & Mikail, 1991). The product is either perfect in its every detail, or it is bad, wrong, a failure. Second, perfectionists are inclined to overgeneralize failures once they are perceived to have occurred (Hewitt & Flett, 1991; Hewitt et al., 1991). From the perspective of a perfectionist, a failure on one task, at one particular point in time, is indicative of a more general and pervasive pattern of failures. The taint of failure spreads and extends across time and domain—and, eventually, from situation or behavior to the person. It is not just the specific job or performance that is a failure; it is the wretched perfectionist him- or herself that is a failure. As Hewitt, Flett, and Ediger (1996) noted, perfectionists are inclined to equate "perfect" performance with self-worth. By the same token, they are apt to view less-than-perfect outcomes (failures, in their eyes) as a sign of worthlessness. Referring back to the discussion of shame versus guilt experiences, this focus on the global self, as opposed to context-specific behavior, lies at the heart of the distinction between shame and guilt. The bottom line is that the idiosyncratic manner in which perfectionists evaluate and interpret their mistakes and failures would appear to lead them inexorably toward the experience of shame.

In contrast to feelings of shame about the self, feelings of guilt about specific behaviors may be less salient in the experience of the perfectionist. When perfectionists err, they focus not merely on a specific mistake or transgression; their failures have broad implications for the self ("with a capital S"). In fact, one might expect an *inverse* relationship between perfectionism and tendencies to experience guilt about specific behaviors, independent of shame about the self.

Dimensions of Perfectionism: Self-Oriented, Socially Prescribed, and Other-Oriented

Thus far, I have discussed the possible affective implications of perfectionism, in general, assuming self-directed perfectionistic standards and cognitions. Recently, Hewitt and Flett (1991) made some intriguing distinctions among different forms of perfectionism, adding new depth to our consideration of this construct. Hewitt and Flett's approach examines the phenomenon of perfectionism from multiple perspectives, in effect varying both the subject and the object of perfectionistic expectations.

Self-oriented perfectionism is what people generally think of when they think of perfectionism. The self-oriented perfectionist holds him- or herself to unusually high standards, demanding perfection in his or her own products and behavior. Thus, in self-oriented perfectionism, the respondent is both the subject and object of often unrealistically high expectations. *Socially prescribed perfectionism* involves the perception that significant others have unrealistically high expectations for oneself. The socially prescribed perfectionist feels compelled to live up to the standards of others; therefore, significant others are the subject and the respondent is the object of expectations. Finally, *other-oriented perfectionism* involves a person's high expectations for significant others: The other-oriented perfectionist holds important *other* people to unrealistically high standards. Thus, in other-oriented perfectionism, the respondent is the subject, but others are the object of perfectionistic expectations.

No doubt, the distinct forms of perfectionism have somewhat different implications for the quality of emotional experience when the object of perfectionistic expectations falls short, matches, or exceeds relevant standards. Specifically, as the winds of fate and fortune shift and the self is evaluated anew, self-oriented and socially prescribed perfectionists would presumably be inclined toward experiences of shame, guilt, embarrassment, or pride. The self-conscious or self-evaluative emotions seem most likely to arise in the context of self-oriented and socially prescribed perfectionism, the two forms of perfectionism in which the self is the object. Other-oriented perfectionism, in contrast, may be more closely linked to non-self-reflective emotions, such as anger, disgust, sadness, disappointment, and so forth.

Moreover, following up on an earlier theme, it is my guess that self-oriented and socially prescribed perfectionists would be especially vulnerable to negative self-evaluative emotions—to shame, in particular—because they evaluate themselves (or believe others evaluate them) against unusually high, often unrealistic standards. As a consequence, the two types of perfectionists inevitably "fail" with considerable regularity. To make matters worse, such failures are construed as signifying general flaws that reflect shamefully on the miserable self of the perfectionist.

The hypothesized link between proneness to shame and perfectionism may be especially pronounced for socially prescribed perfectionists because of their common concern with others' evaluations. As noted earlier, when considering the objective nature of emotion-eliciting situations, no evidence indicates that shame is more likely than guilt to involve an observing audience (Tangney et al., 1994, 1996). In fact, both emotions are typically experienced in the presence of others. Subjectively, however, shame- and guilt-eliciting situations are experienced differently. Phenomenological studies (e.g., Lewis, 1971; Lindsay-Hartz, 1984; Lindsay-Hartz, de Rivera, & Mascolo, 1995; Miller & Tangney, 1994; Tangney, 1993; Tangney et al., 1994, 1996; Wicker, Payne, & Morgan, 1983) have indicated that shame is often associated with the imagery of an evaluating, disapproving other. Put another way, shame and guilt experiences are social emotions; they each involve a focus on other people as well as the self. The nature of the concern differs, however. In a shame experience, people are differentially concerned with others' evaluation of themselves; in a guilt experience, people are more concerned with their (presumably negative) effect on others.

Along the same lines as shame, socially prescribed perfectionism is steeped in a preoccupation with other people's standards, opinions, and evaluations. In fact, Hewitt and Flett (1991) found that socially prescribed perfectionism (but not self-oriented perfectionism) is related to fear of negative evaluation. The common focus on external evaluation suggests that socially prescribed perfectionism, even more so than self-oriented perfectionism, should be associated with a vulnerability to shame experiences. Similarly, one might anticipate a close link between socially prescribed perfectionism and proneness to embarrassment. Embarrassment, too, involves a focus on others' reactions to and evaluations of one's hapless missteps and blunders.

Previous Empirical Studies of Perfectionism, Shame, and Guilt (and Closely Related Constructs)

Actual empirical research on perfectionism and the self-evaluative emotions has so far been pretty sketchy. Several studies have attempted to examine directly the relationship between perfectionism and proneness to shame and guilt. Interpretation of the studies, however, is difficult because of problems in the measurement of shame and guilt. For example, using the Dimensions of Conscience Questionnaire (DCQ; Johnson et al., 1987), Christensen, Danko, and Johnson (1993) found that proneness to shame and guilt were negligibly related to perfectionism. In contrast, embarrassability was moderately positively correlated with perfectionism. The DCQ assesses the degree to which respondents would react to a range of "shame-inducing" versus "guilt-inducing" situations. Ratings for shame-inducing and guilt-inducing situations are aggregated to create indices of shame proneness and guilt proneness, respectively. A critical assumption underlying this approach is that the types of situations that elicit shame and guilt differ significantly—that shame and guilt are distinguished precisely by differences in the content of eliciting situations. As discussed earlier, however, much theoretical and empirical work challenges this notion, beginning with Lewis (1971) and extending to Taylor (1985); Tangney (1992); Tangney et al. (1994); and Niedenthal, Tangney, and Gavanski (1994). Therefore, the basic premise of this type of measure is, at best, questionable. Moreover, Christensen et al. (1993) used Hewitt and Flett's Multidimensional Perfectionism Scale (MPS) (1991) to assess perfectionism but did not report results for the three dimensions of perfectionism (self-oriented, socially prescribed, and other-oriented). It appears that they combined items from all three domains (the methods section is rather sketchy) into a single index of perfectionism, an approach that is questionable as well, given the evidence that the dimensions are theoretically and empirically distinct.

In their comprehensive evaluation of the validity of the MPS, Hewitt and Flett (1991) also examined the relationship of perfectionism to individual differences in shame proneness and guilt proneness. Results showed modest positive correlations between all three dimensions of perfectionism and indices of both shame and guilt, as assessed by Klass's (1987) Problem Situation Questionnaire. (Only the correlation between guilt and self-oriented perfectionism was statistically significant, but the other correlations were only marginally lower in magnitude.) Similarly, Rickner and Tan (1994) found a positive correlation between perfectionism and guilt, as assessed by the Klass measure. Unfortunately, here, too, the results are difficult to interpret because of conceptual limitations with the assessment of shame and guilt. Like the DCQ, Klass's Problem Situation Questionnaire assesses the degree to which respondents would react to a range of shame-inducing versus guilt-inducing situations. Again, the critical assumption underlying this approach—that shame and guilt can be distinguished by the content of eliciting situations—is highly questionable in light of more recent theory and research (Lewis, 1971; Tangney, 1992; Tangney et al., 1994; Taylor, 1985).

Several other studies, although not assessing shame and guilt directly, provide evidence suggesting that perfectionistic tendencies may be differentially related to shame-proneness but not guilt-proneness. Frost et al. (1995, 1997) examined in considerable depth the dynamics, concerns, and beliefs associated with Concern Over Mistakes (CM), a key dimension of perfectionism assessed by their measure. In both studies, the researchers found that, compared with low-CM participants, participants who scored high on CM were more inclined to hide their mistakes from others (a motivation also closely associated with shame). Evidence from Frost et al. (1997) suggested that the tendency toward concealment is rooted in self-evaluative, self-presentational concerns. High-CM participants were more worried than low-CM participants about other people's reactions to their mistakes, and that worry did not appear to result from any other-oriented concerns about the welfare of others. That is, high-CM participants did not differ from low-CM participants in the types of mistakes they made or reported, or in the degree to which they believed their mistakes were harmful to others. Rather, compared with low-CM participants, high-CM participants believed that their mistakes caused more harm to themselves, personally—presumably because of the negative evaluations they anticipated from others. In short, high-CM perfectionists show the same pattern of egocentric concerns displayed by people in the midst of a shame experience (e.g., Tangney et al., 1994). Like shamed people, high-CM perfectionists are not so much concerned about the harmful effect of their mistakes on others but rather about the effect of their mistakes on other people's evaluations of themselves.

Taking an entirely different approach, Hankin, Roberts, and Gotlib (1997) examined the links between perfectionism and self-discrepancies, drawing on Higgins's (1987) framework and measures. To fully appreciate Hankin et al.'s (1997) results, a little background on self-discrepancy theory and shame and guilt may be helpful. At the heart of self-discrepancy theory (Higgins, 1987) is the notion that different types of self-discrepancies (i.e., between one's actual self and several distinct types of "self-guides"[2]) are differentially associated with distinct forms of negative affect. Most relevant to our interests, Higgins (1987) predicted that actual–own versus ideal–other discrepancies would result in a tendency to experience shame, whereas actual–own versus ought–own discrepancies would lead to a tendency to experience guilt.

On the basis of recent theory and research concerning shame and guilt, we recently proposed and tested an alternative hypothesis (Tangney, Niedenthal, Covert, & Barlow, 1998). We reasoned that because shame involves a negative evaluation of the self, whereas guilt involves a negative evaluation of a specific behavior, self-discrepancies of all kinds should be highly relevant to the experience of shame but only tangentially relevant to the experience of guilt. That is, the recognition that one's actual self falls short of any aspired-to self-guide should render one vulnerable to feelings of shame—since the object of shame is the self. Conversely, self-discrepancies assessed without reference to any specific, regretted behavior should be less relevant to guilt. Our results were clearly consistent with our predictions: Proneness to shame, but not to guilt, was associated with self-discrepancies of all sorts. In general, little evidence indicated that specific types of self-discrepancies are associated with specific types of negative affect (Tangney et al., 1998).

Turning back to the Hankin et al. (1997) study, the investigators focused on the links between perfectionism (using Hewitt & Flett's MPS) and self-discrepancies (using Higgins's Selves Questionnaire, but assessing only two of the four standard self-guides—ideal–own judgments, which involve the discrepancy between ideal characteristics and personal characteristics, and ought–other judgments, which involve prescribed expectations from other people). Socially prescribed perfectionism was positively related to both actual own/ideal–own and actual–own/ought–other discrepancies. (The actual–own/ought–other correlation itself narrowly missed statistical significance, but it was not reliably different from the

---

[2]According to Higgins (1987), there are three basic domains of the self: (a) the *actual* self—attributes that either a person or a significant other believes that the person actually possesses; (b) the *ideal* self—attributes that a person or significant other would like the person, ideally, to possess; and (c) the *ought* self—attributes that a person or significant other believes the person should or ought to possess. The standpoint dimension represents the point of view or source of evaluation of the self: (a) one's *own* standpoint, or (b) the standpoint (or point of view) of significant *others*. Combining the *domains of the self* with the *standpoints on the self*, six basic types of self–state representations result: actual–own, actual–other, ideal–own, ideal–other, ought–own, and ought–other. The first two, the actual self-representations, comprise what is usually referred to as the self-concept. The remaining four combinations represent "self-guides."

actual–own/ideal–own correlation.) In contrast, self-oriented perfectionism was negatively but not significantly correlated with the two types of self-discrepancies. Given the theoretical and empirical links between shame and self-discrepancies (Tangney et al., 1998), the findings suggest that a special link may exist between shame and perfectionism, particularly socially prescribed perfectionism.

Dimensions of Perfectionism and Proneness to Self-Evaluative Emotions: New Data From Three Studies

To more directly examine the relationship between dimensions of perfectionism and the self-evaluative emotions using theoretically consistent measures of shame and guilt, I have drawn on data from three independent studies of college undergraduates recently conducted in our lab. In all, 249, 243, and 149 students participated in Studies 1, 2, and 3, respectively. In each sample, approximately 70% of the participants were female, and the majority were White.

Participants in each study completed our Test of Self-Conscious Affect (TOSCA; Tangney, Wagner, & Gramzow, 1989), which assesses individual differences in proneness to shame and guilt, externalization of blame, detachment and unconcern, alpha pride (pride in the entire self), and beta pride (pride in specific behaviors). The TOSCA is a scenario-based, paper-and-pencil measure that presents respondents with a range of situations that they are likely to encounter in day-to-day life. Each scenario is followed by responses that capture phenomenological aspects of shame, guilt, and other theoretically relevant experiences (e.g., externalization and pride). Respondents are asked to imagine themselves in each situation and to then rate their likelihood of reacting in each of the manners indicated. For example, in the adult TOSCA, participants are asked to imagine, "You make a big mistake on an important project at work. People were depending on you and your boss criticizes you." People then rate their likelihood of reacting with a shame response ("You would feel like you wanted to hide"), a guilt response ("You would think 'I should have recognized the problem and done a better job.'"), and so forth. Across the various scenarios, the responses capture affective, cognitive, and motivational features associated with shame and guilt, respectively, as described in the theoretical, phenomenological, and empirical literature. The measures are not forced choice; respondents are asked to rate each of the responses on a 5-point Likert-type scale. This approach allows for the possibility that some respondents may experience shame, guilt, both, or neither emotion in connection with a given situation. Tangney (1996) and Tangney et al. (1996) presented a summary of research supporting the reliability and validity of the TOSCA.

Participants in each study also completed Hewitt and Flett's MPS, a 45-item measure that assesses self-oriented perfectionism (e.g., "When I'm working on something, I cannot relax until it is perfect"), socially prescribed perfectionism (e.g., "I feel that people are too demanding of me"), and other-oriented perfectionism (e.g., "I have high expectations for the people who are important to me"). In addition, participants in Study 2 completed Modigliani's (1968) 26-item Embarrassability Scale.

Our preparations for Study 1 were somewhat imperfect: We inadvertently omitted the second page of the MPS. Thus, in Study 1, the Self-Oriented, Socially Prescribed, and Other-Oriented Perfectionism scales were composed of 8, 5, and 7 items, respectively, rather than the standard 15 items per scale. We straightened out this problem in Studies 2 and 3. As it turned out, an analysis of Study 2 and 3 data suggested that the results from Study 1 were likely close to what they would have been if we had administered the entire MPS. Using data from Studies 2 and 3, we created MPS subscales that were based only on items administered in Study 1 (i.e., from the first page). Correlations between the abbreviated and full versions of the scales were .96 and .94 for self-oriented perfectionism, .81 and .88 for socially prescribed perfectionism, and .86 and .86 for other-oriented perfectionism, in Studies 2 and 3, respectively.

Results across the three studies were quite consistent (Table 8.1). The most striking findings centered on shame: In all three studies, a dispositional tendency to experience shame across a range of situations was reliably linked to socially prescribed perfectionism. People who feel burdened by unrealistically high standards imposed upon them by others also

Table 8.1. Dimensions of Perfectionism and Proneness to Shame, Guilt, and Pride in Three Independent Samples of Undergraduates

Affective style	Study	Dimensions of perfectionism		
		Self-oriented	Socially prescribed	Other-oriented
Shame	Study 1	.08	.33***	.00
	Study 2	.14*	.26***	.03
	Study 3	−.02	.15$^+$	−.06
Shame residuals	Study 1	.05	.30***	−.01
	Study 2	.12	.33***	.04
	Study 3	−.01	.20*	−.05
Embarrassability	Study 2	.10	.31***	.04
Guilt	Study 1	.09	.13*	.01
	Study 2	.10	−.16*	−.04
	Study 3	−.02	−.06	−.03
Guilt residuals	Study 1	.05	−.05	.02
	Study 2	.05	−.26***	−.05
	Study 3	−.02	−.14$^+$	−.01
Alpha pride	Study 1	.02	−.04	.02
	Study 2	.08	.05	.22***
	Study 3	.06	.14$^+$	.14$^+$
Beta pride	Study 1	.09	−.00	.11
	Study 2	.02	−.01	.16*
	Study 3	.08	.12	.03

Note. Study 1, N = 249; Study 2, N = 243–248; Study 3, N = 149.
^+p < .10. *p < .05. **p < .01. ***p < .001.

are vulnerable to frequent and repeated experiences of shame. In contrast, the other two dimensions of perfectionism—self-oriented and other-oriented perfectionism—were largely uncorrelated with tendencies to experience shame. Similar findings were observed for embarrassability, assessed in Study 2.

The findings regarding guilt were less clear cut. Considering first the bivariate relationships, proneness to guilt about specific behaviors showed a modest but statistically significant positive correlation with socially prescribed perfectionism in Study 1 but a negative correlation in Study 2. Subsequent part-correlational analyses (see "Guilt Residuals") revealed that the positive correlation between guilt and socially prescribed perfectionism in Study 1 was largely a result of the influence of shame. Not surprisingly, proneness to shame and proneness to guilt are positively correlated—generally about .42 to .48 among college students and adults. This covariation no doubt reflects the fact that shame and guilt share several common features (e.g., both are dysphoric affects and involve internal attributions of one sort or another) and that the emotions can co-occur with respect to the same situation.

In addition to bivariate correlations, we generally conduct part correlations, in which we factor out shame from guilt and vice versa, to refine our analysis. In effect, the part correlations isolate the unique variance of shame and guilt, respectively, so that we can examine individual differences in a tendency to experience "shame-free" guilt and "guilt-free" shame (i.e., guilt residuals and shame residuals). As shown clearly in Table 8.1, people who are prone to feelings of guilt about specific behaviors that are uncomplicated by feelings of shame about the self are, if anything, disinclined toward socially prescribed perfectionism. Shame-free guilt was negligibly related to socially prescribed perfectionism in Study 1 and was significantly negatively correlated with socially prescribed perfectionism in Study 2; an analogous trend was found in Study 3. In contrast, self-oriented and other-oriented perfectionism were unrelated to guilt proneness according to both bivariate and part correlations.

Turning to the brighter side of self-evaluative emotions, tendencies to experience alpha pride and beta pride were unrelated to perfectionism vis-à-vis the self. Neither self-oriented nor socially prescribed perfectionism was linked to the TOSCA measures of pride. Some findings, however, particularly in Study 2, suggested that pridefulness is linked with other-oriented perfectionism. That is, people who experience feelings of pride with some regularity also are inclined to hold significant others to unusually high standards.

Summary and Conclusion

This chapter has focused on the affective implications of perfectionism, with a special emphasis on the self-evaluative emotions—shame, guilt, embarrassment, and pride. Perfectionists, by their very nature, engage in frequent and vigorous self-evaluation, the outcome of which is likely to significantly color their emotional lives. Little empirical research has directly examined the relationship between perfectionism and tendencies to experience the self-evaluative emotions. In light of theory and related lines of research, however, I hypothesized that self-oriented and, especially, socially prescribed perfectionists would be particularly vulnerable to feelings of shame as well as embarrassment. In contrast, theory suggests that feelings of guilt may be less salient in the experience of the perfectionist. In fact, one might expect an inverse relationship between perfectionism and tendencies to experience guilt about specific behaviors, independent of shame about the self.

Empirical results from three independent studies neatly confirmed this predicted pattern of findings for socially prescribed perfectionism but not for self-oriented perfectionism. Compared with the average person, socially prescribed perfectionists are indeed more prone to painful feelings of shame and embarrassment, and they are less inclined toward adaptive feelings of guilt about specific behaviors. Surprisingly (to me), self-oriented perfectionism was largely unrelated to tendencies to experience self-evaluative emotions.

Why are self-oriented perfectionists somehow able to elude the pervasive, painful tendencies to experience shame and embarrassment that haunt socially prescribed perfectionists? As described in greater detail in subsequent chapters, research suggests that socially prescribed perfectionism is the more maladaptive form of perfectionism when viewed in multiple domains. For example, compared with self-oriented perfectionism, socially prescribed perfectionism is more strongly and consistently linked to indices of maladjustment, including depression, anxiety, obsessive–compulsive symptoms, and somatic complaints (Hewitt & Flett, 1991, 1993). One possibility is that self-oriented perfectionists are more selective in the domains in which they demand perfection. The range may be narrower, and the domains may be more ego syntonic (i.e., consistent with the self's strengths and goals). In short, self-oriented perfectionists may select a more "doable" task. In contrast, socially prescribed perfectionists may feel that they have little choice in the types of standards they must meet and succeed. Standards and goals are experienced as externally imposed; moreover, because multiple "others" may be viewed as prescribing excellence in multiple domains, specific goals and standards may be likely to conflict with one another. In short, socially prescribed perfectionists may be handed (or perceive that they have been handed) an impossible task. In their case, shame and failure may seem inevitable.

Hewitt and Flett have broadened and enriched our conceptualization of perfectionism by distinguishing among three types of perfectionistic strivings. This chapter has focused most heavily on self-oriented and socially prescribed forms of perfectionism, but other-oriented perfectionism is an intriguing dimension in its own right, especially in its implications for interpersonal relationships. Our studies of undergraduates suggested a link between tendencies to experience pride and other-oriented perfectionism: It seems that prideful people feel especially entitled to demand perfection from significant others. The results are consistent with Hewitt,

Flett, and Turnbull's (1992) observation of a link between narcissism and other-oriented perfectionism, and they lend some support for Lewis's (1993) notion that the tendency to experience pride is a "mixed bag": Hubris is not an attractive trait in the interpersonal world. Finally, all things being equal, one might do well to avoid the burden of socially prescribed perfectionism imposed by a prideful, other-oriented perfectionistic significant other.

References

Babcock, M. K., & Sabini, J. (1990). On differentiating embarrassment from shame. *European Journal of Social Psychology, 20,* 151–169.

Barrett, K. C. (1995). A functionalist approach to shame and guilt. In J. P. Tangney & K. W. Fischer (Eds.), *Self-conscious emotions: Shame, guilt, embarrassment, and pride* (pp. 25–63). New York: Guilford.

Benedict, R. (1946). *The chrysanthemum and the sword.* Boston: Houghton Mifflin.

Borg, I., Staufenbiel, T., & Scherer, K. R. (1988). On the symbolic basis of shame. In K. R. Scherer (Ed.), *Facets of emotion: Recent research* (pp. 79–98). Hillsdale, NJ: Erlbaum.

Buss, A. H. (1980). *Self-consciousness and social anxiety.* San Francisco: W. H. Freeman and Company.

Christensen, B. J., Danko, G. P., & Johnson, R. C. (1993). Neuroticism and the belief that one is being scrutinized and evaluated by others. *Personality and Individual Differences, 15,* 349–350.

Cupach, W. R., & Metts, S. (1992). The effects of type of predicament and embarrassability on remedial responses to embarrassing situations. *Communications Quarterly, 40,* 149–161.

Frost, R. O., Trepanier, K. L., Brown, E. J., Heimberg, R. G., Juster, H. R., Makris, G. S., & Leung, A. W. (1997). Self-monitoring of mistakes among subjects high and low in perfectionistic concern over mistakes. *Cognitive Therapy and Research, 21,* 209–222.

Frost, R. O., Turcotte, T. A., Heimberg, R. G., Mattia, J. I., Holt, C. S., & Hope, D. A. (1995). Self-monitoring of mistakes among subjects high and low in perfectionistic concern over mistakes. *Cognitive Therapy and Research, 19,* 195–205.

Gehm, T. L., & Scherer, K. R. (1988). Relating situation evaluation to emotion differentiation: Nonmetric analysis of cross-cultural questionnaire data. In K. R. Scherer (Ed.), *Facets of emotion: Recent research* (pp. 61–77). Hillsdale, NJ: Erlbaum.

Hankin, B. L., Roberts, J., & Gotlib, I. H. (1997). Elevated self-standards and emotional distress during adolescence: Emotional specificity and gender differences. *Cognitive Therapy and Research, 21,* 663–679.

Hewitt, P. L., & Flett, G. L. (1991). Perfectionism in the self and social context: Conceptualization, assessment, and association with psychopathology. *Journal of Personality and Social Psychology, 60,* 456–470.

Hewitt, P. L., & Flett, G. L. (1993). Dimensions of perfectionism, daily stress, and depression: A test of the specific vulnerability hypothesis. *Journal of Abnormal Psychology, 102,* 58–65.

Hewitt, P. L., Flett, G. L., & Ediger, E. (1996). Perfectionism and depression: Longitudinal assessment of a specific vulnerability hypothesis. *Journal of Abnormal Psychology, 105,* 276–280.

Hewitt, P. L., Flett, G. L., & Turnbull, W. (1992). Perfectionism and Multiphasic Personality Inventory (MMPI) indices of personality disorder. *Journal of Psychopathology and Behavioral Assessment, 14,* 323–335.

Hewitt, P. L., Flett, G. L., Turnbull-Donovan, W., & Mikail, S. F. (1991). The Multidimensional Perfectionism Scale: Reliability, validity, and psychometric properties in a psychiatric sample. *Psychological Assessment: A Journal of Consulting and Clinical Psychology, 3,* 464–468.

Higgins, E. T. (1987). Self-discrepancy: A theory relating self and affect. *Psychological Review, 94,* 319–340.

Izard, C. E. (1977). *Human emotions.* New York: Plenum.

Johnson, R. C., Danko, G. P., Huang, Y. H., Park, J. Y., Johnson, S. B., & Nagoshi, C. T. (1987). Guilt, shame and adjustment in three cultures. *Personality and Individual Differences, 8,* 357–364.

Kaufman, G. (1989). *The psychology of shame: Theory and treatment of shame-based syndromes.* New York: Springer.

Klass, E. T. (1987). Situational approach to the assessment of guilt: Development and validation of a self-report measure. *Journal of Psychopathology and Behavioral Assessment, 9,* 35–48.

Klass, E. T. (1990). Guilt, shame, and embarrassment: Cognitive–behavioral approaches. In H. Leitenberg (Ed.), *Handbook of social and evaluation anxiety* (pp. 385–414). New York: Plenum.

Lewis, H. B. (1971). *Shame and guilt in neurosis.* New York: International Universities Press.

Lewis, M. (1992). *Shame: The exposed self.* New York: Free Press.

Lewis, M. (1993). Self-conscious emotions: Embarrassment, pride, shame, and guilt. In M. Lewis & J. Haviland (Eds.), *Handbook of emotions* (pp. 563–573). New York: Guilford.

Lindsay-Hartz, J. (1984). Contrasting experiences of shame and guilt. *American Behavioral Scientist, 27,* 689–704.

Lindsay-Hartz, J., de Rivera, J., & Mascolo, M. (1995). Differentiating shame and guilt and their effects on motivation. In J. P. Tangney & K. W. Fischer (Eds.), *Self-conscious emotions: Shame, guilt, embarrassment, and pride* (pp. 274–300). New York: Guilford.

Manstead, A. S. R., & Tetlock, P. E. (1989). Cognitive appraisals and emotional experience: Further evidence. *Cognition and Emotion, 3,* 225–240.

Mascolo, M. F., & Fischer, K. W. (1995). Developmental transformation in appraisals for pride, shame, and guilt. In J. P. Tangney & K. W. Fischer (Eds.), *Self-conscious emotions: Shame, guilt, embarrassment, and pride* (pp. 64–113). New York: Guilford.

Miller, R. S. (1992). The nature and severity of self-reported embarrassing circumstances. *Personality and Social Psychology Bulletin, 18,* 190–198.

Miller, R. S. (1995). Embarrassment and social behavior. In J. P. Tangney & K. W. Fischer (Eds.), *Self-conscious emotions: Shame, guilt, embarrassment, and pride* (pp. 322–339). New York: Guilford.

Miller, R. S., & Tangney, J. P. (1994). Differentiating embarrassment and shame. *Journal of Social and Clinical Psychology, 13,* 273–287.

Modigliani, A. (1968). Embarrassment and embarrassability. *Sociometry, 31,* 313–326.

Mosher, D. L., & White, B. B. (1981). On differentiating shame and shyness. *Motivation and Emotion, 1,* 61–74.

Niedenthal, P. M., Tangney, J. P., & Gavanski, I. (1994). "If only I weren't" versus "If only I hadn't": Distinguishing shame and guilt in counterfactual thinking. *Journal of Personality and Social Psychology, 67,* 585–595.

Ortony, A., Clore, G. L., & Collins, A. (1988). *The cognitive structure of emotions.* Cambridge, UK: Cambridge University Press.

Parrott, W. G., & Smith, S. F. (1991). Embarrassment: Actual vs. typical cases, classical vs. prototypical representations. *Cognition and Emotion, 5,* 467–488.

Rickner, R. G., & Tan, S. (1994). Psychopathology, guilt, perfectionism, and family of origin functioning among Protestant clergy. *Journal of Psychology and Theology, 22,* 29–38.

Shott, S. (1979). Emotion and social life: A symbolic interactionist analysis. *American Journal of Sociology, 84,* 1317–1334.

Tangney, J. P. (1990). Assessing individual differences in proneness to shame and guilt: Development of the self-conscious affect and attribution inventory. *Journal of Personality and Social Psychology, 59,* 102–111.

Tangney, J. P. (1992). Situational determinants of shame and guilt in young adulthood. *Personality and Social Psychology Bulletin, 18,* 199–206.

Tangney, J. P. (1993). Shame and guilt. In C. G. Costello (Ed.), *Symptoms of depression* (pp. 161–180). New York: John Wiley.

Tangney, J. P. (1996). Conceptual and methodological issues in the assessment of shame and guilt. *Behaviour Research and Therapy, 34,* 741–754.

Tangney, J. P., Marschall, D. E., Rosenberg, K., Barlow, D. H., & Wagner, P. E. (1994). *Children's and adults' autobiographical accounts of shame, guilt and pride experiences: An analysis of situational determinants and interpersonal concerns.* Unpublished manuscript, George Mason University, Fairfax, VA.

Tangney, J. P., Miller, R. S., Flicker, L., & Barlow, D. H. (1996). Are shame, guilt and embarrassment distinct emotions? *Journal of Personality and Social Psychology, 70,* 1256–1269.

Tangney, J. P., Niedenthal, P. M., Covert, M. V., & Barlow, D. H. (1998). Are shame and guilt related to self-discrepancies? A test of Higgins's (1987) hypotheses. *Journal of Personality and Social Psychology, 75,* 256–268.

Tangney, J. P., Wagner, P., & Gramzow, R. (1989). *The Test of Self-Conscious Affect* (TOSCA). Unpublished measure, George Mason University, Fairfax, VA.

Taylor, G. (1985). *Pride, shame and guilt: Emotions of self-assessment.* Oxford, UK: Clarendon Press.

Wicker, F. W., Payne, G. C., & Morgan, R. D. (1983). Participant descriptions of guilt and shame. *Motivation and Emotion, 7,* 25–39.

9

The Role of Irrational Beliefs in Perfectionism

Albert Ellis

The importance of perfectionism in helping people become anxious, depressed, and otherwise emotionally disturbed was at least vaguely seen by the Stoics and Epictetus (Epictetus, 1899; Xenakis, 1969) and has been pointed out by pioneering cognitive therapists such as Alfred Adler (1926, 1927), Pierre Dubois (1907), and Pierre Janet (1898) for more than a century. It also was noted by the non-Freudian psychoanalyst Karen Horney (1950) in her concept of the idealized image.

I was the first cognitive–behavioral therapist to specifically include perfectionism as an irrational, self-defeating belief in my original paper on rational–emotive behavior therapy (REBT), presented at the annual convention of the American Psychological Association in Chicago on August 31, 1956 (Ellis, 1958). Thus, among 12 basic irrational ideas that I included in this paper, I listed *perfectionism* as

> The idea that one should be thoroughly competent, adequate, intelligent, and achieving in all possible respects—instead of the idea that one should *do* rather than desperately try to do well and that one should accept oneself as an imperfect creature, who has general human limitations and specific fallibilities. (p. 41)

In my first book for the public, *How To Live With a Neurotic* (1957), I included among the main irrational ideas leading to disturbance,

> A person should be thoroughly competent, adequate, talented, and intelligent in all possible respects; the main goal and purpose of life is achievement and success; incompetence in anything whatsoever is an indication that a person is inadequate or valueless. (p. 89)

I also noted, "*Perfectionism.* . . . Excessive striving to be perfect will invariably lead to disillusionment, heartache, and self-hatred" (p. 89).

In 1962, after practicing, lecturing, and writing on REBT for seven years, I included in my first book for the psychological profession, *Reason and Emotion in Psychotherapy*, among 11 main irrational ideas that cause and maintain emotional disturbances:

217

2. The idea that one should be competent, achieving, and adequate in all possible respects if one is to consider oneself worthwhile. . . . 4. The idea that it is awful and catastrophic when things are not the way one would very much like them to be. . . . 11. The idea that there is invariably a right, precise, and perfect solution to human problems and that it is catastrophic if this perfect solution is not found. (pp. 69–88)

Obviously, REBT has particularly stressed the irrationality and self-defeatism of perfectionism from its start. Scores of REBT articles and books have made this point endlessly, including many of my own publications (Ellis, 1988; Ellis & Dryden, 1997; Ellis, Gordon, Neenan, & Palmer, 1997; Ellis & Harper, 1997; Ellis & Tafrate, 1997; Ellis & Velten, 1998) and publications by other leading REBTers (Bernard, 1993; Dryden, 1998; Hauck, 1991; Walen, DiGuiseppe, & Dryden, 1992). Following REBT's identification of perfectionism as an important irrational belief, the vast literature has been devoted in recent years to the findings and treatment of perfectionism; cognitive–behavioral therapy also has frequently emphasized the psychological harm and the treatment of perfectionism. A. Beck (1976) and Burns (1980) particularly emphasized its importance, and many other cognitive behaviorists have described it and its treatment (Barlow, 1989; J. Beck, 1995; Flett, Hewitt, Blankstein, & Koledin, 1991; Flett, Hewitt, Blankstein, Solnik, & Van Brunschot, 1996; Freeman & DeWolf, 1993; Goldfried & Davison, 1994; Hewitt & Flett, 1993; Lazarus, Lazarus, & Fay, 1993).

Although I have been one of the main theorists and therapists to emphasize the importance of perfectionism in emotional and behavioral disturbance, I now see that I have never described what the rational or self-helping elements in perfectionism are, how they accompany the irrational and self-defeating elements, and why they probably "naturally" exist and impede humanity's surrendering its strong perfectionistic tendencies. Because this entire book is about perfectionism, it might be good if I were more specific than I have been about these important aspects of it.

The main idea of rationality and irrationality in human behavior stems from the ancient notion that humans, in order to stay alive and well-functioning, have several basic desires, goals, and preferences—which are often incorrectly called *needs* or *necessities*—that help them do so. Thus, people are commonly said to survive better and be more effective when they

1.   have a sense of self-efficacy or self-mastery (ego satisfactions);
2.   actually succeed in getting what they want and avoiding what they don't want (goal or accomplishment satisfaction);
3.   get approval and minimal disapproval of other people whom they consider important (love and approval satisfaction); and
4.   are safe and sound, and not likely to be diseased, hurt, or killed (safety satisfaction).

It is not that people *cannot* exist or *must be* completely miserable if they don't fulfill any or all of these desires and goals; therefore, we had better not call them *needs* or *dire necessities*. But it is usually agreed—and we can tentatively accept for the sake of the following discussion—that humans tend to be better off (happier) and live longer (survive) when they achieve those four goals than when they fail to achieve them.

Assuming—for the sake of discussion and not to posit any absolute truth—that people are more likely to survive and to be glad they're alive if they satisfy the four basic urges or wants mentioned above, then they can probably justifiably take the first of these urges or goals—ego satisfaction—and rationally reach the following conclusion:

> If I have self-inefficacy and view myself as only being able to function badly, and definitely to function imperfectly, I actually will tend to function less well than I am theoretically able to function. Therefore,
>
> 1. I will probably actually get less of what I want and more of what I don't want as I go through life (because I think I am unable to perform well).
> 2. I will probably get less approval and love from significant other people (because, again, I think I am unable to get it).
> 3. I will probably be in more danger of being harmed and killed by dangerous conditions (because I think I am unable to take precautions and cope with threat).

If, in other words, failing to perform well or perfectly well and succeeding in performing badly or imperfectly *will* likely get you less of what you want; less approval from others; and make you less likely to be safe from disease, harm, and death, and if your sense of self-inefficacy will impede you from performing well or perfectly well, then it is quite rational (i.e., self-helping) to have a sense of self-efficacy—as many studies by Bandura (1997) and his followers tend to show. Your *wish* or *desire* to have a sense of self-efficacy, and thereby improve your chances of performing well, being approved by others, and being safe from harm or death, is therefore a rational belief, not an irrational belief.

You also may have an irrational, self-defeating belief about self-efficacy, however, such as, "Because I *desire* to have a sense of self-efficacy, I *absolutely must* have it, else I am a worthless, unlovable, hopelessly endangered person!" To go one step further, your irrational belief about self-efficacy may be, "Because I desire to have it, I *absolutely must,* under all conditions at all times perfectly have it!" Lots of luck with that belief!

What I have said about the goal of self-efficacy also goes for the desire to *be* efficacious, productive, efficient, and accomplished. Such aims are usually rational in that if you perform well and, perhaps, perfectly well, you will *in all likelihood* in most of today's world (although who knows about tomorrow's?) get more of what you want, greater approval (and also envy and jealousy!), and more security and longer life. So under most conditions—although hardly all—if you want to achieve those goals, you try to achieve them. As long as you merely *wish for,* but not *demand,* their achievement, you will (says REBT theory) feel frustrated, sorry, and disappointed but not depressed, anxious, or angry when you do not achieve them.

Escalating your *desire* for success and accomplishment to a *demand,* and especially to a *perfectionistic* demand, is quite another matter! Listen to this: "I *absolutely must*—or under all conditions at all times—*perfectly achieve* my goals!" Or else? Or else you will tend to conclude that you'll *never* get what you want. Or else you'll be *totally* unworthy of approval and love by significant others. Or else you will be in *continual danger* of harm and annihilation. Quite a series of "horrors" you've predicted—and helped bring on yourself.

If what I have been saying so far is correct, you can easily and legitimately have rational, sane, self-helping *desires* for success and achievement—and even for perfect achievement. For example, you can wish for a 100% grade on a test or the approval of all the people you find significant. That would be nice. But don't make it necessary!

Once again, you can have desires—even strong desires—for others' approval. It probably would be great if you acted the way they wanted you to act—and if they always, under all conditions, perfectly favored you. They might well give you more of what you want and less of what you dislike. Fine! But if you *need* others' approval, and especially if you need their undying, perfect approval, watch it! Raising your want to a necessity is your irrationality. Quite a difference!

What about your striving for safety, security, good health, and longevity? By all means strive—but not desperately, compulsively. If you distinctly want security measures like these, you will, perhaps, also notice their disadvantages and restrictions. The safer you make yourself, the more you may sacrifice adventure and experimentation. So you have a choice. A safe, long life is not necessarily a merry one. Caution and concern, as wants and choices, may have real value for you. But to *absolutely need* safety is to make yourself anxious and panicked. And, quite probably, it is likely to bring on some needless dangers.

What I have been saying so far shows that having self-efficacy, competence, lovability, and safety tend to aid human living. Not always, of course, and with some exceptions. For most of the people most of the time, they are characteristics that seem to have more advantages than disadvantages. Therefore, few individuals and groups do not strive for these goals. If they are, in fact, more beneficial than harmful, you are rational or self-helping when you aim for them. Why, then, should you irrationally and self-sabotagingly do yourself in by frequently escalating your desires to unrealistic and often perfectionistic demands? Why do you often turn them into foolish, absolutistic musts?

The usual answer psychologists give to this paradox is a combination of innate, biological tendencies of humans and their early conditioning or rearing. First, for evolutionary, survival reasons they are born wishers *and* demanders, instead of mere wishers. Second, their parents and teachers reinforce their wishing and demandingness and often help make them worse. Third, they practice both wishing and demanding and become habituated to and comfortable with both behaviors; hence, they continue desiring and insisting for the rest of their lives.

These all are probably good reasons why both rational preferring and irrational demanding are so common among practically all people and lead to great benefits and detriments. Over the past 55 years of doing psychotherapy with thousands of people, I have figured out some more specific reasons why humans are "demanders" and "musturbators" when they would probably be much less disturbed if they were mainly "preferrers" and "unimperative goal seekers." Let me present the following ideas as hypotheses that are yet to be tested but will possibly add to our understanding of perfectionism if they are tested and receive some creditable empirical support:

1. People have little difficulty in distinguishing their weak or moderate desires from their demands, but they frequently have great difficulty distinguishing their strong, forceful wishes from insistences. When they have a weak or moderate desire to succeed at an important task, to gain social approval, or to be safe from harm, they rarely or occasionally think that they *absolutely must* achieve those goals, but when they have strong desires to do those things, they frequently insist that they *have* to have them. *Why* they have weak or strong desires depends on many factors, both biological and environmental. But my theory says that once, for any reason, they *do* have powerful wishes—or what Wolcott Gibbs, a *New Yorker* writer, called "a whim of iron"—they frequently think, and especially *feel,* that they *must* attain them.

2. A mild or moderate preference to perform well or win others' approval implies the legitimacy of alternative behaviors. Thus: "I would moderately like to win this tennis match *but* if I lose it's no big deal, and I can probably go on and win the next one." "I would moderately prefer to have Mary like me, *but* if she doesn't, I can live without her approval and probably get Jane, who is not much different from Mary, to like me." If you *mildly* want something and don't get it, there is a good chance that you can get something almost equally desirable instead.

    A strong preference, however, often leaves few alternative choices of equal valence. Thus: "I *greatly* want to win the tennis match, and thereby become champion, so if I lose it I will lose the championship—which I also *strongly* want to win—and never gain it at *all*. Therefore, I *must* win this match to get what I *really* want." "I greatly want to have Mary like me, because she is a *special* person with whom I could be *notably* happy. Therefore, if Mary doesn't like me, and I could be close to Jane instead of her, this is a poor alternative, and it will not really satisfy me. Therefore, I *must* get Mary to like me."

    Strong preferences, consequently, leave little room for alternative choices—or, at least, *equally* satisfying ones—and imply that because alternatives don't exist, you *must* have your strong preferences fulfilled. By their very *strength*, they prejudice you against alternative choices and make your particular choice seem mandatory instead of preferential.

3. Strong desires encourage you, just because of their strength, to focus, sometimes almost obsessive–compulsively, on *one* choice or a *special* choice and to ignore or disparage alternative choices. Thus, if you *mildly* want to win a tennis match, you are free to think of many other things—such as the pleasure your opponent will have if he or she wins instead of you or the fact that he or she will dislike you if you win. So, you consider, again, alternative plans to winning the match and may even deliberately lose it. Or you may decide to play golf instead of tennis.

    If, however, you *strongly* desire to win the tennis match—as well as, perhaps, win the championship along with it—you will tend to focus, focus, focus on the gains to be achieved by winning and the "horrible" consequences of losing, and your (obsessive–compulsive?) focus will discourage alternative thoughts and selectively prejudice you against seriously considering such alternatives. Strong desires, in other words, frequently lead to focused thinking and to prejudiced overgeneralization—not always, of course, but significantly more frequently than mild or moderate desires do. If so, the prejudiced overgeneralization that strong desire encourages leads to the belief that because some other performance goal, approval aim, or safety seeking is *highly* preferable, it is also necessary. Overfocusing on its desirability encourages seeing it as a dire necessity.

Assuming that my hypothesis that strong desires more often lead to demandingness and musturbation than do weak desires is supported by empirical findings, what has all this got to do with perfectionism? My theory goes one step further and says that the beliefs "I would *like* to perform well and often to perform perfectly well" are rational and self-helping in human societies that define certain performances as "good" and then reward the performer—which seems to be the case in practically all cultures that survive. But the beliefs "I *absolutely must* perform well and indeed *must* perform perfectly well" are often irrational and self-defeating because, being a fallible human and living with social restrictions, you frequently will *not* perform well (according to personal and social standards) and you certainly won't be able to function perfectly well.

Moreover, your demand for a guarantee of good or perfect performance may well create feelings of anxiety about performing that will interfere with your succeeding; your demand for a guarantee, "I must not be anxious! I must not be anxious!" will likely make you even more anxious. So demanding, rather than preferring, again won't work too well to aid your purpose. To insist that you *must* get something you desire seems "logical" (in terms of motivation). Paradoxically, it is illogical and tends to create anxiety.

My theory about desire hypothesizes that your strong, rather than weak, desires (a) make you more likely to think that those desires *absolutely must* be fulfilled and (b) make you more likely to think that they must be *perfectly* fulfilled. If their successful fulfillment is rationally beneficial to you and if perfect fulfillment is also rationally beneficial to you —as I have noted above—then it is logical for you to jump from "I absolutely *must* fulfill my strong desires just because they are so strong"— which actually is a complete non sequitur—to "I *absolutely must* fulfill my strong desires perfectly just because they are so strong"—which again, is a complete non sequitur.

I am theorizing, then, that strong desires, rather than weak desires, are profound prejudices—that is, they are cognitive–emotional biases— that for various reasons often encourage people to think, "Because I *strongly* want success, approval, or safety, and it would be beneficial for me to have them, I *absolutely must* have them." This is a fairly grandiose and perfectionistic idea itself, because you and I obviously don't run the universe, so whatever we desire, no matter how strongly we prefer it, doesn't have to exist.

Humans are, however, prone to grandiosity, to demanding that their strong desires absolutely must be fulfilled. They often think wish-fulfillingly—as Freud (1965) and his psychoanalytic followers have pointed out. More to the point, they often think and feel wish-demandingly: "Because I *strongly* want it so, it *should be* that way!" Once they escalate their powerful wishes to dire necessities, they frequently take them one step further: "Because my most important desires are sacred and *absolutely must* be fulfilled, they must be thoroughly, completely, and perfectly fulfilled!" Then they really have emotional and behavioral problems!

Perfectionism, Irrational Beliefs, and Anxiety Sensitivity

Let me consider one more important point. I noted in *Reason and Emotion in Psychotherapy* (Ellis, 1962) that people who are anxious, particularly those who experience panic, frequently make themselves quite anxious about their anxiety and thus have a secondary disturbance about their original disturbance. Why is this so common among humans? According to REBT theory, they are forcefully thinking "I must not be anxious! It's terrible to be anxious! I am an inadequate person for being anxious!"

For several years, Reiss and his coworkers (Reiss & McNally, 1985) have theorized that some people have unusual sensitivity to their own feelings of anxiety, as I hypothesized in 1962. They have conducted many studies of this secondary symptom of anxiety, which they called *anxiety sensitivity*, and have confirmed some of my observations and other clinicians' observations about it (Cox, Parker, & Swinson, 1996; Taylor, 1995; Wachtel, 1994). Reiss's theory of anxiety sensitivity somewhat overlaps with my theory of strong desire in that it implies that some people who experience anxiety about anxiety find their anxious feeling *so* uncomfortable that they "awfulize" about them and thereby produce panic states. Their desire for relief from anxiety is so intense that they *demand* that they not have it and thereby escalate it.

What, we may ask, makes anxiety-sensitive people so *demanding* about their anxiety? My theory answers this question as follows:

1. Anxiety, and particularly panic, is uncomfortable. It feels bad, disrupts competence, may lead to social disapproval, and often brings on physical symptoms—such as shortness of breath and rapid heartbeat—that make you think you are in real physical danger, even that you are dying.
2. Because it is *so* uncomfortable, you *strongly* wish that it not exist —disappear—and that all its disadvantages disappear with it.
3. Because you *strongly* desire it to go, you insist and demand "I must not be anxious! I must not be panicked!"
4. Then, logically (and perversely enough), you make yourself anxious about your anxiety, panicked about your panic.
5. Consequently, you increase your uncomfortable symptoms—especially your physical symptoms of suffocating and heart pounding.
6. You become more panicked than ever.
7. Your vicious cycle continues.
8. Finally, because your slightest feelings of panic bring on *great* discomfort, you may frequently conclude "I must never panic *at all*! I must be *perfectly* free from anxiety and panic!" The moral: By being *acutely aware of your discomfort* (and other disadvantages) of your feeling of panic, you may demand *perfect* freedom from panic and may therefore increase the likelihood of your panicking.

My explanations of anxiety about anxiety and panic about panic in the preceding paragraph fit nicely into my theory about strong desire and its relationship to demandingness and perfectionism. However, beware! The explanatory power of my theory is interesting but may have little connection with empirical findings. Many psychoanalytic theories fit brilliantly together and support their derived postulates, but they appear to be little connected with hard-headed facts.

So I believe in and present this theory that when people's weak desires are thwarted, they commonly lead to healthy negative feelings of disappointment, regret, and frustration, but when their strong desires are thwarted, they more often lead to absolutistic musts and demands and thereby to unhealthy feelings of anxiety, depression, rage, and self-pity. It seems to me a plausible and testable theory. It also seems to explain some reasons for human perfectionism. Now all we have to do is check my theories and explanations to see if any evidence backs them. Theorizing is fun. Evidence gathering is harder.

Perfectionism and Irrational Beliefs in Couples

So far in this chapter I have considered individualistic demands for achievement, approval, and safety but, of course, they exist in couples, in families, and in social respects as well. Take couples therapy, which I have done extensively along REBT lines for more than 40 years. Are husbands, wives, and other partners as demanding and perfectionistic about their mates as they are about themselves? Frequently, yes, and with frightful results for their relationships.

John, a 36-year-old accountant, gave himself a perfectionistic hard time about his work and made himself exceptionally anxious if it wasn't wholly accurate. He excused his perfectionism in this respect by saying that of course it had to be perfectly accurate—because it was accounting and that *meant* accuracy. But John was also perfectionistic about his dress, his tennis game, and several other aspects of his life. Because, however, he worked mightily to keep his accounting, his appearance, and his tennis game in order, he succeeded fairly well in doing so and was only temporarily anxious when things got a bit beyond his control. His compulsive striving kept things pretty much in line.

John, however, was equally perfectionistic about his wife Sally and his two accounting partners. They, too, had to—yes, had to—perform well, dress well, and even play tennis well. And often they didn't, those laggards! John, of course, couldn't control others as he strove for his own perfection, so he was frequently enraged against his "careless" wife and partners, much more than he was anxious about his own performances.

I saw John for therapy because his wife and partners insisted that he go—or else. He was set for a double divorce. I had a rough time, at first, showing him the folly of his own performance-oriented perfectionism, because he was willing to strive mightily to achieve it and suffer occasional panic attacks when he didn't. It was easier to show him that his demands on others just wouldn't work. He had little control over others, and they were going to continue to be just as abominably unperfectionistic—not to mention downright sloppy—as they chose. They *shouldn't* be that way—but they are.

After several sessions of REBT, John was able to *prefer* without *demanding* perfect behavior from Sally and his partners and therefore to be keenly disappointed but not enraged when they made accounting, tennis, or other errors. He lived with their imperfections, and no one divorced him. He only slightly gave up his own perfectionistic demands on himself and continued to perform well in most ways, but he was decidedly more anxious than he need have been.

John's wife Sally, whom I also saw for a few sessions, was nondemanding of herself for the most part but *couldn't stand* the obsessive–compulsiveness of John and their 12-year-old daughter Electra. They were both carved from the same perfectionistic family block (as were John's father and sister) and had to do many things absolutely perfectly. Sally couldn't take their frantically pushing themselves to achieve (which was bad enough) and their insistence that she, too, be faultlessly on the ball (which was impossible!). Although usually easygoing, in this respect she kept inwardly demanding "They *must not* be that scrupulous! They *have to* be more tolerant! I can't bear their intolerance!"

I showed Sally—and she was much easier to work with than was John —that her intolerance of John's and Electra's intolerance was not going to work. Her rage was going to be exceptionally self-upsetting, was not going to change John or Electra, and might lead to her divorcing John (not so bad) but also to her divorcing Electra (not so good!) and to her own psychosomatic horrors (still worse!).

Sally saw the light and soon gave up her intolerance of John's and Electra's intolerance. She still *wanted* them to but didn't insist that they be more reasonable, and she worked with me to change her own demands that her family be less perfectionistic. So John improved in his demands on Sally (and his own partners), and Sally distinctly improved in her perfectionistic demands on John and on Electra. John kept some of his perfectionistic demands on his own performance but did not let them interfere too seriously with his family and business relationships.

Perfectionism and Hypercompetitiveness

One reason why John kept insisting that he must perform outstandingly was because he was fixated on the kind of competitiveness that I described about perfectionists in the original edition of *Reason and Emotion in Psychotherapy* (1962). I said at that time,

> The individual who *must* succeed in an outstanding way is not merely challenging himself and testing his own powers (which may well be beneficial); but he is invariably comparing himself to and fighting to best *others*. He thereby becomes other- rather than self-directed and sets himself essentially impossible tasks (since no matter how outstandingly good he may be in a given field, it is most likely that there will be others who are still better). (pp. 63–64)

After practicing REBT for almost 50 years and after studying the results obtained in scores of studies of irrational beliefs, I find this hypothesis more tenable than ever. Hypercompetitiveness is a common trait of "normal" musturbators and especially of perfectionists. They mainly have unhealthy *conditional* self-acceptance instead of healthy *unconditional* self-acceptance. Their main condition for being a "good person" is notable achievement, and to be a "better person" than others requires outstanding achievement.

Actually, to strive desperately to best others and thereby to gain "better" worth as a person is an undemocratic, fascist-like philosophy. Fascists like Hitler and Mussolini are seen by many of their followers to be not only better (i.e., more competent) in some traits, such as physical prowess or blondeness, but are viewed as being superior *people*. Their *essence* is supposedly outstandingly good. They are almost diametrically opposed to the concept of unconditional self-acceptance, which means fully accepting and respecting yourself *whether or not* you are achieving (Ellis, 1962, 1988; Ellis & Harper, 1997; Ellis & Velten, 1998; Hauck, 1991).

Perfectionists, then, tend to be highly conditional self-acceptors who base their worth as persons on hypercompetitively besting others—and, in the process, often lose out on discovering what they personally want to do—and who tend to fascistically denigrate others. These hypotheses, for which I have found much clinical evidence over the years, merit considerable research efforts.

Perfectionism and Stress

How are perfectionists affected by stressful conditions? More so, I would say, than are run-of-the-mill nonperfectionists. First, they may demand that stress be minimal—or perfectly nonexistent. Second, they may insist that they get perfect solutions to practical problems that create stress—such as how to have a perfect job interview, how to get a perfect job, how to deal with bosses or employees perfectly well, and so forth. Third, when stressful conditions—such as business difficulties—occur, they may demand that they have perfect solutions for them. They not only greatly prefer these conditions of solutions to them but require that they be easily and quickly available—which they normally are not. Therefore, under conditions that are equally stressful to others, perfectionists "find" more stress, less satisfactory solutions, and more prolonged difficulties than nonperfectionists find. Their perfectionism contradicts realistic and probabilistic expectations about the number and degree of stressors that should exist and often results in their making a hassle into a holocaust.

About the stressors of their lives, they have the usual irrational beliefs of disturbed people but hold them more vigorously and rigidly. Thus, they tend to believe that stressful situations *absolutely must not* exist; that it is *utterly awful and horrible* (as bad as it could be) when they do; that they *completely can't stand them* (can't enjoy life *at all* because of them); are *quite powerless* to improve them; and rightly should damn themselves and other people for not removing them or coping beautifully with them.

According to REBT theory, practically all disturbed people *at times* hold these self-defeating beliefs. But perfectionists seem to hold them more frequently and insistently—and cling to them as *fixed ideas*. Consequently, they often require long-term treatment—as Blatt (1995) showed —and, if REBT is used with them, will frequently require several cognitive, emotive, and behavioral methods before they will surrender their beliefs. Why? Because a single method of disputing and acting against their irrational beliefs doesn't seem convincing enough. So a therapist's use of several techniques may finally work better.

By the same token, I have found that if perfectionists who react badly to stressful conditions are placed in cognitive–behavioral group therapy, in which several group members in addition to the therapist actively try to help them give up their rigid beliefs and behaviors, it works better than if they are in individual therapy with only a single therapist to counter their perfectionism. Again, the issue seems to be that compared with nonperfectionists, perfectionists have (a) a stronger desire or preference to do well; (b) a stronger and more rigid demand that they do well; (c) a stronger insistence that they do perfectly well under one or more conditions; and (d) a long-term habit of perfectionistic thinking, feeling, and behaving that resists short-term change. For all these reasons, they frequently are difficult customers, who can use intensive, prolonged therapy.

My hypothesis, then, is that perfectionists are more rigid and persistent in their irrational beliefs than what I call the "nice neurotics." Many of them—not all—have severe personality disorders. They have *idées fixes* (fixed ideas), as Pierre Janet said of many severely disturbed people a century ago. And let us honestly admit this before we try to fix them.

References

Adler, A. (1926). *What life should mean to you*. New York: Greenberg.

Adler, A. (1927). *Understanding human nature*. Garden City, NY: Greenberg.

Bandura, A. (1997). *Self-efficacy: The exercise of control*. New York: Freeman.

Barlow, D. H. (1989). *Anxiety and its disorders: The nature and treatment of anxiety and panic*. New York: Guilford.

Beck, A. T. (1976). *Cognitive therapy and the emotional disorders*. New York: International Universities Press.

Beck, J. S. (1995). *Cognitive therapy: Basics and beyond*. New York: Guilford.

Bernard, M. E. (1993). *Staying rational in an irrational world*. New York: Carol.

Blatt, S. J. (1995). The destructiveness of perfectionism: Implications for the treatment of depression. *American Psychologist, 50,* 1003–1020.

Burns, D. D. (1980). *Feeling good: The new mood therapy*. New York: New American Library.

Cox, B. J., Parker, J. D. A., & Swinson, R. P. (1996). Anxiety sensitivity: Confirmatory evidence for a multidimensional construct. *Behaviour Research and Therapy, 34,* 592–598.

Dryden, W. (1998). *A course in overcoming self-esteem*. Chichester, England: Wiley.

Dubois, P. (1907). *The psychiatric treatment of nervous disorders*. New York: Funk & Wagnalls.

Ellis, A. (1957). *How to live with a neurotic: At work and at home*. New York: Crown.

Ellis, A. (1958). Rational psychotherapy. *Journal of General Psychology, 59,* 35–49.

Ellis, A. (1962). *Reason and emotion in psychotherapy*. New York: Lyle Stuart.

Ellis, A. (1988). *How to stubbornly refuse to make yourself miserable about anything—Yes, anything!* Secaucus, NJ: Lyle Stuart.

Ellis, A., & Dryden, W. (1997). *The practice of rational emotive behavior therapy* (rev. ed.). New York: Springer.

Ellis, A., Gordon, J., Neenan, M., & Palmer, S. (1997). *Stress counseling: A rational emotive behavior approach*. London: Cassell.

Ellis, A., & Harper, R. A. (1997). *A guide to rational living* (3rd rev. ed.). North Hollywood, CA: Melvin Powers.

Ellis, A., & Tafrate, R. C. (1997). *How to control your anger before it controls you*. Secaucus, NJ: Birch Lane Press.

Ellis, A., & Velten, E. (1998). *Optimal aging*. Chicago: Open Court.

Epictetus. (1899). *The works of Epictetus*. Boston: Little, Brown.

Flett, G. L., Hewitt, P. L., Blankstein, K. R., & Koledin, S. (1991). Dimensions of perfectionism and irrational thinking. *Journal of Rational–Emotive and Cognitive–Behavior Therapy, 9,* 185–201.

Flett, G. L., Hewitt, P. L., Blankstein, K. R., Solnik, M., & Van Brunschot, M. (1996). Perfectionism, social problem-solving ability, and psychological distress. *Journal of Rational–Emotive and Cognitive–Behavior Therapy, 14,* 245–275.

Freeman, A., & DeWolf, R. (1993). *The ten dumbest mistakes smart people make and how to avoid them*. New York: Perennial.

Freud, S. (1965). *Standard edition of the complete psychological works of Sigmund Freud*. New York: Basic Books.

Goldfried, M. R., & Davison, G. (1994). *Clinical behavior therapy* (3rd ed.). New York: Wiley.

Hauck, P. A. (1991). *Overcoming the rating game: Beyond self-love—Beyond self-esteem*. Louisville, KY: Westminster/John Knox.

Hewitt, P. L., & Flett, G. L. (1993). Dimensions of perfectionism, daily stress, and depression: A test of the specific vulnerability hypothesis. *Journal of Abnormal Psychology, 102*, 58–65.

Horney, K. (1950). *Neurosis and human growth*. New York: Norton.

Janet, P. (1898). *Neurosis et idees fixes*. Paris: Alcan.

Lazarus, A. A., Lazarus, C., & Fay, A. (1993). *Don't believe it for a minute: Forty toxic ideas that are driving you crazy*. San Luis Obispo, CA: Impact.

Reiss, S., & McNally, R. J. (1985). Expectancy model of fear. In S. Reiss & R. R. Bootzin (Eds.), *Theoretical issues in behavior therapy* (pp. 107–122). New York: Academic Press.

Taylor, S. (1995). Anxiety sensitivity: Theoretical perspectives and recent findings. *Behaviour Research and Therapy, 33*, 243–258.

Wachtel, P. L. (1994). From eclecticism to synthesis: Toward a more seamless psychotherapeutic integration. *Journal of Psychotherapeutic Integration, 1*, 43–54.

Walen, S., DiGiuseppe, R., & Dryden, W. (1992). *A practitioner's guide to rational–emotive therapy*. New York: Oxford University Press.

Xenakis, J. C. (1969). *Epictetus: Philosopher–therapist*. The Hague, Netherlands: Martinus Nijhoff.

10

Dysfunctional Attitudes, Perfectionism, and Models of Vulnerability to Depression

Gary P. Brown and Aaron T. Beck

The past 30 years have seen a fundamental shift in how psychopathology is understood, from a reliance on symptom-based psychiatric definitions to a greater emphasis on the phenomenology and basic mental operations underlying various forms of emotional disturbance. Much of the change in theory and therapy was set in motion by the original cognitive formulation of depression (Beck, 1967), an approach that over time has been extended to virtually the entire range of clinical problems. Specific domains within this general movement toward a greater phenomenological understanding of psychopathology have attracted considerable research interest and have developed into discrete domains of inquiry. Such is the case with the study of perfectionism, which is amply documented in the current volume.

The aim of this chapter is to examine the advances made in the study of perfectionism against the background of the cognitive model and to consider whether some of the ideas emphasized in the model can shed additional light on the issues discussed in this book. In contrast to much of the material in this book, the cognitive model developed almost wholly out of clinical observation and owes relatively less to the trait psychology and personality theory traditions. Furthermore, although global constructs like perfectionism, hopelessness, low self-esteem, and so on, are important components of the cognitive view of psychopathology, they typically are understood in reference to the basic mental operations they entail and the manner in which those operations are carried out.

With respect to the emphasis on basic mental operations, a recurring observation in cognitive formulations of various emotional difficulties is that people undergoing such problems—and, often, those at risk—are likely to reason, problem solve, and interpret certain experiences in a rigid and arbitrary way. This mode of thinking manifests itself through several avenues, and perfectionism is just one of them, albeit an important one. Furthermore, as an outgrowth of the emphasis on basic processes, the cognitive model has evolved in continual contact with developments in applied and basic psychology (see, e.g., Williams, Watts, MacLeod, & Mathews, 1988) and in this respect might also complement the other work presented in this book.

Overview of the Cognitive Model

Haaga, Dyck, and Ernst (1991) offered a useful condensation of the central elements of Beck's original cognitive model of depression and traced the evolution of those ideas over the years. We draw on their account for the following overview of the model.

First, Haaga et al. distinguished between the descriptive aspects of the model, on the one hand, and the predictions made about causation, on the other. With respect to description, Beck's model begins with the basic observation that the thought content of people with depression is more negative than that of nondepressed people both in terms of the overall negative tone and the virtual exclusion of all positive content. The nature of the thinking is also distinctive in that it is automatic, perseverative, and intrusive. Beck further suggested that the negative thought content coalesces around three main themes—negative views of the self, the world, and the future—which Beck collectively called the *cognitive triad.* In addition, whereas negative thinking is found in other emotional disorders, the content of depressive thinking is distinguished by themes of irreversible loss and failure (as opposed to, e.g., the themes of impending danger associated with anxiety; Beck & Emery, 1985). Finally, depressive cognition is characterized by a pervasive and systematic negative bias in information processing. This bias is evident in virtually all aspects of thinking, including reasoning, problem solving, memory, and, potentially, even perception.

The foregoing account of cognitive content in depression applies mainly to moment-to-moment, stream-of-consciousness thinking. A more enduring level of cognition consisting of underlying assumptions and attitudes toward ongoing experience is also an integral part of the model and was developed to account for the thematic regularities observed in depressed people during successive depressive episodes. As Beck, Rush, Shaw, and Emery (1979) noted, "It does not seem plausible to us that the aberrant cognitive mechanisms are created *de novo* every time an individual experiences a depression. It appears more credible that he has some relatively enduring anomaly in his psychological system" (p. 20). Conceptually, this level of cognition has been closely associated in cognitive formulations with the operation of underlying depressogenic schemas that bias information processing during the active phase of a depressive episode and, among people predisposed to relapse, remain present in a latent form, potentially to be triggered by relevant experiences (Kovacs & Beck, 1978).

In an addition to the model, Beck (1983) proposed a basic distinction in the types of events that would be sufficiently meaningful to a given person so as to interact with a preexisting cognitive vulnerability to give rise to depression. For people categorized as *sociotropic,* threats to social affiliation are more potent stressors, whereas for those categorized as *autonomous,* threats to independent functioning have the greater impact.

Various schemes have been proposed for simultaneously representing the various aspects of the model outlined above. A basic distinction between surface-level and deep-level cognition often is considered (Hollon & Bemis, 1981; Kwon & Oei, 1995), whereas Beck, Epstein, and Harrison (1983) proposed a more detailed classification that also arrays various cognitive constructs along a depth dimension, ranging from fleeting surface cognition to more enduring deep structures and personality traits. Hollon and Kriss (1984) and Hammen and Krantz (1985) both proposed a different type of classification that is based on structure, content, and process that cuts across the levels described above. These different classification systems will not be evaluated here but are mentioned because they potentially parallel, at least partially, the recent development of comprehensive, modular models of cognition relevant to psychopathology (e.g., the Interacting Cognitive Subsystems [ICS; Teasdale & Barnard, 1993] and Schematic Propositional Associative and Analogical Representational Systems [SPAARS; Power & Dalgleish, 1997] models).

These classification schemes also are useful for an initial consideration of how perfectionism would be understood within the cognitive model. For the most part, perfectionist beliefs, to the extent that they are an enduring aspect of a person's ongoing view of his or her experience, would be reflected at the level of underlying assumptions. Perfectionistic people also might be expected to be overrepresented within the autonomous, as opposed to the sociotropic, type. Most of the remaining discussion will restrict itself to the level of underlying assumptions. In the next section we try to provide a better sense of this level of the cognitive model by reviewing the development of the most widely used measure of underlying assumptions, the Dysfunctional Attitude Scale (DAS; Weissman & Beck, 1978; Weissman, 1979).

Development and Psychometric Analysis of the DAS

The level of underlying assumptions has received a considerable share of attention from researchers interested in depression because it is seen as an enduring aspect of a person's ongoing representation of his or her experience and, therefore, the likely source of persistent maladaptive appraisals in people experiencing repeated episodes of low mood and depression. A large body of research exists in this area, mainly using the DAS to test various predictions following from the cognitive model.

Weissman and Beck (Weissman & Beck, 1978; Weissman, 1979) developed the DAS. Potential items for the scale were generated from the suggestions of practicing clinicians on the basis of their experiences with depressed people seeking treatment (Weissman, 1979). The items were further refined by the authors to resemble more closely the ideational content of depressed patients described by Beck (1967, 1976). Specifically, maladaptive thinking patterns were reflected in the wording of items using inflexible and absolute language, such as rigid quantifiers ("all," "always," "never"), categorical imperatives ("must," "ought," "have to"), and preemptive class assignments ("nothing-but"; Weissman, 1979).

DAS items are rated on a 7-point Likert-type scale ranging from *totally agree* to *totally disagree*. Possible responses are scored from 1 to 7, the direction depending on whether agreement or disagreement with a particular belief is judged to be the maladaptive response. Higher scores indicate greater dysfunctionality in terms of more arbitrary, rigid, and extreme thinking patterns. Research over the ensuing years has typically used the DAS-A, one of the two 40-item parallel forms (along with the DAS-B) that Weissman (1979) derived from the original 100-item scale, although some recent studies have reverted to the original 100-item scale, and still others have proposed their own shortened forms.

The DAS thus was originally conceived of as a global measure of dysfunctional thinking of the type thought to predispose people to depression. Because items were compiled by polling clinicians, they reflect the typical themes and preoccupations of affiliation, achievement, and self-worth encountered in day-to-day clinical contexts; consequently, an understandable interest developed in identifying the underlying dimensions of the DAS.

Numerous factor-analytic studies of the different forms of the DAS have been completed; little consensus has been reached on an accepted number of factors or factor content, and this body of research needs to be summarized and reviewed in its own right. Most of the studies have been carried out in undergraduate and community samples. For example, Cane, Olinger, Gotlib, and Kuiper (1986) analyzed DAS Form A in an undergraduate sample and found two factors, which they named Performance Evaluation and Approval by Others. Oliver and Baumgart (1985) administered both DAS forms to a sample of hospital workers and their spouses and found a lack of factorial equivalence between the two forms. Finally, Parker, Bradshaw, and Blignault (1984) administered both short forms to two samples of Australian general-practice patients and found four factors, which they named Externalized Self-Esteem, Anaclitic Self-Esteem, Tentativeness, and Need for Approval.

To date, no study can lay claim to uncovering the definitive factor solution of the DAS. The factor solution we will use in referring to the dimensions of the DAS in the remainder of this chapter was reported by Beck, Brown, Steer, and Weissman (1991). That study is distinctive in that it used the original 100-item DAS form and was based on a large clinical sample ($N = 2,023$ consecutive outpatient admissions to a psychiatric clinic). Using both exploratory and confirmatory analytic strategies, Beck et al. (1991) found nine factors similar but not identical to those found in undergraduate samples, as follows: Vulnerability, Need for Approval, Success–Perfectionism, Need to Please Others, Imperatives, Need to Impress, Avoidance of Appearing Weak, Control Over Emotions, and Disapproval–Dependence.

Several subsequent factor analyses of the DAS have been reported. Power, Duggan, Lee, and Murray (1994), also using a clinical sample, did not replicate the Vulnerability factor Beck et al. (1991) described but did reproduce several of the content-specific factors, including Success–Perfectionism and Disapproval–Dependence. Dyck (1992), using a student sample, derived factors quite similar to those of Beck et al. (1991). Calhoon (1996) performed a confirmatory factor analysis of the Beck et al. (1991) structure in a student sample and was unable to demonstrate an adequate fit for the nine-factor solution, suggesting instead a three-factor solution that better fit the data and incorporated the nine Beck et al. factors.

Rigid Thinking and the Dimensions of the DAS

Although the different factor-analytic studies reviewed above do not converge on a single-factor solution, they substantially agree on the general themes embodied in the DAS. Notably, nearly all the studies found factors having to do with perfectionistic achievement and concerns with social affiliation. A further possibility that bears examination in a more detailed way is that other sources of covariance underlie the DAS items besides their manifest content. Specifically, recall that the primary goal of the creators of the DAS in writing items was not to reflect specific content themes but to embody the thinking patterns evident during depression. As we attempt to show below, a closer examination of the wording of items on the factors reveals that they are approximately homogeneous not only in content but also in the mode of thought they reflect. Statistically, this dual basis for items to covary could result in multicollinearity, which in turn could explain the observed difficulty in finding a stable factor solution invariant across different samples and populations.

With respect to mode of thinking, the bulk of DAS items take the form of condition–action rules (i.e., if–then statements); this item form predominates on the Perfectionism factor that Beck et al. (1991) reported. An example is, "If I am not a success then my life is meaningless." Items from both the Approval factor (e.g., "If others dislike you, you cannot be happy") and Disapproval–Dependence factor (e.g., "If people whom I care about do not care for me, it is awful") also reflect this type of thinking and logic, in that the attitudes on those factors also are couched in terms of rigid if–then contingencies. The difference is that the conditional ("if") part of the attitude has to do with desirable or undesirable social (rather than achievement) concerns. The argument thus can be made that, to the extent that extreme and unrealistic outcomes are seen as necessary and intermediate outcomes are considered to be unacceptable, the factors also reflect a sort of perfectionism about social affairs. Thus, the thinking has a common form, although the content varies; the latter maps onto the broad domains of self-definition described by Beck (i.e., autonomy vs. sociotropy; Beck, 1983) and by Blatt (i.e., self-criticism vs. dependency; Blatt, Quinlan, Chevron, McDonald, & Zuroff, 1982).

Another type of perfectionism is evident in the Imperatives factor of Beck et al.'s (1991) solution. Items on this factor reflect self-coercive attitudes (e.g., "I should always have complete control over my feelings"). They are distinguished by the use of modal verbs of obligation, such as "should," "ought," and "must." The recognition of the centrality of this type of thinking to the development of emotional problems is shared by a broad range of theoretical perspectives (see Brown & Beck, 1989, for a brief review) and has been variously called "the tyranny of the shoulds" (Horney, 1950) and "musturbation" (e.g., Ellis, 1985). In contrast to the if–then rigidity discussed above, imperative attitudes are ones that, although rigid and arbitrary, are unconditional rather than conditional—that is, no ifs are involved. The extreme and unrealistic outcomes that "shoulds" require are not tied to environmental contingencies, which may be why they are so strongly implicated in psychopathology.

It thus can be argued that the DAS is, to a substantial degree, a measure of perfectionism, if perfectionism is construed in broad terms. Regarded in this way, it also provides a window into the cognitive underpinning of perfectionism. Furthermore, the foregoing analysis has clear affinities to the developing understanding of perfectionism covered elsewhere in this book. For example, in terms of Hewitt and Flett's (1990, 1991) basic formulation, the clearest parallel is between their self-oriented perfectionism and the construct that is measured by the DAS Perfectionism factor. Less readily apparent is the similarity of Hewitt and Flett's socially prescribed perfectionism to the construct measured by the DAS Imperatives factor: Both constructs have to do with the internalization of socially dictated norms. Finally, although items on the DAS deal with expectations of others' behavior (e.g., "If I put other people's needs before my own they should help me when I need them"), they are, at best, indirectly related to Hewitt and Flett's concept of other-oriented perfectionism.

Dysfunctional Attitudes in Depression and Other Forms of Psychopathology

Since its development, the DAS has been used in diverse research contexts to test and potentially refine various aspects of the cognitive model of depression. It is well accepted that dysfunctional attitudes are elevated in people who are depressed compared with those who are not depressed (e.g., Nelson, Stern, & Chicchetti, 1992; Power, Katz, McGuffin, Duggan, Lam, & Beck, 1994). Furthermore, when pretest–posttest comparisons are made in the course of treatment outcome studies, elevated dysfunctional attitudes appear to predict poor response to treatment in response to both psychological (Blatt, Quinlan, Pilkonis, & Shea, 1995; Jarret, Eaves, Grannemann, & Rush, 1991; Scott, Harrington, House, & Ferrier, 1996) and pharmacological (Fava, Bless, Otto, Pava, & Rosenbaum, 1994; Peselow, Robins, Block, & Barouche, 1990) interventions. Some evidence, however, exists for treatment-specific response as a function of initial levels of dysfunctional attitudes. For example, in a detailed analysis of treatment process, DeRubeis et al. (1990) found that change in cognitive variables, including the DAS, differentially predicted change in depressive symptoms at midtreatment for participants treated with cognitive therapy but not for those treated pharmacologically.

Whereas depressed groups are characterized by elevated dysfunctional attitudes, high levels of dysfunctional attitudes, as measured by the DAS, generally have not been shown to be specific to depression, and elevations typically are found in other clinical groups (e.g., Hollon, Kendall, & Lumry, 1986). That finding does not necessarily pose a problem for the general cognitive model of emotional disorders (Beck, 1976) because comorbid depression is characteristic of many, if not most, clinical disorders. Moreover, cognitive formulations for different psychological disorders tend to emphasize that it is the content, rather than the form, of dysfunctional thinking that changes for different disorders, a claim termed the *cognitive content–specificity* hypothesis (Beck, 1976; Beck, Brown, Steer, Eidelson, & Riskind, 1987). This approach implies that elevations on particular types of dysfunctional attitudes also might be predicted for other disorders on the basis of the hypothesized characteristic content of those disorders.

Several studies have documented elevations in dysfunctional attitudes in groups that would be expected to be characterized by rigid and extreme thought patterns. Poulakis and Wertheim (1993) found a relationship between the DAS and other cognitive measures and scores on a measure of bulimia, a relationship that remained after the level of depression was statistically controlled; Kuehnel and Wadden (1994) reported comparable results. Similarly, Martin, Kuiper, and Westra (1989) found associations between subscales of the DAS and measures of Type A behavior. In an Italian study, a sample of male professional workers classified as fitting the Type A behavior pattern scored higher on factors of the DAS than participants in the same cohort who did not fit the pattern (Sibilia, Picozzi, & Nardi, 1995). Finally, consistent with the cognitive formulation of specific personality disorders (Beck, Freeman, et al., 1990), O'Leary et al. (1991) found higher DAS scores in participants diagnosed with borderline personality disorder with and without major depression than in control participants without a personality disorder, although the groups with and without major depression did not differ from each other.

The different disorders reviewed above each would be independently predicted to involve some form of perfectionistic ideation; separate confirmation for a role for perfectionism in eating disorders, Type A behavior pattern, and borderline personality disorder can be found in the work of Flett and Hewitt using their Multidimensional Perfectionism Scale (Flett, Hewitt, Blankstein, & Dynin, 1994; Hewitt, Flett, & Ediger, 1995; Hewitt, Flett, & Turnbull, 1994).

The disorders discussed above have not yet been subjected to as extensive a cognitive analysis as depression has. However, it is likely that our grasp of these problems would be enhanced if we understood perfectionism not only in terms of unrealistic standards but also in terms of rigid and arbitrary thinking patterns. This point can be illustrated with respect to perfectionism and suicidality. Blatt (1995) recently reviewed extensive findings of a link between perfectionism and suicidal intent, threat, and ideation but noted that a conclusive link has not yet been established between perfectionism and actual suicidal behavior. Because the link between cognitive factors and suicide has been amply documented (Beck, Brown, Berchick, Stewart, & Steer, 1990; Beck, Brown, & Steer, 1989; Beck, Steer, Kovacs, & Garrison, 1985), it is worth considering what additional insight a cognitive analysis can lend to this topic.

Within the cognitive formulation of suicidality, rigid thinking is seen as impairing problem solving, which gives rise to hopelessness over time. Hopelessness, in turn, has been shown to mediate the relationship between depression and suicidality (Kovacs, Beck, & Weissman, 1975). MacLeod, Pankhania, Lee, and Mitchell (1997) provided a detailed sense of how that process may take place. MacLeod et al. compared a group of patients who had recently attempted suicide, who were interviewed shortly after hospital admission, with a group of nonsuicidal depressed patients and a group of community controls. Cognitive rigidity was operationalized within a verbal-fluency paradigm: Participants were asked to come up with as many anticipated future positive and negative events as possible within a set period of time. MacLeod et al. found that those who had attempted suicide reported fewer anticipated positive events coming to mind than the depressed non-suicide-attempters and control participants (they found no differences for negative events). This bias in future-oriented thinking is consistent with the cognitive formulation summarized above and with elevations on more global indicators, such as measures of hopelessness.

The foregoing illustrates how conceptualizing a phenomenon like suicidality in terms of underlying mental processes can complement understandings of the same phenomenon at a global level. It can be further argued that a more basic understanding can better inform the development of methods to address problems like suicidality, which has a significant cognitive component.

Developmental Perspectives

As we describe in a subsequent section, the main focus of research using the DAS has been on delineating a cognitive vulnerability to depression, and conjectures about the developmental origins of a putative vulnerability have been included in most cognitive theoretical formulations (Beck et al., 1979; Kovacs & Beck, 1978). It is surprising, then, as Charlton and Power (1995) remarked, that relatively little research has been undertaken to document the beginnings of dysfunctional thinking in children. In one study, Garber and Robinson (1997) compared 11- and 12-year-old children of mothers with a history of unipolar depression to matched control children. They reported differences between the groups on a set of cognitive measures but not on a simplified version of the DAS. The authors speculate that this finding may have occurred because children at that age are not yet cognitively mature enough to have developed the types of beliefs measured by the DAS.

In lieu of long-term prospective studies capable of documenting a developing vulnerability, efforts instead have been geared to establishing a link between potential cognitive vulnerability variables and retrospective perception of attachment to one's primary caregivers. Whisman and McGarvey (1994), using an undergraduate sample, found an association between perceived attachment and levels of dysfunctional attitudes. They also found that the performance evaluation and approval factors from the Cane et al. (1986) factor solution partially mediated the relationship between attachment and dysphoric mood. In a cross-sectional study that also used a sample of undergraduates, Whisman and Kwon (1992) found that low perceived parental care was related to current depressive symptoms and that the relationship was mediated by levels of dysfunctional attitudes. Finally, Roberts, Gotlib, and Kassel (1996) found that insecure adult attachment was related directly to elevated dysfunctional attitudes and that the relationship served to predispose research participants to lower self-esteem and eventual depressive symptoms.

Further efforts documenting the course of developing dysfunctional beliefs would be welcome, particularly longitudinal studies with young people that can complement the findings of retrospective research being conducted in adult samples.

Cognitive Mediation and Environmental Stress

The approaches represented in this book implicitly share a mediational view of emotional problems—people are seen as reacting emotionally to how they subjectively represent the events that transpire in their lives. This basic premise is not shared by all researchers in this area, however, and the alternative perspective that emphasizes the direct impact of life stress was the basis for a series of influential critiques (Coyne & Gotlib, 1983, 1986). It is therefore worth digressing briefly to review this controversy with the benefit of hindsight before our subsequent discussion of tests of the diathesis–stress predictions of the cognitive model.

A central contention of Coyne and Gotlib's critiques was that cognitive formulations are exclusively mentalistic and completely ignore the role of the environment. The authors also represented the cognitive model as postulating a main effect for cognitive factors in the development of depression. This contention is unfounded, as is evident in the earliest formulations of Beck's theory. For example, Beck (1967, p. 319) noted that fluctuations in negative cognitions are closely tied to environmental events, and Beck (1976, p. 108) provided a classification of the types of events that evoke depressive reactions. More recently, Beck (1987) proposed that "the longitudinal cognitive model should probably be restricted to the so-called reactive depressions; that is, those that are brought about by socially relevant events" (p. 24).

By erecting a false dichotomy between the cognitive and environmental stances, Coyne and Gotlib were able to depict the approaches as being competitive so that the failure of one implied support for the other. Research on environmental factors, however, has turned up only a weak direct relationship to depression, with only 4% to 15% of the variance in symptoms accounted for by life stress alone (Hammen, 1988). Related to this finding, although particular negative life events have been shown to precede the onset of depression (Brown & Harris, 1978), people who become depressed represent a small fraction of the population experiencing such events. Thus, it appears that a main effect for environmental stress is as unlikely as a main effect for cognition. A more realistic position is that neither cognitions nor the environment alone is capable of giving an adequate account of vulnerability to depression (Hammen, 1988). As Segal and Shaw (1986) remarked,

> Coyne and Gotlib may be accurate in their conjecture that future theorists would find it odd that cognitive processes were being explored without reference to environmental factors, yet would these same theorists find interpersonal accounts, bereft of the role of cognitive mediations of behavior, any more complete? (p. 711)

In fact, it is difficult to imagine how an account of the impact of the environment can fail to take into account how events are represented, which is the subject we now take up.

Dysfunctional Attitudes and Vulnerability to Depression

Haaga et al. (1991) summarized four causal elements of the cognitive model, as follows:

1. *Stability.* Dysfunctional beliefs should be stable (albeit varying in degree of accessibility) before, during, and after a depressive episode.
2. *Subjective valuation.* Event valuations can be predicted from personality modes (i.e., sociotropy vs. autonomy).
3. *Onset.* Initial episodes of nonendogenous unipolar depression can be predicted by the interaction of dysfunctional beliefs, event valuations, and vulnerability–congruent negative events.
4. *Recurrence.* Subsequent episodes of nonendogenous depression are predictable in the same way as initial ones (p. 217).

The clearest support for the causal hypotheses of the cognitive model comes from outcome studies that have included long-term follow-up assessments. In those studies, people who eventually relapse typically are found retrospectively to have had residual DAS elevations at the end of treatment (Evans et al., 1985; Scott, Williams, Brittlebank, & Ferrier, 1995; Simons, Murphy, Levine, & Wetzel, 1986; Thase, Simons, McGeary, & Cahalane, 1992). At odds with the predictions of the model, however, is the finding that remitted groups generally are indistinguishable from never-depressed participants during remission (Hamilton & Abramson,

1983; Reda, 1984; Silverman, Silverman, & Eardley, 1984; Simons, Garfield, & Murphy, 1984). The exception is a study by Reda, Carpiniello, Secchiaroli, and Blanco (1985), in which residual elevations on particular DAS items (including some perfectionism items) were found in a pharmacologically treated group during remission.

A more compelling case for cognitive vulnerability could be made if initial onset of depression could be shown to be predictable on the basis of the predictions of the cognitive model. As Haaga et al. (1991) persuasively showed, however, an adequate test would be almost prohibitively difficult to accomplish. They observed

> Using a prospective longitudinal design, one would have to assess personality modes (sociotropy and autonomy); measure dysfunctional beliefs under appropriately challenging conditions; monitor stressors and depression status during a follow-up period; and all this among enough never-before-depressed subjects to permit statistically powerful tests of interaction terms as predictors of a rare discrete outcome (subject does or does not develop a nonendogenous depressive syndrome during follow-up. . . .). (p. 227)

We could add to this the expectation that the stressors occurring during the course of the study would need to be congruent with the presumed underlying vulnerability, not to mention noting the notorious difficulty of validly quantifying stress in the first place (see, e.g., Monroe & Simons, 1991).

Because of the prohibitive difficulty of designing studies that adequately operationalize the theory, it is difficult to reach a conclusion concerning the validity of the causal hypotheses of the cognitive model. Whereas studies purporting to test those hypotheses generally have yielded negative or ambiguous results (see reviews by Barnett & Gotlib, 1988; Charlton & Power, 1995; Coyne & Gotlib, 1983; Haaga et al., 1991; Segal, 1988), we can never be sure that the lack of confirmatory findings is not the result of discrepancies between the underlying theory and the manner in which it is operationalized. Indeed, Haaga et al. stated that none of the studies they reviewed incorporated all the elements needed for an adequate test.

In response to this state of affairs, one approach has been to selectively relax the requirements of adequately testing the full model in a manner that potentially provides informative results that partially support the model. Such a strategy was pursued by Brown, Hammen, Craske, and Wickens (1995), who used an undergraduate sample and a naturalistic stressor, the discrepancy between expected and actual performance on an examination. The degree of performance discrepancy interacted with scores on the Perfectionism factor of the DAS to predict a modest increment in depressive symptoms at posttest. Similar results using a comparable design were reported by Metalsky, Joiner, Hardin, and Abramson (1993), who used measures derived from the hopelessness model of depression but not of perfectionism specifically.

Other features of the Brown et al. (1995) study are worth noting. First, using a naturally occurring and predictable stressor, particularly one like an examination grade, which does not need to be independently quantified and is restricted to a particular domain of experience (in this case, academic achievement), obviates many of the pitfalls of stress measurement. Furthermore, the use of fine-grained measures of vulnerability is consistent with concerns that a potential factor obscuring underlying effects in previous research was the use of overly global measures of vulnerability (see Barnett & Gotlib, 1988; Hammen, 1988).

The use of fine-grained measures of vulnerability also brings research on the cognitive model to the same level of analysis as work done on constructs such as perfectionism. In a study comparable in design to that of Brown et al. (1995), Flett, Hewitt, Blankstein, and Mosher (1995) found that self-oriented perfectionism interacted with stressful life events to predict depressive symptoms 3 months later. Hewitt, Flett, and Ediger (1996) reported similar results in an outpatient sample and found evidence for vulnerability–stress congruency.

The foregoing results should be regarded as preliminary pending replication in further, preferably clinical, samples. Because the studies specifically incorporated design features that had been recommended on the basis of careful review of previous negative or ambiguous findings (Barnett & Gotlib, 1988; Hammen, 1988), one might expect that they are worth pursuing. With respect to those recommendations, at least four key elements should probably be standard features of further research in this area: (a) the use of longitudinal designs; (b) explicit, preferably prospective, measurement of stress or use of contextual-threat methodology (Brown & Harris, 1978); (c) the use of fine-grained measures of vulnerability; and (d) vulnerability–stress matching.

Theoretical Developments and Prospects for Future Research

To summarize, the DAS appears to be quite adequate in helping to characterize the form and content of beliefs during depression, and the evidence is fairly good that the constructs the DAS measures play a contributory role in the risk of relapse among those recovering from depression. Moreover, convincing evidence indicates that elevations on the DAS reflect psychological impairments that presumably are reversed in the course of recovery. Finally, the possibility remains that better research designs will shed more light on the prediction of depression among people who currently are not depressed. In the meantime, we can try to clarify some of the current issues facing researchers in this area while highlighting recent theoretical developments.

Clearly, the issue of cognitive vulnerability to depression is complex, but for the sake of further discussion, it may be worthwhile to try to distill it to two simpler questions: When does the shift take place between nondepressed and depressed thinking, and what are the mechanisms that bring about the shift? The seminal cognitive formulations (Beck, 1967; Kovacs & Beck, 1978) described something of a bootstrap process: Dysfunctional attitudes, or at least latent depressogenic schemata, predispose a person to respond adversely to particular types of events. Once a relevant stressor occurs, a vicious cycle is set in motion, whereby subsequent information processing, including the representation of further experiences, becomes increasingly biased, leading to a further downward spiral in mood.

A critical question is, To what extent must a negative mood be present for the activation of dysfunctional attitudes to take place? Research by Miranda, Persons, and colleagues (Miranda & Persons, 1988; Miranda, Persons, & Byers, 1990) using a mood-induction manipulation suggested that increased dysfunctional attitudes only are apparent among people who were once depressed after a negative mood has been established, whereas those who never have been depressed have no corresponding changes following mood induction. If true, this finding would go some way toward explaining the pattern of findings indicating that elevations on dysfunctional attitudes only accompany lowered mood and would confirm that an enduring vulnerability exists.

Because of the implications of this line of research, the results should be interpreted with care. The studies typically are understood to show that remitted depressives endorse a greater number of dysfunctional attitudes after induction of low mood. The actual finding is that dysfunctional attitudes *correlate* with mood following induction among the previously depressed, leaving open the alternative explanation that the lack of correlation in the never-depressed group was simply the result of restricted range on the mood measure. Other potential artifacts within the design, such as practice effects, other order effects, and demand characteristics, never have been adequately ruled out.

Moreover, even if it were to be reliably found that once-depressed participants more strongly endorse dysfunctional attitudes following mood induction, we would need to question what the responses meant. The instructions for the DAS ask respondents to base their ratings on what is true of them most of the time. For responses to change on a momentary basis either the respondents were disregarding (or not following) the instructions or a fundamental shift in the way they viewed themselves had actually taken place as a result of the mood induction. If the latter were found to be tenable, such a robust manipulation should be demonstrable using other outcome measures than the DAS, which is a rather clumsy change variable given the basis on which responses are expected. If we add to this issue the well-known problems with mood-induction studies as well as the other limitations discussed by Miranda and Gross (1997), the conclusion must be that the results of such priming studies should be interpreted in a highly qualified manner.

The idea that negative mood is the initial prime for dysfunctional thinking is consistent with a recent theoretical formulation set forth by Teasdale (1988). According to that account, people who are to develop depression initially experience a low mood in reaction to stressors capable of producing such a mood in anyone. In people at risk for depression, low mood sets into motion incipient dysfunctional cognitive processes that then contribute to the downward spiral into depression. This theory does not require detectable changes between people at risk and those not at risk and so comports with the available evidence. As a consequence, however, it also minimizes the role that cognitive mediation might play in the initial appraisal of events and is therefore implicitly consistent with the position of Coyne and Gotlib (1986), discussed above, that people react to the inherent impact of events. It thus falls short of explaining the commonplace observation that particular events evoke varied reactions in different people.

One possible modification to this theory is to restrict the hypothetical process Teasdale described to events that actually have been shown to cause a low mood in most people, such as so-called "fateful events" (Dohrenwend, 1992). This formulation would be consistent with findings within the study of traumatic stress. For example, Foy, Rueger, Sipprelle, and Carroll (1984) found that most of the Vietnam veterans they studied who were exposed to particularly harsh conditions during active duty developed posttraumatic stress reactions but that the development of such reactions in veterans exposed to low levels of stress was mediated by premorbid psychological factors. This modification of Teasdale's (1988) theory is still silent about the differences we would expect to find between people at risk and not at risk outside of periods of low mood.

Teasdale and Barnard (1993) proposed a comprehensive framework for integrating the diverse cognitive processes involved in transitions between different mental states: the Interacting Cognitive Subsystems (ICS) approach. According to ICS, information about ongoing experience is encoded in different forms within different subsystems. For example, one subsystem encodes proprioceptive feedback from various physical states, whereas a separate subsystem encodes propositional knowledge. A key feature of this framework is the supposition of a generic level of cognitive processing that synthesizes patterns of information encoded within the different subsystems into a holistic mental model of ongoing experience. Significantly, emotional reactions are related directly to the model of reality at this abstract level of representation rather than to what is represented at the level of any one of the contributory subsystems.

The ICS model has several important implications for our present discussion. First, propositional knowledge, such as dysfunctional attitudes, influences emotional states only through its contribution to the pattern of representation at the highest level. Second, the ICS framework applies equally to all mental states, including depressed and nondepressed states. As such, it can provide a framework for jointly considering the relationship between cognitive processing before and after depressed mood begins.

In a recent study, Teasdale, Taylor, Cooper, Hayhurst, and Paykel (1995) used modified DAS items to pit predictions of the ICS model against those of the associative network theory of mood (Bower, 1981). The latter theory attributes the increased negativity of cognitive content in depressed states to the previous association of such material to depressed mood, which makes the material more accessible when depressed mood is subsequently reinstated. Condition-action (i.e., if–then) items from the DAS were rewritten in the form of sentence stems (e.g., "If I could always be right then others would _____ me."), such that completions consistent with the operation of a depressive mental model would be positive in affective tone (e.g., "like"), which is opposite to the associative network model's prediction that negative material would be more accessible. Consistent with the predictions of the ICS model, Teasdale et al. found that depressed patients gave a greater number of positive completions than nondepressed controls did and that the rate of positive completions diminished with the remission of depression but increased among participants whose mood worsened.

Besides supporting the ICS model, aspects of the Teasdale at al. (1995) study have many implications for our discussion. First, it is worth noting that Teasdale et al. found that the decrease in the rate of positive completions was paralleled by a reduction in DAS scores, implying that the standard DAS indexes the waxing and waning of depressive schematic processing, as it is intended to do. Second, in rewriting the DAS items, their basic form was retained: The sentence stems still reflected the rigid, absolute, and extreme thinking originally built into the DAS. Significantly, then, the results of the study do not exclude the possibility that this form of thinking persists with remission of symptoms.

Finally, the portion of the DAS statements that was left free to vary was the content of the implicational part of the attitude (the "then" portion of the condition–action rule). Teasdale et al. (1995) stated that the ICS analysis "proposes that, in patients, the mental models that become 'switched in' with the depressed state imply a much closer dependence of social worth on social approval or personal success than the models that prevail in the nondepressed state" (pp. 500–501). With remission, social approval and personal success had fewer, or at least less inflexible, implications for self-worth, as reflected in the lower rate of positive completions. Teasdale et al. did not report having conducted exploratory analyses of potential differences in content between the completions of remitted depressives and those of the never-depressed control participants; that type of analysis was, in any case, beyond the scope of the study. Such an analysis, however, would be consistent with similar studies reviewed above that used the standard DAS and examined differences between remitted and never-depressed participants and would be relevant to the central question of whether an enduring cognitive difference detectable outside of symptomatic states could be shown to characterize people who are prone to depression.

The ICS approach provides a useful framework for further consideration of the intricate issues involved in identifying a vulnerability at play during nonsymptomatic states that can predict what may be a fundamentally changed state of affairs during symptomatic states. The essential question is what the relationship is between the mental models that operate under normal circumstances and the ones that begin to operate during symptomatic periods. It is not unreasonable to suppose that depression-prone mental models share certain features that make them depressogenic but are more heterogeneous than the models that are observed to operate during symptomatic phases. The DAS, which is tailored to the relative homogeneity of those who are already depressed, is sensitive to changes that take place within the symptomatic range but fails to capture meaningful variance among the attitudes of those not yet and never to be depressed, which differ not only in degree but in kind.

The limitations mentioned above are not confined to the DAS but are shared by all questionnaire-based methods, which are suited to confirmatory research but can serve as the proverbial procrustean bed when applied to newer areas of exploration. Teasdale et al.'s (1995) approach, using sentence stems derived from the DAS permits less constrained, "bottom-up" responses and can potentially serve as a tool for systematically extending what we know about depressed information processing to the thinking processes of not-yet-depressed people. This approach could be applied quite flexibly: For example, as noted above, the DAS-derived stems that Teasdale et al. retained the rigid language of the DAS items but permitted open responses to the conditioned part of the if–then statements. Other parts of the DAS statements, such as the syntax that lends them their inflexibility, could equally well be cast into an open-response format.

Of course, it also is possible to take a completely unconstrained approach to mapping the differences in mental models of vulnerable and nonvulnerable people, such as content analysis of relevant natural-language protocols. Here again, the goal would be to be guided, rather than constrained, by the existing knowledge we have about depressive thinking during symptomatic periods. Consider the following passage from Blatt's (1995) article on perfectionism, in which he quoted from a speech given by President Bill Clinton's aide Vince Foster before his suicide:

> The reputation you develop for intellectual and ethical integrity will be your greatest asset or your worst enemy. . . . Treat every pleading, every brief, every contract, every letter, every daily task as if your career will be judged on it. . . . I cannot make this point to you too strongly. There is no victory, no advantage, no fee, no favor, which is worth even a blemish on your reputation for intellect and integrity. . . . Dents to the reputation in the legal profession are irreparable. (p. 1004)

The type of rigid, absolute, and extreme thinking we have been emphasizing is quite apparent in this passage. Methods suitable to the analysis of such natural discourse are appearing with increasing frequency in psychology in general and within the study of psychopathology (Brown, MacLeod, Tata, & Goddard, in press; Davidson, Vogel, & Coffman, 1997).

Summary and Conclusion

This chapter has reviewed the literature on enduring aspects of thought processes that are believed to predispose certain people to emotional difficulties from the standpoint of the cognitive model of emotional disorders. The development of the cognitive model signaled a new era in the study of depression; it supplanted the prevailing theories, which understood depression in terms of simple causes, such as early loss or dysfunction in single neurotransmitter systems. The basic principles of the cognitive model can contribute to the study of specific constructs, such as perfectionism, by emphasizing underlying basic mechanisms that can inform and enrich the study of those constructs at a more global level.

This chapter has focused on the underlying assumptions and core beliefs thought to represent enduring aspects of individual representations of experience and on the DAS, the measure most commonly used to test aspects of the cognitive model related to this level of cognitive processing. The DAS appears to reflect not only heightened concerns within specific content areas that typify depression but also the operation of characteristically rigid thinking patterns.

The research reviewed in this chapter is in some ways a testament to the durability of the DAS. Despite being periodically pronounced moribund, the DAS has continued to serve as an important research tool for investigators interested in studying the phenomenology of depression and other forms of emotional disturbance, and it often continues to be used by the very people arguing for its obsolescence. Perhaps because the DAS was developed on the basis of accumulated clinical experience, it appears to embody complex factors that are still to be discovered and understood. Indeed, the research reviewed in this chapter might be seen as representing an "unpacking" of the multidimensionality of the DAS. The use of the DAS in research on psychopathology has tracked the evolution of the cognitive model, following it as it has expanded into new areas of psychology and psychiatry, translated into different languages as cognitive therapy has spread around the world, and remaining a touchstone for successive theoretical developments.

References

Barnett, P. A., & Gotlib, I. H. (1988). Psychosocial functioning and depression: Distinguishing among antecedents, concomitants, and consequences. *Psychological Bulletin, 104,* 97–126.

Beck, A. T. (1967). *Depression: Clinical, experimental, and theoretical aspects.* New York: Harper & Row.

Beck, A. T. (1976). *Cognitive Therapy and the emotional disorders.* New York: International Universities.

Beck, A. T. (1983). Cognitive therapy of depression: New perspectives. In P. Clayton & J. E. Barrett (Eds.), *Treatment of depression: Old controversies and new approaches* (pp. 265–290). New York: Raven Press.

Beck, A. T. (1987). Cognitive models of depression. *Journal of Cognitive Psychotherapy, 1,* 5–37.

Beck, A. T., Brown, G., Berchick, R. J., Stewart, B. L., & Steer, R. A. (1990). Relationship between hopelessness and ultimate suicide: A replication with psychiatric outpatients. *American Journal of Psychiatry, 147,* 190–195.

Beck, A. T., Brown, G., & Steer, R. A. (1989). Prediction of eventual suicide in hospitalized patients by clinical ratings of hopelessness. *Journal of Consulting and Clinical Psychology, 57,* 309–310.

Beck, A. T., Brown, G., Steer, R. A., Eidelson, J. I., & Riskind, J. H. (1987). Differentiating depression and anxiety: A test of the cognitive content specificity hypothesis. *Journal of Abnormal Psychology, 96,* 179–183.

Beck, A. T., Brown, G., Steer, R. A., & Weissman, A. N. (1991). Factor analysis of the Dysfunctional Attitude Scale in a clinical population. *Psychological Assessment, 3,* 478–483.

Beck, A. T., & Emery, G. (1985). *Anxiety disorder and phobias: A cognitive perspective.* New York: Basic Books.

Beck, A. T., Epstein, N., & Harrison, R. (1983). Cognitions, attitudes and personality dimensions in depression. *British Journal of Cognitive Psychotherapy, 1,* 1–16.

Beck, A. T., Freeman, A., & Associates. (1990). *Cognitive therapy of personality disorders.* New York: Guilford.

Beck, A. T., Rush, A. J., Shaw, B. F., & Emery, G. (1979). *Cognitive therapy of depression.* New York: Guilford.

Beck, A. T., Steer, R. A., Kovacs, M., & Garrison, B. (1985). Hopelessness and eventual suicide: A 10-year prospective study of patients hospitalized with suicidal ideation. *American Journal of Psychiatry, 142,* 559–563.

Blatt, S. J. (1995). The destructiveness of perfectionism: Implications for the treatment of depression. *American Psychologist, 50,* 1003–1020.

Blatt, S. J., Quinlan, D. M., Chevron, E. S., McDonald, C., & Zuroff, D. C. (1982). Dependency and self-criticism: Psychological dimensions of depression. *Journal of Consulting and Clinical Psychology, 50,* 113–124.

Blatt, S. J., Quinlan, D. M., Pilkonis, P. A., & Shea, M. T. (1995). Impact of perfectionism and need for approval on the brief treatment of depression: The National Institute of Mental Health Treatment of Depression Collaborative Research Program revisited. *Journal of Consulting and Clinical Psychology, 63,* 125–132.

Bower, G. H. (1981). Mood and memory. *American Psychologist, 36,* 129–148.

Brown, G., & Beck, A. T. (1989). The role of imperatives in psychopathology: A reply to Ellis. *Cognitive Therapy and Research, 13,* 315–321.

Brown, G. P., Hammen, C. L., Craske, M. G., & Wickens, T. D. (1995). Dimensions of dysfunctional attitudes as vulnerabilities to depressive symptoms. *Journal of Abnormal Psychology, 104,* 431–435.

Brown, G. P., MacLeod, A. K., Tata, P., & Goddard, L. (in press). Worry and the simulation of future events. *Anxiety, Stress, and Coping.*

Brown, G. W., & Harris, T. (1978). *Social origins of depression.* New York: Free Press.

Calhoon, S. K. (1996). Confirmatory factor analysis of the Dysfunctional Attitude Scale in a student sample. *Cognitive Therapy and Research, 20,* 81–91.

Cane, D. B., Olinger, L. J., Gotlib, I. H., & Kuiper, N. A. (1986). Factor structure of the Dysfunctional Attitude Scale in a student population. *Journal of Clinical Psychology, 42,* 307–309.

Charlton, P., & Power, M. J. (1995). The assessment of dysfunctional attitudes and their role in the onset, persistence and recurrence of clinical depression. *European Journal of Personality, 9,* 379–400.

Coyne, J. C., & Gotlib, I. H. (1983). The role of cognitions in depression: A critical appraisal. *Psychological Bulletin, 94,* 472–505.

Coyne, J. C., & Gotlib, I. H. (1986). Studying the role of cognition in depression: Well-trodden paths and cul-de-sacs. *Cognitive Therapy and Research, 10,* 695–705.

Davidson, G. C., Vogel, R. S., & Coffman, S. G. (1997). Think-aloud approaches to cognitive assessment and the articulated thoughts in simulated situations paradigm. *Journal of Consulting and Clinical Psychology, 65,* 950–958.

DeRubeis, R. J., Evans, M. D., Hollon, S. D., Garvey, M. J., Grove, W. M., Tuason, V. B., & Vye, C. (1990). How does cognitive therapy work? Cognitive change and symptom change in cognitive therapy and pharmacotherapy for depression. *Journal of Consulting and Clinical Psychology, 58,* 862–869.

Dohrenwend, B. (1992, September–October). *A life-stress research approach.* Paper presented at the Science of Refugee Mental Health: New Concepts and Methods Conference. Boston.

Dyck, M. J. (1992). Subscales of the Dysfunctional Attitude Scale. *British Journal of Clinical Psychology, 31,* 333–335.

Ellis, A. (1985). Expanding the ABC's of RET. In M. J. Mahoney & A. Freeman (Eds.), *Cognition and psychotherapy* (pp. 313–323). New York: Plenum.

Evans, M. D., Hollon, S. D., DeRubeis, R. J., Piasecki, J. M., Tuason, V. B., & Vye, C. (1985). Differential relapse following cognitive therapy and pharmacotherapy for depression. *Archives of General Psychiatry, 49,* 802–808.

Fava, M., Bless, E., Otto, M. W., Pava, J. A., & Rosenbaum, J. F. (1994). Dysfunctional attitudes in major depression: Changes with pharmacotherapy. *Journal of Nervous and Mental Disease, 182,* 45–49.

Flett, G. L., Hewitt, P. L., Blankstein, K. R., & Dynin, C. B. (1994). Dimensions of perfectionism and Type A behaviour. *Personality and Individual Differences, 16,* 477–485.

Flett, G. L., Hewitt, P. L., Blankstein, K. R., & Mosher, S. W. (1995). Perfectionism, life events, and depressive symptoms: A test of a diathesis–stress model. *Current Psychology, 14,* 112–137.

Foy, D. W., Rueger, D. B., Sipprelle, R. C., & Carroll, E. M. (1984). Etiology of posttraumatic stress disorder in Vietnam veterans: Analysis of premilitary, military, and combat exposure influences. *Journal of Consulting and Clinical Psychology, 52,* 79–87.

Garber, J., & Robinson, N. S. (1997). Cognitive vulnerability in children at risk for depression. *Cognition and Emotion, 11,* 619–635.

Haaga, D. A., Dyck, M. J., & Ernst, D. (1991). Empirical status of cognitive theory of depression. *Psychological Bulletin, 110,* 215–236.

Hamilton, E. W., & Abramson, L. Y. (1983). Cognitive patterns and major depressive disorder: A longitudinal study in a hospital setting. *Journal of Abnormal Psychology, 92,* 173–184.

Hammen, C. L. (1988). Depression and cognitions about personal stressful life events. In L. Alloy (Ed.), *Cognitive processes in depression* (pp. 77–108). New York: Guilford.

Hammen, C. L., & Krantz, S. E. (1985). Measures of psychological process in depression. In E. E. Beckham and W. R. Leber (Eds.), *Handbook of depression: Treatment, assessment, and research* (pp. 408–444). Homewood, IL: Dorsey Press.

Hewitt, P. L., & Flett, G. L. (1990). Perfectionism and depression: A multidimensional analysis. *Journal of Social Behavior and Personality, 5,* 423–438.

Hewitt, P. L., & Flett, G. L. (1991). Dimensions of perfectionism in unipolar depression. *Journal of Abnormal Psychology, 100,* 98–101.

Hewitt, P. L., Flett, G. L., & Ediger, E. (1995). Perfectionism traits and perfectionistic self-presentation in eating disorder attitudes, characteristics, and symptoms. *International Journal of Eating Disorders, 18,* 317–326.

Hewitt, P. L., Flett, G. L., & Ediger, E. (1996). Perfectionism and depression: Longitudinal assessment of a specific vulnerability hypothesis. *Journal of Abnormal Psychology, 105,* 276–280.

Hewitt, P. L., Flett, G. L., & Turnbull, W. (1994). Borderline personality disorder: An investigation with the Multidimensional Perfectionism Scale. *European Journal of Psychological Assessment, 10,* 28–33.

Hollon, S. D., & Bemis, K. M. (1981). Self-report and the assessment of cognitive functions. In M. Hersen & A. S. Bellack (Eds.), *Behavioural assessment: A practical handbook* (2nd ed., pp. 125–174). New York: Pergamon Press.

Hollon, S. D., Kendall, P. C., & Lumry, A. (1986). Specificity of depressotypic cognitions in clinical depression. *Journal of Abnormal Psychology, 95,* 52–59.

Hollon, S. D., & Kriss, M. R. (1984). Cognitive factors in clinical research and practice. *Clinical Psychology Review, 4,* 35–76.

Horney, K. (1950). *Neurosis and human growth.* New York: Norton.

Jarret, R. B., Eaves, G. G., Grannemann, B. D., & Rush, J. A. (1991). Clinical, cognitive, and demographic predictors of response to cognitive therapy for depression: A preliminary report. *Psychiatry Research, 37,* 245–260.

Kovacs, M., & Beck, A. T. (1978). Maladaptive cognitive structures in depression. *American Journal of Psychiatry, 135,* 524–533.

Kovacs, M., Beck, A. T., & Weissman, A. N. (1975). Hopelessness: An indicator of suicidal risk. *Suicide, 5,* 98–103.

Kuehnel, R. H., & Wadden, T. A. (1994). Binge eating disorder, weight cycling, and psychopathology. *International Journal of Eating Disorders, 15,* 321–329.

Kwon, S., & Oei, T. P. S. (1995). The roles of two levels of cognitions in the development, maintenance, and treatment of depression. *Clinical Psychology Review, 14,* 331–358.

MacLeod, A. K., Pankhania, B., Lee, M., & Mitchell, D. (1997). Parasuicide, depression and the anticipation of positive and negative future experiences. *Psychological Medicine, 27,* 973–977.

Martin, R. A., Kuiper, N. A., & Westra, H. A. (1989). Cognitive and affective components of the Type A behavior pattern: Preliminary evidence for a self-worth contingency model. *Personality and Individual Differences, 10,* 771–784.

Metalsky, G. I., Joiner, T. E., Jr., Hardin, T. S., & Abramson, L. Y. (1993). Depressive reactions to failure in a naturalistic setting: A test of the hopelessness and self-esteem theories of depression. *Journal of Abnormal Psychology, 102,* 101–109.

Miranda, J., & Gross, J. J. (1997). Cognitive vulnerability, depression, and the mood–state dependent hypothesis: Is out of sight out of mind? *Cognition & Emotion, 11,* 585–605.

Miranda, J., & Persons, J. B. (1988). Dysfunctional attitudes are mood–state dependent. *Journal of Abnormal Psychology, 97,* 76–79.

Miranda, J., Persons, J. B., & Byers, C. N. (1990). Endorsement of dysfunctional beliefs depends on current mood state. *Journal of Abnormal Psychology, 99,* 237–241.

Monroe, S. M., & Simons, A. D. (1991). Diathesis–stress theories in the context of life stress research: Implications for the depressive disorders. *Psychological Bulletin, 110,* 406–425.

Nelson, L. D., Stern, S. L., & Chicchetti, D. V. (1992). The dysfunctional attitude scale: How well can it measure depressive thinking. *Journal of Psychopathology and Behavioral Assessment, 14,* 217–223.

O'Leary, K. M., Cowdry, R. W., Gardner, D. L., Leibenluft, E., Lucas, P. B., and deJong-Meyer, R. (1991). Dysfunctional attitudes in borderline personality disorder. *Journal of Personality Disorders, 5,* 233–242.

Oliver, J. M., & Baumgart, E. P. (1985). The Dysfunctional Attitude Scale: Psychometric properties and relation to depression in an unselected adult population. *Cognitive Therapy and Research, 9,* 161–167.

Parker, G., Bradshaw, G., & Blignault, I. (1984). Dysfunctional attitudes: Measurement, significant constructs and links with depression. *Acta Psychiatrica Scandinavica, 70,* 90–96.

Peselow, E. D., Robins, C. J., Block, P., & Barouche, F. (1990). Dysfunctional attitudes in depressed patients before and after clinical treatment and in normal control subjects. *American Journal of Psychiatry, 147,* 439–444.

Poulakis, Z., & Wertheim, E. H. (1993). Relationships among dysfunctional cognitions, depressive symptoms, and bulimic tendencies. *Cognitive Therapy and Research, 17,* 549–559.

Power, M. J., & Dalgleish, T. (1997). *Cognition and emotion: From order to disorder.* Hove, England: Erlbaum.

Power, M. J., Duggan, C. F., Lee, A. S., & Murray, R. M. (1994). Dysfunctional attitudes in depressed and recovered depressed patients and their first-degree relatives. *Psychological Medicine, 25,* 87–93.

Power, M. J., Katz, R., McGuffin, P., Duggan, C. F., Lam, D., & Beck, A. T. (1994). The Dysfunctional Attitude Scale (DAS): A comparison of forms A and B and proposals for a new subscaled version. *Journal of Research in Personality, 28,* 263–276.

Reda, M. A. (1984). Cognitive organization and antidepressants: Attitude modification during amitriptyline treatment in severely depressed individuals. In M. A. Reda & M. J. Mahoney (Eds.), *Cognitive Psychotherapies* (pp. 119–149). Cambridge, MA: Ballinger.

Reda, M. A., Carpiniello, B., Secchiaroli, L., & Blanco, S. (1985). Thinking, depression, and antidepressants: Modified and unmodified depressive beliefs during treatment with amitriptyline. *Cognitive Therapy and Research, 9,* 135–143.

Roberts, J. E., Gotlib, I. H., & Kassel, J. D. (1996). Adult attachment security and symptoms of depression: The mediating roles of dysfunctional attitudes and low self-esteem. *Journal of Personality and Social Psychology, 70,* 310–320.

Scott, J., Harrington, J., House, R., & Ferrier, I. N. (1996). A preliminary study of the relationship among personality, cognitive vulnerability, symptom profile, and outcome in major depressive disorder. *Journal of Nervous and Mental Disease, 184,* 503–505.

Scott, J., Williams, J. M. G., Brittlebank, A., & Ferrier, I. N. (1995). The relationship between premorbid neuroticism, cognitive dysfunction and persistence of depression: A 1-year follow-up. *Journal of Affective Disorders, 33,* 167–172.

Segal, Z. V. (1988). Appraisal of the self-schema construct in cognitive models of depression. *Psychological Bulletin, 103,* 147–162.

Segal, Z. V., & Shaw, B. F. (1986). When cul-de-sacs are more mentality than reality: A rejoinder to Coyne and Gotlib. *Cognitive Therapy and Research, 10,* 707–714.

Sibilia, L., Picozzi, R., & Nardi, A. (1995). Identifying a psychological profile of Type A behaviour pattern. *Stress Medicine, 11,* 263–270.

Silverman, J. S., Silverman, J. A., & Eardley, D. A. (1984). Do maladaptive attitudes cause depression? *Archives of General Psychiatry, 41,* 28–30.

Simons, A. D., Garfield, S. L., & Murphy, G. E. (1984). The process of change in cognitive therapy and pharmacotherapy for depression—Changes in mood and cognition. *Archives of General Psychiatry, 41,* 45–51.

Simons, A. D., Murphy, G. E., Levine, J. L., & Wetzel, R. D. (1986). Cognitive therapy and pharmacotherapy for depression: Sustained improvement over one year. *Archives of General Psychiatry, 43,* 43–48.

Teasdale, J. D. (1988). Cognitive vulnerability to persistent depression. *Cognition and Emotion, 2,* 247–274.

Teasdale, J. D., & Barnard, P. J. (1993). *Affect, cognition, and change: Re-modelling depressive thought.* Hove, England: Erlbaum.

Teasdale, J. D., Taylor, M. J., Cooper, Z., Hayhurst, H., & Paykel, E. S. (1995). Depressive thinking: Shifts in construct accessibility or in schematic mental models. *Journal of Abnormal Psychology, 104,* 500–507.

Thase, M. E., Simons, A. D., McGeary, J., & Cahalane, J. F. (1992). Relapse after cognitive behavior therapy of depression: Potential implications for longer courses of treatment. *American Journal of Psychiatry, 149,* 1046–1052.

Weissman, A. N. (1979). The Dysfunctional Attitude Scale: A validation study. *Dissertation Abstracts International, 40,* 1389B–1390B. (UMI No. 79-19, 533)

Weissman, A. N., & Beck, A. T. (1978, November). *Development and validation of the Dysfunctional Attitude Scale: A preliminary investigation.* Paper presented at the meeting of the Association for the Advancement of Behavior Therapy, Chicago.

Whisman, M. A., & Kwon, P. (1992). Parental representations, cognitive distortions, and mild depression. *Cognitive Therapy and Research, 16,* 557–568.

Whisman, M. A., & McGarvey, A. L. (1994). Attachment, depressotypic cognitions, and dysphoria. *Cognitive Therapy and Research, 19,* 633–650.

Williams, J. G., Watts, F. N., MacLeod, C., & Mathews, A. (1988). *Cognitive psychology and emotional disorders.* New York: Wiley.

Part III

Perfectionism, Stress, and Coping in Maladjustment

11

Perfectionism and Stress Processes in Psychopathology

Paul L. Hewitt and Gordon L. Flett

The marked increase in research on the perfectionism construct over the past decade reflects the importance of the concept. The research from various laboratories has shown the clinical relevance of the construct not only in association with a variety of phenomena, including anxiety, depression, eating disorders, personality disorders, interpersonal problems, and marital difficulties, but also for how perfectionistic behavior can influence the clinical assessment process (Habke, 1997) and treatment issues (Blatt, 1995; Hewitt, Flynn, Mikail, & Flett, 2001b). Although an impressive list of psychopathological correlates of perfectionism has been developed, most of the research has been conducted without explicit reference to models of perfectionistic behavior and how perfectionism comes to be associated with those disorders. The purpose of this chapter is not only to describe our multidimensional conceptualization of perfectionism traits but also to outline a model that examines how perfectionism functions as both a mediating and a moderating variable in influencing stress and producing or maintaining various psychological disorders and symptoms. Finally, because most of the research on perfectionism has focused on depression as an outcome, we discuss some of that research to illustrate the associations among perfectionism traits, stress, and psychopathology.

Dimensions of Perfectionism

In response to dissatisfaction with the unidimensional conceptualizations of perfectionism that appeared sporadically in the literature over the years, both our research group (Hewitt & Flett, 1989, 1991a, 1991b; Hewitt, Mittelstaedt, & Wollert, 1989) and the research group led by Frost and colleagues (Frost, Marten, Lahart, & Rosenblate, 1990) have conceptualized perfectionism as a multidimensional construct. Although the conceptualizations differ, the need to differentiate facets of perfectionistic behavior is a common theme. In addition, the models suggest that focusing solely on the cognitive components was too restrictive and that interpersonal and motivational factors must be taken into account (see Hewitt & Flett, 1990, 1991b).

Our work has focused on three major trait dimensions of perfectionism: Self-oriented perfectionism, other-oriented perfectionism, and socially prescribed perfectionism (Hewitt & Flett, 1991b). The dimensions are personality traits in the sense that they are stable, ingrained personality styles. Moreover, they are regarded as distinguishable dimensions that are each associated with different psychopathological states. Although the behaviors exhibited are frequently the same or similar among the dimensions (e.g., motivation to actually *be* perfect, maintenance of markedly unrealistic expectations, stringent and critical evaluations, and equating performance with worth), the distinguishing features among the dimensions involve either whom the perfectionistic expectations derive from (i.e., self or others) or to whom the perfectionistic behaviors are directed (i.e., toward self or others).

Self-oriented perfectionism is an intraindividual dimension involving perfectionistic behaviors that both derive from the self and are directed toward the self. That is, the person with self-oriented perfectionism derives his or her own perfectionistic expectations and requires only him- or herself to be perfect. The important facets of self-oriented perfectionism include strong motivations for the self to be perfect, maintaining unrealistic self-expectations in the face of failure, stringent self-evaluations that focus on one's own flaws and shortcomings, and generalization of unrealistic expectations and evaluations across behavioral domains. This dimension is related to disorders and symptoms that involve the self-concept, such as depression and eating disorders.

Other-oriented perfectionism is an interpersonal dimension of perfectionism that also stems from the self, but perfectionistic demands are directed toward others. That is, other-oriented perfectionism entails strong motivations for having others be perfect (e.g., one's children, spouse, subordinates, employees, and so forth), unrealistic expectations, and stringent evaluations of others. Other-oriented perfectionists require others to be perfect in many domains of functioning. This dimension may not necessarily produce self-related disorders or symptoms for the perfectionist him- or herself, but it should produce dissatisfaction or difficulties for the targets of the other-oriented perfectionist. Such perfectionists may experience distress to the extent that the standards they prescribe for others involve a failure on the part of others to provide the other-oriented perfectionist with social support or recognition. Similarly, other-oriented perfectionists may experience difficulties to the extent that the targets of the perfectionistic expectancies feel criticized and express their resentment about being treated in a hostile manner. Thus, the other-oriented perfectionist may experience interpersonal problems and the loss of important relationships.

Socially prescribed perfectionism is another interpersonal dimension. It involves perfectionistic demands that are perceived to derive from others yet are directed toward the self. For example, socially prescribed perfectionism involves the belief in one's inability to meet the perceived perfectionistic demands and expectations imposed by others. Thus, socially prescribed perfectionism entails the perception that others impose unrealistic demands and perfectionistic motives for oneself and will be satisfied only when those demands are met. This dimension of perfectionism is a self-related dimension in the sense that it involves concern with one's own lack of perfection; thus, it should be associated with self-related disorders and symptoms. Perhaps more important, however, is the strong concern over obtaining and maintaining the approval and care of other people and a sense of belonging that could be attained if it were possible to be perfect in the eyes of others.

The three perfectionism dimensions act as core vulnerability factors and are associated differentially with various types of psychopathology (see Hewitt & Flett, 1991b). The dimensions may be involved in either the direct onset of psychological disorders or the exacerbation of symptom severity because they reflect specific vulnerabilities to particular disorders that become manifest in the presence of specific environmental events, situations, or personality features. The trait facets also can function to maintain elevated levels of symptoms by influencing coping mechanisms or by influencing how the person actually deals with stressful events or symptoms. Hence, we suggest that the trait dimensions can play a mediating or a moderating role in the development and maintenance of psychopathology by influencing perceived stressful failures.

Our Multidimensional Perfectionism Scale[1] (MPS; Hewitt & Flett, 1989, 1991b) was developed to assess those dimensions. The measure was created in accordance with widely accepted test construction approaches (e.g., Jackson, 1970); item content was based on case descriptions and theories in the literature as well as on the clinical experience of Paul Hewitt, who has worked extensively with perfectionistic people. Items were retained or rejected on the basis of several criteria; for instance, items were discarded if they had content that might actually represent symptoms of depression or stress-related reactions. Items were retained in the final version of the MPS only after passing several statistical criteria (see Hewitt & Flett, 1991b, for a detailed description).

Perfectionism and Stress in Psychopathology

A primary assumption guiding our work with the MPS is that perfectionistic behavior is associated with psychopathology through its association with and influence on stress. Perfectionists are more likely than nonperfectionists to experience various kinds of stress in a variety of forms, including the experience of daily hassles and a constant pressure to attain high standards that emanate from inside or outside the self. Perfectionists who already are experiencing a high level of daily pressures will be particularly vulnerable to the disruptive effects associated with the experience of negative life events.

The connection between perfectionism and stress in influencing psychopathology can be quite complex. For example, trait dimensions of per-

---

[1]Unless otherwise noted, all references to the MPS refer to the version developed by Hewitt & Flett (1991b).

Table 11.1. Hypothesized Stress Mechanisms in Perfectionism
and Psychopathology

Stress mechanism	Description
Stress generation	A tendency to engage in behavior, make choices, or pursue unrealistic goals that creates stressful events or circumstances
Stress anticipation	A future orientation that involves a preoccupation with possible stressors and problems of personal importance
Stress perpetuation	A tendency to activate maladaptive tendencies (e.g., a ruminative response orientation) that maintain and prolong stressful episodes
Stress enhancement	The magnification of stress due to self-defeating styles of cognitive appraisal (e.g., interpreting minor mistakes and setbacks as personal failures of great importance, overgeneralizing negative outcomes to aspects of the self, and so forth) and maladaptive coping and problem-solving skills

fectionism can play a moderating role in producing psychopathological states by enhancing or exacerbating the aversiveness of experienced stressors or failures. Perfectionistic behavior also can play a mediating role in its association with psychopathology by influencing the generation of stressful failures, the perpetuation of the negative effects of stressors or failures, and the anticipation of future stressors and failures.

Our approach in this chapter is generally consistent with the framework put forth by Bolger and Zuckerman (1995), who acknowledged that personality factors are involved both in the amount of exposure to stressors and in differences in stress reactivity (i.e., coping choice and coping effectiveness). According to our formulation, perfectionism can influence or interact with stress to produce or maintain psychopathological states in at least four ways: (a) stress generation, (b) stress anticipation, (c) stress perpetuation, and (d) stress enhancement. A description of each mechanism and related processes is presented in Table 11.1. Stress generation, stress anticipation, and stress perpetuation all relate to the degree or amount of stress exposure, whereas stress enhancement involves the manner in which a person reacts to stress. We maintain that perfectionists are prone to experiencing psychological distress because they experience high levels of stress exposure and have maladaptive ways of reacting to that stress. The following sections describe the role of perfectionism in each of the four stress processes along with summaries of the research in each area.

Perfectionism and Stress Generation

In recent years, research on stress and maladjustment has expanded considerably by addressing the possibility that certain people are susceptible to adjustment problems because they have a personality orientation that is associated with increased exposure to stress. That is, some people take an active role in creating or generating stress for themselves and for those around them. People can create stressful circumstances for themselves in various ways, such as by associating with "difficult" people or engaging in excessive reassurance seeking to the point that it alienates possible providers of support (see Depue & Monroe, 1986; Hammen, 1991). Monroe and Simons (1991) have suggested that a personality vulnerability factor actually may create the stress with which the vulnerability factor then interacts, producing depression.

We believe that perfectionists, relative to nonperfectionists, are exposed to a greater number of stressful or failure events simply as a result of their unrealistic approach to life. In addition to the usual stressors or failures that can befall any person, stressors or failures actually will be produced by people who are perfectionistic because they seek perfection in many or all spheres of behavior. Perfectionistic behavior can generate stress that stems, in part, from perfectionists' tendencies to stringently evaluate themselves and others, focus on negative aspects of performance, and experience little satisfaction.

Differences should be evident among the various dimensions of perfectionism in terms of their role in the generation of stress. A person with a high level of self-oriented perfectionism can turn a relatively successful experience into a personal failure by striving for impossibly high standards and becoming dissatisfied and disappointed by the level of performance. For example, the excessively perfectionistic student who views an A+ in a course as his or her expected performance will view anything but the A+ as a failure and will experience stress as a result. The tenor who sings beautifully throughout an aria but falters only slightly during the high C will view the entire piece of work as a total failure. In addition, even if a perfectionistic person performs some task flawlessly, little satisfaction may be experienced because he or she still views the performance at least somewhat as a failure. As an illustration, one of Hewitt's patients obtained a coveted A+ in a difficult course he was taking; after receiving the A+, he continued to denigrate himself, stating that he should have been able to get the A+ without studying so hard and that his situation simply reflected that he was not as bright as he thought he should be. Thus, in this situation, even the A+ was not seen as a success that produced satisfaction because the amount of effort required then became an issue. This example underscores the point that extreme perfectionists may be self-critical either for failing to attain an impossible goal or for expending too much effort in an attempt to reach this goal.

Several studies have shown that highly perfectionistic people experience greater dissatisfaction with their performance than do people who are not highly perfectionistic (e.g., Frost & Henderson, 1991). For example, Flynn, Hewitt, Flett, and Weinberg (2001) found that people scoring high on self-oriented perfectionism experienced less satisfaction with performance on a challenging task than those low on self-oriented perfectionism did, even after controlling for actual performance. Likewise, in a sample of professional artists, Mor, Day, Flett, and Hewitt (1995) found that both self-oriented and socially prescribed perfectionism were associated with decreased goal satisfaction and less happiness over performances, even though many of the perfectionists were highly accomplished professionals with international reputations.

The goals that perfectionists pursue should be associated with the generation of stress because extreme perfectionists pursue standards that are beyond attainment. Research in achievement settings has confirmed that some people tend to pursue goals that involve the creation of discrepancies between those goals and current levels of performance (Phillips, Hollenbeck, & Ilgen, 1996). Although trait perfectionism and discrepancy creation has not been investigated directly, a tendency for self-oriented perfectionists to create discrepancies would be in keeping with general evidence that people with high levels of achievement motivation tend to set more difficult goals than do people with lower levels of achievement motivation, even though they do not differ in performance level (Phillips et al., 1996).

Much of the stress generation in achievement situations can be traced back to the perfectionists' unwillingness to lower their expectations, even when provided with feedback suggesting that lowering the standard is the prudent thing to do. In an unpublished study, we established a link between perfectionism and goal inflexibility by administering our perfectionism measure, along with Brandtstadter and Renner's (1990) measures of flexible goal adjustment and tenacious goal pursuit, to a sample of 294 university students. Significant negative correlations were evident between flexible goal adjustment and self-oriented perfectionism ($r = -.18$, $p < .01$), other-oriented perfectionism ($r = -.26$, $p < .01$), and socially prescribed perfectionism ($r = -.32$, $p < .01$). Tenacious goal pursuit was associated with self-oriented perfectionism ($r = .35$, $p < .01$) and other-oriented perfectionism ($r = .18$, $p < .01$).

The link between perfectionism and an unwillingness to change goals may reflect a tendency for perfectionists to be high in cognitive rigidity. Ferrari and Mautz (1997) used a measure of behavioral rigidity and showed that attitudinal inflexibility was associated with all three MPS dimensions. They suggested that this inflexibility could undermine perfectionists' ability to cope effectively with change. We suggest further that goal inflexibility and cognitive inflexibility may create stress and problematic situations for extreme perfectionists.

Not only is it the case that perfectionists may be unwilling or unable to modify their goals, it also appears that perfectionists may sometimes make things difficult for themselves in an attempt to provide themselves with an excuse for failing. That is, perfectionists may add to their difficulties by engaging in self-handicapping behavior in task situations. Experimental research by Hobden and Pliner (1995) found that both self-oriented and socially prescribed perfectionism were associated with self-handicapping behavior—in other words, perfectionists appear to take a situation and make it more difficult for themselves. This behavior can be regarded as taking a relatively less threatening situation and making it more threatening and stressful. Subsequent research has confirmed that socially prescribed perfectionism and self-oriented perfectionism are associated with trait self-handicapping (Sherry, Flett, & Hewitt, 2001).

Another way to generate stress is for people such as perfectionists to put too much pressure on themselves. Beck (1993) alluded to this form of stress as the *internal stressor,* which includes "the demands the individuals place on themselves, their repetitive self-nagging, and their self-reproaches" (p. 350). According to Beck, internal stressors are common among people who set high goals for themselves and drive themselves to achieve those goals.

Weiten (1988, 1998) conducted research on pressure as a particular form of stress and discussed two subtypes of pressure: (a) pressure to successfully perform tasks and carry out responsibilities and (b) pressure to conform to expectations about how one ought to think and act. Weiten (1988) noted that although pressure typically stems from interpersonal sources, it also is important to consider self-imposed pressure. Accordingly, Weiten's Pressure Inventory (1988) includes a subscale that measures putting pressure on oneself.

If perfectionism is linked with stress generation, then it should be associated with self-imposed pressure. Recently, we examined this hypothesis by administering Weiten's Pressure Inventory, a daily hassles inventory, and a battery of perfectionism measures to 100 university students (see Flett, Parnes, & Hewitt, 2001). The correlational findings are shown in Table 11.2, which show that almost all the perfectionism measures were correlated significantly with levels of pressure and self-imposed pressure. Our new measure of automatic, perfectionistic thoughts, the Perfectionism Cognitions Inventory (Flett, Hewitt, Blankstein, & Gray, 1998), had the strongest associations with the measures of pressure and of self-imposed pressure. Thus, it appears that many perfectionists experience significant levels of self-imposed pressure as they strive to meet impossibly high

Table 11.2. Correlations Between Stress and Perfectionism Measures

Perfectionism scale	Stress measure		
	Pressure	Self-pressure	Hassles
Self-Oriented Perfectionism[1]	.29**	.30**	.19
Other-Oriented Perfectionism[1]	.08	.17	.07
Socially Prescribed Perfectionism[1]	.45***	.33***	.39***
Perfectionism Cognitions[2]	.65***	.52***	.47***
Concern Over Mistakes[3]	.38***	.37***	.25*
High Standards[3]	.31***	.26**	.08
Doubts About Actions[3]	.34***	.15	.24*
Organization[3]	−.23*	−.24*	.16
Parental Expectations[3]	.27**	.18	.22*
Parental Criticism[3]	.41***	.37***	.47***

Note. *p < .05. **p < .01. ***p < .001.
[1]From the Multidimensional Perfectionism Scale (Hewitt & Flett, 1991b).
[2]From the Perfectionism Cognitions Inventory (Flett et al., 1998).
[3]From the Multidimensional Perfectionism Scale (Frost et al., 1990).

goals; that pressure is associated with an internal dialogue that involves thoughts about the inability to attain perfection.

Most of our discussion has focused thus far on self-oriented perfectionism, but the interpersonal dimensions of perfectionism are especially important because they may contribute to stress by leading to interpersonal conflict and other interpersonal problems. Other-oriented perfectionists are highly focused on other people's shortcomings and will create interpersonal discord if their disappointment with others is openly expressed. A tendency to be openly critical of others will cause extensive tension in relationships, as in a case study of a 45-year-old businessman who had chronic hypertension:

> [He] interpreted anything less than optimum efficiency on the part of his employees as "negligence," and he would experience hostility toward that employee. Since he considered it unwise to scold his employees, he carried a constant load of hostility. Thus, any performance below his standards (mistakes, delays, etc.) would contribute to the stress he experienced. (Beck, 1993, p. 365)

Some would interpret this stress as originating in the poor performance of the employees, but we view this as stress that emanates from the self because its origin is the intolerant, other-oriented standards of the perfectionist.

Similarly, socially prescribed perfectionism may contribute to conflict and interpersonal problems because socially prescribed perfectionists are highly sensitive to criticism and high in interpersonal sensitivity (see Hewitt & Flett, 1991b, 1993). Mounting evidence supports the role of interpersonal sensitivity in vulnerability to depression (see Boyce, Hickie, & Parker, 1991; Boyce, Parker, Barnett, Cooney, & Smith, 1991). Recently, we evaluated the link between perfectionism and interpersonal sensitivity by administering the MPS and the Interpersonal Sensitivity Measure (IPSM; Boyce & Parker, 1989) to 196 undergraduate students (Flett, Velyvis, & Hewitt, 2001). Socially prescribed perfectionism was associated with total IPSM scores ($r = .32$, $p < .001$) and various facets of interpersonal sensitivity, including separation anxiety ($r = .41$, $p < .001$), a fragile inner self ($r = .32$, $p < .001$), and interpersonal awareness ($r = .29$, $p < .001$). No such associations were evident in this sample for self-oriented or other-oriented perfectionism and levels of interpersonal sensitivity.

The data indicate that socially prescribed perfectionists who have a high level of interpersonal sensitivity are especially likely to overreact to perceived slights and may even respond to ambiguous feedback from another person as if it were negative. One possibility is that people characterized by elevated socially prescribed perfectionism and interpersonal sensitivity will interpret ambiguous interpersonal feedback in a threatening manner and will turn a relatively benign situation into a stressful encounter. Socially prescribed perfectionists also could generate stress for themselves by engaging in excessive reassurance seeking, which would be a reflection of the dependency needs associated with this perfectionism dimension (see Hewitt & Flett, 1993). In fact, the established association between socially prescribed perfectionism and frequent negative social interactions (see Flett, Hewitt, Garshowitz, & Martin, 1997) may be a by-product of core interpersonal needs that actually produce interpersonal problems or losses that again precipitate a depressive episode.

Finally, an indirect link between perfectionism and stress generation may occur because the three MPS dimensions are associated with chronic forms of depression (Hewitt, Flett, Ediger, Norton, & Flynn, 1998). Work by Hammen (1991) and others has shown that chronic forms of depression are associated with stress generation.

Although several possible links exist between perfectionism and stress generation, only indirect evidence presently supports the link between perfectionism and generation of interpersonal stress. As noted earlier, perfectionism is likely to create stress through its association with self-defeating tendencies such as inflexibility and self-handicapping. Some evidence of stress generation was obtained in a prospective study conducted in our laboratory (Hewitt, Flett, & Ediger, 1996). A sample of 124 psychiatric patients completed the MPS; 3 months later, they completed the Life Events Inventory (Cochrane & Robertson, 1973) with respect to the preceding 3 months. Two independent raters indicated which events on the inventory were independent (i.e., definitely not self-generated, such as the death of a family member) and which were possibly dependent (i.e., possibly generated as a result of the participant's personality, such as being fired from a job). We found that, although self-oriented perfectionism was correlated significantly with the number of possibly dependent events, it was not correlated with independent events. Similarly, socially prescribed perfectionism was correlated with the number of possibly dependent events but not with independent events. Finally, other-oriented perfectionism was not associated with either dependent or independent events. The data provide some initial support for the idea that perfectionists may generate some of their own stress.

Recent research in our laboratory is focusing on the associations among perfectionism, interpersonal problems, and depression. One recent study examined this issue in a sample of 72 people undergoing group treatment for difficulties stemming from perfectionism (Hewitt, Flynn, Mikail, & Flett, 2001a). Measures of trait perfectionism, interpersonal problems, and depression were administered prior to the beginning of treatment. Analyses confirmed that interpersonal problems mediated the link between socially prescribed perfectionism and depression, and the general pattern of findings was consistent with the view that perfectionistic behavior can produce interpersonal problems that, in turn, contribute to depression. A goal for future research is to explore those associations in prospective research.

Perfectionism and the Anticipation of Stress

The second mechanism we have proposed is the tendency for perfectionists to anticipate stress or failure and then respond as though the anticipated stress has already occurred. The notion of anticipatory stress is based on the observation that certain people experience stress not only as it happens but also in the here-and-now because they actively anticipate the experience of future stressors of importance (see Peacock & Wong, 1996). This form of stress stems from intrapersonal factors involving the person's future orientation (see Wong, 1993). The anticipated experience of negative emotions in response to possible stress can have a profound influence on the willingness to pursue goals and subsequent goal-based emotions (see Bagozzi, Baumgartner, & Pieters, 1998).

A growing body of evidence indicates that certain perfectionists are preoccupied with the possibility that stressful events will occur and do not necessarily do anything to prevent the stress. Perfectionism has been linked with persistent worry and fear of failure (Flett, Hewitt, Blankstein, & Mosher, 1991; Frost et al., 1990); although the fear of failure is primarily a reflection of the achievement orientation of perfectionists, anticipated stress also may reflect the interpersonal orientation of perfectionists. In this instance, anticipated stress would involve negative expectations among socially prescribed perfectionists about the likelihood of criticism and other forms of mistreatment.

As indicated above, several studies have demonstrated that various facets of perfectionism are associated with a fear of failure, a motivation that reflects the anticipation of failure in performance. In a study of female athletes, Frost and Henderson (1991) assessed cognitive reactions to athletic competition and found that perfectionistic athletes had more of a failure orientation toward athletic performances. Similarly, Flett, Hewitt, Blankstein, and Mosher (1991) showed that the three trait MPS dimensions were associated with decreased tolerance and fear of failure. In a study of perfectionism and procrastination, Flett, Blankstein, Hewitt, and Koledin (1992) found that the trait dimensions of perfectionism were associated with a pervasive fear of failure that seemed to drive the dilatory behavior. Moreover, in one of the only existing tests of perfectionism and the anticipation of future stress, Fry (1995) found that perfectionistic women executives were more likely than other groups of women executives to anticipate that the future would bring stressful mistakes.

The anticipation of future negative events can be viewed as a form of pessimism or hopelessness that involves expectations about negative occurrences in the future. This hopelessness over future events is seen as a central component in several theories of depression. For example, in Beck's (1967) cognitive theory of depression, negative expectations regarding the future, the self, and the world are said to be key factors in the development of depression. Moreover, in the model described by Brown and Harris (1978), the specific and generalized hopelessness that arises from important losses are integral in producing depressive episodes. Finally, in their model of hopelessness depression, Abramson, Metalsky, and Alloy (1989) pointed to the importance of specific and generalized hopelessness in producing and exacerbating depression.

We have noted elsewhere that socially prescribed perfectionism has an inherent element of helplessness and hopelessness associated with it (e.g., Flett, Hewitt, Blankstein, & Koledin, 1991; Hewitt & Flett, 1991a, 1991b). A significant proportion of socially prescribed perfectionists seem to be people who not only anticipate the possibility of negative events but also become quite certain that such events will indeed be experienced. The perceived certainty of those events makes them especially stressful. Andersen (1990) has labeled this phenomenon the "inevitability of future suffering." If negative events are perceived as certain to occur and a person perceives that he or she is unable to do anything to avoid those negative events (i.e., low self-efficacy), then it is likely that the same person will experience hopelessness and related symptoms of hopelessness depression (see Abramson et al., 1989).

As noted above, socially prescribed perfectionism is the perfectionism dimension that should be linked most closely with negative expectations about the future. Theoretical descriptions of the cognitive aspects of concepts, such as attachment style (Bowlby, 1980) and relational schemata (Baldwin, 1992), include the notion that certain people have a working model that includes expectations about future interpersonal events and an insecure attachment style that includes the expectation of negative interpersonal events involving abandonment and rejection. Similarly, socially prescribed perfectionism can be conceptualized as a social–cognitive variable that includes negative expectations about the likelihood of being the target of criticism and mistreatment due to the certainty of experiencing unfair expectancies in the future. In essence, then, we are suggesting that socially prescribed perfectionism includes a "negative future events" schema that is chronically accessed among depressed people.

Empirical research has confirmed the association between socially prescribed perfectionism and negative outcome expectancies. Research with university students indicates that socially prescribed perfectionism is associated with trait pessimism as assessed by the Life Orientation Test (see Martin, Flett, Hewitt, Krames, & Szantos, 1996). This study also found that levels of self-reported depressive symptoms are higher among socially prescribed perfectionists with low levels of general self-efficacy (i.e., beliefs that one cannot control important outcomes).

Other empirical research on hopelessness and the trait dimensions of perfectionism has shown that socially prescribed perfectionism is associated consistently with hopelessness in all the studies that have tested this association, including research with adult psychiatric patients, adolescents, and university students (Chang & Rand, 2000; Dean & Range, 1996; Dean, Range, & Goggin, 1996; Hewitt, Flett, & Turnbull-Donovan, 1992; Hewitt, Newton, Flett, & Callander, 1997; Hewitt, Norton, Flett, Callander, & Cowan, 1998; Ohtani & Sakurai, 1995). The studies' unequivocal findings suggest that socially prescribed perfectionism is indeed an aspect of perfectionism associated with generalized hopelessness.

The association between other dimensions of perfectionism and hopelessness is less clear. For example, Sakurai and Ohtani (1997) developed a multidimensional measure of self-oriented perfectionism that measures four components—desire for perfection, concern over mistakes, high personal standards, and doubting of actions. They found in a sample of 178

Japanese students that concern over mistakes and doubts about actions were associated positively with hopelessness, whereas high personal standards were associated negatively with hopelessness.

In contrast to the many studies of perfectionism and hopelessness, relatively few studies have investigated whether perfectionists anticipate a greater number of difficulties when asked to make predictions about the likelihood of experiencing negative events. Hewitt, Flett, and Weber (1994) provided initial evidence of an association between perfectionism and anticipated stressful events: They reported that both socially prescribed perfectionism and self-oriented perfectionism were associated with predictions of the likelihood of attempting suicide in the future.

Flett, Levy, and Hewitt (2001) directly investigated the proposed association between perfectionism and depressive predictive certainty. In this research, a sample of 100 university students completed the MPS, indices of depression and anxiety, and a battery of measures assessing current stress and anticipated stress in the future. Current stress was assessed by having participants complete a measure of current daily hassles and the Inventory of Negative Social Interactions (Lakey, Tardiff, & Drew, 1994). Future stress was assessed by having participants complete measures of expected hassles over the next 3 months, expected negative social interactions over the next 3 months, and depressive predictive certainty. Analyses of measures of current stress showed that socially prescribed perfectionism was correlated with daily hassles and that both socially prescribed perfectionism and self-oriented perfectionism were associated with the frequency of negative social interactions. A similar pattern emerged for future hassles and future negative social interactions; that is, socially prescribed perfectionism was associated with future hassles and future negative social interactions, and self-oriented perfectionism was associated with future negative social interactions. Finally, higher levels of depressive predictive certainty were associated with both socially prescribed perfectionism and self-oriented perfectionism. Taken together, the findings indicate that perfectionists experience elevated levels of stress, which is accompanied by a tendency to anticipate chronic stress, including negative social interactions in the future. For some perfectionists, an element of predictive certainty is associated with these cynical perceptions. Thus, it appears that certain perfectionists do indeed have a negative future-event schema (Andersen, Spielman, & Bargh, 1992; Reich & Weary, 1998) and a sense of the inevitability of future suffering, as described by Andersen (1990).

Additional evidence of a link between perfectionistic tendencies and the anticipation of stress was obtained in our ongoing investigation of personality and coping with the transition to parenthood. Our sample of 150 women in the final month of their pregnancies were asked to estimate how much stress would be experienced during the rest of the pregnancy and during the first few postpartum months. Participants also indicated how much threat was associated with eight possible negative events taken from a perinatal stress measure, including pregnancy complications, delivery complications, change in relationships, and a change in professional or job status. The items were adapted from a recent study of coping with pregnancy (see Bernazzani, Saucier, David, & Borgeat, 1997). The results showed that the trait MPS dimensions had little association with these measures; however, the trait MPS dimensions were associated with a measure of concern with parenting mistakes, which was patterned after the Frost et al. (1990) general measure of concern over mistakes. In turn, this measure of concern with parenting mistakes was associated with negative predictions about the stress during the remainder of the pregnancy ($r = .26$, $p < .01$), anticipated stress during the initial postpartum months ($r = .28$, $p < .001$), and a composite threat index of possible stressors ($r = .33$, $p < .001$). Thus, the findings suggest that the link between trait perfectionism and anticipated stress about becoming a parent is mediated by an excessive concern with making parenting mistakes.

Perfectionism and Stress Perpetuation

Various dimensions of perfectionism are associated with the perpetuation or maintenance of stress or failures and the attendant distress because perfectionistic people are characterized by maladaptive styles that have the effect of prolonging stressful episodes. Much research supports this idea.

Three interrelated cognitive tendencies appear to be at work here. First, the trait dimensions of perfectionism are associated with self-blame and perseveration regarding failure (e.g., Hewitt & Flett, 1991b; Hewitt, Flett, Turnbull-Donovan, & Mikail, 1991), both of which are inappropriate methods of dealing cognitively with stress and failures. This tendency to engage in failure perseveration would contribute to both prolonging and exacerbating the experience of stress.

Second, certain perfectionists have a cognitive style that involves the frequent experience of automatic, perfectionistic thoughts. Recently, we have shown that perfectionists experience negative automatic thoughts with perfectionistic themes and that the frequent experience of perfectionism cognitions is associated with psychological distress in the form of dysphoria and anxiety, with the tendency to perseverate when confronted with a personal failure (see Flett et al., 1998). Our research with the Perfectionism Cognitions Inventory is based on the premise that certain perfectionists are prone to experiencing perfectionistic thoughts and that one of the contributing factors is the experience of negative life outcomes that highlight the discrepancy between the actual self and the ideal, perfect self. Blatt and Shichman (1983) observed that introjective people ruminate excessively about failures to meet personal standards and maintain a sense of control. A tendency to ruminate about an inability to attain perfectionistic standards is also in keeping with evidence indicating that the ideal self can operate as a self-schema that facilitates the recall of perfectionistic content (Hewitt & Genest, 1990). According to Hewitt and Genest, the ideal self-schema is especially likely to encode and process information that indicates that perfection has not been attained. In the current formulation, stress is a signal that one's life is not perfect; the stress will be prolonged by automatic thoughts involving the failure to attain perfection.

It has been suggested (see Flett et al., 1998) that once a failure or stressful event occurs, perfectionistic people will engage in rumination relating to their needs to be perfect and that by doing so, they will continually highlight the discrepancy between their real and ideal selves. The effect of this repetitive tendency is to increase the salience of the discrepancy and maintain depressive symptoms (Strauman, 1989). Flett et al. (1998) found that elevated automatic perfectionistic cognitions were indeed associated with depression symptoms in four separate samples, including a clinical sample of psychiatric patients. Moreover, the perfectionistic cognitions continued to be significant predictors of depression after partialing out other perfectionism traits and personality variables. The findings suggest that ruminations regarding themes of perfection are associated with depression and may help maintain or even exacerbate the distress that follows from the experience of stressful events.

Third, we maintain that the ruminative style exhibited by certain perfectionists includes that described in the work by Nolan-Hoeksema and her associates, who identified a ruminative response orientation that contributes to the persistence of pathological states—notably, depression (see Nolen-Hoeksema, Morrow, & Frederickson, 1993). Rather than engage in task-focused attempts to alleviate distress or distract themselves, those with the ruminative orientation tend to focus cognitively on their experience of distress and ruminate about the nature and causes of that distress.

A recent study by Flett and Hewitt (2000) generated empirical evidence that certain perfectionists have the ruminative response orientation to depression. In this research, a sample of 146 women in their final month of pregnancy and 138 fathers-to-be completed the MPS, the Perfectionism Cognitions Inventory, and a measure of concern over parenting mistakes. Participants also completed a battery of coping measures, including Butler and Nolen-Hoeksema's (1994) measure of ruminative response style and indices of stress, depression, and anxiety. Initial analyses of the data show that a ruminative response orientation to depression was associated significantly with self-oriented perfectionism, socially prescribed perfectionism, perfectionism cognitions, and concern over parenting mistakes in both women and men (r values ranged from .26 to .49). The data suggest that elements of perfectionism may be associated with persistent depression through an association with a maladaptive, ruminative response orientation.

In addition to cognitive features of perfectionism that may influence stress perpetuation, interpersonal styles of perfectionists can influence the perpetuation and maintenance of stress. For example, one form of dealing appropriately with stressors or with distress involves accessing social support networks (Finch, Okun, Pool, & Ruehlman, 1999) or seeking professional help for personal difficulties (see Bergin & Garfield, 1994). We have suggested that a major facet of perfectionistic behavior is a general inability to demonstrate or admit to one's imperfection (Hewitt et al., 2001a). We have found that perfectionistic people find it quite difficult to ask others for help or support; any request for help will communicate to others that the perfectionist is not perfectly able to cope, has personal problems, or is generally not the perfect person he or she has been trying to portray. Thus, perfectionistic people can lose opportunities to obtain social support or engage in obtaining information or professional help that may be useful in solving problems (e.g., Belsher & Costello, 1991). Not accessing support or professional help, of course, prolongs or even exacerbates the distress, both of which result in maintaining the difficulties or symptoms the person is experiencing.

Although no extensive research has been conducted on perfectionism dimensions and either social or professional support, evidence for the propositions described above can be found in several sources. With respect to seeking social forms of support, Hewitt, Flett, and Endler (1995) reported that socially prescribed perfectionism in women was associated with decreased social diversion, a form of coping that involves seeking people out in order to deal with problems. Similarly, Flett, Blankstein, Hewitt, and Obertynski (1994) found that self-oriented and other-oriented perfectionism were associated with low social support from friends and that socially prescribed perfectionism was associated with low support from family, friends, and significant others. Finally, Hewitt, Flynn, Flett, Nielsen, Parking, Han, and Tomlin (2001) administered measures of social support and perfectionism to one of several samples of university students. Socially prescribed perfectionism was associated with low support from family and with low availability of supportive people, but self-oriented and other-oriented perfectionism were not associated with perceived social support.

This study also yielded several findings that are directly relevant to the issue of whether perfectionists will seek treatment when distressed. We used a multidimensional measure by Fischer and Turner (1970) to assess attitudes and behaviors regarding seeking professional help for distress. Across student and community samples, the three trait MPS dimensions were associated with negative attitudes such as decreased recognition of need for help, stigma tolerance, interpersonal openness, and confidence in mental health professionals. Moreover, all three dimensions were associated with greater fears of psychotherapy and dysfunctional help-seeking attitudes. Finally, analyses that focused on a subset of people ($n = 31$) who had sought help at some point revealed that socially prescribed perfectionism was associated negatively ($r = -.50$) with ratings of comfort in seeking help and positively with ratings of difficulty continuing with treatment ($r = .54$). Self-oriented and other-oriented perfectionism also were associated with increased ratings of difficulty continuing with treatment. The findings from this work support the idea that p ⤍ple who score high on perfectionism traits tend to be less open to seeking professional help for psychological problems and that perfectionism can have a deleterious influence on the continuation of the treatment among those who actually receive help. The results are in keeping with previous research indicating that perfectionists may have a negative orientation toward treatment and the establishment of a working alliance with their therapists (see Blatt & Zuroff, chapter 16, this volume).

A corollary of the proposed link with stress perpetuation is that perfectionism is a personality construct that is likely associated with long-lasting and pernicious forms of maladjustment, such as chronic depression. Hewitt et al. (1998) evaluated the association between trait perfectionism and chronic symptoms of depression by having a sample of 121 current and formerly depressed patients complete the MPS; the Beck Depression Inventory, as a measure of concurrent depression symptoms; and the General Behavior Inventory (Depue, Krauss, Spoont, & Arbisi, 1989), a measure of chronicity of unipolar and bipolar depression symptoms. Regression analyses showed that only self-oriented perfectionism accounted for significant variance in chronic unipolar symptoms, after controlling for chronic bipolar, state unipolar, and other perfectionism dimensions. In predicting chronic bipolar symptoms, other-oriented and socially prescribed perfectionism both accounted for unique variance. The results supported the position that self-oriented perfectionism may function as a vulnerability factor in unipolar depression and is associated with persistent and chronic unipolar depression symptoms. In contrast, the interpersonal trait dimensions appeared to be associated with persistence of manic symptoms.

Some evidence, then, indicates that perfectionism is associated with cognitive and interpersonal factors involved in the perpetuation of stress and related forms of distress. Moreover, perfectionism is associated with chronic dysphoria and, at least to some degree, this association likely reflects persistent and high exposure to stress.

Perfectionism and Stress Enhancement

Research on stress generation and stress reactivity by Bolger and Zuckerman (1995) demonstrated that, although stress generation accounts for substantial variation in adjustment outcomes, stress reactivity is even more important. The individual differences in stress reactivity account for substantially more variance in poor psychological adjustment. In Bolger and Zuckerman's formulation, stress reactivity includes the coping choices made in response to stress and coping effectiveness (i.e., the extent to which coping works by reducing the negative outcomes of the stressful event).

We have conducted extensive research on the association between perfectionism and stress reactivity, as measured by coping choices. This research is based on the assumption that perfectionists have a difficult time accepting failure and have strong negative reactions to the actual or perceived experience of stressful events. In essence, the presence of perfectionism serves to enhance or intensify the negative impact of stress, which may lead to maladjustment.

The enhancement of the aversiveness of stressors can occur because of the manner in which a person evaluates and appraises the meaning of a particular life event (Folkman, Lazarus, Gruen, & DeLongis, 1986). This is especially the case with ego-involving stressful events (Hewitt & Flett, 1993): Stressors that are perceived as more important to the self tend to elicit more extreme reactions (Gruen, Folkman, & Lazarus, 1988). Recent research has confirmed the depressogenic effects of events that are seen as high in personal, contextual threat involving core aspects of the self (see Kendler, Karkowski, & Prescott, 1998).

In the case of perfectionism, stressors that are congruent with a particular perfectionistic style are experienced as more aversive than noncongruent stressors are: The congruent stressors are ego involving, and the aversive negative impact is enhanced, leading to increased symptomatology (Hewitt & Dyck, 1986; Hewitt & Flett, 1993). This tendency to magnify the negative impact of stress stems from equating perfect performance with self-worth, whereby performances other than perfect are interpreted as significant failures and as indications of one's worthlessness. Moreover, these particular types of disruptions, stressors, or failures are interpreted as a lack of competence or as an inability to control outcomes that interferes with the all-important attainment of perfection.

It follows that perfectionists will have especially strong responses to the extent that stressors are appraised as being relevant and important to the self-concept. Given that self-oriented perfectionism involves attaining self-related achievement goals of importance, achievement stressors or failures should be experienced as particularly aversive, relative to other stressors. In contrast, because socially prescribed perfectionism involves maintaining others' approval and a sense of belonging by being perfect, stressors that impinge on one's ability to meet others' expectations may be experienced as more aversive than other stressors. This may be especially the case for the person who perceives that others are placing great worth or meaning on a particular event, performance, or task.

If a link exists between perfectionism and stress enhancement, then it should be the case that a person will experience a particular event or stressor as more distressing if he or she is perfectionistic. Recently, Flynn et al. (2001) assessed the link between stress reactivity and self-oriented perfectionism. It was found that people high in self-oriented perfectionism rated a difficult intellectual task as more distressing and rated their own performance as less satisfactory than did those low in self-oriented perfectionism. The relationships held even when actual performance levels were controlled.

Similarly, Fry (1995) suggested that perfectionists view stressful events as more ego-involving, thereby increasing their perception of the stressfulness of those events. Fry compared women executives who had high or low levels of perfectionism and found that highly perfectionistic women executives rated their events as higher in "primary centrality" (i.e., the perception that a stressful event has significant personal consequences). In related research, Frost et al. (1995) had students engage in either a relatively easy or a more challenging Stroop task and found that compared with low-scoring participants, those who scored high on the Concern Over Mistakes subscale reacted to the challenging condition in which more mistakes were made with more negative mood, lowered confidence, and a greater sense that they should have done better (also see Frost et al., 1997). These investigations provide evidence that perfectionism can influence the aversiveness of events or performances and augment distress.

A heightened level of stress reactivity also would be expected given that elements of perfectionism are associated with a tendency to engage in overgeneralization, a maladaptive cognitive orientation in which negative outcomes are seen globally as reflecting the entire self (Beck, 1967). Thus, a mistake in one area becomes translated into a sweeping negative self-judgment in many or all areas of functioning. Research with subclinical and clinical participants has identified a characteristic tendency for perfectionists to overgeneralize failure to all aspects of the self (Flett, Russo, & Hewitt, 1994; Hewitt et al., 1991; Hewitt, Mittelstaedt, & Wollert, 1989).

Most of our discussion on stress enhancers has focused thus far on self-oriented perfectionism. Regarding the interpersonal dimensions, stress enhancement is a reflection of the high level of interpersonal sensitivity that is at the core of socially prescribed perfectionism. Clearly, the acute interpersonal sensitivity inherent in socially prescribed perfectionism (see Hewitt & Flett, 1991b) suggests that such people will be highly reactive to evaluative feedback from others.

Although past research has established that perfectionism is associated with depression symptoms, research that simply confirms the association between perfectionism and depression does not shed light on the mechanisms involved in producing or exacerbating depression symptoms. We have posited a diathesis–stress conceptualization of the relationships between dimensions of perfectionism and depression that is consistent with the stress-enhancement component of our model (Hewitt & Dyck, 1986; Hewitt & Flett, 1993). Self-oriented perfectionism and socially prescribed perfectionism are proposed as vulnerability factors in depression; a precipitating event, such as a stressful event or a perceived failure experience, must occur for depression to ensue. Moreover, as discussed above, stressors that are congruent with either self-oriented perfectionism (i.e., self-related achievement stressors) or socially prescribed perfectionism (i.e., social stressors) will be experienced as more aversive than noncongruent stressors because the congruent stressors are ego-involving; the aversive negative impact will be enhanced, thereby leading to depression symptoms (Hewitt & Dyck, 1986; Hewitt & Flett, 1993). This specific-vulnerability hypothesis is based on an extension of Oatley and Bolton's (1985) contention that stressors are especially likely to produce depression if those stressors pose a particular threat to a central aspect of the self.

Although some early research on the topic found evidence that attitudes related to self-oriented perfectionism interacted with general stress to predict depression (e.g., Hewitt & Dyck, 1986; Hewitt et al., 1989), recent work addressed the specific-vulnerability hypothesis with respect to perfectionism traits and depression. Hewitt and Flett (1993) assessed levels of self-oriented and socially prescribed perfectionism, specific daily stressors, and concurrent depression symptom severity in a sample of people with unipolar depression and in a heterogeneous sample of psychiatric patients. In the sample of those with unipolar depression, self-oriented perfectionism interacted only with self-related achievement hassles to predict concurrent depression; socially prescribed perfectionism interacted only with social hassles to predict concurrent depression. In both cases, high levels of perfectionism and stress resulted in increased depression. The data support the diathesis—stress model and suggest that the two perfectionism dimensions interact only with congruent stressors to predict concurrent symptom severity. In this study, the same measures were used in a heterogeneous sample of psychiatric patients in an attempt to replicate the results (see Hewitt & Flett, 1993). The findings involving self-oriented perfectionism were replicated in the sample, thereby further supporting the specific-vulnerability hypothesis. In contrast, the findings with socially prescribed perfectionism were not replicated; in fact, it was found that socially prescribed perfectionism interacted with both achievement and interpersonal stressors in the heterogeneous clinical sample. The findings suggest that first, self-oriented perfectionism acts as a diathesis that is robust across clinical samples and that elevated depression will ensue only in the presence of achievement stressors. Conversely, the findings with socially prescribed perfectionism seem to indicate that the findings of congruency are specific to people diagnosed with depression or that specific stressors are not always necessary for socially prescribed perfectionism to be related to depression (Hewitt & Flett, 1991a).

Although the findings of the above studies provided consistent support for the idea that self-oriented perfectionism is a relevant factor in depression, the findings were based on concurrent relationships. An important way to support the notion that self-oriented perfectionism and socially prescribed perfectionism are vulnerability factors to depression is to use a longitudinal research design. Flett, Hewitt, Blankstein, and Mosher (1995), in a college student sample, conducted an initial test of the issue of whether perfectionism is a vulnerability factor that predicts depression symptoms over time. Both self-oriented and socially prescribed perfectionism were correlated with concurrent levels of depressive symptoms, but only self-oriented perfectionism predicted increases in levels of depressive symptoms over a 3-month time period after controlling for initial levels of depression severity. The findings indicated that self-oriented perfectionism is a relevant personality variable in depression both concurrently and over time but that socially prescribed perfectionism may be more relevant for concurrent levels of depression. In another study, Hewitt et al. (1996) assessed whether the perfectionism dimensions interacted with specific stressors to predict depression over time in a large heterogeneous sample of depressed patients. The participants completed measures of perfectionism and depression at Time 1 and measures of specific life-event stress (for the 4-month lag) and depression 4 months later. After controlling for depression at Time 1, self-oriented perfectionism interacted only with achievement stress to predict depression at Time 2, suggesting again that self-oriented perfectionism confers a vulnerability to depression that is evident over time. Socially prescribed perfectionism did not interact with achievement or social stress to predict depression at Time 2. The results indicate that self-oriented perfectionism may be the perfectionism dimension that is most important as a stress-vulnerability factor in depression (Hewitt & Flett, 1993).

In another study, Joiner and Schmidt (1995) attempted to replicate Hewitt et al.'s (1996) findings in a sample of college students. They used six items culled from the Eating Disorders Inventory (Garner, Olmstead, & Polivy, 1983) to represent measures of self-oriented perfectionism and socially prescribed perfectionism. They found that both self-oriented and socially prescribed perfectionism interacted with stress to predict depression over time, although no evidence supported the specific-vulnerability hypothesis. This study provided some support for our general diathesis–stress model but little support was found for the predicted specific interactions between the two perfectionism dimensions and congruent stress. The differences between studies could be the result of several factors, including sample differences and differences in the measures of perfectionism.

More recently, Hewitt et al. (in press) examined perfectionism, stress, depression, anxiety, and anger in a sample of 114 children and adolescents. Correlational analyses indicated that self-oriented perfectionism was associated significantly with depression and anxiety and that socially prescribed perfectionism was associated significantly with depression, anxiety, interpersonal stress, anger suppression, and outwardly directed anger. Regression analyses showed further that self-oriented perfectionism interacted with achievement stress and interpersonal stress to predict levels of depression.

The studies described above are consistent with our contention that perfectionism (i.e., self-oriented perfectionism and, perhaps, socially prescribed perfectionism) may be associated with depression through their influence on stress. The findings are in keeping with the idea that perfectionistic behavior may enhance or exacerbate the negative effects of stress and, in this case, produce an increase in depression symptoms.

Although support is growing for the diathesis–stress model (see also Cheng, 2001), not all research provides evidence for it. For instance, Dean and Range (1996) conducted a test of the diathesis–stress model as part of their research on an escape theory of perfectionism and suicide. Their cross-sectional research with 132 clinical outpatients found that neither self-oriented perfectionism nor socially prescribed perfectionism interacted with negative life events to predict depression. One possible problem with the study is that it was based on a measure of negative life events that asked participants to recall events over a long period (i.e., 2 years), so the accuracy of the life events measured is questionable.

Recently, Chang and Rand (2000) found partial support for a diathesis–stress model of perfectionism and distress. They administered the MPS (Hewitt & Flett, 1991b) and the four-item short form of the Perceived Stress Scale (PSS; Cohen, Kamarck, & Mermelstein, 1983) to a sample of 256 college students. The PSS measures self-reported stress over the past month. The same respondents completed measures of hopelessness and the Depression, Hostility, and Anxiety subscales of the Symptom Check List-90–Revised (SCL-90-R; Derogatis, 1983) approximately 4 to 5 weeks later. The three SCL-90-R subscales were combined into a measure of general distress. Chang and Rand found no significant interactions involving self-oriented or other-oriented perfectionism; however, socially prescribed perfectionism and perceived stress interacted such that greater distress was reported by people with elevated perfectionism and stress scores.

Unfortunately, the results of this study are difficult to interpret in at least two respects. First, as a measure of stress, the PSS has been criticized because it includes item content that reflects both distress and inability to cope (for a summary, see Hewitt, Flett, & Mosher, 1992). Second, Chang and Rand (2000) did not readminister the PSS at the second time point, so no apparent measure of the stress experienced was obtained at the time when the distress measures were obtained. Nevertheless, the Chang and Rand study attests to the general usefulness of a diathesis–stress approach when conceptualizing perfectionism and distress.

The observations outlined above about the nature and assessment of stress lead us to an important caveat: Existing research is limited by the fact that all previous studies used self-report measures of stress and that thus far, no research has investigated the perfectionism–stress association with an interviewer-based measure of stress. In addition, relatively little research has examined perfectionism, stress, and depression in clinically diagnosed depressives. Clearly, longitudinal research using more sophisticated methods of assessment is needed to more rigorously test the diathesis–stress model.

Perfectionism and Coping Responses to Stress

It has been suggested that people with excessive levels of perfectionism traits use deficient forms of problem solving and maladaptive styles of coping when attempting to deal with stressful circumstances (Hewitt et al., 1995); in this way, the impact of stressors can become magnified. In one of the first attempts to assess perfectionism and coping styles, Flett, Hewitt, Blankstein, Solnik, and Van Brunschot (1996) administered the MPS and a measure of social problem-solving (D'Zurilla & Nezu, 1990). Both self-oriented perfectionism and other-oriented perfectionism were associated with positive problem-solving orientations, whereas socially prescribed perfectionism was associated with negative problem-solving orientations.

In one of our initial studies (Flett, Hewitt, Blankstein, & O'Brien, 1991), we had a sample of students complete the MPS, a measure of learned resourcefulness or general coping ability, and measures of depression and self-esteem. Self-oriented and other-oriented perfectionism, but not socially prescribed perfectionism, were associated with increased learned resourcefulness. Collectively, the Flett et al. (1991, 1996) studies suggest that, although evidence indicates that socially prescribed perfectionism is associated with maladaptive coping styles that may maintain maladjustive states such as depression, self-oriented and other-oriented perfectionism are associated with relatively more adaptive forms of coping that, at least theoretically, should help reduce stress and not produce or maintain symptoms. The findings with self-oriented perfectionism appear to be at odds with our model that the coping styles of perfectionism help to perpetuate stress and, by doing so, produce or maintain symptoms.

Finally, in another study with college students, Flett, Russo, and Hewitt (1994) administered the MPS and the Constructive Thinking Inventory (Epstein, 1992), a measure that includes subscale measures of both adaptive (e.g., active behavioral coping) and maladaptive coping (e.g., emotional coping). Once again, socially prescribed perfectionism was associated with less adaptive coping and more maladaptive coping, and less constructive thinking. Self-oriented perfectionism was associated both with active forms of behavioral coping and with maladaptive coping, in the form of emotional coping and reduced self-acceptance. Finally, other-oriented perfectionism was associated with low self-acceptance but active forms of behavioral coping.

In the one study assessing perfectionism and coping in a clinical sample, Hewitt, Flett, and Endler (1995) examined the perfectionism dimensions and coping styles as assessed by the Coping Inventory of Stressful Situations (Endler & Parker, 1990) in a heterogeneous clinical sample. Evidence for maladaptive coping was found with both self-oriented and socially prescribed perfectionists. Self-oriented perfectionism was associated with increased levels of emotion-oriented coping for women, and socially prescribed perfectionism was associated with low levels of social diversion in women and increased emotion-focused coping in men. Other-oriented perfectionism was associated with increased task-oriented coping.

The studies described above indicate that self-oriented perfectionism might involve both adaptive (i.e., task-focused coping strategies) and maladaptive coping (i.e., emotion-oriented strategies) components. Although the maladaptive components are consistent with our contentions, the findings involving adaptive forms of coping are not so consistent. The issue of whether a particular coping is adaptive or maladaptive is complex. Research testing the goodness-of-fit hypothesis underscores the need to examine coping within the context of situational and task parameters. Investigations by Compas and associates (Compas, Malcarne, & Fondacaro, 1988; Forsythe & Compas, 1987) indicated that task-focused coping is adaptive when confronted with controllable situations but maladaptive when confronted with uncontrollable situations. Problem-focused efforts to deal with uncontrollable situations ultimately prove to be self-defeating.

Flett et al. (1994) suggested that the link between self-oriented perfectionism and adaptive coping may reflect, in part, the persistence of self-oriented perfectionists in dealing with issues or completing tasks. Certainly, persistence and perseveration have been associated with self-oriented and socially prescribed perfectionism (Hewitt et al., 1991). The recent Flynn et al. (2001) study, however, sheds some light on the supposed adaptiveness of the coping of self-oriented perfectionists. Flynn et al. (2001) found that self-oriented perfectionism was associated both with emotion-oriented and task-oriented coping. Moreover, it was found that self-oriented perfectionism interacted with task-oriented coping; that is, those high in self-oriented perfectionism and high in task-oriented coping showed both increased and more enduring heart-rate elevations. In contrast, those low in perfectionism and high in task-oriented coping did not show increased heart rates. The findings imply either that the stress response remains elevated in self-oriented perfectionists when using task-oriented coping or that self-oriented perfectionists are trying more actively to succeed on tasks.

Additional analyses revealed that higher heart rates were detected among participants high in self-oriented perfectionism and the thought the task was irrelevant or invalid. In contrast, elevated heart rates were not experienced by participants who were low in self-oriented perfectionism and the thought the task was irrelevant. The findings indicate that although self-oriented perfectionists may use what are defined as generally adaptive coping strategies, using those strategies in certain situations actually may perpetuate or accentuate distress because self-oriented perfectionists may put a great deal of effort into tasks that are irrelevant or unimportant. They may not know when to stop the task focus or may use task-oriented strategies indiscriminately or in inappropriate situations in which a task-focused approach may be maladaptive.

Finally, other-oriented perfectionism seems not to be consistently associated with particular coping styles. In some cases, it is associated with task-oriented coping, and in others, with emotion-oriented coping; in most cases, however, it is not associated with any particular coping style. One reason may be, as we have argued, that it is the person who is the target of the other-oriented perfectionist who requires coping strategies in relation to perfectionistic behavior (Hewitt, Flett, & Mikail, 1995). Additional research is needed to clarify the link between other-oriented perfectionism and coping. Specifically, research remains to be conducted on how other-oriented perfectionists cope when they are disappointed by other people who do not meet their excessive expectations.

Bolger and Zuckerman (1995) incorporated a focus on coping effectiveness as part of the link between personality and stress reactivity. Unfortunately, little research has investigated the issue of whether perfectionism has a direct impact on coping effectiveness. Nevertheless, the studies conducted thus far have provided some evidence supporting the idea that perfectionism moderates the association between coping and maladjustment.

For instance, the Hewitt, Flett, and Endler (1995) study described above found that self-oriented perfectionism moderated the association between emotion-oriented coping and depression. Analyses indicated that patients who were characterized jointly by elevated levels of self-oriented perfectionism and emotion-oriented coping reported the highest depression scores. Similarly, Flett, Hewitt, Blankstein, and O'Brien (1991) found that socially prescribed perfectionism moderated the association between learned resourcefulness and depression. The study found that the highest depression scores were associated with low levels of learned resourcefulness and high levels of socially prescribed perfectionism. Although both studies indicated that the presence of both increased perfectionism and maladaptive coping tends to result in increased depression symptoms, caution is needed in generalizing the results because this issue has not been investigated systematically from a longitudinal perspective.

Perfectionism and Treatment

Given the stated link between perfectionism and elevated levels of stress generation and stress reactivity, perfectionists should be candidates for stress management, stress inoculation training, or other forms of treatment that focus directly on teaching coping strategies. For example, treatments that focus on enhancing problem-solving and coping skills might be quite beneficial in reducing stress reactions and the accompanying symptoms. Although those approaches may be useful in dealing with the sequelae or outcomes of perfectionistic behavior and may help perfectionists cope with attendant stress, it is extremely important to recognize that perfectionism is a deeply ingrained core vulnerability factor and that the negative impact of this intransigent personality style is the true source of the stress that people experience. We believe that the best treatment choice involves psychotherapy that focuses on the core issues in perfectionism (see Hewitt, Flynn, Mikail, & Flett, 2001b). This approach involves an intensive course of treatment (see also Blatt, 1995) that focuses on the motivations for and the precursors of perfectionistic behavior in an attempt to deal with the source of the perfectionism.

Our approach focuses on the interpersonal precursors of perfectionism and fragile identity issues as the most relevant factors in treating perfectionism. These interpersonal precursors involve core needs of the person (i.e., the need to obtain respect, caring, and love and to avoid censure, humiliation, or punishment) that propel perfectionistic behavior in an effort to create an acceptable identity. Our approach focuses on the factors that motivate the perfectionism in the first place because dealing with or focusing on stress, cognitions and attitudes, or critical evaluations may not change the specific underlying issues that create difficulties. Clearly, the treatment is quite challenging given the reticence of perfectionists to seek professional help and to maintain compliance and therapeutic relationships. In addition, perfectionists' fears associated with changing their perfectionistic tendencies and the serious psychopathology that sometimes can result from the perfectionism can complicate treatment. A complete description of the interpersonal psychotherapy treatment approach that we have used is beyond the scope of this chapter; see Hewitt et al. (2001b) for a detailed description.

Conclusion

We have suggested that perfectionistic behavior is associated with maladjustment and distress, in part, because of its influence on stress and failure as well as on coping mechanisms. Although research on this construct has been increasing, as attested by the various chapters in this volume, it is evident from our analysis that many issues remain to be addressed. For example, at the outset of this chapter we mentioned that perfectionism can play both a moderating and a mediating role in relation to stress and psychopathology. Most of the existing research has focused on the moderating role of perfectionism in the stress–pathology link (i.e., the stress-enhancement component) by looking at the interaction of perfectionism and stress in predicting various outcomes; little work has assessed the mediating role of perfectionism in the perpetuation, anticipation, and generation of stress. Two recent studies suggested that mediational models involving perfectionism and stress are highly relevant (see Blankstein & Dunkley, chapter 12, this volume; Chang, 2000), so a dual focus on mediators and moderators is appropriate. Moreover, in complex models, such as the model whereby perfectionism can both generate and interact with stressors in producing psychopathology (e.g., Monroe & Simons, 1991), fairly sophisticated research strategies need to be used.

In summary, we have proposed a model of perfectionism and psychopathology in which different facets of perfectionistic behavior or different kinds of perfectionism influence stressful events, circumstances, or failures and produce or maintain psychopathological states through that influence. Although much research has accumulated over the past decade, research is needed that is theory-driven and based on a framework or theory of the mechanisms involved. We hope that our model will spawn this kind of research and that, ultimately, insights will be gained about how to best help people who have decidedly distressing lives as a result of their perfectionistic tendencies.

References

Abramson, L., Metalsky, G. I., & Alloy, L. B. (1989). Hopelessness depression: A theory-based subtype of depression. *Psychological Review, 96,* 358–372.

Andersen, S. M. (1990). The inevitability of future suffering: The role of depressive predictive certainty in depression. *Social Cognition, 8,* 203–228.

Andersen, S. W., Spielman, L. A., & Bargh, J. H. (1992). Future-event schemas and certainty about the future: Automaticity in depressives' future-event predictions. *Journal of Personality and Social Psychology, 63,* 711–723.

Bagozzi, R. P., Baumgartner, H., & Pieters, H. (1998). Goal-directed emotions. *Cognition and Emotion, 12,* 1–26.

Baldwin, M. W. (1992). Relational schemas and the processing of social information. *Psychological Bulletin, 112,* 461–484.

Beck, A. T. (1967). *Depression: Clinical, experimental, and theoretical aspects.* New York: Harper & Row.

Beck, A. T. (1993). Cognitive approaches to stress. In P. M. Lehrer & R. L. Woolfolk (Eds.), *Principles and practice of stress management* (Vol. 2; pp. 333–372). New York: Guilford.

Belsher, G., & Costello, C. G. (1991). Do confidants of depressed women provide less social support than confidants of nondepressed women? *Journal of Abnormal Psychology, 100,* 516–520.

Bergin, A. E., & Garfield, S. L. (1994). *Handbook of psychotherapy and behavior change.* New York: Wiley.

Bernazzani, O., Saucier, J.-F., David, H., & Borgeat, F. (1997). Psychosocial factors related to emotional disturbances during pregnancy. *Journal of Psychosomatic Research, 42,* 391–402.

Blatt, S. J. (1995). The destructiveness of perfectionism: Implications for the treatment of depression. *American Psychologist, 50,* 1003–1020.

Blatt, S. J., & Shichman, S. (1983). Two primary configurations of psychopathology. *Psychoanalysis and Contemporary Thought, 6,* 187–254.

Bolger, N., & Zuckerman, A. (1995). A framework for studying personality in the stress process. *Journal of Personality and Social Psychology, 69,* 890–902.

Bowlby, J. (1980). *Attachment and loss, Vol. 3: Loss: Sadness and depression.* New York: Basic Books.

Boyce, P., Hickie, I., & Parker, G. (1991). Parents, partners or personality? Risk factors for post-natal depression. *Journal of Affective Disorders, 21,* 245–255.

Boyce, P., & Parker, G. (1989). Development of a scale to measure interpersonal sensitivity. *Australian and New Zealand Journal of Psychiatry, 23,* 341–351.

Boyce, P., Parker, G., Barnett, B., Cooney, M., & Smith, F. (1991). Personality as a vulnerability factor to depression. *British Journal of Psychiatry, 159,* 106–114.

Brandtstadter, J., & Renner, G. (1990). Tenacious goal pursuit and flexible goal adjustment: Explication and age-related analysis of assimilative and accommodative strategies of coping. *Psychology and Aging, 5,* 58–67.

Brown, G. W., & Harris, T. O. (1978). *Social origins of depression: A study of psychiatric disorder in women.* New York: Free Press.

Chang, E. C. (2000). Perfectionism as a predictor of positive and negative psychological adjustment outcomes: Examining a mediational model in younger and older adults. *Journal of Counseling Psychology, 47,* 18–26.

Chang, E. C., & Rand, K. L. (2000). Perfectionism as a predictor of subsequent adjustment: Evidence for a specific diathesis–stress mechanism among college students. *Journal of Counseling Psychology, 47,* 129–137.

Cheng, S. K. (2001). Life stress, problem solving, perfectionism, and depressive symptoms in Chinese. *Cognitive Therapy and Research, 25,* 303–310.

Cochrane, R., & Robertson, A. (1973). The Life Events Inventory: A measure of the relative severity of psychosocial stressors. *Journal of Psychosomatic Research, 17,* 135–139.

Cohen, S., Kamarck, T., & Mermelstein, R. (1983). A global measure of perceived stress. *Journal of Health and Social Behavior, 24,* 386–396.

Compas, B. E., Malcarne, V. L., & Fondacaro, K. M. (1988). Coping with stressful events in older children and younger adults. *Journal of Consulting and Clinical Psychology, 56,* 405–411.

Dean, P. J., & Range, L. M. (1996). The escape theory of suicide and perfectionism in college students. *Death Studies, 20,* 415–424.

Dean, P. J., Range, L. M., & Goggin, W. C. (1996). The escape theory of suicide in college students: Testing a model that includes perfectionism. *Suicide and Life-Threatening Behavior, 26,* 181–186.

Depue, R. A., Krauss, S., Spoont, M. R., & Arbisi, P. (1989). General Behaviour Inventory identification of unipolar and bipolar affective conditions in a nonclinical university population. *Journal of Abnormal Psychology, 98,* 117–126.

Depue, R. A., & Monroe, S. M. (1986). Conceptualization and measurement of human disorder in light stress research: The problem of chronic disturbance. *Psychological Bulletin, 99,* 36–51.

Derogatis, L. R. (1983). *The SCL-90-R: Administration, scoring, and procedures manual II.* Baltimore: Clinical Psychometric Research.

D'Zurilla, T. J., & Nezu, A. M. (1990). Development and preliminary evaluation of the Social Problem-Solving Inventory (SPSI). *Psychological Assessment, 2,* 156–163.

Endler, N. S., & Parker, J. D. A. (1990). Multidimensional assessment of coping: A critical evaluation. *Journal of Personality and Social Psychology, 58,* 844–854.

Epstein, S. (1992). CTI (108-item version) scoring key. Unpublished document.

Ferrari, J. R., & Mautz, W. T. (1997). Predicting perfectionism: Applying tests of rigidity. *Journal of Clinical Psychology, 53,* 1–6.

Finch, J. F., Okun, M. A., Pool, G. J., & Ruehlman, L. S. (1999). A comparison of the influence of conflictual and supportive social interactions on psychological distress. *Journal of Personality, 67,* 584–597.

Fischer, E. H., & Turner, J. I. (1970). Orientations to seeking professional help: Development and research utility of an attitude scale. *Journal of Consulting and Clinical Psychology, 35,* 79–90.

Flett, G. L., Blankstein, K. R., Hewitt, P. L., & Koledin, S. (1992). Components of perfectionism and procrastination in college students. *Social Behavior and Personality, 20,* 85–94.

Flett, G. L., Blankstein, K. R., Hewitt, P. L., & Obertynski, M. (1994, November). *Personality and coping in depression: A comparison of sociotropy, autonomy, and perfectionism.* Paper presented at the annual convention of the Association for the Advancement of Behavior Therapy, San Diego, CA.

Flett, G. L., & Hewitt, P. L. (2000, May). *Perfectionism and coping with the transition to parenthood.* Paper presented at the 77th annual meeting of the Midwestern Psychological Association, Chicago.

Flett, G. L., Hewitt, P. L., Blankstein, K., & Gray, L. (1998). Frequency of perfectionistic thinking in depression. *Journal of Personality and Social Psychology, 75,* 1363–1381.

Flett, G. L., Hewitt, P. L., Blankstein, K., & Koledin, S. (1991). Dimensions of perfectionism and irrational thinking. *Journal of Rational–Emotive and Cognitive–Behavior Therapy, 9,* 185–201.

Flett, G. L., Hewitt, P. L., Blankstein, K. R., & Mosher, S. W. (1991). Perfectionism, self-actualization, and personal adjustment. *Journal of Social Behavior and Personality, 6,* 147–160.

Flett, G. L., Hewitt, P. L., Blankstein, K. R., & Mosher, S. W. (1995). Perfectionism, life events, and depressive symptoms: A test of a diathesis–stress model. *Current Psychology, 14,* 112–137.

Flett, G. L., Hewitt, P. L., Blankstein, K., & O'Brien, S. (1991). Perfectionism and learned resourcefulness in depression and self-esteem. *Personality and Individual Differences, 12,* 61–68.

Flett, G. L., Hewitt, P. L., Blankstein, K. R., Solnik, M., & Van Brunschot, M. (1996). Perfectionism, social problem-solving ability, and psychological distress. *Journal of Rational–Emotive and Cognitive–Behavior Therapy, 14,* 245–275.

Flett, G. L., Hewitt, P. L., Garshowitz, M., & Martin, T. R. (1997). Personality, negative social interactions, and depressive symptoms. *Canadian Journal of Behavioural Science, 29,* 28–37.

Flett, G. L., Levy, L., & Hewitt, P. L. (2001). *Perfectionism, stress, and negative predictive certainty.* Manuscript in preparation.

Flett, G. L., Parnes, J., & Hewitt, P. L. (2001). *Perfectionism and perceived pressure.* Manuscript in preparation.

Flett, G. L., Russo, F. A., & Hewitt, P. L. (1994). Dimensions of perfectionism and constructive thinking as a coping response. *Journal of Rational–Emotive and Cognitive–Behavior Therapy, 12,* 163–179.

Flett, G. L., Velyvis, V., & Hewitt, P. L. (2001). *Dimensions of perfectionism and interpersonal sensitivity.* Manuscript in preparation.

Flynn, C. A., Hewitt, P. L., Flett, G. L., & Weinberg, J. (2001). *Perfectionism, achievement stress, and physiological reactivity.* Manuscript submitted for publication.

Folkman, S., Lazarus, R. S., Gruen, R. J., & DeLongis, A. (1986). Appraisal, coping, health status, and psychological symptoms. *Journal of Personality and Social Psychology, 50,* 571–579.

Forsythe, C. J., & Compas, B. E. (1987). Interaction of cognitive appraisals of stressful events and coping: Tests of the goodness of fit hypothesis. *Cognitive Therapy and Research, 11,* 473–485.

Frost, R. O., & Henderson, K. J. (1991). Perfectionism and reactions to athletic competition. *Journal of Sport and Exercise Psychology, 13,* 323–335.

Frost, R. O., Marten, P., Lahart, C., & Rosenblate, R. (1990). The dimensions of perfectionism. *Cognitive Therapy and Research, 14,* 449–468.

Frost, R. O., Trepanier, K. L., Brown, E. J., Heimberg, R. G., Juster, H. R., Makris, G. S.,

& Leung, A. W. (1997). Self-monitoring of mistakes among subjects high and low in perfectionistic concern over mistakes. *Cognitive Therapy and Research, 21,* 209–222.

Frost, R. O., Turcotte, T. A., Heimberg, R. G., Mattia, J. I., Holt, C. S., & Hope, D. A. (1995). Reactions to mistakes among subjects high and low in perfectionistic concern over mistakes. *Cognitive Therapy and Research, 19,* 207–226.

Fry, P. S. (1995). Perfectionism, humor, and optimism as moderators of health outcomes and determinants of coping styles of women executives. *Genetic, Social, and General Psychology Monographs, 121,* 211–245.

Garner, D. M., Olmstead, M. P., & Polivy, J. (1983). Development and validation of a multidimensional Eating Disorder Inventory for anorexia nervosa and bulimia. *International Journal of Eating Disorders, 2,* 15–34.

Gruen, R. J., Folkman, S., & Lazarus, R. S. (1988). Centrality and individual differences in the meaning of daily hassles. *Journal of Personality, 56,* 743–762.

Habke, A. M. (1997). The manifestations of perfectionistic self-presentation in a clinical sample. *Dissertation Abstracts International, 59,* 02B. (UMI No. 872)

Hammen, C. L. (1991). Generation of stress in the course of unipolar disorder. *Journal of Abnormal Psychology, 100,* 55–61.

Hewitt, P. L., Caelian, C. F., Flett, G. L., Sherry, S. B., Collins, L., & Flynn, C. A. (in press). Perfectionism in children: Associations with depression, anxiety, and anger. *Personality and Individual Differences.*

Hewitt, P. L., & Dyck, D. G. (1986). Perfectionism, stress, and vulnerability to depression. *Cognitive Therapy and Research, 10,* 137–142.

Hewitt, P. L., & Flett, G. L. (1989). The Multidimensional Perfectionism Scale: Development and validation [Abstract]. *Canadian Psychology, 30,* 339.

Hewitt, P. L., & Flett, G. L. (1990). Dimensions of perfectionism and depression: A multidimensional analysis. *Journal of Social Behavior and Personality, 5,* 423–438.

Hewitt, P. L., & Flett, G. L. (1991a). Dimensions of perfectionism in unipolar depression. *Journal of Abnormal Psychology, 100,* 98–101.

Hewitt, P. L., & Flett, G. L. (1991b). Perfectionism in the self and social contexts: Conceptualization, assessment, and association with psychopathology. *Journal of Personality and Social Psychology, 60,* 456–470.

Hewitt, P. L., & Flett, G. L. (1993). Dimensions of perfectionism, daily stress, and depression: A test of the specific vulnerability hypothesis. *Journal of Abnormal Psychology, 102,* 58–65.

Hewitt, P. L., Flett, G. L., & Ediger, E. (1996). Perfectionism and depression: Longitudinal assessment of a specific vulnerability hypothesis. *Journal of Abnormal Psychology, 105,* 276–281.

Hewitt, P. L., Flett, G. L., Ediger, E., Norton, G. R., & Flynn, C. A. (1998). Perfectionism in chronic and state symptoms of depression. *Canadian Journal of Behavioural Science, 30,* 234–242.

Hewitt, P. L., Flett, G. L., & Endler, N. S. (1995). Perfectionism, coping, and clinical depression. *Journal of Clinical Psychology and Psychotherapy, 2,* 47–58.

Hewitt, P. L., Flett, G. L., & Mikail, S. F. (1995). Perfectionism and relationship maladjustment in chronic pain patients and their spouses. *Journal of Family Psychology, 9,* 335–347.

Hewitt, P. L., Flett, G. L., & Mosher, S. W. (1992). The Perceived Stress Scale: Factorial structure and relation to depression symptoms in a psychiatric sample. *Journal of Psychopathology and Behavioral Assessment, 14,* 247–257.

Hewitt, P. L., Flett, G. L., Sherry, S. B., Habke, A. M., Parkin, M., Lam, R. W., McMurtry, B., Ediger, E., Fairlie, P., & Stein, M. (2001). *The interpersonal expression of perfectionism: Perfectionistic self-presentation and psychological distress.* Manuscript submitted for publication.

Hewitt, P. L., Flett, G. L., & Turnbull-Donovan, W. (1992). Perfectionism and suicide potential. *British Journal of Clinical Psychology, 31,* 181–190.

Hewitt, P. L., Flett, G. L., Turnbull-Donovan, W., & Mikail, S. F. (1991). The Multidimensional Perfectionism Scale: Reliability, validity, and psychometric properties in psychiatric sample. *Psychological Assessment, 3,* 464–468.

Hewitt, P. L., Flett, G. L., & Weber, C. (1994). Dimensions of perfectionism and suicide ideation. *Cognitive Therapy and Research, 18,* 439–460.

Hewitt, P. L., Flynn, C. A., Flett, G. L., Nielsen, A. D., Parking, M., Han, H., & Tomlin, M. (2001). *Perfectionism and seeking support from friends, family, and mental health professionals.* Manuscript in preparation.

Hewitt, P. L., Flynn, C. A., Mikail, S. F., & Flett, G. L. (2001a). Perfectionism, interpersonal problems, and depression in psychodynamic/interpersonal group treatment [Abstract]. *Canadian Psychology, 42,* 141.

Hewitt, P. L., Flynn, C. A., Mikail, S. F., & Flett, G. L. (2001b). *Treatment of perfectionism: An interpersonal/psychodynamic group approach.* Manuscript in preparation.

Hewitt, P. L., & Genest, M. (1990). The ideal-self: Schematic processing of perfectionistic content in dysphoric university students. *Journal of Personality and Social Psychology, 59,* 802–808.

Hewitt, P. L., Mittelstaedt, W. M., & Wollert, R. (1989). Validation of a measure of perfectionism. *Journal of Personality Assessment, 53,* 133–144.

Hewitt, P. L., Newton, J., Flett, G. L., & Callander, L. (1997). Suicide ideation in adolescent psychiatric patients: Perfectionism and hopelessness. *Journal of Abnormal Child Psychology, 25,* 95–101.

Hewitt, P. L., Norton, G. R., Flett, G. L., Callander, L., & Cowan, T. (1998). Dimensions of perfectionism, hopelessness, and attempted suicide in a sample of alcoholics. *Suicide and Life Threatening Behaviour, 28,* 395–406.

Hobden, K., & Pliner, P. (1995). Self-handicapping and dimensions of perfectionism: Self-presentation vs. self-protection. *Journal of Research in Personality, 29,* 461–474.

Jackson, D. N. (1970). A sequential system for personality scale development. In C. D. Spielberger (Ed.), *Current topics in clinical and community psychology* (pp. 61–96). San Diego, CA: Academic Press.

Joiner, T. E., Jr., & Schmidt, N. B. (1995). Dimensions of perfectionism, life stress, and depressed and anxious symptoms: Prospective support for diathesis–stress but not specific vulnerability among male undergraduates. *Journal of Social and Clinical Psychology, 14,* 165–183.

Kendler, K. S., Karkowski, L. M., & Prescott, C. A. (1998). Stressful life events and major depression: Risk period, long-term contextual threat, and diagnostic specificity. *Journal of Nervous and Mental Disease, 186,* 661–669.

Lakey, B., Tardiff, T. A., & Drew, J. B. (1994). Negative social interactions: Assessment and relations to social support, cognitions, and psychological distress. *Journal of Social Clinical Psychology, 13,* 42–62.

Martin, T. R., Flett, G. L., Hewitt, P. L., Krames, L., & Szantos, G. (1996). Personality in depression and health symptoms: A test of a self-regulation model. *Journal of Research in Personality, 31,* 264–277.

Monroe, S. M., & Simons, A. D. (1991). Diathesis–stress theories in the context of life stress research: Implications for the depressive disorders. *Psychological Bulletin, 110,* 406–425.

Mor, S., Day, H. I., Flett, G. L., & Hewitt, P. L. (1995). Perfectionism, control, and components of performance stress in professional artists. *Cognitive Therapy and Research, 19,* 207–226.

Nolen-Hoeksema, S., Morrow, J., & Frederickson, B. L. (1993). Response styles and the duration of episodes of depressed mood. *Journal of Abnormal Psychology, 102,* 20–28.

Oatley, K., & Bolton, W. (1985). A social–cognitive theory of depression in reaction to life events. *Psychological Review, 92,* 372–388.

Ohtani, Y., & Sakurai, S. (1995). Relationship of perfectionism to depression and hopelessness in college students. *Japanese Journal of Psychology, 66,* 41–47.

Peacock, E. J., & Wong, P. T. P. (1996). Anticipatory stress: The relation of locus of control, optimism, and control appraisals to coping. *Journal of Research in Personality, 30,* 204–222.

Phillips, J. M., Hollenbeck, J. R., & Ilgen, D. R. (1996). Prevalence and prediction of positive discrepancy creation: Examining a discrepancy between two self-regulation theories. *Journal of Applied Psychology, 81,* 498–511.

Reich, D. A., & Weary, G. (1998). Depressives' future event schemas and the social inference process. *Journal of Personality and Social Psychology, 74,* 1133–1145.

Sakurai, S., & Ohtani, Y. (1997). Relations of "self-oriented perfectionism" to depression and hopelessness. *Japanese Journal of Psychology, 68,* 179–186.

Sherry, S. B., Flett, G. L., & Hewitt, P. L. (2001). Perfectionism and self-handicapping [Abstract]. *Canadian Psychology, 42,* 78.

Strauman, T. J. (1989). Self-discrepancies in clinical depression and social phobia: Cognitive structures that underlie emotional disorders. *Journal of Abnormal Psychology, 98,* 14–22.

Weiten, W. (1988). Pressure as a form of stress and its relationship to psychological symptomatology. *Journal of Social and Clinical Psychology, 6,* 127–139.

Weiten, W. (1998). Pressure, major life events, and psychological symptoms. *Journal of Social Behavior and Personality, 13,* 51–68.

Wong, P. T. P. (1993). Effective management of life stress: The resource-congruence model. *Stress Medicine, 9,* 51–60.

Evaluative Concerns, Self-Critical, and Personal Standards Perfectionism: A Structural Equation Modeling Strategy

Kirk R. Blankstein and David M. Dunkley

Freud (1926/1959) described the development of a harsh punitive superego that can be a driving force for superior achievement and conduct but also can result in little satisfaction in accomplishments and, through self-criticism and vulnerability to failure, in an increased risk for depression and suicide (Blatt, 1995). Readers of this volume will undoubtedly reach two conclusions. First, consistent with Freud's speculations, perfectionism is related to a variety of adaptational outcomes—some that would typically be construed as negative and maladaptive with links to a variety of disorders, problems, and conflicts, and others as possibly positive and adaptive because they reflect competence and successful achievement. Second, more recent theoretical approaches construe perfectionism to be a multidimensional construct with different components related to maladaptive or adaptive correlates and consequences in different ways.

This chapter examines the link between perfectionism components and distress in the context of links with factors such as daily stress, coping, and social support. Is the link between perfectionism components and psychological outcomes a direct link, or is it more indirect and mediated by constructs such as stressful events, coping styles or social support? This

This chapter is based on theses and research projects conducted by students who worked under the supervision of the first author. The research was supported in part by General Research grants from the Social Sciences and Humanities Research Council of Canada and by Internal Research grants from the University of Toronto at Mississauga awarded to the first author. The authors wish to thank the following students who assisted in the design of the studies, collected data, and helped to prepare the data sets for SEM analyses: Sylvia Ghobranios, Jennifer Halsall, Denise Hui, Sandra Lecce, Sharry Taylor, Meredith Williams, and Gary Winkworth. The authors also extend their appreciation to Yoshio Takane for his expert statistical assistance.

chapter reviews the research linking perfectionism to those factors and then reports findings from three new large sample studies. We analyzed the data using structural equation modeling (SEM) because associations between different components of perfectionism and adaptational outcomes are probably more complex than can be captured with relatively simple correlational or multiple regression analyses. However, we also examined the possible role of moderator variables (i.e., interactions between perfectionism factors and other variables), in the prediction of distress. We first review recent conceptualizations from a multidimensional perspective and links to related personality constructs, examine the distinction between what we refer to as *evaluative concerns, self-critical,* and *personal standards perfectionism,* and introduce the reader to our theoretical and data analytic strategy.

Evaluative Concerns, Self-Critical, and Personal Standards Perfectionism: The Multidimensional Perspective

Hamachek (1978) described perfectionism as neurotic when a person has unrealistic standards, is unable to derive satisfaction from performance, and fears negative judgments from others. He characterized perfectionism as normal when a person derives pleasure from striving for excellence yet is able to accept personal and environmental limitations. Although conceptualized traditionally as a unidimensional personality trait, current investigators characterize perfectionism as a multidimensional construct. Research has determined that different components are differentially related to some adaptive and maladaptive qualities (see Enns & Cox, chapter 2, this volume; Mills & Blankstein, 2000; Shafran & Mansell, 2001; Slaney & Ashby, 1996; Slaney, Rice, & Ashby, chapter 3, this volume, for recent reviews).

Two recent conceptualizations that have generated considerable research are those of Hewitt and Flett and colleagues (see Flett & Hewitt, chapter 1, this volume) and Frost and colleagues. Hewitt and Flett (1991a, 1991b) described perfectionism as a three-dimensional personality construct comprising self-oriented, socially prescribed, and other-oriented perfectionism and they developed a self-report instrument—the Multidimensional Perfectionism Scale (MPS), to measure the three components. The Frost version of the MPS (Frost, Marten, Lahart, & Rosenblate, 1990) measures the dimensions of excessive concern over making mistakes, high personal standards, perception of high parental expectations and criticism, doubt regarding the quality of one's actions, and a preference for order and organization.

The two conceptualizations are complementary, and the measured components overlap in meaningful ways that map onto a hypothesized distinction between neurotic, negative, maladaptive components and normal, potentially positive and adaptive aspects of perfectionism. As Frost et al. (1990) stated, the perfectionist's self-imposed "setting of and striving for high standards is certainly not in and of itself pathological" (p. 450).

In a factor analytic examination of the relation between the MPS instruments, Frost, Heimberg, Holt, Mattia, and Neubauer (1993) found that the items on both measures loaded onto two primary factors, which they named *maladaptive evaluative concerns* and *positive achievement striving*. The subscales most related to dysphoria and negative affect were Hewitt and Flett's socially prescribed perfectionism and Frost's concern over mistakes. However, the subscales most related to positive affect were Hewitt and Flett's self-oriented perfectionism and Frost's personal standards. Similar factor solutions were reported by Slaney, Ashby, and Trippi (1995). Thus, both maladaptive and adaptive components of perfectionism have been identified empirically.

Recently, others have distinguished between perfectionism components that may have adaptive and maladaptive correlates and consequences (e.g., Adkins & Parker, 1996; Lynd-Stevenson & Hearne, 1999; Mills & Blankstein, 2000; Terry-Short, Owens, Slade, & Dewey, 1995). For example, Adkins and Parker proposed that high *active* perfectionism (as assessed by Frost's personal standards and related subscales), in contrast to *passive* perfectionism (as assessed by concern over mistakes and doubt about actions), indicates people "who appear not to be predisposed to suicidal preoccupation, are those for whom perfectionistic strivings motivate rather than paralyze; for whom perfectionism spurs rather than inhibits achievement" (p. 539). In the revision of the Almost Perfect Scale–Revised (APS–R), Slaney and his colleagues (Slaney, Rice, & Ashby, chapter 3, this volume; Slaney, Rice, Mobley, Trippi, & Ashby, 2001) developed a measure of discrepancy, defined as "the perception that one consistently fails to meet the high standards one has set for oneself" (Slaney et al., chapter 3, this volume, p. 69). They proposed that it is the "essential defining negative dimension" of perfectionism. Standards and order are presumed to represent normal, or adaptive, perfectionism. We refer to what appears to be two major and distinct dimensions of perfectionism as *evaluative concerns* perfectionism and *personal standards* perfectionism.

Blatt (1974) and Beck (1983) proposed specific cognitive-personality styles that also reflect a "maladaptive" form of perfectionism and are conceptually similar and empirically related to socially prescribed perfectionism (see Blatt, 1995). Blatt presented self-criticism from a psychodynamic orientation, whereas Beck proposed autonomy from a cognitive perspective. Self-critical people are assumed to be concerned with achievement-related events and with convincing themselves and significant others that they are worthy of approval and acceptance. They are critical and demanding of themselves, unsatisfied with their current status, competitive, and concerned about their inability to reach goals and satisfy the expectations of others (Blatt & Zuroff, 1992). The Depressive Experiences Questionnaire (DEQ; Blatt, D'Afflitti, & Quinlan, 1976) is the most widely used measure of self-criticism. An autonomous person strives for independence from others, is concerned with achievement and possible failure, has high standards and goals, prefers solitary activities, and tries to maximize control over the environment in order to reduce the probability of failure and criticism. The most widely used measure of autonomy has been the autonomy scale of the Sociotropy–Autonomy Scale developed by Beck, Epstein, Harrison, and Emery (1983). Recent revisions (Clark & Beck, 1991; Clark, Steer, Beck, & Ross, 1995) have identified solitude—a preference for solitary activities and insensitivity to or lack of awareness of others' needs and wishes, as the vulnerability dimension of autonomy.

The similarities among socially prescribed perfectionism, self-criticism, and autonomy have been demonstrated empirically. For example, studies have reported significant, positive correlations among measures of these constructs (e.g., Clark et al., 1995; Hewitt & Flett, 1993). Each construct also has been associated with the neuroticism factor of the Big Five factor model of personality (Dunkley, Blankstein, & Flett, 1997; Hill, McIntire, & Bacharach, 1997; Zuroff, 1994). Additionally, they have been associated with factors that reflect possible interpersonal maladjustment (Alden & Bieling, 1996; Dunkley et al., 1997; Hill, Zrull, & Turlington, 1997; Zuroff, 1994). Moreover, personality disorders (avoidant, schizoid, schizotypal) associated with socially prescribed perfectionism (Hewitt & Flett, 1991b) also have been associated with self-criticism and autonomy (Ouimette, Klein, Anderson, Riso, & Lizardi, 1994). Of course, conventionally these constructs were conceptualized and studied as specific vulnerabilities to depression. We refer to the shared variance among socially prescribed perfectionism, self-criticism, and autonomy as *self-critical* perfectionism (after Blatt, 1995) and assume that this construct shares significant variance with evaluative concerns perfectionism.

Evaluative Concerns Perfectionism

The distinction between evaluative concerns and personal standards forms of perfectionism can be illustrated by research on the socially prescribed and self-oriented perfectionism constructs. Socially prescribed perfectionism has been associated with such maladaptive characteristics as irrational thinking, self-criticism, self- and other-blame, fear of negative evaluation, procrastination, overgeneralization of failure, low self-efficacy, maladaptive motivation and learning strategies, decreased likelihood of help-seeking, negative social characteristics or interpersonal problems, and psychological maladjustment, including depression, suicide behavior, anxiety, test anxiety, fears reflecting social evaluative concerns, paranoia, obsessive–compulsiveness, Type A behavior, strain on personal projects, and somatization (e.g., Blankstein, Flett, Hewitt, & Eng, 1993; Flett, Blankstein, Hewitt, and Koledin, 1992; Flett, Hewitt, Blankstein, & Dynin, 1994; Flett, Hewitt, Blankstein, & Koledin, 1991; Hewitt & Flett, 1991b; Hewitt, Flett, Ediger, Norton, & Flynn, 1998; Hill, Zrull, & Turlington, 1997; Martin, Flett, Hewitt, Krames, & Szantos, 1996; Mills & Blankstein, 2000; Mosher, Flett, Blankstein, & Hewitt, 2001). In short, the strongest associations with maladjustment involve the socially prescribed perfectionism dimension. Furthermore, this dimension has lacked an association with adaptive personality characteristics (e.g., Hill, McIntire, & Bacharach, 1997).

Personal Standards Perfectionism

Past research on self-oriented perfectionism focused on self-critical, destructive characteristics (see Blatt, 1995) and promoted a negative view of this component. Slaney and Ashby (1996) questioned this negative view and argued for a different approach: the study of criterion groups. High personal standards and orderliness appeared to be central to self-defined and other-defined perfectionism. Slaney and Ashby (1996) reported that participants evaluated their perfectionism positively and were disinclined to give it up, although most found it somewhat distressing. Blankstein (1998) confirmed that dimensions used in this selection strategy are strongly, positively related to self-oriented perfectionism (and unrelated to socially prescribed perfectionism). Self-oriented perfectionism has been associated with numerous positive, adaptive qualities and attributes including constructive achievement striving, positive affect, self-esteem, self-efficacy, self-actualization, resourcefulness, perceived control, adaptive coping with stress, positive appraisals of personal projects, adaptive learning strategies, good academic performance, and positive or successful interpersonal characteristics, such as self-assurance, assertiveness, and altruistic social attitudes (e.g., Blankstein, Halsall, Williams, & Winkworth, 1997; Blankstein & Paduada, 2001; Brown, Heimberg, Frost, Makris, Juster, & Leung, 1999; Flett, Blankstein, Hewitt, & Heisel, 2001; Flett, Hewitt, Blankstein, & Mosher, 1991; Flett, Hewitt, Blankstein, & O'Brien, 1991; Hill, McIntire, & Bacharach, 1997; Hill, Zrull, & Turlington, 1997; Martin et al., 1996; Mills & Blankstein, 2000; Mosher et al., 2001). Although self-oriented perfectionism has been reported to be associated with maladaptive characteristics, such as self-blame, narcissicism, and distress symptoms (e.g., Hewitt & Flett, 1991b), the association with adaptive characteristics suggests a relatively controlled experience of negative characteristics and states (see Hill, McIntire, & Bacharach, 1997). Further, Mills and Blankstein (2000) demonstrated that when partial correlation is used to examine the unique relation between specific perfectionism subscales and motivation and learning measures, self-oriented perfectionism is strongly related to motivation and learning strategies in positive, adaptive ways.

The Role of Hassles, Coping, and Social Support

We have been investigating the link among different components of perfectionism, adaptational outcomes, and other factors related to psychological and physical health. For present purposes we focus on perceived stressful events, particularly daily stress, or "hassles," the dispositional strategies used by people to cope with stress, and perceived social support. We are interested in answering questions such as the following:

- Does perfectionism affect outcomes directly, controlling for possible links to factors such as perceived stress, coping, and support, which also could have direct effects on predicted variables (an additive model)?

- Is the relation between perfectionism and outcomes mediated by its link with factors such as coping (a mediational model)?
- Does perfectionism interact with stressful life events, coping, or social support to produce, maintain, or minimize maladaptive behavior (an interactive model)?

Some conceptual approaches actually are versions of a diathesis–stress or specific-vulnerability perspective which typically is evaluated by testing the interaction effects of perfectionism and some other variable (usually stressful events, e.g., failure experiences) in predicting adaptational outcomes.

Several points can be made about the current status of perfectionism research:

1. Most published papers have simply correlated perfectionism dimensions with variables that are hypothesized to be related to the construct (e.g., dysphoria).
2. Several studies have tested mediational and interactive models, with mixed results.
3. No logical necessity directs that only one model can best explain the link between perfectionism dimensions and the predicted variable of interest. For example, perhaps a mediational model could help explain the link between socially prescribed perfectionism and distress, whereas an interactive model could demonstrate a link between self-oriented perfectionism and distress.
4. It is logically possible that more than one of these models could be valid for predictions of interest involving the same perfectionism dimension (see Baron & Kenny, 1986). With few exceptions, perfectionism researchers have not systematically examined this possibility.
5. Investigators have rarely examined the latter possibility within the context of several variables in addition to perfectionism dimensions (e.g., hassles, coping, social support). Thus, although a few studies tested a diathesis–stress or specific vulnerability model and examined the interaction of perfectionism dimensions and stressful events in relation to dysphoria, they did not assess coping or social support.
6. Past studies that used path analytic or SEM approaches are compromised because they relied on small samples (see Rice, Ashby, & Slaney, 1998, for an example of large sample SEM analyses of perfectionism, self-esteem, and depression).

Several mediating mechanisms could account for a relation between perfectionism and distress. One mechanism concerns the possibility that perfectionists experience a great amount of stress, including stress generated or instigated by their perfectionism. A second mechanism concerns how perfectionists respond to and cope with stressful events, people, and situations. Perfectionists may appraise otherwise ordinary events as if they are major distressing events and have poor strategies for coping with these events. A perceived lack of support is a third potential mediator of the link between perfectionism and distress. The sections that follow present a brief overview of some of the recent research on perfectionism, stress, coping, and social support.

Perfectionism, Stress, and Distress

Perfectionists are assumed to experience chronic daily stress, and some of this stress is probably self-generated, that is, perfectionists play an active role in causing personally stressful events (see Hewitt & Flett, chapter 11, this volume). Evaluative concerns/self-critical perfectionists may perceive that they are under chronic pressure to satisfy unrealistic demands imposed on them by others, whereas personal standards perfectionists' stringent self-evaluations also might instigate stress on a daily basis. Thus, the study of hassles is particularly relevant. Hassles are irritants that can range in severity from minor annoyances (e.g., being late for class), to more upsetting minor pressures (e.g., a disagreement with a friend; Kanner, Coyne, Schaefer, & Lazarus, 1981). Support has been found for the hypothesis that high levels of perceived hassles are predictive of psychological adjustment and health (e.g., Blankstein & Flett, 1992; DeLongis, Folkman, & Lazarus, 1988; Kanner et al., 1981). Further, daily hassles can be better predictors of adjustment difficulties than major life events (e.g., Chamberlain & Zika, 1990; Kanner et al., 1981). Given a hypothesized relation between both evaluative concerns/self-critical perfectionism and personal standards perfectionism and daily stress and the demonstrated relation between hassles and distress, we hypothesized that hassles mediate the link between perfectionism components and distress.

Past theory and research has focused on stress as a moderator rather than a mediator. For example, Hewitt, Flett, and Ediger (1996) proposed that, "self-oriented and socially prescribed perfectionism may be viewed as specific vulnerability factors that require congruent stressors to produce depression symptoms" (p. 276). Self-oriented perfectionism should interact with achievement stress to predict depression, whereas socially prescribed perfectionism should interact with social stress to predict depression. Several recent studies have tested diathesis–stress and specific-vulnerability models. In one such study, Flett, Hewitt, Blankstein, and Mosher (1995) reported that self-oriented and socially prescribed perfectionism interacted significantly with major life stress to produce higher levels of dysphoria in university students. A second sample completed the same measures at two time points separated by a 3-month interval. Self-oriented perfectionism at Time 1 was associated with depression symptoms 3 months later for the students who had experienced a major life event. In contrast to the first sample, socially prescribed perfectionism was a significant predictor of depression as a main effect term, but it did not interact with stress to predict unique variance in depression scores. Unfortunately, interactions with congruent life stress were not evaluated. In contrast, Lynd-Stevenson and Hearne (1999) reported that "passive" perfectionism (but not "active" perfectionism) moderated the impact of stressful events on dysphoria.

Joiner and Schmidt (1995) also reported some prospective support for a diathesis–stress model (but not a specific-vulnerability model that tested congruent perfectionism–life stress interactions); however, the designation of self-oriented or socially prescribed perfectionism was based on just six items from the Eating Disorders Inventory (Garner, Olmstead, & Polivy, 1983). Hewitt and Flett (1993) examined a vulnerability model in depressed and general psychiatric patients. "Achievement" and "interpersonal" hassles were selected from the Revised Hassles Scale (DeLongis et al., 1988). In both samples, self-oriented perfectionism interacted only with achievement stressors to predict depression. Little consistent evidence was found for socially prescribed perfectionism as a specific-vulnerability factor. Hewitt et al. (1996) used a sample of former and current patients to test whether perfectionism dimensions interact with specific stress to predict depression over time. After controlling for initial depression, self-oriented perfectionism interacted with achievement stress (e.g., unemployment) but not with interpersonal stress (e.g., death of a family member) to predict depression 4 months later. Socially prescribed perfectionism did not interact with stress to predict depression at Time 2, but it did predict it as a main effect.

Note, although these studies provide some support for an interactional model with respect to findings involving the predicted interaction between self-oriented perfectionism and life stress, in each instance the interaction accounted for, at most, a few percentage points of variance in depression symptoms. Conversely, socially prescribed perfectionism typically accounted for significant variance as a main effect. Perhaps self-oriented perfectionism is relatively adaptive in situations of low stress but the link between socially prescribed perfectionism and dysphoria is less influenced by moderating factors. Detecting moderator effects, however, is difficult when product terms have high measurement error. McClelland and Judd (1993) indicated that such interactions typically account for only 1% to 3% of unique variance and that amount of variance accounted for is not an adequate indicator of effect magnitude.

Perfectionism, Coping, and Distress

How do perfectionists cope with events? Do they react to major losses and actual failures with maladaptive coping and to minor events as if they are major rejections or failures? Past accounts speculate that they cope in self-defeating ways such as by engaging in all-or-none thinking, ruminative thought, self-blame, and overgeneralization of failure and that they experience a sense of helplessness or hopelessness (Hewitt & Flett, 1993; Hewitt & Flett, 1996). Coping plays a key role in adjustment outcomes (see Endler & Parker, 1990) and is a potential mediator of the perfectionism–

distress link. It also is possible that coping moderates this link. Although there have been many approaches to conceptualizing coping (see Suls, David, & Harvey, 1996), most distinguish between strategies oriented toward approaching or confronting the situation (i.e., approach or problem-focused coping) and strategies oriented toward reducing tension and avoiding the problem (i.e., avoidance or emotion-focused coping).

A few studies have examined perfectionism and aspects of coping from a multidimensional perspective. Thus, Flett, Hewitt, Blankstein, and O'Brien (1991) reported that self-oriented perfectionism was associated with greater learned resourcefulness (i.e., task-oriented coping) as assessed by the Self-Control Schedule (SCS; Rosenbaum, 1980). Although socially prescribed perfectionism and the SCS were not significantly correlated, the combination of socially prescribed perfectionism and low personal resourcefulness was associated with high levels of depression. Flett, Hewitt, Blankstein, Solnik, and Van Brunschot (1996) reported that self-oriented perfectionism was associated with positive self-appraisals of problem solving skills, as assessed by the Social Problem-Solving Inventory (D'Zurilla & Nezu, 1990). In contrast, socially prescribed perfectionism was associated with negative perceptions of problem-solving orientation.

Hewitt, Flett, and Endler (1995) examined perfectionism and coping as assessed by the Coping Inventory for Stressful Situations (CISS; Endler & Parker, 1990) in a mixed diagnosis sample of psychiatric patients. Self-oriented perfectionism was associated with task-oriented coping in both men and women and emotion-focused coping in women, whereas socially prescribed perfectionism was associated with emotion-focused coping in men and the absence of social diversion in women. Although the interaction of self-oriented perfectionism and emotion-oriented coping accounted for unique variance (3%) in depression, none of the other possible interactions were significant. Flett, Russo, and Hewitt (1994) examined relations between the MPS and general coping ability assessed by Epstein and Meier's (1989) Constructive Thinking Inventory (CTI) in college students. Self-oriented perfectionism was associated with active forms of behavioral coping and with a form of emotional coping involving reduced self-acceptance. Socially prescribed perfectionism was associated with less constructive thinking and more negative coping.

Recently, Blankstein and Paduada (2001) examined the link between perfectionism components (Hewitt & Flett, 1991b) and defense styles as assessed by the Defense Styles Questionnaire (Andrews, Pollock, & Stewart, 1989). They predicted that self-oriented perfectionism would be associated with a mature defense style and only weakly associated with a neurotic or immature defense style. In fact, the results showed that self-oriented perfectionism was not strongly correlated with any defense style. Conversely, socially prescribed perfectionism was strongly associated with immature defense styles (i.e., projection, splitting, somatization, and isolation), in partial support of hypotheses proposed by Blatt (1995).

Taken together, the results of a limited number of studies suggest that personal standards perfectionism is associated primarily with adaptive coping tendencies (which possibly decreases the frequency or duration of the hassles experienced), whereas a pervasive link has been found between evaluative concerns/self-critical perfectionism and more avoidant and less active coping (which might further increase the persistence of the daily stress experienced).

Perfectionism, Social Support, and Distress

A growing research literature demonstrates that personality traits (e.g., Cohen, Hettler, & Park, 1997), stressors (e.g., Flett, Blankstein, Hicken, & Watson, 1995), and coping (e.g., Holahan, Moos, & Bonin, 1997) are related to social support. Could social support also mediate the link between perfectionism and distress? Could social support buffer or moderate this link? Although social support can be operationalized in many ways, generally it has been concluded (e.g., Procidano & Smith, 1997) that perceived social support, particularly perceived emotional support (beliefs that significant others offer sympathy, understanding, caring, love, and value and esteem), is the most consistent predictor of well-being and distress and that it buffers, or moderates, the impact of life stress. Social support is assumed to promote adaptive coping strategies. Thoits (1995), for example, conceptualized social support as a coping resource, as "a social 'fund' from which people may draw when handling stressors" (p. 64). People high in adaptive coping skills also should have adaptive social skills, which should increase the probability that social support is available or increase the perception that a support network is in place.

Unfortunately, little research has been conducted on the relations between perfectionism and different aspects of social support. Blankstein (1996) found that perfectionism dimensions are linked to various indices of social support. For example, the Hewitt and Flett (1991b) MPS and the Multidimensional Scale of Perceived Social Support (Zimet, Dahlem, Zimet, & Farley, 1988) were administered to large samples of students. The findings were straightforward: Self-oriented perfectionists perceived that they had adequate social support from family, friends, and significant others, whereas socially prescribed perfectionists perceived that their support was inadequate. Also, it is assumed that socially prescribed perfectionists have a general unwillingness to seek help for their problems (Flett, Hewitt, Blankstein, & Mosher, 1995). We believe that evaluative concerns and self-critical perfectionists experience a fear of criticism and unsatisfactory, conflicted relationships which gives rise to low social support, real or imagined. Indeed, college students with elevated levels of socially prescribed perfectionism and autonomy reported more negative social interactions (Flett, Hewitt, Garshowitz, & Martin, 1997). Socially prescribed perfectionism also has been associated with loneliness, shyness, fear of negative evaluation, and low social self-esteem (Flett, Hewitt, & De Rosa, 1996). In laboratory studies, Mongrain, Vettese, Shuster, and Kendal (1998) and Zuroff and Duncan (1999) videotaped college romantic couples while they attempted to resolve conflicts. The findings illustrate how the stable cognitive structures of self-critical perfectionistic people can generate stressful interpersonal interactions that possibly result in less social support. Mongrain et al. (1998), for example, found that self-critical women were rated objectively as less loving and more hostile, and their partners also were rated as less loving. Mongrain (1998) also reported that self-critics made fewer requests for social support over a 21-day self-monitoring period. She noted that they do not believe others view them highly, do not feel integrated within a social network, and cannot count on others for help.

In perceiving a lack of social support, the evaluative concerns or self-critical perfectionist lacks a vital resource to encourage adaptive coping and reduce a sense of helplessness associated with stressful situations (see Holahan et al., 1997). To our knowledge, no published studies have examined the links among perfectionism, daily stress, coping, social support, and distress, nor have they examined social support as a mediator or moderator of the perfectionism–distress link.

Perfectionism and Multiple Pathways to Adaptational Outcomes: The Promise of SEM

We tested hypotheses about the mediation of links between perfectionism and distress using SEM with several relatively large data sets. The tests of mediation with SEM are particularly relevant to the evaluative concerns and self-critical perfectionism dimensions because these dimensions consistently have the strongest direct association with distress. The primary purpose of our SEM analyses was to illuminate potentially relevant mechanisms, such as hassles, coping, and social support, in the relation between perfectionism dimensions and distress.

In each study, we administered multiple measures of perfectionism, hassles, coping, and distress. Because researchers have expressed the need for the development of specific hassles scales for different populations (e.g., Blankstein & Flett, 1992; Blankstein, Flett, & Koledin, 1991; Chamberlain & Zika, 1990), we used measures of hassles developed for our target population of students (Blankstein & Flett, 1993; Flett, Blankstein, & Martin, 1995). Academic and social hassles are particularly relevant to college students (Flett, Blankstein, Occhiuto, & Koledin, 1994). We also used disposition-oriented instruments to assess coping (e.g., the COPE) based on a conceptualization of coping that assumes that people can be characterized by some preferred ways of coping with adversity, and that they continue to apply the same strategies over time. In the third study, we also included a widely used measure of social support, the Social Provisions Scale (SPS) (Cutrona & Russell, 1987; Cutrona, 1989). The findings from the first study are summarized in Dunkley and Blankstein (2000), while the findings from the third study are summarized in Dunkley, Blankstein, Halsall, Williams, and Winkworth (2000).

Structural Equation Modeling

There are two main advantages to using SEM to test our mediational hypotheses. First, SEM uses conceptual (i.e., latent) factors comprised of two or more correlated predictors (i.e., observed or indicator variables) that enable one to separate error variance from the more meaningful common variance among measures (Newcomb, 1990). The measurement model specifies relations of the observed measures (e.g., socially prescribed perfectionism, concern with mistakes, and doubts about actions) to their underlying constructs or latent variables (e.g., evaluative concerns perfectionism) and is tested using confirmatory factor analysis. In testing mediational hypotheses, controlling for measurement error gives a more accurate estimate of the magnitude of the effects of the predictor and mediator variables on the dependent variable. As noted by Baron and Kenny (1986) "the presence of measurement error in the mediator tends to produce an underestimate of the effect of the mediator variable and an overestimate of the effect of the independent variable on the dependent variable" (p. 1177). A second advantage of SEM is that the techniques also allow one to model relations among the independent and dependent variables and the results reflect a system of dependent relationships (Newcomb, 1990). This advantage is especially useful here because the predictors were expected to covary. Thus, the structural equation model specifies the causal relations among the latent variables. This approach is analogous to fitting several regression equations simultaneously and allows us to test several mediational hypotheses simultaneously (Newcomb, 1990).

Model testing was conducted using the program AMOS (Arbuckle, 1997). It uses the maximum likelihood method to examine the overall fit of the models to the corresponding observed variance–covariance matrices. We used multiple indexes of fit to evaluate measurement and structural equation models, including the chi-square to degrees of freedom ratio (Carmines & McIver, 1981), the goodness of fit index (Joreskog & Sorbom, 1984), the incremental fit index (Bollen, 1989), and the comparative fit index (Bentler, 1990; see Hoyle & Panter, 1995 for a description and discussion of indexes of fit).

The structural models were developed to perform tests of mediation in the relation between perfectionism, particularly evaluative concerns or self-critical perfectionism, and distress. It is theoretically possible that coping, hassles, social support, or all three could fully mediate the relation between perfectionism and distress; however, the possibility that perfectionism has direct effects on distress unique from the mediating effects of coping, hassles, and social support also was tested. Perhaps people who are perfectionistic have other cognitive or behavioral qualities (e.g., self-esteem) that would result in a relation between perfectionism and distress, controlling for coping, hassles, and social support. In SEM and nested-modeling terms, initial models were tested that included direct effects from perfectionism to distress and the indirect effects (i.e., mediated paths) from perfectionism to each of coping, hassles, and social support, respectively, to distress. Tests of mediation were performed by constraining the direct path from perfectionism to distress to zero, eliminating the path from the model. Whether or not there were differences between the partially mediated model (e.g., one that includes the direct effect from perfectionism to distress) and the fully mediated models (e.g., ones that eliminated the direct effect) was then examined using chi-square difference tests.

The Akaike information criterion (Akaike, 1987) and the Bayes information criterion (Schwarz, 1978) also were used to compare competing structural models because they take into account the degree of parsimony in the model (see Hoyle & Panter, 1995). In each comparison in which no significant difference was found, the more constrained of the two models was tentatively accepted (Anderson & Gerbing, 1988).

In summary, we used the two-step approach recommended by Anderson and Gerbing (1988) in which the measurement model should be tested and, when necessary, respecified before testing the structural model. In all three studies, the convergent validity of our indicators to their respective latent constructs was supported. We then tested and compared various structural models.

Study 1. Self-critical perfectionism and distress: Coping and hassles as mediators. In our first study with 233 participants, we used four latent variables in the structural equation model testing: self-critical perfectionism, coping, hassles, and distress. We previously highlighted some of the conceptual and empirical parallels among socially prescribed perfectionism, self-criticism, and autonomy. Although clearly not identical, they all reflect a similar maladaptive form of perfectionism that overlaps our evaluative concerns perfectionism construct. The self-critical perfectionism latent construct was assessed using the socially prescribed perfectionism subscale of the Hewitt and Flett MPS, the solitude subscale of the revised Sociotropy-Autonomy Scale, and the self-criticism subscale of the DEQ. Coping was assessed using the emotion-oriented and task-oriented subscales, and the distraction subscale of the avoidance-oriented subscale of the CISS (Endler & Parker, 1999) because previous research (see Endler & Parker, 1990, 1999) suggested that high levels of emotion-oriented and distraction coping and low levels of task-focused coping are associated with distress. Daily hassles were assessed using the general, academic, and social scales of the General, Academic, and Social Hassles Scales for Students (GASHSS; Blankstein & Flett, 1993). Participants assessed the "persistence" (i.e., frequency, duration, or both) of hassles during the past month. Finally, distress was assessed using the Center for Epidemiological Studies Depression Scale (Radloff, 1977), the state anger scale from the State–Trait Anger Expression Inventory (Spielberger, 1991) modified to assess anger over the past week, and the State University of New York at Albany Revision of the Psychosomatic Symptom Checklist (Cox, Freundlich, & Meyer, 1975) as a measure of psychosomatic distress (Attanasio, Hirschfield, & Yerevanian, 1984).

Confirmatory factor analysis was used to test the measurement model that included the four latent variables, each with two or more indicators, and the results supported the convergent and construct validity of the model. Factor loadings ranged from .32 to .94 in general and, particularly, from .65 to .75 for the self-critical perfectionism measures (see Dunkley & Blankstein, 2000). Furthermore, the intercorrelations among the latent constructs, corrected for measurement error, ranged from .45 to .73 and were all highly significant. These findings support the simple correlation requirements for the presence of mediator effects (see Baron & Kenny, 1986). Thus, both coping and hassles were good preliminary candidates to mediate the relationship between self-critical perfectionism and distress prior to testing the structural models that controlled for the influence on distress of the other variables in the model (see Baron & Kenny, 1986).

Analyses and comparisons of three nested, competing structural models (Anderson & Gerbing, 1988) led to acceptance of the most parsimonious, best-fitting model—the fully mediated model. The final model removed a nonsignificant regression path from self-critical perfectionism to hassles. Standardized parameter estimates for the significant paths of the final model are presented in Figure 12.1. The coefficients at each arrowhead indicate the proportion of variance unaccounted for in each endogenous variable by other variables in the model. These results suggest that the effect of self-critical perfectionism on hassles and distress, respectively, is mediated through coping. That is, self-critical perfectionism was associated with maladaptive coping, which in turn was associated with high levels of hassles and distress. Furthermore, these results suggest that has-

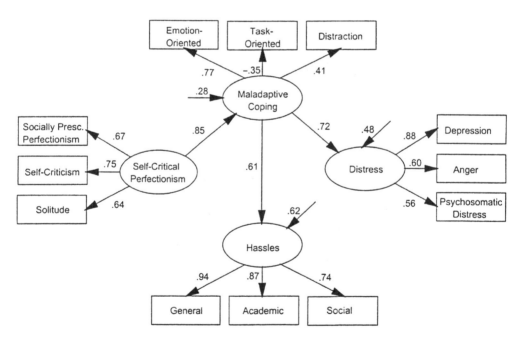

Figure 12.1.   Final modified structural model relating self-critical perfectionism, avoidant coping, hassles, and distress. All standardized parameters are significant. The coefficients at coping, hassles, and distress denote the proportions of variance in the endogenous variable that was not explained by other variables in the model. From "Self-Critical Perfectionism, Coping, Hassles, and Current Distress: A Structural Equations Modeling Approach," by D. M. Dunkley & K. R. Blankstein, 2000, *Cognitive Therapy and Research, 24*, p. 724. Copyright 2000 by Kluwer Academic/Plenum Publishers. Reprinted with permission.

sles and self-critical perfectionism do not have an effect on distress after controlling for the effect of coping on distress. The results are most easily grasped by referring to Figure 12.1 and considering the paths leading from self-critical perfectionism to distress and hassles. These findings suggest that coping mediates the association between self-critical perfectionism and both distress and hassles.

Study 2. Evaluative concerns versus personal standards perfectionism and distress: Coping and hassles as mediators. In our second study, 357 students completed measures of perfectionism, coping, hassles, and distress. There were six latent factors in the model, each with two or more indicators: evaluative concerns and personal standards perfectionism, positive emotional and active coping, hassles, and distress. Evaluative concerns perfectionism was assessed using the socially prescribed perfectionism subscale of the Hewitt and Flett MPS, two subscales from the Frost MPS, concern over mistakes and doubts about actions, and the discrepancy subscale from the APS–R. Personal standards perfectionism was assessed using the self-oriented perfectionism subscale from the Hewitt and Flett MPS, the personal standards subscale from the Frost MPS, and the standards subscale from the APS–R. Daily hassles were assessed using the GASHSS subscales. A latent construct that we refer to as active, or adaptive coping was assessed using the behavioral coping subscales of the CTI (Epstein, 1992): positive thinking, action orientation, and conscientiousness. A coping construct referred to as positive emotional (or, conversely, negative emotional) coping was assessed using the emotional coping subscales of the CTI: self-acceptance, lack of overgeneralization, nonsensitivity, and absence of dwelling. We assessed distress using the primary subscales of the Mood and Anxiety Symptom Questionnaire (Watson, Clark, Weber, Assenheimer, Strauss, & McCormick, 1995): general distress: anxious symptoms, and depressive symptoms, anxious arousal, and anhedonic depression. The confirmatory factor analysis supported the construct validity of the measurement model.

To avoid suppressor effects (see Cohen & Cohen, 1983) and perform strict tests of the hypothesized relations for each perfectionism dimension, we established structural models that fit the data well for each perfectionism dimension separately. Each latent variable in the structural submodels had hypothesized links with each of the other latent variables. We eliminated the nonsignificant paths from these submodels making the estimation of the full structural model (i.e., all causal relations specified for the six latent variables simultaneously) more practical. Next, both perfectionism latent factors, and the significant paths of their respective submodels, were included in the same model to see which paths remained significant controlling for the influence of the other perfectionism variable. Personal standards and evaluative concerns perfectionism factors were permitted to correlate freely. The resulting model and the significant standardized parameter estimates for the paths of this model are presented in Figure 12.2.

The results suggest that the effects of evaluative concerns perfection-

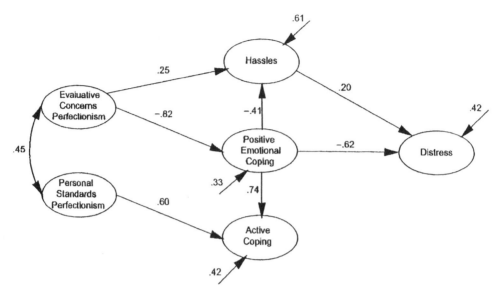

Figure 12.2. Final modified structural model relating evaluative concerns and personal standards perfectionism, emotional and active coping, hassles, and distress. All standardized parameters are significant. The coefficients at coping, hassles, and distress denote the proportions of variance in the endogenous variable that was not explained by other variables in the model.

ism on distress are indirect and mediated through both coping and hassles, because the direct effect of evaluative concerns perfectionism on distress was not supported. That is, evaluative concerns perfectionism was negatively associated with adaptive, positive emotional coping, which was negatively related to distress. Also, evaluative concerns perfectionism was positively associated with hassles, which was positively associated with distress after controlling for the effect of coping. Furthermore, the relation between evaluative concerns perfectionism and hassles was direct but also was mediated by coping. The results are most easily grasped by referring to Figure 12.2 and considering the paths leading from evaluative concerns perfectionism to distress and hassles. With respect to personal standards, although it was negatively related to positive emotional coping when it was tested separate from the influence of evaluative concerns perfectionism, only the path with active coping was unique controlling for the influence of evaluative concerns perfectionism. The fact that personal standards perfectionism became positively related to positive emotional coping, controlling for evaluative concerns perfectionism, was due to a suppressor effect. That is, the relation between personal standards perfectionism and emotional coping changed direction and the relation between evaluative concerns perfectionism and emotional coping was enhanced (correlation = .82 without personal standards perfectionism in the model) after the relation between personal standards and evaluative concerns perfectionism suppressed the irrelevant variance of the other perfectionism dimension in predicting emotional coping (see Cohen & Cohen, 1983). This finding indicates that personal standards are related to an active, adaptive, problem-focused form of coping, but only weakly related to more maladaptive factors such as less positive emotional coping, hassles, and distress.

Study 3. Evaluative concerns versus personal standards perfectionism and distress: The addition of social support as a mediator. In our third study, the large sample size (N = 443) permitted us to randomly split the sample into two halves. One half was used to test the structural model, and the other half was used to cross-validate the SEM results from the first set of analyses. Our mediational models posited hassles, coping, and perceived social support as key mechanisms in the relation between evaluative concerns perfectionism and distress.

Seven latent variables were used in the model testing: evaluative concerns and personal standards perfectionism, active and avoidant coping, social support, hassles, and distress. Evaluative concerns perfectionism was assessed as it was in Study 2 except that the discrepancy subscale of the APS–R was not available. Personal standards perfectionism was assessed using the self-oriented perfectionism subscale of the Hewitt and Flett MPS, and the personal standards subscale from the Frost MPS. Hassles and distress were assessed as they were in our second study. We assessed active coping using three subscales of the COPE (Carver, Scheier, & Weintraub, 1989) that reflect active, problem-focused coping: active coping, planning, and suppression of competing activities. Avoidant coping was assessed using three subscales that reflect maladaptive coping: behavioral disengagement, mental disengagement, and denial. This study was unique because we introduced social support into the analyses for the first time, thereby increasing the complexity of the models. Social support was assessed using Cutrona and Russell's (1987) SPS. In contrast to global measures of perceived support, the SPS taps the extent to which respondents feel that each of six provisions of social relationships is currently available to them. Consistent with Cutrona (1989), we used three of the provisions: reliable alliance, attachment, and guidance, which assess assurance that others can be counted on for help, an emotional closeness that provides a sense of security, and the availability of advice or information, respectively. Confirmatory factor analysis was first used to test the measurement model and produced acceptable indexes of fit (see Dunkley, Blankstein, Halsall, Williams, & Winkworth, 2000).

As in the previous study, the sequence of structural model analyses that was performed with the evaluative concerns latent variable was repeated with the personal standards variable. Because nonsignificant paths had been eliminated and good fitting models had been obtained for each perfectionism dimension separately, the purpose of these analyses was to determine which significant paths in the evaluative concerns and personal standards perfectionism models remained significant controlling for the influence of the other perfectionism dimension. Figure 12.3 presents the significant standardized parameter estimates of the final structural model. The results are most easily grasped by considering the paths leading from evaluative concerns perfectionism to distress. The findings

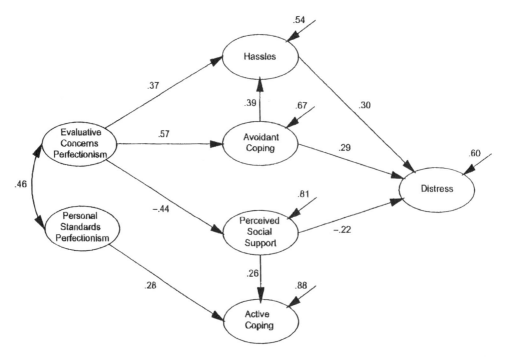

Figure 12.3. Final modified structural model relating evaluative concerns and personal standards perfectionism, avoidant and active coping, perceived social support, hassles, and distress. All standardized parameters are significant. The coefficients at coping, social support, hassles, and distress denote the proportions of variance in the endogenous variable that were not explained by other variables in the model. Reprinted from "The Relation between Perfectionism and Distress: Hassles, Coping, and Perceived Social Support as Mediators and Moderators," by D. M. Dunkley, K. R. Blankstein, J. Halsall, M. Williams, & G. Winkworth, 2000, *Journal of Counseling Psychology, 47,* p. 445. Copyright 2000 by American Psychological Association. Reprinted with permission.

provide clear support for a fully mediated model to explain the relation between evaluative concerns perfectionism and distress. That is, evaluative concerns perfectionism was associated with hassles, avoidant coping, and perceived social support, respectively, each of which was uniquely associated with distress. Moreover, the explanatory power was not reduced by deleting the evaluative concerns perfectionism-to-distress path from the model. Further, although personal standards perfectionism was positively related to hassles, when it was tested separate from the influence of evaluative concerns perfectionism, as in the previous study, only the personal standards perfectionism path with active coping was unique controlling for the effect of evaluative concerns perfectionism. Additionally, perceived social support uniquely positively predicted active coping. Avoidant coping had a unique positive association with hassles.

The findings are consistent with the results of the first two studies and suggest that evaluative concerns perfectionists typically engage in dysfunctional, avoidant kinds of coping, such as disengagement and denial, which may exacerbate both their levels of daily stress and distress. Hassles also mediated the link between evaluative concerns perfectionism and distress. Perceived social support was a third unique mediator in this relation. The negative relation between evaluative concerns perfectionism and the perception that others are available for assistance during stress is consistent with our hypothesis that evaluative concerns or self-critical people have lower perceptions of social support.

Tests of Moderator Hypotheses

We wanted to test interactional (i.e., diathesis stress, specific vulnerability) models of the relations between perfectionism dimensions and both stressful events and coping strategies. Further, it is logical to predict interactions with social support (i.e., stress-buffering hypothesis). However, SEM researchers have not made wide use of interaction factors due to various complexities, including the fact that it is difficult to arrive at clear, unambiguous interpretations (see Newcomb, 1990). Therefore, in each sample, we performed a series of post hoc hierarchical multiple regression analyses to determine whether various moderator hypotheses could account for unique variance in distress scores over and above the variance predicted by main effect variables. Measured variables were standardized and the factor scores of the indicator variables to their latent variables were used to form predictor variables used for the analyses. We evaluated the unique effects of a series of two-way and three-way interactions tested separately while controlling for the main effects of all the predictor variables. This is the procedure typically used to evaluate moderator hypotheses by Hewitt and Flett and their colleagues (e.g., Hewitt et al., 1996) and involves an incremental partitioning of variance (see Cohen & Cohen, 1983). These analyses were particularly relevant to personal standards perfectionism, in our second and third studies, to determine if, or when, this dimension is related to distress.[1]

Our first study of self-critical perfectionism revealed no significant interactions involving self-critical perfectionism and the hassles and coping latent constructs, respectively, predicting distress. In our second study, one significant effect supported our hypothesis: Evaluative concerns perfectionism interacted with coping such that the highest levels of distress were found in perfectionists with relatively less positive emotional coping strategies.

Our third study supported the hypothesis of an interaction with hassles for *both* personal standards and evaluative concerns perfectionists. Although inconsistent with the first two studies, these findings are con-

---

[1]We also tested various versions of *specific* vulnerability hypotheses in all of our studies. For example, the hypothesis that achievement stress moderates the relation between self-oriented perfectionism and distress (Hewitt & Flett, 1993; Hewitt et al., 1996) was assessed by entering the interaction of self-oriented perfectionism with academic hassles into the regression equation following the entry of both variables as main effects. This interaction was significant in Study 3 only.

sistent with a few other studies that have reported significant interactions between dimensions of perfectionism and stress (e.g., Flett, Hewitt, Blankstein, & Mosher, 1995; Hewitt & Flett, 1993; Hewitt et al., 1996; Lynd-Stevenson & Hearne, 1999). Moreover, the interaction between personal standards perfectionism and hassles suggests that high levels of perceived stress can lead to distress in such perfectionists. Although evaluative concerns or personal standards perfectionism did not interact with coping to predict distress, we found that there was a significant increase in distress as perceived social support decreased from high to low levels for *both* evaluative concerns and personal standards perfectionists. This study was unique because we were able to test a series of stress–buffering hypotheses by examining whether, for people experiencing high levels of stress, perfectionism and either social support or coping interacts to predict distress. Only one 3-way interaction predicted unique variance in distress scores: personal standards perfectionism × hassles × social support. For personal standards perfectionists experiencing high levels of stress, there was a negative relation between social support and distress suggesting that low perceptions of social support can exacerbate the impact of high levels of stress on distress.

Consistent with the work of McClelland and Judd (1993), the significant interactions found each accounted for relatively small amounts of variance (1–2%) in distress scores. Further, support for moderator hypotheses was evident only if the interaction terms were analyzed separate from the influence of one another. Although this could be interpreted as failure to support moderator hypotheses, it is reasonable to argue that high interrelations among the interaction terms dissipated the effect of each interaction term (Jaccard, Turrisi, & Wan, 1990).

Summary, Future Research Directions, and Treatment Implications

Our primary purpose in using SEM was to attempt to explain the nature of the relation between different components and dimensions of perfectionism and current distress symptoms. The use of SEM allowed us to test more complex models with as many as four mediating variables while controlling for measurement error, because each variable in the model had multiple indicators (see Baron & Kenny, 1986). Specifically, we sought to determine whether partially mediated models (i.e., models that included the direct effects of self-critical or evaluative concerns perfectionism on distress) would be better fitting models than fully mediated models (i.e., models that eliminated the direct effect on distress) in explaining the link between perfectionism and distress.

The Role of Perfectionism in Adaptational Outcomes: Curse or Blessing?

The link between self-critical or evaluative concerns perfectionism and distress was fully mediated by the relations of perfectionism to coping, hassles, and, in our third study, social support. Maladaptive avoidant or emotional coping in stressful situations, such as disengagement and denial, appears to be an integral part of the self-critical and evaluative concerns perfectionist's existence. In all three studies, self-critical or evaluative concerns perfectionism was strongly related to maladaptive coping which was, in turn, related to distress. Hassles (Studies 2 and 3) and perceived available social support (Study 3) also mediated the link between evaluative concerns perfectionism and distress, controlling for the effect of coping on distress. There was no support for a unique direct effect of these maladaptive forms of perfectionism on distress.

The mediational role of avoidant or emotion-focused coping also helps explain the relationship between maladaptive dimensions of perfectionism and hassles. In each of the studies, high levels of self-critical or evaluative concerns perfectionism were associated with maladaptive coping, and maladaptive coping was associated with the experience of daily hassles. This consistent finding suggests that evaluative concerns or self-critical perfectionists experience higher levels of daily stressful events because they cope maladaptively when encountering difficult or upsetting situations. The two studies involving evaluative concerns perfectionism also supported a direct effect of this form of maladaptive perfectionism on hassles, after controlling for the effect of coping on hassles. This finding is consistent with a hypothesis that the generation, or instigation, of stress is influenced by high levels of perfectionism. Thus, the nature of the relationship between evaluative concerns perfectionism and the experience of hassles appears to be both direct and mediated by coping. The addition of social support was informative. Evaluative concerns perfectionism was associated with a perception of a lack of social support, which was, in turn, associated with reports of less distress.

A demonstration of moderator effects in the relationship between self-critical or evaluative concerns perfectionism and distress proved somewhat elusive. However, there were a few significant and meaningful interaction effects. For example, in our third study evaluative concerns perfectionists reported increased distress when they experienced higher levels of hassles. Our findings are consistent with cognitive theories of psychological stress and coping, such as presented by Lazarus and his colleagues (e.g., Lazarus & Folkman, 1984).

Although personal standards perfectionists tend to be achievement oriented and successful (e.g., Blatt, 1995; Brown, Heimberg, Frost, Makris, Juster, & Leung, 1999; Mills & Blankstein, 2000), we expected to find some emotional "cost" as a consequence of their high standards and drive for perfection. This was not completely accurate, especially when we controlled for the role of evaluative concerns perfectionism. Personal standards perfectionists use adaptive, problem-focused coping and did not experience distress. Nonetheless, the post hoc analyses of interaction effects suggested that personal standards perfectionism can be associated with distress under some circumstances, such as when high levels of hassles overwhelm a perfectionist's ability or desire to engage in active, problem-focused coping. Furthermore, personal standards perfectionists who experience high levels of stress may be at risk for negative outcomes when they also perceive that they lack social support.

Research Directions

It will be important in future work to use multiple outcomes of, for example, distress and achievement in the same studies in order to place the present findings in a broader perspective (see Brown et al., 1999). It also will be important to include social support variables in order to have more complete models of the link between perfectionism and maladjustment. Researchers should examine different aspects of social support, such as practical as opposed to emotional support (see Flett, Blankstein, Hicken, & Watson, 1995). In addition, it also will be of value to incorporate measures of major life events and appraisals of the impact of these events in these more complex models (see Holahan et al., 1997). It has been suggested that a "threshold" may exist such that perfectionism conveys vulnerability only when more severe types of negative events occur (e.g., Clark & Oates, 1995). It also will be necessary to examine the more specific stress processes and mechanisms that can help explain the perfectionism–distress link, including stress anticipation, generation, enhancement, and perpetuation (see Hewitt & Flett, chapter 11, this volume).

It is often concluded that temporal consistency of coping is greater than cross-situational consistency (Compas, Forsythe, & Wagner, 1988). However, the cross-situational stability issue needs to be examined in perfectionists. The measures of coping used in our studies were disposition-oriented and, therefore, cover only one facet of coping. Studies using more situation-oriented measures would be useful. Indeed, given hypotheses that different perfectionism dimensions are related to different types of stressors, it is important to determine whether or not evaluative concerns or self-critical and personal standards perfectionists use different coping strategies with different types of stressors. We recently completed a study in which perfectionists responded to current, personally selected interpersonal and achievement stressors. Analyses of this data will provide us with greater insight into the current coping strategies, cognitions, and behavior of both "normal" and "neurotic" perfectionists when they are confronted with salient stressors. We also will be able to determine whether or not these state (as opposed to dispositional) coping strategies differ for different types of stressors. Following the lead of Aldwin and Revenson (1987), we also are examining both the *effectiveness* of the perfectionist's coping (i.e., how well coping reduces stress) and the *efficacy* of coping (i.e., the perception that coping efforts will be effective). Because it is often reported that there are gender differences in coping (e.g., Nolen-Hoeksema, 1987), in future studies, it will be important to examine the role of gender. Finally, it will be necessary to examine the relationship between our self-criticism perfectionism construct derived from three somewhat different theoretical frameworks, and our evaluative concerns construct based on the multidimensional perfectionism literature.

We acknowledge certain limitations of our studies that also suggest future research. First, a longitudinal study is needed in order to determine whether causal relationships exist among our latent constructs of perfectionism, coping, hassles, social support, and distress. Second, we do not know whether the same relationships would emerge with more objective methods of data collection such as peer ratings, behavioral observations, and clinical judgments. Finally, our findings may not generalize to college students from different locations, or to members of different age or sociocultural groups, or to community and clinical populations. It will be especially important to replicate our findings in clinical samples.

Treatment Implications

The broader implication of our findings is a potential appeal to clinicians and health psychologists who desire a scientific basis for interventions to help manage stress and promote health and psychological well-being. Few studies have examined the effect of evaluative concerns or self-critical perfectionism variables on therapy process and outcome. However, in analyses of the data from the National Institute of Mental Health Treatment of Depression Collaborative Research Program (TDCRP), Blatt and his colleagues (e.g., Blatt, Zuroff, Bondi, Sanislow, & Pilkonis, 1998; Zuroff et al., 2000) reported that Dysfunctional Attitude Scale Perfectionism (Weissman & Beck, 1978) interfered with the development of the therapeutic alliance and was associated with poor outcomes irrespective of the brief treatment received. Blatt (1995) concluded that perfectionists possibly require long-term psychodynamic psychotherapy, and suggested that "one of the primary tasks in treatment would be to enable these patients to begin to relinquish aspects of their identification with harsh, judgmental, parental figures who have set excessively high standards" (p. 1014). This suggestion is consistent with our conceptualization of the evaluative concerns and self-critical perfectionist. Is it possible, however, to achieve the goal without resorting to long-term therapy?

Each path in our models identifies a component that is potentially alterable. For example, in treating self-critical or evaluative concerns perfectionists, our findings suggest that clinicians should direct their attention to the characteristically negative, maladaptive, and dysfunctional ways they respond to and attempt to cope with salient situations (past and present), including interactions with "parental figures" and achievement situations. Thus, modifying both primary and secondary stress appraisal processes (see Lazarus & Folkman, 1984) may be critical factors in effective treatment. A goal of treatment would be to help perfectionists appraise people and events differently such that not so much is at stake, and to develop more adaptive and effective coping strategies to deal with situations that trigger distress. The focus should be on helping clients to develop strategies and skills that emphasize problem-focused, task oriented, active, adaptive coping, instead of a reliance on approaches such as emotion-focused coping, avoidance, overgeneralization, sensitivity, rumination, mental and physical disengagement, and denial that can contribute to the experience and probable recurrence of distress.

It will be vital to help perfectionists learn how to appraise differently, manage, and cope with events in their day-to-day lives that trigger self-engendered stress. Although most previous research has focused on the impact on perfectionists of major life events such as the death of a loved one or the loss of a job, and these are important issues that must be addressed in therapy, our findings point up the importance of a focus in treatment on the hassles of everyday life. Minor events (e.g., independent objective appraisals) appear to exact a heavy toll on some perfectionists. It also will be the task of the clinician to determine whether a client's experience of hassles cuts across various domains and is, therefore, a general problem as our findings suggest or whether the perceived hassles tend to be specific to a particular domain (e.g., interpersonal or achievement). It will be necessary to focus in treatment on areas that are salient to the client. Thus, it will be important to help the client to manage his or her everyday life in such a way that the appraised frequency and duration of daily hassles is reduced or minimized, such as by restructuring a schedule to reduce the demands on the client's time. It also will be appropriate to facilitate a change in the client's perception or appraisals of the people, situations, and events that are a "hassle." It will be critical to work with the client on the development of a perception of coping self-efficacy and a repertoire of efficient and effective coping strategies that can be matched to the demands of actual or perceived stressful events. For example, while it is usually the case that active or problem-focused coping is the most adaptive strategy, under some circumstances (e.g., when changing the situation is beyond personal control) avoidant or emotion-focused coping would be appropriate. It also may be important to work with the evaluative concerns and self-critical perfectionist's appraisal and coping strategies for working through and resolving historically significant relationship and achievement events. Thus, interventions aimed at the development of coping skills and the reduction of perceived hassles could help to minimize the negative effects that evaluative concerns or self-critical perfectionism has on distress.

Because a perceived lack of available social support also mediates the link between evaluative concerns perfectionism and current distress, clinicians should assess the perceived and actual quantity and quality of social support in the perfectionist's life. Evaluative concerns perfectionists perceive that they cannot count on others for help, that they are missing a sense of security based on emotional closeness, and that others are not available to give them advice or information. It will be helpful to work on ways that maximize social support extended to the client by family, friends, and significant others. For example, a component of a social support intervention might be to help perfectionists reconceptualize relationships with their family of origin (see Blatt, 1995), especially because parental expectations and criticism are assumed to play a key role in the development of self-critical and evaluative concerns perfectionism (e.g., Frost et al., 1990). It also may be necessary to modify negative biases in interpreting supportive behaviors and to facilitate social competence (see Brand, Lakey, & Berman, 1995). In the event that support is not available or sources prove counterproductive, it may be useful to involve the client in a group therapy program in which members provide support to each other. As part of a comprehensive, multifaceted intervention plan clients could be encouraged to join community self-help groups and to make use of empirically based self-help books (e.g., Antony & Swinson, 1998).

Regarding personal standards perfectionists in treatment, a challenge will be to develop interventions that will help them find ways to minimize any negative consequences of their perfectionism, such as a cost in terms of appraised daily stress, and emotional distress or conflicted relationships. At the same time, it would be appropriate to help them pursue and enjoy the positive, adaptive, cognitive and motivational aspects of their perfectionism that can lead to effective functioning and success, especially in achievement situations and interpersonal contexts. As Slaney et al. (chapter 3, this volume) pointed out, an increasing emphasis on the adaptive aspects of perfectionism provides the practicing psychologist with a tool that can enhance clients' potential strengths while modifying the deleterious consequences of maladaptive perfectionism. However, it will first be the task of researchers to determine clearly under what circumstances personal standards perfectionism is, in fact, adaptive. Until such time as the adaptive correlates and consequences have been determined, therapists should focus on the evaluative concerns and self-critical components because our research provides additional evidence of "the destructiveness of perfectionism" (Blatt, 1995). Also, it should be recognized that "adaptive" dimensions of perfectionism are typically moderately correlated with "maladaptive" dimensions.

A final proposed direction for future research would be the development and evaluation of a relatively brief treatment intervention for evaluative concerns and self-critical perfectionists. This new, multifaceted intervention could be patterned on a combination of the elements of the cognitive–behavioral and interpersonal therapies evaluated in the TDCRP with an added focus on the careful assessment of evaluative concerns and self-critical perfectionism and on integrating the various strategies outlined above.

Conclusion

Our results demonstrate the central role that coping styles can play in the experience of distress and hassles in perfectionistic people. Maladaptive coping serves a mediating role in the relationship between evaluative concerns and self-critical perfectionism and both the experience of psychological distress symptoms and daily stress. The appraisal of daily hassles and perceived social support also play a mediating role in the perfectionism–distress relationship, at least for evaluative concerns perfectionism. Personal standards perfectionism is linked only to active, adaptive coping after controlling for the influence of evaluative concerns perfectionism on hassles and distress. The structural equation modeling strategy will allow researchers to test out the more complex models that will facilitate our understanding of factors that mediate links between perfectionism and adaptational outcomes. The results of these investigations will, in turn, facilitate the clinician's approach to assessing and treating both the perfectionist concerned about criticism and negative evaluation by self or others and the perfectionist who has stringent personal standards. Our findings are a further demonstration of the importance to both the researcher and the clinician of studying perfectionism from a multidimensional perspective.

References

Adkins, K., & Parker, W. D. (1996). Perfectionism and suicidal preoccupation. *Journal of Personality, 64*, 529–543.

Akaike, H. (1987). Factor analysis and AIC. *Psychometrica, 52*, 317–332.

Alden, L. E., & Bieling, P. J. (1996). Interpersonal convergence of personality constructs in dynamic and cognitive models of depression. *Journal of Research in Personality, 30*, 60–75.

Aldwin, C. M., & Revenson, T. A. (1987). Does coping help? A reexamination of the relation between coping and mental health. *Journal of Personality and Social Psychology, 53*, 337–348.

Anderson, J. C., & Gerbing, D. W. (1988). Structural equation modeling in practice: A review and recommended two-step approach. *Psychological Bulletin, 103*, 411–423.

Andrews, G., Pollock, C., & Stewart, G. (1989). The determination of defense style by questionnaire. *Archives of General Psychiatry, 46*, 450–460.

Antony, M. M., & Swinson, R. P. (1998). *When perfect isn't good enough: Strategies for coping with perfectionism.* Oakland: New Harbinger Publications.

Arbuckle, J. (1997). *AMOS users' guide version 3.6.* Chicago: Small Waters Corporation.

Attanasio, H., Hirschfield, R., & Yerevanian, B. (1984). Psychometric properties of the SUNYA Revision of the Psychosomatic Symptom Checklist. *Journal of Behavioral Medicine, 7*, 247–258.

Baron, R. M., & Kenny, D. A. (1986). The mediator-moderator variable distinction in social psychological research: Conceptual, strategic, and statistical considerations. *Journal of Personality and Social Psychology, 51*, 1173–1182.

Beck, A. T. (1983). Cognitive therapy of depression: New perspectives. In P. J. Clayton & J. E. Barrett (Eds.), *Treatment of depression: Old controversies and new approaches* (pp. 265–290). New York: Raven.

Beck, A. T., Epstein, N., Harrison, R. P., & Emery, G. (1983). *Development of the Sociotropy-Autonomy Scale: A measure of personality factors in psychopathology.* Unpublished manuscript, Center for Cognitive Therapy, University of Pennsylvania Medical School.

Bentler, P. M. (1990). Comparative fit indices in structural models. *Psychological Bulletin, 107*, 238–246.

Blankstein, K. R. (1996). Dimensions of perfectionism and the perception of practical and emotional social support from family, friends, and significant other. Unpublished raw data.

Blankstein, K. R. (1998). Correlates and consequences of self-defined perfectionism. Unpublished raw data.

Blankstein, K. R., & Flett, G. L. (1992). Specificity in the assessment of daily hassles: Hassles, locus of control, and adjustment in college students. *Canadian Journal of Behavioural Science, 24*, 382–398.

Blankstein, K. R., & Flett, G. L. (1993). *Development of the General, Academic, and Social Hassles Scales for Students (GASHSS).* Unpublished manuscript, University of Toronto at Mississauga.

Blankstein, K. R., Flett, G. L., Hewitt, P. L., & Eng, A. (1993). Dimensions of perfectionism and irrational fears: An examination with the fear survey schedule. *Personality and Individual Differences, 15*, 323–328.

Blankstein, K. R., Flett, G. L., & Koledin, S. (1991). The Brief College Student Hassles Scale: Development, validation, and relation with pessimism. *Journal of College Student Development, 32*, 258–264.

Blankstein, K. R., Halsall, J., Williams, M., & Winkworth, G. (1997). Dimensions of perfectionism and cumulative grade point average. Unpublished raw data.

Blankstein, K. R., & Paduada, M. (2001). *Multidimensional perfectionism and defense styles: Relations with negative affectivity and positive affectivity.* Manuscript submitted for publication.

Blatt, S. (1974). Levels of object representation in anaclitic and introjective depression. *Psychoanalytic Study of the Child, 29*, 107–157.

Blatt, S. (1995). The destructiveness of perfectionism: Implications for the treatment of depression. *American Psychologist, 50*, 1003–1020.

Blatt, S. J., D'Afflitti, J. P., & Quinlan, D. M. (1976). Experiences of depression in normal young adults. *Journal of Abnormal Psychology, 85*, 383–389.

Blatt, S. J., & Zuroff, D. C. (1992). Interpersonal relatedness and self-definition: Two prototypes for depression. *Clinical Psychology Review, 12*, 527–562.

Blatt, S. J., Zuroff, D. C., Bondi, C. M., Sanislow, C. A., & Pilkonis, P. A. (1998). When and how perfectionism impedes the brief treatment of depression: Further analyses of the National Institute of Mental Health Treatment of Depression Collaborative Research Program. *Journal of Consulting and Clinical Psychology, 66*, 423–428.

Bollen, K. A. (1989). A new incremental fit index for general structural equation models. *Sociological Methods and Research, 17*, 303–316.

Brand, E. F., Lakey, B., & Berman, S. (1995). A preventive, psychoeducational approach to increase perceived social support. *American Journal of Community Psychology, 23*, 117–135.

Brown, E. J., Heimberg, R. G., Frost, R. O., Makris, G. S., Juster, H. R., & Leung, A. W. (1999). Relationship of perfectionism to affect, expectations, attributions and performance in the classroom. *Journal of Social and Clinical Psychology, 18*, 98–120.

Carmines, E., & McIver, J. (1981). Analyzing models with unobserved variables: Analysis of covariance structures. In G. Bohrnstedt & E. Borgatta (Eds.), *Social measurement: Current issues* (pp. 65–115). Beverly Hills, CA: Sage.

Carver, C. S., Scheier, M. F., & Weintraub, J. K. (1989). Assessing coping strategies: A theoretically based approach. *Journal of Personality and Social Psychology, 56*, 267–283.

Chamberlain, K., & Zika, S. (1990). The minor events approach to stress: Support for the use of daily hassles. *British Journal of Psychology, 81*, 469–481.

Clark, D. A., & Beck, A. T. (1991). Personality factors in dysphoria: A psychometric refinement of Beck's Sociotropy–Autonomy scale. *Journal of Psychopathology and Behavioral Assessment, 13*, 369–388.

Clark, D. A., & Oates, T. (1995). Daily hassles, major and minor life events, and their interaction with sociotropy and autonomy. *Behaviour Research and Therapy, 33*, 819–823.

Clark, D. A., Steer, R. A., Beck, A. T., & Ross, L. (1995). Psychometric characteristics of revised sociotropy and autonomy scales in college students. *Behaviour Research and Therapy, 33*, 325–334.

Cohen, J., & Cohen, P. (1983). *Applied multiple regression: Correlational analyses for the behavioral sciences.* Hillsdale, NJ: Lawrence Erlbaum Associates, Inc.

Cohen, L. H., Hettler, T. R., & Park, C. L. (1997). Social support, personality, and life stress adjustment. In G. R. Pierce, B. Lakey, I. G. Sarason, & B. R. Sarason (Eds.), *Sourcebook of social support and personality.* New York: Plenum Press.

Compas, B. E., Forsythe, C. J., & Wagner, B. M. (1988). Consistency and variability in causal attributions and coping with stress. *Cognitive Therapy and Research, 12*, 305–320.

Cox, D. J., Freundlich, A., & Meyer, R. G. (1975). Differential effectiveness of electromyograph feedback, verbal relaxation instructions and medication placebo with tension headaches. *Journal of Consulting and Clinical Psychology, 43*, 892–898.

Cutrona, C. E. (1989). Ratings of social support by adolescents and adult informants: Degree of correspondence and prediction of depressive symptoms. *Journal of Personality and Social Psychology, 57,* 723–730.

Cutrona, C. E., & Russell, D. (1987). The provisions of social relationships and adaptation to stress. In W. H. Jones & D. Perlman (Eds.), *Advances in personal relationships* (Vol. 1, pp. 37–68). Greenwich, CT: JAI Press.

DeLongis, A., Folkman, S., & Lazarus, R. S. (1988). The impact of daily stress on health and mood: Psychological and social resources as mediators. *Journal of Personality and Social Psychology, 54,* 486–495.

Dunkley, D. M., & Blankstein, K. R. (2000). Self-critical perfectionism, coping, hassles, and current distress: A structural equations modeling approach. *Cognitive Therapy and Research, 24,* 713–730.

Dunkley, D. M., Blankstein, K. R., & Flett, G. L. (1997). Specific cognitive-personality vulnerability styles in depression and the five-factor model of personality. *Personality and Individual Differences, 23,* 1041–1053.

Dunkley, D. M., Blankstein, K. R., Halsall, J., Williams, M., & Winkworth, G. (2000). The relation between perfectionism and distress: Hassles, coping, and perceived social support as mediators and moderators. *Journal of Counseling Psychology, 47,* 437–457.

D'Zurilla, T. J., & Nezu, A. M. (1990). Development and preliminary evaluation of the Social Problem-Solving Inventory (SPSI). *Psychological Assessment, 2,* 156–163.

Endler, N. S., & Parker, J. D. A. (1990). Multidimensional assessment of coping: A critical evaluation. *Journal of Personality and Social Psychology, 58,* 844–854.

Endler, N. S., & Parker, J. D. A. (1999). *Coping inventory for stressful situations (CISS): Manual.* Toronto: Multi-Health Systems, Inc.

Epstein, S. (1992). Constructive thinking and mental and physical well-being. In L. Montada, S. Filipp, & M. J. Lerner (Eds.), *Life crises and experiences of loss in adulthood.* Hillsdale, NJ: Lawrence Erlbaum Associates.

Epstein, S., & Meier, P. (1989). Constructive thinking: A broad coping variable with specific components. *Journal of Personality and Social Psychology, 57,* 332–350.

Flett, G. L., Blankstein, K. R., Hicken, D. J., & Watson, M. S. (1995). Social support and help-seeking in daily hassles versus major life events stress. *Journal of Applied Social Psychology, 25,* 49–58.

Flett, G. L., Blankstein, K. R., Hewitt, P. L., & Heisel, M. J. (2001). *Perfectionism, affect, and domains of psychological well-being.* Manuscript submitted for publication.

Flett, G. L., Blankstein, K. R., Hewitt, P. L., & Koledin, S. (1992). Components of perfectionism and procrastination in college students. *Social Behavior and Personality, 20,* 85–94.

Flett, G. L., Blankstein, K. R., & Martin, T. R. (1995). Procrastination, negative self-evaluation, and stress in depression and anxiety: A review and preliminary model. In J. R. Ferrari, J. L. Johnson, & W. G. McCown (Eds.), *Procrastination and task avoidance: Theory, research, and treatment* (pp. 137–167). New York and London: Plenum Press.

Flett, G. L., Blankstein, K. R., Occhiuto, M., & Koledin, S. (1994). Depression, self-esteem, and complex attributions for life problems. *Current Psychology, 13,* 263–281.

Flett, G. L., Hewitt, P. L., Blankstein, K. R., & Dynin, C. B. (1994). Dimensions of perfectionism and Type A behavior. *Personality and Individual Differences, 16,* 477–485.

Flett, G. L., Hewitt, P. L., Blankstein, K. R., & Koledin, S. (1991). Dimensions of perfectionism and irrational thinking. *Journal of Rational–Emotive & Cognitive–Behavior Therapy, 9,* 185–201.

Flett, G. L., Hewitt, P. L., Blankstein, K. R., & Mosher, S. W. (1991). Perfectionism, self-actualization, and personal adjustment. *Journal of Social Behavior and Personality, 6,* 147–160.

Flett, G. L., Hewitt, P. L., Blankstein, K. R., & Mosher, S. W. (1995). Perfectionism, life events, and depressive symptoms: Test of a diathesis–stress model. *Current Psychology, 14,* 112–137.

Flett, G. L., Hewitt, P. L., Blankstein, K. R., & O'Brien, S. (1991). Perfectionism and learned resourcefulness in depression and self-esteem. *Personality and Individual Differences, 12,* 61–68.

Flett, G. L., Hewitt, P. L., Blankstein, K. R., Solnik, M., & Van Brunschot, M. (1996). Perfectionism, social problem-solving ability, and psychological distress. *Journal of Rational–Emotive & Cognitive–Behavior Therapy, 14*, 245–274.

Flett, G. L., Hewitt, P. L., & DeRosa, T. (1996). Dimensions of perfectionism, psychosocial adjustment, and social skills. *Personality and Individual Differences, 20*, 143–150.

Flett, G. L., Hewitt, P. L., Garshowitz, M., & Martin, T. R. (1997). Personality, negative social interactions, and depressive symptoms. *Canadian Journal of Behavioural Science, 29*, 28–37.

Flett, G. L., Russo, F. A., & Hewitt, P. L. (1993). Dimensions of perfectionism and constructive thinking as a coping strategy. *Journal of Rational–Emotive & Cognitive–Behavior Therapy, 12*, 163–179.

Flett, G. L., Russo, F. A., & Hewitt, P. L. (1994). Dimensions of perfectionism and constructive thinking as a coping response. *Journal of Rational-Emotive and Cognitive-Behavior Therapy, 12*, 163–179.

Flett, G. L., Sawatzky, D. L., & Hewitt, P. L. (1995). Dimensions of perfectionism and goal commitment: A further comparison of two perfectionism measures. *Journal of Psychopathology and Behavioral Assessment, 17*, 111–124.

Freud, S. (1959). Inhibitions, symptoms and anxiety. In J. Strachey (Ed. and Trans.), *The standard edition of the complete psychological works of Sigmund Freud* (Vol. 20, pp. 77–175). London: Hogarth Press. (Original work published 1926)

Frost, R. O., Heimberg, R. G., Holt, C. S., Mattia, J. I., & Neubauer, A. L. (1993). A comparison of two measures of perfectionism. *Personality and Individual Differences, 14*, 119–126.

Frost, R. O., Marten, P., Lahart, C., & Rosenblate, R. (1990). The dimensions of perfectionism. *Cognitive Therapy and Research, 14*, 449–468.

Garner, D. M., Olmstead, M. P., & Polivy, J. (1983). Development and validation of a multidimensional Eating Disorder Inventory for anorexia nervosa and bulimia. *International Journal of Eating Disorders, 2*, 15–34.

Hamachek, D. E. (1978). Psychodynamics of normal and neurotic perfectionism. *Psychology, 15*, 27–33.

Hewitt, P. L., & Flett, G. L. (1991a). Dimensions of perfectionism in unipolar depression. *Journal of Abnormal Psychology, 100*, 98–101.

Hewitt, P. L., & Flett, G. L. (1991b). Perfectionism in the self and social contexts: Conceptualization, assessment, and association with psychopathology. *Journal of Personality and Social Psychology, 60*, 456–470.

Hewitt, P. L., & Flett, G. L. (1993). Dimensions of perfectionism, daily stress, and depression: A test of the specific vulnerability hypothesis. *Journal of Abnormal Psychology, 102*, 58–65.

Hewitt, P. L., & Flett, G. L. (1996). Personality traits and the coping process. In M. Zeidner and N. S. Endler (Eds.), *Handbook of coping* (pp. 410–437). London: Wiley.

Hewitt, P. L., Flett, G. L., & Ediger, E. (1996). Perfectionism and depression: Longitudinal assessment of a specific vulnerability hypothesis. *Journal of Abnormal Psychology, 105*, 276–280.

Hewitt, P. L., Flett, G. L., Ediger, E., Norton, G. R., & Flynn, C. A. (1998). Perfectionism in chronic and state symptoms of depression. *Canadian Journal of Behavioural Science, 30*, 234–242.

Hewitt, P. L., Flett, G. L., & Endler, N. S. (1995). Perfectionism, coping, and depression symptomatology in a clinical sample. *Clinical Psychology and Psychotherapy, 2*, 47–58.

Hill, R. W., McIntire, K., & Bacharach, V. R. (1997). Perfectionism and the big five factors. *Journal of Social Behavior and Personality, 12*, 257–270.

Hill, R. W., Zrull, M. C., & Turlington, S. (1997). Perfectionism and interpersonal problems. *Journal of Personality Assessment, 69*, 81–103.

Holahan, C. J., Moos, R. H., & Bonin, L. (1997). Social support, coping, and psychological adjustment: A resources model. In G. R. Pierce, B. Lakey, I. G. Sarason, & B. R. Sarason (Eds.), *Source book of social support and personality* (pp. 169–186). New York: Plenum Press.

Hoyle, R. H., & Panter, A. T. (1995). Writing about structural equation models. In R. H. Hoyle (Ed.), *Structural equation modeling* (pp. 158–176). Thousand Oaks, CA: Sage.

Jaccard, J., Turrisi, R., & Wan, C. K. (1990). *Interaction effects in multiple regression.* Newbury Park, CA: Sage.

Joiner, T. E. Jr., & Schmidt, N. B. (1995). Dimensions of perfectionism, life stress, and depressed and anxious symptoms: Prospective support for diathesis–stress but not specific vulnerability among male undergraduates. *Journal of Social and Clinical Psychology, 14*, 165–183.

Joreskog, K. G., & Sorbom, D. (1984). *LISREL–VI User's Guide* (3rd ed.). Mooresville, IN: Scientific Software.

Kanner, A. D., Coyne, J. C., Schaefer, C., & Lazarus, R. S. (1981). Comparison of two modes of stress measurement: Daily hassles and uplifts versus major life events. *Journal of Behavioral Medicine, 4*, 189–194.

Lazarus, R. S., & Folkman, S. (1984). *Stress, appraisal, and coping.* New York: Springer.

Lynd-Stevenson, R. M., & Hearne, C. M. (1999). Perfectionism and depressive affect: The pros and cons of being a perfectionist. *Personality and Individual Differences, 26*, 549–562.

Martin, T. R., Flett, G. L., Hewitt, P. L., Krames, L., & Szantos, G. (1996). Personality correlates of depression and health symptoms: A test of a self-regulation model. *Journal of Research in Personality, 31*, 264–277.

McClelland, G. H., & Judd, C. M. (1993). Statistical difficulties of detecting interactions and moderator effects. *Psychological Bulletin, 114*, 376–390.

Mills, J. S., & Blankstein, K. R. (2000). Perfectionism, intrinsic versus extrinsic motivation, and motivated strategies for learning: A multidimensional analysis of university students. *Personality and Individual Differences, 29*, 1191–1204.

Mongrain, M. (1998). Parental representations and support-seeking behaviors related to dependency and self-criticism. *Journal of Personality, 66*, 151–173.

Mongrain, M., Vettese, L. C., Shuster, B., & Kendal, N. (1998). Perceptual biases, affect, and behavior in the relationships of dependents and self-critics. *Journal of Personality and Social Psychology, 75*, 230–241.

Mosher, S. W., Flett, G. L., Blankstein, K. R., & Hewitt, P. L. (2001). *Dimensions of perfectionism and personal projects appraisals in symptoms of depression.* Manuscript submitted for publication.

Newcomb, M. D. (1990). What structural equation modeling can tell us about social support. In I. G. Sarason, B. R. Sarason, and G. R. Pierce (Eds.), *Social support: An interactional view* (pp. 26–63). New York: Wiley.

Nolen-Hoeksema, S. (1987). Sex differences in unipolar depression: Evidence and theory. *Psychological Bulletin, 101*, 259–282.

Ouimette, P. C., Klein, D. N., Anderson, R., Riso, L. P., & Lizardi, H. (1994). Relationship of sociotropy/autonomy and dependency/self-criticism to DSM–III–R personality disorders. *Journal of Abnormal Psychology, 103*, 743–749.

Procidano, M. E., & Smith, W. W. (1997). Assessing perceived social support. In G. R. Pierce, B. Lakey, I. G. Sarason, & B. B. Sarason (Eds.), *Sourcebook of social support and personality* (pp. 93–106). New York: Plenum Press.

Radloff, L. S. (1977). The CES–D scale: A self-report depression scale for research in the general population. *Applied Psychological Measurement, 1*, 385–401.

Rice, K. G., Ashby, J. S., & Slaney, R. B. (1998). Self-esteem as a mediator between perfectionism and depression: A structural equations analysis. *Journal of Counseling Psychology, 45*, 304–314.

Rosenbaum, M. (1980). A schedule for assessing self-control behaviors: Preliminary findings. *Behavior Therapy, 11*, 109–121.

Schwarz, G. (1978). Estimating the dimensions of a model. *The Annals of Statistics, 6*, 461–464.

Shafran, R., & Mansell, W. (2001). Perfectionism and psychopathology: A review of research and treatment. *Clinical Psychology Review, 21*, 879–906.

Slaney, R. B., & Ashby, J. A. (1996). Perfectionists: Study of a criterion group. *Journal of Counseling and Development, 74*, 393–398.

Slaney, R. B., Ashby, J. S., & Trippi, J. (1995). Perfectionism: Its measurement and career relevance. *Journal of Career Assessment, 3*, 279–297.

Slaney, R. B., Rice, K. G., Mobley, M., Trippi, J., & Ashby, J. S. (2001). The Almost Perfect

Scale–Revised. *Measurement and Evaluation in Counseling and Development, 34,* 130–145.

Spielberger, C. D. (1991). *State–Trait Anger Expression Inventory professional manual.* Odessa, FL: Psychological Assessment Resources.

Suls, J., David, J. P., & Harvey, J. H. (1996). Personality and coping: Three generations of research. *Journal of Personality, 64,* 711–735.

Terry-Short, L. A., Owens, R. G., Slade, P. D., & Dewey, M. E. (1995). Positive and negative perfectionism. *Personality and Individual Differences, 18,* 663–668.

Thoits, P. A. (1995). Stress, coping, and social support processes: Where are we? What next? [Extra issue]. *Journal of Health and Social Behavior, 36,* 53–79.

Watson, D., Clark, L. A., Weber, K., Assenheimer, J. S., Strauss, M. E., & McCormick, R. A. (1995). Testing a tripartite model: II. Exploring the symptom structure of anxiety and depression in student, adult, and patient samples. *Journal of Abnormal Psychology, 104,* 15–25.

Weissman, A. N., & Beck, A. T. (1978, August–September). *Development and validation of the Dysfunctional Attitudes Scale: A preliminary investigation.* Paper presented at the 86th Annual Convention of the American Psychological Association, Toronto, Ontario, Canada.

Zimet, G. D., Dahlem, N. W., Zimet, S. G., & Farley, G. K. (1988). The Multidimensional Scale of Perceived Social Support. *Journal of Personality Assessment, 52,* 30–41.

Zuroff, D. C. (1994). Depressive personality styles and the five-factor model of personality. *Journal of Personality Assessment, 63,* 453–472.

Zuroff, D. C., Blatt, S. J., Sotsky, S. M., Krupnick, J. L., Martin, D. J., Sanislow, C. A., & Simmens, S. (2000). Relation of therapeutic alliance and perfectionism to outcome in brief outpatient treatment of depression. *Journal of Consulting and Clinical Psychology, 68,* 114–124.

Zuroff, D. C., & Duncan, N. (1999). Self-criticism and conflict resolution in romantic couples. *Canadian Journal of Behavioural Science, 31,* 137–149.

Part IV _____

Perfectionism and Clinical Disorders

13

Perfectionism and Eating Disorders

Elliot M. Goldner, Sarah J. Cockell, and Suja Srikameswaran

The eating disorders, as conceptualized in current diagnostic nomenclature (American Psychiatric Association, 1994; World Health Organization, 1997), include anorexia nervosa, bulimia nervosa, and related disorders. Anorexia nervosa is characterized by a relentless pursuit of thinness marked by excessively stringent standards. Bulimia nervosa is characterized by cycles of strict dieting and recurrent binge eating and purgative behaviors. A common preoccupation in both anorexia and bulimia nervosa is the quest for the perfect diet, low in fat and other unwanted foods. When the perfect diet, perfect exercise regime, perfect body shape, or perfect weight elude them, people with an eating disorder often experience intense feelings of shame and self-deprecation. Thus, core features of anorexia nervosa and bulimia nervosa appear to be inherently perfectionistic in nature.

Early writings emphasized the obsessional nature of anorexia nervosa, suggesting that people with anorexia refused to eat because of a fear of becoming fat and of achieving psychosexual maturity (Janet, 1929). Other authors have emphasized the theme of asceticism: Food restriction represents such spiritual ideals as self-sacrifice and control over bodily urges (Casper, 1983). Casper suggested that over the past century, the theme of asceticism has become less central and the fear of weight gain and drive for thinness have gained prominence. Bulimia nervosa has a more recent history as a diagnostic entity and was first described in the third edition of the *Diagnostic and Statistical Manual of Mental Disorders* (*DSM-III*; American Psychiatric Association, 1980). People with bulimia and anorexia nervosa share a drive for thinness, but the former experience a rebound from dietary restraint and resort to binge eating and compensatory behaviors. Although some authors (e.g., Casper, 1983) have argued that people with bulimia nervosa differ in character from those with anorexia nervosa, others contend that they share perfectionistic traits and that those traits play a crucial role in the development and maintenance of both disorders (Beebe, 1994; Heatherton & Baumeister, 1991; Slade, 1982).

This chapter describes models of eating disorders that attend to the role of perfectionism and relevant empirical findings. It outlines the contribution that an understanding of perfectionism provides to treatment initiatives in the eating disorders.

Formulations of Perfectionism and the Eating Disorders

This section examines theoretical formulations that include perfectionism (Bruch, 1973, 1977, 1978; Casper, 1983; Garner, 1986; Hewitt, Flett, & Ediger, 1995; Slade, 1982; Strober, 1991) in the development of eating disorders.

Historical and Religious Perspectives

A quest for perfection has been identified in the earliest known cases of eating disorders. In a historical treatise on the eating disorders, Brumberg (1988) described a link between the pursuit of perfection and the restrictive eating behavior that had been a known practice among female saints and ascetics in medieval Europe: "In Catholicism in the thirteenth to sixteenth centuries . . . control of appetite was linked to piety and belief; through fasting, the medieval ascetic strove for perfection in the eyes of her God" (p. 46). Many authors have suggested that the eating behavior of religious figures constituted early cases of anorexia nervosa (Bell, 1985), because the physical manifestations and behaviors appear to be so similar to those observed in anorexic patients. In contrast, Brumberg (1988) argued that the retrospective diagnosis of anorexia nervosa is mistaken in those cases, and she instead identified a historical form of eating disorder distinct to its time and culture. Although she conceived the eating disorders of historical figures to differ from modern-day cases of anorexia and bulimia nervosa, Brumberg saw a significant relationship of those conditions across time and tied the eating behavior in various eras to a pursuit of perfection.

In current times, people with eating disorders often list themes of purity, cleanliness, godliness, and stoicism as important values (Rampling, 1985). Foods, especially fats, are sometimes experienced as toxins and impurities that must be avoided or purged from the body. Some people with eating disorders convey a wish to attain an ethereal state in which they might rise above base appetites and earthly needs.

Psychodynamic and Developmental Models

Psychodynamic theorists have noted the presence of perfectionism in people with anorexia nervosa, but the specific role of this personality variable has not been outlined clearly in theoretical models. Hilde Bruch (1978), in describing her young patients with anorexia nervosa, identified specific perfectionistic behaviors, such as excessive compliance and studiousness. She wrote:

Those in charge of the well-being, care and education of these young-sters need to become alerted to the fact that the "never-giving-any-trouble" child is already in trouble, that the overconscientious, overstudious, and compliant performance is a warning sign of something wrong. In many ways these children fulfill every parent's and teacher's idea of perfection, but they do it in an exaggerated way. It is the extra push, the being not good but "better," that makes the significant difference between these unhappy youngsters who starve themselves and other adolescents who are capable of enjoying life. True prevention requires that their pleasing superperfection is recognized early as a sign of inner misery. (p. 59)

Thus, according to Bruch (1973, 1977, 1978), although many adolescent girls watch their weight, those who go on to develop anorexia nervosa possess a more compliant, perfectionistic, approval-seeking disposition. Bruch (1973, 1978) ascribed such needs for control and perfection to a deep and pervasive sense of ineffectiveness or a response to inner deficits arising from problems in early child development.

Theorists and clinicians elaborated on Bruch's work and, using object relations and self psychology perspectives, proposed that people with eating disorders frequently develop a *false self*: a psychological mask that is donned when interacting with others (Goodsitt, 1997; Johnson & Connors, 1987; Sours, 1980; Striegel-Moore, Silberstein, & Rodin, 1993). The false self portrays a perfect person who is capable and confident—one who never makes mistakes but instead says and does all the right things. Behind the false mask, however, is a person who feels frightened, empty, and isolated by his or her false relationship with peers. Psychodynamic models further link disordered eating behavior and perfectionism as compensatory mechanisms that serve to temporarily obscure feelings of emptiness and deficits in the self.

Psychobiological Models

Strober (1991) proposed that genetic and biological factors are important determinants of eating disorders and may operate through temperamental and personality variables. Drawing on Cloninger's (1987) psychobiological model of temperament and character, he suggested that extreme tendencies toward harm avoidance, low novelty seeking, and high reward dependence constitute the core of anorexia nervosa. *Harm avoidance* refers to the intensity of response to uncertainty and threat; people who are extreme in this dimension demonstrate poor adaptability to change, extreme worry even over minor things, and slow recovery from emotional distress. *Novelty seeking* refers to the intensity with which one responds to novel stimuli. People who are low in this dimension prefer stable, invariant, and emotionally temperate environments. *Reward dependence* refers to the degree to which a person conditions easily to signals of reinforcement. People who are extreme on this dimension tend to be dependent on others for emotional support. They also are hypersensitive to signals of approval and rejection and prone to highly driven and repetitive reward-seeking behavior.

In support of Strober's (1991) model, Casper (1990) found that women who had recovered from restrictive anorexia nervosa rated higher on harm avoidance and lower on novelty seeking than did age-matched non-psychiatric control women. Reward dependence was elevated, but not significantly. The recovered women also rated lower on novelty seeking than their biological siblings did. These findings provide preliminary support for the theory that a temperamental disposition toward control and reserve (i.e., harm avoidance), combined with a preference for safe routine (i.e., low novelty seeking), may characterize people who develop restrictive anorexia nervosa.

Hewitt, Flett, and Ediger (1995) argued that the configuration of personality variables in Strober's (1991) psychobiological model is consistent with a multidimensional model of perfectionism (described later in this chapter). In particular, the authors postulated that perfectionism is linked to harm avoidance because highly perfectionistic people tend to worry about negative evaluations. Furthermore, they proposed that perfectionism is associated with reward dependence because highly perfectionistic people tend to be sensitive to the approval of others. Low levels of novelty seeking can be linked to perfectionism because highly perfectionistic people tend to avoid activities that are novel or unfamiliar for fear of less than excellent performance. Hewitt et al. (1995) concurred with Strober's (1991) suggestion that perfectionistic personality traits may have a genetic basis.

Cognitive–Behavioral Models

Cognitive–behavioral models of the eating disorders have described the critical role of both cognitive and behavioral factors in the maintenance of the disorder (Fairburn, 1981; Fairburn, Shafran, & Cooper, 1999; Garner, Vitousek, & Pike, 1997; Vitousek, 1996). The role of positive and negative cognitive contingencies in symptom formation and maintenance has been identified as a key explanatory factor (Fairburn, Marcus, & Wilson, 1983; Garner, 1986; Vitousek, 1996).

In describing anorexia nervosa, Garner (1986) emphasized that "relentless dieting is maintained by *cognitive self-reinforcement* from the sense of mastery, virtue, and self-control that it provides" (p. 303). Determinants of those positive and negative contingencies are found in logical errors, such as dichotomous reasoning, overgeneralization, personalization, magnification, and arbitrary inference. Two such reasoning errors are closely linked to perfectionism (Barrow & Moore, 1983). First, dichotomous thinking involves approaching experiences in extreme, all-or-none terms. For people with anorexia nervosa, eating anything beyond a preset calorie limit is interpreted as complete loss of control over eating. Second, overgeneralization involves applying a principle or outcome of one event to dissimilar situations. This reasoning error is typical of women with anorexia nervosa, who interpret any deviations from a desired weight goal as indicative of failure as a person in general.

Cognitive–behavioral therapy for eating disorders involves addressing the idiosyncratic beliefs associated with shape and weight, issues of motivation for change, the interaction between physical and psychological facets of the disorder, and self-concept and self-esteem deficits. Thus, the role of perfectionism in cognitive–behavioral models of eating disorders appears to be linked to the development and maintenance of faulty cognitions that reflect unrealistic standards about shape and weight and to the interpretation of "failures" to achieve desired weight loss.

Multifaceted Models

Slade (1982) described the importance of perfectionism as one of two main "setting conditions" for the development of anorexia nervosa. He hypothesized that perfectionistic tendencies, combined with a general dissatisfaction with life and the self, generate a need within the person to "control completely some aspect of the life situation and/or attain total success in some area" (p. 172). Slade reasoned that such complete control would only seem feasible in efforts to target one's own behavior and that weight control would be a prime subject in modern society, particularly for women. Once in place, dieting would be reinforced positively with feelings of success and negatively through fear of weight gain and avoidance or escape from other life difficulties.

In bulimia nervosa, Heatherton and Baumeister (1991) posited that binge eating offers people who have stringent expectations for thinness, high self-awareness, and low self-esteem an opportunity to reduce negative self-awareness. The central hypothesis of their model is that binge eating is an escape from negative affect. Beebe's (1994) integrative model asserted that negative self-awareness triggers dieting. This dieting, however, is generally unsuccessful as it increases negative affect and negative self-awareness, leading to continued dieting and a heightened sensitivity to factors that might break restraint. Thus, a spiraling effect of increasingly disordered eating patterns may result. The integrative model suggests that perfectionism may be a cause of both dieting behavior and aversive self-awareness. Beebe added to Heatherton and Baumeister's (1991) model by arguing that hopelessness, which also has been linked to perfectionism (Blatt, 1995), underlies the chaotic eating patterns that cause or contribute to negative affect. The integrative model suggests that intervention can be made at several points in the cycle, including modifying cognitions through cognitive therapy and increasing self-esteem and reducing aversive self-awareness through interpersonal therapy.

Joiner, Heatherton, Rudd, and Schmidt (1997) proposed a diathesis–stress model that describes the nature of the relationship between perfectionism and bulimic symptoms. Their model evolves from the literature demonstrating the association between perfectionism and depression (Frost, Heimberg, Holt, Mattia, & Neubauer, 1993; Hewitt & Flett, 1991a).

The diathesis−stress model suggests that perfectionism is a risk factor for bulimic symptoms in the presence, and not in the absence, of negative life stress. In this model, negative life stress refers to failed efforts to meet unrealistic standards for shape and weight.

Empirical Findings

A review of the literature reveals that research on eating disorders and perfectionism has evolved from measuring a unidimensional trait to multidimensional conceptualizations of the construct. Whereas in early research, the primary interest was in determining the prevalence of perfectionistic traits in people with eating disorders, current research is exploring the role of perfectionism in the etiology and maintenance of anorexia nervosa and bulimia nervosa.

Early research examining the characteristics of people with anorexia nervosa confirmed that perfectionism was a common premorbid personality characteristic among a substantial number of women with anorexia. For example, Dally (1969) assessed 140 women with anorexia nervosa and found that nearly 75% of patients demonstrated behaviors, cognitive styles, and emotional reactions suggestive of perfectionistic dispositions. The women worried obsessively about their performance on examinations and were excessively fearful of failure. In another study, Halmi, Goldberg, Eckert, Casper, and Davis (1979) interviewed the parents of 44 women with anorexia nervosa and found that 61% were described by parents to have perfectionistic personality characteristics prior to the onset of their illness. Note, however, that those early studies relied on clinical interview data and retrospective reports from parents rather than on standardized measures of personality traits. Furthermore, Sohlberg and Strober (1994) observed that diagnoses in the early studies were not well defined and that three-quarters of the participants could have had other disorders. Although the findings suggest a role for perfectionism in the etiology of anorexia nervosa, they should be interpreted with caution.

Subsequent studies on perfectionism in people with eating disorders were derived from studies using the Eating Disorder Inventory (EDI; Garner, Olmstead, & Polivy, 1983a, 1983b; Garner, 1991), a self-report instrument that has been used widely to study clinical and personality variables in eating disorders. Its Perfectionism subscale comprises six items that sample cognitive and behavioral elements of perfectionism (e.g., "I feel I must do things perfectly, or not do them at all" and "Only outstanding performance is good enough in my family").

Many studies have found significant elevations on the EDI Perfectionism subscale in patients with eating disorders compared with nonaffected populations (Bastiani, Rao, Weltzin, & Kaye, 1995; Bourke, Taylor, & Crisp, 1985; Garner et al., 1983a, 1983b; Rosch, Crowther, & Graham, 1991; Srinivasagam et al., 1995; Thompson, Berg, & Shatford, 1987; Toner, Garfinkel, & Garner, 1986). At least three studies, however, found no significant differences in EDI Perfectionism scores of patients with eating disorders and either patients with other medical or psychiatric illnesses or nonaffected control participants. Blouin, Bushnik, Braaten, and Blouin (1989) found that people with bulimia had levels of perfectionism similar to those with diabetes. Hurley, Palmer, and Stretch (1990) found no difference between levels of perfectionism in patients with eating disorders and patients with general psychiatric disturbance. Finally, Garner, Olmstead, Polivy, and Garfinkel (1984) found no differences between people with anorexia nervosa and weight-preoccupied control participants.

No significant differences in EDI Perfectionism scores have been found when comparing patients with anorexia nervosa and patients with bulimia nervosa (Garner, Olmsted, & Polivy, 1983a). Additionally, patients with restrictive and binge–purge types of anorexia nervosa have not been found to differ on EDI Perfectionism scores (Garner et al., 1983a; Toner, Garfinkel, & Garner, 1986). EDI Perfectionism scores have been found to be elevated in weight-restored anorexia nervosa patients in two studies (Bastiani et al., 1995; Srinivasagam et al., 1995), suggesting that perfectionism might be a persistent trait superordinate to the presence or absence of eating disorder. An earlier study (Garner et al., 1983b), however, found no difference in the EDI Perfectionism scores of people who recovered from anorexia nervosa and normal control individuals.

To test the validity of a diathesis–stress model in bulimia nervosa, Joiner et al. (1997) investigated a total of 890 women from two separate nonclinical samples. The diathesis tested was perfectionism, as measured by the EDI Perfectionism subscale. The stress component of the model was perceived weight. Joiner et al. found that perfectionistic women experienced bulimic symptoms, but only when they perceived themselves as overweight, thus lending support to the diathesis–stress model.

To evaluate Slade's (1982) model of anorexia nervosa, Slade and Dewey (1986) developed the Setting Conditions for Anorexia Nervosa Scale (SCANS), a 40-item self-report measure with five subscales: General Dissatisfaction, Social and Personal Anxiety, Perfectionism, Adolescent Problems, and Weight Control. In a study of 424 students, Kiemle, Slade, and Dewey (1987) found an association among elevated SCANS scores, food avoidance, and preoccupation with weight. They concluded that the hypothesized risk factors "dissatisfaction and lack of control" and "perfectionist tendencies" are closely related to abnormal eating attitudes and behaviors, thus lending support to Slade's (1982) model of etiology. In another study, however, perfectionism, as measured by the SCANS, was not associated with disturbed eating attitudes (Waller, Wood, Miller, & Slade, 1992).

In a study of 286 female students, Fryer, Kroese, and Waller (1997) used the SCANS, together with measures of life stressors and emotion-focused coping, to test Slade's (1982) prediction that the experience of stress results in low self-esteem which in combination with perfectionism, leads to eating disorders. Using path analysis modeling, they found that life stressors and emotion-focused coping were associated with low self-esteem, which in turn was strongly associated with disturbed eating attitudes and behavior. This finding supports some aspects of Slade's (1982) model. Data from this study, however, challenge Slade's (1982) model in two ways. First, no association was found between disturbed eating attitudes and perfectionism. Second, the study suggested that self-esteem is an imperfect mediator between stress and eating psychopathology, whereas Slade's model predicts that self-esteem should mediate perfectly.

Multidimensional Conceptualization of Perfectionism

Trait Perfectionism

With an increased interest in perfectionism and its relationship to eating disorders and other forms of psychopathology, investigators sought a more elaborate understanding of perfectionism than provided by the unidimensional models measured by the EDI and the SCANS. Two groups of investigators independently developed multidimensional conceptualizations of perfectionism containing both personal and interpersonal components (Frost, Marten, Lahart, & Rosenblate, 1990; Hewitt & Flett, 1990).

The 35-item Multidimensional Perfectionism Scale developed by Frost and colleagues (MPS-FROST; Frost, Marten, Lahart, & Rosenblate, 1990) identifies six dimensions of perfectionism: Concern Over Mistakes, Personal Standards, Parental Criticism, Parental Expectations, Doubt About Actions, and finally, Organization. Of note, this measure contains four of the six EDI items on perfectionism.

The Hewitt and Flett Multidimensional Perfectionism Scale (MPS-H&F; 1991b) is a 45-item scale that has demonstrated good reliability and validity (Frost et al., 1993; Hewitt, Flett, Turnbull-Donovan, & Mikail, 1991). In this measure, Hewitt and Flett (1990, 1991b) distinguished three trait dimensions of perfectionism corresponding to three subscales: Self-Oriented, Other-Oriented, and Socially Prescribed Perfectionism (see Flett & Hewitt, chapter 1, this volume, for a broader description).

Hewitt et al. (1995) used the MPS-H&F to assess the relevance of trait dimensions of perfectionism to eating disorder behaviors in a sample of 81 female college students. They found evidence to support an association between perfectionism and eating disorder symptoms. Their results indicated that eating disorder symptoms are driven by the motivation to meet unrealistic standards set by the self (i.e., Self-Oriented Perfectionism), whereas related issues, such as self-esteem and concerns about appearance, appeared to be driven by the motivation to meet standards that are perceived to be set by others (i.e., Socially Prescribed Perfectionism).

Bastiani and co-workers (Bastiani et al., 1995) used both the MPS-FROST and the MPS-H&F to assess levels of perfectionism in 11 women with restrictive anorexia nervosa who were underweight and in 8 women who formerly met criteria for restrictive anorexia nervosa shortly after weight restoration. In addition, 10 women who were free of eating disorder symptoms and psychiatric disorders were investigated as a comparison group. Bastiani et al. found statistically significant differences between people with anorexia (whether underweight or weight restored) and the control group on both MPS measures. The investigators, however, described the women who volunteered for the healthy comparison group as "supernormal controls," which may have increased the likelihood of a Type I error. Furthermore, the small sample size in the study underscores the need for replication.

Srinivasagam et al. (1995) used the MPS-FROST to investigate 20 women who had recovered from anorexia nervosa and 16 healthy women. They found that, when compared with the healthy women, the recovered women had elevations on perfectionism and appeared to have certain obsessive–compulsive personality traits, particularly excessive concern with symmetry and exactness.

Cockell, Hewitt, Goldner, Srikameswaran, and Flett (1996) used the MPS-H&F to examine levels of trait perfectionism among women with anorexia nervosa ($n = 22$) and bulimia nervosa ($n = 13$). Compared with age-matched normal control women ($n = 22$), women with anorexia and bulimia scored significantly higher on the Self-Oriented and Socially Prescribed Perfectionism subscales, but the two groups did not differ from one another. In addition, both Self-Oriented and Socially Prescribed Perfectionism were significantly related to a composite score of purging behaviors, including fasting, exercising, vomiting, and abusing laxatives and diuretics. A multiple regression analysis revealed that only Socially Prescribed Perfectionism predicted the purging behaviors.

To further investigate perfectionism in people with eating disorders, Slade and his colleagues developed two additional measures. The first measure, the Neurotic Perfectionism Scale (NPS; Mitzman, Slade, & Dewey, 1994), was designed to measure the degree to which people set unrealistically high goals, are overly concerned about making mistakes, and are driven by a fear of failure. The second measure was designed to identify both positive (or "normal") and negative (or "neurotic") perfectionism (Terry-Short, Owens, Slade, & Dewey, 1995), following the ideas introduced by Hamachek (1978). Other authors, however, such as Pacht (1984), have disagreed with the concept of normal perfectionism, arguing that perfectionism is a psychopathological personality trait and that identifying types of perfectionism as normal or positive is a misconstrual of other personality variables, such as achievement striving and conscientiousness.

Davis (1997) investigated women with anorexia nervosa ($n = 42$), bulimia nervosa ($n = 59$), and eating disorder not otherwise specified ($n = 22$) using the MPS-H&F and the NPS. No differences were found among the three diagnostic groups on any measures of perfectionism. In addition, Davis sought to study the interaction of normal and neurotic perfectionism and examine the relationship of each to eating disorder pathology and body esteem. In this study, the MPS-H&F Self-Oriented Perfectionism subscale was construed to represent a measure of normal perfectionism, following suggestions by Frost and colleagues (Frost et al., 1993) that the subscale represents "positive strivings." The MPS-H&F subscale was not developed for that purpose, however, and was intended to be a measure of a maladaptive and, hence, neurotic component of trait perfectionism (Hewitt & Flett, 1991b). Inadequate evidence supports the interpretation by Davis (1997) that "body-image perceptions are best understood as an interactive function of normal and neurotic perfectionism which accounts for a substantial proportion of the variance in body esteem" (p. 425) because the measures used in this study have not provided an opportunity to adequately investigate such hypotheses.

In a recent study, Cockell and colleagues (Cockell, Hewitt, Goldner, & Flett, 2001) investigated 21 women with anorexia nervosa and compared their levels of perfectionism, using the MPS-H&F, with that of two control groups. Women with anorexia nervosa reported higher scores on the MPS-H&F Self-Oriented Perfectionism and Socially Prescribed Perfectionism subscales than both the psychiatric and normal control groups. Perfectionism scores of the two control groups were not significantly different from those of the women with anorexia. The investigators found that the results were unchanged when levels of depression, self-esteem, and psychological distress were controlled across the three groups and concluded that perfectionism accounts for unique aspects of anorexic symptomatology independent of other variables related to psychological disturbance. Thus, although dimensions of trait perfectionism have been shown to play an important role in severe psychopathology (e.g., Hewitt et al., 1991; Hewitt & Flett, 1991a, 1991b, 1993; Hewitt, Flett, & Turnbull-Donovan, 1992), the results of the study by Cockell et al. suggest that they are most pronounced among women with anorexia nervosa. For instance, mean scores reported by women with anorexia nervosa were more than one standard deviation higher than mean scores previously reported (Hewitt & Flett, 1991a) for Self-Oriented and Socially Prescribed Perfectionism among people with depression.

Finally, in an innovative study by Pliner and Haddock (1995), perfectionism was examined in an experimental setting involving a goal-setting task. They found that women who were concerned with their weight adhered more strongly to unrealistically high standards of others than did women who were not excessively concerned with their weight. However, the weight-concerned women set lower standards for themselves. In addition, the researchers found that weight-concerned women were more adversely affected by failure feedback and more positively affected by success feedback than their non-weight-concerned counterparts. Based on these findings, the authors suggested that weight-concerned women are socially prescribed perfectionists and they set lower goals for themselves to maintain self-esteem.

Perfectionistic Self-Presentation and Eating Disorders

In addition to the three trait dimensions of perfectionism that reflect the need for the self or others to *be* perfect, Hewitt and colleagues (Hewitt et al., 2001) posited that perfectionism includes self-presentational styles that reflect the need to *appear* to be perfect. The promotion of one's perfection, known as Perfectionistic Self-Promotion, typically involves displaying one's accomplishments, goals, and aspirations. The attempts to appear capable, competent, and successful arise from a need for respect and admiration from others. By contrast, striving to conceal imperfections, or the Nondisplay of Imperfection, involves neither demonstrating nor admitting to perceived shortcomings to avoid criticism and protect self-esteem. People who avoid displaying their imperfections typically do not engage in situations in which personal shortcomings, mistakes, and limitations may be revealed. Here the focus is on avoiding the display of behavior viewed by others. Another pattern of concealing imperfection involves the avoidance of verbal disclosure of imperfections, known as the Nondisclosure of Imperfection. People who adopt this interpersonal style will not communicate personal mistakes and shortcomings because they fear being known as imperfect. The emphasis of this style of self-presentation is on not verbally revealing one's perceived shortcomings to others. Hewitt and his colleagues developed the 27-item Perfectionistic Self-Presentation Scale (PSPS; Hewitt et al., 2001) to measure the three dimensions of perfectionistic self-presentation described above.

There is a growing body of research demonstrating a relationship between perfectionistic self-presentation and eating disorders. In a female college sample, Hewitt et al. (1995) found that all three dimensions of the PSPS were related to eating disorder symptoms, body image dissatisfaction, and low appearance self-esteem. These findings were extended to a clinical sample by Cockell et al. (1996, August) who found that compared to women without eating disorders, those with anorexia and bulimia nervosa endorsed stronger needs to present to others an image of perfection and to avoid displaying or disclosing imperfection to others. Cockell et al. (1996) also found that the need to avoid disclosing imperfection was significantly related to purging behaviors, suggesting that people who avoid talking about aspects of themselves that they perceive to be imperfect tend to actively pursue weight loss by vomiting, abusing laxatives, or exercising excessively. In order to examine the extent to which perfectionistic self-presentation was related to eating disorders specifically, as oppose to general psychopathology, a follow-up study was conducted by Cockell et al. (2001). Comparisons revealed that for all three dimensions of perfectionistic self-presentation, women with anorexia nervosa reported significantly higher scores than women with other Axis I disorders and those with no psychiatric history. The two control groups did not statistically differ from one another. These findings did not change when comparisons were controlled statistically for differences in depression, self-esteem, and global psychological adjustment.

In summary, empirical studies have found elevated perfectionism scores in clinical samples of women with eating disorders. Women who meet diagnostic criteria for eating disorders consistently have been found to have markedly elevated scores on dimensions of trait and self-presentation perfectionism compared with nonaffected control participants. Women with anorexia nervosa also have been found to have notably elevated perfectionism scores when compared with a psychiatric control group with mood disorders.

No significant differences have been found between women with anorexia and bulimia nervosa on measures of trait perfectionism. In addition, women with restrictive and binge–purge types of anorexia nervosa have not been found to differ on levels of perfectionism. Some evidence indicates that women who previously met criteria for anorexia nervosa have elevated perfectionism scores following weight restoration, an indication that trait perfectionism may persist following recovery. Other studies have not found women who have recovered from anorexia nervosa to be more perfectionistic than control women.

Empirical examination of models of eating disorder development involving the interaction of perfectionism and other variables has yielded mixed results. Support has been found for a diathesis–stress model of eating pathology that involves an interaction of perfectionism and perceived weight. Findings are contradictory as to the role of perfectionism in producing eating pathology in interaction with life stressors and coping ability. Support has been found for the hypothesis that Self-Oriented Perfectionism may be specifically linked to eating concerns and dietary restraint, whereas Socially Prescribed Perfectionism may be more important to concerns about appearance and self-esteem.

An Integrative Model of Perfectionism and Eating Disorders

The following section advances a model of the relationship between perfectionism and eating disorders. The current model builds on previous conceptualizations of the etiology and development of eating disorders (Beebe, 1994; Bruch, 1973; Crisp, 1980; Fairburn et al., 1999; Garner & Bemis, 1982; Heatherton & Baumeister, 1991; Sohlberg & Strober, 1994; Vitousek & Manke, 1994; Wonderlich & Mitchell, 1991) and incorporates components of previously advanced models of the specific relationship between perfectionism and eating disorders (e.g., Slade, 1982; Hewitt et al., 1995).

In the current model, perfectionism is considered a personality trait, corresponding to the *DSM-IV* definition: "[an] enduring [pattern] of perceiving, relating to, and thinking about the environment and oneself that [is] exhibited in a wide range of social and personal contexts" (American Psychiatric Association, 1994, p. 630). The *DSM-IV* definition further notes that such traits constitute personality disorder only when inflexible and maladaptive and when they cause significant functional impairment and subjective distress. Furthermore, in the current model, perfectionism is considered a phenotype that most likely is determined by multiple genetic and environmental factors. To date, no investigations have reported genetic contributions to perfectionism. Genetic epidemiological studies, however, have demonstrated that most personality dimensions receive approximately equal contributions from genetic and environmental determinants (Jang, Livesley, Vernon, & Jackson, 1996). If, as anticipated, a substantial genetic contribution is involved in the determination of perfectionism, some people may be prone to developing perfectionistic characteristics. Furthermore, when combined with certain environmental conditions, a genetic proclivity for perfectionism may be intensified. One environmental factor thought to promote perfectionism is family and peer modeling of perfectionistic behavior (Barrow & Moore, 1983; Frost, Lahart, & Rosenblate, 1991). Common genetic pools in families will increase the likelihood of perfectionism in many members; thus, some family climates may be strongly perfectionistic. Additionally, exposure to people with high levels of Other-Oriented Perfectionism may exacerbate Socially Prescribed Perfectionism and perfectionistic self-presentation and, if internalized, may intensify Self-Oriented Perfectionism. People who are high in Other-Oriented Perfectionism will maintain elevated expectations for those around them; if those expectations are manifested in the realm of physical appearance and conformity to cultural ideals of physical beauty, those expectations may be transmitted to others. The interaction of perfectionism and the importance of physical appearance (specifically shape and weight) in modulating self-esteem is significant; we provide a description of this interaction later in the model. Other environmental factors that may promote perfectionism include inconsistent or critical responses from parents or caretakers during development, traumatic incidents, and other insults to self-esteem.

Figure 13.1 provides a schematic outline of the current model. As Slade (1982) described in his model, we also have identified perfectionism as a necessary setting condition for the development of an eating disorder. As described above, the current model defines the genetic and environmental roots of perfectionism and accounts for their potential interaction. Additionally, the current model acknowledges that perfectionism may predispose a person to many psychiatric disorders, such as depression and social phobia, and to eating disorders. This approach is consistent with the general model of perfectionism and maladjustment advanced by Hewitt and Flett (1993), in which they suggested that perfectionism can influence both the frequency and the impact of distressing events. Compulsive behavior problems (e.g., "workaholism" and compulsive exercise) and eating disorders may be invoked when a perfectionistic person makes a concerted attempt at self-improvement. It is not surprising that perfectionistic people undertake attempts at self-improvement, given their frequent self-critical evaluation and exceedingly high expectations. Commonly, a mission of self-improvement follows an insult to self-esteem, such as the loss of a friendship or a failed venture. At times, a specific goal will be set and sought with fervor (e.g., "I will obtain A grades in every course this semester"). Such goals may spring from areas of perceived self-deficit (sometimes following abuse, neglect, or excessive criticism), but that is not necessarily their origin. In fact, self-improvement goals may build on perceived "strengths" (e.g., "I have always been complimented on my slim, athletic body, and I would now like to become even more slim and athletic").

In addition to self-improvement, the desire to escape from aversive and burdensome self-awareness may invoke compulsive behavior problems

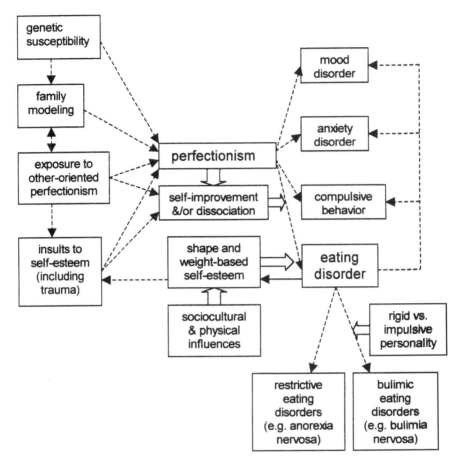

Figure 13.1.   Model of the relationship between the development of perfectionism and eating disorders. Factors that predispose a person to perfectionism and eating disorders are related schematically in a model that is based on clinical and empirical observations. Black arrowheads denote the potential for direct influence; unfilled arrows indicate moderating influence. Broken lines connote the possibility of a direct effect in some cases and not others.

and eating disorders in patients who are binge eating and purging, as described by Heatherton and Baumeister (1991). Additionally, people with restrictive anorexia nervosa often describe relief from noxious thoughts and memories as a welcome accompaniment of starvation. People who have experienced profound neglect or trauma (e.g., abuse and loss) may be more likely to develop compulsive behaviors, including eating disorders, as a means of diminishing aversive awareness (Briere & Runtz, 1988).

To this point, the current model defines perfectionism as a setting condition and describes two factors that can, either separately or together, invoke compulsive behavior or an eating disorder: a concerted attempt at self-improvement and a need for diminution of self-awareness. Perfectionism, in turn, has a moderating influence on each factor. Highly perfectionistic people may be more likely to approach self-improvement in an intensified and unrealistic manner. Furthermore, their need for diminished self-awareness may be magnified by the intense shame and self-reproach they experience when negative memories or thoughts about themselves enter awareness (i.e., they feel so very imperfect).

To explain the specific development of an eating disorder (as opposed to other compulsive behaviors), we must return to the interaction between perfectionism and shape- and weight-based self-esteem. In the current model, sociocultural and physical influences are moderators of shape and weight-based self-esteem. In fact, strong feelings about body shape and weight are prevalent in most societies, and it is common for a person's perception of his or her body shape and weight to significantly affect self-esteem. Certainly, some subcultures, occupations, and endeavors are likely to further intensify shape- and weight-based self-esteem (e.g., fashion industry and elite athletic pursuits). Furthermore, during specific developmental periods, rapid or profound changes in body shape and weight increase the susceptibility of people to feelings about themselves in this regard (e.g., puberty and pregnancy). Sociocultural norms and attitudes also may intensify the focus on the shape and weight of specific groups (e.g., adolescent girls). In addition, a history of having been overweight (or having family members who are overweight) has been found to be a risk factor in the development of eating disorders (Fairburn et al., 1995). Thus, in the current model, many sociocultural and physical factors moderate the degree of shape- and weight-based self-esteem for any person. If shape and weight concerns constitute a relatively insignificant component of a person's self-esteem, it is unlikely that that person will develop an eating disorder, even if perfectionistic. However, when a perfectionistic person experiences his or her shape or weight as a substantial contributor to self-esteem (as a result of demographic, sociocultural, or physical influences), that person is at risk. It is likely that a mission of body shape or weight "improvement" (through dieting, fasting, or exercise) will escalate. Reinforcement may occur as a result of successful restriction or weight loss (leading to increased self-esteem). In other situations, perceived failures (e.g., binge eating or inadequate restriction) will serve to further intensify the perfectionist's efforts toward self-improvement. Alternatively, temporary relief from distressing thoughts or memories achieved through starvation or binge eating may be followed by a noxious return, driving the person to increase the frequency or intensity of disturbed eating behavior.

The current model also accounts for the common finding of comorbid mood or anxiety disorder in people affected by eating disorders. In our model, perfectionism is a risk factor for each disorder. Furthermore, the experience of having an eating disorder may invoke depression stemming from diminished social contacts, self-reproach at symptomatic behavior (e.g., changes in weight, binge eating, and purging), and physical determinants (e.g., starvation and electrolyte and metabolic disruptions). Certain anxiety disorders also may be precipitated by psychological and physical features of the eating disorder.

Finally, we believe that differentiation into restrictive or bulimic types of eating disturbance occurs primarily on the basis of individual personality factors. This assertion is based on robust findings of a characteristic personality configuration associated with restrictive eating disorders (i.e., rigid and overcontrolled) that contrasts with the impulsive personality dimensions found in patients with bulimic eating disorders. Although it is likely that other factors contribute to differentiation into type of eating disorder, the current model contends that personality style is the most salient determinant.

Implications for Treatment

Perfectionism has been described as having a potentially adverse effect on individual, intrapersonal, and interpersonal resources (Ferguson & Rodway, 1994). In an analysis of data gathered in a National Institute for Mental Health multisite study on depression, Blatt and colleagues (Blatt, Quinlan, Pilkonis, & Shea, 1995) found that intense perfectionism had a significantly negative relationship to therapeutic outcome in all four treatment modalities used in the study (i.e., clinical maintenance and imipramine; clinical maintenance and placebo; interpersonal therapy; and cognitive–behavioral therapy). Conversely, patients with relatively low levels of perfectionism were responsive to all four forms of brief treatment for depression.

To date, limited exploration of therapeutic approaches that specifically aim to reduce perfectionism has taken place, and the extent to which perfectionism is mutable is not known. Burns (1980) described a cognitive–behavioral approach to treatment that involves challenging distortions and automatic thoughts, role-playing, and behavioral exercise. Barrow and Moore (1983) recommended a group intervention that combines positive effects of group treatment (e.g., the universalization effect and identification with peers) with a cognitive–behavioral orientation. Sorotzkin (1985) contended that traditional psychodynamic and cognitive–behavioral methods are indicated when perfectionism is associated with a "harsh superego" or overly strong ideals. He noted that people with narcissistic deficits require an approach that bolsters their self-structure and avoids provoking narcissistic injury.

Perfectionism may have an impact on the treatment of people with eating disorders in several ways. Relatively high levels of perfectionism may reduce the likelihood of help seeking (Habke, 1997; Neilsen et al., 1997). Perfectionistic self-presentational styles, such as nondisplay and nondisclosure of imperfection, will make it extremely difficult for many people with eating disorders to accept treatment for a "disorder" or "problem." Often, the first approach to treatment is the result of pressure from family members or employers and is not welcomed (Goldner, Birmingham, & Smye, 1996). Once a person with an eating disorder does approach treatment, perfectionism may interfere with the development of a therapeutic alliance. Perfectionistic self-presentational styles may be strong impediments to the self-disclosure required to establish a therapeutic relationship. Self-oriented perfectionists also tend to be high in self-reported levels of self-criticism (Hewitt & Flett, 1993); thus, a discussion of problems may be experienced as intensely painful and noxious. Furthermore, the ego-syntonic nature of certain eating disorder symptoms, particularly those of restricting and losing weight, may add to the difficulties in establishing a therapeutic alliance. The therapist may be viewed as supportive of failure (i.e., gaining weight and giving up one's resolve).

Once treatment has begun, people with eating disorders may have difficulties setting realistic and appropriate treatment goals. They may be susceptible to perceived failures and prone to "all-or-nothing" thinking with respect to their treatment progress. Furthermore, they may become frustrated and dissatisfied with imperfect results and reluctant to persist with treatments that do not yield quick cures. Some patients may leave treatment prematurely rather than be exposed repeatedly to what they perceive as personal failures.

Accordingly, many therapeutic approaches have attempted to address specific challenges in the treatment of patients with eating disorders. Recently, increased attention has been paid to ambivalence regarding change in the treatment of people with anorexia nervosa (Vitousek & Hollon, 1990), and the use of motivational enhancement training and narrative approaches (Garner, Vitousek, & Pike, 1997; Madigan & Goldner, 1998) is being explored. In those approaches, the patient is helped to reframe his or her relationship to anorexia nervosa by evaluating its pros and cons and is asked to consider the possibility of giving up the exhausting task of being perfect.

Cognitive–behavioral treatments have been effective interventions in the treatment of the eating disorders (Fairburn et al., 1995; Garner et al., 1997). Such approaches challenge cognitive distortions related to eating and weight-related concerns and address distorted thoughts regarding self-concept. Perfectionistic thoughts and behaviors often are addressed as a component of a cognitive–behavioral approach to treatment. In addition to efforts aimed at diminishing perfectionistic thoughts and behaviors, we often assist people in shifting the object of their perfectionistic pursuits. Significantly less harm may result from a perfectionistic approach to schoolwork than a perfectionistic effort to lose as much weight as possible. Such shifts often are facilitated by improvements in a patient's social networks and supports.

Interpersonal therapy is a focal psychotherapy whose effectiveness in the treatment of bulimia nervosa has been empirically validated (Fairburn et al., 1995). The treatment does not directly address eating- and weight-related symptoms, rather, current interpersonal problems are the focus of this time-limited, noninterpretive, nondirective therapy (Fairburn, 1997). Eating disorder symptoms often serve an interpersonal function; they can communicate, in a seemingly "safe" way, feelings such as anger and disappointment that may be difficult to articulate directly. Research on self-critical college students suggests that such people are distrustful and dissatisfied in their romantic relationships and are avoidant and non-self-disclosing because of their expectations of being hurt in close relationships (Zuroff & Fitzpatrick, 1995). Distrust, fear, and an avoidant style, in combination with perfectionistic standards and beliefs that others have high standards or expectations, can interact with the communication function of eating disorder symptoms and maintain the vicious cycle of restricting, bingeing and purging, and avoidance of emotional intimacy. Interpersonal therapy aims to ameliorate specific interpersonal problems and, thus, diminish the triggers of eating disorder symptoms.

A psychodynamically influenced interpersonal approach also is being used to treat people who are perfectionistic (Flynn & Hewitt, 2000). This treatment model focuses on helping affected people identify the origins, function, and interpersonal consequences of perfectionism. This treatment intervention is now being operationalized for empirical investigation.

Summary

This chapter has outlined the history of the role of perfectionism in the eating disorders, spanning from a time when the "quest for perfection" represented an ascetic ideal to current conceptualizations suggesting that perfectionism is a multidimensional construct that may play a significant role in the etiology and maintenance of anorexia and bulimia nervosa. The chapter has presented relevant empirical research and an integrative biopsychosocial model of eating disorders that describes a potential role for perfectionism.

Although extensive research has been conducted in this area, numerous issues still need to be addressed in future research. For instance, it is vital that research examine the role of perfectionism in vulnerability to eating disorders. A clear need remains for prospective research on the link between eating disorders and perfectionism from a multidimensional perspective. In addition, the treatment of perfectionism as it occurs in people with eating disorders is in the early stages of development and represents an important area for future investigation. Finally, the proposed biopsychosocial model would benefit from empirical testing to determine whether it could advance our understanding and inform our treatment of people with eating disorders.

References

American Psychiatric Association. (1980). *Diagnostic and statistical manual of mental disorders* (3rd ed.). Washington, DC: American Psychiatric Association.

American Psychiatric Association. (1994). *Diagnostic and statistical manual of mental disorders* (4th ed.). Washington, DC: American Psychiatric Association.

Barrow, J. C., & Moore, C. A. (1983). Group interventions with perfectionistic thinking. *The Personnel and Guidance Journal, 61,* 612–615.

Bastiani, A. M., Rao, R., Weltzin, T. E., & Kaye, W. H. (1995). Perfectionism in anorexia nervosa. *International Journal of Eating Disorders, 17,* 147–152.

Beebe, D. W. (1994). Bulimia nervosa and depression: A theoretical and clinical appraisal in light of the binge-purge cycle. *British Journal of Clinical Psychology, 33,* 259–276.

Bell, R. (1985). *Holy anorexia.* Chicago: University of Chicago Press.

Blatt, S. J. (1995). The destructiveness of perfectionism: Implications for the treatment of depression. *American Psychologist, 50,* 1003–1020.

Blatt, S. J., Quinlan, D. M., Pilkonis, P. A., & Shea, M. T. (1995). The effects of need for approval and perfectionism on the brief treatment of depression. *Journal of Consulting and Clinical Psychology, 63,* 125–132.

Blouin, A. G., Bushnik, T., Braaten, J., & Blouin, J. H. (1989). Bulimia and diabetes: Distinct psychosocial profiles. *International Journal of Eating Disorders, 8,* 93–100.

Bourke, M. P., Taylor, G., & Crisp, A. H. (1985). Symbolic functioning in anorexia nervosa. *Journal of Psychiatric Research, 19,* 273–278.

Briere, J., & Runtz, M. (1988). Symptomatology associated with childhood sexual victimization in a nonclinical adult sample. *Child Abuse and Neglect, 12,* 51–59.

Bruch, H. (1973). *Eating disorders: Obesity, anorexia nervosa and the person within.* New York: Basic Books.

Bruch, H. (1977). Psychological antecedents of anorexia nervosa. In R. A. Vigersky (Ed.), *Anorexia nervosa* (pp. 1–10). New York: Raven Press.

Bruch, H. (1978). *The golden cage: The enigma of anorexia nervosa.* Cambridge, MA: Harvard University Press.

Brumberg, J. J. (1988). *Fasting girls: The history of anorexia nervosa.* Cambridge, MA: Harvard University Press.

Burns, D. D. (1980). *Feeling good: The new mood therapy.* New York: New American Library.

Casper, R. C. (1983). Some provisional ideas concerning the psychological structure in anorexia nervosa and bulimia. In P. L. Darby, P. E. Garfinkel, D. M. Garner, & D. V. Coscina (Eds.), *Anorexia nervosa: Recent developments in research* (pp. 387–392). New York: Alan R. Liss.

Casper, R. C. (1990). Personality features of women with good outcome from restricting anorexia nervosa. *Psychosomatic Medicine, 52,* 156–170.

Cloninger, C. R. (1987). A systematic method for clinical description and classification of personality variants. *Archives of General Psychiatry, 44,* 573–588.

Cockell, S. J., Hewitt, P. L., Goldner, E. M., & Flett, G. L. (2001). Trait and self-presentation dimensions of perfectionism in women with anorexia nervosa. Manuscript in preparation.

Cockell, S. J., Hewitt, P. L., Goldner, E. M., Srikameswaran, S., & Flett, G. L. (1996, August). *Levels of perfectionism among women with anorexia and bulimia nervosa.* Poster presented at the 26th International Congress of Psychology, Montreal, Quebec, Canada.

Crisp, A. H. (1980). *Anorexia nervosa: Let me be.* New York: Grune & Stratton.

Dally, P. (1969). *Anorexia nervosa.* London: William Heinemann Medical Books Limited.

Davis, C. (1997). Normal and neurotic perfectionism in eating disorders: An interactive model. *International Journal of Eating Disorders, 22,* 421–426.

Fairburn, C. G. (1981). A cognitive-behavioural approach to the management of bulimia. *Psychological Medicine, 11,* 707–711.

Fairburn, C. G. (1997). Interpersonal psychotherapy for bulimia nervosa. In D. M. Garner & P. E. Garfinkel (Eds.), *Handbook of treatment for eating disorders* (2nd ed., pp. 278–294). New York: Guilford Press.

Fairburn, C. G., Marcus, M. D., & Wilson, G. T. (1983). Cognitive-behavioral therapy for binge eating and bulimia nervosa: A comprehensive treatment manual. In C. G. Fairburn & G. T. Wilson (Eds.), *Binge eating: Nature, assessment, and treatment* (pp. 361–404). New York: Guilford Press.

Fairburn, C. G., Norman, P. A., Welch, S. L., O'Connor, M. E., Doll, H. A., & Peveler, R. C. (1995). A prospective study of outcome in bulimia nervosa and the long-term effects of three psychological treatments. *Archives of General Psychiatry, 52,* 304–312.

Fairburn, C. G., Shafran, R., & Cooper, Z. (1999). A cognitive behavioural theory of anorexia nervosa. *Behaviour Research and Therapy, 37,* 1–13.

Ferguson, K. L., & Rodway, M. R. (1994). Cognitive behavioral treatment of perfectionism: Initial evaluation studies. *Research on Social Work Practice, 4,* 283–308.

Flynn, C. A., & Hewitt, P. L. (2000, October). Perfectionism and interpersonal facets of group therapy process. In S. F. Mikail (chair), *Interpersonal Process in Group Therapy.* Symposium presented at the annual convention of the Canadian Group Psychotherapy Association, Vancouver, BC.

Frost, R. O., Heimberg, R. G., Holt, C. S., Mattia, J. I., & Neubauer, A. L. (1993). A comparison of two measures of perfectionism. *Personality and Individual Differences, 14,* 119–126.

Frost, R. O., Lahart, C., & Rosenblate, R. (1991). The development of perfectionism: A study of daughters and their parents. *Cognitive Therapy and Research, 15,* 469–489.

Frost, R. O., Marten, P., Lahart, C., & Rosenblate, R. (1990). The dimensions of perfectionism. *Cognitive Therapy and Research, 14,* 449–468.

Fryer, S., Kroese, B. S., & Waller, G. (1997). Stress, coping, and disturbed eating attitudes in teenage girls. *International Journal of Eating Disorders, 22,* 427–436.

Garner, D. M. (1986). Cognitive therapy for anorexia nervosa. In K. D. Brownell & J. P. Foreyt (Eds.), *Handbook of eating disorders: Physiology, psychology, and treatment of obesity, anorexia, and bulimia* (pp. 301–327). New York: Basic Books.

Garner, D. M. (1991). *Eating Disorder Inventory-2 professional manual.* Odessa, FL: Psychological Assessment Resources.

Garner, D. M., & Bemis, K. (1982). A cognitive-behavioral approach to anorexia nervosa. *Cognitive Therapy and Research, 6,* 123–150.

Garner, D. M., Olmstead, M. P., & Polivy, J. (1983a). The Eating Disorder Inventory: A measure of cognitive-behavioral dimensions of anorexia nervosa and bulimia. In P. L. Darby, P. E. Garfinkel, D. M. Garner, & D. V. Coscina (Eds.), *Anorexia nervosa: Recent developments in research* (pp. 173–184). New York: Alan R. Liss.

Garner D. M., Olmstead, M. P., & Polivy, J. (1983b). The development and validation of a multidimensional eating disorder inventory for anorexia and bulimia. *International Journal of Eating Disorders, 1,* 15–34.

Garner, D. M., Olmstead, M. P., Polivy J., & Garfinkel, P. E. (1984). Comparison between weight-preoccupied women and anorexia nervosa. *Psychosomatic Medicine, 46,* 255–266.

Garner, D. M., Vitousek, K. M., & Pike, K. M. (1997). Cognitive-behavioral therapy for anorexia nervosa. In D. M. Garner & P. E. Garfinkel (Eds.), *Handbook of treatment for eating disorders* (2nd ed., pp. 94–144). New York: Guilford Press.

Goldner, E. M., Birmingham, C. L., & Smye, V. (1996). Addressing treatment refusal in anorexia nervosa: Clinical, ethical, and legal considerations. In D. M. Garner & P. E. Garfinkel (Eds.), *Handbook of treatment for eating disorders* (pp. 450–461). New York: Guilford Press.

Goodsitt, A. (1997). Eating disorders: A self-psychological perspective. In D. M. Garner & P. E. Garfinkel (Eds.), *Handbook of treatment for eating disorders* (2nd ed.; pp. 205–228). New York: Guilford Press.

Habke, A. M. (1997). The manifestations of perfectionistic self-presentation in a clinical sample. *Dissertation Abstracts International, 59,* 02B (UMI No. 872).

Halmi, K. D., Goldberg, S. C., Eckert, E., Casper, R., & Davis, J. M. (1979). Unique features associated with age of onset of anorexia nervosa. *Psychiatry Research, 1,* 209–215.

Hamachek, D. E. (1978). Psychodynamics of normal and neurotic perfectionism. *Psychology, 15,* 27–33.

Heatherton, T. F., & Baumeister, R. F. (1991). Binge eating as escape from self-awareness. *Psychological Bulletin, 110,* 86–108.

Hewitt, P. L., & Flett, G. L. (1990). Perfectionism and depression: A multidimensional analysis. *Journal of Social Behavior and Personality, 5,* 423–438.

Hewitt, P. L., & Flett, G. L. (1991a). Dimensions of perfectionism in unipolar depression. *Journal of Abnormal Psychology, 100,* 98–101.

Hewitt, P. L., & Flett, G. L. (1991b). Perfectionism in the self and social contexts: Conceptualization, assessment, and association with psychopathology. *Journal of Personality and Social Psychology, 60,* 456–470.

Hewitt, P. L., & Flett, G. L. (1993). Dimensions of perfectionism, daily stress, and depression: A test of the specific vulnerability hypothesis. *Journal of Abnormal Psychology, 102,* 58–65.

Hewitt, P. L., Flett, G. L., & Ediger, E. (1995). Perfectionism trait and perfectionistic self-presentation in eating disorder attitudes, characteristics, and symptoms. *International Journal of Eating Disorders, 18,* 317–326.

Hewitt, P. L., Flett, G. L., Sherry, S. B., Habke, A. M., Parkin, M., Lam, R. W., McMurtry, B., Ediger, E., Fairlie, P., & Stein, M. (2001). *The interpersonal expression of perfection-*

ism: Perfectionistic self-presentation and psychological distress. Manuscript submitted for publication.

Hewitt, P. L., Flett, G. L., & Turnbull-Donovan, W. (1992). Perfectionism and Multiphasic Personality Inventory (MMPI) indices of personality disorder. *Journal of Psychopathology and Behavioral Assessment, 14,* 323–335.

Hewitt, P. L., Flett, G. L., Turnbull-Donovan, W., & Mikail, S. F. (1991). The Multidimensional Perfectionism Scale: Reliability, validity, and psychometric properties in psychiatric samples. *Psychological Assessment, 3,* 464–468.

Hurley, J. B., Palmer, R. L., & Stretch, D. (1990). The specificity of the Eating Disorder Inventory: A re-appraisal. *International Journal of Eating Disorders, 9,* 419–424.

Janet, P. (1929). *The major symptoms of hysteria* (2nd ed.). New York: Macmillan.

Jang, K. L., Livesley, W. J., Vernon, P. A., & Jackson, D. N. (1996). Heritability of personality disorder traits: A twin study. *Acta Psychiatrica Scandinavica, 94,* 438–444.

Joiner, T. E., Jr., Heatherton, T. F., Rudd, M. D., & Schmidt, N. B. (1997). Perfectionism, perceived weight status, and bulimic symptoms: Two studies testing a diathesis–stress model. *Journal of Abnormal Psychology, 106,* 145–153.

Johnson, C., & Connors, M. E. (1987). *The etiology and treatment of bulimia nervosa.* New York: Basic Books.

Kiemle, G., Slade, P. D., & Dewey, M. E. (1987). Factors associated with abnormal eating and behaviors: Screening individuals at risk of developing an eating disorder. *International Journal of Eating Disorders, 6,* 713–724.

Madigan, S. P., & Goldner, E. M. (1998). A narrative appraisal to anorexia: Discourse, reflexivity, and questions. In N. F. Hoyt (Ed.), *The handbook of constructive therapies: Innovative appraisals from leading practitioners* (pp. 380–400). San Francisco: Jossey-Bass.

Mitzman, S. F., Slade, P. D., & Dewey, M. E. (1994). Preliminary development of a questionnaire designed to measure neurotic perfectionism in eating disorders. *International Journal of Eating Disorders, 18,* 317–326.

Neilsen, A., Hewitt, P. L., Han, H., Habke, A. M., Cockell, S. J., Stager, G., & Flett, G. L. (1997, August). *Perfectionistic self-presentation styles and attitudes toward professional help seeking.* Paper presented at the annual meeting of the Canadian Psychological Association, Toronto, Ontario.

Pacht, A. R. (1984). Reflections on perfection. *American Psychologist, 39,* 386–390.

Pliner, P., & Haddock, G. (1995). Perfectionism in weight-concerned and -unconcerned women: An experimental approach. *International Journal of Eating Disorders, 19,* 381–389

Rampling, D. (1985). Ascetic ideals and anorexia nervosa. *Journal of Psychiatric Research, 19,* 89–94.

Rosch, D. S., Crowther, J. H., & Graham, J. R. (1991). MMPI-derived personality description and personality subtypes in an undergraduate bulimic population. *Psychology of Addictive Behaviors, 5,* 15–22.

Slade, P. D. (1982). Towards a functional analysis of anorexia nervosa and bulimia nervosa. *British Journal of Clinical Psychology, 21,* 167–179.

Slade, P. D., & Dewey, M. E. (1986). Development and preliminary validation of SCANS: A screening instrument for identifying individuals at risk for developing anorexia and bulimia nervosa. *International Journal of Eating Disorders, 5,* 517–538.

Sohlberg, S., & Strober, M. (1994). Personality in anorexia nervosa: An update and a theoretical integration. *Acta Psychiatrica Scandinavica, 89*(Suppl. 378), 1–15.

Sorotzkin, B. (1985). The quest for perfection: Avoiding guilt or avoiding shame? *Psychotherapy, 3,* 564–571.

Sours, J. A. (1980). *Starving to death in a sea of objects.* New York: Jason Aronson.

Srinivasagam, N. M., Kaye, W. H., Plotnicov, K. H., Greeno, C., Weltzin, T. E., & Rao, R. (1995). Persistent perfectionism, symmetry, and exactness after long-term recovery from anorexia nervosa. *American Journal of Psychiatry, 152,* 1630–1634.

Striegel-Moore, R. H., Silberstein, L. R., & Rodin, J. (1993). The social self in bulimia nervosa: Public self-consciousness, social anxiety, and perceived fraudulence. *Journal of Abnormal Psychology, 102,* 297–303.

Strober, M. (1991). Disorders of the self in anorexia nervosa: An organismic-developmental paradigm. In C. Johnson (Ed.), *Psychodynamic treatment of anorexia nervosa and bulimia nervosa* (pp. 354–373). New York: Guilford Press

Terry-Short, L. A., Owens, R. G., Slade, P. D., & Dewey, M. E. (1995). Positive and negative perfectionism. *Personality and Individual Differences, 18,* 663–668.

Thompson, D. A., Berg, K. M., & Shatford, L. A. (1987). The heterogeneity of bulimic symptomatology: Cognitive and behavioral dimensions. *International Journal of Eating Disorders, 6,* 215–234.

Toner, B. B., Garfinkel, P. E., & Garner, D. M. (1986). Long-term follow-up of anorexia nervosa. *Psychological Medicine, 48,* 520–529.

Vitousek, K. M. (1996). The current status of cognitive-behavioral models of anorexia nervosa and bulimia nervosa. In P. M. Salkovskis (Ed.), *Frontiers of cognitive therapy* (pp. 383–418). New York: Guilford Press.

Vitousek, K. M., & Hollon, S. D. (1990). The investigation of schematic content and processing in eating disorders. *Cognitive Therapy and Research, 14,* 191–214.

Vitousek, K. M., & Manke, F. (1994). Personality variables and disorders in anorexia nervosa and bulimia nervosa. *Journal of Abnormal Psychology, 103,* 137–147.

Waller, G., Wood, A., Miller, J., & Slade, P. D. (1992). The development of neurotic perfectionism: A risk factor for unhealthy eating attitudes. *British Review of Bulimia and Anorexia Nervosa, 6,* 57–62.

Wonderlich, S. A., & Mitchell, J. E. (1991). Eating disorders and personality disorders. In J. Yager, H. E. Gwirtsman, & C. E. Edelstein (Eds.), *Special problems in managing eating disorders* (pp. 51–86). Washington, DC: American Psychiatric Association Press.

World Health Organization. (1997). *Multiaxial presentation of the ICD-10 for use in adult psychiatry.* New York, NY: Cambridge University Press.

Zuroff, D. C., & Fitzpatrick, D. A. (1995). Depressive personality styles: Implications for adult attachment. *Personality and Individual Differences, 18,* 253–265.

14

Perfectionism, Anxiety, and Obsessive–Compulsive Disorder

Randy O. Frost and Patricia Marten DiBartolo

Early speculation and recent findings have linked perfectionism with a wide variety of disorders, including depression (Blatt, 1995; Hewitt & Dyck, 1986); eating disorders (Bastiani, Rao, Weltzin, & Kaye, 1995); and physical conditions, such as ulcerative colitis and irritable bowel syndrome (Pacht, 1984). From the beginning of the 20th century, theorists also have suggested that perfectionism plays a role in the experience of anxiety and anxiety disorders, especially obsessive–compulsive disorder (OCD). Before beginning this review, we discuss the ways in which perfectionism has been defined in the empirical literature.

Much of the recent research on perfectionism has been based on conceptualizations that emphasize the multidimensional nature of the construct. Hewitt and Flett (1991b) posited three dimensions of perfectionism on the basis of the locus or target of excessively high expectations: self-oriented perfectionism, socially prescribed perfectionism, and other-oriented perfectionism (for a description, see Flett & Hewitt, chapter 1, this volume). Another conceptualization of perfectionism has focused on distinguishing the setting of high personal standards, which may have both positive and negative ramifications, from excessive concern over making mistakes and doubting the quality of one's actions (Frost, Marten, Lahart, & Rosenblate, 1990). This conceptualization envisions five primary dimensions of perfectionism. Concern Over Mistakes reflects the degree to which a person will interpret mistakes as indicators of failure, respond negatively to mistakes, and assume that others would also evaluate their mistakes negatively. Doubts About Actions measures how confident people are about their ability to complete tasks. Parental Expectations and Parental Criticism are related to one's perceptions that one's parents set extremely high standards and were overly critical of one's efforts, respectively. The Personal Standards dimension indicates the degree to which people set excessive standards for themselves and base their self-evaluation on their ability to achieve those standards. A sixth dimension of perfectionism (Organization) is ancillary. Organization reflects the tendency to place importance on order, organization, and orderliness.

Both conceptualizations of perfectionism have been accompanied by the development of a multidimensional measure (Frost et al., 1990; Hewitt

& Flett, 1991b); interestingly, both are called the Multidimensional Perfectionism Scale (MPS). Considerable reliability and validity data are available for each measure. The Hewitt and Flett conceptualization and the Frost et al. conceptualization are complementary in that the major negative dimensions of Frost et al. (Concern Over Mistakes and Doubts About Actions) have to do with the nature of perfectionistic thoughts and evaluations, whereas the Hewitt and Flett dimensions have to do with whom or by whom these thoughts are directed.

Two studies have found that the dimensions reflected in the two conceptualizations overlap in predictable ways. Frost, Heimberg, Holt, Mattia, and Neubauer (1993) compared the responses of a large sample of college students on the two measures. Both Hewitt and Flett's Self-Oriented Perfectionism and Socially Prescribed Perfectionism subscales were significantly correlated with Frost et al.'s total MPS score. Scores on Hewitt and Flett's Self-Oriented Perfectionism subscale were most strongly related to those on Frost et al.'s Personal Standards subscale, whereas their Socially Prescribed Perfectionism subscale was correlated with many Frost et al. subscales, including Concern Over Mistakes, Parental Expectations, and Parental Criticism. Consistent with those findings, Flett, Sawatzky, and Hewitt (1995) also found self-oriented perfectionism to be most closely associated with Personal Standards, whereas socially prescribed perfectionism was most closely correlated with Concern Over Mistakes, Parental Expectations, and Parental Criticism among a large sample of college students (for additional results, see Enns & Cox, chapter 2, this volume).

In the Frost et al. (1993) study, a factor analysis including all the subscales of the two separate measures revealed two factors: Positive Achievement Striving and Maladaptive Evaluation Concerns. Subscale loadings on the Positive Achievement Striving factor were Personal Standards and Organization from the Frost et al. measure and Self-Oriented Perfectionism and Other-Oriented Perfectionism from the Hewitt and Flett MPS. In contrast, the Hewitt and Flett Socially Prescribed Perfectionism subscale and four Frost et al. subscales (i.e., Concern Over Mistakes, Doubts About Actions, Parental Expectations, and Parental Criticism) loaded on the Maladaptive Evaluation Concerns factor. Each factor evidenced a unique relationship with measures of affect. Particularly, the Positive Achievement Striving factor was correlated with positive affect but not with measures of negative affectivity. The maladaptive evaluation factor was not correlated with positive affect but was associated with depression and negative affectivity scores. Consistent with this finding, other researchers (e.g., Terry-Short, Owens, Slade, & Dewey, 1995) have suggested drawing a distinction between positive and negative perfectionism.

With these conceptualizations in mind, this chapter reviews four areas of research linking perfectionism and anxiety. First, it reviews research on the association between perfectionism and general measures of anxiety. This research has relied on trait anxiety measures, and more clinically derived anxiety scales. Studies of life stress form the second area for review. Third, our review examines studies of situations involving evaluative threat, including laboratory-induced and naturally occurring stress. Finally, the chapter discusses the association between perfectionism and OCD, an anxiety disorder long thought to be closely tied to perfectionism.

Perfectionism and General Anxiety

Numerous studies have linked perfectionism to trait anxiety. Among a sample of college students, Deffenbacher, Zwemer, Whisman, Hill, and Sloan (1986) examined the relationship between the trait version of the Spielberger State–Trait Anxiety Inventory (STAI; Spielberger, Gorsuch, & Lushene, 1970) and three subscales of the Irrational Beliefs Test (Jones, 1969) that reflect perfectionistic themes (i.e., Demand for Approval, Personal Perfection, and Personal Solutions). Significant positive correlations were found between trait anxiety and both the Demand for Approval and Personal Perfection subscales. Similarly, Christensen, Danko, and Johnson (1993) reported a significant correlation between perfectionism and trait anxiety using the STAI. Unfortunately, the exact measure of perfectionism used in their study was not specified, but it would appear that the authors used one of the dimensions of Hewitt and Flett's MPS (either Socially Prescribed Perfectionism or Self-Oriented Perfectionism) or a composite of the two dimensions.

Other studies have suggested that the relationship between trait anxiety and perfectionism is a result of the maladaptive evaluation concerns associated with perfectionism, particularly its socially prescribed aspects. For example, Hankin, Roberts, and Gotlib (1997) reported that socially prescribed perfectionism (but not self-oriented perfectionism) was positively correlated with STAI scores among high school students. Similarly, Flett, Hewitt, Endler, and Tassone (1994–1995) found that two trait-anxiety subscales of the Endler Multidimensional Anxiety Scales (EMAS; Endler, Edwards, & Vitelli, 1991) were positively correlated with socially prescribed perfectionism. In contrast, no other relationship was found between any of the EMAS trait-anxiety subscales and self-oriented perfectionism. Finally, Juster et al. (1996) examined trait anxiety and Frost et al. (1990) MPS scores among 61 participants with social phobia. Trait anxiety (Spielberger et al., 1970) was significantly correlated with two MPS subscales reflecting evaluative concerns (Concern Over Mistakes and Doubt About Actions); the correlations remained significant even when depression scores were partialed out.

Two other studies provided data regarding the relative importance of self-oriented and socially prescribed perfectionism in accounting for the relationship between trait anxiety and perfectionism. In an early study, Flett, Hewitt, and Dyck (1989) administered the STAI along with the Burns Perfectionism Scale (BPS; Burns, 1980) to a sample of college students. The authors described the BPS as a measure of self-oriented perfectionism and found that it was significantly and positively correlated with trait anxiety. A similar finding was reported in a subsequent study by Flett et al. (1994–1995): In that investigation, the BPS was correlated with two dimensions of trait anxiety as measured by the EMAS. Although the authors of both studies (Flett et al., 1989, 1994–1995) originally interpreted the BPS as a measure of self-oriented perfectionism, Flett et al. (1995) noted that the measure is characterized by many items that reflect both social and self-evaluative concerns. In fact, the BPS is highly correlated with the Concern Over Mistakes subscale of the Frost MPS (Frost et al., 1990), which has been found to be closely related to socially prescribed perfectionism (Frost et al., 1993). Concern over mistakes is also a major component of the maladaptive evaluation concern feature of perfectionism. Thus, if the BPS is interpreted as more analogous to a measure of socially prescribed perfectionism (or maladaptive evaluation concern), the above data seem to provide consistent evidence of the association of trait anxiety to social evaluative aspects of perfectionism.

The studies' findings are sufficiently consistent to conclude that perfectionism is associated with measures of trait anxiety, albeit the magnitude of those correlations typically has been low to moderate. The research to date suggests that the relationship between perfectionism and trait anxiety may be explained by the social and maladaptive evaluation aspects of perfectionism (i.e., Socially Prescribed Perfectionism, Concern Over Mistakes, and Doubts About Actions).

A few studies have found correlations between perfectionism and measures of more specific types of anxiety. For example, Penn State Worry Questionnaire (PSWQ; Meyer, Miller, Metzger, & Borkovec, 1990) scores were positively correlated with perfectionism levels, as reflected by scores on the BPS. Frost and Roberts (1997) further examined the relationship between worry and perfectionism dimensions among college students. Concern Over Mistakes, Personal Standards, Doubts About Actions, and Parental Criticism from the Frost MPS all were significantly and positively correlated with scores on the PSWQ. Concern Over Mistakes and Doubts About Actions showed the most substantial correlations, which ranged from .53 to .64.

Interestingly, the subscales capturing the maladaptive evaluation concerns (Concern Over Mistakes and Doubts About Actions) and positive achievement striving (Personal Standards) dimensions of perfectionism each had unique relationships with worry. When partial correlations were calculated between worry and either Concern Over Mistakes and Doubts About Actions (controlling for Personal Standards), the correlations remained significant. Likewise, when the correlation between worry and Personal Standards was calculated (controlling for Concern Over Mistakes and Doubts About Actions), Personal Standards remained significantly correlated with worry. This finding is consistent with other research on both clinical (Borkovec, 1994) and nonclinical (Tallis, Davey, & Capuzzo, 1994) samples and suggests that worry can function as a motivational force.

Studies using other general measures of anxiety also support an association between perfectionism and anxiety; however, many investigations have detected a relationship between perfectionism and a variety of measures of nonanxiety psychopathology as well. Frost et al. (1990) reported significant correlations of Concern Over Mistakes and Doubts About Actions with the Brief Symptom Inventory (BSI; Derogatis & Mesilaratos, 1983) Anxiety subscale scores among college students. Similarly, Hewitt and Flett (1991b) found that both Self-Oriented Perfectionism and Socially Prescribed Perfectionism were correlated with the Anxiety subscale of the SCL-90 among college students. In both studies (Frost et al., 1990; Hewitt & Flett, 1991b), however, dimensions of perfectionism also were correlated with all or nearly all the other SCL-90 subscales.

Some findings indicate that perfectionism is more generally associated with negative affectivity and not just trait anxiety. For example, Minarik and Ahrens (1996) reported significant correlations between both Concern Over Mistakes and Doubts About Actions and Beck Anxiety Inventory (BAI; Beck, Epstein, Brown, & Steer, 1988) scores and Beck Depression Inventory (BDI; Beck, Ward, Mendelson, Mock, & Erbaugh, 1961) scores. Frost et al. (1993) found significant correlations of Concern Over Mistakes, Doubts About Actions, and Socially Prescribed Perfectionism with negative affect on the Positive and Negative Affect Schedule (PANAS; Watson, Clark, & Tellegen, 1988). Likewise, Brown et al. (1999) also found Concern Over Mistakes to be positively correlated with negative affect and negatively correlated with positive affect. Note that negative affect is not a pure measure of anxiety but a mixture of anxiety and depression symptoms.

The data raise an important question in studying the relationship between perfectionism and anxiety. That is, to what extent is this relationship specific or unique? For example, it seems that perfectionism is associated with increased risk for a wide range of psychopathological symptoms in addition to clinical anxiety (see Frost et al., 1990; Hewitt & Flett, 1991a, 1991b; Kawamura, Hunt, Frost, & DiBartolo, 2001). In addition, because considerable overlap exists between anxiety and depressive symptoms and it is well known that perfectionism measures are associated with depressive symptoms (Hewitt & Flett, 1993), how much of the variance in perfectionism's relationship with anxiety is shared with depression?

Hewitt and Flett (1991a) examined perfectionism levels, as measured by their MPS, in patients with depression, patients with anxiety disorder, and nonpatient control participants. The anxious patients and nonpatient control participants were not significantly different from one another on Self-Oriented Perfectionism, although both groups scored significantly lower on this subscale than the depressed group. On Socially Prescribed Perfectionism, both the anxious and the depressed patient groups had significantly higher scores than the nonpatient group, but they were not significantly different from each other. Similar to our earlier arguments, the data suggest that anxiety may be characterized by socially prescribed perfectionism, rather than self-oriented perfectionism; however, the relationship of anxiety to socially prescribed perfectionism may not be unique given that the depressed patients were not significantly different from the anxious patients on this dimension.

Further data supporting the nonspecific relationship between nonclinical anxiety and perfectionism were generated by Alden, Bieling, and Wallace (1994) in a study of anxious and dysphoric college students. Using a 2 (Socially Anxious vs. Nonanxious) × 2 (Dysphoric vs. Nondysphoric) design, the data revealed main effects of both anxiety and dysphoria on Socially Prescribed Perfectionism scores. That is, both socially anxious and dysphoric participants reported significantly higher levels of socially prescribed perfectionism than nonanxious and nondysphoric participants did. In contrast, no group effects were found on Self-Oriented Perfectionism scores. Again, the findings suggest that both anxiety and depression are related to socially prescribed perfectionism.

Some studies have statistically controlled for other symptoms to determine whether the relationship between perfectionism and anxiety is unique. Most such studies have suggested that the relationship between anxiety and perfectionism is not specific. For example, Westra and Kuiper (1996; Study 2) found that socially prescribed perfectionism was related to both depression and anxiety (and to bulimic and Type A symptoms), although it was not uniquely correlated with any one particular type of psychopathology. Minarik and Ahrens (1996) examined the relationship between the Frost MPS subscales and BAI scores, controlling for depression (i.e., BDI scores) among college students. Although Concern Over Mistakes, Doubts About Actions, and Personal Standards subscale scores were significantly correlated with BAI scores (Personal Standards negatively so), when BDI scores were controlled in a regression analysis, none of the perfectionism measures predicted anxiety. Meanwhile, when BAI scores were controlled in a similar regression analysis, Concern Over Mistakes and Doubts About Actions remained significant predictors of BDI scores, suggesting that those dimensions of perfectionism are more specifically related to depression than anxiety. The other study using the BAI failed to find any relationship between either self-oriented or socially prescribed perfectionism and anxiety scores (Saddler & Buckland, 1995).

The Hewitt and Flett (1991a) study described earlier, which used samples of clinically depressed and clinically anxious patients and a nonpatient control group, reported results similar to those obtained by Minarik and Ahrens (1996). Among all the participants in Hewitt and Flett's study, both self-oriented and socially prescribed perfectionism were correlated with a measure of anxiety (EMAS–State Anxiety); however, the relationships were no longer significant when BDI scores were controlled in a regression equation. In contrast, when anxiety scores were controlled, depression scores were significantly related to both self-oriented and socially prescribed perfectionism.

Two studies have provided evidence suggesting a unique relationship between certain features of perfectionism and anxiety. Westra and Kuiper (1996; Study 1) measured four types of psychopathology (i.e., depression, anxiety, bulimia, and Type A behavior) and several types of related dysfunctional cognitions among college students. They used two subscales of the Dysfunctional Attitudes Scale (DAS; Weissman, 1979) that are conceptually related to perfectionism (i.e., Performance Evaluation and Approval by Others). The DAS Performance Evaluation subscale appears somewhat analogous to the dimension of self-oriented perfectionism in that it measures self-expectations for performance, whereas the DAS Approval by Others subscale appears to be similar to socially prescribed perfectionism. Results indicated that the Performance Evaluation scores were not correlated with anxiety symptoms; the Approval by Others subscale scores, however, were significantly related to anxiety, even when Type A, depression, and bulimia symptoms were controlled. The conclusions are somewhat tenuous given the uncertainty about how the DAS corresponds to the better validated dimensions of perfectionism.

Two other investigations using the Frost MPS have provided evidence of a unique association between perfectionism and trait anxiety after controlling for depression levels. Juster et al. (1996) found the relationship of Concern Over Mistakes and Doubts About Actions to trait anxiety to be independent of depression levels (as measured by the BDI) among a sample of patients with social phobia. Similarly, Kawamura et al. (2001) found in a sample of students that a Perfectionism factor comprising Concern Over Mistakes, Doubts About Action, Parental Criticism, and Parental Expectations was related to an Anxiety factor comprising scales assessing social anxiety, worry, and trait anxiety, after controlling for the BDI.

The weight of evidence suggests that, although anxiety is associated primarily with the maladaptive evaluation concern dimensions of perfectionism (i.e., socially prescribed perfectionism, concern over mistakes, and doubts about actions), rather than its other dimensions (i.e., self-oriented perfectionism, parental expectations, parental criticism, and personal standards), this relationship may not be unique. That is, socially prescribed perfectionism, concern over mistakes, and doubts about actions are related to a broad range of psychopathology, including anxiety. In fact, only Juster et al. (1996) provided clear evidence of a unique relationship of perfectionism to anxiety once depression levels had been controlled. It was noted earlier that this study used a pure sample of social phobia patients. It is possible that perfectionism is uniquely related to social anxiety, particularly at clinically significant levels. This possibility may help explain why the unique relationship of perfectionism to trait anxiety was found only among participants with social phobia. A study conducted by Antony, Purdon, Huta, and Swinson (1998) provided some evidence that perfectionism levels in people diagnosed with social phobia were significantly higher than those found in patients with other anxiety disorders. They found that patients with social phobia had significantly higher scores on the maladaptive evaluation concern aspects of perfectionism than did patients with either panic disorder or OCD.

Indeed, investigators have found consistent relationships between the dimensions of perfectionism associated with social evaluative concerns (e.g., Concern Over Mistakes and Socially Prescribed Perfectionism) and measures of social anxiety in recent research. DiBartolo, Dixon, Almodovar, and Frost (1998) found that people high in Concern Over Mistakes had high fear of negative evaluation scores, high public and private self-consciousness scores, and high social anxiety scores. Juster et al. (1996) also found Concern Over Mistakes and Doubts About Actions scores to be correlated with fear of negative evaluation, scores on a questionnaire assessing social phobia, and an interview-based social anxiety measure among social phobia patients. Blankstein, Flett, Hewitt, and Eng (1993) found that socially prescribed perfectionism was correlated with social fears as measured by the Fear Survey Schedule (Wolpe & Lang, 1964), whereas self-oriented and other-oriented perfectionism were not. Similarly, Flett, Hewitt, and DeRosa (1996) found that socially prescribed perfectionism, but not self-oriented perfectionism, was correlated with many indices of social anxiety, including fear of negative evaluation, social self-esteem, shyness, and loneliness. Furthermore, Alden et al. (1994) reported that the frequency of self-appraisal during a social interaction was a significant predictor of participants' Socially Prescribed Perfectionism scores. Given that self-consciousness and fear of negative evaluation in social situations are cardinal features of the social phobia diagnosis, it would appear likely that this specific dimension of perfectionism would be strongly associated with social phobia.

In sum, the studies on perfectionism and general anxiety suggest that dimensions of perfectionism, particularly Concern Over Mistakes, Doubts About Actions, and Socially Prescribed Perfectionism, are correlated with trait anxiety and with measures of anxiety as a symptom of psychopathology (i.e., BAI, SCL-90, PANAS, and PSWQ scores). Personal standards and self-oriented perfectionism do not appear to be strongly related to anxiety. In addition, the research literature does not provide support for a unique relationship between anxiety and perfectionism. Some preliminary data, however, suggest that perfectionism may be particularly associated with social anxiety. This potential relationship deserves attention in future research.

Perfectionism and Life Stress

Beyond the issue of whether perfectionism is associated with trait or general measures of anxiety symptoms is the question of the extent to which perfectionism is associated with the everyday experience of anxiety and stress. The overly critical self-evaluations that are part of perfectionism in all likelihood lead perfectionists to experience anxiety in response to everyday situations that other people do not find stressful. It could be hypothesized that perfectionists perceive a greater frequency of stressors in their lives and react more strongly to them, perhaps because of their perception that the occurrence of life stressors indicates failure (Flett et al., 1989; Hewitt, Flett, & Weber, 1994).

Some evidence supports an association between perfectionism and the report of daily stress. Daily stress measures (e.g., hassles scales) typically focus on the minor annoyances, irritants, and problems of everyday life (e.g., headaches, concerns about weight, and fear of rejection). Using a sample of female executives, Fry (1995) found a positive correlation between perfectionism scores (using a composite of Hewitt and Flett MPS subscales) and a measure of daily hassles. Likewise, in a study of adjustment to college for entering students, Van Cleve, Frost, and DiBartolo

(1997) found that Frost MPS total scores and Concern Over Mistakes scores were correlated with the reported intensity of hassles but not their frequency. Other subscales reflecting the maladaptive evaluation concerns typical of perfectionism (e.g., Doubts About Actions) were correlated with both the intensity and frequency of hassles.

Other data indicate that perfectionism is associated with the reported experience of significantly more stressful life events that have a negative impact. For example, Flett, Hewitt, and Hallett (1995) found socially prescribed perfectionism to be associated with many indices of stress among teachers. Using the Teacher Stress Inventory (Fimian, 1984), they found that socially prescribed perfectionism was correlated with the frequency and intensity of professional distress and both emotional and physiological manifestations of stress. Socially Prescribed Perfectionism also was negatively correlated with job satisfaction. Other-oriented and self-oriented perfectionism showed few significant correlations with measures of stress or satisfaction among teachers.

Furthermore, Hewitt, Flett, and Ediger (1996) found that both self-oriented perfectionism and socially prescribed perfectionism were correlated with interpersonal stressful life events but not with achievement-related stressful life events. Additionally, Dean, Range, and Goggin (1996) reported a correlation between negative life events as measured by the Life Experiences Survey (LES; Sarason, Johnson, & Siegel, 1978) and socially prescribed perfectionism. Flett, Hewitt, Blankstein, and Mosher (1995) reported this same association across two separate samples. Note that the LES requires respondents to indicate the impact (positive to negative) of a variety of life events such that negative LES scores reflect the degree to which participants perceive their life experiences as having an adverse effect on their lives. Thus, the association between the LES and perfectionism levels may be a result of the cognitive–appraisal style characteristic of perfectionism rather than any real difference in the frequency of negative life events.

Finally, two studies have examined the hypothesis that perfectionism interacts with stress to produce high levels of anxiety. Flett et al. (1989) tested whether perfectionism is a diathesis that produces high levels of neuroticism and trait anxiety when paired with increased life stress. Using the BPS, they failed to find any direct association between perfectionism and scores on the Social Readjustment Rating Scale (Holmes & Rahe, 1967), a measure of the occurrence of negative life events. They did find, however, that perfectionism and life stress interacted to predict both high levels of neuroticism and trait anxiety. People who were high in perfectionism and were experiencing high levels of life stress had higher levels of neuroticism and trait anxiety than those with low levels of life stress —or even nonperfectionists who had high levels of life stress—did.

Joiner and Schmidt (1995) further examined the vulnerability hypothesis among a sample of college students in a prospective design. They predicted that socially prescribed perfectionism would interact with interpersonal (but not achievement) stress to predict anxiety and depression. They also predicted that self-oriented perfectionism would not predict anxiety. To test their hypotheses, Joiner and Schmidt used the Eating Disorders Inventory (Garner, Olmstead, & Polivy, 1983) Perfectionism subscale and divided it into self-oriented and socially prescribed perfectionism items using a LISREL model analysis. Although the item content may reflect these aspects of perfectionism, the small number of items in each scale (three) and the absence of any direct correlation to the Hewitt and Flett measures leaves the validity of the scales questionable. A further cause for concern is the weak pattern of correlations of the perfectionism measures with measures of depression and anxiety among the participants. Nevertheless, Joiner and Schmidt's findings were quite interesting. For the whole sample, no correlations were found between the two perfectionism subscales and either achievement or interpersonal life stressors. They did, however, find modest support for their vulnerability hypothesis. Specifically, socially prescribed perfectionism interacted with Negative Life Events Questionnaire scores (Saxe & Abramson, 1987) to predict anxiety, but only in men. In contrast, self-oriented perfectionism did not predict anxiety.

Although some evidence supports the hypothesis that perfectionists report greater frequency of daily or life stress, the findings have been somewhat inconsistent. This inconsistency may be due, in part, to method variance. Measures of negative life events, such as the Negative Life Events Questionnaire (Saxe & Abramson, 1987) and Social Readjustment Rating Scale (Holmes & Rahe, 1967), failed to show any relationship with measures of perfectionism (Flett et al., 1989; Joiner & Schmidt, 1995). Conversely, measures of the impact of life events, such as the LES, and measures of daily stress, such as the Hassles Scale (DeLongis, Folkman, & Lazarus, 1988), were correlated with various perfectionism dimensions in several studies (Dean et al., 1996; Flett, Hewitt, Blankstein, & Mosher, 1995; Fry, 1995; Van Cleve et al., 1997). Measures of daily hassles have been criticized for their overlap with measures of psychopathology; hassles are not simply the occurrence of an event but a stress-related interpretation of an everyday event. Although this criticism of hassles as a measure of stressful events is valid, it is consistent with the hypothesis presented above that perfectionists will interpret daily events in such a way that more of them are defined as stressors.

The findings from the studies described in this section suggest that Socially Prescribed Perfectionism, Concern Over Mistakes, Doubts About Actions, and Parental Criticism are associated with the experience of daily hassles and stress. These dimensions of perfectionism reflect its maladaptive evaluation aspects. In contrast, relatively little support can be found for the relationship between self-oriented perfectionism and personal standards and the frequency or intensity of daily hassles. Furthermore, some data provide tentative support for the vulnerability hypothesis and thereby suggest that perfectionism interacts with stressful events to predict anxiety.

Perfectionism and Reactions to Threat

In addition to the two areas just reviewed, a third line of research on the relationship between anxiety and perfectionism involves the study of situations with various levels of evaluative threat. Given that one defining feature of perfectionism is the tendency to engage in overly critical self-evaluation (Frost et al., 1990), perfectionists are likely to believe that any performance that is less than perfect is equivalent to failure (Hamachek, 1978; Missildine, 1963). Accordingly, any situation with an evaluative component is viewed as an opportunity for failure. As a result, perfectionists may "feel anxious, confused, and emotionally drained before a new task ever begins" (Hamachek, 1978, p. 28). Some research on this issue focuses on reactions to naturally occurring evaluative threat, and some involves laboratory-induced evaluative threat. In general, the studies examine whether perfectionists show more negative affective, cognitive, and behavioral responses to evaluative threat than nonperfectionists do.

One way of examining reactions to threats involves studying people who experience high evaluative threat situations on a routine basis, such as athletes and performance artists. Frost and Henderson (1991) studied the retrospective accounts of 40 female varsity athletes' cognitive and affective reactions to athletic competition. Athletes high in perfectionism (as measured by Frost MPS total scores and scores on Concern Over Mistakes) reported lower levels of confidence in their ability to succeed in sports and higher levels of cognitive and physiological anxiety prior to athletic competition. Frost and Henderson also found that high levels of Concern Over Mistakes were associated with high levels of anticipatory anxiety in the 24 hours before a competition.

Perfectionists' anxiety about performance may be related to their cognitions in anticipation of and in response to mistakes during competition. The nature of perfectionistic thought processes before and during competition suggests that athletes high in Concern Over Mistakes engage in much thinking about the threatening nature of competition, the likelihood of failure, and the negative consequences of failure. For example, Concern Over Mistakes and Doubts About Actions were correlated with participants' increased endorsement of items reflecting a view of competition as an opportunity for failure and feelings of disappointment in response to making a mistake during competition. Furthermore, in the hours before a competition, athletes high in Concern Over Mistakes reported greater fear, and more frequent images of making mistakes during their upcoming game or meet than their counterparts not scoring high on the subscale did. Finally, athletes high in Concern Over Mistakes or Doubts About Actions reported greater difficulty forgetting about their mistakes during competition and focused more attention on them than other athletes. This pattern of rumination about mistakes was corroborated by coaches' ratings of perfectionistic players' having more difficulty recovering from mistakes during competition. Interestingly, no relationship was found between any dimension of perfectionism and coaches' ratings of player ability.

In a recent, retrospective study of perfectionism in athletics, Gould, Udry, Tuffey, and Loehr (1996) examined perfectionism in the context of burnout in competitive tennis players. Participants for the study were highly competitive junior tennis players who either had burned out on tennis or continued to play at a competitive level. Compared with the active players, players with burnout had higher self-reported levels of Concern Over Mistakes, Parental Criticism, and Parental Expectations and lower levels of Personal Standards. In fact, a discriminant function analysis entering Frost MPS scores and measures of trait sport anxiety and athletic self-identity indicated that certain MPS subscales (i.e., Parental Criticism, Parental Expectations, and Personal Standards) could be used to correctly classify 70% of the participants.

Using a different group of performers, Mor, Day, Flett, and Hewitt (1995) examined perfectionism and anxiety among a sample of professional performing artists. The performers completed measures of perfectionism, anxiety, personal control, and performance evaluation. Among this sample, self-oriented perfectionism and socially prescribed perfectionism were correlated positively with debilitating performance anxiety and somatic anxiety. Those perfectionism dimensions were negatively correlated with happiness while performing and satisfaction with career progress. Socially prescribed perfectionism also was correlated negatively with facilitative performance anxiety. The study is important because its findings suggest that personal control moderated the link between perfectionism and anxiety: Performers with high levels of self-oriented perfectionism and low levels of personal control had high levels of debilitating anxiety and low levels of facilitating anxiety. The same was true for self-oriented perfectionism and socially prescribed perfectionism in relation to goal satisfaction.

In addition to retrospective studies of perfectionists' reactions to evaluative situations, prospective studies examining reactions to ongoing evaluative situations (e.g., students in a course) have been conducted. Using a prospective methodology, Frost et al. (1997) asked participants either high or low in perfectionistic Concern Over Mistakes (CM) to keep a journal of their mistakes for 5 consecutive days. In their journal, participants answered a series of questions about each mistake they made, including its description, its perceived seriousness, their emotional and cognitive reactions to it, and their concerns about other people seeing the mistake.

The quantity and quality of mistakes reported by perfectionists and nonperfectionists were similar. High- and low-CM participants reported a similar number of mistakes in their journals and remembered a similar number of mistakes when contacted by telephone at follow-up 2 weeks later. Furthermore, ratings made by independent judges of the importance, "wrongness," and harmfulness of each mistake revealed no differences between high- and low-CM participants.

Many differences, however, were found between high- and low-CM participants in their reactions to and beliefs about their mistakes. In response to their mistakes, those high in CM reported experiencing significantly more negative affect and more "should" statements (e.g., "I should have known better" and "I should not have allowed this to happen") than their low-CM counterparts. They also were more "bothered" by their mistakes and rated them as more serious, more "wrong," and more "morally reprehensible" than low-CM participants.

Regarding beliefs about the consequences of their mistakes, it appears as though high-CM participants' concern for the harm of their mistakes has a specific locus. Participants were asked several questions about whom each mistake would harm (i.e., self or others). High-CM participants believed that their mistakes would cause significantly greater harm to themselves than did low-CM participants, but no difference was found between high- and low-CM participants on their reports of the extent to which their mistakes would harm others. This finding suggests that despite finding that their mistakes were morally wrong, high-CM participants did not worry as much about their mistakes' effects on other people.

As has been seen in most of the other research on reactions to evaluative threat, high-CM participants were more worried about other peoples' reaction to their mistakes than were low-CM participants. It is clear that this worry was not because the mistakes would cause harm to other people. Instead, the worries appear to concern the possibility that others would think badly of them for their mistakes. This finding may explain why in this study, as in several studies that have asked this question (Frost, Turcotte, Heimberg, & Mattia, 1995, Frost et al., 1997), high-CM participants wanted to keep their mistakes secret.

This study indicates that perfectionists, especially those high in CM, react more emotionally and negatively to their mistakes in performance. It also provides some information about how mistakes affect people long after they occur. Two weeks after participants completed their mistake journals, no group differences were found in the number of mistakes recalled; however, high-CM participants reported more thoughts about their most important mistake and being more bothered by thoughts about that mistake than low-CM participants.

In another prospective investigation, Brown et al. (1999) examined the correlates of personal standards and CM in the context of an ongoing college course. PS and CM were measured at the beginning of a semester, and indices of anxiety, attributions for performance, and actual performance were measured throughout the semester. CM was associated with high levels of initial anxiety about the course grade and was predictive of anxiety 1 week after the midterm and final exams. Furthermore, CM was associated with disappointment with performance, the perception of greater course difficulty, negative attributions about one's performance on the midterm exam, and a lack of willingness to disclose performance on the final exam. In contrast, Personal Standards was associated with high grade point average and final exam grade. Additionally, when Personal Standards was combined with surpassing expected performance standards on the midterm exam, it was associated with less perceived midterm difficulty, more willingness to disclose midterm exam scores, and less attribution of performance to negative factors.

Finally, in addition to retrospective and prospective studies of naturally occurring threat, laboratory stressors provide another methodology for studying the reactions of perfectionists to threat. In one of the first studies using a laboratory stressor, Frost and Marten (1990) assigned participants who scored high or low on the Frost MPS to high- or low-evaluative-threat conditions in a writing task. Evaluative threat was manipulated by telling participants that they were part of a nationwide writing evaluation project in which their writing ability would be compared with that of other students across the country and that a printout comparing their writing level with other students' would be made available to them. Low-threat participants were asked to do the writing task, but nothing was said about evaluation of their writing. Cognitive, affective, and behavioral responses to the writing task were compared.

Perfectionism interacted with level of threat in determining affective responses to the task. When the evaluation of threat was minimized, no differences were found between perfectionists and nonperfectionists in negative affect. Among participants for whom the evaluative component of the task was salient, perfectionists had significantly greater negative affect than nonperfectionists. Furthermore, perfectionists experienced greater negative affect in the high-evaluative-threat condition than in the low-threat condition, whereas no differences were found in affective responses of people scoring low on the MPS across threat conditions. The findings illustrate the importance of the evaluative-threat domain for perfectionists. When engaged in a task in which the evaluative threat is salient, perfectionists respond with increased anxiety and depression. The data also suggest that the evaluative-threat manipulation was relatively weak and only affected people high in perfectionism; the threshold for detecting evaluative threat may be lower for perfectionists than nonperfectionists.

Regardless of the level of threat, perfectionists approached and responded differently to the writing task. First, independent judges rated perfectionists' writing quality as poorer than nonperfectionists' writing quality across both threat conditions. The finding was not a result of the effect of anxiety because perfectionists in the low threat condition were not particularly anxious and yet they wrote essays of lesser quality than nonperfectionists. Additionally, prior to the task, perfectionists rated the task as more important than nonperfectionists did. After the task, the perfectionists were more likely to believe that they should have done better than were the nonperfectionists; that belief was not mediated by how they actually performed on the task (as rated by independent judges).

In a subsequent laboratory study, we examined perfectionists' responses to a task involving the manipulation of the frequency of mistakes (Frost et al., 1995). Two groups of participants were used in this study: those who scored in the highest and lowest quartiles of the distribution of CM scores. Using a Stroop task, we then created two conditions: one in which participants made a high number of mistakes (naming the color of antagonistic color names) and one in which participants made a low number of mistakes (naming the color of a series of Xs). We then monitored reactions to the tasks. The manipulation of threat (i.e., high-mistake vs. low-mistake task) clearly worked. All participants in the high-mistake task condition reported higher negative affect, had lower confidence in their performance, took longer to complete the task, and reported having committed a larger number of mistakes than did their low-mistake counterparts.

As found in the Frost and Marten (1990) study, a significant interaction occurred between perfectionism and threat for experience of anxiety. In the low-mistake task, no group differences in negative affect were found. In the high-mistake (i.e., high-threat) task, high-CM participants reported significantly greater negative affect than low-CM participants did. Despite the affective differences, no differences in performance occurred between high- and low-CM participants.

The findings regarding the cognitive responses of high-CM compared with low-CM scorers mirrored those reported in other studies. Again, participants high in CM had lower confidence following the high-mistake task than did low-CM participants, but high- and low-CM participants did not differ in the low-mistake task. Also, consistent with the Frost and Marten (1990) study, high-CM participants reported thinking that they should have done better to a significantly greater extent than did low-CM participants, regardless of the level of threat.

Regarding their beliefs about how other people would evaluate their performance, no differences were found between high- and low-CM participants in the low-mistake-frequency task in the extent to which they believed others would view them as less intelligent on the basis of their performance. In the high-mistake-frequency task, however, high-CM participants were more likely to feel that others would think of them as less intelligent as a result of their performance. For both the low- and high-mistake-frequency task, high-CM participants were less willing to share their results with others than were low-CM participants. A significant interaction between CM and task, however, indicated that this effect was significantly greater in the high-mistake-frequency condition.

Flett et al. (1994–1995) also examined the components of state anxiety under conditions of high and low ego threat. To manipulate ego threat, Flett et al. told half of the participants that they were to participate in a "test" that was highly predictive of success and ability; the other half were told that the test was in the initial stages of development and was not predictive of ability. The manipulation seemed to have minimal impact on participants' anxiety, however. That is, no differences were found between high- and low-ego-threat conditions on measures of state anxiety or perception of threat. Nevertheless, under high-ego-threat conditions, socially prescribed perfectionism was significantly correlated with both worry and autonomic arousal (as well as state anxiety). Under the no-ego-threat condition, however, no correlations were found between measures of state anxiety (i.e., worry and autonomic arousal) and perfectionism. Despite the weakness of the threat manipulation, it produced an increase in anxiety among only socially prescribed perfectionists. Also in this study, participants scoring high in Socially Prescribed Perfectionism perceived greater threat (in both the high- and low-threat conditions) even in the low-ego-threat condition. Like the Frost and Marten (1990) study, the findings suggest that perfectionists have a different threshold for the detection of threat.

Finally, DiBartolo et al. (2001) examined reactions of high- and low-CM participants to a public-speaking task, presumably a high-evaluative-threat condition. In response to this task, high-CM participants showed differences in appraisal, anxiety, and self-evaluation before, during, and after the speech. During the speech, their ratings of anxiety and distress tended to be significantly higher than those of low-CM participants. In addition, significant group differences were found in negative affect as measured by the PANAS in response to the task. Participants high in CM reported significantly greater negative affect both immediately before and after the speech than did low-CM participants.

In addition, many interesting cognitive differences were found. Before the speech, high-CM participants were more likely to report believing that others would do better on the speech than they would and that it was more important to do well on the speech task than were participants low in CM. Both before and after the task, high-CM participants reported a greater number of negative cognitions associated with the speech (e.g., "I will run out of things to say," "I will sound really stupid") than low-CM participants did. Compared with low-CM participants, they also estimated the probability of a disastrous outcome during the speech and the "horribleness" of such an outcome as significantly higher. Interestingly, despite the affective and cognitive differences, audience ratings failed to reveal any group differences in observable anxiety or quality of the speech.

All participants were contacted 1 week later to assess the extent to which their experience still affected them. High-CM participants were significantly more bothered by thoughts about the speech and were less satisfied with their performance than the low-CM participants were. They also reported enjoying the task less and rated themselves as less able to communicate their ideas.

In sum, the research literature on the effects of evaluative threat on perfectionists has many important implications. First, it is clear that people high in perfectionistic thinking (i.e., Concern Over Mistakes and Socially Prescribed Perfectionism) experience more anxiety before, during, and after performing an evaluative task than their nonperfectionistic counterparts. It may be that every task has enough of an evaluative component that perfectionists give it special importance and respond with increased anxiety. For example, as noted earlier, Flett et al. (1994–1995) found that participants high in socially prescribed perfectionism perceived more threat than low socially prescribed perfectionist participants did in both the high- and low-threat conditions. Only perfectionists reported more anxiety in the high-threat condition than in the low-threat condition. This finding is consistent with Frost and Marten's (1990) speculation that perfectionists are more likely to view situations as being important than nonperfectionists are and with Missildine's (1963) suggestion that all tasks carry with them the "opportunity for failure" and are therefore threatening to perfectionists. As suggested earlier, perfectionists may have a low threshold for evaluative threat. It is clear from this research that when perfectionists perceive evaluative threat, they experience not only increased anxiety but also many other cognitive and behavioral events.

The increase in anxiety and negative affectivity that is characteristic of perfectionistic people is associated with a consistent pattern of cognitive responses. First, perfectionists believe that doing well on evaluative tasks is important (Frost & Marten, 1990), and they endorse more personal imperatives, or should statements, in relation to their performance (Frost et al., 1997). The data are consistent with earlier theorizing, which suggested that perfectionists are plagued by thoughts that they should have done better at their daily tasks (Burns, 1980; Ellis, 1962, chapter 9, this volume; Hamachek, 1978; Pacht, 1984). Horney (1950) suggested that these should statements are a strategy to avoid mistakes; such imperatives may motivate the perfectionist to work hard at avoiding mistakes. Frost et al. (1997) suggested that they are part of a review process that high-CM people use to evaluate their behavior. They may form an automatic self-evaluative and self-corrective process in which performance is compared with an ideal (i.e., perfection) and self-instructions (i.e., personal imperatives) are formed in an attempt to achieve the ideal.

Higgins (1987) has proposed such a process for explaining attempts at self-correction. In his theory, two beliefs are used as *self-guides*, or standards. *Ideal self* refers to beliefs about what one hopes to be. *Ought self* refers to the beliefs about what one has a moral duty to be. The self-guides are compared with beliefs about the actual self. The discrepancy between the self-guides and the actual self forms the basis of self-evaluation and regulatory behavior. Self-discrepancies appear to be differentially related to emotional distress. In both clinical and nonclinical samples, discrepancies between actual and ideal self were associated with depression and depressed mood, whereas discrepancies between actual and ought self were associated with anxiety disorders and anxiety symptoms (Higgins, Klein, & Strauman, 1985; Scott & O'Hara, 1993; Strauman, 1989; Strauman & Higgins, 1987). In a recent study combining discrepancy measures and the Hewitt and Flett MPS, the discrepancy between the actual and ought self was not related to self-oriented and socially prescribed perfectionism, but the larger discrepancies between the actual and ideal self were correlated with socially prescribed perfectionism (Hankin et al., 1997). Further research on the relationship between discrepancy measures and dimensions of perfectionism is needed.

Perfectionists' post-task regret about the quality of their performance, as reflected by should statements, appears to result in a rumination effect (DiBartolo et al., 2001; Frost et al., 1997). In fact, Guidano and Liotti (1983) suggested that rumination about mistakes is a key feature of perfectionism. The follow-up data from the DiBartolo et al. (1998) and Frost et al. (1997) studies suggested that part of the phenomenon of perfectionism is rumination about mistakes and failures in performance long after the evaluative threat is over. Both studies indicated that for perfectionists, perceived mistakes or failures occur no more frequently than those experienced by nonperfectionists, nor are their mistakes any more serious; however, rumination over mistakes or failure may provide a sort of cognitive rehearsal that sensitizes perfectionists to evaluative threat.

In several studies, participants high in CM were less willing than low-CM participants to disclose their performance to others (Brown et al., 1999; Frost et al., 1995, 1997). This behavior may be part of a pattern of avoidance of possible criticism from others. Burns (1980) hypothesized that perfectionists have a phobia about disclosing anything about themselves that could be subject to criticism. In a more direct study of this issue, Samolewicz, DiBartolo, and Prins (1996) administered the Frost MPS, the Self-Concealment Scale (Larson & Chastain, 1990), and a trauma-specific concealment scale to a group of undergraduate women. Perfectionism was positively correlated with concealment scores and trauma-specific concealment. The tendency of perfectionists to avoid disclosure and to actively conceal personal information from others may play an important role in the relationship between perfectionism and anxiety disorders. Avoidance of fear-evoking situations is a key element in the development of many anxiety disorders. It is likely that perfectionism has an impact beyond the issue of concealment, however. For instance, in the Samolewicz et al. study, perfectionism was correlated with posttraumatic stress disorder symptoms even when the variance due to trauma-specific concealment was controlled.

The anxiety and cognitive preoccupation that are characteristic of perfectionists when performing under conditions of evaluative threat could potentially lead to decrements in performance (Meyers, Cooke, Cullen, & Liles, 1979) and, possibly, motivation (Deci & Ryan, 1985; McAuley & Tammen, 1989). Focusing attention on mistakes during competition may distract a person from task-relevant processing, and performance may suffer. To date, only one study has found a significant difference between perfectionists and nonperfectionists in the quality of their performance (Frost & Marten, 1990). In the context of this study, we hypothesized that differences in writing quality may reflect skill deficiencies that are secondary to perfectionistic behavior. We hypothesized that perfectionists avoid writing tasks, procrastinate about them, and avoid having others review and comment on their work to a greater extent than nonperfectionists do. As a result, they neither practice nor receive constructive feedback about their writing. Consistency, practice, and feedback are key to the development of writing skills (Boice, 1983). It will be important for future studies to elucidate what types of conditions and tasks result in behavioral disruptions in performance for perfectionists.

Most of the studies of this type have used evaluative threat to induce anxiety. Although we have noted that perfectionists respond to evaluative threat with increased anxiety relative to nonperfectionists, we would make no such prediction for other types of threat (e.g., physical threat). Further research is needed to test the hypothesis that evaluative threat alone will increase anxiety for perfectionists.

Perfectionism and OCD

Although Hewitt and Flett (1991a) found higher socially prescribed perfectionism in a mixed-diagnosis group of patients with anxiety disorders, few studies have examined differences in perfectionism across anxiety disorders. The exceptions are studies of social phobia and OCD. Because the relationship between perfectionism and social phobia is covered elsewhere in this book (see Alden, Ryder, & Mellings, chapter 15, this volume), we will review the literature on perfectionism and OCD here.

Perfectionism has been closely tied to OCD since the writings of Janet in the early 1900s (Janet, 1903; as cited in Pitman, 1987). Janet suggested three stages in the development of OCD. The first stage, the *psychasthenic state*, was hypothesized to be common to all forms of psychopathology. Characteristic of this state is the sense of never performing actions in exactly the right way, even though the behavior meets acceptable standards to an observer. This tormenting perfectionism was thought to have its roots in childhood and to form the basis of later psychopathology, including OCD. In the second stage, *forced agitations*, perfection in perceptions and behavior is necessary to overcome feelings of uncertainty. The perfectionistic features of the psychasthenic state and forced agitations are necessary precursors to the development of full-blown *obsessions and compulsions*, the third and final stage of the process.

Psychoanalytic writers also have emphasized notions of perfectionism in their descriptions and theoretical accounts of OCD. Jones (1918) described the core of OCD as a "pathologically intolerant insistence on the absolute necessity of doing things in exactly the 'right way'" (p. 417). Straus (1948) emphasized the intolerance of uncertainty in characterizing patients with OCD and related it to the development of perfectionism. Humans expect their actions to have a planned effect, but they do so with the knowledge that unforeseen possibilities may alter the outcome. To cope with the fear of uncertainty, the obsessive person avoids criticism by engaging in no behavior that might provoke it. Another way to overcome this impasse is to make one's actions above criticism and reproach. By being perfect, one can obtain immunity from criticism. According to Straus, the elaborate symptomatology of the patient with OCD is a direct result of this perfectionism.

Similarly, other analytic theorists have emphasized the role of perfectionism in the attempts of people with OCD to attain and maintain control over the environment (Mallinger, 1984; Mallinger & DeWyze, 1992; Salzman, 1979). These writers suggested that the central goal of such people is to maintain control over events in their life to feel safe from harm. This view is similar to Straus's but emphasizes the perception of control rather than uncertainty. People with OCD attempt to control their own thoughts and feelings and the thoughts, feelings, and actions of others toward them. One manifestation of this attempt at control is perfectionism. By being perfect (i.e., eliminating mistakes), the risk of harm (i.e., criticism) is minimized. Of course, it is impossible to be perfect. Recognition of this leaves people with OCD doubtful about the quality of their actions and anxious about the amount of risk to which they are exposed. The illusion of control over these events, which cannot be controlled by "perfection," is attained by cognitive distortions, such as superstitions and obsessions, and by compulsive behavior. The implication of this analysis is that perfectionism is symptomatic of an excessive need for control to avoid risk. In short, milder forms of excessive need for control would manifest themselves in perfectionism without obsessions and compulsions. More extreme forms of excessive need for control would produce not only perfectionism but also obsessions and compulsions. Although Mallinger's (1984) and Salzman's (1979) focus is on OCD, the analysis suggests that the origin of perfectionism is an excessive need for control.

In addition to dynamic theories, the issues of control, security, and concern over criticism have been heavily emphasized in cognitive theories (Beck, Emery, & Greenberg, 1985) and behavioral theories (McAndrews, 1989) of OCD. McFall and Wollersheim (1979) proposed a cognitive model of OCD that focuses on the cognitive appraisal of threat; they suggested that people with OCD have learned a core set of four assumptions or beliefs that lead them to perceive the world as a dangerous and threatening place; two of the assumptions reflect perfectionistic thinking styles. One assumption is that "one should be perfectly competent, adequate, and achieving in all possible respects" (p. 335). McFall and Wollersheim suggested that people with OCD believe that they must be perfect to feel good about themselves and to avoid criticism and disapproval from others. In this respect, the theory is identical to Salzman's (1979) and Mallinger's (1984) in that perfectionism is used to control how the environment (i.e., other people) reacts. The other perfectionistic assumption is that mistakes or failures to meet goals are catastrophic and deserving of punishment. This assumption has more to do with the meaning of mistakes, and other cognitive theorists (e.g., Beck et al., 1985) have suggested that it is important in the development of many forms of psychopathology.

In yet another cognitive theory, Guidano and Liotti (1983) suggested that perfectionism is one of the fundamental traits in the development of OCD among people with obsessional personality. Like McFall and Wallersheim (1979), they suggested that OCD symptoms result from certain core beliefs or assumptions. The underlying cognitive structure or set of beliefs of people with OCD is characterized by three things: perfectionism, a need for certainty, and a belief in perfect solutions. Those beliefs lead the patient with OCD to ruminate over mistakes (both past and future) and reject any solution that is not "the perfect one"; if a less than perfect solution is achieved, it is viewed as a failure. This type of dichotomous thinking is frequently described in the cognitive-therapy literature. In many ways, this model is similar to the models of Salzman (1979) and Mallinger (1984). Here, however, instead of emphasizing the need for control, what is emphasized is perfectionism and a need for certainty (see Straus, 1948). For Salzman (1979) and Mallinger (1984), perfectionism and the need for certainty are products of a need for control.

More recently, Freeston and colleagues (Freeston & Ladouceur, 1997; Freeston, Rheaume, & Ladouceur, 1996) suggested that perfectionism is one of five types of faulty beliefs and appraisals of intrusive thoughts that characterize OCD. Similar to Guidano and Liotti (1983), Freeston and colleagues suggested that perfectionistic appraisals are based on the notion that a perfect state is possible. Like other theorists, they observe that the need for certainty, the need to know, and the need for control (especially of thoughts) are the perfectionistic appraisals typically found in OCD.

Other types of OCD symptoms may qualify as perfectionism driven, such as obsessions of symmetry, completeness, and "not just right" phenomena in which things are experienced as somehow not right, as though a mistake has been made but is not apparent (Leckman, Walker, & Goodman, 1994).

This analysis has been expanded by the Obsessive Compulsive Cognitions Working Group (OCCWG, 1997) in an attempt to generate common measuring instruments for obsessive–compulsive thoughts. Using an expert-consensus strategy, the OCCWG identified six domains of obsessional beliefs. One of the domains was perfectionism, defined as "the tendency to believe there is a perfect solution to every problem, that doing something perfectly (i.e., mistake free) is not only possible, but also necessary, and that even minor mistakes will have serious consequences" (p. 678). The OCCWG generated a measure of perfectionism and is currently in the process of examining the reliability and validity of the measure in normal and clinical samples.

The different theories tying perfectionism to OCD share several common themes. The predominant one is that perfectionistic thinking and perfectionistic behavior represent attempts to avoid something unpleasant (i.e., criticism, disaster, uncertainty, or lack of control). Either perfectionism develops in an attempt to avoid uncertainty or in an attempt to establish control, or perfectionism is at the core and produces uncertainty and a desire for control over one's environment. In either case, the major feature is the avoidance of mistakes rather than the achievement of goals. This finding is consistent with recent research suggesting that Concern Over Mistakes is the main dimension of perfectionism (Frost et al., 1990).

Until recently, most of the literature on this topic has consisted of clinical observations of perfectionistic tendencies. Unfortunately, perfectionism has not been well defined or adequately measured in these studies, but they form a consistent pattern of clinical evidence for a connection between perfectionism and OCD. Both Adams (1973) and Rasmussen and Tsuang (1986) reported perfectionistic characteristics in large numbers of patients with OCD. Other authors have described the perfectionistic traits of individual patients (Anonymous & Tiller, 1989). Those descriptions have mirrored the theoretical accounts of OCD-related perfectionism. Patients with OCD see imperfections everywhere, and they cope with the accompanying anxiety through compulsive behavior. The patients described in these reports engaged in excessive striving to meet other people's standards and, when they could not be met, they experienced feelings of failure.

Several other clinical studies suggested that families of patients with OCD are characterized by perfectionism. Examining the case notes of a set of 44 adolescent patients with OCD, Allsopp and Verduyn (1990) found that perfectionism and precision were the characteristics noted most frequently in the patients' parents. Honjo, Hirano, and Murase (1989) conducted a chart review of children with OCD symptoms. Perfectionism and other obsessive–compulsive personality disorder (OCPD) characteristics were evident in more than half of the parents. Lo (1967) found that 29% of parents of patients with OCD had parents who were perfectionistic, whereas only 5% of the parents of people with schizophrenia did. Hoover and Insel (1984) studied a large number of relatives of patients with OCD and concluded that OCD families are solitary and isolated and emphasize cleanliness and perfectionism. Balslev-Olesen and Geert-Jorgensen (1959) reported that nearly half of their sample of 62 people with obsessive–compulsive neuroticism had perfectionistic parents or siblings. Nearly half of the patients were reported to have had a "perfectionistic or rigorous" upbringing. Their report suggested that perfectionistic upbringing may be especially prevalent among male patients with OCD. Clark and Bolton (1985) found that patients with OCD perceive greater demands from their parents. Rasmussen and Eisen (1989) described perfectionism as one of eight developmental antecedents of OCD.

Lo (1967) developed a model to explain the relationship between perfectionistic parents and the emergence of OCD symptoms in their children on the basis of his examination of a series of patients with OCD and their parents. Extrapolating from his findings, he contended that perfectionism (defined as "demanding of oneself and others a higher quality of performance than is required by the situation"; Hollender, 1965, p. 94) leads to compulsive symptoms in the following way. Perfectionistic parents expect a high standard of performance, which the child feels pressured to meet. The child, needing acceptance from parents and needing to feel secure, will strive to meet those standards. With time, the need to please parents changes, and the child internalizes this striving. The child must strive to meet his or her own standards of performance; the perfectionistic standards get higher and higher, and the child becomes anxious when they are not maintained. Perfectionism turns into compulsive symptoms when extra demands are placed on the maturing child. Although the details of how this process works are not spelled out by Lo, it is consistent with other suggestions that the development of OCD is associated with demanding and critical parents (see Rachman & Hodgson, 1980) and is part of a process in which perfectionism plays a role (Pitman, 1987).

In addition to these clinical observations, some empirical research has examined the link between perfectionism and OCD, but most of it has used samples of subclinical participants. Using nonclinical participants, Ferrari (1995) found perfectionism scores, as measured by the Perfectionism Cognitions Inventory (PCI; Flett, Hewitt, Blankstein, & Gray, 1998), to be positively correlated with the Lynfield Obsessive–Compulsive Questionnaire (LOCQ; Allen & Turner, 1975). Similarly, Frost et al. (1990) found significant correlations among most of the subscales of the Frost MPS, the Maudsley Obsessive–Compulsive Inventory (MOCI; Rachman & Hodgson, 1980), and the Everyday Checking Behavior Scale (Sher, Frost, & Otto, 1983) among college women. Concern Over Mistakes and Doubts About Actions were the subscales most closely associated with the OCD measures. Rheaume, Freeston, Dugas, Letarte, and Ladouceur (1995), using the Padua Inventory (Sanavio, 1988) and the Frost MPS among college students, likewise found that Concern Over Mistakes and Doubts About Actions were correlated with OCD symptoms. Personal Standards had a small correlation with OCD symptoms, whereas Parental Criticism and

Parental Expectations were not correlated. Of note in this study was the finding that perfectionism accounted for a significant proportion of the variance in OCD scores even after the influence of "responsibility" was controlled.

Frost, Steketee, Cohn, and Griess (1994) identified people with sub-clinical compulsiveness as those who had high scores on two of three screening measures: the MOCI, the Compulsive Activity Checklist—Revised (Steketee & Freund, 1993), and the Obsessive Thoughts Checklist (Bouvard, Mollard, Cottraux, & Guerin, 1989). In both undergraduate and graduate student samples, participants who were subclinically compulsive scored higher than their noncompulsive counterparts on Concern Over Mistakes, Personal Standards, and Doubts About Actions. Parental Criticism and Parental Expectation scores were higher for subclinical obsessive–compulsive participants in the undergraduate sample only. Some evidence suggested that parents of subclinical compulsive participants had more perfectionistic traits, especially for fathers (Frost et al., 1994).

Furthermore, several studies have reported associations between perfectionism and specific obsessive–compulsive symptoms (i.e., washing, checking, and hoarding). Tallis (1996) suggested that a specific form of washing compulsion has at its core a type of perfectionism. For such patients, the washing is not to remove the contamination but to achieve a perfect state of cleanliness in either one's self or one's possessions. Ferrari (1995) found no relationship, however, between frequency of perfectionistic cognitions and compulsive washing behavior. He did find that compulsive checking was associated with perfectionistic cognitions. Gershuny and Sher (1995) also found higher perfectionism scores among a group of non-clinical compulsive checkers than among noncheckers. They hypothesized that perfectionism leads some people to try to exert control over events through checking rituals. This hypothesis is similar to Salzman's (1979) theorizing about the relationship between perfectionism and control, although Salzman indicated that the need for control leads to perfectionism rather than vice versa.

In our research, we have found that most of the dimensions of perfectionism, especially Concern Over Mistakes and Doubts About Actions, are correlated with compulsive hoarding. Among college students, community samples, and people with problem hoarding, those dimensions of perfectionism were associated with hoarding symptoms (Frost & Gross, 1993). Those dimensions also have been associated with compulsive indecisiveness (Frost & Shows, 1993; Gayton, Clavin, Clavin, & Broida, 1994). Ferrari (1995), however, failed to find a correlation between indecisiveness and the frequency of perfectionistic cognitions among college students.

Despite the varied data indicating a relationship between perfectionism and subclinical obsessive–compulsive symptomatology, relatively little empirical research compares patients with OCD with nonclinical control participants. Ferrari (1995) was the first to examine empirically the relationship between perfectionism and OCD in a clinical population. This study used the PCI as a measure of perfectionism. The PCI was created as a measure of the frequency of perfectionistic thoughts rather than as a measure of perfectionistic traits, as is the case with the more widely used measures of perfectionism. He reported a significant correlation between the PCI and the LOCQ and the Decisional Procrastination Scale (Mann, 1982) among a group of patients with OCD symptoms, although it was not entirely clear whether those patients had OCD or OCPD. Ferrari (1995) also found that this clinical sample of patients with OCD had significantly higher scores on the PCI than two nonclinical college student samples did.

Frost and Steketee (1997) compared Frost MPS scores of 34 patients diagnosed with OCD, 14 patients diagnosed with panic disorder with agoraphobia, and 35 community control participants. Patients with OCD differed from the community control participants on total perfectionism, Concern Over Mistakes, and Doubts About Actions. The group that had panic disorder with agoraphobia, however, also had higher scores than community control participants on total perfectionism and Concern Over Mistakes, and the group did not differ from patients with OCD on those dimensions. Patients with OCD had higher Doubts About Actions scores than panic-disorder patients did with panic disorder. Together, the studies suggest that perfectionism, particularly Concern Over Mistakes and Doubts About Actions, is elevated among patients with OCD. Antony et al. (1998) also found elevated Frost MPS dimensions among patients with OCD, panic disorder, and social phobia; the patients had relatively few differences among them.

The findings of Frost and Steketee (1997) and Antony et al. (1998) raise a question about the specificity of the relationship between perfectionism and OCD, however. Perfectionism scores appear to be elevated not only in patients with OCD but also in patients with panic disorder (Frost & Steketee, 1997). Findings from the Juster et al. (1996) study suggest that perfectionism is elevated among patients with social phobia as well (see Alden et al., chapter 15, this volume). It is possible that certain features of perfectionism may distinguish patients with OCD from patients with other anxiety disorders. Doubts About Actions scores distinguished patients with OCD from patients with panic disorder in the Frost and Steketee (1997) study, and the scores of the patients with OCD on that dimension were higher than those Juster et al. (1996) reported for patients with social phobia. Further research is needed to determine what dimensions might differentiate OCD from other anxiety disorders. Rheaume et al. (1995) suggested that it might be the belief that perfection is possible. Another possibility is what some OCD theorists have called not just right experiences (Leckman, Walker, & Goodman, 1994). Ongoing data collection by the OCCWG that compares patients with OCD with patients with other anxiety disorders on a newly developed measure of perfectionistic beliefs thought to be related to OCD may provide much-needed information about the features of perfectionism that are specific to OCD.

Conclusions and Future Directions

Many lines of empirical data are converging indicating that the maladaptive evaluation aspects of perfectionism are associated with anxiety. First,

Concern Over Mistakes, Doubts About Actions, and Socially Prescribed Perfectionism typically are correlated with measures of trait anxiety. Those dimensions of perfectionism also are associated with daily hassles. Second, perfectionists have a tendency to interpret daily life events as more threatening or stressful than do nonperfectionists. Third, people who are high in maladaptive evaluation aspects of perfectionism respond to potentially evaluative tasks with greater distress and anxiety. Those affective responses are accompanied by a characteristic cognitive pattern of interpreting good task performance as being important and pressuring oneself with personal imperatives or should statements. Finally, in addition to the anecdotal clinical evidence that suggests a link between perfectionism and the development of OCD, studies using both clinical and nonclinical samples have provided evidence that the maladaptive evaluation concern aspects of perfectionism are associated with OCD symptomatology.

Despite the research data, many questions concerning the relationship of perfectionism to anxiety have yet to be fully addressed. First, it is unclear how (or whether) the two constructs are causally related. It may be that perfectionism serves as a risk factor for the later development of anxiety or anxiety disorders. Conversely, people may develop perfectionistic tendencies in response to anxiety as a means of controlling it or coping with it. Finally, it is equally plausible that a third variable (e.g., depression) accounts for the relationship between the two phenomena.

The above possibilities raise many important conceptual problems. First, although perfectionism often is considered an enduring cognitive or personality style, no longitudinal research has studied its course over the life span or under what conditions it will fluctuate. It also is unclear how its fluctuations are related to the development of the various types of psychopathology, including anxiety. Certain developmental milestones (e.g., becoming a new parent) or treatment interventions (e.g., cognitive therapy) may change perfectionistic thinking. Understanding how perfectionism changes with age and circumstance may provide clues for how it develops.

Recent treatment outcome data suggest that perfectionism may need to be targeted separately from other foci of treatment (e.g., depression and eating-disordered behavior) for improvement to occur. Srinivasagam et al. (1995) found that women who were judged to be recovered from anorexia still had significantly higher Frost MPS scores than a comparison group of normal women. Additionally, Blatt, Quinlan, Pilkonis, and Shea (1995) reported that high perfectionism scores were associated with poor outcome across all four treatment conditions of the National Institute of Mental Health Treatment of Depression Collaborative Research Program. Although some preliminary data indicate that intervention strategies specifically targeting perfectionistic tendencies may be useful in ameliorating this problem (e.g., Broday, 1989; Ferguson & Rodway, 1994), none of the existing studies of this kind have been controlled clinical trials.

Finally, the research data on the relationship of perfectionism to anxiety have provided little support for a unique relationship between the two constructs. Specifically, it seems that the maladaptive evaluation aspects of perfectionism are associated with negative affectivity rather than anxiety per se. Perfectionism also appears to be significantly elevated in people experiencing clinical levels of emotional distress. For example, little evidence indicates that anxiety disorders can be differentiated from other types of psychopathology on the basis of perfectionism scores. Similarly, few studies have found that particular dimensions of perfectionism are uniquely related to specific anxiety disorders. Indeed, evidence indicates that the maladaptive evaluation concern aspects of perfectionism are associated with OCD, social phobia, and panic disorder (Frost & Steketee, 1997; Juster et al., 1996). Other evidence suggests that perfectionism may play a role in posttraumatic stress disorder (Samolewicz et al., 1996), excessive worry (Van Cleve et al., 1997) and, perhaps, generalized anxiety disorder. Research on perfectionism in those disorders is much needed.

The little evidence that does suggest a unique relationship between perfectionism and anxiety appears to center on studies that have specifically examined social anxiety or social phobia (e.g., Antony et al., 1998; Juster et al., 1996). Additionally, studies inducing social evaluative threat have found reliable and differential affective and cognitive responses of perfectionists compared with nonperfectionists.

Note that self-consciousness and fear of negative evaluation are cardinal features of the process of social anxiety and, at excessive levels, are characteristic of the diagnosis of social phobia. Given that Concerns Over Mistakes and Evaluative Preoccupation also are defining features of the pathological aspects of perfectionism, it is not surprising that social anxiety and social phobia may be most strongly associated with perfectionistic tendencies. The exact nature of those social concerns needs further exploration. That is, perfectionists are not any more concerned than nonperfectionists that their mistakes will cause harm to others.

Several studies have suggested that perfectionists ruminate about mistakes long after they are over (DiBartolo et al., 1998; Frost et al., 1997). Further research on the nature of this rumination is needed. Understanding the course of rumination and what events interrupt it will be important for the development of treatments for perfectionism.

In conclusion, the research to date suggests an association between perfectionism and anxiety. Further empirical work needs to focus on how the two constructs are causally related, whether specific dimensions of perfectionism are associated with anxiety or anxiety disorders, and how we can best provide adequate interventions to lessen the negative effects of perfectionism. Only through such research will we be able to develop clinical innovations that will have an impact on the lives of people who struggle with their perfectionism and concomitant emotional distress.

References

Adams, P. (1973). *Obsessive children*. New York: Brunner/Mazel.

Alden, L. E., Bieling, P., & Wallace, S. T. (1994). Perfectionism in an interpersonal context:

A self-regulation analysis of dysphoria and social anxiety. *Cognitive Therapy and Research, 18,* 297–316.

Allen, J. J., & Turner, G. S. (1975). The Lynfield Obsessive–Compulsive Questionnaire. *Scottish Medical Journal, 20,* 21–24.

Allsopp, M., & Verduyn, C. (1990). Adolescents with obsessive–compulsive disorder: A case note review of consecutive patients referred to a provincial regional adolescent unit. *Journal of Adolescence, 13,* 157–169.

Anonymous, & Tiller, J. (1989). Obsessive–compulsive disorder: A sufferer's viewpoint. *Australian and New Zealand Journal of Psychiatry, 23,* 279–281.

Antony, M. M., Purdon, C. L., Huta, V., & Swinson, R. P. (1998). Dimensions of perfectionism across the anxiety disorders. *Behaviour Research and Therapy, 36,* 1143–1154.

Balslev-Olesen, T., & Geert-Jorgensen, E. (1959). The prognosis of obsessive compulsive neurosis. *Acta Psychiatrica et Neurologica Scandinavica, 136,* 232–291.

Bastiani, A. M., Rao, R., Weltzin, T. E., & Kaye, W. H. (1995). Perfectionism in anorexia nervosa. *International Journal of Eating Disorders, 17,* 147–152.

Beck, A. T., Emery, G., & Greenberg, R. (1985). *Anxiety disorders and phobias: A cognitive perspective.* New York: Basic Books.

Beck, A. T., Epstein, N. A., Brown, G., & Steer, R. A. (1988). An inventory for measuring clinical anxiety: Psychometric properties. *Journal of Consulting and Clinical Psychology, 56,* 893–989.

Beck, A. T., Ward, C. H., Mendelson, M., Mock, J., & Erbaugh, J. (1961). An inventory for measuring depression. *Archives of General Psychiatry, 4,* 561–571.

Blankstein, K. R., Flett, G. L., Hewitt, P. L., & Eng, A. (1993). Dimensions of perfectionism and irrational fears: An examination with the Fear Survey Schedule. *Personality and Individual Differences, 15,* 323–328.

Blatt, S. J. (1995). The destructiveness of perfectionism: Implications for the treatment of depression. *American Psychologist, 50,* 1003–1020.

Blatt, S. J., Quinlan, D. M., Pilkonis, P. A., & Shea, M. T. (1995). Impact of perfectionism and need for approval on the brief treatment of depression: The National Institute of Mental Health Treatment of Depression Collaborative Research Program revisited. *Journal of Consulting and Clinical Psychology, 63,* 125–132.

Boice, R. (1983). Observational skills. *Psychological Bulletin, 93,* 3–29.

Borkovec, T. (1994). The nature, functions, and origins of worry. In G. C. L. Davey & F. Tallis (Eds.), *Worrying: Perspectives on theory, assessment, and treatment* (pp. 5–33). New York: Wiley.

Bouvard, M., Mollard, E., Cottraux, J., & Guerin, J. (1989). Etude preliminaire d'une liste de pensees obsedantes. *L'Encephale, XV,* 351–354.

Broday, S. F. (1989). A short-term group for perfectionists. *Journal of College Student Development, 30,* 183–184.

Brown, E. J., Makris, G. S., Juster, H. R., Leung, A. W., Heimberg, R. G., & Frost, R. O. (1999). Relationship of perfectionism to affect, expectations, and attributions and performance in the classroom. *Journal of Social and Clinical Psychology, 18,* 98–120.

Burns, D. (1980). The perfectionist's script for self-defeat. *Psychology Today, November,* 34–52.

Christensen, B. J., Danko, G. P., & Johnson, R. (1993). Neuroticism and the belief that one is being scrutinized and evaluated by others. *Personality and Individual Differences, 15,* 349–350.

Clark, D., & Bolton, D. (1985). Obsessive compulsive adolescents and their parents: A psychometric study. *Journal of Child Psychology and Psychiatry, 26,* 267–276.

Dean, P. J., Range, L. M., & Goggin, W. C. (1996). The escape theory of suicide in college students: Testing a model that includes perfectionism. *Suicide and Life-Threatening Behaviors, 26,* 181–186.

Deci, E. L., & Ryan, R. M. (1985). *Intrinsic motivation and self-determination in human behavior.* New York: Plenum Press.

Deffenbacher, J., Zwemer, W., Whisman, M. A., Hill, R. W., & Sloan, R. (1986). Irrational beliefs and anxiety. *Cognitive Therapy and Research, 10,* 281–292.

DeLongis, A., Folkman, S., & Lazarus, R. S. (1988). The impact of daily stress on health and mood: Psychological and social resources as mediators. *Journal of Personality and Social Psychology, 54,* 486–495.

Derogatis, L. R., & Mesilaratos, N. (1983). The Brief Symptom Inventory: An introductory report. *Psychological Medicine, 13,* 595–605.

DiBartolo, P. M., Dixon, A., Almodovar, S., & Frost, R. O. (2001). Can cognitive restructuring reduce the disruption associated with perfectionistic concerns? *Behavior Therapy, 32,* 167–184.

Ellis, A. (1962). *Reason and emotion in psychotherapy.* New York: Lyle Stuart.

Endler, N. S., Edwards, J. M., & Vitelli, R. (1991). *Endler Multidimensional Anxiety Scale (EMAS): Manual.* Los Angeles, CA: Western Psychological Services.

Ferguson, K. L., & Rodway, M. R. (1994). Cognitive behavioral treatment of perfectionism: Initial evaluation studies. *Research on Social Work Practice, 4,* 283–308.

Ferrari, J. R. (1995). Perfectionism cognitions with nonclinical and clinical samples. *Journal of Social Behavior and Personality, 10,* 143–156.

Fimian, M. J. (1984). The development of an instrument to measure occupational stress in teachers: The Teacher Stress Inventory. *Journal of Occupational Psychology, 57,* 277–293.

Flett, G. L., Hewitt, P. L., Blankstein, K. R., & Gray, L. (1998). Psychological distress and the frequency of perfectionistic thinking. *Journal of Personality and Social Psychology, 75,* 1363–1381.

Flett, G. L., Hewitt, P. L., Blankstein, K. R., & Mosher, S. W. (1995). Perfectionism, life events, and depressive symptoms: A test of a diathesis–stress model. *Current Psychology, 14,* 112–137.

Flett, G. L., Hewitt, P. L., & DeRosa, T. (1996). Dimensions of perfectionism, psychosocial adjustment, and social skills. *Personality and Individual Differences, 20,* 143–150.

Flett, G. L., Hewitt, P. L., & Dyck, D. G. (1989). Self-oriented perfectionism, neuroticism, and anxiety. *Personality and Individual Differences, 10,* 731–735.

Flett, G. L., Hewitt, P. L., Endler, N. S., & Tassone, C. (1994–1995). Perfectionism and components of state and trait anxiety. *Current Psychology, 13,* 326–350.

Flett, G. L., Hewitt, P. L., & Hallett, C. J. (1995). Perfectionism and job stress in teachers. *Canadian Journal of School Psychology, 11,* 32–42.

Flett, G. L., Sawatzky, D. L., & Hewitt, P. L. (1995). Dimensions of perfectionism and goal commitment: A further comparison of two perfectionism measures. *Journal of Psychopathology and Behavioral Assessment, 17,* 111–124.

Freeston, M. H., & Ladouceur, R. (1997). *The cognitive behavioral treatment of obsessions: A treatment manual.* Quebec, Canada: University of Laval.

Freeston, M. H., Rheaume, J., & Ladouceur, R. (1996). Correcting faulty appraisals of obsessive thoughts. *Behaviour Research and Therapy, 34,* 443–446.

Frost, R. O., & Gross, R. (1993). The hoarding of possessions. *Behaviour Research and Therapy, 31,* 367–381.

Frost, R. O., Heimberg, R. G., Holt, C. S., Mattia, J. I., & Neubauer, A. L. (1993). A comparison of two measures of perfectionism. *Personality and Individual Differences, 14,* 119–126.

Frost, R. O., & Henderson, K. (1991). Perfectionism and reactions to athletic competitions. *Journal of Sport Psychology, 13,* 323–335.

Frost, R. O., & Marten, P. (1990). Perfectionism and evaluative threat. *Cognitive Therapy and Research, 14,* 559–572.

Frost, R. O., Marten, P., Lahart, C., & Rosenblate, R. (1990). The dimensions of perfectionism. *Cognitive Therapy and Research, 14,* 449–468.

Frost, R. O., & Roberts, J. (1997). *Perfectionism and daily hassles among college students.* Unpublished manuscript.

Frost, R. O., & Shows, D. L. (1993). The nature and measurement of compulsive indecisiveness. *Behaviour Research and Therapy, 31,* 683–692.

Frost, R. O., & Steketee, G. (1997). Perfectionism and obsessive compulsive disorder. *Behaviour Research and Therapy, 35,* 291–296.

Frost, R. O., Steketee, G., Cohn, L., & Griess, K. (1994). Personality traits in subclinical and non-obsessive–compulsive volunteers and their parents. *Behaviour Research and Therapy, 32,* 47–56.

Frost, R. O., Trepanier, K. L., Brown, E. J., Heimberg, R. G., Juster, H. R., & Makris, G. S. (1997). Self-monitoring of mistakes among subjects high and low in concern over mistakes. *Cognitive Therapy and Research, 21*, 209–222.

Frost, R. O., Turcotte, T., Heimberg, R. G., & Mattia, J. I. (1995). Reactions to mistakes among subjects high and low in perfectionistic concern over mistakes. *Cognitive Therapy and Research, 19*, 195–205.

Fry, P. S. (1995). Perfectionism, humor, and optimism as moderators of health outcomes and determinants of coping styles of women executives. *Genetic, Social, and General Psychology Monographs, 121*, 211–245.

Garner, D. M., Olmstead, M. P., & Polivy, J. (1983). The Eating Disorder Inventory: A measure of cognitive–behavioral dimensions of anorexia and bulimia. In P. L. Darby, P. E. Garfinkel, D. M. Garner, & D. V. Coscina (Eds.), *Anorexia nervosa: Recent developments in research* (pp. 173–184). New York: Alan R. Liss.

Gayton, W. F., Clavin, R. H., Clavin, S. L., & Broida, J. (1994). Further validation of the indecisiveness scale. *Psychological Reports, 75*, 1631–1634.

Gershuny, B., & Sher, K. (1995). Compulsive checking and anxiety in a nonclinical sample: Differences in cognition, behavior, personality and affect. *Journal of Psychopathology and Behavioral Assessment, 17*, 19–38.

Gould, D., Udry, E., Tuffey, S., & Loehr, J. (1996). Burnout in competitive junior tennis players: I. A quantitative psychological assessment. *Sport Psychologist, 10*, 322–340.

Guidano, V., & Liotti, G. (1983). *Cognitive processes and emotional disorders*. New York: Guilford Press.

Hamachek, D. E. (1978). Psychodynamics of normal and neurotic perfectionism. *Psychology, 15*, 27–33.

Hankin, B. L., Roberts, J., & Gotlib, I. H. (1997). Elevated self-standards and emotional distress during adolescence: Emotional specificity and gender differences. *Cognitive Therapy and Research, 21*, 663–680.

Hewitt, P. L., & Dyck, D. G. (1986). Perfectionism, stress, and vulnerability to depression. *Cognitive Therapy and Research, 10*, 137–142.

Hewitt, P. L., & Flett, G. L. (1991a). Dimensions of perfectionism in unipolar depression. *Journal of Abnormal Psychology, 100*, 98–101.

Hewitt, P. L., & Flett, G. L. (1991b). Perfectionism in the self and social contexts: Conceptualization, assessment, and association with psychopathology. *Journal of Personality and Social Psychology, 60*, 456–470.

Hewitt, P. L., & Flett, G. L. (1993). Dimensions of perfectionism, daily stress, and depression: A test of the specific vulnerability hypothesis. *Journal of Abnormal Psychology, 102*, 58–65.

Hewitt, P. L., Flett, G. L., & Ediger, E. (1996). Perfectionism and depression: Longitudinal assessment of a specific vulnerability hypothesis. *Journal of Abnormal Psychology, 105*, 276–280.

Hewitt, P. L., Flett, G. L., & Weber, C. (1994). Dimensions of perfectionism and suicide ideation. *Cognitive Therapy and Research, 18*, 439–460.

Higgins, E. T. (1987). Self-discrepancy: A theory relating self and affect. *Psychological Review, 94*, 319–340.

Higgins, E. T., Klein, R., & Strauman, T. J. (1985). Self-concept discrepancy theory: A psychological model for distinguishing among different aspects of depression and anxiety. *Social Cognition, 3*, 51–76.

Hollender, M. H. (1965). Perfectionism. *Comprehensive Psychiatry, 6*, 94–103.

Holmes, T., & Rahe, H. (1967). The Social Readjustment Rating Scale. *Journal of Psychosomatic Research, 11*, 213–218.

Honjo, S., Hirano, C., & Murase, S. (1989). Obsessive compulsive symptoms in childhood and adolescence. *Acta Psychiatrica, 80*, 83–91.

Hoover, C. F., & Insel, T. R. (1984). Families of origin in obsessive–compulsive disorder. *The Journal of Nervous and Mental Disease, 172*, 207–215.

Horney, K. (1950). *Neurosis and human growth: The struggle toward self-realization*. New York: Norton.

Joiner, T. E., Jr., & Schmidt, N. B. (1995). Development of perfectionism, life stress, and depressed and anxious symptoms: Prospective support for diathesis stress but not specific vulnerability among male undergraduates. *Journal of Social and Clinical Psychology, 14*, 165–183.

Jones, E. (1918). Anal–erotic character traits. *Journal of Abnormal Psychology, 13*(5), 261–284.

Jones, R. G. (1969). A factorial measure of Ellis' irrational belief systems with personality and maladjustment correlates. *Dissertation Abstracts, 29*, 4379B–4380B. (UMI No. 69-6443)

Juster, H. R., Heimberg, R. G., Frost, R. O., Holt, C. S., Mattia, J. I., & Faccenda, K. (1996). Social phobia and perfectionism. *Personality and Individual Differences, 21*, 403–410.

Kawamura, K. Y., Hunt, S. L., Frost, R. O., & DiBartolo, P. M. (2001). Perfectionism, anxiety, and depression: Are the relationships independent? *Cognitive Therapy and Research, 25*, 291–301.

Larson, D. G., & Chastain, R. L. (1990). Self-concealment: Conceptualization, measurement and health implications. *Journal of Social and Clinical Psychology, 9*, 439–455.

Leckman, J. F., Walker, D., & Goodman, W. (1994). "Just right" perceptions associated with compulsive behavior in Tourette's Syndrome. *American Journal of Psychiatry, 151*, 675–680.

Lo, W. H. (1967). A follow-up study of obsessional neurotics in Hong Kong Chinese. *British Journal of Psychiatry, 113*, 823–832.

Mallinger, A. E. (1984). The obsessive's myth of control. *Journal of the American Academy of Psychoanalysis, 12*, 147–165.

Mallinger, A. E., & DeWyze, J. (1992). *Too perfect: When being in control gets out of control.* New York: Clarkson Potter Club.

Mann, L. (1982). *Decision-making questionnaire.* Unpublished inventory. Flinders University of South Australia, Bedford Park, Australia.

McAndrews, J. F. (1989). Obsessive–compulsive disorder: A behavioral case formulation. *Journal of Behavior Therapy and Experimental Psychiatry, 20*, 311–318.

McAuley, E., & Tammen, V. V. (1989). The effects of subjective and objective competitive outcomes on intrinsic motivation. *Journal of Sport and Exercise Psychology, 11*, 84–93.

McFall, M., & Wollersheim, J. (1979). Obsessive–compulsive neurosis: A cognitive–behavioral formulation and approach to treatment. *Cognitive Therapy and Research, 3*, 333–348.

Meyer, T., Miller, M., Metzger, R. L., & Borkovec, T. (1990). Development and validation of the Penn State Worry Questionnaire. *Behaviour Research and Therapy, 28*, 487–495.

Meyers, A., Cooke, C., Cullen, J., & Liles, L. (1979). Psychological aspects of athletic competition: A replication across sports. *Cognitive Therapy and Research, 3*, 361–366.

Minarik, M. L., & Ahrens, A. (1996). Relations of eating behavior and symptoms of depression and anxiety to the dimensions of perfectionism among undergraduate women. *Cognitive Therapy and Research, 20*, 155–169.

Missildine, W. H. (1963). *Your inner child of the past.* New York: Simon & Schuster.

Mor, S., Day, H. I., Flett, G. L., & Hewitt, P. L. (1995). Perfectionism, control, and components of performance anxiety in professional performers. *Cognitive Therapy and Research, 19*, 207–225.

Obsessive Compulsive Cognitions Working Group. (1997). Cognitive assessment of obsessive compulsive disorder. *Behavior Research and Therapy, 35*, 667–681.

Pacht, A. R. (1984). Reflections on perfection. *American Psychologist, 39*, 386–390.

Pitman, R. (1987). Pierre Janet on obsessive–compulsive disorder (1903): Review and commentary. *Archives of General Psychiatry, 44*, 226–232.

Rachman, S. J., & Hodgson, R. (1980). *Obsessions and compulsions.* Englewood Cliffs, NJ: Prentice-Hall.

Rasmussen, S., & Eisen, J. L. (1989). Clinical features and phenomenology of obsessive compulsive disorder. *Psychiatric Annals, 19*, 67–73.

Rasmussen, S., & Tsuang, M. (1986). Clinical characteristics and family history in DSM-III obsessive–compulsive disorder. *American Journal of Psychiatry, 143*, 317–322.

Rheaume, J., Freeston, M. H., Dugas, M. J., Letarte, H., & Ladouceur, R. (1995). Perfectionism, responsibility, and obsessive–compulsive symptoms. *Behaviour Research and Therapy, 33*, 785–794.

Saddler, C. D., & Buckland, R. L. (1995). The Multidimensional Perfectionism Scale: Correlations with depression in college students with learning disabilities. *Psychological Reports, 77*, 483–490.

Salzman, L. (1979). Psychotherapy of the obsessional. *American Journal of Psychotherapy, 33*, 32–40.

Samolewicz, A., DiBartolo, P. M., & Prins, A. (1996, November). *The measurement of trauma concealment and its relationship to perfectionism.* Paper presented at the International Society of Traumatic Stress Studies, San Francisco.

Sanavio, E. (1988). Obsessions and compulsions: The Padua inventory. *Behaviour Research and Therapy, 26*, 169–177.

Sarason, I. G., Johnson, J. H., & Siegel, J. M. (1978). Assessing the impact of life changes: Development of the Life Experiences Survey. *Journal of Consulting and Clinical Psychology, 46*, 932–946.

Saxe, L. L., & Abramson, L. Y. (1987). *The Negative Life Events Questionnaire: Reliability and validity.* Unpublished manuscript.

Scott, L., & O'Hara, M. W. (1993). Self-discrepancies in clinically anxious and depressed university students. *Journal of Abnormal Psychology, 102*, 282–287.

Sher, K., Frost, R. O., & Otto, R. (1983). Cognitive-deficits in compulsive checkers: An exploratory study. *Behaviour Research and Therapy, 21*, 357–363.

Spielberger, C. D., Gorsuch, R. L., & Lushene, R. E. (1970). *Manual for the State–Trait Anxiety Inventory.* Palo Alto, CA: Consulting Psychologists Press.

Srinivasagam, N. M., Kaye, W. H., Plotnicov, K. H., Greeno, C., Weltzin, T. E., & Rao, R. (1995). Persistent perfectionism, symmetry, and exactness after long-term recovery from anorexia nervosa. *American Journal of Psychiatry, 152*, 1630–1634.

Steketee, G., & Freund, B. (1993). Compulsive Activity Checklist (CAC): Further psychometric analyses and revision. *Behavioural Psychotherapy, 21,* 13–25.

Strauman, T. J. (1989). Self-discrepancies in clinical depression and social phobia: Cognitive structures that underlie emotional disorders? *Journal of Abnormal Psychology, 101*, 87–95.

Strauman, T. J., & Higgins, E. T. (1987). Automatic activation of self-discrepancies and emotional syndromes: When cognitive structures influence affect. *Journal of Personality and Social Psychology, 53*, 1004–1014.

Straus, E. W. (1948). On obsession: A clinical and methodological study. *Nervous and Mental Disease Monograph, 73,* 26–51.

Tallis, F. (1996). Compulsive washing in the absence of phobic and illness anxiety. *Behaviour Research and Therapy, 34*, 361–362.

Tallis, F., Davey, G. C. L., & Capuzzo, N. (1994). The phenomenology of nonpathological worry: A preliminary investigation. In G. C. L. Davey & F. Tallis (Eds.), *Worrying: Perspectives on theory, assessment and treatment* (pp. 61–90). New York: Wiley.

Terry-Short, L. A., Owens, R. G., Slade, P. D., & Dewey, M. E. (1995). Positive and negative perfectionism. *Personality and Individual Differences, 18*, 663–668.

Van Cleve, K., Frost, R. O., & DiBartolo, P. M. (1997). *Perfectionism and perceived self-competence in college students.* Unpublished manuscript.

Watson, D., Clark, L. A., & Tellegen, A. (1988). Development and validation of brief measures of positive and negative affect: The PANAS scales. *Journal of Personality and Social Psychology, 54*, 1063–1070.

Weissman, A. N. (1979). The Dysfunctional Attitudes Scale: A validation study. Unpublished dissertation, University of Pennsylvania. *Dissertation Abstracts International, 40*, 1389–1390.

Westra, H. A., & Kuiper, N. A. (1996). Communality and specificity of dysfunctional cognitions, and the prediction of four different forms of psychological maladjustment. *Personality and Individual Differences, 20*, 575–588.

Wolpe, J., & Lang, P. J. (1964). Fear Survey Schedule for use in behavior therapy. *Behaviour Research and Therapy, 9*, 401–410.

Perfectionism in the Context of Social Fears: Toward a Two-Component Model

Lynn E. Alden, Andrew G. Ryder, and Tanna M. B. Mellings

People with social anxiety are their own worst critics. They closely monitor their social behavior, take note of every mistake or small disfluency, and berate themselves for their inadequacies. Because they believe that others will share their negative views, they anticipate rejection, pity—even disgust—from those with whom they interact. When socially anxious patients enter therapy, they typically begin with a litany of their social inadequacies rather than an expression of their loneliness and despair, which are more likely to be the impetus for seeking treatment.

On closer observation, the socially anxious person's self-derogation often has a curious quality—it is excessive when compared with the person's abilities and social experiences. Moreover, self-criticism can occur even when the person handled a social situation well and others responded positively. Observations of this sort have led many writers to speculate that socially anxious people may be perfectionists, whose high performance standards and concern with mistakes contribute to their social distress and self-criticism. Exploring and expanding on this hypothesis is the central focus of this chapter. The research literature on social anxiety and perfectionism contains some puzzling inconsistencies; at the end of the chapter, we propose a two-component model that we believe might resolve those issues. We begin by describing the various conditions in which social evaluative fears are prominent features.

Social Evaluative Anxiety

Although social anxiety and avoidance play a role in many clinical conditions, they are definitive characteristics of two disorders included in the fourth edition of the *Diagnostic and Statistical Manual of Mental Disorders* (*DSM-IV*; American Psychiatric Association, 1994): social phobia and avoidant personality disorder. *Social phobia* is defined as a "marked and persistent fear of one or more social or performance situations in which

. . . the individual fears that he or she will act in a way that will be humiliating or embarrassing" (p. 416). The situations that elicit social anxiety are divided into those that involve public performance, such as eating, drinking, writing, or speaking in public, and those that involve social interaction, such as initiating conversations, attending parties, or dating (e.g., Habke, Hewitt, Norton, & Asmundson, 1997). The phobic person's fears may be confined to only one or two situations or may be generalized across most social situations. This syndrome is now believed to be one of the more common psychiatric conditions, with a lifetime prevalence rate estimated to be as high as 13% of the general population.

Avoidant personality disorder (APD) is defined as "a pervasive pattern of social inhibition, feelings of inadequacy, and hypersensitivity to negative evaluation that begins by early adulthood and is present in a variety of contexts" (American Psychiatric Association, 1994, p. 662). Clinical depictions of APD emphasize the characterological nature of this condition, namely, its early onset, stability, and pervasiveness. Although personality types characterized by social sensitivity and withdrawal appear in early clinical descriptions of personality disorders (e.g., Kretschmer, 1925), APD was first included in the *DSM* system in 1980. The current conceptualization of APD had its origins in Millon's (1981) biosocial learning theory, which proposed that the avoidant pattern develops when a child with a fearful or anxious temperament is exposed to early social experiences characterized by persistent deprecation, rejection, and humiliation. APD is a common comorbid personality condition among patients who experience mood disorders and anxiety disorders. The lifetime prevalence rate for APD is estimated at 1% of the general population, and APD is found in approximately 10% of outpatients seeking psychiatric treatment (American Psychiatric Association, 1994).

Even this cursory overview reveals the similarity between social phobia and APD. Although the two disorders arose from different clinical traditions—social phobia from anxiety disorders and APD from the context of personality theories—empirical studies indicate that considerable overlap exists between the two. Nearly all patients with APD also meet diagnostic criteria for generalized social phobia (GSP), and approximately 44% of patients with GSP also meet criteria for APD (Brown, Heimberg, & Juster, 1995). The high rate of comorbidity and similarity in clinical presentation and treatment response indicate that APD and GSP are either different ways to conceptualize the same underlying condition or represent different points along a continuum of symptom severity.

Concern with social evaluation also is believed to contribute to several anxiety-related problems that arise in work situations, specifically, procrastination and professional performance fears. Procrastination involves the prospect of indirect social evaluation. As with socially anxious people, procrastinators have been shown to fear negative social evaluation and to engage in self-monitoring and self-criticism (Ferrari, 1991, 1992). Although procrastination involves factors in addition to concern with negative evaluation (e.g., negativism), some procrastination studies are relevant to our discussion of perfectionism and social anxiety. Some performing artists, such as professional musicians and actors, experience crippling fears of evaluation when faced with the prospect of performing in public. From a diagnostic standpoint, performance anxiety of this type is considered a type of circumscribed social phobia; however, enough distinct features warrant separate consideration. For one thing, people who make their living as performing artists face more overt pressures for perfection than does the average person who engages in a casual social interaction (Dews & Williams, 1989). After all, few job opportunities exist for a pianist who consistently misses notes or an actor who blows his or her lines.

Social anxiety and avoidance also have been studied in nonclinical populations. In the clinical literature, the term *socially anxious* is used to describe people with chronic social anxiety and is often used to denote a subclinical variant of social phobia or APD. Developmental psychologists use the term *social timidity*, or *reticence*, to describe an innate tendency toward autonomic hypersensitivity in response to changes in the environment (see, e.g., Jerome Kagan's classic studies of social reticence in children; Kagan, Reznick, & Snidman, 1988). Personality and social psychologists study shyness, a personality trait that predisposes people toward anxiety and reticence in social situations (e.g., Briggs, Cheek, & Jones, 1986). Although the way in which the various constructs are conceptualized and the measures used to assess them vary, more similarities than differences can be found across these research domains (e.g., Briggs & Smith, 1986).

We now turn to an examination of the role of perfectionism in social phobia, APD, and social anxiety. For efficiency, we use the term *socially anxious* to refer to all of those groups unless further delineation is necessary. We begin with a discussion of the nature of perfectionism and then outline theoretical models of social anxiety that refer to perfectionism or related constructs. Next, we review empirical literature to see what is known concerning the link between social anxiety and perfectionism, noting inconsistencies and unresolved issues in existing studies. Finally, we consider a model of perfectionism that we believe might reconcile some of those inconsistencies.

Perfectionism

The literature most commonly defines *perfectionism* as the tendency to establish excessively high personal standards of performance (Burns, 1980; Hamachek, 1978; Hollender, 1965; Pacht, 1984). Recent writings place equal emphasis on cognitive and emotional factors that can accompany stringent standards, such as sensitivity to mistakes and the tendency to blame or criticize (e.g., Frost, Marten, Lahart, & Rosenblate, 1990; Hewitt & Flett, 1991). In the context of social anxiety, the most frequently used perfectionism measures are the Frost Multidimensional Perfectionism Scale (MPS) and the Hewitt and Flett MPS (Frost et al., 1990; Hewitt & Flett, 1991). Because the measures have been described elsewhere in this volume, we will outline them only briefly here.

Frost and colleagues proposed that perfectionism consists of five core features: (a) high personal standards, (b) concern over mistakes, (c) doubt about the quality of one's performance, (d) perceptions of parental expectations, and (e) perceptions of parental criticism (Frost et al., 1990). Their MPS was developed to tap those factors. Although the dimensions can be combined into a total perfectionism score, results of a recent factor-analytic study indicated that the five dimensions fall into two clusters: maladaptive evaluation concerns, as reflected in the Concern Over Mistakes, Doubts About Actions and, to a lesser extent, Parental Criticism subscales, and positive striving, as reflected in the Personal Standards subscale (Frost, Heimberg, Holt, Mattia, & Neubauer, 1993). It is notable that the subscales reflecting maladaptive evaluation concerns are consistently associated with psychopathology (e.g., Antony, Purdon, Huta, & Swinson, 1998). Personal Standards, however, appears to be more complex, conceptually: In some situations, the scale appears to reflect positive achievement striving, whereas in others it is associated with psychopathology (Frost et al., 1990).

Hewitt and Flett (1991) proposed that perfectionism has both personal and social components. They distinguished three components of perfectionism, which are based on the person who establishes the perfectionistic standards or is the target of them. *Self-oriented perfectionism* involves self-directed perfectionistic standards, *other-oriented perfectionism* involves having unrealistic standards for significant others, and *socially prescribed perfectionism* involves a person's belief that others exert pressure on him or her to be perfect. The three dimensions are largely independent and display distinct patterns of correlations with various types of psychopathology. High scores on the Socially Prescribed Perfectionism (SPP) subscale of the Hewitt and Flett MPS have been shown to be associated with a wide range of psychological disorders, including social anxiety, whereas the Self-Oriented Perfectionism (SOP) and Other-Oriented Perfectionism (OOP) subscales display greater specificity (e.g., Antony et al., 1998; Hewitt & Flett, 1991; Hewitt, Flett, Turnbull-Donovan, & Mikail, 1991).

Theoretical Perspectives

Four sets of writers allude to perfectionism or similar constructs in the context of social anxiety. Each provides a different perspective on this issue and uses somewhat different terminology, including high standards (e.g., Clark & Wells, 1995; Leary & Kowalski, 1995), rigid social rules (Beck & Emery, 1985), and perfectionistic beliefs (e.g., Heimberg & Becker, in press). We discuss each approach in turn.

In their self-presentational model, Schlenker and Leary (1982) proposed that social anxiety arises when people doubt their ability to make the social impression they desire to give. Initially developed to explain why people experience state social anxiety, this model has now been extended to chronic social anxiety and social phobia (Arkin, Lake, & Baumgardner, 1986; Leary & Kowalski, 1995). These writers view social anxiety as a secondary emotion—one that arises from situations or characteristics that heighten people's self-presentation concerns or lower their expectations of success—and devote particular attention to personality characteristics, such as excessive need for social approval, low social skills, and public self-consciousness, which are believed to lead to self-presentational concerns and, ultimately, to social anxiety. One such personality factor is the tendency to establish excessively high and rigid standards for evaluating social performance. "People whose standards for judging their social performances and others' reactions to them are too high believe that they consistently fail to make a satisfactory impression on others, even though, by most people's standards, they come across fine" (Leary, 1987, p. 133). It is notable that Leary identified high standards as only one of many individual differences that contribute to self-presentational doubts. One implication of this point is that high standards and social anxiety are not inevitably linked. Thus, one would expect to find high standards among only a subset of people who are socially anxious or have a social phobia.

Clark and Wells (1995) included passing reference to high standards in their cognitive model of social phobia, which asserts that people with social phobia hold negative assumptions that lead them to anticipate that they will behave in an inept and unacceptable fashion. Some of those assumptions include the notion of high standards (e.g., "I must not show any signs of weakness" and "I must not let anyone see I am anxious"). This cognitive set automatically activates an "anxiety program" designed to protect the person from harm. One aspect of this program is the tendency of socially anxious people to focus attention on detailed monitoring of themselves; another is the adoption of "safety behaviors" to prevent negative outcomes. Thus, phobic patients might grip a glass tightly to stop their hands from shaking. Unfortunately, however, both processes increase the salience of interoceptive anxiety-related cues and the likelihood that the feared outcome will actually occur (e.g., the person's hand trembles more). In this model, high standards are clearly secondary to other processes, such as self-focused attention, judgmental biases, and the adoption of safety behaviors, factors purported to directly affect social anxiety.

Standards are more extensively dealt with in Beck and Emery's (1985) schematic-processing model of social evaluative anxiety. According to this theory, social anxiety depends on the person's cognitive appraisal of a social situation as potentially dangerous. In socially anxious patients, schemata used for processing social danger are hypervalent and readily activated by social scrutiny. Embedded in the schemata are assumptions about the world and rules that guide one's behavior in response to it (e.g., "Other people are evaluators who look for weakness and pounce on every flaw" and "Nothing I can do will be good enough to live up to the expectations or demands of others"). The element of the Beck–Emery model most closely related to perfectionism is the socially anxious person's putative belief that social situations are governed by rigid rules. The anxious person believes that "he must adhere to stringent rules regarding the volume and tone of his voice, his articulateness, and speed of speaking, his fluency and control of speech. . . . Any departure from the rules may make him susceptible to disapproval and devaluation" (p. 149). Schematic activation results in preferential processing of negative information about the self and the social situation, which in turn leads to misinterpretations of social events. Thus, anxious people perceive themselves and their social encounters to be more negative than they actually are. Schematic activation also leads to behavioral inhibition and heightened anxiety, which interfere with effective social performance. Moreover, anxiety is itself interpreted as a sign of not meeting the social rules, which further increases the person's sense of vulnerability and so on, in a vicious cognitive–emotional cycle. In this model, belief in rigid social rules is an integral component of social evaluative fears.

In a similar vein, Heimberg and his colleagues proposed that perfectionistic beliefs are key features of social phobia (e.g., Heimberg & Becker, in press; Juster et al., 1996). Heimberg suggested that an interaction of genetic susceptibility and early experience leads to the development of three core beliefs: that social situations are potentially dangerous, that negative outcomes can be averted only by performing perfectly, and that the phobic person is not capable of achieving the necessary standard of behavior (e.g., Juster et al., 1996). The person's concern with mistakes is believed to lead to excessive self-evaluation and to an exaggeration of the importance of any mistakes that do occur, even if such mistakes are within normal limits. Essentially the person equates mistakes with total failure and assumes that others do as well. Ongoing self-evaluation and preoccupation with mistakes lead to increased anxiety and pressure to make up for the mistakes that do occur. This process also is believed to distract attention from the social task and increase the likelihood of making further mistakes. Heimberg's theory is unique in its emphasis on the developmental roots of perfectionistic beliefs in parental standards and criticism (see Bruch, Heimberg, Berger, & Collins, 1989). Indeed, the anxious person's strivings for perfection are painted as strategies designed to compensate for an internalized image of oneself as inadequate.

The above theories have obvious similarities. In all four, the socially anxious person is concerned about falling short of some idealized standard of evaluation and that concern contributes to the person's discomfort in social interactions. The theories also differ, however. For instance, the notion of excessively high standards is of secondary importance in the Clark–Wells and Leary models, whereas rigid rules and perfectionistic beliefs are central features of both the Beck–Emery and Heimberg models.

More important, however, are differences in the way these writers envision the basic nature of perfectionistic tendencies. Leary emphasized high standards themselves, whereas the Beck–Emery and Heimberg models place equal emphasis on the person's concern about the social consequences of mistakes. As we will see, the same two themes—high standards and concern with mistakes—permeate the empirical literature. A second, although less explicit, distinction is that of the relative roles of self and others' standards. Leary appeared to talk about the person's high standards for his or her own behavior, whereas Beck and Emery's and Heimberg's emphasis on negative responses from others reflects an inter-

personal interpretation of perfectionism, although not to the extent articulated in Hewitt and Flett's framework. A final difference concerns the
enmeshment of perfectionistic standards, or rigid rules, and social anxiety.
In the Leary system, the two factors have a degree of independence: Not
all socially anxious people have high standards, and presumably not
everyone with high standards becomes socially anxious. In both the Beck–
Emery and Heimberg models, rigid rules and perfectionistic beliefs form
an integral part of social phobia, thereby playing an essential role in the
dynamic processes that underlie social fears. Thus, one would expect that
without the belief in rigid rules or the need to achieve perfect performance,
social anxiety would be considerably less severe. In our review of the empirical literature, we pay particular attention to these three issues and
note where the scientific evidence supports one or another feature of the
four theories.

Empirical Studies

Four bodies of literature are relevant to our discussion of perfectionism,
two of which indirectly address the perfectionism–social anxiety relationship. Self-criticism and negative biases in self-judgments sometimes are
used to infer the existence of perfectionistic tendencies, and those factors
have been assessed in people who are socially anxious. Other studies have
indicated that discrepancies in various self-representations (e.g., between
one's actual and ideal self) are associated with negative affective states.
Such discrepancies raise the possibility that people prone to negative affect have perfectionistic self-structures that serve as standards of reference or evaluation. The remaining two bodies of literature examine the
theoretical issues raised above in a more straightforward manner because
they directly assess social standards and perfectionistic personality traits.

Self-criticism and judgmental biases. Among the lay public, people
who are preoccupied with self-appraisal and who are prone to self-criticism
often are called perfectionistic, particularly when self-criticism appears to
be unwarranted. Socially anxious people display all those tendencies. During social encounters, their attention is focused on monitoring their own
behavior and emotions, and they engage in a process of ongoing self-
appraisal (e.g., Alden, Teschuk, & Tee, 1992; Woody, Chambless, & Glass,
1997). They also report a greater number of self-critical thoughts before
and during social situations than do nonanxious people (e.g., Glass, Merluzzi, Biever, & Larsen, 1982; Mahone, Bruch, & Heimberg, 1993; Stopa
& Clark, 1993). Following social interactions, they are prone to ruminate
about their perceived inadequacies, even when an interaction was brief
and involved others who are unimportant to their lives and whom they
will never see again (Mellings & Alden, 2000).

Socially anxious people also display negative biases in their self-
related social judgments; that is, they underestimate themselves. Although socially phobic patients often are perceived as less socially skilled

and more anxious than control groups, they rate themselves even more negatively than do objective observers (e.g. Alden & Wallace, 1995; Rapee & Lim, 1992; Stopa & Clark, 1993). They also underestimate others' liking for them (Alden & Wallace, 1995). Indeed, socially anxious people have been found to rate themselves negatively even when their behavior is indistinguishable from that of normal comparison groups (McEwan & Devins, 1983). For example, Rapee and Lim (1992) found that socially phobic patients rated themselves negatively in a public-speaking task even though the audience could not distinguish their performances from those of nonanxious people. Thus, their self-criticism is excessive or exaggerated.

The presence of frequent self-criticism and negative judgmental biases is consistent with the notion that socially anxious people evaluate their behavior in reference to stringent standards. Other explanations, however, can be found for both tendencies. As noted above, socially anxious people do indeed perform less well at times than do nonanxious people. Thus, one could argue that their negative self-thoughts are an accurate reflection of their less-than-stellar behavior. Another possibility is that socially anxious people are overly critical, but for reasons other than comparison to perfectionistic standards. For example, Clark and Wells (1995) proposed that self-focused attention results in an exaggeration of anxiety-related sensations and behaviors. As a result, those factors are theorized to be processed more deeply and thereby to loom large in judgments about such situations. In support of this notion, several empirical studies found that socially anxious participants' appraisals of social situations were more strongly influenced by their subjective discomfort than by their objective performances (McEwan & Devins, 1983). If judgmental distortions can arise because of selective attention to and processing of certain types of self-related information, it is not necessary to posit the existence of perfectionistic standards per se to account for this phenomenon. Taken together, this group of studies does not provide a definitive answer to the relationship between perfectionism and social anxiety.

Self-discrepancy studies. In self-discrepancy theory, self-regulation is viewed as a function of the dynamic relationships between various self-state representations (Higgins, 1987). According to Higgins, self-representations fall into three domains: (a) the *actual self*, (b) the *ideal self*, and (c) the *ought self*, which can be considered from either one's own perspective or the perceived perspectives of others. The ideal and ought selves are viewed as standards, or *self-guides*, for the regulation of the actual self. When the person perceives a significant discrepancy between the actual self and those guides, he or she may experience emotional distress and attempt to reduce the discrepancy. Higgins and Strauman demonstrated that discrepancies between the actual self and the ought-other self (the self the person believes others feel he or she ought to be) were uniquely predictive of arousal as opposed to depression (e.g., Higgins, Klein, & Strauman, 1985; Strauman & Higgins, 1987). Furthermore, actual-self and ought-other discrepancies were found to distinguish patients with social phobia from those with depression (Strauman, 1989,

1992). Thus, people with social phobia were prone to experiencing a sense of incongruency between how they viewed themselves and their self-representations of parental expectations.

This depiction of social phobia brings to mind Heimberg's suggestion that social phobia emerges in part from a background of parental expectations and criticism. It is easy to envision how such experiences could lead to internalized representations of others' expectations as divergent from and, possibly, more demanding than one's sense of self. What this work does not address, however, is the basis of the divergence between representations of the actual self and the ought-other self. The two self states may diverge because the ought-other self contains particularly stringent, or perfectionistic, features or because the actual self contains negative features. Although the notion of an internalized representation of perfectionistic parental expectations is one possible explanation of self-state discrepancies, this pattern is equally well explained by the long-established observation that people who are socially phobic have negative views of themselves. Again, this work does not answer our central question.

Standard-setting in social situations. A more direct examination of the relative contributions of perfectionistic standards and negative self-appraisals is possible within the framework of self-regulation theory. In this perspective, social anxiety is said to arise when people perceive a discrepancy between their social performance and various relevant standards of comparison in the social situation. This discrepancy leads them to expect negative social outcomes and to disengage from the interaction (Alden & Wallace, 1991; Carver & Scheier, 1986). In a series of studies in our laboratory, we assessed social standards independently of social self-efficacy (i.e., one's judgment about one's own social ability; Alden, Bieling, & Wallace, 1994; Wallace & Alden, 1997). We measured two types of standards: (a) *self-standards*, or the level of social performance the person him- or herself wanted to meet, and (b) *others' standards*, or the person's perception of the level of performance various other people (e.g., one's partner) expected from him or her.

As one would expect, the studies revealed that both socially anxious students and socially phobic patients rated their social ability lower than did comparison groups. Interestingly, we found no evidence of higher self-standards. Indeed, both socially anxious students and socially phobic patients established personal standards that were significantly lower than those established by nonanxious control groups. In addition, we found no support for the notion that socially anxious people perceived others as having stringent standards: Neither the socially anxious students nor the socially phobic patients rated others' standards for them higher than did comparison groups.

It is notable, however, that the socially anxious groups displayed a significant discrepancy between their self-efficacy ratings and their ratings of others' standards. That is, they doubted their ability to meet others' expectations. This discrepancy in large part was a result of their low ratings of ability, not high ratings of others' standards. No such discrepancy emerged between their perceived ability and their own standards, primarily because the goals they set for themselves in the social interaction were low and within the range of their perceived ability. Recent work has suggested that this discrepancy between ability and others' standards distinguishes people who are socially anxious and phobic from those with depressive disorders (Alden et al., 1994; Alden & Papsdorf, 1999), results reminiscent of Strauman's self-discrepancy studies. Taken together, this body of work indicates that social anxiety may be associated less with high standards than with a pervasive sense of inadequacy that leads to the belief that one will fall short of others' expectations.

Perfectionistic personality features. The studies most relevant to our central question are those that directly measured perfectionistic personality traits. Most of the studies either examined the correlations between perfectionism and various measures of social anxiety or compared socially anxious groups to nonanxious control participants. A few researchers, however, attempted to explore the factors that underlie the perfectionism–social anxiety relationship. The later results raise some questions about the nature of this association.

Several studies examined social anxiety within Frost's five-dimensional conceptualization of perfectionism. One study found that patients with social phobia obtained high mean scores on three of Frost's core dimensions, Concern Over Mistakes, Doubts About Actions, and Parental Criticism. No differences were found on Personal Standards or Parental Expectations (Juster et al., 1996). The results were confirmed in two separate investigations conducted by independent researchers, both of which found between-group differences on Concern Over Mistakes, Doubts About Actions, and Parental Criticism (Antony et al., 1998; Lundh & Ost, 1996). Finally, Concern Over Mistakes and Doubts About Actions were found to correlate with a variety of social anxiety measures, whereas Personal Standards and Parental Expectations did not (Saboonchi & Lundh, 1997).

Several aspects of this work should be noted. First, socially anxious people were characterized by maladaptive evaluation concerns but not by high standards. As a result, when one considers the total perfectionism score, which sums the two factors, no relationship is found between perfectionism and social anxiety in either clinical or nonclinical populations (Lundh & Ost, 1996). Second, Saboonchi and Lundh (1997) found that only Doubts About Actions was related to social threat interference on the Stroop task, a nonobtrusive measure believed to be specific to social anxiety. Finally, maladaptive evaluation concerns also were associated with other types of anxiety, such as agoraphobic fears, obsessive–compulsive disorder, and panic disorder (Antony et al., 1998; Saboonchi & Lundh, 1997), suggesting that such concerns are shared with other anxiety-related conditions. We examine the significance of those findings later in this chapter.

More studies have examined social anxiety within Hewitt and Flett's three-factor framework. This work consistently has revealed an association between social anxiety and the SPP subscale. Alden et al. (1994) found that socially anxious participants were significantly higher on SPP than were nonanxious control participants, whereas no differences emerged for SOP. The same pattern was found in patients with social phobia (Bieling & Alden, 1997; Wallace & Alden, 1995). Similarly, Flett, Hewitt, and DeRosa (1996) found that SPP displayed low but statistically significant correlations with measures of loneliness, shyness, fear of negative evaluation, and social self-esteem, whereas SOP did not. Finally, Saboonchi and Lundh (1997) found significant correlations between SPP and a variety of measures of social anxiety in a student sample, although they found no relationship between SPP and social threat interference on the Stroop task. The same pattern emerged in studies of procrastination (i.e., in general, procrastination was significantly correlated with SPP but not SOP; Flett, Blankstein, Hewitt, & Koledin, 1992; Saddler & Sacks, 1993). These results indicate that people who are socially anxious do not expect themselves to be perfect but feel that others have excessive expectations for them.

These studies raise an interesting issue: On the one hand, socially anxious people perceive others as having perfectionistic expectations; on the other hand, they rate others' standards for them no higher than control groups do (e.g., Wallace & Alden, 1991, 1997). To explore this apparent paradox, we measured perfectionism and standards in the same study (Alden et al., 1994). Anxious and nonanxious participants completed the Hewitt and Flett MPS and rated their own and their perceptions of others' standards for them prior to a social interaction. Both findings were replicated: Socially anxious participants scored higher on SPP but rated others' standards for them no higher than did control participants. Bieling and Alden (1997) found similar results with socially phobic patients. The findings suggest that the perception that others have high standards does not explain the association between social anxiety and SPP.

Two other studies also examined the SPP–social anxiety relationship. Saboonchi and Lundh (1997) found that nearly all the significant correlations between SPP and various measures of social anxiety were lost when public self-consciousness was controlled. Similarly, Jackson, Towson, and Narduzzi (1997) examined various predictors of shyness in a regression analysis. Expectations of rejection and perceived interpersonal incompetence significantly predicted shyness scores, but neither SOP nor SPP entered into the prediction equation. Thus, once variance attributable to negative expectations and self-rated social ability was removed, SPP was no longer associated with shyness. The findings suggest that the shared variance between SPP and social anxiety is a result of the sense of personal inadequacy, self-focused attention, and neurotic self-criticism found in many types of psychopathology.

Do the above findings mean that SPP contributes nothing to our understanding of social anxiety apart from the long-established observation that such people feel inadequate and are self-critical? If so, should we conclude that concepts such as rigid rules and perfectionistic beliefs should be eliminated from theories of social anxiety? Not necessarily, as described below.

Other findings need explanation as well. Most notably, the meaning (i.e., correlates) of perfectionism measures varies in different settings and populations. For example, SPP is associated with ratings of others' standards in clinical populations but not in nonclinical populations (Alden et al., 1994; Bieling & Alden, 1997). Similarly, Frost found that his Personal Standards subscale at times predicts positive achievement striving and at other times predicts impairment (Frost et al., 1993). Why do perfectionism scores predict psychological problems sometimes but not always, and for some people but not others?

Second, if perfectionism is integral to social anxiety, one would expect most socially anxious people to obtain high perfectionism scores. Correlations between perfectionism measures and social anxiety, however, typically are modest (but see Saboonchi & Lundh, 1997) and, although socially anxious groups display higher average perfectionism scores than nonanxious groups do, the two populations overlap considerably (Bieling & Alden, 1997). Another nagging problem is that, as with the Frost Concern Over Mistakes scale, SPP is related to many types of pathology and to other types of anxiety (e.g., Antony et al., 1998; Saboonchi & Lundh, 1997). Theories postulating that perfectionism is integral to social anxiety must be able to explain why one perfectionist develops social phobia whereas another develops, say, agoraphobia or depression.

Perfectionism and Performing Artists

Somewhat different findings emerge in the few studies that examined social evaluative concerns in performing artists and writers. Dews and Williams (1989) found that many university music students expressed a need for perfection (i.e., no mistakes) in their musical performances. This perfectionism in music students was linked both to social pressures from within the music community and to self-imposed performance standards socialized from an early age (Dews & Williams, 1989). Consistent with this idea, Mor, Day, Flett, and Hewitt (1995) found that both self-oriented and SPP were associated with performance anxiety in a sample of professional musicians and actors. Furthermore, both types of perfectionism led to an increase in debilitating anxiety as well as to a decrease in facilitating anxiety (Mor et al., 1995). Thus, in contrast to the studies of social anxiety discussed above, evaluation anxiety in performing artists does appear to be linked to SOP, and there is also reason to believe that perfectionistic standards for performance may be integral to this condition. Theories of social anxiety must be able to account for these differences.

Two-Component Model of Perfectionism

We believe that many of the issues that arise in the social anxiety literature can be resolved if one formally adopts a two-component model of perfectionism. Elsewhere, we have described such a model (Alden, Ryder, & Mellings, 1999). To summarize briefly, pathological perfectionism appears to comprise two distinct elements. Component 1, *performance expectations*, reflects a tendency to strive for or evaluate oneself in reference to high standards. This is the classic definition of perfectionism articulated by early writers (Burns, 1980; Hamachek, 1978). One of Hewitt and Flett's (1991) important contributions was to demonstrate that in the context of perfectionism, high standards either can be established by oneself or perceived to be established by others. Component 2, *maladaptive self-appraisal*, includes a sense of personal inadequacy and neurotic self-doubt accompanied by a pathological self-appraisal system that operates to accentuate the significance of small behavioral disfluencies and internal sensations of anxiety. Readers will recognize that this second component shares much with such long-established constructs as neuroticism, low self-esteem, and low self-efficacy. It also is similar to Frost's higher order factor of Maladaptive Evaluation Concerns (Frost et al., 1993).

One can envision all combinations of the two components (see Figure 15.1). People who are low in both components—that is, who are not concerned about meeting high standards and do not engage in maladaptive self-appraisal—can be viewed as self-accepting. Those who are characterized only by maladaptive self-appraisal would be expected to display per-

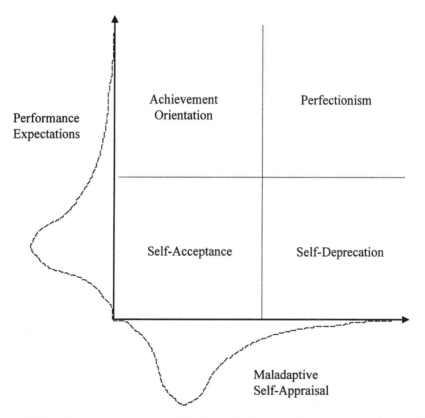

Figure 15.1.   Two-component model of perfectionism: Performance expectations and maladaptive self-appraisal.

severative self-monitoring, self-doubt and deprecation, and fear of negative evaluation. In the personality literature, such people would be viewed as high in neuroticism, one of five basic dimensions of personality (e.g., Mc-Crae & Costa, 1987). People who evaluate their efforts in comparison to stringent standards but do not engage in ongoing negative self-appraisal could be viewed as high in achievement motivation, which can be an adaptive feature. Such people might embody what Hamachek (1978) labeled "normal" perfectionism. Finally, those who score high in both components, that is, who evaluate themselves in comparison to high standards but also are prone to self-doubt and negative self-appraisal, represent what Hamachek called "neurotic" perfectionists. This last category captures the pathological form of perfectionism associated with psychopathology.

One implication of this model is that high standards will or will not be pathological depending on the presence of Component 2. Another implication is that people can display various degrees of each characteristic. Extant measures of perfectionism appear to have been explicitly designed to measure a combination of both components, perhaps because the instruments were developed to examine the role of perfectionism in psychopathology. The measures contain items that reflect high standards, items that reflect neurotic self-appraisal, and items whose content reflects both components simultaneously. This composition suggests that moderate elevations on perfectionism scales may reflect different combinations of the underlying elements. One would expect, however, that high scorers would display both high standards and maladaptive self-appraisal.

To make sense of the social anxiety literature, it is useful to consider the two components separately. We propose that maladaptive self-appraisal is inherent to social anxiety. The tendency in and of itself causes problems for socially anxious people, and indeed, in the opinion of some cognitive writers, maladaptive self-appraisal is the defining feature of social phobia (e.g., Clark & Wells, 1995). Conversely, following Leary's earlier writings, we propose that the tendency to compare oneself to high standards, established either by oneself or by others, is independent of social anxiety. Thus, we would expect that some socially anxious people would be characterized by high standards, whereas others would not. Socially anxious people who obtain particularly high scores on perfectionism measures, such as the SPP subscale, would be those who display both underlying components. Consistent with this reasoning, Bieling and Alden (1997) found that people who are socially phobic who had particularly high SPP scores perceived others to have high standards for them in a social task, whereas those with low scores did not.

This two-component model resolves many of the apparent inconsistencies in the social anxiety literature. First, the model explains results showing that perfectionism subscales that reflect high standards do not correlate with objective measures of social anxiety, such as social threat Stroop interference, in contrast to scales that more purely measure negative self-appraisal (Saboonchi & Lundh, 1997). The model also clarifies why Frost's maladaptive evaluation scales correlate with social anxiety, whereas his total perfectionism score, which includes Personal Standards, does not.

Furthermore, this model reconciles the apparently paradoxical findings that socially anxious groups report somewhat higher SPP than control groups but do not differ on average in their ratings of others' standards (Bieling & Alden, 1997). Moderately elevated SPP scores could arise in part from the maladaptive self-appraisal that characterizes socially anxious people and in part because some in this group perceive others as having high standards.

Another issue this model resolves is that of the findings indicating that the association between SPP and social anxiety disappears when variance attributable to neurotic appraisal (i.e., low self-evaluation, fear of negative evaluation) is controlled (Jackson et al., 1997; Saboonchi & Lundh, 1997). Namely, if SPP elevations in part are due to endorsement of items reflecting maladaptive self-appraisal, removing that variance would significantly reduce the SPP–social anxiety correlation. The two-component model also accounts for findings that perfectionism scales have different correlates in clinical and nonclinical samples. For one thing, people with social phobia generally display lower social self-efficacy and more negative self-appraisal than their nonclinical socially anxious counterparts, suggesting that clinical populations are generally higher on Component 2 than nonclinical samples are. Consistent with this reasoning, some writers have proposed that patients with social phobia are less able to override pathological self-appraisal than are nonclinically shy people (Stopa & Clark, 1993). The higher perfectionism scores in clinical samples may reflect greater neuroticism.

This model also reconciles the results of studies with performing artists with those of studies of general social anxiety. People who are successful as musicians or actors are likely to be those who were socialized to establish high performance standards, standards that are maintained by social pressures within their professional communities (Dews & Williams, 1989). Some of them, however, also have tendencies toward neurotic self-appraisal which, combined with high standards, results in debilitating anxiety when faced with an audience.

An additional advantage of a two-component model of perfectionism is that it explicitly allows the discrimination between so-called normal and neurotic perfectionism (Hamachek, 1978). Although most researchers give a nod to the distinction, it has not been fully integrated into empirical studies. The model also is consistent with Frost's important factor-analytic study of various perfectionism measures that identified two higher order factors in those instruments (Frost et al., 1993). Finally, the two-component model provides a framework that integrates the self-regulation and perfectionism literatures and work on self-appraisal processes in people who are socially anxious (e.g., Clark & Wells, 1995).

Summary

It is clear from the research literature that socially anxious and socially phobic people do not set high standards for their behavior in social situations. Indeed, if anything, they establish lower standards for themselves in social interactions than do comparison groups. People who are socially anxious, however, do perceive themselves as falling short of others' expectations, a conclusion that is supported by three separate bodies of literature on self-discrepancies, self-regulation, and perfectionistic traits. Empirical studies also indicate that this discrepancy is primarily due to the pervasive sense of inadequacy that characterizes the self-perceptions of people who are socially anxious. For some socially anxious people, however, the belief that others have stringent expectations also plays a role in their distress and avoidance.

Research to date has confirmed and disconfirmed elements of all four theories of social anxiety. Particularly, we agree with Leary's view that high standards and social anxiety are distinct features and that high standards contribute to social anxiety for some people. Our review also confirms the Beck–Emery and Heimberg emphasis on the interpersonal nature of self-criticism (i.e., that socially phobic people are primarily concerned about falling short of what others expect, not what they themselves expect). Finally, the developmental aspects of Heimberg's model and his proposition that concern with mistakes is an integral element to social phobia also received empirical support.

All in all, our reading of this literature points to a complex view of perfectionism as it relates to social anxiety. We believe that many of the inconsistencies in the social anxiety literature can be resolved by adopting a two-component model of perfectionism that distinguishes the tendency to compare oneself to high standards from the tendency to engage in maladaptive self-appraisal. The two-component model provides a useful framework for integrating previous and current theoretical perspectives. If the model is accurate, people who display a combination of the two components should display a distinct pattern of cognitive and behavioral qualities compared with those who display either tendency alone. Preliminary work on the model is supportive (Alden, Ryder, & Mellings, 1999), but more research is necessary.

References

Alden, L. E., Bieling, P. J., & Wallace, S. T. (1994). Perfectionism in an interpersonal context: A self-regulation analysis of dysphoria and social anxiety. *Cognitive Therapy and Research, 18*, 297–316.

Alden, L. E., & Papsdorf, M. (1999). Social feedback and changes in self and social judgements in social phobia or depression. Unpublished manuscript.

Alden, L. E., Ryder, A. G., & Mellings, T. M. B. (1999). Perfectionism: A two component perspective. Unpublished manuscript.

Alden, L. E., Teschuk, M., & Tee, K. (1992). Public self-awareness and withdrawal from social interactions. *Cognitive Therapy and Research, 16*, 249–267.

Alden, L. E., & Wallace, S. T. (1991). Social standards and withdrawal from social situations. *Cognitive Therapy and Research, 15*, 85–100.

Alden, L. E., & Wallace, S. T. (1995). Social phobia and social appraisal in successful and unsuccessful interactions. *Behaviour Research and Therapy, 33*, 497–506.

American Psychiatric Association. (1994). *Diagnostic and statistical manual of mental disorders* (4th ed.). Washington, DC: Author.

Antony, M. M., Purdon, C. L., Huta, V., & Swinson, R. P. (1998). Dimensions of perfectionism across the anxiety disorders. *Behaviour Research and Therapy, 36*, 1143–1154.

Arkin, R. M., Lake, E. A., & Baumgardner, A. H. (1986). Shyness and self-presentation. In W. H. Jones, J. M. Cheek, & S. R. Briggs (Eds.), *Shyness: Perspectives on research and treatment* (pp. 189–204). New York: Plenum Press.

Beck, A. T., & Emery, G. (1985). The evaluation anxieties. In *Anxiety disorders and phobias: A cognitive perspective* (pp. 146–166). New York: Basic Books.

Bieling, P. J., & Alden, L. E. (1997). The consequences of perfectionism for patients with social phobia. *British Journal of Clinical Psychology, 36*, 387–395.

Briggs, S. R., Cheek, J. M., & Jones, W. H. (1986). Introduction to shyness. In W. H. Jones, J. M. Cheek, & S. R. Briggs (Eds.), *Shyness: Perspectives on research and treatment* (pp. 1–16). New York: Plenum Press.

Briggs, S. R., & Smith, T. G. (1986). Measurement of shyness. In W. H. Jones, J. M. Cheek, & S. R. Briggs (Eds.), *Shyness: Perspectives on research and treatment* (pp. 47–62). New York: Plenum Press.

Brown, E. J., Heimberg, R. G., & Juster, H. R. (1995). Social phobia subtype and avoidant personality disorder: Effect on severity of social phobia, impairment, and outcome of cognitive behavioral treatment. *Behavior Therapy, 26*, 467–486.

Bruch, M. A., Heimberg, R. G., Berger, P., & Collins, T. M. (1989). Social phobia and perceptions of early parental and personal characteristics. *Anxiety Research, 2*, 57–65.

Burns, D. D. (1980). *Feeling good: The new mood therapy*. New York: New American Library.

Carver, C. S., & Scheier, M. F. (1986). Analyzing shyness: A specific application of broader self-regulatory principles. In W. H. Jones, J. M. Cheek, & S. R. Briggs (Eds.), *Shyness: Perspectives on research and treatment* (pp. 173–188). New York: Plenum Press.

Clark, D. M., & Wells, A. (1995). A cognitive model of social phobia. In R. G. Heimberg, M. R. Liebowitz, D. A. Hope, & F. R. Schneier (Eds.), *Social phobia: Diagnosis, assessment and treatment* (pp. 69–93). New York: Guilford Press.

Dews, C. L., & Williams, M. S. (1989). Student musicians' personality styles, stresses, and coping patterns. *Psychology of Music, 17*, 37–47.

Ferrari, J. R. (1991). Compulsive procrastination: Some self-reported characteristics. *Psychological Reports, 68*, 455–458.

Ferrari, J. R. (1992). Procrastinators and perfect behavior: An exploratory factor analysis of self-presentation, self-awareness, and self-handicapping components. *Journal of Research in Personality, 26*, 75–84.

Flett, G. L., Blankstein, K. R., Hewitt, P. L., & Koledin, S. (1992). Components of perfectionism and procrastination in college students. *Social Behavior and Personality, 20*, 85–94.

Flett, G. L., Hewitt, P. L., & DeRosa, T. (1996). Dimensions of perfectionism, psychosocial adjustment, and social skills. *Personality and Individual Differences, 20*, 143–150.

Frost, R. O., Heimberg, R. G., Holt, C. S., Mattia, J. I., & Neubauer, A. L. (1993). A comparison of two measures of perfectionism. *Personality and Individual Differences, 14*, 119–126.

Frost, R. O., Marten, P., Lahart, C., & Rosenblate, R. (1990). The dimensions of perfectionism. *Cognitive Therapy and Research, 14*, 449–468.

Glass, C. R., Merluzzi, T. V., Biever, J. L., & Larsen, K. H. (1982). Cognitive assessment of social anxiety: Development and validation of a self-statement questionnaire. *Cognitive Therapy and Research, 6*, 37–55.

Habke, A. M., Hewitt, P. L., Norton, G. R., & Asmundson, G. (1997). The Social Phobia and Social Interaction Anxiety Scales: An exploration of the dimensions of social anxiety and sex differences in structure and relations with pathology. *Journal of Psychopathology and Behavioral Assessment, 19*, 21–39.

Hamachek, D. E. (1978). Psychodynamics of normal and neurotic perfectionism. *Psychology, 15*, 27–33.

Heimberg, R. G., & Becker, R. E. (in press). *Treatment of social fears and phobia*. New York: Guilford Press.

Hewitt, P. L., & Flett, G. L. (1991). Perfectionism in the self and social contexts: Conceptualization, assessment, and association with psychopathology. *Journal of Personality and Social Psychology, 60*, 456–470.

Hewitt, P. L., Flett, G. L., Turnbull-Donovan, W., & Mikail, S. F. (1991). The Multidimensional Perfectionism Scale: Reliability, validity, and psychometric properties in psychiatric samples. *Psychological Assessment, 3*, 464–468.

Higgins, E. T. (1987). Self-discrepancy: A theory relating self and affect. *Psychological Review, 94*, 319–340.

Higgins, E. T., Klein, R., & Strauman, T. J. (1985). Self-concept discrepancy theory: A psychological model for distinguishing among different aspects of depression and anxiety. *Social Cognition, 3*, 51–76.

Hollender, M. H. (1965). Perfectionism. *Comprehensive Psychiatry, 6*, 94–103.

Jackson, T., Towson, S., & Narduzzi, K. (1997). Predictors of shyness: A test of variables associated with self-presentational models. *Social Behavior and Personality, 25*, 149–154.

Juster, H. R., Heimberg, R. G., Frost, R. O., Holt, C. S., Mattia, J. I., & Faccenda, K. (1996). Social phobia and perfectionism. *Personality and Individual Differences, 21*, 403–410.

Kagan, J., Reznick, S., & Snidman, N. (1988). Biological bases of childhood shyness. *Science, 240*, 167–171.

Kretschmer, E. (1925). *Physique and character*. London: Kegan Paul.

Leary, M. R. (1987). A self-presentational model for the treatment of social anxieties. In J. E. Maddux, C. D. Stoltenberg, & R. Rosenwein (Eds.), *Social processes in clinical and counseling psychology* (pp. 126–138). New York: Springer-Verlag.

Leary, M. R., & Kowalski, R. M. (1995). The self-presentation model of social phobia. In R. G. Heimberg, M. R. Liebowitz, D. A. Hope, & F. R. Schneier (Eds.), *Social phobia: Diagnosis, assessment and treatment* (pp. 94–112). New York: Guilford Press.

Lundh, L.-G., & Ost, L.-G. (1996). Stroop interference, self-focus and perfectionism in social phobics. *Personality and Individual Differences, 20*, 725–731.

Mahone, J. E., Bruch, M. A., & Heimberg, R. G. (1993). Focus of attention and social anxiety: The role of negative self-thoughts and perceived positive attributes of the other. *Cognitive Therapy and Research, 17*, 209–224.

McCrae, R. R., & Costa, P. T., Jr. (1987). Validation of the five-factor model of personality across instruments and observers. *Journal of Personality and Social Psychology, 52*, 81–90.

McEwan, K. L., & Devins, G. M. (1983). Is increased arousal in social anxiety noticed by others? *Journal of Abnormal Psychology, 92*, 417–421.

Mellings, T. M. B., & Alden, L. E. (2000). Cognitive processes in social anxiety: The effects of self-focus, rumination, and anticipatory processing. *Behaviour Research and Therapy, 38*, 243–257.

Millon, T. (1981). *Disorders of personality: DSM III: Axis II*. New York: Wiley-Interscience.

Mor, S., Day, H. I., Flett, G. L., & Hewitt, P. L. (1995). Perfectionism, control, and components of performance anxiety in professional artists. *Cognitive Therapy and Research, 19*, 207–225.

Pacht, A. R. (1984). Reflections on perfection. *American Psychologist, 39*, 386–390.

Rapee, R. M., & Lim, L. (1992). Discrepancy between self and observer ratings of performance in social phobics. *Journal of Abnormal Psychology, 101*, 728–731.

Saboonchi, F., & Lundh, L.-G. (1997). Perfectionism, self-consciousness and anxiety. *Personality and Individual Differences, 22*, 921–928.

Saddler, C. D., & Sacks, L. A. (1993). Multidimensional perfectionism and academic procrastination: Relationships with depression in university students. *Psychological Reports, 73*, 863–871.

Schlenker, B. R., & Leary, M. R. (1982). Social anxiety and self-presentation: A conceptualization and model. *Psychological Bulletin, 92*, 641–669.

Stopa, L., & Clark, D. M. (1993). Cognitive processes in social phobia. *Behaviour Research and Therapy, 31*, 255–267.

Strauman, T. J. (1989). Self-discrepancies in clinical depression and social phobia: Cognitive structures that underlie emotional disorders? *Journal of Abnormal Psychology, 98*, 14–22.

Strauman, T. J. (1992). Self-guides, autobiographical memory, and anxiety and dysphoria:

Toward a cognitive model of vulnerability to emotional distress. *Journal of Abnormal Psychology, 101*, 87–95.

Strauman, T. J., & Higgins, E. T. (1987). Automatic activation of self-discrepancies and emotional syndromes: Cognitive structures influence affect. *Journal of Personality and Social Psychology, 53*, 1004–1014.

Wallace, S. T., & Alden, L. E. (1991). Discrepancies between standards and perceived ability in social interactions. *Cognitive Therapy and Research, 15*, 257–274.

Wallace, S. T., & Alden, L. E. (1995). Social anxiety and standard-setting following social success and failure. *Cognitive Therapy and Research, 19*, 613–631.

Wallace, S. T., & Alden, L. E. (1997). Social phobia and positive social events: The price of success. *Journal of Abnormal Psychology, 106*, 1–10.

Woody, S. R., Chambless, D. L., & Glass, C. R. (1997). Self-focused attention in the treatment of social phobia. *Behaviour Research and Therapy, 35*, 117–129.

16

Perfectionism in the Therapeutic Process

Sidney J. Blatt and David C. Zuroff

The personality variable of perfectionism is related to adaptive capacities as well as to a wide range of symptoms and various forms of psychopathology, especially depression and suicide (Blatt, 1995). Important contributions have been made to the research literature on perfectionism over the past decade by two research teams, one led by Randy Frost and the other by Gordon Flett and Paul Hewitt who, at about the same time, developed what each called a Multidimensional Perfectionism Scale (MPS). Although the two scales were based on somewhat different conceptualizations, a wide range of research using the scales developed by Frost and colleagues (e.g., Frost, Marten, Lahart, & Rosenblate, 1990) and by Hewitt and Flett (e.g., Hewitt & Flett, 1989, 1991a, 1991b) has contributed to an impressive emerging literature. The purpose of this chapter is to integrate extensive findings that indicate that a patient's proclivity toward perfectionism, or self-criticism, plays a major role in psychological treatment. Not only does perfectionism contribute significantly to therapeutic outcome, but we have been able to identify some of the mechanisms or processes through which perfectionism affects treatment outcome.

The theoretical contributions of Blatt and colleagues (e.g., Blatt, 1974, 1991, 1995; Blatt & Blass, 1990, 1996; Blatt & Shichman, 1983) place perfectionism in a broad theoretical context, enabling us to understand more fully why perfectionism is such a powerful psychological variable and why it plays a pivotal role in the therapeutic process. Blatt and colleagues view psychological development as evolving through a complex dialectic transaction between two fundamental processes: (a) a *relatedness* (or *anaclitic*) developmental line, which leads to increasingly mature, mutually satisfying, reciprocal, interpersonal relationships, and (b) a *self-definitional* (or *introjective*) developmental line, which leads to a consolidated, realistic, essentially positive, differentiated, and integrated identity. The two developmental processes (relatedness and self-definition) evolve throughout life in a reciprocal, mutually facilitating, dialectic transaction. An increasingly differentiated, integrated, and mature sense of self emerges out of satisfying interpersonal relationships; conversely, the continued development of increasingly mature and satisfying interpersonal relationships depends on the development of an increasingly mature self-concept or identity (Blatt, 1990, 1995; Blatt & Blass, 1990, 1996; Blatt & Shichman, 1983). These formulations are consistent with a wide range of personality theories, from psychoanalytic conceptualizations to empirical investigations, that consider the dimensions of relatedness and self-definition as central processes in psychological development (e.g., Angyal, 1951; Bakan, 1966; Balint, 1952; Benjamin, 1990; Bowlby, 1988; Freud, 1930/1957; McAdams, 1985; McClelland, 1986; Shor & Sanville, 1978; Wiggins, 1991).

Extensive research has demonstrated important differences between people who, within the normal range, place somewhat greater emphasis on either of the two personality dimensions (see Blatt & Zuroff, 1992, for a review). In addition, various forms of psychopathology evolve from severe disruptions of the normal developmental processes; they result in exaggerated preoccupations with one of these developmental dimensions and the defensive avoidance of the other. Exaggerated preoccupation with either relatedness or self-definition identifies two distinctly different configurations of psychopathology, each of which contains several types of disordered behavior that range from relatively severe to relatively mild (Blatt, 1974, 1990, 1991, 1995; Blatt & Shichman, 1983).

Based on developmental and clinical considerations, one configuration of disorders, *anaclitic psychopathologies*, involves primary preoccupation with interpersonal relations, such as issues of merger, trust, caring, intimacy, and sexuality. Patients with anaclitic disorders are intensely preoccupied with issues of relatedness at different developmental levels, ranging from a lack of differentiation between self and other to dependent attachments to difficulties in more mature, intimate relationships. Anaclitic disorders, which range developmentally from more to less disturbed, include nonparanoid schizophrenia, borderline personality disorder, infantile (or dependent) personality disorder, anaclitic depression, and hysterical disorders. The disorders not only share a basic preoccupation with libidinal issues of relatedness but also tend to use primarily avoidant defenses to cope with psychological conflict and stress (e.g., withdrawal, denial, and repression).

In contrast, a series of disorders can be identified as *introjective psychopathologies*, in which patients are primarily preoccupied with establishing and maintaining a viable sense of self at different developmental levels, ranging from a basic sense of separateness, through concerns about autonomy and control, to more complex internalized issues of self-worth. Introjective disorders, ranging developmentally from more to less severely disturbed, include paranoid schizophrenia, the schizotypic or overideational borderline personality, paranoia, obsessive–compulsive personality disorder, introjective (i.e., guilt-ridden) depression, and phallic narcissism. Introjective psychopathology involves preoccupations with issues of self-definition at the expense of development of capacities for interpersonal relatedness and ranges from primitive concerns about self-definition in paranoid schizophrenia and the overideational borderline personality (Blatt & Auerbach, 1988), to concerns about separateness and power in paranoia, to issues of autonomy and control in obsessive–compulsive disorders, to more internalized concerns about self-worth in guilt-ridden depression and phallic narcissism. Perfectionism, or self-criticism, is an essential dimension in each form of introjective psychopathology: Paranoid patients are preoccupied with issues of blame, fault, and responsibility; patients with obsessive–compulsive disorders are concerned about details, errors, and control; and patients with introjective depression focus on issues of failure and transgression.

Introjective patients are ideational and are more concerned with establishing, protecting, and maintaining a viable self-concept than they are about the quality of their interpersonal relations and achieving feelings of trust, warmth, and affection. Issues of anger and aggression, directed toward the self or others, are usually central to their difficulties. Patients with these disorders not only share a preoccupation with issues of self-definition and an instinctual focus on aggression but also tend to use primarily counteractive defenses that transform conflicts rather than avoid them (e.g., projection, rationalization, intellectualization, doing and undoing, reaction formation, and overcompensation; Blatt, 1974, 1990, 1991, 1995; Blatt & Shichman, 1983).

Perfectionism and self-criticism are essential qualities within the introjective configuration. In normal (i.e., nonclinical) people, those qualities contribute to adaptive functioning. In the extreme, the qualities are linked to various forms of introjective psychopathology, particularly paranoia, obsessive–compulsive disorders, introjective depression, and phallic narcissism.

In contrast to the atheoretical diagnostic taxonomy established in the *Diagnostic and Statistical Manuals* of the American Psychiatric Association, which is based primarily on differences in manifest symptoms and on the implicit assumption that psychopathology is a series of diseases derived from malfunctioning biological processes (Blatt & Levy, 1998), the diagnostic differentiation between anaclitic and introjective psychopathologies derives from psychoanalytic theory, including observations about differences in primary instinctual focus (i.e., libidinal vs. aggressive), types of defensive organization (i.e., avoidant vs. counteractive), and predominant character style (e.g., emphasis on object vs. self-orientation and on affects vs. cognition; Blatt, 1991, 1995).

This theoretical model of personality development and psychopathology enabled us to introduce patient dimensions into the study of therapeutic change. Almost a half century ago, Lee Cronbach (Cronbach, 1953, 1957; Cronbach & Gleser, 1953; Edwards & Cronbach, 1952) observed that different types of patients might respond differently to various forms of treatment and change in different, but equally desirable, ways. Despite the cogency of Cronbach's argument, research in psychotherapy has continued to emphasize randomized clinical trials and the comparison of the efficacy of different treatments for particular focal symptoms. Cronbach and others (e.g., Shoham-Salomon & Hannah, 1991) urged psychotherapy investigators to adopt more complex research designs that differentiate among patients and to study the interaction between types of patients and their response to different types of treatment, possibly leading to somewhat different outcome (Blatt & Felsen, 1993).

Few studies in the past 45 years, however, have successfully integrated patient variables in the research design or in the data analyses. One of the primary reasons for this failure has been, as Cronbach (1967) cautioned, that the study of the interactions between patient and type of treatment and type of outcome (what Cronbach called "aptitude-treatment" and "aptitude-outcome" interactions) depends on the selection of appropriate individual qualities of patients out of the potentially infinite array of personal characteristics that might be relevant to the treatment process. Cronbach and others stressed that patient variables need to be theoretically derived, empirically justified, or both, or the investigators could be drawn into what Cronbach (1975) described as a "hall of mirrors" (Beutler, 1991; Smith & Sechrest, 1991; Snow, 1991).

The conceptualization of relatedness and self-definition in personality development and the two configurations of psychopathology discussed above provide a theoretical matrix for introducing patient variables into studies of the treatment process. These patient dimensions were introduced in three recent treatment studies: (a) an investigation of therapeutic change in seriously disturbed, treatment-resistant patients in long-term, intensive, inpatient treatment; (b) a comparison of the differential effects of psychoanalysis and long-term supportive-expressive psychotherapy in outpatients; and (c) an extensive evaluation of several brief outpatient treatments for patients with serious levels of depression.

In the two studies that evaluated therapeutic response in long-term intensive treatment (Blatt, 1992; Blatt & Ford, 1994; Blatt, Ford, Berman, Cook, & Meyer, 1988), the two types of patients (i.e., anaclitic and introjective) were reliably differentiated on the basis of descriptions of the patients in clinical case records prepared at the beginning of treatment. Findings in both studies—of outpatients in two forms of treatment and of seriously disturbed, treatment-resistant patients in long-term, intensive, inpatient treatment—indicated that anaclitic and introjective patients come to treatment with different needs, respond differentially to different types of therapeutic intervention, and demonstrate different treatment outcomes.

Therapeutic change was studied in a sample of seriously disturbed, treatment-resistant patients in long-term, intensive, psychodynamically oriented, inpatient treatment in an open therapeutic facility (including at least four times weekly psychoanalytically oriented psychotherapy; Blatt & Ford, 1994; Blatt et al., 1988). Systematic differences were found in the therapeutic response of anaclitic and introjective patients according to several independent measures of change derived from clinical case records and psychological test protocols assessed at the outset of treatment and again after 15 months of intensive inpatient treatment. In general, patients demonstrated significant improvement, but introjective patients (those patients preoccupied primarily with issues of self-definition, autonomy, self-control, and self-worth) consistently had greater improvement than anaclitic patients. Independent of the degree of therapeutic gain, anaclitic and introjective patients changed (i.e., regressed or progressed) in different ways. Introjective patients changed primarily in their clinical symptoms (as reliably rated from clinical case reports) and cognitive functioning (as independently assessed on psychological tests), including thought disorder on the Rorschach and IQ. In contrast, anaclitic patients (those patients preoccupied primarily with concerns about disruptions of interpersonal relatedness) changed primarily in the quality of their interpersonal relationships (as reliably rated from clinical case reports) and in the representation of the human form on the Rorschach. Thus, anaclitic and introjective patients appear to change primarily in the modalities that express their basic concerns and preoccupations. Anaclitic patients changed primarily in dimensions assessing interpersonal relationships; change in introjective patients occurred primarily in cognitive functioning and clinical symptoms (Blatt & Ford, 1994).

The distinction between anaclitic and introjective patients also was applied to data from the Menninger Psychotherapy Research Project (MPRP; Blatt, 1992). The MPRP was designed to compare the effects of psychoanalysis and long-term, psychodynamically oriented psychotherapy in outpatients. Extensive prior analyses of data derived from clinical evaluations and psychological test assessments, conducted both before and after treatment in the MPRP, failed to find any systematic differences between the two types of therapeutic intervention (Wallerstein, 1986). Using the distinction of two configurations of psychopathology, further analysis of the data, however, indicate that anaclitic and introjective patients are differentially responsive to psychotherapy and psychoanalysis. Independent evaluation of psychological test data, gathered at the beginning and end of treatment, indicated that anaclitic patients in psychotherapy had significantly greater improvement than did anaclitic patients in psychoanalysis. Introjective patients in psychoanalysis, in contrast, had significantly greater improvement than introjective patients in psychotherapy. Not only was the therapeutic response of the two groups of patients significantly different within the two types of treatment, but the patient-by-treatment interaction term indicated a significant ($p < .001$) crossover interaction (Blatt, 1992). Thus, the relative therapeutic efficacy of psychoanalysis and psychotherapy seems contingent, to a significant degree, on the nature of the patient's pretreatment pathology and character structure. It seems consistent that the relatively dependent, interpersonally oriented, anaclitic patients should be more responsive in a therapeutic context that provided more direct personal interaction with the therapist and that the relatively ideational, introjective patients, who are preoccupied with separation, autonomy, and independence, would be more responsive to psychoanalysis (Blatt, 1992).

The differential response of anaclitic and introjective patients in these two studies of long-term treatment suggested that this diagnostic distinction might be useful in evaluating the differential efficacy of the brief outpatient treatments for depression evaluated in the Treatment for Depression Collaborative Research Program (TDCRP) sponsored by the National Institute of Mental Health (NIMH). The differentiation between interpersonally oriented, dependent, anaclitic patients and ideational, perfectionistic, self-critical introjective patients seemed that it might be especially relevant to the TDCRP because the distinction between anaclitic and introjective psychopathology has been particularly useful in identifying two major types of depression (Blatt, 1974, 1998; Blatt, D'Affliti, & Quinlan, 1976; Blatt, Quinlan, & Chevron, 1990; Blatt, Quinlan, Chevron, McDonald, & Zuroff, 1982). Investigators from both psychodynamic (e.g., Arieti & Bemporad, 1978, 1980; Blatt, 1974; Bowlby, 1988) and cognitive–behavioral (Beck, 1983) perspectives have discussed two major types of experiences that result in two types of depression: (a) disruptions of gratifying interpersonal relationships (e.g., loss of a significant figure) and (b) disruptions of an effective and essentially positive sense of self (e.g., feelings of failure, guilt, and worthlessness).

The distinction between anaclitic (dependent) and introjective (self-critical) depressed patients has been made in a wide range of studies using several well-established scales: the Depressive Experiences Questionnaire (DEQ; Blatt et al., 1976, 1979), the Sociotropy-Autonomy Scale (SAS; Beck, 1983), The Personal Styles Inventory (Robins & Luten, 1991), and the Dysfunctional Attitudes Scale (DAS; Weissman & Beck, 1978). Studies using these scales demonstrate important differences between patients with anaclitic and introjective depression (e.g., Blatt et al., 1982).

In attempting to introduce this distinction into analyses of data from the TDCRP, we reviewed the extensive TDCRP research protocol and noted that the DAS had been administered during intake and screening (as well as during and following treatment). Several factor-analytic studies, including an analysis of the DAS in the TDCRP, identified two major dimensions in the DAS: (a) Need for Approval (NFA) and (b) Perfectionism (PFT). Because several studies demonstrated that the two DAS factors are related to the anaclitic and introjective dimensions as assessed on the DEQ, we decided to explore the impact of pretreatment patient differences on NFA and PFT on treatment outcome and on aspects of the treatment process in the TDCRP.[1]

---

[1]Several factor-analytic studies of the DAS have consistently identified two major and stable factors in the DAS: one focused on issues of relatedness and the other on issues of self-definition. Those factors have been labeled, respectively, Need for Approval by Others and Performance Evaluation (Self-Worth or Perfectionism; Cane, Olinger, Gotlib, & Kuiper, 1986; Imber et al., 1990; Oliver & Baumgart, 1985). Pilon (1987), conducting a discriminant analysis based on three of the measures of two types of depression (DEQ, SAS, and DAS), the Beck Depression Inventory (BDI), and the Personality Research Form (PRF; Jackson, 1974), identified two fundamental dimensions, which he labeled (a) *relatedness-to-others*, which included appealing to others for support, help, and advice; seeking to be loved and valued by others; and craving affection and being overly dependent and fearful of abandonment and (b) *self-definition*, which included feeling unsatisfied and critical of oneself, feeling a failure for not meeting expectations, needing to be outstanding and avoid feeling inferior, and feeling ambivalent about interpersonal relationships. Pilon noted the congruence of the two dimensions with the Dependency and Self-Criticism scales of the DEQ and with the Need for Approval and Perfectionism scales of the DAS. Blaney and Kutcher (1991) also evaluated the relationships among these measures of dimensions of depression (DEQ, SAS, and DAS) and found high congruence among the three scales that assessed interpersonal

The multisite TDCRP, an extensive, carefully designed and conducted, randomized clinical trial, compared two forms of manual-directed brief outpatient psychotherapy (cognitive–behavioral and interpersonal therapy) for the treatment of depression with imipramine plus clinical management, as a standard control, and with a double-blind placebo, also with clinical management. Comparison of the effects of 16 weeks of treatment indicated that medication (imipramine) resulted in more rapid reduction in symptoms, but at termination no significant differences were found among the three active treatment conditions (e.g., Elkin, 1994). In contrast to the marginal differences among treatments at termination, highly significant relations were found between pretreatment level of perfectionism, as measured by one of the two factors identified on the DAS (Weissman & Beck, 1978), and treatment outcome across all four treatment conditions (Blatt, Quinlan, Pilkonis, & Shea, 1995).

In our analyses of the TDCRP data, we discovered that introjective qualities, assessed by the PFT factor of the DAS, significantly impeded treatment outcome at both termination (Blatt et al., 1995) and follow-up 18 months after termination (Blatt, Zuroff, Bondi, Sanislow, & Pilkonis, 1998). Although NFA and PFT did not interact significantly with the different forms of treatment in predicting outcome, PFT significantly predicted ($p = .031$ to .001) less positive outcome, as assessed by residualized gain scores of all five primary measures of clinical change (i.e., Hamilton Rating Scale for Depression [Hamilton, 1960], BDI [Beck, Ward, Mendelson, Mock, & Erbaugh, 1961], Global Assessment Scale [Endicott, Spitzer, Fleiss, & Cohen, 1976], Symptom Check List-90 [SCL-90; Derogatis, Lipman, & Covi, 1973], and the Social Adjustment Scale [Weisman & Paykel, 1974]) in the TDCRP, across all four treatment groups (Blatt et al., 1995). Combining all five outcome measures into a single factor, PFT predicted the combined residualized gain score at termination at a highly significant level ($r = .29$, $p < .001$). Not only did PFT predict less improvement from pretreatment to posttreatment, it also was the case that patients who were highly perfectionistic at the beginning of treatment were more vulnerable to experiencing depressive symptoms in response to stress during the 18-month follow-up period (Zuroff, Blatt, Krupnick, & Sotsky, 2001).

In contrast, NFA had a consistent marginal positive relationship to treatment outcome on all five outcome measures as well as to the combination of all five residualized gain scores ($p = .114$). Thus, preoccupation with introjective issues of self-definition and self-worth, as measured by the PFT scale of the DAS, significantly impeded response to short-term treatment for depression, whether the treatment was pharmacotherapy, psychotherapy, or placebo (Blatt et al., 1995).

---

relatedness (DEQ Dependency, SAS Sociotropy, and DAS Need for Approval). The relationships among the three scales that assess individuality (DEQ Self-Criticism, SAS Autonomy, and DAS Perfectionism) were more complex, primarily because the Autonomy scale of the SAS appears to measure primarily counterdependency rather than individuality. The relationship between the DEQ Self-Criticism and DAS Perfectionism scales, however, was substantial, and both have robust correlations with independent measures of depression (Blaney & Kutcher, 1991; Nietzel & Harris, 1990).

Pretreatment PFT also had consistent and significant negative relationships with ratings made by the therapists, independent clinical evaluators, and the patients themselves at termination. Pretreatment PFT also correlated significantly with ratings at termination by clinical evaluators of the patients' clinical condition and the patients' need for further treatment as well as with ratings by patients of their satisfaction with treatment (Blatt et al., 1998). These disruptive effects of pretreatment PFT on therapeutic outcome persisted even at a follow-up evaluation conducted 18 months after the termination of treatment.

Therapeutic progress had been assessed every 4 weeks during the 16-week treatment process in the TDCRP; therefore, we were able to evaluate when and how PFT disrupted therapeutic progress (Blatt et al., 1998). Patients at three levels of perfectionism were compared on an aggregate measure of maladjustment at each of the four evaluation points in the treatment process. Repeated measures of analysis of variance of this composite measure of maladjustment using one between-subjects variable (i.e., level of perfectionism) and one within-subjects variable (i.e., time: intake, 4 weeks, 8 weeks, 12 weeks, and termination) indicated a significant Perfectionism × Time interaction. This significant Perfectionism × Time interaction was probed by two additional repeated measures of ANOVA: one including the three time periods from intake to mid-treatment (8 weeks) and the other including the three time periods from mid-treatment to termination. No significant Perfectionism × Treatment interaction was found in the first analysis, that is, during the first half of treatment. The interaction during the second half of treatment, however, was significant. Thus, pretreatment PFT had little effect on therapeutic gain during the first 8 weeks of treatment, but a significant difference emerged during the second half of treatment: Low-perfectionism patients continued to improve, whereas moderate- and high-perfectionism patients made only slight additional progress. The findings suggest that perfectionistic patients may be negatively affected by the anticipation of an arbitrary, externally imposed termination. As perfectionistic patients begin to confront the end of treatment, they "may experience a sense of personal failure, dissatisfaction, and disillusionment" with themselves and with the treatment (Blatt et al., 1998, p. 428). Because perfectionistic people often need to maintain control and preserve their sense of autonomy (Blatt, 1974, 1995; Blatt & Zuroff, 1992), they may react negatively to a unilateral, externally imposed termination date (Blatt et al., 1998).

Additional analyses of data from the TDCRP indicated that pretreatment level of perfectionism affected therapeutic outcome by disrupting the patients' quality of interpersonal relations both in the treatment process and in social relationships outside of treatment. Zuroff et al. (2000), using ratings of the therapeutic alliance in the TDCRP developed by Krupnick et al. (1996) that were based on a modified version of the Vanderbilt Therapeutic Alliance Scale (Hartley & Strupp, 1983), found that patients' (but not the therapists') contributions to the therapeutic alliance mediated the effect of pretreatment perfectionism on treatment outcome at termination. Highly perfectionistic patients failed to continue to participate actively in the development of the therapeutic alliance, especially in the latter half of the treatment process, and the disrupted therapeutic alliance led to poorer therapeutic response (Zuroff et al., 2000, p. 121).

Shahar, Blatt, Zuroff, Krupnick, and Sotsky (2001) found that pre-treatment perfectionism also was related to impaired social support outside of treatment and that this impaired social support significantly mediated the relationship of perfectionism to treatment outcome. Clinical evaluators in the TDCRP used the Social Network Form (Elkin, Parloff, Hadley, & Autry, 1985) to assess patients' social network; patients with high levels of pretreatment perfectionism reported less satisfying social relationships over the course of treatment, which in turn predicted poorer therapeutic outcome. Thus, perfectionistic patients appear to have greater interpersonal difficulty both within and external to the treatment process. They have a poorer therapeutic alliance (Zuroff et al., 2000) and a more limited social network (Shahar et al., 2001) during treatment than their nonperfectionistic counterparts. The disruptive effects of an arbitrary, externally determined, termination on perfectionistic patients appears to be accompanied by a disruption of their interpersonal relationships.

The extensive data gathered as part of the TDCRP also provided an opportunity to evaluate circumstances within the various treatments in the TDCRP that served to reduce the negative effects of pretreatment perfectionism. We explored whether the quality of the therapeutic relationship as experienced by the patient might mitigate the negative effects of PFT on treatment outcome (Blatt, Zuroff, Quinlan, & Pilkonis, 1996). The Barrett-Lennard Relationship Inventory (B-L RI; Barrett-Lennard, 1962) had been administered as part of the TDCRP research protocol to assess the quality of the therapeutic relationship at the beginning of treatment (i.e., after two sessions) and at termination. The B-L RI is based on the view of Carl Rogers (1951, 1957, 1959) that the therapist's empathic understanding, unconditional positive regard, and congruence are the "necessary and sufficient conditions" for therapeutic change. On the basis of those formulations, Barrett-Lennard (1962) developed four scales (Empathic Understanding, Level of Regard, Unconditionality of Regard, and Congruence) to assess the patient's perception of the therapeutic relationship. Several reviews (Barrett-Lennard, 1986; Gurman, 1977) indicated acceptable levels of reliability and validity for the four scales of the B-L RI. Prior research, for example, indicated that the four scales predict therapeutic change and are related significantly to independent estimates of the therapist's competence (Barrett-Lennard, 1962).

The degree to which patients in the TDCRP perceived their therapist at the end of the second treatment hour as empathic, caring, open, and sincere, as assessed by the B-L RI, had a significant ($p < .05$) relationship to therapeutic outcome as assessed by four of the five outcome measures (BDI, SCL-90, GAS, and SAS; Blatt et al., 1996). This finding is consistent with a report by Krupnick et al. (1996), who, using the Vanderbilt Therapeutic Alliance Scale, found that the mean of therapeutic alliance (assessed in the 3rd, 9th, and 15th sessions) was significantly related to outcome across treatment groups. This relationship was determined, however, primarily by the patient's, rather than by the therapist's, contributions to the therapeutic alliance.

The perceived level of the therapeutic relationship at the end of the second treatment hour, as measured by the B-L RI, was independent of the patients' pretreatment level of DAS Perfectionism ($r = -.09$). Although highly perfectionistic patients appeared to be capable of perceiving their therapist positively, they were relatively less able to benefit from treatment. Because PFT and B-L RI scores were not significantly correlated, they each appeared to contribute independent variance to the prediction of therapeutic outcome. Surprisingly, however, the interaction of PFT and B-L RI did not add significantly to the prediction of therapeutic outcome. Exploratory analyses indicated a significant curvilinear (quadratic) component to the interaction between PFT and the B-L RI in predicting therapeutic outcome. The level of B-L RI at the end of the second hour had only marginal effects on the relation of PFT to therapeutic outcome at low and high levels of perfectionism ($p < .10$ and $.15$, respectively), but the level of the B-L RI significantly ($p < .001$) reduced the negative effects of perfectionism on treatment outcome at the midlevel of perfectionism (Blatt et al., 1996).

The various analyses indicated that the effects of brief treatment for depression, as assessed in the TDCRP, are significantly determined by patient dimensions, especially by pretreatment level of perfectionism or self-criticism, independent of the type of treatment the patient was provided. This negative effect of PFT on therapeutic outcome in brief treatment stands in contrast to the findings that perfectionistic, self-critical, introjective outpatients did relatively well in long-term, intensive, outpatient treatment (Blatt, 1992) as well as in long-term, intensive, inpatient treatment (Blatt & Ford, 1994).

Summary

In summary, the findings in the study of brief and long-term treatment indicate that patient characteristics significantly influence the relative efficacy of therapeutic interventions. The distinction between two primary dimensions of personality development—relatedness and self-definition—and between two types of psychopathology—anaclitic and introjective—enabled us to introduce dimensions of the patient into studies of treatment outcome and of the treatment process and to evaluate the interaction of patient variables with mutative factors that potentially exist in both short- and long-term treatment. The results both confirm the cogency of Cronbach's emphasis almost 50 years ago of the need to include patient characteristics in studies of the therapeutic process and outcome and stress the importance of perfectionism, or introjective personality characteristics more generally, as central dimensions that play a significant role in individual responses to the treatment process.

References

Angyal, A. (1951). *Neurosis and treatment: A holistic theory*. New York: Wiley.

Arieti, S., & Bemporad, J. R. (1978). *Severe and mild depression: The therapeutic approach*. New York: Basic Books.

Arieti, S., & Bemporad, J. R. (1980). The psychological organization of depression. *American Journal of Psychiatry, 137*, 1360–1365.

Bakan, D. (1966). *The duality of human existence: An essay on psychology and religion*. Chicago: Rand McNally.

Balint, M. (1952). *Primary love and psychoanalytic technique*. London: Hogarth Press.

Barrett-Lennard, G. T. (1962). Dimensions of therapist responses as causal factors in therapeutic change. *Psychological Monographs, 76* (43, Whole No. 562).

Barrett-Lennard, G. T. (1986). The Relationship Inventory now: Issues and advances in theory, method, and use. In L. S. Greenberg & W. M. Pinsof (Eds.), *The psychotherapeutic process: A research handbook* (pp. 439–476). New York: Guilford Press.

Beck, A. T. (1983). Cognitive therapy of depression: New perspectives. In P. J. Clayton & J. E. Barrett (Eds.), *Treatment of depression: Old controversies and new approaches* (pp. 265–290). New York: Raven.

Beck, A. T., Ward, C. H., Mendelson, M., Mock, J., & Erbaugh, J. (1961). An inventory for measuring depression. *Archives of General Psychiatry, 4*, 561–571.

Benjamin, J. (1990). An outline of intersubjectivity: The development of recognition. *Psychoanalytic Psychology, 7*, 33–46.

Beutler, L. E. (1991). Have all won and must all have prizes? Revisiting Luborsky et al.'s verdict. *Journal of Consulting and Clinical Psychology, 59*, 226–232.

Blaney, P. H., & Kutcher, G. S. (1991). Measures of depressive dimensions: Are they interchangeable? *Journal of Personality Assessment, 56*, 502–512.

Blatt, S. J. (1974). Levels of object representation in anaclitic and introjective depression. *Psychoanalytic Study of the Child, 29*, 107–157.

Blatt, S. J. (1990). Interpersonal relatedness and self-definition: Two personality configurations and their implications for psychopathology and psychotherapy. In J. L. Singer (Ed.), *Repression and dissociation: Implications for personality theory, psychopathology, and health* (pp. 299–335). Chicago: University of Chicago Press.

Blatt, S. J. (1991). A cognitive morphology of psychopathology. *Journal of Nervous and Mental Disease, 179*, 449–458.

Blatt, S. J. (1992). The differential effect of psychotherapy and psychoanalysis on anaclitic and introjective patients: The Menninger Psychotherapy Research Project revisited. *Journal of the American Psychoanalytic Association, 40*, 691–724.

Blatt, S. J. (1995). Representational structures in psychopathology. In D. Cicchetti & S. Toth (Eds.), *Rochester symposium on developmental psychopathology: Vol. 6. Emotion, cognition, and representation* (pp. 1–33). Rochester, NY: University of Rochester Press.

Blatt, S. J. (1998). Contributions of psychoanalysis to the understanding and treatment of depression. *Journal of the American Psychoanalytic Association, 46*, 723–752.

Blatt, S. J., & Auerbach, J. S. (1988). Differential cognitive disturbances in three types of "borderline" patients. *Journal of Personality Disorders, 2*, 198–211.

Blatt, S. J., & Blass, R. B. (1990). Attachment and separateness: A dialectic model of the products and processes of psychological development. *Psychoanalytic Study of the Child, 45*, 107–127.

Blatt, S. J., & Blass, R. (1996). Relatedness and self definition: A dialectic model of personality development. In G. G. Noam & K. W. Fischer (Eds.), *Development and vulnerabilities in close relationships* (pp. 309–338). Hillsdale, NJ: Erlbaum.

Blatt, S. J., D'Afflitti, J. P., & Quinlan, D. M. (1976). Experiences of depression in normal young adults. *Journal of Abnormal Psychology, 85*, 383–389.

Blatt, S. J., D'Afflitti, J. P., & Quinlan, D. M. (1979). *Depressive Experiences Questionnaire*. Unpublished research manual, Yale University, New Haven, CT.

Blatt, S. J., & Felsen, I. (1993). "Different kinds of folks may need different kinds of strokes": The effect of patients' characteristics on therapeutic process and outcome. *Psychotherapy Research, 3*, 245–259.

Blatt, S. J., & Ford, R. Q. (1994). *Therapeutic change: An object relations perspective.* New York: Plenum Press.

Blatt, S. J., Ford, R. Q., Berman, W., Cook, B., & Meyer, R. G. (1988). The assessment of change during the intensive treatment of borderline and schizophrenic young adults. *Psychoanalytic Psychology, 5,* 127–158.

Blatt, S. J., & Levy, K. N. (1998). A psychodynamic approach to the diagnosis of psychopathology. In J. W. Barron (Ed.), *Making diagnosis meaningful* (pp. 73–109). Washington, DC: American Psychological Association Press.

Blatt, S. J., Quinlan, D. M., & Chevron, E. S. (1990). Empirical investigations of a psychoanalytic theory of depression. In J. Masling (Ed.), *Empirical studies of psychoanalytic theories* (Vol. 3, pp. 89–147). Hillsdale, NJ: Analytic Press.

Blatt, S. J., Quinlan, D. M., Chevron, E. S., McDonald, C., & Zuroff, D. C. (1982). Dependency and self-criticism: Psychological dimensions of depression. *Journal of Consulting and Clinical Psychology, 50,* 113–124.

Blatt, S. J., Quinlan, D. M., Pilkonis, P. A., & Shea, M. T. (1995). Impact of perfectionism and need for approval on the brief treatment of depression: The National Institute of Mental Health Treatment of Depression Collaborative Research Program Revisited. *Journal of Consulting and Clinical Psychology, 63,* 125–132.

Blatt, S. J., & Shichman, S. (1983). Two primary configurations of psychopathology. *Psychoanalysis and Contemporary Thought, 6,* 187–254.

Blatt, S. J., & Zuroff, D. C. (1992). Interpersonal relatedness and self-definition: Two prototypes for depression. *Clinical Psychology Review, 12,* 527–562.

Blatt, S. J., Zuroff, D. C., Bondi, C. M., Sanislow, C. A., & Pilkonis, P. A. (1998). When and how perfectionism impedes the brief treatment of depression: Further analyses of the NIMH TDCRP. *Journal of Consulting and Clinical Psychology, 66,* 423–428.

Blatt, S. J., Zuroff, D. C., Quinlan, D. M., & Pilkonis, P. A. (1996). Interpersonal factors in brief treatment of depression: Further analyses of the National Institute of Mental Health Treatment of Depression Collaborative Research Program. *Journal of Consulting and Clinical Psychology, 64,* 162–171.

Bowlby, J. (1988). *A secure base: Clinical applications of attachment theory.* London: Routledge & Kegan Paul.

Cane, D. B., Olinger, L. J., Gotlib, I. H., & Kuiper, N. A. (1986). Factor structure of the Dysfunctional Attitude Scale in a student population. *Journal of Clinical Psychology, 42,* 307–309.

Cronbach, L. J. (1953). Correlation between persons as a research tool. In O. H. Mowrer (Ed.), *Psychotherapy: Theory and research* (pp. 376–389). New York: Ronald.

Cronbach, L. J. (1957). The two disciplines of scientific psychology. *American Psychologist, 12,* 671–684.

Cronbach, L. J. (1967). Instructional methods and individual differences. In R. Gagne (Ed.), *Learning and individual differences* (pp. 23–39). Columbus, OH: Charles E. Merrill.

Cronbach, L. J. (1975). Beyond the two disciplines of scientific psychology. *American Psychologist, 30,* 116–127.

Cronbach L. J., & Gleser, G. G. (1953). Assessing similarity between profiles. *Psychological Bulletin, 50,* 456–474.

Derogatis, L. R., Lipman, R. S., & Covi, L. (1973). SCL-90: An outpatient psychiatric rating scale–preliminary report. *Psychopharmacology Bulletin, 9,* 13–28.

Edwards, A. L., & Cronbach, L. J. (1952). Experimental design for research in psychotherapy. *Journal of Clinical Psychology, 8,* 51–59.

Elkin, I. (1994). The NIMH Treatment of Depression Collaborative Research Program: Where we began and where we are now. In A. E. Bergin & S. L. Garfield (Eds.), *Handbook of psychotherapy and behavior change* (4th ed., pp. 114–135). New York: Wiley.

Elkin, I., Parloff, M. B., Hadley, S. W., & Autry, J. H. (1985). NIMH Treatment of Depression Collaborative Research Program: Background and research plan. *Archives of General Psychiatry, 42,* 305–316.

Endicott, J., Spitzer, R. L., Fleiss, J. L., & Cohen, J. (1976). The Global Assessment Scale: A procedure for measuring overall severity of psychiatric disturbance. *Archives of General Psychiatry, 33,* 766–771.

Freud, S. (1957). Civilization and its discontents. In J. Strachey (Ed. and Trans.), *The stan-*

dard edition of the complete psychological works of Sigmund Freud (Vol. 21, pp. 64–145). London: Hogarth Press. (Original work published 1930)

Frost, R. O., Marten, P., Lahart, C., & Rosenblate, R. (1990). The dimensions of perfectionism. *Cognitive Therapy and Research, 14,* 449–468.

Gurman, A. S. (1977). The patient's perception of the therapeutic relationship. In A. S. Gurman & A. M. Razin (Eds.), *Effective psychotherapy: A handbook of research* (pp. 503–543). New York: Pergamon.

Hamilton, M. A. (1960). A rating scale for depression. *Journal of Neurology, Neurosurgery, and Psychiatry, 6,* 56–62.

Hartley, D. E., & Strupp, H. H. (1983). The therapeutic alliance: Its relationship to outcome in brief psychotherapy. In J. Masling (Ed.), *Empirical studies of psychoanalytic theories* (pp. 1–27). Hillsdale, NJ: Erlbaum.

Hewitt, P. L., & Flett, G. L. (1989). The Multidimensional Perfectionism Scale: Development and validation [Abstract]. *Canadian Psychology, 30,* 339.

Hewitt, P. L., & Flett, G. L. (1991a). Dimensions of perfectionism in unipolar depression. *Journal of Abnormal Psychology, 100,* 98–101.

Hewitt, P. L., & Flett, G. L. (1991b). Perfectionism in the self and social contexts: Conceptualization, assessment, and association with psychopathology. *Journal of Personality and Social Psychology, 60,* 456–470.

Imber, S. D., Pilkonis, P. A., Sotsky, S. M., Elkin, I., Watkins, J. T., Collins, J. F., Shea, M. T., Leber, W. R., & Glass, D. R. (1990). Mode-specific effects among three treatments for depression. *Journal of Consulting and Clinical Psychology, 58,* 352–359.

Jackson, D. N. (1974). *Personality research form.* Goshen, NY: Research Psychologists Press.

Krupnick, J. L., Sotsky, S. M., Simmens, S., Moyer, J., Elkin, I., Watkins, J., & Pilkonis, P. A. (1996). The role of the therapeutic alliance in psychotherapy and pharmacotherapy outcome: Findings in the NIMH Treatment of Depression Collaborative Research Program. *Journal of Consulting and Clinical Psychology, 64,* 532–539.

McAdams, D. P. (1985). *Power, intimacy, and the life story: Personological inquiries into identity.* Homewood, IL: Dorsey.

McClelland, D. C. (1986). Some reflections on the two psychologies of love. *Journal of Personality, 54,* 334–353.

Nietzel, M. T., & Harris, M. J. (1990). Relationship of dependency and achievement/autonomy to depression. *Clinical Psychology Review, 10,* 279–297.

Oliver, J. M., & Baumgart, E. P. (1985). The Dysfunctional Attitude Scale: Psychometric properties in an unselected adult population. *Cognitive Theory and Research, 9,* 161–169.

Pilon, D. (1987, August). *Validation of Beck's sociotropic and autonomous modes of depression.* Paper presented at the annual meeting of the American Psychological Association, New York.

Robins, C. J., & Luten, A. G. (1991). Sociotropy and autonomy: Differential patterns of clinical presentation in unipolar depression. *Journal of Abnormal Psychology, 100,* 74–77.

Rogers, C. R. (1951). *Client-centered therapy.* Boston: Houghton Mifflin.

Rogers, C. R. (1957). The necessary and sufficient conditions of therapeutic personality change. *Journal of Consulting Psychology, 21,* 95–103.

Rogers, C. R. (1959). A theory of therapy, personality, and interpersonal relationships as developed in the client-centered framework in psychology: A study of science. In S. Koch (Ed.), *Formulations of the person and the social context* (pp. 184–256). New York: McGraw-Hill.

Shahar, G., Blatt, S. J., Zuroff, D. C., Krupnick, J. L., & Sotsky, S. M. (2001). *Disruptive effects of perfectionism on interpersonal relations in brief treatment for depression.* Manuscript submitted for publication.

Shoham-Salomon, V., & Hannah, M. T. (1991). Client-treatment interactions in the study of differential change processes. *Journal of Consulting and Clinical Psychology, 59,* 217–225.

Shor, J., & Sanville, J. (1978). *Illusions in loving: A psychoanalytic approach to intimacy and autonomy.* Los Angeles: Double Helix.

Smith, B., & Sechrest, L. (1991). The treatment of Aptitude X Treatment interactions. *Journal of Consulting and Clinical Psychology, 59*, 233–244.

Snow, R. E. (1991). Aptitude-treatment interactions as a framework for research on individual differences in psychotherapy. *Journal of Consulting and Clinical Psychology, 59*, 205–216.

Wallerstein, R. S. (1986). *Forty-two lives in treatment: A study of psychoanalysis and psychotherapy*. New York: Guilford Press.

Weisman, M. M., & Paykel, E. S. (1974). *The depressed woman: Study of social relationships*. Chicago: University of Chicago Press.

Weissman, A. N., & Beck, A. T. (1978, August–September). *Development and validation of the Dysfunctional Attitudes Scale: A preliminary investigation*. Paper presented at the 86th annual meeting of the American Psychological Association, Toronto.

Wiggins, J. S. (1991). Agency and communion as conceptual coordinates for the understanding and measurement of interpersonal behavior. In W. W. Grove & D. Cicchetti (Eds.), *Thinking clearly about psychology, Vol. 2: Personality and psychotherapy* (pp. 89–113). Minneapolis: University of Minnesota Press.

Zuroff, D. C., Blatt, S. J., Krupnick, J. L., & Sotsky, S. M. (2001). *Vicissitudes of life after short-term treatment of depression: Stress reactivity and its moderators*. Manuscript submitted for publication.

Zuroff, D. C., Blatt, S. J., Sotsky, S. M., Krupnick, J. L., Martin, D. J., Sanislow, C. A., & Simmens, S. (2000). Relation of therapeutic alliance and perfectionism to outcome in brief outpatient treatment of depression. *Journal of Consulting and Clinical Psychology, 68*, 114–124.

Author Index

Numbers in italics refer to listings in the reference sections.

Subject Index

About the Editors

Gordon L. Flett is professor of psychology at York University in Toronto. He received his PhD from the University of Toronto in 1988. His research interests include the role of personality factors in depression as well as the continuity of depression. In 1991 he teamed with Paul L. Hewitt to create the Multidimensional Perfectionism Scale. They have collaborated on 38 refereed journal articles on perfectionism and on numerous conference presentations. This work has been supported by major research grants from Health Canada and the Social Sciences and Humanities Research Council of Canada. In 1999 Dr. Flett received the Dean's Award for Outstanding Research from the Faculty of Arts at York University, and in 1996 he was recognized in an American Psychological Society survey as being among the top 25 authors in psychology in terms of current research productivity.

Paul L. Hewitt is clinical psychologist and associate professor of psychology at the University of British Columbia in Vancouver. He received his PhD from the University of Saskatchewan in 1988 and completed his clinical internship at the University of Washington Health Sciences Center. Dr. Hewitt has been conducting research on perfectionism and psychopathology since his undergraduate training and has published extensively in the perfectionism field as well as in suicide literature. He has conducted numerous workshops, symposia, and educational media presentations regarding perfectionism and has served on editorial boards. Dr. Hewitt consults with a variety of professional groups and, since the late 1980s, he has had a private practice, focusing on clinical work with people experiencing perfectionistic behavior.